Lecture Notes in Computer Science   **13931**

Founding Editors

Gerhard Goos
Juris Hartmanis

Editorial Board Members

The series Lecture Notes in Computer Science (LNCS), including its subseries Lecture Notes in Artificial Intelligence (LNAI) and Lecture Notes in Bioinformatics (LNBI), has established itself as a medium for the publication of new developments in computer science and information technology research, teaching, and education.

LNCS enjoys close cooperation with the computer science R & D community, the series counts many renowned academics among its volume editors and paper authors, and collaborates with prestigious societies. Its mission is to serve this international community by providing an invaluable service, mainly focused on the publication of conference and workshop proceedings and postproceedings. LNCS commenced publication in 1973.

Cristina David · Meng Sun

Editors

Theoretical Aspects of Software Engineering

17th International Symposium, TASE 2023
Bristol, UK, July 4–6, 2023
Proceedings

 Springer

Editors
Cristina David
University of Bristol
Bristol, UK

Meng Sun
Peking University
Beijing, China

ISSN 0302-9743   ISSN 1611-3349 (electronic)
Lecture Notes in Computer Science
ISBN 978-3-031-35256-0   ISBN 978-3-031-35257-7 (eBook)
https://doi.org/10.1007/978-3-031-35257-7

This Springer imprint is published by the registered company Springer Nature Switzerland AG
The registered company address is: Gewerbestrasse 11, 6330 Cham, Switzerland

Preface

The International Symposium on Theoretical Aspects of Software Engineering (TASE) gathers researchers and practitioners interested by the new results on innovative advances in software engineering. It records the latest developments in formal and theoretical software engineering methods and techniques. TASE 2023 was the 17th International Symposium on Theoretical Aspects of Software Engineering, a series of symposia started in 2007 with the aim to bring together researchers and developers from academia and industry with interest in the theoretical aspects of software engineering. In past years, TASE took place in Shanghai (2007), Nanjing (2008), Tianjing (2009), Taipei (2010), Xi'an (2011), Beijing (2012), Birmingham (2013), Changsha (2014), Nanjing (2015), Shanghai (2016), Sophia Antipolis (2017), Guangzhou (2018), Guilin (2019), Hangzhou (2020), Shanghai (2021), and Cluj-Napoca (2022).

TASE 2023 was held in Bristol, United Kingdom during July 4–6, 2023. This year we received 49 submissions covering different areas of theoretical software engineering. Each paper was single-blind reviewed by at least three reviewers and the Program Committee accepted 19 regular long papers and 2 short papers, leading to an attractive scientific program. This edition of TASE was enhanced by the presence of 3 keynote speakers, Stefan Kiefer (University of Oxford, UK), Peter Schrammel (Diffblue Ltd., UK), and Naijun Zhan (Chinese Academy of Sciences, China).

TASE 2023 would not have succeeded without the deep investment and involvement of the Program Committee members and the external reviewers who evaluated (with about 150 reviews) and selected the best contributions. This event would not exist without the authors and contributors who submitted their proposals. We address our thanks to everyone—reviewers, authors, Program Committee members, and organization committee members—involved in the success of TASE 2023.

The EasyChair system was set up for the management of TASE 2023, supporting submission, review, and volume preparation processes. It proved to be a powerful framework. We thank Springer for the smooth cooperation in the production of this proceedings volume.

TASE 2023 was hosted and sponsored by University of Bristol, UK. The local organization committee offered all the facilities to run the event in a lovely and friendly atmosphere. Many thanks to all the local organizers.

Lastly, we wish to express our special thanks to the steering committee members, in particular Shengchao Qin and Huibiao Zhu, for their valuable support.

May 2023

Meng Sun
Cristina David

Organization

Program Committee

Bernhard K. Aichernig	TU Graz, Austria
Yamine Ait Ameur	Université de Toulouse, France
Toshiaki Aoki	JAIST, Japan
Guangdong Bai	University of Queensland, Australia
Richard Banach	University of Manchester, UK
Luís Soares Barbosa	University of Minho, Portugal
Marcello Bonsangue	Leiden University, The Netherlands
Martin Brain	City, University of London, UK
Liqian Chen	National University of Defense Technology, China
Zhenbang Chen	National University of Defense Technology, China
Wei-Ngan Chin	National University of Singapore, Singapore
Lucas Cordeiro	University of Manchester, UK
Andreea Costea	National University of Singapore, Singapore
Florin Craciun	Babeş-Bolyai University, Romania
Cristina David	University of Bristol, UK
Guillaume Dupont	Institut de Recherche en Informatique de Toulouse, France
Flavio Ferrarotti	Software Competence Centre Hagenberg, Austria
Simon Foster	University of York, UK
Marc Frappier	Université de Sherbrooke, Canada
Kim Guldstrand	Larsen Aalborg University, Denmark
Matthias Güdemann	UAS Munich, Germany
Fei He	Tsinghua University, China
Thai Son Hoang	University of Southampton, UK
Zolt So HorvvSon	Eötvös Loránd University, Hungary
Zhe Hou	Griffith University, Australia
Xiaowei Huang	University of Liverpool, UK
Fuyuki Ishikawa	National Institute of Informatics, Japan
Andreas Katis	KBR Inc. at NASA Ames Research Center, USA
Pascal Kesseli	Lacework Ltd., Switzerland
Olga Kouchnarenko	University of Franche-Comté, France
Regine Laleau	Paris-Est Creteil University, France
Quang Loc Le	University College London, UK

Guoqiang Li	Shanghai Jiao Tong University, China
Dorel Lucanu	Alexandru Ioan Cuza University, Romania
Frederic Mallet	Côte d'Azur University, France
Diego Marmsoler	University of Exeter, UK
Kazutaka Matsuda	Tohoku University, Japan
Dominique Mery	Universit de Lorraine, LORIA, France
Alan Mycroft	University of Cambridge, UK
Kazuhiro Ogata	JAIST, Japan
Dominic Orchard	University of Kent, UK
Jun Pang	University of Luxembourg, Luxembourg
Geguang Pu	East China Normal University, China
Shengchao Qin	Teesside University, UK
Adrian Riesco	Universidad Complutense de Madrid, Spain
Cristina Seceleanu	Mälardalen University, Sweden
Neeraj Singh	University of Toulouse, France
Meng Sun	Peking University, China
Cong Tian	Xidian University, China
Jaco van de Pol	Aarhus University, Denmark
Rob van Glabbeek	University of Edinburgh, UK
Xiaofei Xie	Nanyang Technological University, Singapore
Naijun Zhan	Institute of Software, Chinese Academy of Sciences, China
Xiyue Zhang	University of Oxford, UK
Yongwang Zhao	Zhejiang University, China
Huibiao Zhu	East China Normal University, China
Xue-Yang Zhu	Institute of Software, Chinese Academy of Sciences, China
Peter Ölveczky	University of Oslo, Norway

Additional Reviewers

Alshmrany, Kaled	Luan, Xiaokun
Bu, Hao	Masson, Pierre-Alain
Chen, Minyu	O'Connor, Liam
Deng, Yuxin	Pferscher, Andrea
González, Senén	Tejfel, Máté
Gu, Rong	Torrens, Paulo
Kitlei, Róbert	Xiong, Jiawen
Lefaucheux, Engel	Xu, Xiong
Li, Jingyang	Xu, Zhiwu
Liu, Ai	Xue, Xiaoyong
Liu, Depeng	Zhao, Hengjun

Contents

Automating Recoverability Proofs for Cyber-Physical Systems with Runtime Assurance Architectures

Vivek Nigam[2,3]([✉]) and Carolyn Talcott[1]

[1] SRI International, Menlo Park, USA
[2] Federal University of Paraíba, João Pessoa, Brazil
vivek.nigam@gmail.com
[3] Huawei Munich Research Center, Munich, Germany

Abstract. Cyber-physical systems (CPSes), such as autonomous vehicles, use sophisticated components like ML-based controllers. It is difficult to provide evidence about the safe functioning of such components. To overcome this problem, Runtime Assurance Architecture (RTA) solutions have been proposed. The RTA's decision component evaluates the system's safety risk and whenever the risk is higher than acceptable the RTA switches to a safety mode that, for example, activates a controller with strong evidence for its safe functioning. In this way, RTAs increase CPS runtime safety and resilience by recovering the system from higher to lower risk levels. The goal of this paper is to automate recovery proofs of CPSes using RTAs. We first formalize the key verification problems, namely, the decision sampling-time adequacy problem and the time-bounded recoverability problem. We then demonstrate how to automatically generate proofs for the proposed verification problems using symbolic rewriting modulo SMT. Automation is enabled by integrating the rewriting logic tool (Maude), which generates sets of non-linear constraints, with an SMT-solver (Z3) to produce proofs

1 Introduction

Cyber-physical systems (CPSes) are increasingly performing complex safety-critical missions in an autonomous fashion, autonomous vehicles (AVs) being a current prime example. Given the complexity of the environment in which such CPSes operate, they often rely on highly complex machine learning (ML) based controllers [1] because of ML's capability of learning implicit requirements about the vehicle operation conditions. It has been notably hard, however, to provide safety arguments using only such ML-based components due to their functional insufficiency [2]. Despite the great amount of effort in building methods for verifying systems with ML-based components, they still present more faults than acceptable [16].

Runtime assurance architectures (RTAs), based on the well-known simplex architecture [29,30], have been proposed [13,19,24] as a means to overcome this challenge. An RTA contains a decision module that evaluates the system's safety risk formalized as a collection of safety properties. Whenever a safety risk is higher than acceptable, the RTA moves the system to a safe state. As illustrated by Fig. 1, RTA

C. David and M. Sun (Eds.): TASE 2023, LNCS 13931, pp. 1–19, 2023.
https://doi.org/10.1007/978-3-031-35257-7_1

increases CPS safety and resilience by dynamically adapting the CPS behavior according to the perceived system risk level, recovering the CPS from a higher-risk situation. We use the symbol dt to denote the sampling interval in which the decision module evaluates the system's level of risk. These levels of risks are formalized as properties tailored according to the operational domain of the system [21]. For example, vehicles on a highway have a different formalization of risk level than vehicles in urban scenarios where pedestrians may be crossing roads. In the diagram in Fig. 1 there are four increasing levels of risk (safer, safe, unsafe, bad), e.g., denoting risks of an accident, from safer denoting the lowest and desirable risk level to bad denoting the highest level of risk that has to be avoided at all costs, to avoid possible accidents.

If the risk is safer, then the decision module uses the output from the primary, unverified controller. However, if a higher risk safe is detected, then the decision module uses the output of the safe controller. The expectation is then that the safe controller recovers eventually from the high risk situation leading the system to return to a situation that is safer. It may be that in the process the CPS will pass through situations that are unsafe, but it definitely shall not pass through situations that are bad, e.g., situations of imminent crash that trigger other safety mechanisms, such as emergency brakes.

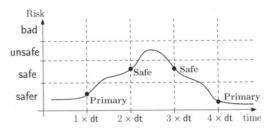

Fig. 1. Illustration of how one expect RTA to maintain safety during runtime. dt is the sampling time of the decision module. **Primary** (respectively, **Safe**) denotes that the decision module switches to the primary (respectively, safe) controller.

There are two key properties about RTAs which engineers have to demonstrate by providing sufficient evidence:

- dt **Adequacy:** the sampling time interval is small enough that bad situations are not missed by the RTA;
- **Time Bounded Recoverability:** if the system risk becomes greater than acceptable (safer) the safe controller can bring the system back to a safer state within a specified time bound, without entering a bad state.

The main goal of this paper is to develop methods to generate formal proofs for these properties for RTA instances in an automated fashion. This is accomplished by using the Symbolic Soft-Agents framework [21] which enables the automated generation of safety proofs for CPS using symbolic rewriting modulo SMT [26]. Our contributions here are in two areas:

- **Formal foundation.** We provide formal definitions for three variants of dt adequacy, and prove the relations among them. We also provide a formal definition of time bounded recoverability. We define a notion of one period recoverability, and prove that one period recoverability together with any one of the dt adequacy properties

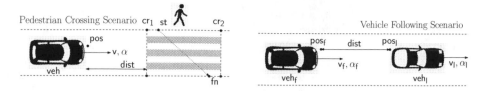

Fig. 2. Pedestrian crossing and vehicle following logical scenarios diagrams. The road is on the Y-axis, so imagine the illustrations rotated counterclockwise.

implies time bounded recoverability. The formal definitions are tailored so that they are amenable to automated verification.

- **Automated Checking of RTA Properties:** Based on the specification of RTA properties and of abstract descriptions of situations in which CPSes operate, called logical scenarios [20, 25], we present algorithms for verifying two forms of dt adequacy and for one period recoverability, and report results of experiments for two logical scenarios. The experiments demonstrate the feasibility of automated proof and also illustrate some of the challenges.

Section 2 describes the logical scenarios of our running examples. Section 3 formalizes the notion of levels of risk using safety properties. These are then used to define several notions of sampling time adequacy in Sect. 4 and recoverability properties in Sect. 5. Section 6 describes experiments based on the logical scenarios in Sect. 2. We conclude with related and future work in Sects. 7 and 8. The companion report [22] contains some missing proofs and more details about the implementation.

2 Logical Scenarios and Motivating Examples

A key step in the development of autonomous CPSes is the definition of the situations in which these systems will operate [20, 25, 34]. These situations are specified as abstract scenarios, called logical scenarios [20, 25], such as lane changing or vehicle following or pedestrian crossing, in which an AV has to avoid harm. These logical scenarios contain details about the situations in which a vehicle shall be able to safely operate such as which types and number of actors, e.g., vehicles, pedestrians, operating assumptions, e.g., range of speeds, and road topology, e.g., number of lanes. Moreover, these logical scenarios are associated with safety metrics that formalize the properties that need to be satisfied by the vehicle. For a comprehensive list of logical scenarios and associated properties we refer to [34] and references therein. Examples of scenario description and generation formalisms can be found in [9, 14]. As a logical scenario may have infinitely many concrete instances, it is challenging to demonstrate that a vehicle will satisfy such safety properties in all instances.

We use two running examples illustrated by the diagrams in Fig. 2: a pedestrian crossing scenario and a vehicle following scenario.

Pedestrian Crossing. In this scenario an ego vehicle, i.e., a vehicle which is of primary interest in testing, trailing or operational scenarios, vh, is at position pos and is approaching with speed v and acceleration α, with a pedestrian crossing situated between the positions cr_1 and cr_2. Moreover, a pedestrian is attempting to cross the road using the pedestrian crossing. As long as the pedestrian does not move outside the pedestrian crossing, the exact shape of the pedestrian crossing is not important as vh shall always stop before the pedestrian crossing whenever a pedestrian is intending to cross it. To keep things simple, assume that the pedestrian is crossing the street at constant speed, v_p, following a straight line as illustrated in Fig. 2 by the dashed line from st to fn.

The operational design domain (ODD) of such a logical scenario is specified by constraints on its parameters (pos, v, α, cr_1, cr_2, v_p). Typically, one specifies the bounds on the speeds and accelerations. Consider for example:
$$0\,m/s \leq v \leq 10\,m/s \quad -8\,m/s^2 \leq \alpha \leq 2\,m/s^2 \quad 1\,m/s \leq v_p \leq 4\,m/s$$
Moreover, $pos.y < cr_1.y$, that is the vehicle is approaching the pedestrian crossing and $cr_1.y \leq st.y, fn.y \leq cr_2.y$, that is st, fn are in the pedestrian crossing area, where for any position $l = (px, py)$, $l.x$ and $l.y$ denote, respectively, px and py.

Vehicle Following. Our second running example is a vehicle following scenario as depicted in Fig. 2. This example commonly appears in the literature and therefore, we do not describe in the same level of detail, but simply refer to [21]. In a nutshell, it consists of two vehicles, a follower vehicle (veh_f) and a leader vehicle (veh_l). Typically, these vehicles are in a highway with multiple lanes at reasonably high speeds, e.g., speeds between 60 km/h and 140 km/h and the same acceleration bounds as in the vehicle in the pedestrian crossing scenario. Moreover, there are only vehicles, i.e., no pedestrians. no bicycles, etc. The following vehicle shall avoid approaching dangerously close to the leader vehicle while still maintaining a reasonable speed.

We assume that from an instance, conf, of a logical scenario (LS), we can compute the function conf $\longrightarrow_\Delta$ $conf_1$, where $conf_1$ is an LS instance specifying the physical attributes, e.g., speeds, directions, accelerations, of the agents obtained according to their speeds, directions and accelerations in conf after a period of $\Delta > 0$ time units. Moreover, we assume that if conf $\longrightarrow_{\Delta_1+\Delta_2}$ $conf_1$, then there exists conf$'$ such that conf $\longrightarrow_{\Delta_1}$ conf$'$ $\longrightarrow_{\Delta_2}$ $conf_1$. Notice that since $\longrightarrow_\Delta$ is a function, conf' is unique. For example, consider the instance of the pedestrian crossing scenario where the vehicle has speed of $10\,m/s$, acceleration of $2m/s^2$, and position $pos.x = 0m$. After $\Delta = 0.1\,s$, the speed of the vehicle will be $10.2\,m/s$ and new position $1.1\,m$. The vehicle is traveling in a constant direction along the road, and we omit it.

3   Safety Properties and Levels of Risk

A key aspect of RTA mechanisms is the ability to check for the level of risk of the system, e.g., whether it is safe or not. We formalize the notion of level of risk as a partial order on safety properties as follows:

Definition 1. *An RTA safety property specification for a logical specification LS is a tuple $\langle S, \prec_1, \mathsf{bad}, \models \rangle$ where*

- $S = \{SP_1, \ldots, SP_n\}$ is a finite set of safety properties;
- $\prec_1 \colon S \times S$ is an asymmetric binary relation over S, where $SP_1 \prec_1 SP_2$ denotes that the safety property SP_2 specifies a less risky condition than the safety property SP_1. Let $\prec$ be the order obtained from $\prec_1$ by applying transitivity. We assume that $\prec$ is a strict pre-order (no cycles).
- the safety property bad $\in S$ is the least element of $\prec$, specifying the condition that shall be avoided, i.e., the highest risk
- $\vDash$ specifies when an instance conf of LS satisfies a property $SP \in S$, written conf $\vDash$ SP. Moreover, we assume that if conf $\vDash SP_1$ and $SP_1 \prec SP_2$ or $SP_2 \prec SP_1$, then conf $\nvDash SP_2$. That is, any instance of a logical scenario can only satisfy one level of risk. We also assume that any instance of a logical scenario is at some level of risk, that is, for all instances conf of LS, there is at least one SP such that conf $\vDash$ SP.

The following two examples illustrate different options of safety properties for the pedestrian crossing and the vehicle following examples described in Sect. 2.

Example 1. Consider the pedestrian crossing shown in Fig. 2. We define the following RTA safety property specification $\langle\{bad, unsafe, safe, safer\}, \prec_1, bad, \vDash\rangle$ with bad $\prec_1$ unsafe $\prec_1$ safe $\prec_1$ safer based on the *time to zebra* metric [34]

$$
\begin{aligned}
\text{safer} \ &:= \text{dist} \geq \text{dStop} + \text{gap}_{safer} * v \\
\text{safe} \ &:= \text{dStop} + \text{gap}_{safer} * v > \text{dist} \geq \text{dStop} + \text{gap}_{safe} * v \\
\text{unsafe} &:= \text{dStop} + \text{gap}_{safe} * v > \text{dist} \geq \text{dStop} + \text{gap}_{unsafe} * v \\
\text{bad} \ &:= \text{dStop} + \text{gap}_{unsafe} * v > \text{dist}
\end{aligned}
\tag{1}
$$

where dist $= cr_1.y - \text{pos}.y$ is the distance between the ego vehicle and the pedestrian crossing, dStop $= -(v * v)/(2 * \text{maxDec})$ is the distance necessary to stop the ego vehicle by applying its maximum deceleration maxDec, e.g., when issuing an emergency brake, and $\text{gap}_{safer} > \text{gap}_{safe} > \text{gap}_{unsafe} > 0$ are used with v to specify a safety margin distance in the safety property. The values for $\text{gap}_{safer}, \text{gap}_{safe}, \text{gap}_{unsafe}$ shall be defined according to the ego vehicle's capabilities, e.g., the sampling time dt, and the ODD specifications, e.g., bounds on acceleration and speed. It is then straightforward to check whether an instance of a pedestrian logical scenario satisfies ($\vDash$) any one of the properties above.

While this may seem like a good candidate safety property specification for the pedestrian crossing, it turns out that it is hard to demonstrate vehicle recoverability as we show in Sect. 6. The problem lies in the fact that the three properties tend to be all the same when the vehicle speed (v) tends to zero, and similarly, when dist is too large. We, therefore, establish an alternative definition for safer as follows:

$$
\text{safer} := \text{dist} \geq \text{dStop} + \text{gap}_{safer} * v \text{ or } v \leq \text{lowSpd or dist} \geq \text{farAway}
\tag{2}
$$

where lowSpd and farAway are constants specifying a maximum speed for which the vehicle is very safe, e.g., the speed lowSpd is less than the speed of a pedestrian, and the distance farAway that is far enough from the pedestrian crossing.

Example 2. One well-known example for vehicle safety assurance for the vehicle following scenario is the Responsibility-Sensitive Safety (RSS) [31,34] safe distance metric. The RSS safety distance drss(react) is specified as follows:

$$\text{drss}(\text{react}) = v \times \text{react} + \frac{\text{maxacc}_f \times \text{react}^2}{2} - \frac{(v + \text{maxacc}_f \times \text{react})^2}{2 \times \text{maxdec}_f} - \frac{v_l^2}{2 \times \text{maxdec}_l}$$

where react is a parameter for the time for the vehicle to react; v and v_l are, respectively, the follower and leader vehicle speeds; maxacc_f is the maximum acceleration of the follower vehicle; and maxdec_f and maxdec_l are, respectively, the maximum deceleration of the follower and leader vehicles. Based on drss(react) two properties are defined: bad when dis $<$ drss and safer otherwise.

As RSS has only two properties, the definition of recoverability using RTA implies that the system must always satisfy the safer property; otherwise it must satisfy bad. This means that the primary controller shall be trusted and that RTA is not necessary from the beginning (and probably not desired as the primary controller is assumed not to be verified). It is possible to adapt the RSS definitions by adding additional levels in between safer and bad based on the react time:

safer := dis $\geq$ drss$(3 \times$ dt$)$ safe := drss$(2 \times$ dt$) \leq$ dis $<$ drss$(3 \times$ dt$)$
unsafe := drss$($dt$) \leq$ dis $<$ drss$(2 \times$ dt$)$ bad := dis $<$ drss$($dt$)$

Intuitively, when a vehicle is in a configuration satisfying safer it can wrongly evaluate safety risk, e.g., due to distance sensor errors, for two cycles before the RSS property is invalidated. Similarly, safe it can evaluate wrongly for one cycle and unsafe it always has to evaluate correctly the risk.

4   Sampling Time (dt) Adequacy

The RTA monitor has to detect when the system risk changes, and even more so when risk increases, that is, when systems satisfy properties SP that are closer to bad, i.e., move lower in the order $\prec$. This means that the sampling time dt plays an important role in the correctness of a RTA system. For example, if the sampling time is $4 \times$ dt in Fig. 1, the RTA monitor may fail to detect elevation of risk from safer to safe thus not activating the trusted controller soon enough to avoid further escalation of risk.

There is a trade-off between the ability of the system to detect changes of risk and therefore its ability to quickly react to changes, and the performance requirements of monitor system in determining risk, i.e., dt time. The lower the dt, the greater is the ability of the system to detect changes and also greater are the performance requirements on the monitoring components.

Moreover, a key challenge is that dt shall be appropriate in detecting risk changes for all instances of the ODD, i.e., all possible instances of speeds and accelerations. Our approach is to use SMT-solvers to generate dt adequacy proofs automatically building on ideas in [21]. Depending on the definition of dt adequacy, the complexity of the problem can increase substantially, making automation difficult or not feasible.

We propose three alternative definitions of requirements on dt, defined below, that illustrate the trade-offs between the capability of the system to detect risk changes and the development and verification efforts. Figure 3 illustrates these definitions. The first definition, called *one transition adequacy*, is illustrated by left-most diagram in Fig. 3. Intuitively, this definition states that the dt shall be fine enough to detect whenever the configuration of the scenario evolves from satisfying a property, SP_1, to satisfying another property, SP_2. As an example, the dotted evolution of the system passing through conf'_d contains multiple property changes within a period of dt.

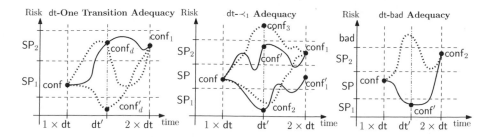

Fig. 3. Illustration of dt adequacy properties. Full line system evolutions illustrate allowed evolutions and dotted evolutions illustrate not allowed evolutions.

Definition 2. *Let* $Spec = \langle \mathcal{S}, \prec_1, \mathrm{bad}, \vDash \rangle$ *be a RTA safety property specification for a logical scenario* LS; *and* dt *be a sampling time.* dt *is one transition adequate with respect to Spec and* LS *if for all instances* conf, conf_1 *of* LS *such that* $\mathrm{conf} \to_{\mathrm{dt}} \mathrm{conf}_1$ *we have:*

– *if* $\mathrm{conf} \vDash SP_1$ *and* $\mathrm{conf}_1 \vDash SP_2$, *then there is a decomposition* $\mathrm{conf} \to_{\mathrm{dt}'}$ $\mathrm{conf}_d \to_{\mathrm{dt-dt}'} \mathrm{conf}_1$ *of* $\mathrm{conf} \to_{\mathrm{dt}} \mathrm{conf}_1$ *for some* $0 \leq \mathrm{dt}' < \mathrm{dt}$, *such that:*
  - *For all decompositions of* $\mathrm{conf} \to_{\mathrm{dt}'} \mathrm{conf}_d$ *as* $\mathrm{conf} \to_{\mathrm{dt}_2} \mathrm{conf}_2 \to_{\mathrm{dt}'-\mathrm{dt}_2} \mathrm{conf}_d$ *where* $0 < \mathrm{dt}_2 < \mathrm{dt}'$, *we have that* $\mathrm{conf}_2 \vDash SP_1$;
  - *For all decompositions of* $\mathrm{conf}_d \to_{\mathrm{dt-dt}'} \mathrm{conf}_1$ *as* $\mathrm{conf}_d \to_{\mathrm{dt}_3}$ $\mathrm{conf}_3 \to_{\mathrm{dt-dt}'-\mathrm{dt}_3} \mathrm{conf}_1$ *where* $0 \leq \mathrm{dt}_3 < \mathrm{dt} - \mathrm{dt}'$, *we have that* $\mathrm{conf}_3 \vDash SP_2$.

The following proposition follows immediately from Definition 2. It states that if dt is one transition adequate, then to check that a configuration satisfying bad is not reachable, it is enough to check whether the configurations during sampling are not bad, instead of checking all decompositions.

Proposition 1. *Let* $Spec = \langle \mathcal{S}, \prec_1, \mathrm{bad}, \vDash \rangle$ *be a RTA safety property specification for a logical scenario* LS. *Let* dt *be one-transition-adequate w.r.t. Spec. For all decompositions* $\mathrm{conf} \to_{\mathrm{dt}'} \mathrm{conf}' \to_{\mathrm{dt-dt}'} \mathrm{conf}_1$ *of* LS, $\mathrm{conf}' \vDash \mathrm{bad}$ *if and only if* $\mathrm{conf} \vDash \mathrm{bad}$ *or* $\mathrm{conf}_1 \vDash \mathrm{bad}$.

Definition 2 is rather complex involving many quantifier alternations thus being very difficult to generate proofs for. In fact, due to limitations on computing time, it is not always possible to guarantee that dt can satisfy one-transition-adequacy. Therefore, we propose two alternative definitions of weaker properties illustrated by the center and right-most diagrams in Fig. 3. These properties are amenable to the automated generation of proofs as we detail in Sect. 6.

The first alternative definition is $\prec_1$ adequacy. Instead of requiring dt to be fine enough to detect when the system satisfies different properties, $\prec_1$ adequacy allows system evolution to migrate within $\prec_1$ range of a safety property multiple times, as illustrated by the system evolution passing through conf'. The system shall be able to detect whenever the risk of the system increases at least two levels.

Definition 3. *Let* $Spec = \langle \mathcal{S}, \prec_1, \text{bad}, \vDash \rangle$ *be a RTA safety property specification for a logical scenario* LS; *and* dt *be a sampling time.* dt *is* $\prec_1$ *adequate with respect to* $Spec$ *and* LS *if for all instances* conf *of* LS *and relations* conf $\rightarrow_{dt}$ conf_1 *if for all* $0 < dt' \le dt$ *and decompositions* conf $\rightarrow_{dt'}$ $\text{conf}' \rightarrow_{dt-dt'}$ conf_1 *we have:*

- *If* conf $\vDash SP_1$ *and* $\text{conf}_1 \vDash SP_2$ *for* $SP_1 \ne SP_2$, *then* $\text{conf}' \vDash SP_1$ *or* $\text{conf}' \vDash SP_2$.
- *If* conf $\vDash SP$ *and* $\text{conf}_1 \vDash SP$, *then* $\text{conf}' \vDash SP$ *or* $\text{conf}' \vDash SP'$ *where* $SP' \prec_1 SP$ *or* $SP \prec SP'$.

One can generalize the definition of $\prec_1$ to allow evolutions on larger ranges of safety properties, e.g. $\prec_n$ adequacy for $n \ge 1$ allow evolutions within n safety risk levels.

The following property of $\prec_1$-adequacy provides a basis for defining recoverability based on $\prec_1$-adequate dt. It is enough to check that no configuration satisfying bad or a property immediately greater to bad is reachable.

Proposition 2. *Let* $Spec = \langle \mathcal{S}, \prec_1, \text{bad}, \vDash \rangle$ *be a RTA safety property specification for a logical scenario* LS; *and* dt *be* $\prec_1$ *adequate sampling time. If* conf $\rightarrow_{dt}$ conf_1 *with* conf $\vDash SP_1$ *and* $\text{conf}_1 \vDash SP_2$ *where* $SP_1 \ne \text{bad}$ *and* $SP_2 \ne \text{bad}$ *and* bad $\not\prec_1 SP_1$ *or* bad $\not\prec_1 SP_2$, *then for all* $0 < dt' \le dt$ *and decompositions* conf $\rightarrow_{dt'}$ $\text{conf}' \rightarrow_{dt-dt'}$ conf_1 *we have* conf' $\not\vDash$ bad.

Consider for example the safety property specification in Example 1 and assume that dt is $\prec_1$-adequate. From Proposition 2, if there is no transition conf $\rightarrow_{dt}$ conf_1 where conf $\vDash$ unsafe and $\text{conf}_1 \vDash$ unsafe, then we can guarantee that the system does not pass through a configuration conf' with conf' $\vDash$ bad including the intermediate configurations that have not been sampled by the vehicle system.

The next adequacy only requires that the dt is fine enough to detect when a system evolution satisfies the bad property. As illustrated by the right-most diagram in Fig. 3, the dotted evolution satisfying bad within dt would invalidate dt adequacy.

Definition 4. *Let* $Spec = \langle \mathcal{S}, \prec_1, \text{bad}, \vDash \rangle$ *be a RTA safety property specification for a logical scenario* LS; *and* dt *be a sampling time.* dt *is bad-adequate with respect to* $Spec$ *and* LS *if for all instances* conf *of* LS *and* conf $\rightarrow_{dt}$ conf_1 *if for all* $0 < dt' \le dt$ *and decompositions* conf $\rightarrow_{dt'}$ $\text{conf}' \rightarrow_{dt-dt'}$ conf_1 *we have:*

- *if* conf $\not\vDash SP$ *and* $\text{conf}_1 \not\vDash SP$ *with* $SP = \text{bad}$ *or* bad $\prec_1 SP$, *then* conf' $\not\vDash$ bad.

The following proposition is similar to Proposition 1 establishing the conditions for verifying for bad-adequacy.

Proposition 3. *Let* $Spec = \langle \mathcal{S}, \prec_1, \text{bad}, \vDash \rangle$ *be a RTA safety property specification for a logical scenario* LS. *Let* dt *be* bad-*adequate w.r.t.* $Spec$. *For all decompositions* conf $\rightarrow_{dt'}$ $\text{conf}' \rightarrow_{dt-dt'}$ conf_1 *of* LS, conf' $\vDash$ bad *if and only if* conf $\vDash SP_0$ *and* $\text{conf}_1 \vDash SP_1$ *with* $\{SP_0, SP_1\} \subseteq \{\text{bad}\} \cup \{SP \mid \text{bad} \prec_1 SP\}$.

The following proposition establishes relations between the different adequacy definitions. Our experiments show that it is possible for dt to be bad-adequate and not $\prec_1$-adequate.

Proposition 4. *Let* $Spec = \langle \mathcal{S}, \prec_1, \mathsf{bad}, \models \rangle$ *be a safety property specification for a logic scenario* LS *and* dt *a sampling time.*

- *If* dt *is one transition adequate, then* dt *is* $\prec_1$-*adequate and* dt *is* bad-*adequate.*
- *If* dt *is* $\prec_1$-*adequate then* dt *is* bad-*adequate.*

5 RTA-Based Recoverability Properties

There are many informal definitions of resilience [3,5,6,17]. In the broadest sense, resilience is "the ability of a system to adapt and respond to changes (both in the environment and internal)" [6]. NIST [27] provides a more precise, but still informal definition of resilience and more focused on attacks: "The ability to anticipate, withstand, recover, and adapt to adverse conditions, stresses, attacks or compromises on systems that use or are enabled by cyber resources."

Intuitively, systems, such as an autonomous vehicle in an LS instance, implementing RTA can be shown to exhibit a basic form of resilience we refer to as recoverability: they detect when a specified risk level is reached and adapt to reduce the risk. Our goal is to formalize this intuition of RTA recoverability with precise definitions.

To accomplish this, we must model the control aspects of the system as well as the change in physical state. Thus we augment the semantic relation $\rightarrow_{\mathsf{dt}}$ (called $\longrightarrow_\Delta$ above) which models the physical aspect of behavior with a relation $\rightarrow_{\mathsf{tasks}}$ that models the control aspect, typically sensing, analyzing, and deciding/planning. Formally, the system behavior is a set of (possibly infinite) execution traces:

$$\mathsf{conf}_0 \rightarrow_{\mathsf{tasks}} \mathsf{conf}_0' \rightarrow_{\mathsf{dt}} \mathsf{conf}_1 \rightarrow_{\mathsf{tasks}} \mathsf{conf}_1' \rightarrow_{\mathsf{dt}} \mathsf{conf}_2 \rightarrow_{\mathsf{tasks}} \cdots$$

where dt is the system's sampling time, $\mathsf{conf}_i' \rightarrow_{\mathsf{dt}} \mathsf{conf}_{i+1}$ is a function, and $\mathsf{conf}_i \rightarrow_{\mathsf{tasks}} \mathsf{conf}_i'$ is an internal transition specifying the behavior of the agents in conf_i, e.g., sensing, updating local knowledge bases, and deciding which actions to take. The exact definition of this transition depends on system specification. Since safety properties are related to the physical attributes of the system, e.g., speed, location, we normally assume that if $\mathsf{conf}_i \models \mathsf{SP}$, then also $\mathsf{conf}_i' \models \mathsf{SP}$. For example, this is the case with the safety properties in Example 1. This assumption is not strictly necessary as the definitions below can be extended to cover cases when this assumption does not hold.

Definition 5. *Let* $Spec = \langle \mathcal{S}, \prec_1, \mathsf{bad}, \models \rangle$ *be a safety property specification for a logical scenario* LS *and* dt *a sampling time, where* $\mathsf{SP}_{\mathsf{safe}} \in \mathcal{S}$ *is the minimal acceptable safe property and* $\mathsf{SP}_{\mathsf{safer}} \in \mathcal{S}$ *is the acceptable safer property where* $\mathsf{SP}_{\mathsf{safe}} \prec \mathsf{SP}_{\mathsf{safer}}$. *Let* t *be a positive natural number. A system* S *is* $\langle \mathsf{SP}_{\mathsf{safe}}, \mathsf{SP}_{\mathsf{safer}}, t \rangle$-*recoverable if for all instances* conf_0 *of* LS *and traces* $\tau = \mathsf{conf}_0 \rightarrow_{\mathsf{tasks}} \mathsf{conf}_0' \rightarrow_{\mathsf{dt}} \mathsf{conf}_1 \rightarrow_{\mathsf{tasks}} \mathsf{conf}_1' \rightarrow_{\mathsf{dt}}$ $\cdots$ *such that* $\mathsf{conf}_0 \models \mathsf{SP}$ *with* $\mathsf{SP} = \mathsf{SP}_{\mathsf{safe}}$ *or* $\mathsf{SP}_{\mathsf{safe}} \prec \mathsf{SP}$:

- *For all* $\mathsf{conf}_i' \rightarrow_{\mathsf{dt}} \mathsf{conf}_{i+1}$ *in* τ, *there is no decomposition* $\mathsf{conf}_i' \rightarrow_{\mathsf{dt}_1} \mathsf{conf} \rightarrow_{\mathsf{dt}-\mathsf{dt}_1}$ conf_{i+1}, *with* $0 \leq \mathsf{dt}_1 \leq \mathsf{dt}$, *such that* $\mathsf{conf} \models \mathsf{bad}$. *That is, the system never reaches a configuration that satisfies* bad.
- *For all* conf_i *in* τ, *such that* $\mathsf{conf}_i \models \mathsf{SP}_{\mathsf{safe}}$, *then* $\mathsf{conf}_{i+t} \models \mathsf{SP}$ *with* $\mathsf{SP}_{\mathsf{safer}} \prec$ SP *or* $\mathsf{SP}_{\mathsf{safer}} = \mathsf{SP}$. *That is, if the system reaches the minimal safety property, it necessarily returns to the acceptable safer property.*

This definition formalizes the ability of the system to recover from a higher level of risk as illustrated by Fig. 1. Intuitively, the property SP_{safe} specifies the highest acceptable risk before the system shall react to reduce risk, i.e., when the RTA instance triggers the safe controller, while SP_{safer} specifies the risk that shall be achieved within t logical ticks of the system, i.e., $t \times dt$, that is when the RTA instance resumes using the output of the primary controller.

There are some subtleties in this definition that are worth pointing out:

– Recovery Period: The time t in Definition 5 specifies the time that the system has to recover. On the one hand, it avoids that the system stays in a higher risk situation, albeit still safe, for a long period of time, thus reducing the chance of safety accidents. On the other hand, if t is too small, it will require a stricter safe controller or not be realizable given the vehicle's capabilities, e.g., maximum deceleration. Therefore, the value of t will depend on situation under consideration. To mitigate this problem, we propose automated ways to prove recoverability in Sect. 6.
– Recoverability Smoothness: Notice that we require that $SP_{safe} \prec SP_{safer}$ and not $SP_{safe} \prec_1 SP_{safer}$, i.e., SP_{safer} can be multiple levels of risk safer than SP_{safe}. By selecting appropriately these properties, e.g., setting SP_{safer} with a much lower risk than SP_{safe}, one can avoid the oscillation of the system between normal operation (using the primary controller) and recovery operation (using the safe controller).

Procedure to Demonstrate Recoverability. A challenge in proving a system resilient as per Definition 5 is that one needs to reason about all traces which may have infinite length and furthermore all decomposition of traces. To address this challenge we demonstrate (Theorem 1 below) that it is enough that the dt is adequate (as in Sect. 3), dt is fine enough not to skip properties (Definition 7 below), and consider only traces of bounded size as specified by the following definition:

Definition 6. *Let* $Spec, LS, SP_{safer}, SP_{safe}, t$ *be as in Definition 5 and* dt *be the sampling time. A system* S *is* $\langle SP_{safe}, SP_{safer}, t \rangle$*–one-period-recoverable if for all traces* $\tau = conf_0 \to_{tasks} conf'_0 \to_{dt} conf_1 \to_{tasks} \cdots \to_{dt} conf_t$ *such that* $conf_0 \vDash SP_{safe}$*:*

1. $conf_t \vDash SP_{safer}$*–the system recovers in t time ticks to a lower risk situation.*
2. *For all* $conf'_i \to_{dt} conf_{i+1}$ *in* τ*, there is no decomposition* $conf'_i \to_{dt_1} conf \to_{dt-dt_1} conf_{i+1}$*, with* $0 \leq dt_1 \leq dt$*, such that* $conf \vDash$ *bad.*

To prove recoverability for unbounded traces (Theorem 1), we also need to ensure that property SP_{safe} that triggers an RTA is not skipped. This is formalized by the following definition.

Definition 7. *Let* $Spec, LS, SP_{safer}, SP_{safe}, t$ *be as in Definition 5 and* dt *be the sampling time. We say that* dt *does not skip a property* SP_{safe} *if there is no transition of the form* $conf \longrightarrow_{dt} conf_1$ *such that* $conf \vDash SP$ *and* $conf_1 \vDash SP_1$ *with* $SP_{safe} \prec SP$ *and* $SP_1 \prec SP_{safe}$*.*

Theorem 1. *Let* dt *be one-transition or* $\prec_1$ *or bad-adequate where* dt *does not skip* SP_{safe}*. A system* S *is* $\langle SP_{safe}, SP_{safer}, t \rangle$*-one-period-recoverable if and only if* S *is* $\langle SP_{safe}, SP_{safer}, t \rangle$*-recoverable.*

Condition for Checking One-Recovery-Period Recoverability: Even when considering only one-recovery-period recoverability, it is still necessary to consider all possible decompositions of dt transitions (item 2 in Definition 6). This can be overcome depending on the type of dt adequacy: using Propositions 1, 2, and 3, it is enough to check that that all configurations $conf_i$ for $0 \leq i \leq t$ do not satisfy bad nor a SP such that bad $\prec_1$ SP.

6 Experimental Results

We carried out a collection of experiments using the symbolic soft agents framework [21] and symbolic rewriting modulo SMT as described in Sect. 6.1. Section 6.2 describes the experiments for automatically proving dt-adequacy. Section 6.3 describes the experiments for automatically proving timed recoverability. We used a value of $dt = 0.1s$ for all experiments. If an answer has not been returned after one hour, an experiment is aborted. All experiments were carried out on a 2.2 GHz 6-Core Intel Core i7 machine with 16 GB memory. The code is available in the folder rta_symbolic_agents at https://github.com/SRI-CSL/VCPublic. We considered the scenarios described as follows:

pedCross(gap$_{safer}$,gap$_{safe}$,gap$_{unsafe}$,senerr) – Pedestrian Crossing using only Relative Distances: This scenario is the pedestrian crossing scenario described in Sect. 2. The safety properties of the scenario are those as described in Eq. 1 using only relative distances and parametrized by the values gap$_{safer}$, gap$_{safe}$, gap$_{unsafe}$. We assume that the sensor that detects pedestrians and their properties, namely, speed, position and direction, may not be perfect. That is, the vehicle's local knowledge base, used to decide which action it will take, may not correspond to the ground truth. In particular, the position of the pedestrian inferred by the vehicle may differ by some amount proportional to the actual distance to the pedestrian.

The error, err, is proportional to the distance (pos_p − pos) between the vehicle and the pedestrian as specified by the formula (err $\leq$ (pos_p − pos) × senerr and err $\geq$ 0.) In this case the safe controller of the vehicle is conservative, e.g., reducing the speed of the vehicle more aggressively, so to still satisfy the timed recoverability property. When senerr = 0, then the sensors are not faulty.

pedCrBnds(gap$_{safer}$,gap$_{safe}$,gap$_{unsafe}$,senerr) – Pedestrian Crossing with safer specified using low speeds and great distances: This is similar to the previous case, but now we are using the safety property for safer as specified by Eq. 2.

folRSS(maxdec$_l$) – Vehicle Following with RSS Properties: This scenario involves the vehicle following scenario using the safety properties based on the RSS property [31] described in Example 2. We parametrize the safety property according to the assumed maximum deceleration of the leader (maxdec$_l$). We follow the analysis carried out in [18]. This work identifies three scenarios based on the expected occurrence of leader vehicle deceleration. The first scenario, which is highly unlikely, is that the leader makes an emergency brake (maxdec$_l = -8\,\mathrm{m/s}^2$); the second when the leader vehicle decelerates heavily (maxdec$_l = -5\,\mathrm{m/s}^2$); and the most likely case when the leader vehicle decelerates normally (maxdec$_l = -2\,\mathrm{m/s}^2$).

folGap(gap_{safer},gap_{safe},gap_{unsafe}) – Vehicle Following with Gap Distances Properties: This scenario is described in more detail in [21]. In particular, we use safety properties based gap distances, similar to the pedestrian crossing.

6.1   Automating Recoverability Proofs Using Symbolic Soft-Agents

Figure 4 depicts the main machinery that has been implemented and used. It is based on the soft-agents framework [32] and the general symbolic libraries described in [21]. The general symbolic soft-agents libraries specify the executable semantics of CPS based on rewriting rules. The symbolic soft-agents rewrite rules correspond directly to the two LS relations $\rightarrow_{tasks}$ and $\rightarrow_{dt}$. We implemented the vehicle-specific libraries for specifying vehicle scenarios. We have also implemented the machinery for checking for dt-adequacy (bad-adequacy and $\prec_1$-adequacy) and Timed Recoverability.

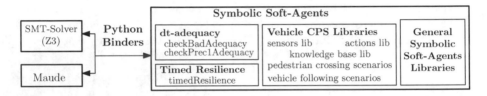

Fig. 4. Key libraries and tools used for automating recoverability proofs.

The symbolic soft-agents are executable specifications. In particular, the execution traces are enumerated by Maude [10] search. The constraints in the traces (non-linear arithmetic formulas) are solved by the SMT-solver (Z3 [12]). We implemented the connection between the symbolic soft-agents libraries and SMT solvers using the Python Binders described in [28], thus enabling easy extensions to additional solvers and other tools in the future.

The basic idea is to search for a counter-example to the property of interest. Because the symbolic search is complete, failure to find a counter-example means that the property holds for all instances of the LS under consideration. Notice that in our scenarios, we consider traces of finite length. There may be infinitely may state, but search terminates as the states finitely represented using symbolic terms.

As an example, to check bad-adequacy, the algorithm follows Proposition 2 by searching for a counter example, i.e. properties $SP_0 \prec_1 SP_1$ (not bad) and LS instances $conf_0$, $conf_1$ such that $conf_0$ satisfies SP_0, $conf_1$ satisfies SP_1, $conf_0 \rightarrow_{dt} conf_1$, and there is dt_0 with $0 < dt_0 < dt$, $conf_2$ such that $conf_0 \rightarrow_{dt_0} conf_2 \rightarrow_{dt-dt_0} conf_1$, where $conf_2$ satisfies bad. If no counterexample is found then bad-adequacy holds for the given LS, dt, and property specification.

Using symbolic rewriting, an arbitrary instance of LS is represented by a term, asys, consisting of a symbolic agent configuration and a symbolic environment. The environment contains knowledge of the physical state and the constraint on symbol values. The assertion that a property SP holds for a configuration is represented by the term enforce(asys, SP) that conjoins the boolean term specifying SP in terms of the symbols of asys to the constraint in the environment. cond(asys) is the constraint in the environment part of asys.

The base case is adequacy for a pair of properties, SP_0, SP_1. The algorithm for this case does the following. First, use symbolic search from $asys_0$ = enforce(asys, SP_0) for some $asys_1$ such that $asys_0 \rightarrow_{dt} asys_1$ and cond(enforce($asys_1$, SP_1))) is satisfiable. If no such $asys_1$ is found, dt-adequacy holds for the given SP_0, SP_1. Otherwise, for some found $asys_1$ do a symbolic search from (a copy of) $asys_0$ for some $asys_2$, dt_0, where dt_0 is symbolic, such that $asys_0 \rightarrow_{dt_0} asys_2$ and

cond(enforce($asys_1$, SP_1)) $\land$ cond(enforce($asys_2$, bad)) $\land$ $0 < dt_0 < dt$

is satisfiable. If such $asys_1$, $asys_2$, dt_0 are found we have a counter-example, otherwise bad-adequacy holds for SP_0, SP_1.

The remaining algorithms for $\prec_1$-adequacy, noSkip property, and t-recoverability follow the same pattern as for bad-adequacy.

6.2 dt-adequacy Experiments

Table 1 presents our main experiments for proving dt-adequacy. Since for each scenario there are four levels of properties (bad, unsafe, safe, safer), there are ten cases to consider, e.g., the case from starting at a configuration satisfying safer and ending at another configuration satisfying safe and so on.

Table 1. Automated proofs for bad and $\prec_1$-adequacy for different scenarios. DNF denotes that the experiment was aborted after one hour.

Pedestrian Crossing Scenarios		
Scenario	bad-adequacy	$\prec_1$-adequacy
pedCross$(3, 2, 1, 0)$	Yes (130 s)	DNF
pedCrBnds$(3, 2, 1, 0)$	Yes (172 s)	No (358 s), failed case from safe to safer
pedCross$(5, 2, 1, 0)$	Yes (89 s)	Yes(149 s)
pedCrBnds$(5, 2, 1, 0)$	Yes (78 s)	No(172s), failed case from safe to safer
folGap$(3, 2, 1)$	DNF	Yes (1413 s)
folGap$(6, 4, 2)$	Yes (51 s)	No (52s), failed case from safe to safe
folGap$(7, 5, 1)$	Yes (55 s)	Yes (83 s)
folRSS(-8)	DNF	DNF
folRSS(-5)	DNF	DNF
folRSS(-2)	Yes (304s)	Yes (533 s)

Pedestrian Crossing Scenarios: The soft-agents machinery is able to prove bad-adequacy in less than 3 min. However, for $\prec_1$-adequacy, the soft-agents machinery fails to return a result for the scenario pedCross$(3, 2, 1, 0)$ (without the explicit bounds). In particular, the SMT-solver cannot prove or find a counter-example within one hour. If we increase the values of gap_{safer} and gap_{safe} to 5 and 2, then the soft-agent machinery terminates positively. While it is hard to formally justify this as the SMT-solver applies several heuristics, this is, intuitively, expected as these new values result in more coarse safety properties.

Moreover, the $pedCrBnds$ scenarios do not satisfy the $\prec_1$-adequacy. In particular, it fails one case, namely, from safe to safer. This seems to suggest that one can merge safe and safer in the analysis of recoverability, as we are still able to detect transitions to the lower properties (unsafe and bad).

Vehicle Following Scenarios: Both sets of scenarios were challenging for the soft-agents machinery. Differently from the pedestrian crossing example, folGap was easier to prove $\prec_1$-adequacy and not terminating for bad-adequacy. Interestingly, when increasing the gap_{safer}, gap_{safe}, gap_{unsafe} bounds to 6,4, and 2, respectively, $\prec_1$-adequacy failed in the case from safe to safe, but increasing further the values to 7,5 and 1, the proof is established. This indicates that the value of 2 for gap_{unsafe} is not adequate as the system is capable of traversing a configuration satisfying bad within a dt. For folRSS, the soft-agents machinery was only able to prove both adequacy properties when assuming a maximum deceleration for the leader vehicle of $-2m/s^2$.

In summary, all the scenarios, except folRSS(-5) and folRSS(-8), the soft-agents machinery is capable of demonstrating automatically bad and $\prec_1$ adequacy. The cases of folRSS(-5) and folRSS(-8) are more challenging and the investigation on how to improve the machinery or CPS modeling to handle them is left to future work.

Table 2. Automated proofs for Timed-Recoverability. The symbol $\star$ denotes that the experiment used a very aggressive controller. As the scenario pedCrBnds$(3, 2, 1, 0)$ is not recoverable for $t = 4$, it is not necessary to carry out experiments for the scenarios marked with –.

$\langle$safe, safer, $t\rangle$-One-Recovery-Period		
Pedestrian Crossing Scenarios		
Scenario	$t = 4$	$t = 5$
pedCross$(3, 2, 1, 0)$	No (34 s)	No (115 s)
pedCrBnds$(3, 2, 1, 0)$	No (27 s)	Yes (621 s)
pedCross$(5, 2, 1, 0)$	No (27 s)	No (93 s)
pedCrBnds$(3, 2, 1, 0.50)$	–	No (103 s)
pedCrBnds$(3, 2, 1, 0.33)$	–	No (104 s)
pedCrBnds$(3, 2, 1, 0.125)$	–	Yes (637 s)
pedCrBnds$(3, 2, 1, 0.1)$	–	Yes (734s)
Vehicle Followin g Scenarios		
Scenario	Recoverability	
folGap$(3, 2, 1)$	$t = 5$	No (12 s)
folGap$(6, 4, 2)$	$t = 5$	No (11 s)
folGap$(7, 5, 1)$	$t = 5$	No (12 s)
folRSS(-5)	$t = 2$	No (5 s)
folRSS(-5)	$t = 3$	No (81 s)
folRSS(-5)	$t = 4$	No (1126 s)
folRSS(-5)	$t = 2$	Yes (38 s) $\star$
folRSS(-2)	$t = 2$	Yes (43 s)

6.3 Time-Bounded Recoverability Experiments

Table 2 summarizes our main experiments for recoverability involving the pedestrian crossing and vehicle following scenarios. Recall that the objective of $\langle safe, safer, t \rangle$-Recoverability is to prove that the safety controller is capable of reducing vehicle risk to safer. For the purpose of illustration, we specified two controllers for the vehicle follower scenarios: a non-aggressive safety controller and an aggressive controller. The latter always activates the emergency brake, i.e., maximum deceleration. Finally, for each scenario, our machinery showed that dt does not skip safe (see Definition 7) in around one second.

Pedestrian Crossing Scenarios: The first observation is that one is not able to establish recoverability with the safety properties used for pedCross. Our machinery returns a counter-example where the vehicle has very low speeds and is very close to the pedestrian crossing with distance around 0.5m. This illustrates the importance of including the bounds to safety properties as done in pedCrBndsas in Eq. 2.

For the scenario pedCrBnds$(3, 2, 1, 0)$, the safety controller always returns to a safer risk situation after 5 ticks, but not 4 ticks. Notice that for pedCrBnds$(5, 2, 1, 0)$ this is no longer the case as it fails also after 5 ticks. This is expected as the "distance" between the properties safe and safer has increased.

Finally, the experiments for pedCrBnds$(gap_{safer}, gap_{safe}, gap_{unsafe}, senerr)$ illustrate how to check the recoverability of safety controllers in the presence of faulty sensors. If we assume faults of 50% or 33% on the pedestrian sensor, the safety controller cannot guarantee that it will always return to a safer risk condition. However, it is able to do so for errors of 12.5% or 10%.

Vehicle Following Scenarios: Our experiments demonstrate that it seems harder to establish recoverability when using time gaps to establish levels of risk. It probably requires a more sophisticated safety controller. On the other hand, when using RSS-based properties, it is possible to establish recoverability, even with small time frames, albeit when assuming normal decelerations of the leader vehicle. It is possible to establish recoverability for scenarios assuming higher values for deceleration, but then a more aggressive controller is required.

7 Related Work

RTAs. Since the first proposal of RTAs, called Simplex Architecture [29], there has been several recent proposals of RTA variants [11,19,24] (to name a few). While there are some differences on their architectures and functions, they all contain a decision module that evaluates the system risk level to decide which controller to use (the safe or the advanced controller). Therefore, all the requirements formalized in this paper, namely, the time sampling adequacy and recoverability are still relevant and applicable. Indeed, we advance the state of the art by providing suitable definitions that are amenable to automated verification.

We have been inspired by [13] that proposes high-level requirements on the recoverability of RTAs based on the level of risk of the system. In particular, the methods for checking adequacy of the sampling and for checking t-recoverability correspond to the safety and liveness requirements of RTA wellformedness. The third condition concerns the minimum time to become unsafe (non-safe) with any controller in charge, needed to ensure that the monitor can switch controllers and the safe controller can react before reaching an unsafe condition. This can be shown using $<_1$-adequacy and continuity of properties in a $<_1$-chain. Summarizing, symbolic rewriting combined with SMT solving provides automated methods to verify correctness of time sampling mechanisms and safety requirements such as those of the RTA framework of [13].

In a similar direction, [19] proposes high-level requirements for the correctness of the decision module based on the definition of what is safe and existence of "permanently safe command sequences", which seems related to our time recoverability property. They do not investigate, however, the effect of the time sampling and the correctness of the decision module.

CPS Verification and Validation. Much of the literature in CPS verification, e.g. [15] to name one, including some of the previous work on RTA [11,19,24], rely on simulation-based methods. These approaches are complementary to the one introduced in this paper. While this paper's approach targets more early phase development by providing proofs that RTA specifications are suitable for all instances of a logical scenario, simulation-based approaches focus on later approaches for validating and testing implementations of RTA systems on particular instances of logical scenarios.

dL, KeYmaera X, and VeriPhy. The KeYmaera X prover [23,33] uses differential dynamic logic (dL) to specify and verify CPS controller designs. It is the starting point of the VeriPhy pipeline [7,8] for producing code from logical specifications. dL specifications and logical scenarios have in common that they are given by terms with constrained variables representing all instances where values of variables satisfy the given constraints. Our methods differ in that dL specifications are not directly executable and therefore, one uses interactive theorem proving methods to verify dl specifications, whereas logical scenarios are executable thus enabling further automation of verification proofs using rewriting modulo SMT.

Formal Definitions of Resilience: Alturki *et al.* [4] propose formal definitions for resilience and show them to be undecidable in general and PSPACE-complete for some cases. While formal connections are left to future work, our definition of timed recoverability seem to specialize their definition so to be applicable for RTA architectures, e.g., considering dt-adequacy.

8   Conclusions

In this paper we present methods to automate proving safety properties using abstract logical scenarios (LS). An LS consists of instances of a pattern satisfying given ODD constraints, together with a two-step transition relation giving the semantics. The first step corresponds to reading sensors, analyzing and deciding on actions (setting control parameters). The second step evolves the system for the sampling time between observations. Towards a formal foundation we introduce a notion of Safety Property Specification for an LS as a set of property (names) with a risk level ordering relation, a unique least (most risky) element, bad, and a satisfaction relation. An adequate sampling time should ensure that nothing important is missed. We define three notions of dt adequacy and show that they are distinct and totally ordered. A system may be allowed to enter a situation that is safe but risky, but a resilient system will recover to an acceptably safe situation. This is formalized in a definition of t-recoverability. A notion of one-period-recovery t-recoverability is defined that is amenable to verification, and shown to be equivalent to t-recoverability for adequate dt using an inductive argument.

Towards automation of proofs, we use symbolic rewriting modulo SMT as the execution and search engine [21]. Algorithms were developed to prove all (infinitely many) instances of an LS satisfy different notions of dt adequacy or t-recoverability (or to provide counter example instances). We report a set of experiments checking dt adequacy and t-recoverability properties for LSs and safety property specifications related to vehicle automation: vehicle following and pedestrian crossing. The experiments show that it possible to find values of dt and safety parameters where adequacy holds and very simple controllers satisfy t-recoverability. They also highlight challengin corner cases.

One direction of future work is to investigate a wider range of case studies to better understand how the different design parameters interact. Another important direction is to develop methods to compose Logical Scenarios and proofs, thus scaling analysis of complex systems.

Acknowledgments. Talcott was partially supported by the U. S. Office of Naval Research under award numbers N00014-15-1-2202 and N00014-20-1-2644, and NRL grant N0017317-1-G002. We also thank the anonymous reviewers for their comments.

References

1. Apollo. An Open Autonomous Driving Platform. https://github.com/ApolloAuto/apollo
2. I. 21448:2019 (2021). https://www.iso.org/standard/70939.html.
3. Allenby, B., Fink, J.: Toward inherently secure and resilient societies. Science **309**(5737), 1034–1036 (2005)
4. Alturki, M.A., Kirigin, T.B., Kanovich, M.I., Nigam, V., Scedrov, A., Talcott, C.L.: On the formalization and computational complexity of resilience problems for cyber-physical systems. In Seidl, H., Liu, Z., Pasareanu, C.S., (eds.) Theoretical Aspects of Computing - ICTAC 2022–19th International Colloquium, Tbilisi, Georgia, 27–29 September 2022, Proceedings, vol. 13572. LNCS, pp 96–113. Springer (2022). https://doi.org/10.1007/978-3-031-17715-6_8
5. Barker, K., Ramirez-Marquez, J.E., Rocco, C.M.: Resilience-based network component importance measures. Reliability Eng. Syst. Safety **117**, 89–97 (2013)
6. Bloomfield, R., et al.: Towards identifying and closing gaps in assurance of autonomous road vehicles-a collection of technical notes part 1. arXiv preprint arXiv:2003.00789 (2020)
7. Bohrer, B., Tan, Y.K., Mitsch, S., Myreen, M.O., Platzer, A.: VeriPhy: Verified controller executables from verified cyber-physical system models. In: Proceedings of 39th ACM SIGPLAN Conference on Programming Language Design and Implementation. ACM New York (2018)
8. Bohrer, B., Tan, Y.K., Mitsch, S., Sogokon, A., Platzer, A.: A formal safety net for waypoint following in ground robots. IEEE Robot. Autom. Lett. (2019). arxiv:1903.15073

9. Bozga, M., Sifakis, J.: Specification and validation of autonomous driving systems: A multilevel semantic framework. CoRR, abs/ arXiv: 1210.90647 (2021)

10. M. Clavel., et al.: All About Maude: A High-Performance Logical Framework, vol. 4350. LNCS. Springer (2007). https://doi.org/10.1007/978-3-540-71999-1

11. Damare, A., Roy, S., Smolka, S.A., Stoller, S.D.: A barrier certificate-based simplex architecture with application to microgrids. In: Dang, T., Stolz, V., (eds.), Runtime Verification - 22nd International Conference, RV 2022, Tbilisi, Georgia, 28–30 September 2022, Proceedings, vol. 13498. LNCS, pp. 105–123. Springer (2022). https://doi.org/10.1007/978-3-031-17196-3_6

12. de Moura, L., Bjørner, N.: Z3: an efficient SMT solver. In: Ramakrishnan, C.R., Rehof, J. (eds.) TACAS 2008. LNCS, vol. 4963, pp. 337–340. Springer, Heidelberg (2008). https://doi.org/10.1007/978-3-540-78800-3_24

13. Desai, A., Ghosh, S., Seshia, S.A., Shankar, N., Tiwari, A.: SOTER: A runtime assurance framework for programming safe robotics systems. In: 49th Annual IEEE/IFIP International Conference on Dependable Systems and Networks, DSN 2019, Portland, OR, USA, 24–27 June 2019, pp. 138–150. IEEE (2019)

14. Fremont, D.J., Dreossi, T., Ghosh, S., Yue, X., Sangiovanni-Vincentelli, A.L., Seshia, S. A.: Scenic: a language for scenario specification and scene generation. In McKinley, K.S., Fisher, K., (eds.) Proceedings of the 40th ACM SIGPLAN Conference on Programming Language Design and Implementation, PLDI 2019, Phoenix, AZ, USA, 22–26 June 2019, pp. 63–78. ACM (2019)

15. Fremont, D.J:. Formal scenario-based testing of autonomous vehicles: From simulation to the real world. In: 23rd IEEE International Conference on Intelligent Transportation Systems, ITSC 2020, Rhodes, Greece, 20–23 September 2020, pp 1–8. IEEE (2020)

16. Jha, S., Rushby, J., Shankar, N.: Model-centered assurance for autonomous systems. In: Casimiro, A., Ortmeier, F., Bitsch, F., Ferreira, P. (eds.) SAFECOMP 2020. LNCS, vol. 12234, pp. 228–243. Springer, Cham (2020). https://doi.org/10.1007/978-3-030-54549-9_15

17. Laprie, J.-C.: From dependability to resilience. In 38th IEEE/IFIP International Conference on dependable systems and networks, pp G8–G9. Citeseer (2008)

18. Luca Mengani, P.D.: Hazard analysis and risk assessment and functional safety concept. Technical report, D2.11 of H2020 project ENSEMBLE (2019). www.platooningensemble.eu

19. Mehmood, U., Sheikhi, S., Bak, S., Smolka, S.A., Stoller, S.D.: The black-box simplex architecture for runtime assurance of autonomous CPS. In: Deshmukh, J.V., Havelund, K., Perez, I., (eds.) NASA Formal Methods - 14th International Symposium, NFM 2022, Pasadena, CA, USA, 24–27 May 2022, Proceedings, vol. 13260. LNCS, pp. 231–250. Springer (2022). https://doi.org/10.1007/978-3-031-06773-0_12

20. Menzel, T., Bagschik, G., Maurer, M.: Scenarios for development, test and validation of automated vehicles. In: 2018 IEEE Intelligent Vehicles Symposium, IV 2018, Changshu, Suzhou, China, 26–30 June 2018, pp. 1821–1827. IEEE (2018)

21. Nigam, V., Talcott, C.: Automating safety proofs about cyber-physical systems using rewriting modulo smt. In: Bae, K., (ed.), 14th International Workshop on Rewriting Logic and its Applications, vol. 13252. LNCS, pp. 212–229. Springer (2022). https://doi.org/10.1007/978-3-031-12441-9_11

22. Nigam, V., Talcott, C.: Technical-report: Automating recoverability proofs for cyber-physical systems with runtime assurance architectures (2023)

23. Quesel, J.-D., Mitsch, S., Loos, S., Aréchiga, N., Platzer, A.: How to model and prove hybrid systems with KeYmaera: a tutorial on safety. Int. J. Softw. Tools Technol. Trans. **18**, 67–91 (2016)

24. Ramakrishna, S., Hartsell, C., Burruss, M.P., Karsai, G., Dubey, A.: Dynamic-weighted simplex strategy for learning enabled cyber physical systems. J. Syst. Archit. **111**, 101760 (2020)

25. Riedmaier, S., Ponn, T., Ludwig, D., Schick, B., Diermeyer, F.: Survey on scenario-based safety assessment of automated vehicles. IEEE Access **8**, 87456–87477 (2020)
26. Rocha, C., Meseguer, J., Muñoz, C.: Rewriting modulo SMT and open system analysis. J. Logical Algebraic Meth. Program., 269–297 (2017)
27. Ross, R., Pillitteri, V., Graubart, R., Bodeau, D., McQuaid, R.: Developing cyber resilient systems: a systems security engineering approach. Technical report, National Institute of Standards and Technology (2019)
28. Rubio, R.: Maude as a library: An efficient all-purpose programming interface. In: Bae, K. (ed.), Rewriting Logic and Its Applications - 14th International Workshop, vol. 13252. LNCS, pp. 274–294. Springer (2022). https://doi.org/10.1007/978-3-031-12441-9_14
29. Seto, D., Krogh, B., Sha, L., Chutinan, A.: The simplex architecture for safe online control system upgrades. In: Proceedings of the 1998 American Control Conference. ACC (IEEE Cat. No.98CH36207), vol. 6, pp. 3504–3508 (1998)
30. Sha, L.: Using simplicity to control complexity. IEEE Softw. **18**(4), 20–28 (2001)
31. Shalev-Shwartz, S., Shammah, S., Shashua, A.: On a formal model of safe and scalable self-driving cars. CoRR, abs/ arXiv: 1708.06374 (2017)
32. Talcott, C., Nigam, V., Arbab, F., Kappé, T.: Formal specification and analysis of robust adaptive distributed cyber-physical systems. In: Bernardo, M., De Nicola, R., Hillston, J. (eds.) SFM 2016. LNCS, vol. 9700, pp. 1–35. Springer, Cham (2016). https://doi.org/10.1007/978-3-319-34096-8_1
33. TKX team, KeYmaera X: An aXiomatic tactical theorem prover for hybrid systems (2022). (Accessed 22 Sept 2022)
34. Westhofen, L., et al.: Criticality metrics for automated driving: A review and suitability analysis of the state of the art. Archives of Computational Methods in Engineering, abs/ arXiv: 2108.02403 (2022)

Verified Transformation of Continuation-Passing Style into Static Single Assignment Form

Siyu Liu[iD] and Yuting Wang$^{(\boxtimes)}$[iD]

John Hopcroft Center for Computer Science,
School of Electronic Information and Electrical Engineering,
Shanghai Jiao Tong University, Shanghai, 200240, China
{liu_siyu,yuting.wang}@sjtu.edu.cn

Abstract. Static Single Assignment form (SSA) is widely adopted as
an intermediate representation (IR) of production compilers as it enables
aggressive compiler optimizations based on data-flow analysis. We are
concerned with developing verified compilers for functional programming
languages that exploit the benefits of SSA. The most obvious approach
to achieving our goal is to verify the transformation from Continuation-
Passing Style (CPS)—an intermediate representation widely adopted by
both production and verified functional compilers—to SSA. In this paper,
we show how to verify the translation from CPS to SSA and how to apply
the verified translation towards building verified functional compilers.
Concretely, we develop and verify a transformation algorithm from PCF
programs in CPS to SSA. By extending the transformation with a verified
CPS transformation from PCF, we get a verified compilation chain from
PCF to SSA. We have also connected this chain with LLVM at the target
level to provide a foundation for building more sophisticated verified
functional compilers targeting SSA IRs.

1 Introduction

Formal verification has been shown highly effective for ensuring the correctness
of compilers. One notable example is the verified C compiler CompCert [16]. It
compiles a significant subset of C into assembly code on multiple architectures
(including PowerPC, ARM, X86, and RISC-V). The correctness of its compilation (i.e., the target assembly code preserves the semantics of source C programs)
is formally verified in the Coq proof assistant.

Continuation-Passing Style (CPS) is an intermediate representation (IR) that
makes explicit the control flow of functional programs and facilities control-flow
analysis and optimizations. It is widely adopted in both production and verified compilers for functional programming languages [4,7,18,19,23]. However,
it means that verified functional compilers cannot be directly supported by
the mainstream compiler infrastructures (e.g., LLVM and GCC) which adopt
Static Single Assignment form (SSA) as their IR. SSA becomes prevalent in
compiler infrastructures as it allows for convenient and accurate data-flow analysis (DFA) by enforcing that every variable could be assigned only once, which

C. David and M. Sun (Eds.): TASE 2023, LNCS 13931, pp. 20–37, 2023.
https://doi.org/10.1007/978-3-031-35257-7_2

in turn enables aggressive optimizations based on DFA. Many popular imperative programming languages (e.g. Rust [2] and Swift [25]) use these compiler infrastructures as their backends to generate code with great performance [15]. Production functional compilers are starting to adopt SSA as well. For example, the newest version of SML-New Jersey has switched from a CPS middle-end to LLVM [10].

In this paper, we investigate the construction of verified compilers for functional programming languages with SSA IRs. In particular, we formalize and verify the transformation from CPS to SSA so as to connect the traditional verified functional compilers targeting CPS with verified backends working on SSA IRs. Although researchers have explored the correspondence between CPS and SSA programs [1,14] and have designed transformations from CPS to SSA [10,12], it is still not clear how to formally verify such transformations.

We summarize our contributions below:[1]

- Our primary contribution is the design and verification of a transformation from CPS to SSA. The source language is the representative functional language PCF (Programming Computable Functions) [21] in CPS. The target language is a simplified version of LLVM IR. Both are given small-step operational semantics. The transformation is designed based on the connection between CPS and SSA [1,12]. It is verified via simulation between source and target semantics. To the best of our knowledge, this is the first verified transformation from CPS functional programs to SSA.
- We have also built a prototype compiler for PCF. It is partially verified and may serve as a basis for verified functional compilers in the future. More specifically, we have designed and verified a CPS transformation for PCF. It is connected to the verified CPS-to-SSA transformation. The SSA IR is then transformed to LLVM IR via the abstract syntax provided by Vellvm—a verified LLVM infrastructure [24].

In the rest of the paper, we first introduce necessary background in Sect. 2. We then discuss the verified transformation of CPS to SSA in Sect. 3. We present the prototype compiler and an evaluation of our work in Sect. 4. We discuss the related work in Sect. 5 and finally conclude in Sect. 6.

2 Background

2.1 Continuation-Passing Style and Static Single Assignment

The defining characteristic of Continuation-Passing Style is the explicit representation of control flow via continuations. A continuation represents the remaining computation after the current execution point. It takes the form of a function with the result of the current execution as its input. A regular function converted into CPS has a continuation as an additional parameter. When a function call

---

[1] The complete artifact in Coq is at https://doi.org/10.5281/zenodo.7882331.

returns, the continuation parameter is called with the return value (i.e., returning the result). For example, Fig. 1 shows a program in the direct style and in CPS. In Fig. 1b, when the function finishes its execution with the result bound to z, $(k\,z)$ 'returns' the result and performs the remaining computation in the continuation k. Note that, in CPS programs every control point is explicitly named, which facilitates control-flow analysis and compiler optimizations.

$$\textbf{function } h(x,y) = \qquad\qquad \textbf{function } h(x,y,k) = \textbf{let } x_1 = x * x \textbf{ in}$$

$$(x * x) \,+\, (y * y) \qquad\qquad \textbf{let } y_1 = y * y \textbf{ in } (\textbf{let } z = x_1 + y_1 \textbf{ in } (k\,z))$$

(a) Direct Style   (b) CPS

Fig. 1. A Functional Program and its CPS Form

Static Single Assignment is widely used in compiler infrastructures. In SSA, each variable is assigned only once, which is similar to name binding in functional languages [14]. To describe multiple assignments (definitions) to the same variable, a variable is divided into different versions so that each assignment gets its own version of the variable. Special statements called ϕ-nodes are inserted at join points for variables to generate new definitions. As an example, Fig. 2 depicts a control-flow diagram in SSA. The predecessor of b_2 may be b_1 or b_2 itself. Therefore, the variable y is given different names in b_1 and b_2. The ϕ-node at the beginning of b_2 merges y_1 and y_3 into a new variable y_2. The value of y_2 is either from y_1 or y_3 according to the control flow during execution. With unique definitions of variables, SSA enables efficient implementation of compiler optimization algorithms based on data-flow analysis [12].

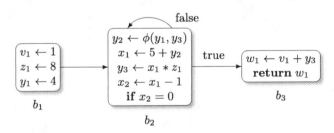

Fig. 2. A Control Flow Diagram in SSA

According to Appel et al. [1], SSA can also be viewed as a functional language, despite their differences in syntactic forms. Beringer [14] presents a functional representation of SSA that relates program constructs in SSA to that of functional programs. For example, let bindings in functional languages are similar to assignments in SSA, and the lexical scopes of bound variables correspond to dominating regions in SSA. Although continuation arguments are not explicitly visible in the control flow graph in SSA, they correspond to locations for storing return addresses upon function calls. Kelsey introduces an approach to converting CPS programs to SSA [12]. It involves labeling λ-binders in CPS programs to distinguish between procedures, jumps, and continuations.

2.2 Compiler Verification via Simulation

We adopt CompCert's simulation-based techniques for our verification of transformations. CompCert is the state-of-the-art verified C compiler. In its framework, compiler correctness is defined as semantics preservation, meaning that target programs behave as prescribed by source programs. Semantics preservation is proved by establishing backward simulation for safe source programs. However, backward simulation is hard to prove directly. Instead, it is obtained by establishing forward simulation from safe source programs to deterministic target language which implies safe backward simulation. Moreover, since forward simulation is transitively composable, it is possible to prove forward simulation for individual compiler passes and compose the results to derive forward simulation for the whole compiler.

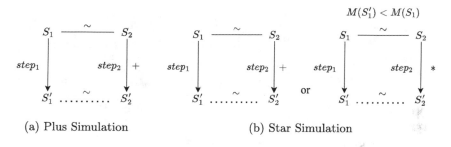

(a) Plus Simulation   (b) Star Simulation

Fig. 3. Different Simulation Diagrams

To prove forward simulation for a compiler pass translating the source language L_1 into target language L_2, the key is to establish an invariant $S_1 \sim S_2$ between the program states of L_1 and L_2 and to show it holds throughout the execution of source and target programs. Following the approach of CompCert, we first need to define the small-step operational semantics for L_1 and L_2. Given any source program P_1 and target program P_2, we then prove that the initial states of P_1 and P_2 satisfy the invariant $\sim$. Finally, we prove that the internal executions are related by $\sim$. That is, assuming $S_1 \sim S_2$ and the source program transits from S_1 to S_1' in one step, then the target program should transit from S_2 to S_2' and $S_1' \sim S_2'$ should be established after the transition. Depending on the transition from S_2 to S_2', there are the following kinds of simulation diagrams:

- Lock-step simulation denotes that S_2 transits to S_2' in one step.
- Plus simulation (Fig. 3a) denotes that S_2 transits to S_2' in one or more steps.
- Star simulation (Fig. 3b) denotes that S_2 transits to S_2' in zero or more steps.
  In this case, it is possible that the source execution takes an infinite number of steps and the target one stays in S_2. To rule out such "infinite stuttering", one need to define a measure function M for source states that is strictly decreasing as source execution goes on. With this restriction, diverging behaviors are also preserved by simulation.

3 Verified Transformation of CPS into SSA

3.1 Source Language: PCF in Continuation-Passing Style

Programming Computable Functions (PCF) is a widely studied functional language [21]. In this section, we define the syntax and small-step operational semantics of PCF in the direct style and in CPS. We also show how to transform the standard PCF to CPS and how to verify this transformation.

Syntax and Semantics PCF presented in this paper is adopted from Dowek and Lévy [9]. It includes the basic λ-calculus, arithmetic, conditional expressions and fixed points. The syntax of PCF and its CPS form is defined in Fig. 4.

$$op := +\ |\ -\ |\ \times\ |\ \div \qquad\qquad v := i\ |\ x$$

$$t := i\ |\ x\ |\ t_1\ t_2\ |\ \textbf{ifz}\ t_1\ t_2\ t_3 \qquad t := \textbf{letval}\ x = v\ \textbf{in}\ t\ |\ k\ v\ |\ \textbf{ifz}\ v\ t_1\ t_2$$

$$|\ op\ t_1\ t_2 \qquad\qquad\qquad\qquad |\ f\ k\ v\ |\ \textbf{letop}\ x = op\ x_1\ x_2\ \textbf{in}\ t$$

$$|\ \textbf{let}\ x = t_1\ \textbf{in}\ t_2 \qquad\qquad\quad |\ \textbf{letcont}\ k\ x = t_1\ \textbf{in}\ t_2$$

$$|\ \textbf{fix}\ f\ x\ t \qquad\qquad\qquad\qquad |\ \textbf{letfun}\ f\ k\ x = t_1\ \textbf{in}\ t_2$$

(a) PCF in the Direct Style   (b) PCF in CPS

Fig. 4. Syntax of PCF

The most basic PCF terms are natural numbers i and variables x. An application is represented as $t_1\ t_2$. We use $\textbf{let}\ x = t_1\ \textbf{in}\ t_2$ to bind variable x in t_2 to the value of t_1. A conditional expression in PCF is written as $\textbf{ifz}\ t_1\ t_2\ t_3$. If the value of t_1 is 0, the whole term is reduced to t_2. Otherwise, it is reduced to t_3. A fixed point in PCF is $\textbf{fix}\ f\ x\ t$ where f may occur in t. As an example, the factorial of 2 is defined in Fig. 5a using PCF in the direct style.

PCF in CPS follows the style proposed by Kennedy [13]. Value v in a CPS term can be introduced by $\textbf{letval}\ x = v\ \textbf{in}\ t$. $k\ v$ applies the continuation k to the argument v. $f\ k\ v$ applies the function f to the argument v and passes the continuation k to accept the result of this call. The statement $\textbf{letop}\ x = op\ x_1\ x_2\ \textbf{in}\ t$ binds x in term t to the result of a binary operation. A continuation k is introduced by $\textbf{letcont}\ k\ x = t_1\ \textbf{in}\ t_2$ where t_1 is the body of continuation k. $\textbf{letfun}\ f\ k\ x = t_1\ \textbf{in}\ t_2$ constructs a function f whose return continuation is k. Figure 5b depicts the factorial of 2 in CPS, in which every computation step is made explicit. In this figure, the top-level continuation k_{init} accepts the result of the whole program and is bound by its context.

We give small-step operational semantics to languages introduced in this paper. A judgement $S \rightarrow S'$ denotes that the program state S' can be reached from the original state S by executing one step. In PCF, the transitions between the program states are represented as $(t_{pcf}, ctx) \rightarrow (t'_{pcf}, ctx')$. t_{pcf} is a PCF term representing the expression under evaluation. ctx is a context containing a

$$\text{letfun } fact \ k \ x = (\textbf{ifz } x \ (\textbf{letval } x_1 = 1 \text{ in } (k \ x_1))$$

$$(\textbf{fix } fact \ x$$
$$\textbf{ifz } x \ 1$$
$$(x * (fact \ (x - 1))))$$
$$2$$

(a) PCF

$$(\textbf{letval } x_2 = 1 \text{ in } (\textbf{letop } x_4 = x - x_2 \text{ in}$$
$$\textbf{letcont } k_1 \ z = (\textbf{letop } x_3 = x * z \text{ in } (k \ x_3))$$
$$\text{in } fact \ k_1 \ x_4))) \text{ in}$$
$$(\textbf{letval } x_5 = 2 \text{ in } (\textbf{letcont } k_2 \ y = k_{init} \ y \text{ in } (fact \ k_2 \ x_5)))$$

(b) PCF in CPS

Fig. 5. Computing Factorials in PCF

$$\frac{t_{pcf} = (\textbf{fix } f \ x \ t_1) \ t_2}{(t_{pcf}, \ ctx) \to (t_2, \ ctx_{seq} \ (\textbf{fix } f \ x \ t_1) \ ctx)} \qquad \frac{t_2 \text{ is a value} \quad t_3 = \textbf{fix } f \ x \ t_1}{(t_2, \ ctx_{seq} \ t_3 \ ctx) \to (t_1[t_2/x, t_3/f], \ ctx)}$$

Fig. 6. Selected Rules of Operational Semantics for PCF

$$\frac{t_{cps} = (\textbf{letval } x = v \text{ in } t)}{(t_{cps}, \ loc_{cps}) \to (t[v/x], \ loc_{cps})} \qquad \frac{t_{cps} = (\textbf{letop } x = op \ v_1 \ v_2 \text{ in } t)}{(t_{cps}, \ loc_{cps}) \to (t[(\textbf{eval}_{op} \ op \ v_1 \ v_2)/x], \ loc_{cps})}$$

$$\frac{t_{cps} = (\textbf{ifz } 0 \ t_1 \ t_2)}{(t_{cps}, \ loc_{cps}) \to (t_1, \ loc_{cps})} \qquad \frac{t_{cps} = (\textbf{letfun } f \ k \ x = t_1 \text{ in } t_2)}{(t_{cps}, \ loc_{cps}) \to (t_2, \ loc_{cps} \ [f \mapsto t_{cps}])}$$

$$\frac{t_{cps} = (\textbf{ifz } n \ t_1 \ t_2) \quad n \neq 0}{(t_{cps}, \ loc_{cps}) \to (t_2, \ loc_{cps})} \qquad \frac{loc_{cps} \ f = (\textbf{letfun } f \ k \ x = t_1 \text{ in } t_2)}{(f \ k_0 \ x_0, \ loc_{cps}) \to (t_1[x_0/x, k_0/k], \ loc_{cps})}$$

$$\frac{loc_{cps} \ k = (\textbf{letcont } k \ x = t_1 \text{ in } t_2)}{(k \ v, \ loc_{cps}) \to (t_1[v/x], \ loc_{cps})} \qquad \frac{t_{cps} = (\textbf{letcont } k \ x = t_1 \text{ in } t_2)}{(t_{cps}, \ loc_{cps}) \to (t_2, \ loc_{cps} \ [k \mapsto t_{cps}])}$$

Fig. 7. Rules of Operational Semantics for PCF in CPS

stack of terms for advancing the execution once the evaluation of t_{pcf} finishes. When $ctx = ctx_{stop}$, the execution ends after t_{pcf} evaluates to a value. Otherwise, $ctx = ctx_{seq} \ t \ ctx$, indicating that the value of t_{pcf} will be used by the following term t to advance the execution. After one step, the new program state contains an updated PCF term t'_{pcf} and context ctx'. Selected transition rules are shown in Fig. 6. When applying a fixed point to a term t_2, t_2 is evaluated first and the fix point is pushed into the context. When the value of t_2 is ready, it is substituted into the fixed point for the parameter x and the evaluation continues.

The small-step operational semantics for PCF in CPS is represented as rules for deriving judgements of the form $(t_{cps}, loc_{cps}) \to (t'_{cps}, loc'_{cps})$. Similarly, t_{cps} is a CPS term under evaluation. loc_{cps} is a mapping from continuation variables or function names to terms that introduce them. t'_{cps} and loc'_{cps} are the updated CPS term and mapping, respectively. Transition rules of the small-step semantics of PCF in CPS are shown in Fig. 7. For a term $(\textbf{letcont } k \ x = t_1 \text{ in } l_2)$, we first evaluate t_2 and update loc_{cps} with the mapping from continuation k to the term. $loc_{cps} \ [k \mapsto t_{cps}]$ denotes this updating operation. When the continuation k is applied to a value v (represented by $k \ v$), $k \ v$ is reduced by substituting v into t_1 for x. Reduction of **letfun** terms is similar.

Algorithm 1: CPS Transformation

$\mathcal{F}_{proc}$:   **Input** : t_{pcf} **Output** : t_{cps}
$\mathcal{F}_{proc}(t_{pcf}) := \mathcal{F}(t_{pcf}, [k_{init}], \lambda x.(k_{init}\ x))$

$\mathcal{F}$:   **Input** : t_{pcf}, l_v, κ **Output** : t_{cps}
(1). $\mathcal{F}(i, l_v, \kappa) :=$ **letval** $x = i$ **in** $\kappa(x)$
(2). $\mathcal{F}(x, l_v, \kappa) := \kappa(x)$
(3). $\mathcal{F}(t_1\ t_2, l_v, \kappa) := \mathcal{F}(t_1, l'_v, \lambda x.\mathcal{F}(t_2, l'_v, \lambda y.(\textbf{letcont}\ k\ z = \kappa(z)\ \textbf{in}\ (x\ k\ y))))$
    where $l'_v = l_v +\!\!\!+\ [k; x; y; z]$
(4). $\mathcal{F}(\textbf{ifz}\ t_1\ t_2\ t_3, l_v, \kappa) := \mathcal{F}(t_1, l'_v, \lambda x.(\textbf{ifz}\ x\ \mathcal{F}(t_2, l'_v, \kappa)\ \mathcal{F}(t_3, l'_v, \kappa)))$
    where $l'_v = l_v +\!\!\!+\ [x]$
(5). $\mathcal{F}(op\ t_1\ t_2, l_v, \kappa) := \mathcal{F}(t_1, l'_v, \lambda x.\mathcal{F}(t_2, l'_v, \lambda y.(\textbf{letop}\ z = op\ x\ y\ \textbf{in}\ \kappa(z))))$
    where $l'_v = l_v +\!\!\!+\ [x; y; z]$
(6). $\mathcal{F}(\textbf{let}\ x = t_1\ \textbf{in}\ t_2, l_v, \kappa) := \mathcal{F}(t_1, l_v, \lambda x.\mathcal{F}(t_2, l_v, \kappa))$
(7). $\mathcal{F}(\textbf{fix}\ f\ x\ t, l_v, \kappa) :=$ **letfun** $f\ k\ x = \mathcal{F}(t, l'_v, \lambda y.(k\ y))$ **in** $\kappa(f)$
    where $l'_v = l_v +\!\!\!+\ [k; y]$

Fig. 8. CPS Transformation Algorithm

CPS Transformation. We now introduce the transformation of PCF terms into CPS terms which follows the general pattern for CPS transformations [6,20]. It is described by the function $\mathcal{F}_{proc}$ in Fig. 8 which makes use of a generalized form $\mathcal{F}$. The input and output of $\mathcal{F}$ are represented as (t_{pcf}, l_v, κ) and t_{cps}, respectively. t_{pcf} is the PCF term to be converted. κ takes the form $\lambda x.t'_{cps}$ and denotes the CPS term (continuation) to be applied after the current term is reduced to a value. t_{cps} is the generated CPS term. We use explicit names for variables in our algorithms. l_v is a list of variables that are already used. The newly generated names should not collide with those in l_v. For example, the new variables k, x, y, z resulting from transforming $t_1\ t_2$ by using Rule (3) in Fig. 8 must be fresh with respect to l_v. They are added to l_v after the transformation. To simplify the transformation rules, we do not specify the operations for generating new variables using l_v which basically represent variables as positive numbers and choose unused positive numbers for new variables.

3.2   Target Language: SSA in the Style of LLVM IR

We define the syntax and semantics of the target SSA language, which is a simplified version of LLVM IR with its most essential program constructs.

$$l := string \quad v := i \mid x \qquad r := \textbf{ret}\ v \mid \textbf{br}_{uc}\ l \mid \textbf{br}_c\ v\ l_1\ l_2$$
$$\phi_a := (l,\ v) \quad \phi := x = \overline{\phi_a} \qquad c := v \mid op\ v_1\ v_2 \mid \textbf{icmp}\ v_1\ v_2 \mid \textbf{call}\ x\ v$$
$$a := x = c; \quad b := l :\ \overline{\phi}\ \overline{a}\ r \quad f := \textbf{define}\ l_1(l_2)\ \overline{b} \qquad t := \overline{f}$$

Fig. 9. Syntax of the SSA Target Language

Syntax and Semantics. The syntax of our SSA language is defined in Fig. 9. The top-level translation unit t consists of a sequence of function definitions. A function f contains the function name l_1, the parameter l_2 and a list of basic blocks $\bar{b}$. A block b consists of block label l, a sequence of ϕ-nodes, a sequence of instructions i and one terminating instruction (terminator) r. An instruction a assigns the value of a command c to a variable x. Commands include binary operations, commands for comparing values, and function calls. Terminators include **ret** and **br** for representing jumping between functions and blocks, respectively. As an example, the factorial of 2 in SSA is shown in Fig. 10.

> **define** $fact\ (x)$
>
> b_1 : $b_0 = $ **icmp** $x\ 0$; **br$_c$** b_0 t_0 f_0;
>
> t_0 : $x_1 = 1$; $r_{t0} = x_1$; **ret** r_{t0};
>
> f_0 : $x_2 = 1$; $x_4 = x - x_2$; $z = $ **call** $fact\ x_4$; **br$_{uc}$** k_1;
>
> k_1 : $x_3 = x * z$; $r_{k1} = x_3$; **ret** r_{k1};
>
> **define** $main\ ()$
>
> b_1 : $x_5 = 2$; $y = $ **call** $fact\ x_5$; **br$_{uc}$** k_2;
>
> k_2 : $r_{k2} = y$; **ret** r_{k2};

Fig. 10. Computing Factorials in SSA

The small-step operational semantics for SSA is represented as rules for deriving judgments of the form $(pc, ppc, loc_{ssa}, s_{ssa}) \rightarrow (pc', ppc', loc'_{ssa}, s'_{ssa})$. pc is a program counter used to locate the current instruction. It has 3 elements (l_f, l_b, n): l_f is the function label, l_b is the block label, and n represents the index of an instruction in a block. **code**$_{at}$ pc fetches the instruction at pc. ppc stores the program counter before the last jump from the preceding block in order to evaluate ϕ-nodes. loc_{ssa} is a mapping of variables to their values. We keep the program counter of the instruction that calls the current function in a stack s_{ssa} so that we can go back to this location when the current function returns.

The most important rules for the SSA operational semantics are shown in Fig. 11. The first rule describes transitions for function calls. The control flow jumps to the beginning of the function f and the return address is stored in s_{ssa}. **arg** f gets the parameters of function f and $loc_{ssa}\ [x \mapsto v_0]$ adds the mapping from x to v_0 to loc_{ssa}. As an example, in Fig. 10, when the main function calls $fact$ the state transits from $((main, b_1, 1), (main, empty, 1), loc_{ssa}, s_{ssa})$ to $((fact, b_1, 0), (main, b_1, 1), loc_{ssa}\ [x \mapsto 2], \textbf{push}\ s_{ssa}\ (main, b_1, 1))$ following the first rule in Fig. 11. The second rule defines the transition that occurs when the current function returns a value to the calling function. It retrieves the return location npc from the top of s_{ssa} and jumps back to it. We elide a discussion of the remaining rules which follow a similar pattern.

$$\frac{\textbf{code}_{at}\ pc\ =\ (y = \textbf{call}\ f\ v_0)\quad \textbf{arg}\ f = x}{(pc,\ ppc,\ loc_{ssa},\ s_{ssa}) \to ((f, b_1, 0),\ pc,\ loc_{ssa}\,[x \mapsto v_0],\ \textbf{push}\ s_{ssa}\ pc)}$$

$$\frac{\textbf{code}_{at}\ pc\ =\ (\textbf{ret}\ v)\quad pc.l_f \neq main\quad npc = \textbf{top}\ s_{ssa}\qquad \textbf{code}_{at}\ npc\ =\ (x = \textbf{call}\ f\ v_0)}{(pc,\ ppc,\ loc_{ssa},\ s_{ssa}) \to (npc+1,\ pc,\ loc_{ssa}\,[x \mapsto v],\ \textbf{pop}\ s_{ssa})}$$

$$\frac{\textbf{code}_{at}\ pc\ =\ (x = \overline{\phi_a})\quad n\ =\ \textbf{eval}_\phi\ \overline{\phi_a}\ ppc}{(pc,\ ppc,\ loc_{ssa},\ s_{ssa}) \to (pc+1,\ ppc,\ loc_{ssa}\,[x \mapsto n],\ s_{ssa})}$$

$$\frac{\textbf{code}_{at}\ pc\ =\ (x = op\ v_1\ v_2)\quad n\ =\ \textbf{eval}_{exp}\ loc_{ssa}\ op\ v_1\ v_2}{(pc,\ ppc,\ loc_{ssa},\ s_{ssa}) \to (pc+1,\ ppc,\ loc_{ssa}\,[x \mapsto n],\ s_{ssa})}$$

$$\frac{\textbf{code}_{at}\ pc\ =\ (x = \textbf{icmp}\ v_1\ v_2)\quad \textbf{if}\ (\textbf{equal}_{val}\ loc_{ssa}\ v_1\ v_2)\ n = 1\ \textbf{else}\ n = 0}{(pc,\ ppc,\ loc_{ssa},\ s_{ssa}) \to (pc+1,\ ppc,\ loc_{ssa}\,[x \mapsto n],\ s_{ssa})}$$

$$\frac{\textbf{code}_{at}\ pc\ =\ (\textbf{br}_{\textbf{uc}}\ l)}{(pc,\ ppc,\ loc_{ssa},\ s_{ssa}) \to ((pc.l_f, l, 0),\ pc,\ loc_{ssa},\ s_{ssa})}$$

$$\frac{\textbf{code}_{at}\ pc\ =\ (\textbf{br}_{\textbf{c}}\ v\ l_1\ l_2)\quad \textbf{if}\ (\textbf{equal}_{val}\ loc_{ssa}\ v\ 0)\ l_n = l_1\ \textbf{else}\ l_n = l_2}{(pc,\ ppc,\ loc_{ssa},\ s_{ssa}) \to ((pc.l_f, l_n, 0),\ pc,\ loc_{ssa},\ s_{ssa})}$$

Fig. 11. Rules of Operational Semantics for SSA

Functions with Free Variables. An important difference between our SSA language and the LLVM IR is that we allow functions to contain free variables that are defined in other functions since loc_{ssa} is a global mapping. This is to accommodate the fact the our source language has higher-order functions with free variables. In a typical compiler for functional languages, a transformation known as *closure conversion* is applied to CPS terms to convert open functions into closed ones which are in turn hoisted to the top level. The formal verification of closure conversion has been investigated extensively [17,23]. For simplicity, we do not include closure conversion into our compilation chain. Instead, we take the view that our SSA language supports both closed and open functions and focus on the essence of CPS to SSA transformation, which we discuss below.

3.3 Transformation Algorithm

We present the transformation algorithm for converting PCF programs in CPS form to SSA programs. In essence, it is a recursive function that takes a source CPS program and an empty SSA program, puts new components (e.g. basic blocks, instructions) into the SSA program, and updates the parameters as it recursively translates the CPS term. Once the translation of the entire CPS program is finished, the resulting SSA program is the target program.

The function $\mathcal{G}_{proc}$ in Fig. 12 translates a CPS term to an SSA top-level translation unit t_{ssa} with a main function. It makes use of function $\mathcal{G}$ which takes $(t_{cps}, t_{ssa}, pc, n, loc)$ as input and (t'_{ssa}, n', loc') as output. t_{cps} is the CPS term to be converted and t_{ssa} is the SSA program already generated. pc represents the current program counter at which we insert new SSA code. To generate new block labels for the branches of conditional statements in SSA, we keep track of the

---

Algorithm 2: CPS→SSA Transformation

$\mathcal{G}_{proc}$:   **Input** : t_{cps} **Output** : t_{ssa}
$\mathcal{G}_{proc}(t_{cps}) := t_{ssa}$
    where $(t_{ssa}, n, loc) = \mathcal{G}(t_{cps}, \mathbf{app}_b \; nil \; main, (main, b_1, 0), 0, loc_{empty})$

$\mathcal{G}$:   **Input** : $t_{cps}, t_{ssa}, pc, n, loc$ **Output** : t'_{ssa}, n', loc'
(1). $\mathcal{G}(\mathbf{letval} \; x = v \; \mathbf{in} \; t, t_{ssa}, pc, n, loc) :=$
        $\mathcal{G}(t, \mathbf{app}_i \; t_{ssa} \; pc \; [x = v;], pc + 1, n, loc)$
(2). $\mathcal{G}(\mathbf{letop} \; x = op \; x_1 \; x_2 \; \mathbf{in} \; t, t_{ssa}, pc, n, loc) :=$
        $\mathcal{G}(t, \mathbf{app}_i \; t_{ssa} \; pc \; [x = op \; x_1 \; x_2;], pc + 1, n, loc)$
(3). $\mathcal{G}(\mathbf{letfun} \; f \; k \; x = t_1 \; \mathbf{in} \; t_2, t_{ssa}, pc, n, loc) := \mathcal{G}(t_2, t', pc, n', loc')$
        where $(t', n', loc') = \mathcal{G}(t_1, \mathbf{app}_p \; t_{ssa} \; f, (f, b_1, 0), 0, loc \; (k \mapsto t_{cps}))$
(4). $\mathcal{G}(\mathbf{letcont} \; k \; x = t_1 \; \mathbf{in} \; t_2, pc, n, loc) :=$
        $\mathcal{G}(t_1, \mathbf{app}_b \; t' \; pc \; k, (pc.l_f, k, 0), n', loc')$
        where $(t', n', loc') = \mathcal{G}(t_2, t_{ssa}, pc, n, loc \; (k \mapsto t_{cps}))$
(5). $\mathcal{G}(\mathbf{ifz} \; x \; t_1 \; t_2, pc, n, loc) := \mathcal{G}(t_2, \mathbf{app}_b \; t' \; pc \; f_n, (pc.l_f, f_n, 0), n', loc')$
        where $t_{br} = \mathbf{app}_i \; t_{ssa} \; pc \; [b_n = \mathbf{icmp} \; x \; 0; \; \mathbf{br_c} \; b_n \; t_n \; f_n;]$
        and $(t', n', loc') = \mathcal{G}(t_1, \mathbf{app}_b \; t_{br} \; pc \; t_n, (pc.l_f, t_n, 0), n + 1, loc)$
(6). $\mathcal{G}(k \; x, t_{ssa}, pc, n, loc) :=$
    $\begin{cases} (\mathbf{app}_i \; t_{ssa} \; pc \; [r_b = x; \; \mathbf{ret} \; r_b;], n, loc) \\ \qquad \textbf{when} \; loc \; k := \mathbf{letfun} \; f \; k \; x_0 = t_1 \; \mathbf{in} \; t_2 \; \text{or} \; k = k_{init} \\ (\mathbf{app}_i \; t_{ssa} \; pc \; [x_0 = x; \; \mathbf{br_{uc}} \; k;], n, loc) \\ \qquad \textbf{when} \; loc \; k := \mathbf{letcont} \; k \; x_0 = t_1 \; \mathbf{in} \; t_2 \end{cases}$
(7). $\mathcal{G}(f \; k \; x, t_{ssa}, pc, n, loc) :=$
    $\begin{cases} (\mathbf{app}_i \; t_{ssa} \; pc \; [r_b = \mathbf{call} \; f \; x; \; \mathbf{ret} \; r_b;], n, loc) \\ \qquad \textbf{when} \; loc \; k := \mathbf{letfun} \; f \; k \; x_0 = t_1 \; \mathbf{in} \; l_2 \; \text{or} \; k = k_{init} \\ (\mathbf{app}_i \; t_{ssa} \; pc \; [x_0 = \mathbf{call} \; f \; x; \; \mathbf{br_{uc}} \; k;], n, loc) \\ \qquad \textbf{when} \; loc \; k := \mathbf{letcont} \; k \; x_0 = t_1 \; \mathbf{in} \; t_2 \end{cases}$

Fig. 12. CPS-to-SSA Transformation Algorithm

number of **ifz** terms encountered in the CPS program with the parameter n. loc is the mapping from continuation variables to CPS terms that define them. We also use it to determine whether k is a local continuation (i.e., continuation variable introduced by **letcont**) or a return continuation (i.e., continuation variable of a function). Note that we store the entire **letcont** or **letfun** term in loc_{cps} to represent local and return continuations, although we do not need their bodies. This is to avoid introducing intermediate terms for representing local and return continuations. The function returns the updated SSA program t'_{ssa}, the new number n' and the updated mapping loc'. In the initial state, t_{ssa} is an empty main function, pc points to the beginning of the main function, n is 0 and loc is empty. **app** operations in Fig. 12 represent appending new components to an SSA program at the location of pc. For instance, $(\mathbf{app}_i \; t_{ssa} \; pc \; [x = v;])$ in Rule (1) means inserting an instruction $[x = v;]$ to the location pc in t_{ssa}.

We demonstrate how the algorithm works with the example of transforming factorial of 2 in CPS shown in Fig. 5b into the SSA program in Fig. 10.

(a) According to Rule (3), we first translate the **ifz** term to an SSA function $fact$ and append it to the initial empty SSA program. Assuming the updated SSA program and parameters are t_0, n_0 and loc_0, the next step is to evaluate $\mathcal{G}(\textbf{letval } x_5 = 2 \textbf{ in} \ldots, t_0, (main, b_1, 0), n_0, loc_0)$.

(b) Following Rule (1), we insert $[x_5 = 2;]$ to $(main, b_1, 0)$ in t_0 and call the new SSA program t_1. Then, the evaluating goal becomes $\mathcal{G}(\textbf{letcont } k_2 \, y = k_{init} \, y \textbf{ in } (fact \, k_2 \, x_5), t_1, n_0, loc_0)$.

(c) Based on Rule (4), we should translate $(fact \, k_2 \, x_5)$ first. By Rule (7), since continuation k_2 is a local continuation, we insert $[y = \textbf{call } fact \, x_5; \textbf{ br}_{uc} \, k_2;]$ to $(main, b_1, 1)$ and $(main, b_1, 2)$ respectively. Then, we append an empty block k_2 to the SSA program and call the new program t_2. We also add the mapping from k_2 to the **letcont** term to loc_0 and call the updated mapping loc_1. The goal finally becomes $\mathcal{G}(k_{init} \, y, t_2, (main, k_2, 0), n_0, loc_1)$.

(d) Following Rule (6), we insert $[r_{k2} = y; \textbf{ ret } r_{k2};]$ to $(main, k_2, 0)$ and $(main, k_2, 1)$. The resulting SSA program is the one shown in Fig. 10.

3.4   Semantics Preservation of the Transformations

Overview of Verification. We discuss the verification of the transformations introduced above. Given a PCF program t_{pcf}, it is first converted into a CPS term by $\mathcal{F}_{proc}$ and then translated to a SSA program t_{ssa} by $\mathcal{G}_{proc}$. The overall transformation function is denoted as $Comp(t_{pcf}) = \mathcal{G}_{proc}(\mathcal{F}_{proc}(t_{pcf}))$. Semantics preservation of the transformations is represented by Theorem 1 and Theorem 2 where $t \Downarrow n$ denotes that t evaluates to a value n and $t \Uparrow$ denotes that t diverges. If the converted SSA program terminates and evaluates to n, the PCF program also terminates and evaluates to n. On the other hand, if the SSA program diverges, the PCF program also diverges.

Theorem 1 (Preservation of Terminating Behaviors).

$\forall \, t_{pcf} \, t_{ssa} \, n, \; t_{ssa} \Downarrow n \, \wedge \, t_{ssa} = Comp(t_{pcf}) \Longrightarrow t_{pcf} \Downarrow n.$

Theorem 2 (Preservation of Diverging Behaviors).

$\forall \, t_{pcf} \, t_{ssa}, \; t_{ssa} \Uparrow \, \wedge \, t_{ssa} = Comp(t_{pcf}) \Longrightarrow t_{pcf} \Uparrow.$

We prove the semantics preservation theorems by using the simulation techniques introduced in Sect. 2.2. We first establish forward simulation for every transformation. We then compose the results into a single forward simulation which is flipped into a backward simulation for safe programs by exploiting the determinism of the target language. Note that the proof depends on the property that a terminating PCF term always evaluates to a value (i.e., does not stuck). We assume this property holds instead of proving it because the proof cannot be completed with the explicit naming of variables. We plan to address this problem by adopting the locally nameless representation in the future. Finally, we derive semantics preservation from the backward simulation.

We are left with proving forward simulation for our transformations. The structure of the proofs are similar for both the CPS transformation and the CPS-to-SSA one, except that the former is verified by using a plus simulation while the latter is verified by using a star simulation (see Sect. 2.2). We discuss the latter proof below as the transformation from CPS to SSA is the focus of this paper and has a more complicated proof.

Forward Simulation of the CPS-to-SSA Transformation. To define a forward simulation, we need an invariant between the program states of CPS and SSA languages which we write as $S_{cps} \sim S_{ssa}$. We shall discuss its precise definition shortly. Given any CPS program t_{cps} and its transformed form t_{ssa} in SSA, we define that t_{cps} forward simulates t_{ssa} if the invariant $\sim$ holds for their initial states and continues to hold throughout the execution. The following theorem states that $\sim$ holds for initial states where $\texttt{initial}\ (t_{cps}) = (t_{cps}, loc_{empty})$ and $\texttt{initial}\ (t_{ssa}) = (t_{ssa}, (main, empty, 0), (main, empty, 0), loc_{empty}, s_{empty})$; we prove this theorem by unfolding definitions in a straightforward manner.

Theorem 3 (Simulation of Initial States).

$$\forall t_{cps}\ t_{ssa},\ t_{ssa} = \mathcal{G}_{proc}(t_{cps}) \implies \texttt{initial}\ (t_{cps}) \sim \texttt{initial}\ (t_{ssa}).$$

The following theorem states that $\sim$ holds for internal executions.

Theorem 4 (Simulation of Internal Executions).

$$\forall S_{cps}\ S_{ssa}\ S'_{cps},\ S_{cps} \to S'_{cps} \wedge S_{cps} \sim S_{ssa} \implies \exists S'_{ssa},\ S'_{cps} \sim S'_{ssa} \wedge$$
$$(S_{ssa} \xrightarrow{+} S'_{ssa} \vee (S_{ssa} \xrightarrow{*} S'_{ssa} \wedge M(S'_{cps}) < M(S_{cps}))).$$

In this theorem, we use star simulation introduced in Sect.2.2 to relate the transitions of CPS and SSA program states as stuttering could happen when a **letcont** term is evaluated: the source CPS term may take one step while the target SSA term takes zero step. To solve the infinite stuttering problem, we need a measure M for source states which is strictly decreasing as the execution goes. In this paper, we use the number of **letcont** structures as the measure. We prove Theorem 4 by induction on $S_{cps} \to S'_{cps}$. In each case of $S_{cps} \to S'_{cps}$, we construct S'_{ssa} that matches S'_{cps} by $\sim$. In the cases where the target execution does not take a step and $S'_{cps} \sim S_{ssa}$, we prove that $M(S'_{cps}) < M(S_{cps})$.

We now discuss $\sim$ in detail. It recursively matches each subterm of a CPS program with corresponding code segment in the generated SSA program. For example, a local continuation k introduced by a **letcont** term corresponds to a basic block named k in the SSA program. The body of the continuation k is related to the SSA code starting from block k. When a local continuation k is applied to a variable x, the corresponding SSA instructions assign x to a variable with the same name as the bound variable of k and jump to the block named k. The most important rules of $\sim$ are shown in Fig. 13. Rules (1) and (3) defines matching states for calls to local continuations and return continuations, respectively. Rules (2) and (4) demonstrates that if a CPS term contains subterms like t and u, the subterms and their corresponding SSA components should be related recursively. Rule (5) defines matching states for function calls.

To understand how $\sim$ works in the proof of forward simulation, we take the CPS and SSA programs that calculate factorial of 2 in Fig. 5b and Fig. 10 as examples. In the beginning, their initial states are related by $\sim$. According to their small-step operational semantics, the next program states are:

- S_{cps1} : $(\textbf{letval}\ x_5 = 2\ \textbf{in}\dots, loc_{empty}\ [k \mapsto fact_{cps}])$
- S_{ssa1} : $(fact_{ssa}, (main, b_1, 0), (main, empty, 0), loc_{empty}\ [x_5 \mapsto 2], s_{empty})$

$$\frac{\begin{array}{c} loc_{cps}\ k = \textbf{letcont}\ k\ x_1 = t\ \textbf{in}\ u \\ \textbf{code}_{at}\ pc\ =\ x_1 = x \quad \textbf{code}_{at}\ (pc+1)\ =\ \textbf{br}_{uc}\ k \end{array}}{(k\ x, loc_{cps}) \sim (t_{ssa}, pc, ppc, loc_{ssa}\ x_1 \mapsto x, s_{ssa})}$$

$$\frac{\begin{array}{c} t_{cps} = \textbf{letcont}\ k\ x_1 = t\ \textbf{in}\ u \quad (u, loc_{cps}) \sim (t_{ssa}, pc, ppc, loc_{ssa}, s_{ssa}) \\ (t, loc_{cps}\ k \mapsto t_{cps}) \sim (t_{ssa}, (pc.l_f, k, 0), pc, loc_{ssa}, s_{ssa}) \end{array}}{(t_{cps}, loc_{cps}\ k \mapsto t_{cps}) \sim (t_{ssa}, pc, ppc, loc_{ssa}, s_{ssa})}$$

$$\frac{\begin{array}{c} loc_{cps}\ k = \textbf{letfun}\ f\ k\ x_1 = t\ \textbf{in}\ u\ \text{or}\ k = k_{init} \\ \textbf{code}_{at}\ pc\ =\ r_b = x \quad \textbf{code}_{at}\ (pc+1)\ =\ \textbf{ret}\ r_b \end{array}}{(k\ x, loc_{cps}) \sim (t_{ssa}, pc, ppc, loc_{ssa}\ r_b \mapsto x, s_{ssa})}$$

$$\frac{\begin{array}{c} t_{cps} = \textbf{letfun}\ f\ k\ x_1 = t\ \textbf{in}\ u \\ (t, loc_{cps}\ k \mapsto t_{cps}) \sim (t_{ssa}, (f, b_1, 0), pc, loc_{ssa}, s_{ssa}) \\ (u, loc_{cps}\ k \mapsto t_{cps}) \sim (t_{ssa}, (main, b_1, 0), pc, loc_{ssa}, s_{ssa}) \end{array}}{(t_{cps}, loc_{cps}\ k \mapsto t_{cps}) \sim (t_{ssa}, pc, ppc, loc_{ssa}, s_{ssa})}$$

$$\frac{\begin{array}{c} loc_{cps}\ k = \textbf{letcont}\ k\ x_1 = t\ \textbf{in}\ u \\ \textbf{code}_{at}\ pc\ =\ x_1 = \textbf{call}\ f\ x \quad \textbf{code}_{at}\ (pc+1)\ =\ \textbf{br}_{uc}\ k \end{array}}{(f\ k\ x, loc_{cps}) \sim (t_{ssa}, pc, ppc, loc_{ssa}, s_{ssa})}$$

Fig. 13. Selected Rules of the $\sim$ Relation

To confirm that $S_{cps1} \sim S_{ssa1}$ holds, we fetch the instruction $[x_5 = 2]$ at $(main, b_1, 0)$. The updated mappings in S_{cps1} and S_{ssa1} are named loc_{cps1} and loc_{ssa1}. After one-step transition, their program states change to:

- S_{cps2} : $(\textbf{letcont}\ k_2\ y = k_{init}\ y\ \textbf{in} \ldots, loc_{cps1})$
- S_{ssa2} : $(fact_{ssa}, (main, b_1, 1), (main, empty, 0), loc_{ssa1}, s_{empty})$

According to Rule (2) in Fig. 13, we need to relate the subterms $(k_{init}\ y)$ and $(fact\ k_2\ x_5)$ with the corresponding segments of SSA code:

- $(k_{init}\ y, loc_{cps1}\ [k_2 \mapsto t_{cps2}]) \sim (fact_{ssa}, (main, b_1, 1), (main, empty, 0), loc_{ssa1}, s_{empty})$
- $(fact\ k_2\ x_5, loc_{cps1}\ [k_2 \mapsto t_{cps2}]) \sim (fact_{ssa}, (main, k_2, 0), (main, b_1, 1), loc_{ssa1}, s_{empty})$

Here, the first relation can be established by using Rule (3) and the second one can be proved using Rule (5). As we can see from the reasoning above, we can reduce these two programs step by step, show the intermediate states are related, and finally draw a conclusion that they both evaluate to the same value.

4 Application to Verified Compilation

4.1 Compilation of PCF to LLVM

We present the application of our verified transformations to construct a compiler from PCF to LLVM IR. The compiler reads PCF programs and generates LLVM IR programs through the compilation passes shown in Fig. 14:

- *PCF Parser.* It transforms PCF programs in text form into a stream of tokens via a lexer and parses these tokens into PCF terms in Coq.
- *CPS Transformation.* As introduced in Sect. 3.1, PCF terms are first converted into their CPS form. The correctness of the CPS transformation is verified, as described in Sect. 3.4.
- *CPS-to-SSA Transformation.* After the CPS transformation, CPS terms are converted to SSA programs as shown in Sect. 3.3. The conversion is also verified as described in Sect. 3.4.
- *SSA-to-LLVM IR.* SSA programs are transformed into the abstract syntax trees of LLVM IR which are then written to a text form. In our prototype, we use the AST in the verified LLVM infrastructure Vellvm [24]. Note that the verification of this pass is left for future work.

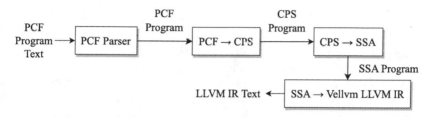

Fig. 14. Overview of the PCF-to-LLVM Compiler

4.2   Implementation and Evaluation

Our entire development is carried out in the interactive theorem prover Coq, with the exception that the PCF parser is implemented in OCaml by using Ocamllex and Ocamlyacc [22]. The lines of code (LOC) for each module and the proportions of code for each category are shown in Table 1. As we can see, more than half of our work is devoted to verification.

5   Related Work

Much work in the field of compiler verification has been carried out based on CompCert, including a lot of work on verification of functional compilers. For instance, the verified functional compiler CertiCoq compiles Gallina (Coq's language) to Clight in CompCert [5] and the verified compiler for miniML targets the Cminor language in CompCert [7]. CompCert's optimizing IR is standard three-address code. The modularity, portability and optimizing potential of SSA IR (e.g., LLVM IR) has attracted attentions of developers of functional compilers. In recent years, functional compilers that do not originally use SSA back-ends have started to switch to them for better performance [10]. Our work is based on these observations and is the first step towards building verified functional compilers that exploit benefits of SSA.

Table 1. Evaluation

Categories	Contents	LOC	Proportion(%)
Language Definitions	PCF	171	23.9
	CPS	228	
	SSA	303	
Transformations	PCF→CPS	148	24.5
	CPS→SSA	251	
	SSA→Vellvm LLVM IR	318	
Verification	PCF→CPS Forward Simulation	364	51.6
	CPS→SSA Forward Simulation	696	
	Combination of Forward Simulation	49	
	Backward Simulation	404	

Translation Algorithms from CPS to SSA. As mentioned in Sect. 2.1, Kelsey has introduced a conversion algorithm from annotated CPS to SSA [12]. However, the CPS and SSA languages in Kelsey's work are quite different from what we use in this paper. Kelsey's CPS language treats parameters of binary expressions and conditions in conditional statements as expressions, making it more like standard functional programs with the added elements of continuations. For example, expression $k((x + y) + z)$ is allowed in Kelsey's work, but it must be converted to **letop** $x_0 = x + y$ **in** (**letop** $x_1 = x_0 + z$ **in** $k\ x_1$) in our work. Additionally, instead of focusing on the flow analysis between procedures, Kelsey's conversion algorithm chooses to first merge CPS procedures and then convert them as a whole. So the top-level unit is a procedure and there is no function call, which are different from the LLVM-based SSA language used in this paper. There have also been other work on relating functional programs with SSA [1,14]. None of the above transformation has been formally verified.

CertiCoq: Verified Compiler for Gallina. CertiCoq compiles Gallina to an intermediate language in CompCert called Clight, in order to link with CompCert and to obtain a complete verified compilation chain [5,18,19]. The compilation passes from CPS to C and their correctness proofs are formalized in Coq, which makes use of big-step operational semantics instead of small-step ones. Its target language is not SSA-based, so it cannot be directly connect to LLVM or exploit optimizations based on SSA.

Vellvm: Verified LLVM IR. Vellvm defines the LLVM abstract syntax tree (AST) in Coq and provides formal semantics for LLVM IR. Older versions of Vellvm that are no longer maintained provide operational semantics [26]. Newer versions have been transferred to semantics based on interaction trees [24]. In this paper, Vellvm AST is used as the compilation target for SSA program and the final LLVM IR code is generated using a compilation pass designed by us.

SML New Jersey's New Backend Based on LLVM. The SML-New Jersey compiler (SML/NJ) is a well-known compiler for Standard ML. It has recently changed its backend to compile its CPS intermediate language to LLVM IR [10]. In this new version, CPS code is first converted to a control flow graph (CFG) intermediate language and then to LLVM IR. It shows that connecting CPS IR to an SSA-based compiler infrastructure enables rich optimizations provided by these infrastructures. Our work is inspired by this recent trend and furthermore tries to verify such connections.

CompCertSSA. Verified compilers are also beginning to support SSA back-ends. CompCertSSA is an extension of CompCert with a SSA middle-end [3]. It provides SSA as an alternative optimizing IR and allows for verified conversion between three-address code and SSA IR. This enables optimizations based on SSA in CompCert [8,11]. The range of optimizations provided by CompCertSSA is still limited and not comparable to LLVM. However, it provides a complete verified compilation chain starting from C, making it a reasonable candidate for developing verified functional compilers targeting SSA. We plan to investigate how to connect our work with CompCertSSA in the future.

6   Conclusion

This paper is a first attempt at developing verified functional compilers that target SSA IR. The key is to provide a verified transformation algorithm from CPS to SSA, thereby linking the verified functional compilers to verified SSA infrastructures. We introduce such an algorithm which takes representative functional programs in CPS as input and generates SSA programs in the style of LLVM as output. We then give the source and target programs small-step operational semantics and verify the correctness of the transformation based on simulation. To the best of our knowledge, this is the first verified transformation from CPS functional programs to SSA. Based on this algorithm, we have also built a prototype compiler for PCF that targets LLVM IR. This provides a foundation for developing verified functional compilers that may exploit the benefits of SSA compilation infrastructures in the future.

Acknowledgments. We would like to thank the anonymous referees for their helpful feedback which improved this paper significantly. This work was supported by the National Natural Science Foundation of China (NSFC) under Grant No. 62002217.

References

1. Appel, A.W.: SSA is functional programming. ACM SIGPLAN Notices **33**(4), 17–20 (1998). https://doi.org/10.1145/278283.278285
2. Balasubramanian, A., Baranowski, M.S., Burtsev, A., Panda, A., Rakamarić, Z., Ryzhyk, L.: System programming in rust: Beyond safety. In: Proceedings of the 16th Workshop on Hot Topics in Operating Systems, pp. 156–161 (2017). https://doi.org/10.1145/3139645.3139660

3. Barthe, G., Demange, D., Pichardie, D.: Formal verification of an SSA-based middle-end for CompCert. ACM Trans. Program. Lang. Syst. **36**(1) (mar 2014). https://doi.org/10.1145/2579080

4. Bélanger, O.S., Monnier, S., Pientka, B.: Programming type-safe transformations using higher-order abstract syntax. In: Gonthier, G., Norrish, M. (eds.) Certified Programs and Proofs - Third International Conference, CPP 2013, Melbourne, VIC, Australia, December 11–13, 2013, Proceedings. Lecture Notes in Computer Science, vol. 8307, pp. 243–258. Springer (2013). https://doi.org/10.1007/978-3-319-03545-1_16

5. Bélanger, O.S., Weaver, M.Z., Appel, A.W.: Certified code generation from CPS to C. preparation. (2019), https://www.cs.princeton.edu/~appel/papers/CPStoC.pdf

6. Danvy, O., Millikin, K., Nielsen, L.R.: On one-pass CPS transformations. BRICS Report Series **14**(6) (2007)

7. Dargaye, Z.: Vérification formelle d'un compilateur optimisant pour langages fonctionnels. Ph.D. thesis, Université Paris-Diderot-Paris VII (2009)

8. Demange, D., Pichardie, D., Stefanesco, L.: Verifying fast and sparse SSA-based optimizations in Coq. In: Franke, B. (ed.) Compiler Construction, pp. 233–252. Springer, Berlin Heidelberg, Berlin, Heidelberg (2015). https://doi.org/10.1007/978-3-662-46663-6_12

9. Dowek, G., Lévy, J.J.: Introduction to the theory of programming languages. Springer Science & Business Media (2010)

10. Farvardin, K., Reppy, J.: A new backend for Standard ML of New Jersey. In: Proceedings of the 32nd Symposium on Implementation and Application of Functional Languages,pp. 55–66 (2020). https://doi.org/10.1145/3462172.3462191

11. Herklotz, Y., Demange, D., Blazy, S.: Mechanised semantics for gated static single assignment. In: Krebbers, R., Traytel, D., Pientka, B., Zdancewic, S. (eds.) Proceedings of the 12th ACM SIGPLAN International Conference on Certified Programs and Proofs, CPP 2023, Boston, MA, USA, January 16–17, 2023, pp. 182–196. ACM (2023). https://doi.org/10.1145/3573105.3575681

12. Kelsey, R.A.: A correspondence between continuation passing style and static single assignment form. ACM SIGPLAN Notices **30**(3), 13–22 (1995). https://doi.org/10.1145/202530.202532

13. Kennedy, A.: Compiling with continuations, continued. In: Proceedings of the 12th ACM SIGPLAN International Conference on Functional Programming, pp. 177–190 (2007). https://doi.org/10.1145/1291151.1291179

14. L. Beringer, J.S., Rastello, F.: Static Single Assignment Book. Springer Science & Business Media (2018)

15. Lattner, C.: Introduction to the LLVM compiler infrastructure. In: Itanium conference and expo (2006)

16. Leroy, X.: A formally verified compiler back-end. J. Autom. Reason. **43**(4), 363–446 (2009). https://doi.org/10.1007/s10817-009-9155-4

17. Paraskevopoulou, Z., Appel, A.W.: Closure conversion is safe for space. Proceedings of the ACM on Programming Languages 3(ICFP), pp. 1–29 (2019). https://doi.org/10.1145/3341687

18. Paraskevopoulou, Z., Grover, A.: Compiling with continuations, correctly. Proc. ACM Program. Lang. **5**(OOPSLA) (oct 2021). https://doi.org/10.1145/3485491

19. Paraskevopoulou, Z., Li, J.M., Appel, A.W.: Compositional optimizations for CertiCoq. Proc. ACM Program. Lang. **5**(ICFP) (aug 2021). https://doi.org/10.1145/3473591

20. Plotkin, G.D.: Call-by-name, call-by-value and the λ-calculus. Theoret. Comput. Sci. **1**(2), 125–159 (1975). https://doi.org/10.1016/0304-3975(75)90017-1
21. Plotkin, G.D.: LCF considered as a programming language. Theoret. Comput. Sci. **5**(3), 223–255 (1977)
22. Smith, J.B.: Ocamllex and Ocamlyacc. Practical OCaml, pp. 193–211 (2007)
23. Wang, Y., Nadathur, G.: A higher-order abstract syntax approach to verified transformations on functional programs. In: Thiemann, P. (ed.) Programming Languages and Systems, pp. 752–779. Springer, Berlin Heidelberg, Berlin, Heidelberg (2016). https://doi.org/10.1007/978-3-662-49498-1_29
24. Zakowski, Y., Beck, C., Yoon, I., Zaichuk, I., Zaliva, V., Zdancewic, S.: Modular, compositional, and executable formal semantics for LLVM IR. Proceedings of the ACM on Programming Languages **5**(ICFP), 1–30 (2021). https://doi.org/10.1145/3473572
25. Zhang, Y., Yang, M., Zhou, B., Yang, Z., Zhang, W., Zang, B.: Swift: a register-based JIT compiler for embedded JVMs. In: Proceedings of the 8th ACM SIGPLAN/SIGOPS conference on Virtual Execution Environments, pp. 63–74 (2012). https://doi.org/10.1145/2365864.2151035
26. Zhao, J., Nagarakatte, S., Martin, M.M., Zdancewic, S.: Formalizing the LLVM intermediate representation for verified program transformations. In: Proceedings of the 39th annual ACM SIGPLAN-SIGACT symposium on Principles of programming languages, pp. 427–440 (2012). https://doi.org/10.1145/2103621.2103709

OAT: An Optimized Android Testing Framework Based on Reinforcement Learning

Mengjun Du[1], Peiyang Li[1], Lian Song[1], W. K. Chan[2], and Bo Jiang[1](✉)

[1] State Key Laboratory of Software Development Environment, School of Computer Science and Engineering, Beihang University, Beijing, China
{dumj,lipeiyang,songlian,jiangbo}@buaa.edu.cn
[2] Department of Computer Science, City University of Hong Kong, Hong Kong, China
wkchan@cityu.edu.hk

Abstract. Automated testing of Android applications is always a challenging task. Deep reinforcement learning can continuously optimize the current exploration strategy through the interaction with the application under test and can explore application states that are difficult to reach in the testing process. However, existing state-of-the-art deep reinforcement learning techniques rely on coarse GUI state definitions, which make them hard to explore interesting application states even with the guidance of reward function. In this work, we propose OAT, an optimized automated testing tool for Android applications based on deep reinforcement learning. OAT is designed with a pair of fine-grained state representation and reward function to provide more effective reward incentives for reinforcement learning. OAT also adopts the Monte Carlo Tree Search (MCTS) strategy to more effectively explore promising GUI states. Our experimental evaluation shows that OAT is more effective than the state-of-the-art Android application testing techniques in terms of both code coverage and fault detection.

Keyword: Android Testing · Deep reinforcement learning · Reward function

1 Introduction

With the popularity of smart phones and tablet computers, the mobile application market has witnessed explosive growth. As the most popular mobile operating system, Android accounts for 70% of the smartphone system market [1]. Google Play is the most popular app market on the Android platform, with more than 2.7 million apps currently available [2]. It is very important to ensure that these apps work correctly to provide good user experience. Effective and automated Android application testing techniques are crucial to achieve this goal.

The Graphical User Interface (GUI) state traversal-based testing techniques have been extensively studied and used in academia and industry. In general, they formulate the Android application testing problem into the GUI state search problem. They try to cover as many GUI states and widgets as possible during the exploration process. Typically, the Graphical User Interface (GUI) is dynamically queried with Android

© The Author(s), under exclusive license to Springer Nature Switzerland AG 2023
C. David and M. Sun (Eds.): TASE 2023, LNCS 13931, pp. 38–58, 2023.
https://doi.org/10.1007/978-3-031-35257-7_3

system APIs to parse the widgets of the current Activity followed by building a GUI state representation based on the widgets information. In general, a more fine-grained GUI state representation is more effective to detect bugs within Android application.

The random testing strategy [3, 4] uses randomly generated events to test an Android application. However, for a complex Android application, the random testing strategy may repeatedly explore some GUI states for a long time since it is not aware of GUI state change. Existing techniques such as Stoat [15] and TimeMachine [5] tool guide the GUI state exploration strategy through continuous code coverage measurement, which can be expensive.

Recently, ARES [6] has transformed the Android application testing problem into the deep reinforcement learning problem. It formulates multiple deep reinforcement learning algorithms including DDPG [21], TD3 [22], and SAC [9]. Among them, SAC is the best performing algorithm. ARES also proposes corresponding reward functions for the Android testing question, which encourages the model to cover more activities or trigger crashes. In general, ARES has achieved comparable or better testing effectiveness than the state-of-the-art Android testing techniques such as Stoat and TimeMachine.

However, ARES fails to capture the structural relationship between an activity and the widgets contained in the activity at the state level in this deep RL strategy, which makes the identification of new GUI state inaccurate. Furthermore, the reward function of ARES can only provide positive feedback when discovering new activities, it does not reward the changes of widgets within the same activity. Finally, the search strategy of ARES is prone to fall into local maxima during GUI state traversal, making it hard to find interesting inputs.

Therefore, this paper proposes Optimized Android Testing framework (OAT), which formulates an optimized deep reinforcement learning model to perform effective Android testing. It proposes fine-grained representation of the states of Android application and uses MCTS [7] exploration strategy to support the exploration process of reinforcement learning. OAT also designs new reward function to give appropriate rewards to the changes within the activity. Finally, only those crashes that have not been detected will be rewarded.

The contribution of this work is threefold. First, it designs a new fine-grained GUI state representation to support effective GUI state exploration with deep reinforcement learning. Second, it designs a novel reward function to give appropriate rewards to fine-grained state changes and unique crashes. Third, our experimental evaluation shows the high effectiveness and feasibility of OAT.

The organization of the remaining sections is as follows. In Sect. 2, we provide an overview of the ARES Android application testing framework and presents its main design decisions. Then we discuss the limitations of ARES to motivate our work. In Sect. 3, we introduce our OAT framework for Android application testing and present its optimized GUI state definitions and search strategies in detail. After that, we report our experiments in Sect. 4 to evaluate OAT in terms of search strategy and reward function. We have also compared OAT with the state-of-the-art tools for Android application testing. We summarize related work in Sect. 5 and conclude the paper in Section 6.

2 The Ares Testing Framework

ARES adopts several reinforcement learning models to learn the exploration strategy and it constantly updates and improves its strategy through the interaction with the Android application under test (i.e., app. Environment). The ARES configured with SAC [8] model performs the best. The current state of the Android application is represented by the information of current activity and widgets. This representation of state is used as the input to the SAC model. The SAC will output the next action to perform on the Android application under test according to the current input. After the corresponding action is performed on the test application, the reward function will return the reward for executing the action to continuously optimize the exploration strategy of the model.

As shown in Eq. (1), the ARES state is composed of the activities that the GUI belongs to and the widgets under the GUI. The substate $(a_0, \ldots a_m)$ uses one hot encoding to indicate whether the activities exist. The substate $(w_0, \ldots w_n)$ uses one hot encoding to indicate whether the widgets exist. If the activities and widgets appear in the current GUI, the corresponding one hot encoding will be set to 1. ARES only considers the type information of the widget, not the text information of the widget. This may cause the GUI state to fail to reflect some fine-grained changes in the app.

$$state = (a_0, \ldots a_m, w_0, \ldots w_n) \tag{1}$$

In the reward function, ARES encourages the discovery of new activities. When new activities are found or crashes occur, the reward function will return a high reward. In other cases, there is no reward. However, ARES did not reward the state changes within the activity, which also led to the failure to get feedback on the fine-grained changes in the app. As shown in Eq. (2), when a new activity of the Android application is found or a crash occurs, the high reward R1 will be returned. Leaving the testing app will return a high penalty. In other cases, a penalty R3 will be returned.

$$Reward = \begin{cases} R1 \; new\, activity\, or\, crash \\ R2 \; leave\, the\, testing\, app \\ R3 \; otherwise \end{cases} \tag{2}$$

The state representation of ARES only remembers whether activities and widgets exist in the state representation. It cannot distinguish the change of properties (e.g., text) of widgets in the GUI state. At the same time, the reward function in ARES returns a certain reward only when a new activity is found or a crash occurs. However, there is no appropriate reward for the state change within the activity. Finally, ARES will also return rewards when the same crash occurs many times, which may make the reinforcement learning model to fall into local optimum.

3 The Design of OAT

In this section, we present the design of OAT. We will first provide an overview of OAT. Then we present its optimization in terms of GUI state definition, search strategy, and reward function.

3.1 Overview of the OAT Framework

The workflow of OAT is shown in Fig. 1. The OAT Android application testing framework is mainly composed of three parts: application running environment, application environment interface and reinforcement learning model. It uses the powerful exploration ability of deep reinforcement learning to systematically traverse the GUI states of Android application and detect hidden bugs within the application.

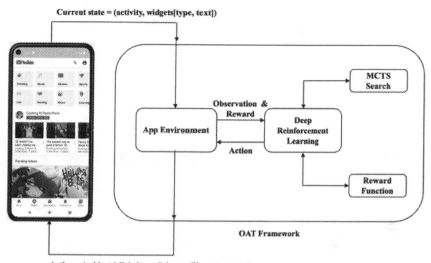

Fig. 1. The Workflow of OAT

The application environment essentially represents the application under test to interact with the Deep Reinforcement Learning-based (DRL) testing algorithm. On the one hand, the App. Environment returns the current state of application as observations to the DRL algorithm. On the other hand, the App. Environment receives the actions from the DRL algorithm and sends them to the application under test.

The DRL algorithm is the core of the entire automated testing framework. OAT uses EfficientZero [9] as the deep reinforcement learning backbone and also uses Monte Carlo Tree Search (MCTS) as the search algorithm to balance the exploration and utilization in the process of state search. The DRL algorithm accepts an application state from the application environment and returns an action to perform. It then receives the new application state and a reward is calculated to update and optimize the model.

3.2 Fine-Grained GUI State Definition

OAT dynamically queries and parses the GUI state to get the properties of the GUI widgets, which describe the type and text of each widget. As shown in Eq. (3), a GUI state is a one hot encoding obtained from the mapping of activities and widgets.

$$GUI\ state = (a_0, \dots a_m, w_0, \dots w_n) \tag{3}$$

As shown in Eq. (4) and Eq. (5), $a_0, \ldots a_m$ indicates the current activity of the app, and $w_0, \ldots w_n$ indicates whether the corresponding widget with the same text and type exists.

$$a_i = \begin{cases} 1 \ if \ GUI \ is \ in \ activity(i) \\ 0 \ otherwise \end{cases} \tag{4}$$

$$w_i = \begin{cases} 1 \ if \ widget[type \ text]_i exists \\ 0 \ otherwise \end{cases} \tag{5}$$

Assume that the current Android application includes login.activity, main.activity, widget[intput, 'user'], widget[button, 'login'] and widget[textView, 'content']. (a_0, a_1) and (w_0, w_1, w_2) can be expressed as follows:

$$(a_0, a_1) = (login.activity, main.activity)$$

$$(w_0, w_1, w_2) =$$
$$\left(widget\left[input,'user'\right], widget\left[button,'login'\right], widget\left[textView,'content'\right] \right)$$

The current GUI is in the login.activity of the application, including widget[intput, 'user'] and widget[button, 'login']. Therefore, a_0, w_0, w_1 are set to 1 and a_1, w_2 are set to 0. The one hot encoding of the GUI state is shown in the Eq. (6):

$$GUI \ state = (a_0, a_1, w_0, w_1, w_2) = (1, 0, 1, 1, 0) \tag{6}$$

With such definition of fine granularity GUI state, the state space explored by OAT is much larger than that of ARES in general.

3.3 Reward Function Based on Fine-Grained GUI State

The DRL algorithm tries to maximize the reward received to effectively guide the testing process. The reward function will return the reward of the action to the reinforcement learning algorithm after the Android application has received the corresponding event.

The goal of Android application testing is to cover as many GUI states as possible, so our reward function encourages the behavior of finding new states. We adopt a more fine-grained state representation, which makes the reward function to return rewards for small changes such as the text of widgets in the GUI state.

$$Reward = \begin{cases} R1 \ new \ state \ or \ new \ crash \ is \ found \\ R2 \ leave \ testing \ app \\ R3 \ otherwise \end{cases} \tag{7}$$

As shown in Eq. (7), when a new state of the Android application is found or a new crash is triggered, the large positive reward $R1$ (1000) will be returned. If the application under test is left during testing, a negative reward $R2$ (-100) will be returned. In other cases, a negative reward $R3$ (-1) will be returned.

In general, the definition of reward function of OAT is different from that of ARES in two aspects. First, the reward function of OAT will use fine-grained GUI state definition to determine whether a new state is found. Second, the reward function of OAT will not return R1 when a duplicated crash is triggered.

3.4 Optimization on Search Strategy

Monte-Carlo Tree Search [42–45], or MCTS, is a heuristic search algorithm. In the reinforcement learning algorithm of EfficientZero [9], Monte Carlo Tree Search (MCTS) is used to get the next optimal action. However, the search process of Efficient Zero is performed on simulated environment, which is quite different from the real Android application in terms of complexity. OAT builds its deep reinforcement learning model with MCTS to perform search directly on top of the GUI state transition graph of the application under testing.

$$USB\,Score = Q(s, a) + P(s, a)\frac{\sqrt{\sum_b N(s,b)}}{1+N(s,a)}\left(c_1 + \log\left(\frac{\sum_b N(s,b)+c_2+1}{c_2}\right)\right) \qquad (8)$$

In OAT, the GUI state transition graph of the application is dynamically built during the testing process for Monte Carlo tree search. The Android application model is represented by a directed graph model. The nodes in the graph are the state embedded in code vectors. Each node stores a list of operable widgets. An operable widget of each node points to the next state (node) to which the current state will jump when operated.

As shown in Eq. (8), $Q(s, a)$ represents the estimated reward value of action a upon state s and $P(s, a)$ represents the selection probability of action a upon state s. $N(s, a)$ represents the cumulative number of selections of action a under state s. The Upper Confidence Bound (UCB) [10] scores tend to encourage the selection of widgets with high cumulative rewards and encourage the selection of widgets with high selection times of neighboring widgets but low selection times of them. In the process of exploration, MCTS will record the reward and the selection times of each action and use UCB [10] score to calculate the probability of each optional action selected. In this way, OAT uses MCTS to search for interesting Android application states, which provides opportunities to explore promising states in the long term to avoid local optimum.

4 Evaluation

In this section, we first systematically evaluate the effectiveness and efficiency of our proposed optimizations in OAT. Then we will compare OAT with peer state-of-the-art techniques for Android application testing.

4.1 Research Questions

We study the following research questions:

RQ1: Do the optimizations proposed by OAT useful improve the effectiveness of Android application testing in terms of code coverage and fault detection?

RQ2: How does OAT compare with existing state-of-the-art techniques in terms of code coverage and fault detection?

Through RQ1, we want to evaluate the impact of each optimization on the effectiveness of Android application testing. With RQ2, we further want to evaluate the relative effectiveness of OAT when compared with state-of-the-art Android testing techniques.

Table 1. F-Droid apps benchmark used as subjects

Id	App. Name	LOC	Code Coverage Tool
1	antennapod	7975	JACOCO
2	aquadroid	1157	JACOCO
3	bookymcbookface	1595	JACOCO
4	camera-roll	6836	JACOCO
5	lightning-browser	11961	JACOCO
6	opentracks	5260	JACOCO
7	passandroid	4569	JACOCO
8	phonograph	8758	JACOCO
9	redreader	12958	JACOCO
10	simple-solitaire	5907	JACOCO
11	slide	30483	JACOCO
12	wifikeyshare	627	JACOCO
13	yalpstore	6734	JACOCO
14	afwall	5130	JACOCO
15	andotp	1560	JACOCO
16	android-anuto	4325	JACOCO
17	wikipedia	23543	JACOCO
18	busybox	540	JACOCO
19	connectbot	3904	JACOCO
20	dns66	1264	JACOCO
21	editor	1547	JACOCO
22	gpslogger	3201	JACOCO
23	lexica	1215	JACOCO
24	card-locker	1228	JACOCO
25	markor	4607	JACOCO
26	micromathematics	10506	JACOCO
27	neurolab-android	3954	JACOCO
28	opentasks	5772	JACOCO
29	tuner	2207	JACOCO
30	vanilla	4747	JACOCO

4.2 Subject Programs

As shown in Table 1, for RQ1, the subject programs used in our experiment are 30 applications randomly selected from the F-Droid benchmark [46], which was also used

Table 2. AndroTest Apps used as subjects

Id	App. Name	LOC	Code Coverage Tool
1	book-catalogue	9857	EMMA
2	countdowntimer	650	EMMA
3	divideandconquer	814	EMMA
4	munchlife	254	EMMA
5	myexpenses	2935	EMMA
6	photostream	1375	EMMA
7	randommusicplayer	400	EMMA
8	ringdroid	2897	EMMA
9	spritemethodtest	1008	EMMA
10	syncmypix	4104	EMMA
11	translate	799	EMMA
12	wordpress_394	10100	EMMA
13	alogcat	901	EMMA
14	aarddict.android	2197	EMMA
15	anymemo-stable	8428	EMMA
16	baterrydog	556	EMMA
17	addi	19945	EMMA
18	evancharltmileage	4628	EMMA
19	autoanswer	479	EMMA
20	multismssender	828	EMMA
21	kvance.nectroid	2536	EMMA
22	cri.sanity	4840	EMMA
23	dalvik-explorer	1375	EMMA
24	hotdeath-debug	3902	EMMA
25	conf.hatalab.mnv	3673	EMMA
26	k9mail	22208	EMMA
27	fercanet.lnm	492	EMMA
28	counter	2454	EMMA
29	beide.bomber	376	EMMA
30	frozenbubble	1706	EMMA
31	passwordmanager	10833	EMMA
32	tippy_1.1.3	1083	EMMA

(continued)

Table 2. (*continued*)

Id	App. Name	LOC	Code Coverage Tool
33	tomdroid	1519	EMMA
34	weight-chart	1116	EMMA
35	whohasmystuff	729	EMMA

by to evaluate different configurations of ARES [6]. For RQ2, since some peer techniques for comparison only supports code instrumentation with EMMA, we randomly select 35 applications from the AndroTest benchmark [14] as subjects due to their better support of EMMA as shown in Table 2. Note that the ARES [6] framework also makes use of the AndroTest benchmark when comparing with peer techniques. It should be noted that the subjects used in our experiment are comparable to previous works [5, 6, 15] in terms of scale. In Table 1 and 2, the column LOC refers to the executable lines of code for each Android game app. The column Code Coverage Tool shows the tool used to collect code coverage.

4.3 Experiment Setup

The experiment setup involves the setup of the training environment as well as the application testing environment. The experiment is carried out on a desktop equipped with 3.40GHz 8 core Intel i7–6700 CPU and 32GB RAM. The operating system used is Ubuntu 18.04. The GPU for training the deep reinforcement learning network is GeForce 1050Ti. The Android application testing environment is an Android emulator [20] with Android 8.1 (API level 27).

OAT is built on the ARES Android testing framework by redesigning the DRL algorithm, the search strategy, the GUI state definition, and the reward function. To be specific, OAT is implemented in Python and the DRL algorithm is based on pytorch. Furthermore, OAT adopts Appium [11] to start and stop the Android emulator and install/uninstall Android applications. OAT also depends on the UiAutomator [19] to query the GUI state of the applications under test to obtain the list of widgets and their properties. To collect code coverage, OAT adopts Emma [12] and JaCoCo [13] to perform code instrumentation and generate code coverage statistics.

4.4 Experimental Procedure

To answer RQ1, we set up five techniques to evaluate the effectiveness of the fine-grained GUI state definition and the MCTS search strategy of OAT. We use Monkey [4] as the baseline technique. We also adopt the original version of ARES tool configured with SAC algorithm. We use the SAC version of ARES in our experiment because it achieves the best fault detection effectiveness in the original ARES [6] work. ARES_FINE introduces fine-grained GUI state definition on top of ARES. OAT_COARSE uses MCTS search strategy without fine-grained GUI state definition. Finally, OAT uses both MCTS

Table 3. Setting of experiment parameters

Experiment	Fine-Grained GUI State Definition	MCTS
OAT_Coarse	×	√
OAT	√	√
ARES	×	×
ARES_FINE	√	×

search strategy and the fine-grained GUI state definition. The configurations in terms of optimization options are shown in Table 3.

The comparison between ARES and ARES_FINE as well as between OAT_COARSE and OAT are used to verify the effectiveness of fine-grained GUI state definition. The comparison between ARES and OAT_COARSE as well as OAT and ARES_FINE is used to verify the effectiveness of MCTS search strategy. Due to the randomness of the evaluated technique, the code coverage and fault detection results are the average of 10 rounds of testing. The testing time in each round is set to 1 h. The experiment for RQ1 takes 1500 h to complete.

To answer RQ2, we compare OAT with existing state-of-the-art testing techniques. We compared OAT with Monkey [4], ARES (SAC version) [6], Stoat [15], and TimeMachine [5]. Monkey is a widely used techniques for evaluating other Android application testing techniques. ARES is a recently proposed Android testing technique based on deep reinforcement learning. Stoat and TimeMachine are two popular and effective state-of-the-art Android application testing techniques. Similar to RQ1, for each round of testing, the testing time for each Android application in the benchmark is 1 h. The code coverage and fault detection results are the average of 10 rounds of testing to mitigate the impact of randomness. The experiment for RQ2 takes 1400 h to complete.

To gather the failure information of each program execution, we collected the system *logcat* files and extracted the exceptions with stack trace information. We wrote a script to parse exceptions and errors triggered in the testing process. We considered two failures as the same if they had the same stack traces and produced the same kind of error messages upon failure. In this way, we were able to measure the number of distinct failures within the experiment.

4.5 Evaluating the Optimization Effectiveness of OAT

The code coverage results of the 30 Android applications from F-Droid are shown in Table 4. OAT has achieved the best results in terms of code coverage. It performs the best code coverage on 19 out of the 30 applications. ARES has the worst performance among all tested techniques. Our analysis on ARES found its reward function with the coarse granularity of GUI state definition cannot provide effective guidance in the training phase. Therefor the model often converges to the same testing strategy without effectively traversing the GUI states of the application under testing.

Table 4. Code coverage experiment results

App.name	Monkey	ARES	ARES_Fine	OAT_coarse	OAT
antennapod	**0.27**	0.2	0.19	0.23	**0.27**
aquadroid	**0.83**	**0.83**	**0.83**	**0.83**	**0.83**
bookymcbookface	**0.47**	0.21	0.24	0.24	0.26
camera-roll	0.28	0.27	0.26	**0.32**	0.30
lightning-browser	**0.33**	0.31	**0.33**	0.27	**0.33**
opentracks	0.46	0.43	0.43	0.45	**0.48**
passandroid	**0.02**	0.01	**0.02**	**0.02**	**0.02**
phonograph	0.16	**0.17**	**0.17**	**0.17**	0.15
redreader	**0.21**	0.19	0.19	0.20	0.20
simple-solitaire	0.29	0.38	**0.39**	0.37	0.37
slide	**0.05**	**0.05**	**0.05**	**0.05**	**0.05**
wifikeyshare	**0.38**	0.36	0.36	0.38	**0.38**
yalpstore	**0.35**	0.27	0.28	**0.35**	**0.35**
afwall	0.18	0.18	0.17	0.18	**0.21**
andotp	0.19	0.12	**0.45**	0.12	0.34
android-anuto	0.57	0.54	0.55	0.56	**0.58**
wikipedia	0.19	0.19	**0.22**	0.15	0.19
busybox	**0.86**	0.82	0.83	0.86	**0.86**
connectbot	0.28	0.26	0.28	**0.29**	**0.29**
dns66	**0.75**	0.74	0.72	**0.75**	0.74
editor	0.49	0.5	0.49	0.42	**0.52**
gpslogger	0.49	0.34	0.32	0.48	**0.50**
lexica	**0.68**	0.59	0.65	**0.68**	**0.68**
card-locker	0.41	0.39	**0.57**	0.53	0.46
markor	0.45	0.37	0.37	0.45	**0.47**
micromathematics	**0.50**	**0.50**	**0.50**	**0.50**	**0.50**
neurolab-android	0.28	0.15	0.30	**0.31**	0.28
opentasks	0.54	0.5	0.51	0.56	**0.57**
tuner	0.80	0.8	0.77	**0.81**	**0.81**
vanilla	**0.41**	0.4	0.32	**0.41**	**0.41**
Average	0.406	0.368	0.392	0.397	**0.413**
Best	14	4	10	13	**19**

In general, the fine-grained GUI state definition can enable better code coverage effectiveness. In particular, the ARES_FINE performs better than ARES on average in terms of code coverage. Furthermore, OAT on average performs better than OAT_COARSE in terms of code coverage. The MCTS search strategy adopted by OAT also has to better code coverage. In particular, OAT on average performs better than ARES_FINE in terms of code coverage. Since they adopt the same granularity of GUI state definition, the use of MCTS search strategy makes the difference. On average, OAT performs the best in terms of code coverage among all evaluated techniques.

Table 5. Test results of fault detection

App. name	Monkey	ARES	ARES_Fine	OAT_coarse	OAT
antennapod	0	0	0	0	0
aquadroid	**2.2**	1	1	1.2	1.6
bookymcbookface	0	0	0	0	0
camera-roll	1.2	2	0	1.6	**1.8**
lightning-browser	0	0	0	0	**0.2**
opentracks	0	0	0	1.2	0.2
passandroid	0	0	0	**0.2**	0
phonograph	0	0	0	0	0
redreader	0	0	0	0	0
simple-solitaire	0.6	2	2	**1.2**	0.8
slide	**1**	1	1	1	1
wifikeyshare	0	1	1	0	0
yalpstore	0	0	0	0	0
afwall	0	0	0	0	**0.2**
andotp	0.6	1	1	0	0.8
android-anuto	0	0	0	0	0
wikipedia	0	0	0	0	**0.2**
busybox	**1**	0	0	1	1
connectbot	**0.2**	0	0	0	0
dns66	1	1	1	1	1
editor	0	0	0	0	**0.2**
gpslogger	**0.8**	0	0	0.6	**0.8**

(*continued*)

Table 5. (*continued*)

App. name	Monkey	ARES	ARES_Fine	OAT_coarse	OAT
lexica	**1.6**	1	1	1	1.4
card-locker	0.2	0	0	**0.6**	**0.6**
markor	6.4	1	3	7	**8**
micromathematics	**0.2**	0	0	0	**0.2**
neurolab-android	2	2	0	2.4	**2.6**
opentasks	**0.4**	0	1	0.2	**0.4**
tuner	**1**	0	1	0.8	**1**
vanilla	1.4	0	**2**	1.8	1.2
Average	0.73	0.43	0.5	0.72	**0.84**
Best	10	4	6	7	**15**

Having compared different techniques in terms of code coverage, we further evaluate their fault detection effectiveness as shown in Table 5. The fault detection result is the average number of crashes found in 10 rounds of experiments. First, fine-grained GUI state definition leads to better fault detection effectiveness. OAT performs significantly better than OAT_COARSE and ARES_FINE performs better than ARES. Second, the MTCS search strategy is also effective to improve fault detection effectiveness. This is supported by the higher fault detection effectiveness of OAT over ARES_FINE and OAT_COARSE over ARES. Finally, although Monkey's fault detection effectiveness is not bad, OAT still performs the best among all techniques in comparison.

4.6   Comparison with the State of Art Techniques

In this section, we continue to compare OAT with other state-of-the-art techniques. Table 6 shows the code coverage results of Monkey, Stoat, TimeMachine and OAT on 35 apps. On the one hand, OAT achieves the best average code coverage result among all techniques. On the other hand, it only reaches the highest code coverage on 10 out of the 35 apps, which is less than that of TimeMachine.

Table 7 shows the fault detection experiment results of Monkey, Stoat, TimeMachine and OAT on the 35 apps. OAT achieves the best performance with detecting 1.19 faults per application on average. The second one is TimeMachine, which detects 0.92 faults on average. And OAT reached the highest fault detection on 14 out of the 35 apps. Finally, Monkey and Stoat detects 0.64 and 0.63 fault on average. The improvement of OAT in terms of fault detection over other techniques is significant.

Stoat builds navigation models for Android applications through dynamic analysis, which is used to effectively explore application states. Stoat uses random FSMs to model application behavior and then extracts test cases from these models. TimeMachine can record and save the state of Android application during the testing process. When necessary, it can return to a certain app state under test to continue the test, saving the

Table 6. Code coverage comparison with State-of-the-ART techniques

App. name	Monkey	Stoat	TimeMachine	OAT
book-catalogue	0.20	0.23	0.16	**0.32**
countdowntimer	0.75	**0.77**	0.75	0.60
divideandconquer	0.56	0.53	**0.77**	0.56
munchlife	0.70	**0.71**	0.62	0.66
myexpenses	**0.58**	0.37	0.22	**0.58**
photostream	0.28	**0.32**	0.29	0.28
randommusicplayer	0.54	0.59	**0.76**	0.54
ringdroid	0.26	0.18	0.22	**0.27**
spritemethodtest	0.68	0.69	**0.82**	0.68
syncmypix	0.24	0.25	**0.27**	0.24
translate	0.47	**0.49**	0.47	0.47
wordpress_394	0.05	0.05	**0.06**	0.05
alogcat	0.80	0.80	0.68	**0.81**
aarddict.android	0.13	0.17	**0.18**	0.13
anymemo-stable	0.37	0.37	0.39	**0.42**
batterydog	0.60	0.61	**0.64**	0.62
addi	0.17	0.17	**0.18**	0.17
evancharltmileage	0.39	**0.42**	0.36	0.32
autoanswer	0.14	0.18	**0.21**	0.14
multismssender	0.64	**0.67**	0.52	0.63
kvance.nectroid	0.45	**0.48**	0.36	0.44
cri.sanity	0.23	**0.26**	0.24	0.22
dalvik-explorer	0.38	0.40	0.47	**0.54**
hotdeath-debug	0.66	0.66	**0.70**	0.61
conf.hatalab.mnv	0.56	0.40	0.42	**0.61**
k9mail	0.07	0.07	**0.08**	0.07
fercanet.lnm	**0.45**	**0.45**	0.44	**0.45**
counter	0.23	0.26	**0.31**	0.23
beide.bomber	0.68	0.72	**0.81**	0.68
frozenbubble	0.64	0.65	**0.74**	0.65
passwordmanager	0.07	0.08	0.06	**0.11**
tippy_1.1.3	**0.81**	0.76	0.78	0.80

(continued)

Table 6. (*continued*)

App. name	Monkey	Stoat	TimeMachine	OAT
tomdroid	0.52	0.54	**0.55**	0.52
weight-chart	0.55	0.47	0.50	**0.70**
whohasmystuff	**0.77**	0.75	0.63	0.76
Average	0.446	0.444	0.447	**0.454**
Best	4	9	**15**	10

Table 7. Fault detection comparison with State-of-the-ART techniques

App.name	Monkey	Stoat	TimeMachine	OAT
book-catalogue	0	0.6	**0.8**	0
countdowntimer	0	0	**0.6**	0
divideandconquer	0	0	0	0
munchlife	0	0	0	0
myexpenses	1	**1.2**	1	0
photostream	1.1	0.8	1.2	**2.2**
randommusicplayer	0	0	0	**1.1**
ringdroid	1.9	2.1	**2.3**	1.8
spritemethodtest	0	0	0	0
syncmypix	0	0	0	**1**
translate	0	0	0	**0.8**
wordpress_394	1	0.7	**1.2**	1
alogcat	0	0	1	**1.3**
aarddict.android	0	0	0	0
anymemo-stable	**2.2**	1.6	1.8	1
baterrydog	0	0	0	**0.7**
addi	1	**1.1**	1	1
evancharltmileage	1	0.8	0.6	**1.5**
autoanswer	1.5	2.9	2.2	**3.4**
multismssender	0	0	0	**1**
kvance.nectroid	0	0	0	0
cri.sanity	**1**	0	**1**	0.6
dalvik-explorer	1	0.6	1.4	**1.8**
hotdeath-debug	**2**	1.4	**2**	0

(*continued*)

Table 7. (*continued*)

App.name	Monkey	Stoat	TimeMachine	OAT
conf.hatalab.mnv	0	0	0	0
k9mail	1	2.6	6.1	**12.4**
fercanet.lnm	**3.2**	2	3	3
counter	0	0	0	**1.4**
beide.bomber	0	0	0	0
frozenbubble	0	0	0	0
passwordmanager	1	0.4	1.2	**1.4**
tippy_1.1.3	0	0	0	0
tomdroid	0	0	1	1
weight-chart	2.6	**3.2**	2.7	2.2
whohasmystuff	0	0	0	0
Average	0.64	0.63	0.92	**1.19**
Best	4	3	7	**14**

traversal time required to reach the state at the cost of additional storage space and the loading time. In addition, TimeMachine needs to calculate code coverage online during testing to determine which parts of Android applications have not been explored. The disadvantage of this method is that its strategy leads to non-trivial computation cost, resulting in a longer testing time.

OAT adopts reinforcement learning algorithm to carry out adaptive learning of exploration strategy. In the process of exploration, it can continuously reach some Android application states that are difficult to traverse before according to previous experience, so as to achieve a high code coverage. OAT has designed a new reward function for the state search process of Android application testing, which can not only reward the state change caused by interface jump, but also reward the fine-grained widget position and text change in the interface. The new reward function makes the exploration strategy learned during the test more comprehensive and detailed. These optimizations in general improve the code coverage and fault detection capabilities of OAT.

5 Related Work

5.1 Random Based Strategy

Because of the complexity and diversity of the Android test environment, the random test strategy can often achieve relatively stable results with high efficiency. Monkey [4] is the most commonly used tool among random testing techniques. It conducts application testing by interacting with randomly selected positions on the screen. Monkey is simple in design and can often achieve good test results.

Dynodroid [3] adds system events to Monkey's random testing strategy. It can obtain corresponding system events through the application's registration behavior in the Android framework. In the selection of random events, Dynodroid adopts the BiasedRandom selection strategy, which prefers to select the events that are least frequently selected. In addition, Dynodroid also supports users to enter account and password during the testing process to pass the authentication interface.

Other tools [38–40] use fuzzing to generate intent inputs rather than exploring the state model of the application. Null intent fuzzer [38] is an open-source intent fuzzer designed to reveal buggy intent handlers of activities that do not properly check input. Although it is quite effective and professional in revealing such problems, it is not effective to detect other problems. Intent Fuzzy [39] mainly tests how an application interacts with other applications installed on the same device. It includes a static analysis component, which is built on FlowDroid [41] to identify the organizational structure of intents so that they can be generated accordingly. The tool has been proved to be effective in revealing security problems.

5.2 Model Based Strategy

Some model based testing technologies [16, 23–25] build the GUI model of the Android application under test and choose the next exploration strategy according to the model. These methods usually assume that the model is a finite state machine and dynamically build the GUI model in the process of testing, with the ultimate goal of exploring all possible states and events in the model.

GUIRipper [16] builds GUI models through dynamic testing. It explores the built models through DFS policies and updates GUI models as well as executable event lists when new states are found. When new state cannot be found for a long time, GUIRipper will restart the searching process from the appropriate states.

Stoat [15] builds navigation models for Android applications through dynamic analysis, which is used to effectively explore application states and then extracts test cases from these models. Stoat uses random FSMs to model application behavior. The application model is built using dynamic analysis and is enhanced through a weighted UI exploration strategy and static analysis.

Hao et al. [17] proposed the PUMA tool, which is a general Android automated testing framework. In addition to providing monkey's random testing strategy, it can also be used for dynamic analysis and test case generation of Android applications. Users can also extend it according to their own needs.

Such methods [35, 36, 37] use genetic algorithms or symbolic execution to generate coverage oriented inputs. Sapienz [18] is an Android application testing tool based on multi-objective search. It uses crossover and mutation in genetic algorithm to continuously optimize test cases, so as to achieve higher code coverage, more accurate fault detection and shorter test cases.

TimeMachine [5] can record and save the Android application test environment during the test process. When necessary, it can return to a certain app state under test to continue the test, saving the traversal time required to reach the state at the cost of additional storage space and the loading time required by the app test state. TimeMachine calculates code coverage online during testing to determine which parts of Android applications have not been explored. When the exploration stops, TimeMachine will choose the previous state to restart and explore again.

5.3 Machine Learning Based Strategy

Machine learning based strategies usually use deep neural networks to learn testing strategies. Some methods [28–30] perform training based on previous testing data, and then testing the learned strategies on new applications. QBE [26] conducts model training and strategy learning based on the code coverage and fault detection data in Android applications. QBE represents the same abstract state of different applications, so that the strategies learned previously can be used on new apps. However, Android application design is flexible, complex and diverse. Therefore, old knowledge may not work on new apps.

Other methods [31–33] train a model for each application separately, or dynamically adjust the model during testing. AutoBlackTest [27] is one of the first works to propose reinforcement learning for GUI testing. This method is based on the simplest form of Q-Learning, and the initial value in the Q table strongly affects its effectiveness.

There are also methods that extend AutoBlackTest without an explicit training process. They only use Q-Learning to guide the testing process of Android applications. Q-testing [34] is also an Android automated testing method based on Q-learning. Q-learning uses Q-table as a lightweight model to learn experience and knowledge, and uses curiosity strategy to explore unknown functions. The reward of Q-learning is calculated from the status similarity of Android app.

6 Conclusion

In this work, we propose OAT, an optimized automated testing tool for Android applications based on deep reinforcement learning. It proposes a fine-grained representation of Android application state and uses MCTS exploration strategy to support the exploration process of reinforcement learning. OAT also designed a new loss function to give appropriate rewards for changes of state within an activity. Finally, only those crashes that have not been detected will be rewarded. Our experiments show that the proposed fine-grained reward function and MCTS exploration strategy can improve code coverage and fault detection capabilities. Furthermore, OAT is more effective than Monkey, Stoat and TimeMachine in terms of both code coverage and fault detection capability.

For future work, we will improve the model design of RL algorithm to better meet the requirements of Android application testing. In addition, we plan to continue to optimize the state representation and reward function to achieve better testing effect and efficiency.

Acknowledgement. This work was supported in part by the CityU MF EXT (project no. 9678180).

References

1. Mobile OS Market Share (2021). https://gs.statcounter.com/os-market-share/mobile/worldwide.
2. Statista. Number of apps available in leading app stores as of July 2014. http://www.statista.com/statistics/276623/number-of-apps-available-in-leading-app-stores/. (Accessed 08 2014)
3. Machiry, A., Tahiliani, R., Naik, M.: Dynodroid: an input generation system for Android apps. In: Proceedings of the 2013 9th Joint Meeting on Foundations of Software Engineering, pp. 224–234. Association for Computing Machinery, Saint Petersburg, Russia (2013)
4. Doyle, J., Saber, T., Arcaini, P., Ventresque, A.: Improving mobile user interface testing with model driven monkey search. In: 2021 IEEE International Conference on Software Testing, Verification and Validation Workshops (ICSTW), pp. 138–145. IEEE (2021)
5. Dong, Z., Böhme, M., Cojocaru, L., Roychoudhury, A.: Time-travel testing of android apps. In: Proceedings of the ACM/IEEE 42nd International Conference on Software Engineering, pp. 481–492 (2020)
6. Romdhana, A., Merlo, A., Ceccato, M., Tonella, P.: Deep reinforcement learning for black-box testing of android apps. ACM Trans. Softw. Eng. Methodol. **31**(4), Article 65 , 29 pages (2022)
7. Coulom, R.: Efficient selectivity and backup operators in monte-carlo tree search. In: Computers and Games: 5th International Conference, CG 2006, Turin, Italy, 29–31 May 2006. Revised Papers 5, pp. 72–83. Springer (2006)
8. Haarnoja, T., Zhou, A., Abbeel, P., Levine, S.: Soft actor-critic: Off-policy maximum entropy deep reinforcement learning with a stochastic actor. In: Proceedings of the Interntional Conference on Machine Learning, pp. 1861–1870. PMLR (2018)
9. Ye, W., Liu, S., Kurutach, T., Abbeel, P., Gao, Y.J.A.i.N.I.P.S.: Mastering atari games with limited data, vol. 34, pp. 25476–25488 (2021)
10. Auer, P., Cesa-Bianchi, N., Fischer, P.J.M.l.: Finite-time analysis of the multiarmed bandit problem, vol. 47, pp. 235–256 (2002)
11. Appium. http://appium.io. (Accessed 25 Sept 2020)
12. Emma, http://emma.sourceforge.net (Accessed 30 Dec 2020)
13. Jacoco Code Coverage. https://www.eclemma.org/jacoco/. (Accessed 15 Nov 2020)
14. Choudhary, S.R., Gorla, A., Orso, A.: Automated test input generation for android: Are we there yet?. In: 2015 30th IEEE/ACM International Conference on Automated Software Engineering (ASE), pp. 429–440 (2015)
15. Su, T., et al.: Guided, stochastic model-based GUI testing of Android apps. In: Proceedings of the 2017 11th Joint Meeting on Foundations of Software Engineering, pp. 245–256 (2017)
16. Amalfitano, D., Fasolino, A.R., Tramontana, P., De Carmine, S., Memon, A.M.: Using GUI ripping for automated testing of Android applications. In: Proceedings of the 27th IEEE/ACM International Conference on Automated Software Engineering, pp. 258–261 (2012)
17. Hao, S., Liu, B., Nath, S., Halfond, W.G., Govindan, R.: Puma: Programmable ui-automation for large-scale dynamic analysis of mobile apps. In: Proceedings of the 12th annual international conference on Mobile systems, applications, and services, pp. 204–217 (2014)
18. Mao, K., Harman, M., Jia, Y.: Sapienz: Multi-objective automated testing for android applications. In: Proceedings of the 25th International Symposium on Software Testing and Analysis, pp. 94–105 (2016)
19. UIAutomator (2021). https://developer.android.com/training/testing/ui-automator
20. Android Emulator. https://developer.android.com/studio/run/emulator/. (Accessed 20 Oct 2020)
21. Lillicrap, T.P., et al.: Continuous control with deep reinforcement learning (2015)

22. Fujimoto, S., Hoof, H., Meger, D.: Addressing function approximation error in actor-critic methods. In: International Conference on Machine Learning, pp. 1587–1596. PMLR (2018)
23. Amalfitano, D., Fasolino, A.R., Tramontana, P., Ta, B.D., Memon, A.M.J.I.s.: MobiGUITAR: Automated model-based testing of mobile apps, vol. 32, pp. 53–59 (2014)
24. Azim, T., Neamtiu, I.: Targeted and depth-first exploration for systematic testing of android apps. In: Proceedings of the 2013 ACM SIGPLAN International Conference on Object Oriented Programming Systems Languages & Applications, pp. 641–660 (2013)
25. Baek, Y.-M., Bae, D.-H.: Automated model-based android gui testing using multi-level gui comparison criteria. In: Proceedings of the 31st IEEE/ACM International Conference on Automated Software Engineering, pp. 238–249 (2016)
26. Koroglu, Y., et al.: QBE: QLearning-based exploration of android applications. In: 2018 IEEE 11th International Conference on Software Testing, Verification and Validation (ICST), pp. 105–115. IEEE (2018)
27. Mariani, L., Pezze, M., Riganelli, O., Santoro, M.: Autoblacktest: Automatic black-box testing of interactive applications. In: 2012 IEEE Fifth International Conference on Software Testing, Verification and Validation, pp. 81–90. IEEE (2012)
28. Borges Jr, N.P., Gómez, M., Zeller, A.: Guiding app testing with mined interaction models. In: Proceedings of the 5th International Conference on Mobile Software Engineering and Systems, pp. 133–143 (2018)
29. Li, Y., Yang, Z., Guo, Y., Chen, X.: Humanoid: A deep learning-based approach to automated black-box android app testing. In: 2019 34th IEEE/ACM International Conference on Automated Software Engineering (ASE), pp. 1070–1073. IEEE (2019)
30. Lin, J.-W., Jabbarvand, R., Malek, S.: Test transfer across mobile apps through semantic mapping. In: 2019 34th IEEE/ACM International Conference on Automated Software Engineering (ASE), pp. 42–53. IEEE (2019)
31. Adamo, D., Khan, M.K., Koppula, S., Bryce, R.: Reinforcement learning for android gui testing. In: Proceedings of the 9th ACM SIGSOFT International Workshop on Automating TEST Case Design, Selection, and Evaluation, pp. 2–8 (2018)
32. Vuong, T.A.T., Takada, S.: Semantic analysis for deep Q-network in android GUI testing. In: 31st International Conference on Software Engineering and Knowledge Engineering(SEKE), pp. 123–128 (2019)
33. Vuong, T.A.T., Takada, S.: A reinforcement learning based approach to automated testing of android applications. In: Proceedings of the 9th ACM SIGSOFT International Workshop on Automating TEST Case Design, Selection, and Evaluation, pp. 31–37 (2018)
34. Pan, M., Huang, A., Wang, G., Zhang, T., Li, X.: Reinforcement learning based curiosity-driven testing of Android applications. In: Proceedings of the 29th ACM SIGSOFT International Symposium on Software Testing and Analysis, pp. 153–164 (2020)
35. Anand, S., Naik, M., Harrold, M.J., Yang, H.: Automated concolic testing of smartphone apps. In: Proceedings of the ACM SIGSOFT 20th International Symposium on the Foundations of Software Engineering, pp. 1–11 (2012)
36. Gao, X., Tan, S.H., Dong, Z., Roychoudhury, A.: Android testing via synthetic symbolic execution. In: Proceedings of the 33rd ACM/IEEE International Conference on Automated Software Engineering, pp. 419–429 (2018)
37. Mahmood, R., Mirzaei, N., Malek, S.: Evodroid: segmented evolutionary testing of android apps. In: Proceedings of the 22nd ACM SIGSOFT International Symposium on Foundations of Software Engineering, pp. 599–609 (2014)
38. NCC group Intent Fuzzer. https://www.nccgroup.trust/us/our-research/intent-fuzzer/. (Accessed 31 Dec 2022)
39. Sasnauskas, R., Regehr, J.: Intent fuzzer: crafting intents of death. In: Proceedings of the 2014 Joint International Workshop on Dynamic Analysis (WODA) and Software and System Performance Testing, Debugging, and Analytics (PERTEA), pp. 1–5 (2014)

40. Ye, H., Cheng, S., Zhang, L., Jiang, F.: Droidfuzzer: Fuzzing the android apps with intent-filter tag. In: Proceedings of International Conference on Advances in Mobile Computing & Multimedia, pp. 68–74 (2013)
41. Arzt, S., et al.: Flowdroid: Precise context, flow, field, object-sensitive and lifecycle-aware taint analysis for android apps, vol. 49, pp. 259–269 (2014)
42. Abramson, B.: The expected-outcome model of two-player games. Morgan Kaufmann (2014)
43. Hafner, D., Lillicrap, T., Norouzi, M., Ba, J.J.a.p.a.: Mastering atari with discrete world models (2020)
44. Silver, D., et al.: Mastering the game of Go with deep neural networks and tree search, vol. 529, pp. 484–489 (2016)
45. Silver, D., et al.: Mastering the game of go without human knowledge, vol. 550, pp. 354–359 (2017)
46. Droid F. F-droid: Free and open source android app repository. https://f-droid.org/. (Accessed 31 Dec 2022)

Decomposing Synthesized Strategies for Reactive Multi-agent Reinforcement Learning

Chenyang Zhu[1(✉)], Jinyu Zhu[1], Yujie Cai[1], and Fang Wang[2(✉)]

[1] Changzhou University, Changzhou Jiangsu, China
zcy@cczu.edu.cn
[2] Brunel University London, London, UK
fang.wang@brunel.ac.uk

Abstract. Multi-Agent Reinforcement Learning (MARL) has been used to solve sequential decision problems by a collection of intelligent agents interacting in a shared environment. However, the design complexity of MARL strategies increases with the complexity of the task specifications. In addition, current MARL approaches suffer from slow convergence and reward sparsity when dealing with multi-task specifications. Linear temporal logic works as one of the software engineering practices to describe non-Markovian task specifications, whose synthesized strategies can be used as a priori knowledge to train the multi-agents to interact with the environment more efficiently. In this paper, we consider multi-agents that react to each other with a high-level reactive temporal logic specification called Generalized Reactivity of rank 1 (GR(1)). We first decompose the synthesized strategy of GR(1) into a set of potential-based reward machines for individual agents. We prove that the parallel composition of the reward machines forward simulates the original reward machine, which satisfies the GR(1) specification. We then extend the Markov Decision Process (MDP) with the synchronized reward machines. A value-iteration-based approach is developed to compute the potential values of the reward machine based on the strategy structure. We also propose a decentralized Q-learning algorithm to train the multi-agents with the extended MDP. Experiments on multi-agent learning under different reactive temporal logic specifications demonstrate the effectiveness of the proposed method, showing a superior learning curve and optimal rewards.

Keywords: Reinforcement Learning · Linear Temporal Logic · GR(1) · Reward Shaping

1 Introduction

A multi-agent system is a distributed computing system in which multiple agents interact in the same environment in a cooperative or adversarial manner to maximize the ability to accomplish tasks and achieve specific goals [7].

Multi-agent Reinforcement learning (MARL) has been used to solve sequential decision-making problems for multi-agent systems, which is widely used in task scheduling, resource allocation, and collaborative decision support in stochastic environments [27]. Reactive MARL is a subfield of MARL that focuses on the problem of training multiple agents to interact with each other to achieve a common goal. The design complexity of reactive MARL strategies increases with the complexity of task specifications. Moreover, the current MARL approaches suffer from slow convergence and reward sparsity when dealing with multi-task specifications [34].

Linear Temporal Logic (LTL) [23] is one of the most commonly used formal methods for specifying the desired properties of a system, such as safety and liveness properties. Using LTL to specify task specifications in multi-agent systems can help to capture the temporal properties of the environment and the interactions between agents. Taking motion planning as an example, LTL can describe task specifications such as avoiding certain obstacle areas and traveling through certain areas with some temporal orders. Several approaches have been used to integrate LTL with MARL. One approach is to use LTL to specify the task specifications of multi-agents and use reinforcement learning approaches to learn the policies of agents that satisfy the LTL specifications [30]. However, this approach is intractable under complicated LTL specifications. There is also research to transform LTL to LDBA (Limit-Deterministic Büchi Automata) and use MARL to learn the optimal policies for the agents that maximize the expected cumulative reward while satisfying the LTL formulas [9]. This kind of approach mainly focuses on satisfying temporal logic specifications with maximum probability in unknown stochastic environments, and less work has been done to decompose the whole task into independent sub-tasks for the multi-agents to accomplish. There also exists approaches that use the synthesized strategies of LTL specifications as a priori knowledge to train the multi-agents to interact with the environment more efficiently [34]. This paper mainly focuses on using this approach to decompose the synthesized strategy into independent sub-tasks so as to improve the performance of multi-agents.

This paper considers multi-agents that react to each other with a high-level reactive temporal logic specification called Generalized Reactivity of rank 1 (GR(1)). We first decompose the synthesized strategy of GR(1) into a set of potential-based reward machines for individual agents. Parallel composition is typically used to combine the behavior of multiple systems into a single system. However, the parallel composition of the decomposed reward machines might not be bisimulation equivalent to the original synthesized strategy. Therefore we provide sufficient conditions to prove that the parallel composition of the reward machines forward simulates the original reward machine, which then can be used to show that the parallel composition of the decomposed reward machines still satisfies the GR(1) specification. Furthermore, the Markov Decision Process (MDP) is extended with the synchronized reward machines. A value-iteration-based approach is developed to compute the potential values of the reward machine based on the strategy structure. We also propose a decentralized Q-learning algorithm to train the multi-agents with the extended MDP.

Experiments on multi-agent learning under different reactive temporal logic specifications have shown that the proposed approach outperforms the state-of-art MARL algorithms in terms of the learning curve and optimal rewards.

The rest of the paper is organized as follows. Section 2 provides an overview of GR(1) specifications and RL with Q-learning and reward shaping. Section 3 presents the framework to decompose the synthesized strategy from GR(1) specification for decentralized training in MARL. Formal proofs and algorithms are presented in this section. Section 4 uses a grid-world case study to illustrate the effectiveness of the proposed approach using four GR(1) specifications. Section 5 discusses related work integrating LTL with RL for training agents to satisfy multi-task specifications in MARL. Section 6 summarizes the contributions of the work and outlines future work.

2 Preliminaries

2.1 Synthesis of Reactive Temporal Logic

LTL is a formalism introduced by Pnueli to specify properties of discrete systems, which extends propositional logic with temporal operators such as eventually operator $\Diamond$, always operator $\Box$, until operator $\mathcal{U}$ and next operator $\bigcirc$ [23]. Reactive properties refer to the desired properties such as safety, liveness, or other temporal properties that must be satisfied in order for the system to function as desired. Reactive properties can be formalized using LTL to ensure that the system behaves in accordance with the desired properties in a reactive environment.

LTL strategy synthesis refers to generating a control strategy that satisfies the LTL specification over infinite traces. With the automata-based approach, the LTL formula is first translated into the Buchi automaton, a finite-state automaton with a single accepting state. Then a Deterministic Finite Automaton (DFA) is constructed to guide the system to reach the accepting state. However, the complexity of LTL synthesis depends on the size of DFA, which is exponential in the number of atomic propositions in the LTL formula. Research has shown that the LTL synthesizing problem is 2EXPTIME-complete [24]. GR(1) is a fragment of LTL for synthesizing controllers for reactive systems, whose control strategies can be synthesized in polynomial time [22]. The GR(1) specifications can be formalized in Formula (1), which consists of:

- φ_I: A Boolean formula characterizing the initial state;
- $\bigwedge_i \Box \psi_i$: The conjunction of LTL formulas that denoting the system invariants, where ψ_i is a Boolean formula presenting the transition relation;
- $\bigwedge_i \Box \Diamond \varphi_i$: The conjunction of LTL formulas that denoting the liveness goals, where φ is a Boolean formula.

$$\phi = (\varphi_I^e \wedge \bigwedge_i \Box \psi_i^e \wedge \bigwedge_i \Box \Diamond \varphi_i^e) \rightarrow (\varphi_I^s \wedge \bigwedge_i \Box \psi_i^s \wedge \bigwedge_i \Box \Diamond \varphi_i^s) \qquad (1)$$

Here $\varphi_I^e, \psi_i^e, \varphi_i^e$ denote the assumptions on the environment, and $\varphi_I^s, \psi_i^s, \varphi_i^s$ characterize the behavior of the system. Given that the environment satisfies the assumptions presented as LTL formulas, the system is supposed to satisfy the specifications.

2.2 Reinforcement Learning with Q-learning and Reward Shaping

In RL, an agent learns the behavior to interact with a dynamic environment through a trial-and-error manner and receives a reward for each action it takes [15]. The agent learns to make decisions during the training process by maximizing the expected cumulative reward. Typically the environment is modeled as an MDP in the form

$$\mathcal{M} = \langle S, s_0, A, P, R, \gamma \rangle$$

where S represents a finite set of states, $s_0 \in S$ denotes the initial states, A denotes a finite set of actions, $P \in S \times A \to Dist(S)$ denotes the transition probability distribution, $R \in S \times A \times S \to \mathbb{R}$ denotes the rewards assigned to the transitions between states, and γ denotes the discount factor. Here we use $\mathbb{R}$ to denote the real numbers. The policy of the agent $\lambda \in S \to Dist(A)$ is the probability distribution of the action $a \in A$ given the current state $s \in S$. At each step the agent selects an action $a \sim \lambda(s)$ based on the current s and receives the reward $R(s, a, s')$ where $s' \sim P(s, a)$. The goal of the agent is to find the optimal policy λ^* that maximizes the expected discounted reward.

Q-learning is a model-free reinforcement learning approach to find the optimal policy λ^* for an agent in an MDP with Bellman equation and value iteration [28]. Q-learning uses a function $Q \in S \times A \to \mathbb{R}$ to evaluate the quality of a state-action combination. Initially, the Q is initialized to the initial values, then at each step t, the agent selects an action $a_t \in A$, enters the state s_{t+1}, and gets the reward $R(s_t, a_t, s_{t+1})$. The Q function is updated with Eq. (2), where $\alpha \in [0, 1]$ is the learning rate. Based on Eq. (2), the Bellman equation can be derived as Eq. (3). The Q-learning algorithm is known for its ability to converge to the optimal policies in MDP [5].

$$Q(s_t, a_t) \leftarrow Q(s_t, a_t) + \alpha(R(s_t, a_t, s_{t+1}) + \gamma max_{a_{t+1}} Q(s_{t+1}, a_{t+1}) - Q(s_t, a_t)) \tag{2}$$

$$Q^*(s, a) = R(s, a, s') + \gamma \sum_{s' \in S} P(s' \mid s, a) \max_{a'} Q^*(s', a') \tag{3}$$

Recent research has shown that it is difficult to specify the rewards when designing the MDP. Usually, a reward is assigned only if the agent has accomplished the tasks, while this approach does not suit scenarios involving multiple sub-tasks and specifications. Reward shaping is used in RL to modify the reward function so that it can be used to guide the agent to learn towards a desired behavior [11]. One approach in reward shaping is to assign a potential functions $\phi \in S \to \mathbb{R}$ to each state s, and the reward function can be designed as Eq. (4) to avoid the transitions from states with high potential values to those with low potential values.

$$R(s_t, a_t, s_{t+1}) \leftarrow R(s_t, a_t, s_{t+1}) + \gamma \phi(s_{t+1}) - \phi(s_t) \tag{4}$$

3 Reactive Multi-Agent Reinforcement Learning with GR(1) Specifications

3.1 Reactive Multi-Agent Reinforcement Learning Framework

In Reactive MARL, agents might need to react to each other or the environment. Designing efficient reward functions for the reactive MARL algorithm is challenging for several reasons. Firstly, it is difficult to define the exact objective and reward functions. The reward function should reflect the desired behavior of the agents, whose goal is to satisfy the reactive specifications. Also, the reward function should be designed to encourage the agents to coordinate their actions effectively. Moreover, the policies of other agents may change during training, leading to non-stationarity environments and difficulties in defining stable reward functions. Here we use an example to illustrate our reactive MARL settings:

```
1  ENV: a;
2  SYS: b c;
3
4  ENVINIT: !a;
5  ENVTRANS: [](!a -> a') ;
6  ENVGOAL:[]<> a;
7
8  SYSINIT: !b&!c;
9  SYSTRANS: [](a&!b -> b')
10 &[](a&!c -> c')
11 &[](b&c -> b'&!c');
12 SYSGOAL: []<> (b&c);
13
```

Fig. 1. The GR(1) specification (left column) with its synthesized strategy (right column), where 1,2,3,4 denote the states and a1,a2,a3,a4,a5,a6,a7 denote the actions. Here state 0={!a,!b,!c}, state 1={a,b,c}, state 2={!a,b,!c}, state 3={a,b,!c}, state 4={!a,!b,!c}, a1=a&b&c, a2=!a&!c, a3=a&c, a4=c, a5=!c, a6=!a&!b&c, a7=a&b.

Example: Given three agents moving around a grid-world, we have different task locations for the agents to accomplish different tasks. Consider a scenario that the agents are required to cooperate to complete the tasks specified by the GR(1) specifications as shwon in Fig. 1. There are three task locations a, b, c used by three agents $agent_1$, $agent_2$ and $agent_3$, respectively. Initially $agent_1$ is not located on location a, $agent_2$ is not located on b and $agent_3$ is not located at c. The system constraints of the three agents can be expressed as:

- $agent_1$ should reach location a if it is not located at a;
- $agent_2$ should reach location b when $agent_1$ has reached location a and stays at a;

- $agent_3$ should reach location c when $agent_1$ has reached location a and stays at a;
- If $agent_2$ is located at b and $agent_3$ is located at c, then $agent_3$ should leave c;

Under these system constraints, the goal of the three agents can be expressed as:

- $agent_1$ should reach location a infinitely often;
- $agent_2$ should reach location b and $agent_3$ should reach location c infinitely often if $agent_1$ has reached location a infinitely often;

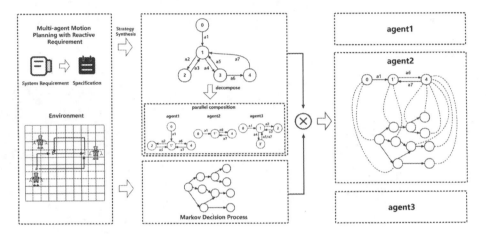

Fig. 2. Overall Framework of Reactive Multi-agent Reinforcement Learning

Figure 2 shows the overall framework of reactive multi-agent reinforcement learning. We first use strategy synthesis tools such as gr1c [18] to construct the synthesized strategy of the GR(1) specification or requirements of the system. The synthesized strategy is then decomposed into individual reward machines for each agent. Here we provide proof to show that the parallel composition of individual reward machines forward simulates the reward machine constructed from the synthesized strategy so that the interactions of these agents still satisfy the GR(1) specification. Also, the original reward machine can reach an accepting state if and only if all the individual reward machines reach their accepting states. At last, the MDP is extended with individual reward machines for decentralized training.

3.2   Synthesized Strategy Decomposition

GR(1) synthesis is based on the idea of constructing a game between the system and its environment, where the goal of the system is to satisfy the specifications and the goal of the environment is to prevent the system from satisfying the specifications. The strategy synthesized from the GR(1) can be presented as a transducer $\langle \mathcal{E}, \mathcal{E}_0, \mathcal{T}, \mathcal{F}, \xi^e, \xi^a \rangle$, where $\mathcal{E}$ is a finite set of states, $\mathcal{E}_0 \in \mathcal{E}$ is the initial state, $\mathcal{T} \subset E$ is the set of accepting state, $\mathcal{F}$ is the set of actions, $\xi^e \in \mathcal{E} \times \mathcal{F} \to \mathcal{E}$ is the transition function between states with corresponding actions, $\xi^a \in \mathcal{E} \to \mathcal{F}$ is the state output function which outputs the actions. We first construct the reward machine $\mathcal{N}$ with potential values that encode the synthesized strategy $\mathcal{S}$ in Definition 1, which introduces the reward function δ^r and potential function ϕ into $\mathcal{S}$. Given the state-action tuple (e, a), the reward function δ^r and the potential function ϕ can be calculated as Eq. (5) and Eq. (6), respectively. In the cases that the next state in the reward machine is one of the accepting states, formally presented as $\xi^e(e, a) \in \mathcal{T}$, then $\delta^r(e, a)$ is assigned with a reward $rv \in \mathbb{R}$, also $\phi(e, a)$ is assigned with some potential value $pv \in \mathbb{R}$. Here we assume that rv and pv are under the same scalar. The accepting states can also indicate that the task specifications have been satisfied. In the cases that the next state in the reward machine is not one of the accepting states, formally presented as $\xi^e(e, a) \notin \mathcal{T}$, then $\delta^r(e, a)$ is assigned with a reward 0, and $\phi(e, a)$ is assigned with a value within the range $(0, pv)$.

Definition 1 (Reward Machine with Potential Values). *Given the synthesized strategy $\mathcal{S} = \langle \mathcal{E}, \mathcal{E}_0, \mathcal{T}, \mathcal{F}, \xi^e \rangle$, the potential-based reward machine is defined as $\mathcal{N} = \langle E, E_0, T, F, \delta^e, \delta^r, \phi \rangle$, where E is a finite set of states, $E_0 \in E$ is the initial state, $T \subset E$ is the set of accepting states, F is the set of actions, $\delta^e \in E \times F \to E$ is the transition function between states, $\delta^r \in E \times F \to \mathbb{R}$ is the rewards function of the state with the transition function, $\phi \in E \to \mathbb{R}$ is the potential function of the states, where: $E = \mathcal{E}, E_0 = \mathcal{E}_0, T = \mathcal{T}, F = \mathcal{F}, \delta^e = \xi^e$;*

$$\delta^r(e, a) = \begin{cases} 0 & \xi^e(e, a) \notin \mathcal{T} \\ rv & \xi^e(e, a) \in \mathcal{T} \end{cases} \tag{5}$$

$$\begin{cases} \phi(e, a) \in (0, pv) & \xi^e(e, a) \notin \mathcal{T} \\ \phi(e, a) = pv & \xi^e(e, a) \in \mathcal{T} \end{cases} \tag{6}$$

The reward machine $\mathcal{N}$ in Definition 1 defines the team task of the agents in the MARL setting, where F defines all the high-level actions for the multi-agent systems. Each individual agent i within the system has a local observation with a subset of the actions $F_i \in F$. The reward machine $\mathcal{N}$ is decomposed into the individual reward machines based on the local action set F_i of each agent i. Definition 2 is used to define the projected states of the local action set F_i in the reward machine $\mathcal{N}$. We first define a mapping function ζ_i from a state $e \in E$ to a set of states $\hat{E} \subseteq E$ in Eq. (7). Given the state $e \in E$, we group all the states transited from e with the action set $F \setminus F_i$ as one set. Then the projected states of $\mathcal{N}$ under the local action set F_i is defined as the set of sets $\zeta_i(e)$ for all the states $e \in E$, which is defined in Eq. (8).

Definition 2 (Projected States of Local Action Set). *Given the reward machine* $\mathcal{N} = \langle E, E_0, T, F, \delta^e, \delta^r, \phi \rangle$ *and the local action set* F_i, *the mapping function* ζ_i *from a state* $e \in E$ *to a set of states* $\hat{E} \subseteq E$ *is defined as:*

$$\zeta_i(e) = \hat{E} = \{e' \in E \mid \forall e' \in E \wedge a \in F \setminus F_i \Rightarrow e' \in \delta^e(e, a)\} \tag{7}$$

The projected states of $\mathcal{N}$ *under the local action set* F_i *is defined as:*

$$E_i = \{\zeta_i(e) \mid e \in E\} \tag{8}$$

Based on Definition 1 and Definition 2, Definition 3 is constructed to define the individual reward machines $\mathcal{N}_i$ for each agent i in the MARL setting. The individual reward machines $\mathcal{N}_i$ are decomposed from the reward machine $\mathcal{N}$ with the local event set F_i. In Definition 3, the states, initial states, and terminal states are mapped with the projected function ζ. The transition relation δ_i^e is preserved only when the transition exists between different projected states. If the transited state is the terminal state, then the reward is set to rv and the potential value is set to pv. Otherwise, the reward is set to 0 and the potential value is set to $(0, pv)$.

Definition 3 (Individual Reward Machine). *Given the reward machine* $\mathcal{N} = \langle E, E_0, T, F, \delta^e, \delta^r, \phi \rangle$ *and the local action set* F_i, *the individual reward machine* $\mathcal{N}_i$ *for agent* i *is defined as* $\mathcal{N}_i = \langle E_i, E_{0i}, T_i, F_i, \delta_i^e, \delta_i^r, \phi_i \rangle$, *where*

- $E_i = \{\zeta_i(e) \mid e \in E\}$;
- $E_{0i} = \{\zeta_i(e) \mid e \in E_0\}$;
- $T_i = \{\zeta_i(e) \mid e \in T\}$;
- $\delta_i^e \in E_i \times F_i \to E_i$ *is defined such that* $e_i' = \delta_i^e(e_i, a)$ *if and only if* $e_i \in \zeta_i(e)$, $e_i' \in \zeta_i(e')$ *and* $e' = \delta^e(e, a)$;
- $\delta_i^r \in E_i \times F_i \to \mathbb{R}$ *is defined such that* $\delta_i^r(e_i, a) = rv$ *if* $\delta_i^e(e_i, a) \in T_i$. *Otherwise,* $\delta_i^r(e_i, a) = 0$;
- $\phi_i \in E_i \to \mathbb{R}$ *is defined such that* $\phi_i(e_i) = pv$ *if* $e_i \in T_i$. *Otherwise,* $\phi_i(e_i) \in (0, pv)$.

Take the example in Fig. 1 as an example, we decompose the strategy into three individual strategies as shown in Fig. 3. Given the local event set F_i, we merge the transited states with events in $F \setminus F_i$. In the example, $F = \{a_1, a_2, a_3, a_4, a_5, a_6, a_7\}$ and $F_2 = \{a_1, a_6, a_7\}$. So state 2 and 3 are merged to state 1 based on Definition 2. In addition, the three agents should synchronize on the same event. For example, action $a1$ should be taken by the three agents simultaneously, or neither of the agents will trigger the state transition between state 0 and state 1.

The reward machine $\mathcal{N}$ is constructed from the synthesized strategy from the GR(1) specification, which guarantees that the corresponding system behaves

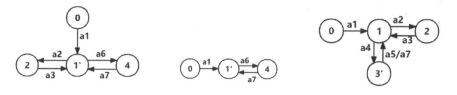

(a) Strategy for Agent 1   (b) Strategy for Agent 2   (c) Strategy for Agent 3

Fig. 3. Decomposed Strategies from the Example of Fig. 1

in accordance with the GR(1) specification. Specifically, the run of the reward machine $\mathcal{N}$ is guaranteed to satisfy the GR(1) specification if the accepting states are visited infinitely often. However, the parallel composition of the decomposed individual reward machines might not be bisimilarly equivalent to the original reward machine [16,17]. Therefore, we first validate that the parallel composition of the decomposed individual reward machines can still satisfy the GR(1) specification.

The forward simulation can be used to verify the refinement of systems with finite and infinite traces [19,32]. We use the definition of forward simulation and parallel composition to verify that the parallel composition of the decomposed reward machines can still preserve the GR(1) specifications. Inspired by the definition of forward simulation [19] and parallel composition [3,16], we define the forward simulation and parallel composition of reward machines in Definition 4 and Definition 5.

Definition 4 (Forward Simulation of Reward Machine).   *Given two reward machines* $\mathcal{M}$ *and* $\mathcal{N}$, $\mathcal{M}$ *is foward simulated by* $\mathcal{N}$, *denoted as* $\mathcal{M} \prec \mathcal{N}$, *if there exists a relation* $J \in E_{\mathcal{M}} \leftrightarrow E_{\mathcal{N}}$ *such that:*

- $(E_{0\mathcal{M}}, E_{0\mathcal{M}}) \in J$;
- $\forall(e_1, e_2) \in J \wedge e'_1 \in \delta^e_{\mathcal{M}}(e_1, a)$, *then* $\exists e'_2$ *such that* $(e'_1, e'_2) \in J$ *and* $e'_2 \in \delta^e_{\mathcal{N}}(e_2, a)$;

Definition 5 (Parallel Composition of Reward Machines).   *Given the reward machines* $\mathcal{N}_1, \mathcal{N}_2, ... \mathcal{N}_n$, *the parallel composition of* $\mathcal{N}_1$ *and* $\mathcal{N}_2$, *denoted as* $\mathcal{N}_1 \parallel \mathcal{N}_2 = \langle \hat{E}, \hat{E}_0, \hat{T}, \hat{F}, \hat{\delta}^e, \hat{\delta}^r, \hat{\phi} \rangle$, *is defined as:*

- $\hat{E} = E_1 \times E_2$;
- $\hat{E}_0 = (E_{01}, E_{02})$
- $\hat{T} = T_1 \times T_2$;
- $\hat{F} = F_1 \cup F_2$;
- $\hat{\delta}$ *is defined for all* $(e_1, e_2) \in E_1 \times E_2$ *and* $a \in F_1 \cup F_2$ *such that:*

$$
\hat{\delta}^e = \begin{cases} (\delta^e_1(e_1, a), \delta^e_2(e_2, a)) & \text{if } \delta^e_1(e_1, a), \delta^e_2(e_2, a) \text{ are defined and } a \in F_1 \cap F_2 \\ (\delta^e_1(e_1, a), e_2) & \text{if } \delta^e_1(e_1, a) \text{ is defined and } a \in F_1 \setminus F_2 \\ (e_1, \delta^e_2(e_2, a)) & \text{if } \delta^e_2(e_2, a) \text{ is defined and } a \in F_2 \setminus F_1 \\ \text{undefined} & \text{otherwise} \end{cases}
$$

– $\hat{\delta}^r$ is defined for all $(e_1, e_2) \in E_1 \times E_2$ and $a \in F_1 \cup F_2$ such that:

$$\hat{\delta}^r((e_1, e_2), a) = \begin{cases} rv & \text{if } \hat{\delta}^e((e_1, e_2), a) \in \hat{T} \\ 0 & \text{otherwise} \end{cases}$$

– $\hat{\phi}$ is defined for all $(e_1, e_2) \in E_1 \times E_2$ such that:

$$\hat{\phi}((e_1, e_2)) = \begin{cases} pv & \text{if } (e_1, e_2) \in \hat{T} \\ (0, pv) & \text{otherwise} \end{cases}$$

The parallel composition of all individual reward machines, denoted as $||_{i=1}^n \mathcal{N}_i$, is defined based on the associativity property of parallel composition [3], formally:

$$||_{i=1}^n \mathcal{N}_i = (((\mathcal{N}_1 \,||\, \mathcal{N}_2) \,||\, \mathcal{N}_3) \cdots) \,||\, \mathcal{N}_n$$

Based on the above definitions, we first use Lemma 3.1 to show that the reward machine $\mathcal{N}$ is forward simulated by the parallel composition of its decomposed reward machines $||_{i=1}^n \mathcal{N}_i$ if the union event set of the decomposed reward machines is equal to the event set of the original reward machine. Then, we construct Theorem 3.2 to show that if the reward machine is constructed from the synthesized strategy of the GR(1) specification, then the parallel composition of the decomposed individual reward machines can visit the accepting states infinitely often.

Lemma 3.1. *Given that $\bigcup_{i=1}^n F_i = F$, the reward machine $\mathcal{N}$ is forward simulated by the parallel composition of its decomposed reward machines, formally presented as $\mathcal{N} \prec ||_{i=1}^n \mathcal{N}_i$.*

Proof. We first prove $\mathcal{N} \prec (\mathcal{N}_1 \,||\, \mathcal{N}_2)$. Let $\mathcal{N} = \langle E, E_0, T, F, \delta^e, \delta^r, \phi \rangle$, $\mathcal{N}_1 \,||\, \mathcal{N}_2 = \langle \hat{E}, \hat{E}_0, \hat{T}, \hat{F}, \hat{\delta}^e, \hat{\delta}^r, \hat{\phi} \rangle$, we prove that there exists a relation $J = \{(e_1, e_2) \in E \times \hat{E} \mid \forall e_1 \in ran(\delta^e) \Rightarrow e_2 = (\zeta_1(e_1), \zeta_2(e_1))\}$ between $\mathcal{N}$ and $\mathcal{N}_1 \,||\, \mathcal{N}_2$. It is obvious that $(E_0, (\zeta_1(E_0), \zeta_2(E_0)))) \in J$. Then we prove for all $i \geq 0$, if $(e_i, \hat{e}_i) \in J$, then $(e_{i+1}, \hat{e}_{i+1}) \in J$.

Based on Definition 2 and Definition 5,

$$\hat{e}_{i+1} = \hat{\delta}^e(\hat{e}_i, a) = \begin{cases} (\delta_1^e(\zeta_1(e_i), a), \delta_2^e(\zeta_2(e_i), a)) & \text{if } a \in F_1 \cap F_2 \\ (\delta_1^e(\zeta_1(e_i), a), e_2) & \text{if } a \in F_1 \setminus F_2 \\ (e_1, \delta_2^e(\zeta_2(e_i), a)) & \text{if } a \in F_2 \setminus F_1 \end{cases}$$

$$\zeta_i(e_{i+1}) = \begin{cases} \delta_i(\zeta_i(e_i), a) & \text{if } a \in F_i \\ \zeta_i(e_i) & \text{if } a \notin F_i \end{cases}$$

Consider the three cases, namely $a \in F_1 \cap F_2$, $a \in F_1 \setminus F_2$ and $a \in F_2 \setminus F_1$, we can prove that $\hat{e}_{i+1} = (\zeta_1(e_{i+1}), \zeta_2(e_{i+1}))$, which can then be used to prove $(e_{i+1}, \hat{e}_{i+1}) \in J$.

Next we extend the above result to n agents: $\mathcal{N} \prec \mathcal{N}_1 \| \mathcal{N}_1'$, where $\mathcal{N}_1'$ is the parallel composition of reward machines whose local event set is $F \setminus F_1$. Then $\mathcal{N}_1' \prec \mathcal{N}_2 \| \mathcal{N}_2'$. So we have the following proof:

$$\mathcal{N} \prec \mathcal{N}_1 \| \mathcal{N}_1' \prec \mathcal{N}_1 \| \mathcal{N}_2 \| \mathcal{N}_2' \prec \cdots \prec \mathcal{N}_1 \| \mathcal{N}_2 \cdots \| \mathcal{N}_n = \|_{i=1}^{n} \mathcal{N}_i$$

Theorem 3.2. *Given reward machine $\mathcal{N}$ and a collection of agents with local action set F_1, F_2,...,F_n such that $\cup_{i=1}^{n} F(i) = F$. Then any event sequence of the system $\|_{i=1}^{n} \mathcal{N}_i$ can visit the accepting states infinitely often.*

Proof. Based on Lemma 3.1, $\mathcal{N} \prec \|_{i=1}^{n} \mathcal{N}_i$. Since the reward machine $\mathcal{N}$ is constructed from the synthesized strategy of the GR(1) specification, then the event sequence π of $\mathcal{N}$ satisfies $(\pi, i) \models \Box \Diamond e \in T$. From Definition 5, if $\mathcal{N}$ is at the terminal state, then $\|_{i=1}^{n} \mathcal{N}$ is also at the terminal state. So $\|_{i=1}^{n} \mathcal{N}$ satisfies $(\hat{\pi}, i) \models \Box \Diamond \hat{e} \in \hat{T}$.

3.3 Extending MDP with Synthesized Strategies of GR(1) Specifications

MDP is used in reinforcement learning to model the environment. However, the Markov property of MDP puts a limit on the RL as it requires that the future states of the system only depends on the current state and not on the history. In this paper, we extend the MDP with the decomposed reward machines $\mathcal{N}_i$ to reward the agents in Definition 6. Here we assume that $\mathcal{M}$ and $\mathcal{N}_i$ share the same labeling function $\mathcal{L}$. If $\langle e, \mathcal{L}(s, a, s') \rangle \in \text{dom}(\delta_i^e)$, then $\mathcal{N}_i$ would move from e to $\delta_i^e(e, \mathcal{L}(s, a, s'))$, otherwise the reward machine will stay in the state e. As the transition probability distribution is defined over $S \times A$, the extended transition probability $\hat{P}$ is the same. As shown in Eq. (9), if the next state in the reward machine is the accepting state, then $\hat{R}$ is updated with the reward function δ_i^r only. In the cases that the next state is not the accepting state, then $\hat{R}$ is updated with both δ_i^r and ϕ_i. Here we assume that δ_i^r and ϕ_i are in the same scale to balance the impact of the reward function and potential function.

Definition 6 (MDP with Individual Reward Machine). *Given the individual reward machine $\mathcal{N}_i = \langle E_i, E_{0i}, T_i, F_i, \delta_i^e, \delta_i^r, \phi_i \rangle$ and the MDP $\mathcal{M} = \langle S, s_0, A, P, R, \gamma \rangle$, where $\mathcal{M}$ and $\mathcal{N}_i$ shares the labeling function $\mathcal{L} \in S \times A \times S \rightarrow F_i$. The extended MDP is defined as $\mathcal{M}_{\mathcal{N}_i} = \langle \hat{S}, \hat{s}_0, A, \hat{P}, \hat{R}, \gamma \rangle$, where:*

- $\hat{S} = S \times E_i$;
- $\hat{s}_0 = s_0 \times E_{0i}$;
- $\hat{P}(\langle s', e_i' \rangle \mid \langle s, e_i \rangle, a) = P(s' \mid s, a)$
- $\hat{R}(\langle s, e_i \rangle, a, \langle s', e_i' \rangle)$ is defined for all $\langle s, e_i \rangle \in S \times E_i$, $a \in A$, such that:

$$
\begin{cases}
\delta_i^r(e_i, \mathcal{L}(s, a, s')) & e_i' \in T_i \\
\delta_i^r(e_i, \mathcal{L}(s, a, s')) + \gamma \phi_i(e_i') - \phi_i(e_i) & e_i' \notin T_i
\end{cases}
\tag{9}
$$

3.4 Multi-Agent Reinforcement Learning with Synchronized Synthesized Strategies

In reactive MARL, the agents are trained to coordinate their actions to achieve the best collective outcome. There are centralized training approaches and decentralized training approaches to train the reactive MARL. Centralized training with decentralized execution can monitor the interactions between actions to handle nonstationarity despite its poor scalability [14]. However, decentralized training has good scalability but might converge to sub-optimal policies [31]. In our reactive MARL setting, the optimal strategy of each agent is to visit the accepting state of its reward machine infinitely often. Based on Definition 3 and Theorem 3.2, the optimal strategy of the team is consistent with the optimal joint strategies of individual agents. Thus in this paper, we propose a decentralized Q-learning algorithm to train the reactive MARL as shown in Algorithm 1.

Algorithm 1: Decentralized Q-learning with extended MDP

input : $\mathcal{M}, \mathcal{N}_i$, where $i \in [1,n], \gamma \in (0,1], \alpha \in (0,1]$
output: $Q_i(\langle s, e_i \rangle, a)$, where $s \in S, e \in E_i, a \in A$
1 For all $i \in [1,n]$, initialize $Q_i(\langle s, e_i \rangle, a)$ arbitrarily;
2 **for** t *from 0 to num_episodes:* **do**
3   Initialize $s \leftarrow s_0, e_i \leftarrow E_{0i}$;
4   **for** *each agent* i: **do**
5   Choose a from s using policy derived from $Q(\langle s, e_i \rangle, a)$ with boltzmann exploration;
6   Take action a with pre-defined probability p and observe the next state $\langle s', e'_i \rangle$;
7   Compute $\hat{R}_i(\langle s, e_i \rangle, a, \langle s', e'_i \rangle)$;
8   **for** $e_i \in E_i$ **do**
9              $Q_i(\langle s, e_i \rangle, a) \leftarrow (1 - \alpha)Q(\langle s, e_i \rangle, a) + \alpha(\hat{R}_i + \gamma max'_a Q(\langle s', e'_i \rangle, a'))$;
10   **end**
11   Update $s \leftarrow s'$ and $e_i \leftarrow e'_i$;
12   **if** $e_i \in T_i$ **then**
13   break
14   **end**
15   **end**
16 **end**
17 **return** $Q_i(\langle s, e_i \rangle, a)$

The algorithm takes in the MDP $\mathcal{M}$, individual reward machine $\mathcal{N}_i$, the learning rate α, an epsilon parameter and outputs the Q value function $Q_i(\langle s, e_i \rangle, a)$ for each agent i. Algorithm 1 follows the standard routine of Q-learning that uses the boltzmann exploration to select actions and calculate the Q values. Under the MARL setting, the agents must synchronize on the shared events between agents. That is, if the chosen event a is the shared event among multiple agents, then a should trigger the transitions in the individual reward machines of these agents. So during the decentralized training of individual agents, the action a will be taken with a pre-defined probability p to observe the next state pair $\langle s', e'_i \rangle$. In this case, a will always be taken after some steps. Then we compute the reward based on Eq. (9) based on the reward function and the potential function. Then for all the states in the individual reward machine, we calculate the Q value function for each state e_i with the Bellman equation.

In typical reinforcement learning, a reward is only given upon completing a task. This approach may not be appropriate in situations with multiple sub-tasks and requirements. Reward shaping is used in reinforcement learning by adding additional rewards to steer the agent towards specific goals [11]. In reward shaping, potential values are utilized to incentivize the agent to perform actions resulting in states with high potential values and deter actions resulting in low potential values. Inspired by work in [13], we propose a value-iteration-based reward shaping algorithm as shown in Algorithm 2 to assign potential values to the reward machine.

Algorithm 2: Value-Iteration Based Reward Shaping Algorithm

    input : $\mathcal{N}_i, \gamma$
    output: ϕ_i

1 **for** $e \in E_i$ **do**
2     $\phi_i(e) \leftarrow 0$
3 **end**
4 $err \leftarrow 1$;
5 **while** $err > \epsilon$ **do**
6     $err \leftarrow 0$;
7   **for** $e \in E_i$ **do**
8        $\phi' \leftarrow max\{\delta_i^r(e,a) + \gamma(\phi_i(\delta_i^e(e,a))) \mid \forall a \in F_i\}$;
9        $err = max\{err, \mid \phi' - \phi_i(e) \mid\}$;
10       $\phi_i(e) \leftarrow \phi'$;
11   **end**
12 **end**
13 **return** ϕ_i

The algorithm takes in the individual reward machine N_i and the discount factor γ. The algorithm aims to find the optimal policy that maximizes the expected discounted cumulative reward. Initially, the potential values of ϕ_i are set to 0. Then for each iteration, we update the value function for each state e as in Eq. (10). The algorithm terminates when the change in the values of the states becomes negligible. Moreover, we use the calculated value function as the potential function of the reward machine.

$$\phi' = max\{\delta_i^r(e,a) + \gamma(\phi_i(\delta_i^e(e,a))) \mid \forall a \in F_i\} \tag{10}$$

4   Experiments

4.1   Experiment Setup

In this section, the proposed algorithms are evaluated empirically with four different environment settings. Algorithm 1 and Algorithm 2 were implemented within the OpenAI Gym environment [1], utilizing the grid-world task configuration depicted in Sect. 3. A grid map of 10×10 size is constructed with randomly generated task locations. We used four GR(1) specifications to specify the reactive specifications of experiment settings with different agents. In these experiment settings, each agent had five available actions: move left, move right, move up, move down, and stay still. The agents should move and cooperate based on the GR(1) specifications.

We compared our proposed algorithm of the decentralized Q-learning with individual reward machines and reward shaping (DQ-iRM+RS) with four other algorithms. The first algorithm is the decentralized Q-learning with individual reward machines (DQ-iRM), which is inspired by work in [20]. The second is the centralized Q-learning with the original reward machine (CQRM), inspired by work in [13,33]. We also implemented the reward shaping technique on the IQL approach [25] (IQL+RS) and h-IL approach [26] (h-IL+RS). All the reward shaping was implemented with the value iteration algorithm.

Regarding the hyperparameter settings, we set the learning rate as 0.8, the discount factor as 0.9, and the error for value iteration as 10^{-7}. Each algorithm was subjected to five independent trials per experiment, and the learning curve for the average reward with deviation per episode was calculated. The experiments were trained with 60 episodes, each episode with 1000 steps.

4.2   Discussions

Figure 4 shows the comparison of learning curves for reactive MARL using different GR(1) specifications under the same hyper-parameter settings. The four approaches, namely DQ-iRM+RS, DQ-iRM, IQL+RS and h-IL+RS, show a steady increase in accumulated reward over time, indicating that the agents trained with these models are consistently improving their performance. However, the CQRM approach does not learn during the training. From the average accumulated reward from four experiments, we can conclude that the DQ-iRM+RS model is the top-performing model, which obtained the highest average accumulated reward with good stability. The second-best model is DQ-iRM, which is followed by IQL+RS and h-IL+RS.

Compared with the other three models, the learning curve of DQ-iRM+RS shows a much faster convergence to the optimal policy, with the agent achieving a high level of performance within a small number of episodes in all the experiments. Lastly, the learning curve of DQ-iRM+RS demonstrates better stability than the DQ-iRM approach, showing that the reward shaping has helped the agents generalize well to different scenarios. Although the IQL+RS approach has the best stability, it has a lower accumulated reward compared with the DQ-iRM+RS model and DQ-iRM model.

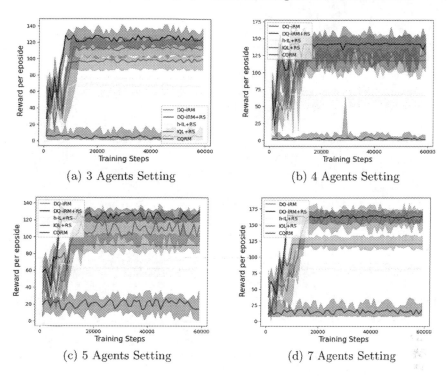

(a) 3 Agents Setting

(b) 4 Agents Setting

(c) 5 Agents Setting

(d) 7 Agents Setting

Fig. 4. Comparison of learning curves for reactive MARL using different GR(1) specifications under the same hyper-parameter settings: $\alpha = 0.8, \gamma = 0.9, \epsilon = 10^{-7}$

5   Related Work

In recent years, there has been research on the application of synthetic strategies through LTL as prior knowledge for reinforcement learning for complex tasks, mainly by constructing non-Markovian reward functions through LTL [4]. Previous works have explored various methods for combining LTL and MDP to obtain optimal control policies that reflect temporal properties. These methods typically start by converting the LTL formula into an automaton, then integrating the automaton with the system MDP so that the resulting product MDP reflects both the MDP and LTL specifications. Common types of automata studied in this context include Deterministic Rabin Automata (DRA), LDBA, and Deterministic Finite Automata (DFA).

Approaches utilizing DRA and LDBA typically design rewards based on the reachability probability of the product MDP [6,10,29]. However, using DRA to construct the product MDP may result in suboptimal strategies and an underestimation of the satisfaction probability of the specifications [8]. Same for the LDBA approaches, the reward function is set according to the repeated reachability of states satisfying the *Büchi* condition. LDBA-based approaches assign rewards only to states satisfying the *Büchi* condition, leading to sparse reward issues. To enhance sampling efficiency, Oura et al. proposed using Limited-Deterministic Generalized *Büchi* Automata to build the product MDP, resulting in a larger set of states satisfying the *Büchi* condition compared to LDBA [21]. This reduces the sparsity of the reward function and improves the efficiency of RL training.

Moreover, some approaches utilize DFA to create the reward machine, allowing for the specification of reward functions and revealing the structure of the reward function [13]. Icarte et al. introduced the QRM and CRM approach, which employs Mealy machines to create reward machines and train the agents with Q-learning [12,13]. Building on this approach, Camacho et al. added value iteration-based reward shaping to calculate potential functions for various states in the reward machine [2]. In the MARL scenarios, Neary et al. proposed to decompose the reward machines with individual reward machines, which shows that the decentralized training learns faster than the centralized training [20]. Their work necessitates certain restrictions for establishing that the original reward machine is bisimilar to the parallel composition of decomposed reward machines. Our approach relaxes these restrictions by using forward simulation to maintain temporal properties. Furthermore, we introduce a reward-shaping technique to speed up the convergence rate.

6   Conclusion and Future Work

In conclusion, this paper addresses the challenge of efficiently training multi-agents to interact in an environment with complex task specifications. The study focuses on using GR(1) as a high-level reactive temporal logic specification and decomposing its synthesized strategy into a set of potential-based reward machines for individual agents. We provide theoretical foundations for the parallel composition of decomposed strategies forward simulates the original strategy. The proposed decentralized Q-learning with reward machines performs better than state-of-art MARL algorithms regarding the learning curve and optimal rewards in experiments with different reactive temporal logic specifications.

There are still several areas for improvement in future research. Firstly, more advanced RL algorithms such as DQN, PPO, and DDPG can be used to adapt to continuous states and action domains. Additionally, the GR(1) specification can be incomplete and unrealizable, from which the strategy can not be synthesized. In this case, a counter-strategy-based approach can be developed to refine the GR(1) specifications and make them realizable.

Acknowledgement. This work was supported by National Natural Science Foundation of China (No.62202067) and Natural Science Foundation of the Higher Education Institutions of Jiangsu Province (No. 22KJB520012).

References

1. Brockman, G., et al.: Openai gym. arXiv preprint arXiv:1606.01540 (2016)

2. Camacho, A., Toro Icarte, R., Klassen, T.Q., Valenzano, R., McIlraith, S.A.: Ltl and beyond: Formal languages for reward function specification in reinforcement learning. In: Proceedings of the Twenty-Eighth International Joint Conference on Artificial Intelligence, (IJCAI), pp. 6065–6073 (7 2019)

3. Cassandras, C.G., Lafortune, S.: Introduction to discrete event systems. Springer (2008)

4. Ding, X., Smith, S.L., Belta, C., Rus, D.: Optimal control of markov decision processes with linear temporal logic constraints. IEEE Trans. Autom. Control $59(5)$, 1244–1257 (2014)

5. Even-Dar, E., Mansour, Y.: Convergence of optimistic and incremental q-learning. In: Advances in Neural Information Processing Systems, vol. 14 (2001)

6. Gao, Q., Hajinezhad, D., Zhang, Y., Kantaros, Y., Zavlanos, M.M.: Reduced variance deep reinforcement learning with temporal logic specifications. In: Proceedings of the 10th ACM/IEEE International Conference on Cyber-Physical Systems(ICCPS), pp. 237–248 (2019)

7. Gronauer, S., Diepold, K.: Multi-agent deep reinforcement learning: a survey. Artif. Intell. Rev. 5, 1–49 (2021). https://doi.org/10.1007/s10462-021-09996-w

8. Hahn, E.M., Perez, M., Schewe, S., Somenzi, F., Trivedi, A., Wojtczak, D.: Omega-regular objectives in model-free reinforcement learning. In: International Conference on Tools and Algorithms for the Construction and Analysis of Systems(TACAS), pp. 395–412. Springer (2019)

9. Hammond, L., Abate, A., Gutierrez, J., Wooldridge, M.: Multi-agent reinforcement learning with temporal logic specifications. In: Adaptive Agents and Multi-Agent Systems (2021)

10. Hasanbeig, M., Kantaros, Y., Abate, A., Kroening, D., Pappas, G.J., Lee, I.: Reinforcement learning for temporal logic control synthesis with probabilistic satisfaction guarantees. In: 2019 IEEE 58th Conference on Decision and Control (CDC), pp. 5338–5343. IEEE (2019)

11. Hu, Y., et al.: Learning to utilize shaping rewards: a new approach of reward shaping. Adv. Neural. Inf. Process. Syst. 33, 15931–15941 (2020)

12. Icarte, R.T., Klassen, T., Valenzano, R., McIlraith, S.: Using reward machines for high-level task specification and decomposition in reinforcement learning. In: International Conference on Machine Learning(ICML), pp. 2107–2116. PMLR (2018)

13. Icarte, R.T., Klassen, T.Q., Valenzano, R., McIlraith, S.A.: Reward machines: exploiting reward function structure in reinforcement learning. J. Artif. Intell. Res. 73, 173–208 (2022)

14. Ikeda, T., Shibuya, T.: Centralized training with decentralized execution reinforcement learning for cooperative multi-agent systems with communication delay. In: 2022 61st Annual Conference of the Society of Instrument and Control Engineers (SICE), pp. 135–140. IEEE (2022)

15. Kaelbling, L.P., Littman, M.L., Moore, A.W.: Reinforcement learning: a survey. J. Artif. Intell. Res. 4, 237–285 (1996)

16. Karimadini, M., Lin, H.: Guaranteed global performance through local coordinations. Automatica $47(5)$, 890–898 (2011)

17. Karimadini, M., Lin, H., Karimoddini, A.: Cooperative tasking for deterministic specification automata. Asian J. Contr. $18(6)$, 2078–2087 (2016)

18. Livingston, S.: Gr1c: A collection of tools for gr(1) synthesis and related activities, https://github.com/tulip-control/gr1c

19. Lynch, N., Vaandrager, F.: Forward and backward simulations. Inf. Comput. $121(2)$, 214–233 (1995)

20. Neary, C., Xu, Z., Wu, B., Topcu, U.: Reward machines for cooperative multi-agent reinforcement learning. In: Proceedings of the 20th International Conference on Autonomous Agents and MultiAgent Systems. pp. 934–942. AAMAS In: 21, International Foundation for Autonomous Agents and Multiagent Systems, Richland, SC (2021)
21. Oura, R., Sakakibara, A., Ushio, T.: Reinforcement learning of control policy for linear temporal logic specifications using limit-deterministic generalized büchi automata. IEEE Contr. Syst. Lett. **4**(3), 761–766 (2020)
22. Piterman, N., Pnueli, A., Sa'ar, Y.: Synthesis of reactive (1) designs. In: International Workshop on Verification, Model Checking, and Abstract Interpretation, pp. 364–380. Springer (2006)
23. Pnueli, A.: The temporal logic of programs. In: 18th Annual Symposium on Foundations of Computer Science (sfcs 1977), pp. 46–57. IEEE, IEEE (Sep 1977). https://doi.org/10.1109/sfcs.1977.32
24. Pnueli, A., Rosner, R.: On the synthesis of a reactive module. In: Proceedings of the 16th ACM SIGPLAN-SIGACT Symposium on Principles of Programming Languages, pp. 179–190 (1989)
25. Tan, M.: Multi-agent reinforcement learning: Independent vs. cooperative agents. In: Proceedings of the Tenth International Conference on Machine Learning, pp. 330–337 (1993)
26. Tang, H., et al.: Hierarchical deep multiagent reinforcement learning with temporal abstraction. arXiv preprint arXiv:1809.09332 (2018)
27. Waqar, N., Hassan, S.A., Pervaiz, H., Jung, H., Dev, K.: Deep multi-agent reinforcement learning for resource allocation in noma-enabled mec. Comput. Commun. **196**, 1–8 (2022)
28. Watkins, C.J., Dayan, P.: Q-learning. Mach. Learn. **8**(3), 279–292 (1992)
29. Wolff, E.M., Topcu, U., Murray, R.M.: Robust control of uncertain markov decision processes with temporal logic specifications. In: 2012 IEEE 51st IEEE Conference on Decision and Control (CDC), pp. 3372–3379. IEEE (2012)
30. Yang, C., Littman, M.L., Carbin, M.: On the (in) tractability of reinforcement learning for ltl objectives. In: Proceedings of the Thirty-First International Joint Conference on Artificial Intelligence, IJCAI, pp. 3650–3658 (2022)
31. Zhang, K., Yang, Z., Liu, H., Zhang, T., Basar, T.: Fully decentralized multi-agent reinforcement learning with networked agents. In: International Conference on Machine Learning, pp. 5872–5881. PMLR (2018)
32. Zhu, C., Butler, M., Cirstea, C., Hoang, T.S.: A fairness-based refinement strategy to transform liveness properties in Event-B models. Sci. Comput. Program. **225**, 102907 (2023)
33. Zhu, C., Cai, Y., Hu, C., Bi, J.: Efficient reinforcement learning with generalized-reactivity specifications. In: 2022 29th Asia-Pacific Software Engineering Conference (APSEC), pp. 31–40. IEEE (2022)
34. Zhu, C., Cai, Y., Zhu, J., Hu, C., Bi, J.: Gr (1)-guided deep reinforcement learning for multi-task motion planning under a stochastic environment. Electronics **11**(22), 3716 (2022)

Contract Based Embedded Software Design

Christian Lidström[(✉)] and Dilian Gurov[(✉)]

KTH Royal Institute of Technology, Stockholm, Sweden
{clid,dilian}@kth.se

Abstract. In embedded systems development, *contract based design* is a design paradigm where a system is divided hierarchically into components and developed in a top-down manner, using contracts as a means to divide responsibilities and manage the complexity of the system. Contract theories provide a formal basis for reasoning about the properties of the system, and of the contracts themselves. In previous work, we have developed a contract theory for sequential, procedural programs, that is defined abstractly, at the semantic level. The theory fulfils well-established, desired properties of system design. In this paper, we present a methodology for applying the contract theory in real embedded software design. We show how to instantiate the contract theory with concrete syntaxes for defining components and contracts, and how the contract theory enables formal reasoning about the resulting objects. In order to cope with the need for different behavioural models at different levels of abstraction in an embedded system, we extend the contract theory through parametrisation on the semantic domain. We illustrate the application of the proposed methodology on a small, but realistic example, where the temporal logic TLA is used for reasoning at the system level, while lower level components are specified using pre- and post-conditions in the form of ACSL, a specification language for C.

1 Introduction

A *contract* for a software component is a means to specify the behaviour (or result) the component has to produce, called the guarantee, provided that the user (or client) of the component fulfils certain constraints on how it interacts with the component, called assumptions. Software contracts were pioneered by the works of Floyd [14] and Hoare [15]. In Hoare logic, meaning is assigned to sequential programs axiomatically, through so-called Hoare triples, allowing the desired relationship between initial and final values of certain variables to be specified. Specifying contracts in this way has been advocated by Meyer with the design methodology Design-by-Contract [23]. The methodology is well-suited for *independent implementation and verification*, meaning that development of software components occurs independently, without knowledge of any implementation details of other components, but instead relying on the contracts of the latter. Contract based design as an approach to *systems design* thus provides a way to deal with the complexity of large systems, making explicit the assumptions on each component's environment. In a top-down design flow, contracts are

C. David and M. Sun (Eds.): TASE 2023, LNCS 13931, pp. 77–94, 2023.
https://doi.org/10.1007/978-3-031-35257-7_5

iteratively decomposed into sub-contracts [7,9,17,28], and the typical task then is to show that the *composition* of the sub-contracts *refines* the original contract. Contract refinement and composition enable the *independent development* and *reuse* of components. Further, contract *conjunction* allows the superimposition of contracts over the same component, when they concern different aspects of its behaviour. *Contract theories* formalise the abstract notion of a contract [8], and define operations and relations on contracts mentioned above.

Motivation. In previous work [21], we proposed a contract theory for reasoning about procedural programs, and takes therefore *procedures* as the basic building block (i.e., component). The theory is abstract in that it is developed purely at the semantic level, in terms of standard *denotational semantics*. We showed, in the context of a simplistic imperative programming language with procedures, that Hoare logic contracts and their procedure-modular verification can be cast naturally in our contract theory. We also showed that the contract theory instantiates the meta-theory of Benveniste et al. [8], and thus fulfils certain well-established and desired properties of embedded systems development. In a follow-up work [2], we showed in practice how to combine state-of-the-art verification tools for different semantic domains, and presented a proof-of-concept tool chain for this purpose. We also sketched how the contract theory can serve as formal basis for this approach, but left out a fully formal justification.

To illustrate the usefulness of the contract theory, the present paper presents a *methodology* of how to apply it in embedded systems development. In embedded systems, the type of behaviour that is of interest typically differs at different levels in the hierarchy of the system. At lower levels, software components are often understood as *state transformers*, i.e., as components the purpose of which is to transform certain initial values to certain final values, where the intermediate values are just implementation details irrelevant to the computed function. Such programs are appropriately specified using Hoare logic contracts in the form of pre- and post-conditions. At higher levels, however, such specifications are usually not sufficient, since the behaviour depends on *interaction* between several software sub-systems. Here, specifications are typically of a *temporal* nature, and the intermediate states of the program execution cannot be ignored. Since our previous work only dealt with the former case, we will show here that our framework is also fit for reasoning about the temporal behaviour of programs. Even more, we extend the contract theory to handle the *combination* of the different notions of behaviour, as needed for embedded systems development.

Example. Embedded systems typically interact with their environment through sensors and actuators, and have the goal to maintain certain temporal properties. Say we want to design a system, which (among other things) uses a sensor to measure the temperature of a part of the system, and displays it to a user. The temperature is measured in the unit of Kelvin, but should be displayed to the user in Celsius. A desired temporal property of this system is:

$$\text{At any point in time, when the temperature is read from the sensor} \atop \text{it must eventually be displayed, in Celsius.} \tag{1}$$

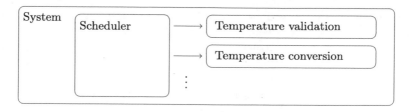

Fig. 1. Division of the example system into components

A formalised specification, or contract, of this property would be the starting point for the design of the system. Then, the system is divided into appropriate proto-components (i.e., components yet to be specified), defining the intended system architecture, and the contract is decomposed into contracts for those components, in such a way that their composition refines the top-level contract. Reasonably, such a system will have a function that reads the sensor value, and checks for potential erroneous inputs, such as in the case of potential hardware faults. The system will then have a function that converts the sanitised sensor value, and displays it (which we will model as writing to a variable). Finally, a main, *scheduling* component will continuously execute the other components. Figure 1 illustrates the system architecture, where the arrows indicate procedure calls between components. As pointed out, the top-level property is of a temporal nature, whereas the two sub-components perform computations of a transformational nature. This has to be reflected by their respective contracts.

Contributions. We present a *methodology* for designing embedded software, formally underpinned by our contract theory [21]. The contract theory provides a formal basis for system design as per the principles of contract based design. The contract theory is *abstract*, allowing instantiations with different specification and implementation languages, and is based on *procedures*, making it fit for software development. To allow the combination of different execution domains, we generalise here the contract theory of [21] through *parametrisation* on the domain of execution behaviour of system components.

We show how to instantiate the parametrised contract theory using, in combination, two semantic domains of executions: state pairs and infinite traces. We use established languages and tools to support this instantiation, such as the Frama-C [18] (whose specification language is ACSL [4]) and TLA [19,20] frameworks. We show how high-level, temporal contracts expressed in TLA can be decomposed into lower-level, state-transformation contracts expressed in ACSL. This enables procedure-modular verification of embedded software implemented in C, relative to procedure contracts, while satisfying the high-level contracts. The whole system design process is exemplified on industrial-like software.

Structure. The paper is organised as follows. Section 2 introduces the concepts of contract based design, contract theories and meta-theories. Section 3 presents our abstract, and parametrised, contract theory. Section 4 describes abstractly how the contract theory can be applied, and what is required to instantiate it. Section 5 shows how the contract theory can be instantiated with concrete languages for specifying contracts, in two different domains. Section 6 shows how components can be concretely defined (that is, implemented) using the C language, and describes procedure-modular verification in the context of the two domains. Section 7 illustrates the application of the contract theory on our running example. Section 8 details the related work. We conclude with Sect. 9.

2   Contract Based Design and Contract Theories

Contract based design [8,23] is a systems design paradigm where the design of a system is performed in a top-down manner, through the use of contracts. Top-level properties are specified as a contract for the system as a whole. The system is then divided, conceptually, into *components* intended to perform specific tasks, defining the system architecture. The top-level contract is *decomposed* into contracts for the components of the system, documenting their intended behaviour. Base components (i.e., components which are not further divided) are then implemented individually and independently, by relying on the contracts of other components. Finally, the components are assembled iteratively, in a bottom-up manner, until the whole system is formed. Contracts must thus expose enough information to the other components about the provided functionality, and state the expectations on the rest of the system.

A common design pattern are *assume-guarantee* contracts. Here, a contract consists of a set of *assumptions* and a set of *guarantees*. The assumptions specify how the component expects the system, or environment, to behave. For example, it may require that certain other components exist, and that they can be interfaced with in a specific way. The guarantees specify how the component obliges itself to behave, e.g., how it can be interfaced with, and what computations it performs, under the condition that the assumptions are adhered to.

Our focus here is on the design of embedded software, where the end-goal is to fulfil some system-wide properties. Thus, as contracts are decomposed and components are implemented to satisfy them, it is important that this is performed so that, when the final system is assembled, the top-level properties hold. Benveniste et al. [8] examined existing system design methodologies, and identified two properties as essential for any design framework: *independent implementation*, and *reuse*, of components. To this end, one should be able to *decompose* and *compose* components as well as contracts. In addition, the framework must also allow for the *refinement* and *abstraction* of contracts, in order to expose only the information appropriate at specific levels of abstraction.

Contract Theories and Meta-Theories. Contract theories provide formal frameworks for contract based system design, defining the basic units of reasoning, and the operations and relations over them. In turn, contract meta-theories systematise such contract theories by axiomatising the desired properties of their relations and operations, instead of defining them explicitly. Benveniste et al. [8]

develop such a meta-theory, which systematises contract theories for system design in cyber-physical systems. As such, it states that a contract theory must have a notion of *component* and a notion of *contract*. Further, there must be *composition* operators over both notions, a binary *refinement* relation between contracts, and a *conjunction* operator over contracts. While their definitions are left abstract, the meta-theory formulates axioms that must be fulfilled by contract theories in order to enable proper design-chain management. For instance, one axiom stated by the meta-theory postulates that when a contract C_1 refines another contract C_2, written $C_1 \preceq C_2$, then every implementation of C_1 must also implement C_2. This ensures that contracts can be extracted and implemented at the appropriate level of abstraction, while not affecting the higher-level contracts. For a comprehensive view of the axioms, see the original monograph [8], or the paper in which our contract theory was originally presented [21]. In Sect. 3, we present an extended version of our contract theory, in which the semantic domain of component behaviour is left as a parameter.

3   An Abstract Parametrised Contract Theory

We have previously proposed an abstract contract theory for procedural languages [21], based on a denotational semantics over the domain **State** $\times$ **State**, where **State** denotes the set of states. The contract theory was solely defined at the semantic level, without proposing any concrete languages for defining contracts and components. In this paper, we generalise the contract theory by parametrising the semantic domain. This enables the use of arbitrary domains, allowing a wider range of concrete syntaxes, and, in turn, types of properties to be specified. As we shall see, the new contract theory supports also the *combination* of several domains, depending on their relevance for the respective component. As in the original work, it supports the design-by-contract methodology developed by Meyer [23], and satisfies the axioms of the meta-theory of Benveniste et al. [8]. Thus, the contract theory satisfies important properties desired in system design methodologies, such as *independent development*, and *reuse*, of components. This section summarises the generalised abstract contract theory, leaving out the technical details not needed to follow this paper. The full definition of the contract theory can be found in [2].

We focus on procedural languages, and assume a finite set of procedure names $\mathcal{P}$. We consider an abstract notion of behaviour, called a *run*, representing a single execution of a system. Let **Run** denote the set of all runs. For any set of procedure names $P \subseteq \mathcal{P}$, a *procedure environment* $\mathbf{Env}_P = P \to 2^{\mathbf{Run}}$ maps procedure names to corresponding sets of runs. We define a partial order relation on procedure environments as point-wise set inclusion: for any $\rho \in \mathbf{Env}_P$ and $\rho' \in \mathbf{Env}_{P'}$, $\rho \sqsubseteq \rho'$ iff $P \subseteq P'$ and $\forall p \in P.\rho(p) \subseteq \rho'(p)$. Let $\mathbf{Env} = \bigcup_{P \subseteq \mathcal{P}} \mathbf{Env}_P$. Then, $(\mathbf{Env}, \sqsubseteq)$ is a complete lattice, since for every subset of **Env** there exists a greatest lower bound (*glb*) and a least upper bound (*lub*). The respective *glb* and *lub* operations on environments are denoted by $\sqcap$ and $\sqcup$. For two environments $\rho_1 \in \mathbf{Env}_{P_1}$ and $\rho_2 \in \mathbf{Env}_{P_2}$, $\rho_1 \sqcap \rho_2$ is the environment $\rho \in \mathbf{Env}_{P_1 \cap P_2}$ such that $\forall p \in P_1 \cap .\rho(p) = \rho_1(p) \cap \rho_2(p)$.

An *interface* $I = (P^-, P^+)$ is a pair of disjoint sets of procedure names. Both *components* and *contracts* are equipped with interfaces. P^+ are the procedures *provided* by a component, i.e., procedures that are (or will be) implemented within it. Conversely, P^- are the procedures *required* by the component, i.e., those called from it but not implemented in it. A *component* m with interface $I_m = (P_m^-, P_m^+)$ is a monotonic mapping of type $m : \mathbf{Env}_{P_m^-} \to \mathbf{Env}_{P_m^+}$, i.e., a function giving the behaviour of provided procedures, depending on the behaviour of required procedures. Two components m_1 and m_2 are *composable* if and only if $P_{m_1}^+ \cap P_{m_2}^+ = \varnothing$, and the (sequential) composition is defined in terms of fixed-points. A *denotational contract* c with interface $I_c = (P_c^-, P_c^+)$ is a pair (ρ_c^-, ρ_c^+), where the required procedure environment $\rho_c^- \in \mathbf{Env}_{P_c^-}$ and the provided procedure environment $\rho_c^+ \in \mathbf{Env}_{P_c^+}$. The rationale behind these definitions is that a component m, when given the environment ρ_c^-, implements the contract, denoted $m \models c$, if the resulting procedure environment is at least as strict as ρ_c^+, under some additional restrictions on their interfaces. Furthermore, contract c *refines* contract c', denoted $c \preceq c'$, if and only if $\rho_{c'}^- \sqsubseteq \rho_c^-$ and $\rho_c^+ \sqsubseteq \rho_{c'}^+$. Contract composition has similar restrictions on the interfaces as for components, and for every procedure required by one contract and provided by the other, the provided behaviour must be at least as strict as the required one. Then, the *composition* of two composable contracts $c_1 = (\rho_{c_1}^-, \rho_{c_1}^+)$ and $c_2 = (\rho_{c_2}^-, \rho_{c_2}^+)$ with interfaces $I_{c_1} = (P_{c_1}^-, P_{c_1}^+)$ and $I_{c_2} = (P_{c_2}^-, P_{c_2}^+)$ is the contract $c_1 \otimes c_2 \overset{\text{def}}{=} (\rho_{c_1 \otimes c_2}^-, \rho_{c_1}^+ \sqcup \rho_{c_2}^+)$, where $\rho_{c_1 \otimes c_2}^-$ is the glb of $\rho_{c_1}^-$ and $\rho_{c_2}^-$, but restricted to those procedures not provided by one of the contracts.

The following two theorems correspond to Theorem 1 and 2 in [21]. Since the original proofs do not rely on any particular domain of runs, they apply also here, and are therefore omitted.

Theorem 1. *Component composition is well-defined, i.e., the involved fixed-points exist, and the resulting components are monotonic mappings.*

Note that for this result to hold, when instantiating with a concrete semantics, one must restrict the base components to be monotonic.

The next result captures the essential properties of composition.

Theorem 2. *For any composable contracts c_1 and c_2, and any implementations $m_1 \models c_1$ and $m_2 \models c_2$, m_1 and m_2 are composable. Furthermore, $c_1 \otimes c_2$ is the least contract w.r.t. the refinement order for which the following holds:*

(i) $m_1 \times m_2 \models c_1 \otimes c_2$, and
(ii) if m is an environment to $c_1 \otimes c_2$, then $m_1 \times m$ is an environment to c_2 and $m \times m_2$ is an environment to c_1.

4   The Contract Theory as Basis for System Design

This section describes how the abstract contract theory can be applied for the design of, and reasoning about, real systems. By *applying* the contract theory, we mean casting the concrete specification and implementation languages in its framework, thus showing that the desired properties of system design methodologies hold. We first describe how the parametrised contract theory can be instantiated with concrete languages, possibly using several semantic domains, and then discuss procedure-modular verification in this setting.

4.1   Instantiating the Contract Theory

Instantiating the parametrised contract theory requires certain steps to be taken. Concretely, the following *elements* must be provided:

1. A *semantic domain* for runs.
2. A syntax for defining components, i.e., a *programming language*.
3. A syntax for defining contracts, i.e., a *specification language*.
4. A *contract-relative* semantics mapping concretely defined components and contracts to abstract ones, as denotations over the chosen semantic domain, under certain conditions.

The last item requires some explanation. We take the view of contracts as being separate from their implementation, and desire a program S to satisfy its contract C, denoted $S \models C$, precisely when $[S] \subseteq [C]$, where $[C] \in 2^{\mathbf{Run}}$ is some given denotational semantics of C. Equivalently, one can require that the denotational semantics for contracts be defined so that the following holds:

$$[C] = \bigcup_{S \models C} [S] \qquad (2)$$

Following the design-by-contract methodology, the semantics of procedures should be given *relative to the contracts* of the other procedures. Assuming that every procedure p is equipped with a contract C_p, we introduce the *contract environment* ρ_c, defined by $\rho_c(p) \overset{\text{def}}{=} [C_p]$ for all $p \in P$, and use it to define a contract-relative semantics $[S]^{cr} \overset{\text{def}}{=} [S]_{\rho_c}$. In particular, the denotation of procedure calls is obtained from this environment (and not from solving fixed-point equations). This semantics naturally induces a contract-relative satisfaction relation $S_p \models^{cr} C_p$, where S_p is a procedure-body and C_p its contract. The contract-relative semantics must fulfil the following *properties*:

1. All base components must be monotonic mappings.
2. For any two disjoint sets of functions P_1^+ and P_2^+, abstracted individually into components m_1 and m_2, respectively, and $P_1^+ \cup P_2^+$ abstracted into component m, we must have $m_1 \times m_2 = m$.
3. For any procedure p with procedure contract C_p, abstracted into component m_p with contract c_p, we must have $S_p \models^{cr} C_p$ whenever $m_p \models c_p$.

The first restriction is needed for Theorem 1 to hold. The second restriction establishes, together with the commutativity and associativity of component composition, that the order in which we choose to abstract and compose components is unimportant. The third restriction establishes that contract satisfaction at the concrete level is consistent with that at the abstract level. The latter two restrictions enable *procedure-modular verification*, which we now discuss.

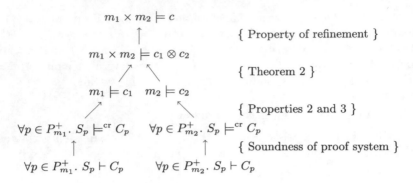

Fig. 2. View of procedure-modular verification, assuming $c_1 \otimes c_2 \preceq c$

4.2 Procedure-Modular Verification

The contract-relative semantics provides a basis for procedure-modular verification, which is performed at the syntactic level. Figure 2 illustrates how procedure-modular verification of concrete implementations against concrete specifications enables us to show, in the end, that the composition of the parts of a system fulfils some higher-level contract. We shall explain the scheme in a top-down manner. Given that $c_1 \otimes c_2 \preceq c$ has already been established (i.e., the top-level contract c has been refined and decomposed), we obtain from the properties of refinement within the contract-theory, and Theorem 2, that for the final result to hold, each sub-component must be shown to implement its contract. The properties listed in Sect. 4.1 entail that this can be shown by establishing contract satisfaction at the concrete level, which in turn follows from (syntactic) verification, assuming that the latter is sound w.r.t. the contract-relative semantics. Thus, the problem of proving high-level properties in a system composed of many, independently implemented components, is reduced to procedure-modular verification (at the syntactic level), and to showing refinement and decomposition of contracts. Syntactic, procedure-modular verification is supported by a variety of existing frameworks such as Frama-C [18] and OpenJML [13]. In the next sections, we will see concretely how, by treating contracts in one domain as a subset of another domain, we can procedure-modularly verify contracts expressing temporal properties relative to transformational contracts.

5   Specifying and Decomposing Contracts

Following the principles of contract based design outlined in Sect. 2, a system is designed in a top-down manner. Many formal languages for specifying contracts already exist, and this section describes how two such languages can be used to instantiate the contract theory. We chose, at the higher hierarchical level, to instantiate it with TLA [20], a well-known high level language for temporal reasoning about systems. On the lower level, we chose ACSL [4], the specification language of Frama-C [18], a mature tool for verification of software written in C, one of the programming languages most commonly used in embedded systems. Frama-C includes plugins for deductive verification of C functions against contracts [5]. The two languages have different semantic domains, and are thus appropriate for specifying different aspects of the system. We show how to combine the two domains within the contract theory, and how to decompose contracts written in one language to contracts written in both.

5.1   Specifying Temporal Contracts with TLA

In embedded systems development, the top-level properties that are of greatest interest are typically of temporal nature, such as various safety and liveness properties. For this reason, we consider the domain of infinite traces (i.e., sequences of states) $\sigma = s_1, s_2, \ldots$, over states $s_i \in \textbf{State}$, which we still leave abstract, but for which we assume that in a particular state we know the values of the variables. We denote the set of all traces by $\textbf{State}^\omega$.

Temporal Logic of Actions. (TLA) [19,20] is a logic for reasoning about the temporal behaviour of (usually concurrent) systems. Central to TLA is the notion of *action*, which is a state predicate containing variables, constants, and logical operators. Variables can be either so-called *flexible* or *rigid* variables. Flexible variables represent the program variables, whereas rigid variables are constant but unknown values, and can be used to express relations between states. Rigid variables are implicitly universally quantified. Actions are evaluated over pairs of states, representing a (transition) relation between the old state and the new state. Flexible (i.e., program) variables can either be primed or unprimed. In an action, unprimed occurrences of a variable are evaluated in the first state, whereas primed occurrences are evaluated in the second. For example, $x' + 1 = x$ is an action asserting that the value of x in the old state is one added to the value of x in the new state. The denotational semantics of an action A, written $[\![A]\!]$, is defined as a set of state pairs as expected.

TLA formulas consist of actions, logical operators, and temporal operators, and are evaluated over infinite traces. To give actions a meaning in the context of traces, we define their trace-semantics as follows:

$$[\![A]\!]^\omega \stackrel{\text{def}}{=} \{s_1, s_2, s_3, \ldots \in \textbf{State}^\omega \mid (s_1, s_2) \in [\![A]\!]\}$$

TLA includes the two temporal operators $\Box$ and $\Diamond$, with their usual meaning, where F is a formula:

$$[\![\Box F]\!]^\omega \stackrel{\text{def}}{=} \{s_1, s_2, s_3, \ldots \in \textbf{State}^\omega \mid \forall n \in \mathbb{N}. s_n, s_{n+1}, s_{n+2}, \ldots \in [\![F]\!]^\omega\}$$

$$[\![\Diamond F]\!]^\omega \stackrel{\text{def}}{=} \{s_1, s_2, s_3, \ldots \in \textbf{State}^\omega \mid \exists n \in \mathbb{N}. s_n, s_{n+1}, s_{n+2}, \ldots \in [\![F]\!]^\omega\}$$

Finally, we define (similarly to e.g. [25]) a *TLA contract* as a pair $C = (P, F)$, where P is a state predicate (the pre-condition), and F a TLA formula as above (the post-condition), with the following semantics:

$$[\![C]\!]^\omega \stackrel{\text{def}}{=} \{\sigma = s_1, s_2, s_3, \ldots \in \textbf{State}^\omega \mid s_1 \models P \to \sigma \in [\![F]\!]^\omega\}$$

5.2   Specifying Hoare-style Contracts with ACSL

For certain system components, one is not interested in their temporal behaviour, but rather in that they compute the correct outputs from the inputs (or formally, in the *state transformer* they embody). For this, it is sufficient to specify a relation between the pre- and post-states of the computation, and $\mathbf{State} \times \mathbf{State}$ is thus a suitable domain of runs. We will therefore use Hoare-style pre- and post-conditions to specify contracts for such components.

In ACSL, contracts are written as annotations in the source code, as C comments beginning with an @-symbol. Here, we shall limit ourselves to three ACSL constructs for writing contracts. The keyword `requires` specifies the precondition P of a function, which callers must satisfy before calling the function. The keyword `ensures` specifies the post-condition Q, which the function must guarantee upon return (w.r.t. partial correctness). The keyword `assigns` specifies the frame condition, i.e., a set of memory locations L that are allowed to change value during the call. In addition, ACSL supports so-called *ghost* variables, or logical variables, which may be used in specifications. Thus, viewing an ACSL contract as a triple $C = (P, Q, L)$, we define its semantics as:

$$[\![C]\!] \stackrel{\text{def}}{=} \{(s, s') \mid \forall \mathcal{I}. (s \models_{\mathcal{I}} P \Rightarrow s' \models_{\mathcal{I}} Q) \wedge \forall l \notin L. s(l) = s'(l)\} \qquad (3)$$

where $\mathcal{I}$ ranges over all possible interpretations of logical variables. We also note that any variables occurring in the pre-condition or frame condition, or parameters occurring in the post-condition, are evaluated in the pre-state. Variables (except parameters) occurring in the post-condition are evaluated in the post-state. The special keyword `\old` is used to enforce evaluation in the pre-state.

5.3   Abstraction to Denotational Contracts

We will now show how the concrete contracts, i.e., the TLA and ACSL contracts, can be abstracted into contracts in our abstract theory. The abstraction is based on the procedures' callees and the semantics defined in Sects. 5.1 and 5.2.

Definition 1 (From concrete to denotational contracts). *For procedure p calling other procedures P^-, equipped with concrete contract C_p, we define its denotational contract $c_p \stackrel{\text{def}}{=} (\rho_{c_p}^-, \rho_{c_p}^+)$ with interface $P_{c_p}^+ \stackrel{\text{def}}{=} \{p\}$ and $P_{c_p}^- \stackrel{\text{def}}{=} P^-$, so that $\rho_{c_p}^+(p) \stackrel{\text{def}}{=} [\![C_p]\!]$, and $\forall p' \in P^-. \rho_{c_p}^-(p') \stackrel{\text{def}}{=} [\![C_{p'}]\!]$.*

In our instantiation of the contract theory, **Run** takes two different meanings, and thus the resulting denotations are over different semantic domains.

6   Implementing and Verifying Components

After having defined the components of the system, and specified them in the form of contracts, they can be implemented. The implementation is performed individually, under the assumption that the other components fulfil their contracts. This section presents a contract-relative semantics for the C language [16], and shows how the example system can be implemented within it.

6.1 Infinite Traces over Program States

While we will not define here a full semantics for the C language (see e.g. [10] for a trace-based operational semantics for a subset of C, or [27] for a denotational-style semantics), this section describes how, given a semantics, the contract theory can be instantiated with C as the concrete implementation language, and specifically how to treat procedures as components. Programs are defined in the context of a finite set $\mathcal{P}$ of declared function names. We assume that function names are unique, i.e., there cannot be functions with the same name but with different types or number of parameters. The set of program states **State** is conventionally defined as the set of mappings from references to memory locations, and from memory locations to contents (as in, e.g., [10, 26]).

For any finite set of function names P, we define the set of *function environments* $\mathbf{Env}_P = P \to 2^{\mathbf{Run}}$ containing the possible mappings from function names to traces, representing the effect of executing the respective function. *Interfaces* for sets of functions are defined as for components in Sect. 3. The semantics of a statement S is then defined in the context of an interface (P^-, P^+) and environments $\rho^- \in \mathbf{Env}_{P^-}$ and $\rho^+ \in \mathbf{Env}_{P^+}$, denoted $[\![S]\!]_{\rho^-}^{\rho^+}$, and $[\![S]\!]_{\rho^-}^{\rho^+} \subseteq \mathbf{Run}$. For example, the semantics of a function call without parameters, $[\![p()]\!]_{\rho^-}^{\rho^+}$, then depends on whether p is provided or required, and is defined as $\rho^+(p)$ if $p \in P^+$, and as $\rho^-(p)$ if $p \in P^-$.

Given an environment $\rho^- \in \mathbf{Env}_{P^-}$, we define the function $\xi : \mathbf{Env}_{P^+} \to \mathbf{Env}_{P^+}$ as $\xi(\rho^+)(p) \stackrel{\text{def}}{=} [\![S_p]\!]_{\rho^-}^{\rho^+}$ for any $\rho^+ \in \mathbf{Env}_{P^+}$ and $p \in P^+$. Then, $(\mathbf{Env}_{P^+}, \sqsubseteq)$ is a complete lattice and ξ is monotonic, and thus, by Tarski's Fixed-Point Theorem [29], ξ has a least fixed-point ρ_0^+. In the context of an interface (P^-, P^+) and environment $\rho^- \in \mathbf{Env}_{P^-}$, we define $[\![S]\!]_{\rho^-} \stackrel{\text{def}}{=} [\![S]\!]_{\rho^-}^{\rho_0^+}$ as the *standard denotation* of statements, where ρ_0^+ is the least fixed-point of ξ. Essentially, this ensures that the denotation of the function body of a procedure p is equal to the denotation of a call to p. In the above setting, we could instantiate **Run** to a variety of different domains (or combination thereof), such as **State** $\times$ **State** or **State**$^\omega$.

6.2 Abstraction to Components

Using the above notation, we can now define an abstraction from C programs to components of our abstract contract theory.

Definition 2 (From C functions to components). *For any set of functions P^+ calling functions P', we define component* $m : \mathbf{Env}_{P_m^-} \to \mathbf{Env}_{P_m^+}$ *with* $P_m^- \stackrel{\text{def}}{=} P' \setminus P_m^+$ *and* $P_m^+ \stackrel{\text{def}}{=} P^+$, *by* $\forall \rho_m^- \in \mathbf{Env}_{P_m^-}.\ \forall p \in P_m^+.\ m(\rho_m^-)(p) \stackrel{\text{def}}{=} [\![S_p]\!]_{\rho_m^-}$.

Following the scheme outlined in Sect. 4.1, we obtain a contract-relative semantics by using ρ_c as the relativising environment for the concrete semantics.

6.3 Procedure-Modular Verification of Components

When the components of the system have been implemented, the components can be verified against their contracts, assuming that the other components satisfy theirs. As long as the full contract-relative semantics of our concrete languages fulfils properties 2 and 3 stated in Sect. 4.1, and we have a proof system that is sound w.r.t. the semantics, the functions can be individually verified, and if this verification succeeds, the composition of all components is guaranteed to implement the top-level contract.

7 Designing the Example System

We now return to the example system introduced in Sect. 1, and design it according to the methodology proposed above.

7.1 Specifying the System

The task is to design a system fulfilling Property (1), and since we have shown how TLA can instantiate the contract theory, we use it to express the property:

$$F_{sys} = \Box((\texttt{in\_temp}' = \texttt{sensor} \wedge \texttt{in\_temp}' = t_0) \rightarrow \Diamond(\texttt{out\_temp} = t_0 - 273))$$

Here, the variables `sensor`, `in_temp` and `out_temp` are (to be) program variables, or flexible variables in TLA terminology. They represent the sensor value, the read sensor value, and the value outputted to be displayed, respectively. The variable t_0 is a rigid variable, meaning that it is implicitly universally quantified, and used to relate read and displayed values in different states. The subformula `in_temp`$' = $ `sensor` $\wedge$ `in_temp`$' = t_0$ is a TLA action, denoting all state pairs where the value of `in_temp` in the second state equals the value of `sensor` in the first, with the intention of capturing that the sensor value has just been read. The subformula (`out_temp` $= t_0 - 273$) is a state predicate, which is a special case of an action, only evaluated in the first state; we model displaying the temperature as writing it to the variable `out_temp`. Thus, the denotation $[\![F_{sys}]\!]^\omega$ will be the set of traces where for every value of `in_temp` read from the sensor, there eventually is a state where `out_temp` is assigned the converted value. In this case we will not impose any particular pre-condition, thus $P_{sys} = \texttt{true}$, forming the TLA contract $C_{sys} = (P_{sys}, F_{sys})$. In the abstracted denotational contract, we will have $P^-_{sys} = \varnothing$, since the full system should not depend on additional functions. For the provided functions, $\rho^+_{C_{sys}}(\texttt{main}) = [\![C_{sys}]\!]$, since `main` is the entry-point to the system, while for all other functions we allow any behaviour, since at the system level we are not interested in how they are implemented. Since displaying the temperature is only part of the system functionality, the full contract would be a conjunction of C_{sys} and several other contracts.

```
/*@ assigns in_temp;                /*@ requires in_temp >= 0;
      ensures in_temp ==                assigns out_temp;
         (value >= 0 ?                  ensures out_temp ==
             value : 0);                    \old(in_temp) - 273;
 */                                  */
```

(a) Contract C_{read} for **read**, reading and sanitising the sensor value

(b) Contract C_{conv} for **convert**, a temperature conversion function

Fig. 3. ACSL contracts for two functions in our system

7.2 Decomposing the System

As the next step, we want to decompose this system-level contract into contracts for the three functions of the system. The main function, which continuously calls the other functions, will be specified by the same contract, i.e. $C_{sys} = C_{main}$. However, in order for the main function to satisfy this, some assumptions (which are different from the precondition) on the helper functions are needed, essentially stating that the called procedures fulfil their respective guarantees. Thus, the two resulting denotational contracts will differ.

Two components then remain to be specified: a function **read**, reading and checking the sensor value, and a function **convert**, converting a temperature from Kelvin to Celsius. Contracts for these components, which we denote C_{read} and C_{conv}, are given in Fig. 3. In the case of **read**, we want the function to read a sensor value, given as a parameter **value**, and store it in **in_temp**, and the frame condition specifies therefore that this is the only variable assigned to. Furthermore, we want it to check that the value is valid, and if it is not lower than 0 (the lowest temperature in Kelvin) it should be written to **in_temp**, and otherwise be saturated to 0, before storing it. In the case of **convert**, we similarly specify its frame condition. As the post-condition we specify that it should store the converted value of **in_temp** in **out_temp**. However, it will not always be possible to compute this value, since there is the possibility of underflow for very small inputs. Thus, we also specify a pre-condition saying that the value must be non-negative, meaning that for negative inputs the result is left undefined.

The denotation $[\![C_{read}]\!]$ will then consist of all state pairs (s, s') such that when $s(\mathtt{value}) \geq 0$ then $s'(\mathtt{in\_temp}) = s(\mathtt{value})$ and otherwise $s'(\mathtt{in\_temp})$ will be 0, where in both cases no other variables are changed. The denotation $[\![C_{conv}]\!]$ will consist of all state pairs (s, s') such that $s(\mathtt{in\_temp}) \geq 0$ and $s'(\mathtt{out\_temp}) = s(\mathtt{in\_temp}) - 273$, or $s(\mathtt{in\_temp}) < 0$ and for all program variables $v \neq \mathtt{out\_temp}$, $s(v) = s'(v)$.

In the abstracted denotational contracts, we will have for the **main** function that $c_{main} = (\rho^-_{main}, \rho^+_{main})$, where $\rho^-_{main}(\mathtt{read}) = [\![C_{read}]\!]$, $\rho^-_{main}(\mathtt{convert}) = [\![C_{conv}]\!]$, and $\rho^+_{main}(\mathtt{main}) = [\![C_{main}]\!]$. The functions **read** and **convert** will have no assumptions in their denotational contracts. Even without referring to a dedicated proof system, it should be obvious that $c_{main} \otimes c_{read} \otimes c_{conv} \preceq c_{sys}$; since both c_{sys} and c_{main} specify the same behaviour for **main**, then so will the

```
volatile int sensor;
int in_temp;
int out_temp;
void main() {
  while (1) {
    // ...
    read(sensor);
    // ...
    convert();
    // ...
  }
}
```

(a) Main program iteratively calling component functions

```
void read(int value) {
  if (value < 0) {
    in_temp = 0;
  } else {
    in_temp = value;
  }
}
```

(b) A function for reading and checking a sensor value

```
void convert() {
  out_temp = in_temp - 273;
}
```

(c) A function performing temperature unit conversion

Fig. 4. A simple C program consisting of three functions

composition, and since the composition restricts the other functions more than c_{sys}. In the composition, the dependencies on other functions will also be resolved, leaving no required functions. Thus, the composition is shown correct, and it remains to implement the components and verify them against their contracts.

7.3   Implementing the System

Figure 4 shows how the functions in the example system can be implemented in C. In a trace semantics setting, considering the three functions as a single program, we can see that calling main will produce strictly infinite traces, where in_temp is continuously assigned some value not less than 0, and shortly after that out_temp is assigned the converted value.

Let us now consider abstraction of components, individually, using different semantic domains as previously discussed. In the example, the read and convert functions do not make any procedure calls, meaning $P_{read}^- = P_{conv}^- = \varnothing$, thus $m_{read}(\rho^-)$ and $m_{conv}(\rho^-)$ are constant for all ρ^-. We then have $m_{read} \models c_{read}$ and $m_{conv} \models c_{conv}$, since their interfaces are compatible and, in the case of read, the denotations of the contract and the function body coincide exactly, i.e., $m_{read}(\text{read}) = c_{read}(\text{read})$, whereas for convert, since the contract leaves out_temp unspecified for in_temp < 0, its denotation is a superset of that of the function body, and $m_{conv}(\text{convert}) \subseteq c_{conv}(\text{convert})$. For the main function we consider a trace-based semantics, but where the mapping from the required functions read and conv has pairs of states as the domain. The scheduling function will then produce traces consisting of pairs of states, where the relation between the states within pairs is dependent on $\rho^-(\text{read})$ and $\rho^-(\text{convert})$, that is, for each function call is the assumed contract taken as a TLA action. Based on this, one can establish that $m_{main} \models c_{main}$ holds.

7.4   Verifying the System

In the example, the functions `convert` and `display_temp` are easily verified against their ACSL contracts using the existing Frama-C framework. This verification is in the context of state pairs, which can be considered the same domain as that of actions in TLA. Thus, considering the contracts for the above functions as TLA actions, the `main` function is verified procedure-modularly using TLC, by transforming such contracts into TLA actions, and, for the rest of the program, using standard procedures for converting programs into TLA specifications, as described, e.g., in [30]. Tools already exist that automate parts of this process, such as the Frama-C plugin C2TLA+ [22], which translates C programs to TLA. In our previous work [2], we extended this method to replace function bodies with their ACSL contracts at certain call sites, and, also with this method, the `main` function is easily verified against its contract. (There exist other tools for verifying C programs against temporal formulas [3,24], but we are not aware of any such tool that is procedure modular.)

We have now shown that the composition of the sub-contracts refines the system contract, and verified that each component implements its contract. By the properties of the contract theory, then, we have established that $m_{main} \times m_{read} \times m_{conv} \models c_{sys}$, utilising existing verification techniques and tools, where components are individually implemented and verified.

8   Related Work

Modular design and formal reasoning about compositions of specifications and components have long been an active area of research. One early study is [1]. We mention here some additional works in the field. One main difference between these works and our work, is our treatment of procedures as the central unit of composition, enabling existing specification and verification frameworks to naturally be cast in our theory.

In [11], a compositional specification theory supporting assume-guarantee reasoning about the temporal ordering of input and output actions is presented. Components can be modelled either operationally, thus closely resembling the actual implementations, or more abstractly through declarative specifications. The theory includes a refinement preorder, enabling reuse of components, and operations such as parallel composition, conjunction, and quotienting, enabling independent and incremental development.

A generic model of contracts for embedded systems design is presented in [7], aimed at supporting a methodology of distributed development of different aspects of a system. The framework supports so-called "rich components", in which a diverse set of functional and non-function aspects can be expressed and reasoned about. The contract-based formalisation of components makes an incremental realisation of components and viewpoints possible.

Inspired by the previous work, an axiomatisation of the notion of specifications is presented in [6], from which it is then shown how a contract framework can be built on such specification theories, by deriving the notion of contracts, and their refinement and composition. The authors show that a trace-based contract theory can fit into this framework.

This is built upon in [12], extending the framework with synchronous and asynchronous (de)composition, with a focus on top-down design. To this end, the authors develop a proof system, in which the decomposition of assume-guarantee contracts generates proof obligations, which can be further reduced to satisfiability problems, and when verified one can conclude the correctness of the system. The framework can be instantiated with various temporal logics.

In [25], a trace-based logic for reasoning about the behaviour of While programs is presented. The framework includes a proof system that is both sound and complete. As a main result, it is shown that the logic subsumes the standard partial and total correctness Hoare logic, in the sense that in one direction, Hoare logic can be embedded in the presented logic, and in the other direction the trace-based logic can be projected onto standard Hoare logic, meaning that derivations in the former can be translated into derivations of the latter.

9   Conclusion

This paper presents a methodology for designing and reasoning about embedded procedural software. The formal basis is a contract theory we previously proposed in [21], generalised here by parametrisation on the semantic domain of runs, which is to be instantiated depending on the given properties of interest. The contract theory is applicable to real software in conjunction with existing formal verification tools, as illustrated by an instantiation with well-known, concrete specification and programming languages.

The proposed methodology follows the principles of *contract based design*, where high-level contracts are specified for the system as a whole, and decomposed into contracts for sub-components of the system, in different concrete languages and semantic domains. The implemented components are then verified *modularly*, thus, by virtue of the properties of the contract theory, ensuring that the high-level contracts are fulfilled.

Future work includes the extension of the theory with mechanisms for *interaction* with the environment, such as input/output, concurrency or message passing, in order for the theory to be useful in wider practical scenarios. This may require our trace semantics to be extended with an explicit notion of events, as well as with parallel composition. We also plan to instantiate the theory with a domain capturing the notion of time, such as timed words. Finally, we plan to develop a proof system for syntactically proving decompositions correct.

References

1. Abadi, M., Lamport, L.: Composing specifications. ACM Trans. Program. Lang. Syst. **15**(1), 73–132 (1993). https://doi.org/10.1145/151646.151649

2. Amilon, J., Lidström, C., Gurov, D.: Deductive verification based abstraction for software model checking. In: Margaria, T., Steffen, B. (eds.) Leveraging Applications of Formal Methods, Verification and Validation. Verification Principles. pp. 7–28. Springer International Publishing, Cham (2022). https://doi.org/10.1007/978-3-031-19849-6_2

3. Baranová, Z., et al.: Model checking of C and C++ with DIVINE 4. In: D'Souza, D., Narayan Kumar, K. (eds.) ATVA 2017. LNCS, vol. 10482, pp. 201–207. Springer, Cham (2017). https://doi.org/10.1007/978-3-319-68167-2_14

4. Baudin, P., Filliâtre, J.C., Marché, C., Monate, B., Moy, Y., Prevosto, V.: ACSL: ANSI/ISO C Specification Language. http://frama-c.com/acsl.html

5. Baudin, P., Bobot, F., Correnson, L., Dargaye, Z., Blanchard, A.: WP Plug-in Manual - Frama-C 23.1 (Vanadium). CEA LIST. https://frama-c.com/download/frama-c-wp-manual.pdf

6. Bauer, S., et al.: Moving from specifications to contracts in component-based design. In: Fundamental Approaches to Software Engineering, pp. 43–58 (2012). https://doi.org/10.1007/978-3-642-28872-2_3

7. Benveniste, A., Caillaud, B., Ferrari, A., Mangeruca, L., Passerone, R., Sofronis, C.: Multiple viewpoint contract-based specification and design. In: Formal Methods for Components and Objects, vol. 5382, pp. 200–225 (Oct 2007). https://doi.org/10.1007/978-3-540-92188-2_9

8. Benveniste, A., et al.: Contracts for System Design, vol. 12. Now Publishers (2018). https://doi.org/10.1561/1000000053

9. Benvenuti, L., Ferrari, A., Mangeruca, L., Mazzi, E., Passerone, R., Sofronis, C.: A contract-based formalism for the specification of heterogeneous systems. In: 2008 Forum on Specification, Verification and Design Languages, pp. 142–147 (Sep 2008). https://doi.org/10.1109/FDL.2008.4641436

10. Blazy, S., Leroy, X.: Mechanized semantics for the Clight subset of the C language. J. Autom. Reason. 43 (2009). https://doi.org/10.1007/s10817-009-9148-3

11. Chen, T., Chilton, C., Jonsson, B., Kwiatkowska, M.: A compositional specification theory for component behaviours. In: Seidl, H. (ed.) ESOP 2012. LNCS, vol. 7211, pp. 148–168. Springer, Heidelberg (2012). https://doi.org/10.1007/978-3-642-28869-2_8

12. Cimatti, A., Tonetta, S.: Contracts-refinement proof system for component-based embedded systems. Sci. Comput. Program. 97 (2015). https://doi.org/10.1016/j.scico.2014.06.011

13. Cok, D.R.: JML and OpenJML for Java 16. In: Proceedings of the 23rd ACM International Workshop on Formal Techniques for Java-like Programs, pp. 65–67. Association for Computing Machinery, New York (2021). https://doi.org/10.1145/3464971.3468417

14. Floyd, R.W.: Assigning meanings to programs. Mathemat. Aspects Comput. Sci. **19**, 19–32 (1967). https://doi.org/10.1007/978-94-011-1793-7_4

15. Hoare, C.A.R.: An axiomatic basis for computer programming. Commun. ACM **12**(10), 576–580 (1969). https://doi.org/10.1145/363235.363259

16. ISO: ISO C standard 1999. Tech. rep. (1999). https://www.open-std.org/jtc1/sc22/wg14/www/docs/n1256.pdf, ISO/IEC 9899:1999 draft

17. Jones, C.: Specification and design of (parallel) programs. In: Proceedings Of IFIP 1983, vol. 83, pp. 321–332 (Jan 1983)

18. Kirchner, F., Kosmatov, N., Prevosto, V., Signoles, J., Yakobowski, B.: Frama-C: A software analysis perspective. Formal Aspects Comput. **27**(3), 573–609 (2015). https://doi.org/10.1007/s00165-014-0326-7

19. Lamport, L.: The temporal logic of actions. ACM Trans. Program. Lang. Syst. **16**(3), 872–923 (1994). https://doi.org/10.1145/177492.177726
20. Lamport, L.: Specifying Systems: The TLA+ Language and Tools for Hardware and Software Engineers. Addison-Wesley (June 2002)
21. Lidström, C., Gurov, D.: An abstract contract theory for programs with procedures. In: Guerra, E., Stoelinga, M. (eds.) Fundamental Approaches to Software Engineering, pp. 152–171. Springer International Publishing, Cham (2021). https://doi.org/10.1007/978-3-030-71500-7_8
22. Methni, A., Lemerre, M., Hedia, B., Haddad, S., Barkaoui, K.: Specifying and verifying concurrent C programs with TLA+. In: Formal Techniques for Safety-Critical Systems, vol. 476, pp. 206–222 (Nov 2014). https://doi.org/10.1007/978-3-319-17581-2_14
23. Meyer, B.: Applying "design by contract". IEEE Comput. **25**(10), 40–51 (1992). https://doi.org/10.1109/2.161279
24. Morse, J., Cordeiro, L., Nicole, D., Fischer, B.: Model checking LTL properties over ANSI-C programs with bounded traces. Softw. Syst. Model. **14**(1), 65–81 (2013). https://doi.org/10.1007/s10270-013-0366-0
25. Nakata, K., Uustalu, T.: A Hoare logic for the coinductive trace-based big-step semantics of While. Logical Meth. Comput. Sci. **11**(1) (2015). https://doi.org/10.2168/LMCS-11(1:1)2015
26. Nielson, H.R., Nielson, F.: Semantics with applications: an appetizer. Springer-Verlag, Berlin, Heidelberg (2007). https://doi.org/10.1007/978-1-84628-692-6
27. Papaspyrou, N.S.: Denotational semantics of ansi c. Comput. Stand. Interfaces **23**(3), 169–185 (2001). https://doi.org/10.1016/S0920-5489(01)00059-9
28. Staden, S.: On rely-guarantee reasoning. In: Hinze, R., Voigtländer, J. (eds.) MPC 2015. LNCS, vol. 9129, pp. 30–49. Springer, Cham (2015). https://doi.org/10.1007/978-3-319-19797-5_2
29. Tarski, A.: A lattice-theoretical fixedpoint theorem and its applications. Pac. J. Math. **5**, 285–309 (1955)
30. Yu, Y., Manolios, P., Lamport, L.: Model checking TLA+ specifications. In: Pierre, L., Kropf, T. (eds.) Correct Hardware Design and Verification Methods, pp. 54–66. Springer, Berlin Heidelberg, Berlin, Heidelberg (1999). https://doi.org/10.1007/3-540-48153-2_60

Verifying Refinement of Probabilistic Contracts Using Timed Automata

Anton Hampus$^{(\boxtimes)}$ and Mattias Nyberg

KTH Royal Institute of Technology, Stockholm, Sweden
{ahampus,matny}@kth.se

Abstract. Compositional verification allows a system to be verified indirectly by verifying the individual components of the system. The key step is to ensure that the decomposition of the system specification into component specifications is correct. That is, it needs to be verified that the composition of the component specifications refines the system specification. In many cyber-physical systems, specifications are probabilistic in nature. For instance, a specification might state that the probability of reaching an unsafe state within 10.000 h shall be less than 0.05. Verifying refinement under such assumptions requires techniques beyond traditional theorem proving. This paper presents a solution where specifications are built up by probabilistic contracts based upon timed automata. In particular, the main contribution is an algorithm for verifying refinement between such specifications. The algorithm utilizes a reduction to the language emptiness problem, making the algorithm terminate after a finite number of computations.

Keywords: Probabilistic Contracts · Automata · Algorithms

1 Introduction

Given a top-level specification ϕ and a system S made up of components $S_1, \ldots S_m$, the goal is to verify that S satisfies ϕ. For a scalable solution to this problem, the principle of *compositional verification* [33] has been proposed. First, the top-level specification ϕ is *decomposed* into component specifications $\phi_1, \ldots \phi_m$. Applying the principle of compositional verification then consists of verifying that (1) each component S_i implements its specification ϕ_i, and (2) the composition of the component specifications $\phi_1, \ldots \phi_m$ *refines* the top-level specification ϕ. The key difficulty, and the topic of the present paper, is (2), which we shall refer to as *verifying refinement*.

We consider the scope of general cyber-physical systems, which encapsulates both safety and cyber-security aspects. To accurately represent and reason about these systems, they are assumed to progress in continuous time with continuous state spaces. Based on formal logic, there already exist several frameworks that allow expressing specifications and verifying refinement between them, see e.g.

Supported by Vinnova FFI through the SafeDim project.

[9,26,29,35]. However, they give no support for reasoning about probabilistic or stochastic behaviors. This is a major limitation considering the stochastic nature of many cyber-physical systems, in particular within safety where specifications typically set limits on the probability of undesired events to occur within certain time intervals. For instance, a specification might state that the probability of reaching an unsafe state within 10.000 h shall be less than 0.05. Also of interest are specifications of software using probabilistic algorithms or running in a probabilistic setting.

Recently, a new trace-based specification theory for stochastic systems has been proposed [18]. Here, *behaviors* of components are expressed as probability measures on trace sets, and specifications are represented as sets of such behaviors. As is usual in specification theories [15], the theory in [18] enables *compositions* of behaviors, *compositions* of specifications, reasoning about behaviors *implementing* a specification, and a specification *refining* another specification. These are all crucial for verifying decompositions. Based on *assume-guarantee contracts* [6,25,37], the syntax of these specifications is built up by *probabilitic contracts* $\mathcal{P}_{>p}(\mathcal{A}, \mathcal{G})$ that give a lower bound p for a linear-time property $\mathcal{G}$, called *guarantee*, given a linear-time property $\mathcal{A}$, called *assumption*.

The two major limitations with the theory in [18] is that (1) it assumes a discrete state space, and (2) the procedure for verifying refinement is not guaranteed to terminate due to an explicit enumeration of infinite sets of paths. To solve (1), the present paper proposes, as a first contribution, an extension of the theory in [18] based on predicates, enabling support for continuous state spaces. To solve (2), as the main contribution of the paper, a new algorithm is proposed for verifying refinement using a reduction to the well-studied language emptiness problem for timed automata. This guarantees an answer in finite time. Furthermore, the present paper augments the syntax of specifications to facilitate more general formulae, and is now based on the well-studied timed Muller automata [3], allowing the reuse of theories and algorithms applying to that class.

The paper is organized as follows. Section 2 recalls the specification theory of [18]. In Sect. 3, the new type of *predicates* are defined and connected to deterministic timed Muller automata (DTMAs). Section 4 presents the syntax and semantics of specifications based on DTMAs. Section 5 presents the new algorithm for verifying refinement between specifications and Sect. 6 demonstrates the algorithm on an example. Lastly, Sect. 7 surveys related work and Sect. 8 concludes the paper.

2   Stochastic Behaviors

In the present paper, we will represent the current state of any given system using a set of *variables*. As a system changes state over time, the variables change values accordingly. Assume a fixed non-empty finite set X of variables, each $x \in X$ ranging over a (possibly uncountable) non-empty set $\texttt{range}(x)$. As part of the first contribution of the paper, we allow these ranges to be arbitrary sets. For instance, variables can range over the integers or reals, thereby permitting both discrete and continuous state spaces. Besides introducing *continuous traces* that capture this generality, the rest of this section recalls important definitions from [18].

2.1 Continuous Traces

The intuition behind a *continuous trace* is to represent how the variables in X change values over time, in a way similar to *signals* of [22,23]. A continuous trace is a function mapping each point in time to the current values assigned to the variables. These value assignments are called *valuations*. Formally, given a set $E \subseteq X$ of variables, a *valuation for* E is a function $\nu^E : E \to \bigcup_{x_i \in E} \mathrm{range}(x_i)$ mapping each $x_i \in E$ to a value in $\mathrm{range}(x_i)$. Let $\mathrm{val}(E)$ denote the set of all possible valuations for E.

Definition 1 (Continuous Trace). *Given a set $E \subseteq X$ of variables, a continuous trace for E is a function $\theta : \mathbb{R}_{\geq 0} \to \mathrm{val}(E)$ mapping each time-point t to a valuation for E.*

In what follows, continuous traces will be referred to simply as *traces*, for short. Let $\mathrm{tr}(E)$ denote the set of all possible traces for E. By convention, let $\mathrm{tr}(\emptyset) = \emptyset$. Furthermore, for any trace $\theta \in \mathrm{tr}(E)$ and set $E' \subseteq E$ of variables, let $\theta|_{E'}$ denote the projection $\theta' : \mathbb{R}_{\geq 0} \to \mathrm{val}(E')$ such that $\forall t \in \mathbb{R}_{\geq 0}. \forall x \in E'. \theta'(t)(x) = \theta(t)(x)$. To define *trace composition*, consider two traces θ_1 and θ_2 for disjoint sets of variables E_1 and E_2, respectively. The *composition of θ_1 and θ_2* is the trace $\theta_1 \parallel \theta_2 : \mathbb{R}_{\geq 0} \to \mathrm{val}(E_1 \cup E_2)$ such that $(\theta_1 \parallel \theta_2)(t)(x)$ equals $\theta_i(t)(x)$ whenever $x \in E_i$, $i \in \{1, 2\}$.

2.2 Input/Output Behaviors

Before we can define *input/output behaviors*, we must first define "ordinary" *behaviors*. In short, these are just probability measures on traces, similar to *trace distributions* of [34,36] but over continuous time and general state spaces. For the following definition of behavior, we assume, for each set $E \subseteq X$, a fixed σ-algebra σ_E such that all trace sets considered in the rest of the paper are measurable. For more details, see [18].

Definition 2 (Behavior). *Given a non-empty set of variables $E \subseteq X$, a behavior over E is a probability measure defined on σ_E.*

Let $\mathrm{beh}(E)$ denote the set of all possible behaviors over a non-empty $E \subseteq X$. Since system components often have control over some variables while being dependent on others, a more general notion of behavior is needed to capture this fact. These are the so-called *input/output behaviors*. They are functions mapping each possible input trace to an "ordinary" behavior over the output variables.

Definition 3 (Input/Output Behavior). *Given two disjoint sets of variables $I \subseteq X$ and $O \subseteq X$, where O is non-empty, an* input/output behavior from I to O *is a function $\beta : \mathrm{tr}(I) \to \mathrm{beh}(O)$.*

Let $\mathtt{beh}(I, O)$ denote the set of all possible I/O behaviors from a set I to a non-empty set O. Given an I/O behavior β from I to O, we call I the set of *input variables* and O the set of *output variables*, denoted $\mathtt{in}(\beta)$ and $\mathtt{out}(\beta)$, respectively.

To be able to compose behaviors, they are assumed to be *compatible*. Formally, two I/O behaviors β_1 and β_2 are said to be *compatible* if $\mathtt{in}(\beta_1) = \emptyset$ and $\mathtt{in}(\beta_2) = \mathtt{out}(\beta_1)$. Note that, although it is possible to create a more general definition of compatibility, these assumptions are made for simplicity.

Definition 4 (Composition of I/O Behaviors). *The composition of two compatible I/O behaviors β_1 and β_2, denoted $\beta_1 \parallel \beta_2$, is the unique I/O behavior from $\emptyset$ to $\mathtt{out}(\beta_1) \cup \mathtt{out}(\beta_2)$, i.e. the probability measure*

$$\beta_1 \parallel \beta_2 \in \mathtt{beh}(\mathtt{out}(\beta_1) \cup \mathtt{out}(\beta_2)) \ ,$$

induced by

$$\beta_1 \parallel \beta_2(\Theta_1 \times \Theta_2) = \int_{\Theta_1} \beta_2(\theta_1)(\Theta_2)\beta_1(d\theta_1) \ . \tag{1}$$

Here, the fact that $\beta_1 \parallel \beta_2$ constitutes a probability measure follows from [32] (Theorem 5.8.1 and Theorem 2.4.3).

2.3   Specifications

Intuitively, we may think of a specification as a set of "allowed" I/O behaviors. However, instead of saying that an I/O behavior β is allowed by a specification Σ, we use the terminology that β *implements* Σ.

Definition 5 (Specification). *Given two disjoint sets of variables $I \subseteq X$ and $O \subseteq X$ such that O is non-empty, a specification Σ from I to O is a subset of the I/O behaviors $\mathtt{beh}(I, O)$, i.e. $\Sigma \subseteq \mathtt{beh}(I, O)$.*

The notation $\mathtt{in}(\cdot)$ and $\mathtt{out}(\cdot)$ is extended also to specifications in the obvious way. An I/O behavior β from I to O is said to *implement* a specification Σ from I to O if $\beta \in \Sigma$. The key notion of the present paper is *refinement* between specifications. A specification Σ refines a specification Σ' if each behavior implementing Σ also implements Σ'. This is captured by the following definition.

Definition 6 (Refines). *A specification Σ_1 from I to O refines a specification Σ_2 from I to O if $\Sigma_1 \subseteq \Sigma_2$.*

Not unlike I/O behaviors, specifications for two components can be composed to form a single specification for the component composition. This is done on the behavior level, by composing each possible pair of behaviors taken from the two specifications. Extending the notion of compatible behaviors, two specifications Σ_1 and Σ_2 are said to be *compatible* if $\mathtt{in}(\Sigma_1) = \emptyset$ and $\mathtt{in}(\Sigma_2) = \mathtt{out}(\Sigma_1)$.

Definition 7 (Parallel Composition of Specifications). *Given two compatible specifications Σ_1 and Σ_2, the parallel composition of Σ_1 and Σ_2, denoted $\Sigma_1 \parallel \Sigma_2$, is the specification $\Sigma_1 \parallel \Sigma_2 = \{\beta_1 \parallel \beta_2 \mid \beta_1 \in \Sigma_1, \beta_2 \in \Sigma_2\}$.*

3   Timed Automata

In the present paper, timed automata as defined by [3,4] are used as a way to represent sets of traces. As we will see later, putting probability bounds on the trace sets of such automata serves as a representation for the type of specifications defined in Sect. 2.3.

3.1   Timed Predicate Sequences

In the present paper, we represent time using a *continuous semantics* [4,5,23] as opposed to the *point-wise semantics* of e.g. timed words used in [2,3]. For a comparison between the two, see e.g. [14,20,30]. Runs of an automaton thus correspond to *timed predicate sequences*, which are a simple extension of the timed state sequences of [4]. More precisely, instead of atomic propositions, we will utilize a more general notion of *predicates* over variables in X.

In accordance with [4], a *time interval* $I \subseteq \mathbb{R}_{\geq 0}$ is a subset of the non-negative real numbers, taking the form (a, b), $(a, b]$, $[a, b)$ or $[a, b]$ where $a, b \geq 0$ such that $a \leq b$ if $I = [a, b]$ and $a < b$ otherwise. For any interval $I \subseteq \mathbb{R}_{\geq 0}$, let $l(I)$ denote the left endpoint of I and $r(I)$ denote the right endpoint of I. Two intervals I_1 and I_2 are said to be *adjacent* if $r(I_1) = l(I_2)$, and either I_1 is right-closed and I_2 is left-open or I_1 is right-open and I_2 is left-closed.

Also in accordance with [4], we now define *interval sequences* partitioning the real timeline. Let $\mathbb{N}$ denote the non-negative integers.

Definition 8 (Interval Sequence [4]). *An* interval sequence *is an infinite sequence of intervals* $I_0 I_1 I_2 \dots$ *partitioning the non-negative real line such that (1)* $0 \in I_0$, *(2) for each* $i \in \mathbb{N}$, I_i *and* I_{i+1} *are adjacent, and (3) the intervals cover all of* $\mathbb{R}_{\geq 0}$, *i.e.* $\bigcup_{i \in \mathbb{N}} I_i = \mathbb{R}_{\geq 0}$.

To express boolean statements about the values of variables, for instance that $x_1 > x_2$, we now define *predicates* over subsets of X. These facilitate the first contribution of the paper, allowing truth statements about both discrete and continuous state spaces. As will be presented later, these predicates can be coupled with timed automata to represent sets of continuous traces.

Definition 9 (Predicate). *Given a set* $E \subseteq X$ *of variables, a* predicate over E *is a function* $q : \mathtt{val}(E) \to \{\mathtt{true}, \mathtt{false}\}$ *mapping each valuation for* E *to a truth value.*

Given a predicate q over some set E of variables, let $\mathtt{var}(q)$ denote the set E. Throughout the rest of the paper, consider a fixed non-empty finite predicate set $\mathcal{Q}$. We extend the $\mathtt{var}(\cdot)$ notation also to predicate sets, so that whenever $Q \subseteq \mathcal{Q}$, $\mathtt{var}(Q) = \bigcup_{q \in Q} \mathtt{var}(q)$.

Definition 10 (Timed Predicate Sequence). *A* timed predicate sequence *is a pair* $\tau = (\bar{Q}, \bar{I})$ *where* $\bar{Q} = Q_0 Q_1 Q_2 \dots$ *is an infinite sequence of predicate sets* $Q_i \subseteq \mathcal{Q}$ *and* $\bar{I} = I_0 I_1 I_2 \dots$ *is an interval sequence.*

Intuitively, in any timed predicate sequence $(Q_0 Q_1 Q_2 \ldots, I_0 I_1 I_2 \ldots)$, each set Q_i represents the predicates that are true throughout the corresponding interval I_i. Given a timed predicate sequence $\tau = (\bar{Q}, \bar{I})$, let $\tau^* : \mathbb{R}_{\geq 0} \rightarrow 2^{\mathcal{Q}}$ be the function such that $\tau^*(t) = Q_i$ for each $i \in \mathbb{N}$ and $t \in I_i$.

3.2   Deterministic Timed Muller Automata

Throughout the rest of the paper, we make use of so-called *deterministic timed Muller automata* (DTMAs) which suit our specific needs. Although strictly less expressive than their non-deterministic counterpart, DTMAs are closed under the two crucial operations intersection and complement, rather than just intersection [3]. The paper also relies heavily on the fact that the language emptiness problem for timed automata is decidable [3]. We consider a fixed set of *clocks*.

Definition 11 (Clock Constraint). *Given a set C of clocks, a clock constraint δ on C is defined inductively by the grammar $\delta ::= c \sim k \mid \delta \wedge \delta \mid \delta \vee \delta \mid \neg \delta$, where c ranges over clocks C, $\sim \in \{<, \leq, \geq, >\}$, and k ranges over rationals $\mathbb{Q}$.*

Note that a constraint `true` can be defined as an abbreviation. Given a set C of clocks, let Δ^C denote the set of all possible clock constraints on C. In accordance with [1,3] and due to their decidability result relying on this, k ranges over rationals instead of e.g. reals. This is a reasonable restriction since any real number can be approximated to arbitrary precision by a rational number.

Given a set C of clocks, a *clock valuation for C* is a function $\nu^C : C \rightarrow \mathbb{R}_{\geq 0}$ mapping each clock $c \in C$ to a non-negative real number $\nu^C(c)$. For any number $t \in \mathbb{R}_{\geq 0}$, let $\nu^C + t$ be the clock valuation for C assigning each clock $c \in C$ to $\nu^C(c) + t$. Given a function f and two values a and v, let $f[a \mapsto v]$ denote the function mapping a to v and agreeing with f on all other values. Extending this to sets $A = \{a_1, \ldots, a_k\}$, let $f[A \mapsto v]$ be shorthand for $f[a_1 \mapsto v] \ldots [a_k \mapsto v]$.

Definition 12 (Satisfy Clock Constraint). *Given a set $C = \{c_1, \ldots, c_m\}$ of clocks, a clock constraint δ on C and a clock valuation ν^C for C, the valuation ν^C satisfies δ if $\delta[c_1 \mapsto \nu^C(c_1)] \ldots [c_m \mapsto \nu^C(c_m)]$ interprets to `true` in the usual logic sense.*

The following definition introduces *predicate constraints*, which are formulae built up by predicates and logic connectives. Note that, since predicates and clocks are different objects, so are predicate constraints and clock constraints.

Definition 13 (Predicate Constraint). *A predicate constraint ψ is defined inductively by the grammar $\psi ::= q \mid \psi \wedge \psi \mid \psi \vee \psi \mid \neg \psi$, where q ranges over predicates $\mathcal{Q}$.*

Once again, a constraint `true` can be defined as an abbreviation. Let Ψ denote the set of all possible predicate constraints.

Definition 14 (Satisfy Predicate Constraint). *A predicate set Q satisfies a predicate constraint ψ if the formula obtained from ψ by substituting `true` for each predicate $q \in Q$ and `false` for each predicate $q \in \mathcal{Q} \setminus Q$ evaluates to `true` in the usual logic sense.*

To define timed Muller automata and their semantics, we will closely follow [4], which also uses a continuous semantics. However, we replace propositional constraints by predicate constraints.

Definition 15 (Timed Muller Automaton). *A timed Muller automaton (TMA) is a tuple* $\mathcal{M} = \langle V, v_0, C, \alpha, \beta, \rightarrow, \mathcal{F} \rangle$ *where*

- *V is a non-empty finite set of* locations,
- *$v_0 \in V$ is the* initial location,
- *C is a non-empty finite set of* clocks,
- *$\alpha : V \rightarrow \Psi$ is a location labeling function associating each $v \in V$ to a predicate constraint $\psi \in \Psi$,*
- *$\beta : V \rightarrow \Delta^C$ is a location labeling function associating each $v \in V$ to a clock constraint $\delta \in \Delta^C$,*
- *$\rightarrow \subseteq V \times 2^C \times V$ is a set of* transitions *where each $(v, R, v') \in \rightarrow$ consists of a source v, a set R of reset clocks, and a destination v',*
- *and $\mathcal{F} \subseteq 2^V$ is the* acceptance family.

For notational convenience, unless otherwise stated, each location v is assumed to have a self-transition of the form $(v, \emptyset, v)$. This is done to enable the automaton to generate infinite runs even when no other outgoing transitions exist. An example TMA is given in Fig. 1a. It has two locations, a clock c, two predicate constraints h and $\neg h$, a clock constraint $c \geq 10^3$, two drawn transitions, and two implicit self-transitions.

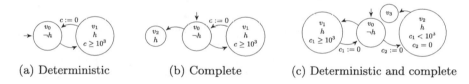

(a) Deterministic   (b) Complete   (c) Deterministic and complete

Fig. 1. Timed Muller automata describing an overheating motor. Omitted constraints are to be understood as constraints that always evaluate to true.

We extend the notation $\mathtt{var}(\cdot)$ such that, given a TMA $\mathcal{M} = \langle V, v_0, C, \alpha, \beta, \rightarrow, \mathcal{F} \rangle$, $\mathtt{var}(M)$ denotes the smallest set of variables E such that $\mathtt{var}(q) \subseteq E$ for each predicate q appearing in α. The semantics of TMAs is defined in terms of *runs*, which represent stepping through the transitions of an automaton subject to the clock constraints. The definition presented here follows closely that of [4].

Definition 16 (Run). *Given a timed Muller automaton $\mathcal{M} = \langle V, v_0, C, \alpha, \beta, \rightarrow, \mathcal{F} \rangle$, a run ρ of $\mathcal{M}$ is an infinite sequence*

$$\rho = \xrightarrow[\nu_0^C]{} (v_0, I_0) \xrightarrow[\nu_1^C]{R_1} (v_1, I_1) \xrightarrow[\nu_2^C]{R_2} (v_2, I_2) \xrightarrow[\nu_3^C]{R_3} \cdots$$

where $\nu_i^C \in \mathtt{val}(C)$ are clock valuations, $v_i \in V$ are locations, $I_0 I_1 I_2 \ldots$ is an interval sequence, and $R_i \subseteq C$ are clock sets, such that

- *for each clock $c \in C$, $\nu_0^C(c) = 0$,*
- *for each $i \in \mathbb{N}$, there exists a transition (v_i, R_{i+1}, v_{i+1}) in $\rightarrow$ that resets the clocks R_{i+1}, i.e. such that $\nu_{i+1}^C = (\nu_i^C + (r(I_i) - l(I_i)))[R_{i+1} \mapsto 0]$,*
- *for each $i \in \mathbb{N}$ and $t \in I_i$, $\nu_i^C + (t - l(I_i))$ satisfies $\beta(v_i)$.*

Given a run ρ, let $\texttt{inf}(\rho)$ denote the set of locations visited an infinite number of times in ρ, i.e. the locations $v \in V$ such that $v = v_i$ for infinitely many i. Using similar notation as for timed predicate sequences, let ρ^* denote the function associating each time with the current location in the run ρ. That is, given a run $\rho = \xrightarrow[\nu_0^C]{} (v_0, I_0) \xrightarrow[\nu_1^C]{R_1} (v_1, I_1) \xrightarrow[\nu_2^C]{R_2} (v_2, I_2) \xrightarrow[\nu_3^C]{R_3} \cdots$ of a TMA $\mathcal{M} = \langle V, v_0, C, \alpha, \beta, \rightarrow, \mathcal{F} \rangle$, $\rho^* : \mathbb{R}_{\geq 0} \rightarrow V$ is the function such that $\rho^*(t) = v_i$ for each $i \in \mathbb{N}$ and $t \in I_i$. In the following definition, we connect automata to corresponding sets of *accepted* timed predicate sequences. A timed predicate sequence τ is *consistent with* a run ρ if for each $i \in \mathbb{N}$ and time $t \in I_i$, the predicate set $\tau^*(t)$ satisfies $\alpha(\rho^*(t))$.

Definition 17 (Accepts). *A timed Muller automaton $\mathcal{M} = \langle V, v_0, C, \alpha, \beta, \rightarrow, \mathcal{F} \rangle$ accepts a timed predicate sequence τ if τ is consistent with some run ρ of $\mathcal{M}$ such that $\texttt{inf}(\rho) \in \mathcal{F}$.*

Given a TMA $\mathcal{M}$, let $L(\mathcal{M})$ denote the set of all timed predicate sequences accepted by $\mathcal{M}$. As a further step, in Sect. 4, we will extend acceptance also to traces, completing the goal of using automata to represent trace sets.

Example 1 (Overheating Motor). Consider a motor that may *overheat*, exceeding 200 °C. A possible requirement is that the motor shall not overheat within the first 10^3 s and, whenever overheated, shall not overheat again within 10^3 s. Let x be a variable representing the current temperature and h be a predicate evaluating to true if and only if $x \geq 200$. A TMA describing this requirement is shown in Fig. 1a. It has two locations and a single clock c keeping track of the current duration of being below 200 °C. The acceptance family is $\mathcal{F} = \{\{v_0\}, \{v_0, v_1\}\}$, accepting exactly the timed predicate sequences for which either (a) there exists a point after which the motor is never overheated, or (b) the motor alternates between overheating and cooling, and is never overheated more often than every 10^3 s. Note that omitting the set $\{v_0\}$ from $\mathcal{F}$ neglects case (a).

3.3   Operations on Timed Automata

To support the later presented algorithm for the refinement problem, we now introduce the two operations *intersection* and *complement* for timed automata. Since non-deterministic TMAs are not closed under complement, we first define *deterministic* TMAs, or *DTMAs* for short. Proofs for all presented propositions are given in the report [17].

Definition 18 (Deterministic TMA). *A timed Muller automaton $\mathcal{M} = \langle V, v_0, C, \alpha, \beta, \rightarrow, \mathcal{F} \rangle$ is deterministic if for each location $v \in V$, predicate set $Q \subseteq \mathcal{Q}$ and clock valuation $\nu^C \in \texttt{val}(C)$, whenever there exist $v', v'' \in V$ such that*

– Q *satisfies both* $\alpha(v')$ *and* $\alpha(v'')$,
– *there exist transitions* (v, R', v') *and* (v, R'', v'') *for some sets* R' *and* R'',
– $\nu^C[R' \mapsto 0]$ *satisfies* $\beta(v')$, *and* $\nu^C[R'' \mapsto 0]$ *satisfies* $\beta(v'')$,

then $v' = v''$.

Figures 1a and 1c are two examples of DTMAs. The automaton of Fig. 1b is not deterministic because whenever the automaton is at v_0, with $c \geq 10^3$, and h turns true, there are two possible locations to enter nondeterministically.

Taking the viewpoint that automata *read* timed predicate sequences as opposed to *generating* them, it is possible that a given DTMA "gets stuck" when arriving at a predicate set for which there exists no corresponding transition. Although not a problem semantically, stuck runs makes it cumbersome to define the complement and intersection operations for automata. Furthermore, given a DTMA $\mathcal{M}$, it is always possible to construct an equivalent automaton $\mathcal{M}'$ with $L(\mathcal{M}) = L(\mathcal{M}')$, preserving determinism and in which runs never get stuck. Such an automaton is said to be *complete*, see e.g. [3] for a completeness construction. In short, the construction works by adding new "trap" locations and corresponding transitions through which all otherwise stuck runs are lead. Without loss of generality, all automata of the present paper are henceforth assumed to be complete. However, we usually omit to explicitly draw trap locations and corresponding transitions to make the illustrations more compact. In our context, completeness is captured by the following definition.

Definition 19 (Complete DTMA). *A DTMA* $\mathcal{M} = \langle V, v_0, C, \alpha, \beta, \rightarrow, \mathcal{F} \rangle$ *is complete if for each timed predicate sequence* τ, *there exists a run* ρ *of* $\mathcal{M}$ *such that* τ *is consistent with* ρ.

Figures 1b and 1c are two examples of complete timed Muller automata. The automaton of Fig. 1a is not complete because whenever the automaton is at location v_0, $c < 10^3$, and h turns true, there is no location to enter.

The intersection operator for complete DTMAs is based on parallel composition as defined in [4] and the intersection construction presented in [3].

Definition 20 (Intersection of Complete DTMA). *Let* $\mathcal{M}_1 = \langle V_1, v_{01}, C_1, \alpha_1, \beta_1, \rightarrow_1, \mathcal{F}_1 \rangle$ *and* $\mathcal{M}_2 = \langle V_2, v_{02}, C_2, \alpha_2, \beta_2, \rightarrow_2, \mathcal{F}_2 \rangle$ *be complete DTMAs such that* $V_1 \cap V_2 = \emptyset$ *and* $C_1 \cap C_2 = \emptyset$. *The intersection of* $\mathcal{M}_1$ *and* $\mathcal{M}_2$ *is the TMA* $\mathcal{M}_1 \sqcap \mathcal{M}_2 = \langle V_1 \times V_2, (v_{01}, v_{02}), C_1 \cup C_2, \alpha, \beta, \rightarrow, \mathcal{F} \rangle$ *where*

– *for each* $(v_1, v_2) \in V_1 \times V_2$, $\alpha((v_1, v_2)) = \alpha_1(v_1) \wedge \alpha_2(v_2)$,
– *for each* $(v_1, v_2) \in V_1 \times V_2$, $\beta((v_1, v_2)) = \beta_1(v_1) \wedge \beta_2(v_2)$,
– $\rightarrow$ *is the smallest set that contains, for each pair of transitions* $(v_1, R_1, v_1') \in \rightarrow_1$ *and* $(v_2, R_2, v_2') \in \rightarrow_2$, *the transition* $((v_1, v_2), R_1 \cup R_2, (v_1', v_2'))$,
– *the acceptance family* $\mathcal{F}$ *is the set* $\boldsymbol{\mathcal{F}}^1 \cap \boldsymbol{\mathcal{F}}^2$, *where*

$$\boldsymbol{\mathcal{F}}^1 = \{F \subseteq V_1 \times V_2 \mid \{v_1 \in V_1 \mid \exists v_2 \in V_2 \;.\; (v_1, v_2) \in F\} \in \mathcal{F}_1\},$$

$$\boldsymbol{\mathcal{F}}^2 = \{F \subseteq V_1 \times V_2 \mid \{v_2 \in V_2 \mid \exists v_1 \in V_1 \;.\; (v_1, v_2) \in F\} \in \mathcal{F}_2\}.$$

Definition 21 (Complement of Complete DTMA [3]). *Let* $\mathcal{M} = \langle V, v_0, C,$ $\alpha, \beta, \rightarrow, \mathcal{F} \rangle$ *be a DTMA. The complement of* $\mathcal{M}$ *is the DTMA* $\mathcal{M}^c = \langle V, v_0, C, \alpha,$ $\beta, \rightarrow, 2^L \setminus \mathcal{F} \rangle$.

Proposition 1. *Suppose that* $\mathcal{M}$ *and* $\mathcal{M}'$ *are complete DTMAs. Then* $L(\mathcal{M} \sqcap$ $\mathcal{M}') = L(\mathcal{M}) \cap L(\mathcal{M}')$ *and* $\mathcal{M}^c = L(\mathcal{M})^c$. *Furthermore, the class of complete DTMAs is closed under intersection and complement.*

4   Specifying Behaviors Using Timed Automata

In this section, we define a specification language and accompanying semantics that allows us to instantiate the type of specification from Definition 5. This language, defined using a formal grammar, consists of so-called *Probabilistic Contract Formulae* (PCFs). The basic building-block is a probabilistic assume-guarantee contract, or *probabilistic contract* for short, of the form $\mathcal{P}_{\sim p}(\mathcal{A}, \mathcal{G})$, consisting of an *assumption* $\mathcal{A}$, *guarantee* $\mathcal{G}$, and *probability bound* p. Both $\mathcal{A}$ and $\mathcal{G}$ represent linear-time properties and are given as DTMAs. Semantically, a probabilistic contract represents the set of all I/O behaviors such that, whenever the assumption is satisfied, the probability of the guarantee respects the probability bound. As will later be defined, these probabilistic contracts can be composed by negation ($\neg$), parallel composition ($\|$), and conjunction ($\wedge$).

We begin by formalizing the way in which automata represent sets of traces, using the notion of *accepted trace*. First, a trace θ for X is said to be *consistent with* a timed predicate sequence τ if for each $t \in \mathbb{R}_{\geq 0}$ and $q \in \mathcal{Q}$, the predicate application $q(\theta|_{\mathtt{var}(q)}(t))$ evaluates to true if and only if $q \in \tau^*(t)$.

Definition 22 (Accepted Trace). *A TMA* $\mathcal{M}$ *accepts a trace* θ *for* X *if there exists a timed predicate sequence* τ *such that* $\mathcal{M}$ *accepts* τ *and* θ *is consistent with* τ.

Given a TMA $\mathcal{M}$, let $L^*(\mathcal{M})$ denote the set of traces accepted by $\mathcal{M}$. Furthermore, if E is a set of variables such that $\mathtt{var}(\mathcal{M}) \subseteq E \subseteq X$, then let $L^E(\mathcal{M})$ denote the set $\{\theta|_E \mid \theta \in L^*(\mathcal{M})\}$ of accepted traces restricted to the variables E. For reasons of convenience, to ensure that $L(\mathcal{M})$ is empty if and only if $L(\mathcal{M}^*)$ is empty, we assume without loss of generality that every predicate $q \in Q$ is *satisfiable*. That is, there exists some trace θ that makes $q(\theta)$ evaluate to true.

Definition 23 (Probabilistic Contract Formula). *A probabilistic contract formula* (PCF) ϕ *is defined inductively using the grammar*

$$\phi ::= P_{\sim p}(\mathcal{A}, \mathcal{G}) \mid \neg \phi \mid \phi \| \phi \mid \phi \wedge \phi \,,$$

where $\sim \in \{<, \leq, \geq, >\}$ *is a comparison operator,* $p \in [0, 1]$ *is the probability bound, and* $\mathcal{A}$ *and* $\mathcal{G}$, *the assumption and guarantee, respectively, are complete DTMAs such that* $\mathtt{var}(\mathcal{G}) \setminus \mathtt{var}(\mathcal{A}) \neq \emptyset$.

Remark 1. Timed predicate sequences, which are an intermediate step between automata and their accepted traces, intrinsically obey the so-called *finite variability* property [4]. This property states that each bounded time interval contains at most finitely many state changes, which according to [4] is an adequate assumption for modelling discrete-state systems. However, the discreteness of timed predicate sequences is merely an abstraction put over traces, which by no means are restricted to obey finite variability. For instance, a trace over real-valued variables can generally change values uncountably many times even within bounded time intervals.

The semantics of a PCF ϕ is defined in terms of its *interpretation* $[\![\phi]\!]$, evaluating to a specification, i.e. a set of I/O behaviors. Since parallel composition is only defined for compatible specifications, we require in the following definition that, for each PCF of the form $\phi_1 \parallel \phi_2$, the specifications $[\![\phi_1]\!]$ and $[\![\phi_2]\!]$ are compatible. Similarly, for each PCF $\phi_1 \wedge \phi_2$, we require that ϕ_1 and ϕ_2 have the same input and output variables.

Definition 24 (PCF Interpretation). *Given a probabilistic contract* $P_{\sim p}(\mathcal{A}, \mathcal{G})$, *as shorthand, let I denote* $\mathtt{var}(\mathcal{A})$, O *denote* $\mathtt{var}(\mathcal{G}) \setminus \mathtt{var}(\mathcal{A})$, *and* $\Theta_{\mathcal{G}}$ *denote* $\{\theta_O \in \mathtt{tr}(O) \mid \theta_I \parallel \theta_O \in L^{I \cup O}(\mathcal{G})\}$. *The interpretation* $[\![\phi]\!]$ *of a PCF* ϕ *is defined inductively by:*

$$[\![P_{\sim p}(\mathcal{A}, \mathcal{G})]\!] = \begin{cases} \{\beta \in \mathtt{beh}(I, O) \mid \beta()(L^O(\mathcal{G})) \sim p\}, & I = \emptyset \\ \{\beta \in \mathtt{beh}(I, O) \mid \forall \theta_I \in L^I(\mathcal{A}) . \ \beta(\theta_I)(\Theta_{\mathcal{G}}) \sim p\}, & I \neq \emptyset \end{cases}$$

$$[\![\neg\phi]\!] = \{\beta \in \mathtt{beh}(\mathtt{in}([\![\phi]\!]), \mathtt{out}([\![\phi]\!])) \mid \beta \notin [\![\phi]\!]\}$$

$$[\![\phi_1 \parallel \phi_2]\!] = [\![\phi_1]\!] \parallel [\![\phi_2]\!]$$

$$[\![\phi_1 \wedge \phi_2]\!] = [\![\phi_1]\!] \cap [\![\phi_2]\!]$$

We extend the notion of *input variables* and *output variables* also to PCFs ϕ such that $\mathtt{in}(\phi) = \mathtt{in}([\![\phi]\!])$ and $\mathtt{out}(\phi) = \mathtt{out}([\![\phi]\!])$. See Sect. 6 for examples of PCFs.

The refinement-verification algorithm in the next section relies on negating the top-level specification to generate its complement. The following proposition states that this works as required, provided that the specification has no input variables. As before, the proof is given in the report [17].

Proposition 2. *Suppose that* $\phi = P_{\sim p}(\mathcal{A}, \mathcal{G})$ *is a probabilistic contract with no input variables. Then* $[\![\neg\phi]\!] = [\![P_{\sim^c p}(\mathcal{A}, \mathcal{G})]\!]$, *where* $\sim^c$ *is the complement of the operator* $\sim$, *so that* $\leq^c$ *is equivalent to* $>$, $>^c$ *is equivalent to* $\leq$, $<^c$ *is equivalent to* $\geq$, *and* $\geq^c$ *is equivalent to* $<$.

5 Algorithm for Verifying Refinement

In this section, we present the main contribution of the paper, namely an algorithm for verifying refinement between PCFs. To guarantee termination, we make a reduction to the well-studied language emptiness problem for timed automata. Note that even though our framework uses timed automata in alignment with the previous attempt [18], the algorithm will work on any specification formalism that admits finite-time complement and intersection and for which language emptiness is decidable. The algorithm takes two inputs ϕ and ϕ_0, each being a PCF, and outputs **true** only if ϕ refines ϕ_0. In this sense, the algorithm is sound. However, it is not complete, as will be discussed in more detail below.

To verify refinement, the strategy is to consider probability measures over the entire trace space directly, and show that none of these respect all of the bounds imposed by both ϕ and $\neg\phi_0$ simultaneously. Note that, since the top-level specification is complemented, this would imply that $[\![\phi]\!] \subseteq [\![\phi_0]\!]$. The key is to encode each such bound as a linear inequality, resulting in a system of linear inequalities and allowing us to find a solution by reduction to linear programming. Each variable z_j in the linear inequalities represents the probability of a corresponding trace subset Θ_j, so the question becomes how to partition the trace space into suitable subsets. Any such partition $\boldsymbol{\Theta} = \{\Theta_j\}_{j=1}^{k}$ needs to be fine-grained enough to allow puzzling the Θ_j together to construct each bound but still finite in order to guarantee termination. A critical property to facilitate the former is that, given any such subset Θ_j, all traces in Θ_j must be accepted by the same set of assumptions and guarantees. Such a partition is always possible, see line 1 of Algorithm 1 where each element ω_j in Ω corresponds to a partition element $\Theta_j = L^*(\omega_j)$. To construct the linear inequalities, consider an arbitrary bound $\mathcal{P}_{\sim p}(\mathcal{A}, \mathcal{G})$ appearing in ϕ or $\neg\phi_0$, and let $\Theta_{j_1}, \ldots, \Theta_{j_l}$ be all partition elements accepted by $\mathcal{A}$ and $\Theta_{i_1}, \ldots, \Theta_{i_{l'}}$ be all partition elements accepted by both $\mathcal{A}$ and $\mathcal{G}$. To encode this bound, we simply add the inequality $\frac{z_{j_1} + \cdots + z_{j_l}}{z_{i_1} + \cdots + z_{i_{l'}}} \sim p$ representing a conditional probability of the guarantee given the assumption, see line 5 of Algorithm 1. To limit the search to true probability measures, we must also add inequalities imposing (i) that the probabilities of all Θ_j sum to 1, (ii) that the probability of each Θ_j is non-negative, and (iii) that the probability of each empty set $\Theta_j = \emptyset$ is 0. Lastly, we look for a solution to the system of linear inequalities using e.g. the simplex method, see [10, 27]. If no real solution is found, we conclude that ϕ refines ϕ_0.

The algorithm is presented in pseudocode below, where we assume that ϕ is a composition of the form $\phi_1 \parallel \phi_2 \parallel \cdots \parallel \phi_m$, each being a probabilistic contract, and that also ϕ_0 is a probabilistic contract. Furthermore, due to the difficulties in solving linear inequalities with non-strict inequalities, we assume that the probability bound of each ϕ_i, $i \geq 1$, is non-strict and the probability bound of ϕ_0 (which will be complemented) is strict. This restriction is often insignificant in practice since any PCF with non-strict bound can be approximated to arbitrary precision by one with a strict bound, and vice versa. Given a list Ω, let ω_j denote its jth element. On line 5, the notation $\mathcal{M} \in \omega_j$, where $\mathcal{M}$ is a DTMA, means that $\mathcal{M}$ appears as part of the intersection ω_j. For each index $0 \leq i \leq m$, let $\sim_i$, p_i, $\mathcal{A}_i$ and $\mathcal{G}_i$ denote the comparison operator, probability bound, assumption and guarantee, respectively, of the PCF ϕ_i. The details of the algorithm are demonstrated in Sect. 6 on an example.

Algorithm 1. Verify that a PCF $\phi_1 \parallel \cdots \parallel \phi_m$ refines a PCF ϕ_0.

1: $\Omega \leftarrow \begin{pmatrix} \mathcal{A}_0 \sqcap \mathcal{G}_0 \sqcap \mathcal{A}_1 \sqcap \mathcal{G}_1 \sqcap \cdots \sqcap \mathcal{A}_m \sqcap \mathcal{G}_m, \\ \mathcal{A}_0 \sqcap \mathcal{G}_0 \sqcap \mathcal{A}_1 \sqcap \mathcal{G}_1 \sqcap \cdots \sqcap \mathcal{A}_m \sqcap \mathcal{G}_m^c, \\ \mathcal{A}_0 \sqcap \mathcal{G}_0 \sqcap \mathcal{A}_1 \sqcap \mathcal{G}_1 \sqcap \cdots \sqcap \mathcal{A}_m^c \sqcap \mathcal{G}_m, \\ \vdots \\ \mathcal{A}_0^c \sqcap \mathcal{G}_0^c \sqcap \mathcal{A}_1^c \sqcap \mathcal{G}_1^c \sqcap \cdots \sqcap \mathcal{A}_m^c \sqcap \mathcal{G}_m^c \end{pmatrix}$

2: Let $z_0, z_1, \ldots, z_{k-1}$ be fresh variables, where $k = |\Omega|$

3: $\texttt{ineqs} \leftarrow \{z_0 + z_1 + \cdots + z_{k-1} = 1\}$

4: **for** $\phi_i \in \{\phi_1, \ldots, \phi_m, \neg\phi_0\}$ **do**

5:     $\texttt{ineqs} \leftarrow \texttt{ineqs} \cup \left\{ \left(\sum\limits_{j:\mathcal{A}_i \sqcap \mathcal{G}_i \in \omega_j} z_j \right) \sim_i p_i \left(\sum\limits_{j:\mathcal{A}_i \in \omega_j} z_j \right) \right\}$

6: **for** $j \in \{0, \ldots, k-1\}$ **do**

7:     **if** $L(\omega_j)$ is empty **then**

8:         $\texttt{ineqs} \leftarrow \texttt{ineqs} \cup \{z_j = 0\}$

9:     **else**

10:         $\texttt{ineqs} \leftarrow \texttt{ineqs} \cup \{z_j \geq 0\}$

11: **return true** if $\texttt{ineqs}$ has no real solutions; **unknown** otherwise

---

Note that, whenever a solution to the system of linear inequalities is found, the algorithm outputs **unknown** rather than **false**. To see why, consider one of the probabilistic contracts ϕ_i of the composition, and suppose that it has both input and output variables. Then the behaviors in $[\![\phi]\!]$ respect the probability bound of ϕ_i on *each* input trace satisfying the assumption. Intuitively, this means that the granularity is fine. On the other hand, since the algorithm considers conditional probabilities rather than individual input traces, any proposed solution only needs to respect this bound *on average*, taken over all input traces satisfying the assumption. Intuitively, the granularity is coarser. This is a weaker condition, potentially resulting in spurious solutions. Since a fine-grained solution always implies a course-grained solution, but not vice versa, the algorithm is sound but not complete. The proof of the following theorem is given in the report [17].

Theorem 1 (Soundness). *Let ϕ_0 be a probabilistic contract and ϕ be a PCF of the form $\phi_1 \parallel \phi_2 \parallel \cdots \parallel \phi_m$, each ϕ_i being a probabilistic contract, such that ϕ_0 and ϕ have the same (non-empty) set of output variables and no input variables. If the procedure $\texttt{Refines}(\phi, \phi_0)$ given by Algorithm 1 returns **true** then ϕ refines ϕ_0.*

6   Illustrative Example

Following the setting of [18], consider a hypothetical power-generating system composed of two components g_1 and g_2 representing the *main* and *backup* generator, respectively. In order for the backup to work properly, it must first have been charged by the main, demonstrating a sort of dependence between the two. Assume that we are given, in natural language, a top-level specification S_0 and two component specifications S_1 and S_2, one for each generator. Our objective is to answer whether or not the decomposition is correct. That is, does the parallel composition $S_1 \parallel S_2$ of the component specifications refine the top-level specification S_0? Let the three specifications be given as follows:

S_0: "total power output shall be at least 1 kW throughout the first 7 h with over 45% probability",

S_1: "main power output shall be at least 1 kW throughout the first 6 h with at least 70% probability",

S_2: "assuming main power output is at least 1 kW throughout the first 3 h, then the first time t it declines below 1 kW, with at least 80% probability, backup power output shall be at least 1 kW throughout the interval $[t, t + 2h]$".

Let us now express the above specifications as PCFs. For each generator g_i, let the real-valued variable x_i represent its current power output. Each possible *trace* for the set of variables $\{x_1, x_2\}$ therefore gives, for each point in time, the power output of the main and backup generator, separately. For $i \in \{1, 2\}$, let q_i be the *predicate* $x_i \geq 1$ kW, asserting that generator g_i outputs at least 1 kW of power. We now express each specification S_j above as a corresponding PCF ϕ_j. For compactness, let $\top$ denote an automaton accepting *all* traces $\mathtt{tr}(X)$, thus acting as a non-assumption. Starting with the top-level specification S_0, let

$$\phi_0 = \mathcal{P}_{>0.45}\left(\top. \quad \rightarrow \boxed{\begin{array}{c} q_1 \vee q_2 \\ c_0 \leq 7 \end{array}} \longrightarrow \boxed{\boxed{c_0 > 7}}\right).$$

Denoting the double-ringed location as l, let the acceptance family of the guarantee be the singleton set $\{\{l\}\}$. We will continue to use this convention whenever there is only one double-ringed location. This PCF puts no assumptions on the environment and contains the guarantee that at least 1 kW is output through the first 7 h by either the main or backup generator, or both. This time limit of 7 h is enforced by the clock c_0 and clock constraint $c_0 > 7$, since the accepting location can only be entered if the constraint $q_1 \vee q_2$ has remained true at all times before then. Otherwise, the run moves to an implicit trap location, see Sect. 3.3. The probability bound states that all traces satisfying this guarantee must have a total probability mass strictly greater than 0.45. For the main generator specification S_1, let

$$\phi_1 = \mathcal{P}_{\geq 0.7}\left(\top. \quad \rightarrow \boxed{\begin{array}{c} q_1 \\ c_1 \leq 6 \end{array}} \longrightarrow \boxed{\boxed{c_1 > 6}}\right).$$

This PCF follows the same pattern as ϕ_0 but, since the predicate q_2 is not used, only constrains the main generator. Note that ϕ_1 by itself neither refines nor is refined by ϕ_0 due to the shorter time limit of 6 h, which is why the backup generator is needed for the decomposition to work.

Since the natural-language specification S_2 for the backup g_2 contains an assumption about the power output of g_1, so must the corresponding PCF:

$$\phi_2 = \mathcal{P}_{\geq 0.8}\left(\left(\begin{array}{c}q_1\\c_{2,1}\leq 3\end{array}\right)\longrightarrow\left(c_{2,1}>3\right),\quad \rightarrow\left(q_1\right)\xrightarrow{c_{2,2}\,:=\,0}\left(\begin{array}{c}\neg q_1\wedge q_2\\c_{2,2}=0\end{array}\right)\longrightarrow\left(\begin{array}{c}q_2\\c_{2,2}\leq 2\end{array}\right)\longrightarrow\left(c_{2,2}>2\right)\right).$$

The assumption, which is put on the main generator, encodes the charging requirement of the backup using the same pattern as before. In the guarantee, let l_1 and l_2 denote the two double-ringed locations, from top to bottom respectively. The acceptance family is the set $\{\{l_1\},\{l_2\}\}$, which captures two scenarios. The first, captured by l_1, is where q_1 never turns false, in which case the backup is not required to do anything. The second, captured by l_2, is where q_1 turns false and the backup compensates, turning q_2 true. The time at which this happens is recorded by the clock reset $c_{2,2} := 0$, and q_2 must then remain true for the next 2 h for the trace to be accepted.

Verifying that this decomposition is correct amounts to evaluating whether $\phi_1 \parallel \phi_2$ refines ϕ_0. This is done following Algorithm 1, by checking emptiness of each possible combination of the four automata or their complements, and reducing to determining a solution for a system of linear inequalities. For example, it is clear that the language $L(\Omega_0) = L(\mathcal{G}_0 \sqcap \mathcal{G}_1 \sqcap \mathcal{A}_2 \sqcap \mathcal{G}_2) = L(\mathcal{G}_0) \cap L(\mathcal{G}_1) \cap L(\mathcal{A}_2) \cap L(\mathcal{G}_2)$ is non-empty because e.g. the constant trace $\theta(t) = \{x_1 \mapsto 1000, x_2 \mapsto 1000\}, t \in \mathbb{R}_{\geq 0}$, in which both the main and backup generator outputs 1 kW constantly, is accepted by each automaton. In contrast, the language $L(\Omega_2) = L(\mathcal{G}_0 \sqcap \mathcal{G}_1 \sqcap \mathcal{A}_2^c \sqcap \mathcal{G}_2) = L(\mathcal{G}_0) \cap L(\mathcal{G}_1) \cap L(\mathcal{A}_2^c) \cap L(\mathcal{G}_2)$ is empty. To see this, note that $\mathcal{G}_1$ specifies 1 kW for at least 6 h while $\mathcal{A}_2$ specifies the same output for the shorter duration of at least 3 h. It is obviously not possible for a trace to uphold 1 kW for 6 h but not for 3 h, implying $L(\mathcal{G}_1) \cap L(\mathcal{A}_2^c) = \emptyset$. Checking emptiness for each combination gives

$$\left\{\begin{array}{llll}L(\Omega_0), & L(\Omega_1), & L(\Omega_2), & L(\Omega_3),\\L(\Omega_4), & L(\Omega_5), & L(\Omega_6), & L(\Omega_7),\\L(\Omega_8), & L(\Omega_9), & L(\Omega_{10}), & L(\Omega_{11}),\\L(\Omega_{12}), & L(\Omega_{13}), & L(\Omega_{14}), & L(\Omega_{15})\end{array}\right\}=\left\{\begin{array}{llll}\cdot, & \cdot, & \emptyset, & \emptyset,\\\cdot, & \cdot, & \cdot, & \emptyset,\\\emptyset, & \cdot, & \emptyset, & \emptyset,\\\cdot, & \cdot, & \cdot, & \cdot\end{array}\right\}.$$

Let us now construct the system of linear inequalities expressing the probability bounds of $[\![\neg\phi_0 \wedge (\phi_1 \parallel \phi_2)]\!]$. For each composition Ω_k, we define a corresponding variable z_k to represent the probability mass of all traces accepted by Ω_k. That is, for a behavior $\beta \in [\![\neg\phi_0 \wedge (\phi_1 \parallel \phi_2)]\!]$, z_k represents the probability $\beta()(L^*(\Omega_k))$. The resulting inequalities are as follows:

$$\left\{\begin{array}{ll}\displaystyle\sum_{j=0}^{15} z_j = 1 & (2)\\[4mm](z_2, z_3, z_7, z_8, z_{10}, z_{11}) = (0,0,0,0,0,0) & (3)\\[2mm](z_0, z_1, z_4, z_5, z_6, z_9, z_{12}, z_{13}, z_{14}, z_{15}) \geq (0,0,0,0,0,0,0,0,0,0) & (4)\\[2mm]z_0 + z_1 + z_2 + z_3 + z_4 + z_5 + z_6 + z_7 \leq 0.45 & (5)\\[2mm]z_0 + z_1 + z_2 + z_3 + z_8 + z_9 + z_{10} + z_{11} \geq 0.7 & (6)\\[2mm]z_0 + z_4 + z_8 + z_{12} \geq 0.8(z_0 + z_1 + z_4 + z_5 + z_8 + z_9 + z_{12} + z_{13}). & (7)\end{array}\right.$$

The equality (2) represents the fact that all variables must sum to 1 to constitute a probability measure. Next, (3) constrains the variables corresponding to empty languages to have probability 0, and (4) constrains the rest to be at least non-negative. Lastly, reconstructing the probability bounds given by the complement of ϕ_0 and by ϕ_1 and ϕ_2 gives the remaining inequalities (5), (6) and (7). Using e.g. the simplex method, we see that this system of linear inequalities has no solution. According to Theorem 1, we conclude that $\phi_1 \parallel \phi_2$ refines ϕ_0.

7   Related Work

A related field is the area of *model checking* [24,31]. However, this is different from the present paper, since the goal of model checking is to verify implementation rather than refinement.

Specification theories for *Probabilistic Automata* have been proposed [21,34, 36] in which the semantics is defined as sets of so-called *trace distributions*, resembling the behaviors of the present paper. A similar notion of *bundles*, which are generated by *probabilistic modules* instead of probabilistic automata, is studied in [11]. Although both of these theories facilitate refinement verification, they assume discrete time and a specific underlying probability structure, while the present paper explicitly supports continuous time and general probability measures. Also in the continuous setting, *probabilistic I/O automata* [38] and *interactive Markov chains* [16] combine exponential distributions with non-deterministic choice, and *constraint Markov chains* [7] can be used as a finite representation of infinite sets of continuous-time Markov chains. While these theories assume the memoryless property, the present paper allows general probability spaces. Also supporting general probability spaces, a stochastic process algebra called *SPADES* [13] has been introduced. However, the focus there is on discrete-event simulation while the present paper studies refinement of specifications.

In the probabilistic contract setting, the papers [12] and [28] present two different compositional contract-based specification theories for stochastic systems. Both theories include refinement verification, although under the assumption of discrete time in contrast to the continuous-time support of the present paper.

The systems of linear inequalities considered in the present paper are essentially instances of generalized probabilistic satisfiability (GenPSAT), which is an NP-complete problem [8,19].

8   Conclusions

For cyber-physical systems, the ability to *specify* probabilistic properties, e.g. related to safety, is fundamental. Also fundamental is the ability to handle systems with continuous state spaces. The present paper has presented a theory for such specifications based upon *probabilistic contracts*. In particular, the main contribution is an algorithm for verification of *refinement* between such specifications. The algorithm utilizes a reduction to the language emptiness problem, making the algorithm terminate after a finite number of computations.

References

1. Alur, R.: Timed automata. In: Halbwachs, N., Peled, D. (eds.) CAV 1999. LNCS, vol. 1633, pp. 8–22. Springer, Heidelberg (1999). https://doi.org/10.1007/3-540-48683-6_3

2. Alur, R., Dill, D.: Automata for modeling real-time systems. In: Paterson, M.S. (ed.) ICALP 1990. LNCS, vol. 443, pp. 322–335. Springer, Heidelberg (1990). https://doi.org/10.1007/BFb0032042

3. Alur, R., Dill, D.L.: A theory of timed automata. Theoret. Comput. Sci. **126**(2), 183–235 (1994). https://doi.org/10.1016/0304-3975(94)90010-8

4. Alur, R., Feder, T., Henzinger, T.A.: The benefits of relaxing punctuality. J. ACM (JACM) **43**(1), 116–146 (1996)

5. Alur, R., Henzinger, T.A.: Logics and models of real time: a survey. In: de Bakker, J.W., Huizing, C., de Roever, W.P., Rozenberg, G. (eds.) REX 1991. LNCS, vol. 600, pp. 74–106. Springer, Heidelberg (1992). https://doi.org/10.1007/BFb0031988

6. Benveniste, A., Caillaud, B., Ferrari, A., Mangeruca, L., Passerone, R., Sofronis, C.: Multiple viewpoint contract-based specification and design. In: de Boer, F.S., Bonsangue, M.M., Graf, S., de Roever, W.-P. (eds.) FMCO 2007. LNCS, vol. 5382, pp 200–225. Springer, Heidelberg (2008). https://doi.org/10.1007/978-3-540-92188-2_9

7. Caillaud, B., Delahaye, B., Larsen, K.G., Legay, A., Pedersen, M.L., Wasowski, A.: Compositional design methodology with constraint Markov chains. In: 2010 Seventh International Conference on the Quantitative Evaluation of Systems, pp. 123–132. IEEE (2010)

8. Caleiro, C., Casal, F., Mordido, A.: Generalized probabilistic satisfiability. Electron. Notes Theor. Comput. Sci. **332**, 39–56 (2017)

9. Cuoq, P., Kirchner, F., Kosmatov, N., Prevosto, V., Signoles, J., Yakobowski, B.: Frama-C. In: Eleftherakis, G., Hinchey, M., Holcombe, M. (eds.) SEFM 2012. LNCS, vol. 7504, pp. 233–247. Springer, Heidelberg (2012). https://doi.org/10.1007/978-3-642-33826-7_16

10. Dantzig, G.B.: Origins of the simplex method. In: A History of Scientific Computing, pp. 141–151 (1990)

11. de Alfaro, L., Henzinger, T.A., Jhala, R.: Compositional methods for probabilistic systems. In: Larsen, K.G., Nielsen, M. (eds.) CONCUR 2001. LNCS, vol. 2154, pp. 351–365. Springer, Heidelberg (2001). https://doi.org/10.1007/3-540-44685-0_24

12. Delahaye, B., Caillaud, B., Legay, A.: Probabilistic contracts: a compositional reasoning methodology for the design of systems with stochastic and/or nondeterministic aspects. Formal Methods Syst. Des. **38**(1), 1–32 (2011)

13. D'Argenio, P.R., Katoen, J.-P., Brinksma, E.: An algebraic approach to the specification of stochastic systems (Extended abstract). In: Gries, D., de Roever, W.-P. (eds.) Programming Concepts and Methods PROCOMET 1998. ITIFIP, pp. 126–147. Springer, Boston, MA (1998). https://doi.org/10.1007/978-0-387-35358-6_12

14. D'Souza, D., Prabhakar, P.: On the expressiveness of MTL in the pointwise and continuous semantics. Int. J. Softw. Tools Technol. Transfer **9**, 1–4 (2007)

15. Fahrenberg, U., Legay, A., Traonouez, L.-M.: Specification theories for probabilistic and real-time systems. In: Bensalem, S., Lakhneck, Y., Legay, A. (eds.) ETAPS 2014. LNCS, vol. 8415, pp. 98–117. Springer, Heidelberg (2014). https://doi.org/10.1007/978-3-642-54848-2_7

16. Gössler, G., Xu, D.N., Girault, A.: Probabilistic contracts for component-based design. Formal Methods Syst. Des. **41**(2), 211–231 (2012)

17. Hampus, A., Nyberg, M.: Verifying Refinement of Probabilistic Contracts Using Timed Automata (With Proofs) (2023). https://urn.kb.se/resolve?urn=urn%3Anbn%3Ase%3Akth%3Adiva-325814

18. Hampus, A., Nyberg, M.: Formally verifying decompositions of stochastic specifications. In: Groote, J.F., Huisman, M. (eds.) International Conference on Formal Methods for Industrial Critical Systems, pp. 193–210. Springer, Cham (2022). https://doi.org/10.1007/978-3-031-15008-1_13

19. Hansen, P., Jaumard, B.: Probabilistic satisfiability. In: Kohlas, J., Moral, S. (eds.) Handbook of Defeasible Reasoning and Uncertainty Management Systems: Algorithms for Uncertainty and Defeasible Reasoning, vol. 5, pp. 321–367 (2000). https://doi.org/10.1007/978-94-017-1737-3_8

20. Konur, S.: Real-time and probabilistic temporal logics: an overview. arXiv preprint arXiv:1005.3200 (2010)

21. Kwiatkowska, M., Norman, G., Parker, D., Qu, H.: Assume-guarantee verification for probabilistic systems. In: Esparza, J., Majumdar, R. (eds.) TACAS 2010. LNCS, vol. 6015, pp. 23–37. Springer, Heidelberg (2010). https://doi.org/10.1007/978-3-642-12002-2_3

22. Maler, O., Nickovic, D.: Monitoring temporal properties of continuous signals. In: Lakhnech, Y., Yovine, S. (eds.) FORMATS/FTRTFT -2004. LNCS, vol. 3253, pp. 152–166. Springer, Heidelberg (2004). https://doi.org/10.1007/978-3-540-30206-3_12

23. Maler, O., Nickovic, D., Pnueli, A.: From MITL to timed automata. In: Asarin, E., Bouyer, P. (eds.) FORMATS 2006. LNCS, vol. 4202, pp. 274–289. Springer, Heidelberg (2006). https://doi.org/10.1007/11867340_20

24. Mereacre, A., Katoen, J.P., Han, T., Chen, T.: Model checking of continuous-time Markov chains against timed automata specifications. Logical Methods Comput. Sci. **7** (2011)

25. Meyer, B.: Applying 'design by contract'. Computer **25**(10), 40–51 (1992)

26. de Moura, L., Bjørner, N.: Z3: an efficient SMT solver. In: Ramakrishnan, C.R., Rehof, J. (eds.) TACAS 2008. LNCS, vol. 4963, pp. 337–340. Springer, Heidelberg (2008). https://doi.org/10.1007/978-3-540-78800-3_24

27. Nash, J.C.: The (Dantzig) simplex method for linear programming. Comput. Sci. Eng. **2**(1), 29–31 (2000)

28. Nuzzo, P., Li, J., Sangiovanni-Vincentelli, A.L., Xi, Y., Li, D.: Stochastic assume-guarantee contracts for cyber-physical system design. ACM Trans. Embed. Comput. Syst. (TECS) **18**(1), 1–26 (2019)

29. Nyberg, M., Westman, J., Gurov, D.: Formally proving compositionality in industrial systems with informal specifications. In: Margaria, T., Steffen, B. (eds.) ISoLA 2020. LNCS, vol. 12478, pp. 348–365. Springer, Cham (2020). https://doi.org/10.1007/978-3-030-61467-6_22

30. Ouaknine, J., Worrell, J.: Some recent results in metric temporal logic. In: Cassez, F., Jard, C. (eds.) FORMATS 2008. LNCS, vol. 5215, pp. 1–13. Springer, Heidelberg (2008). https://doi.org/10.1007/978-3-540-85778-5_1

31. Paolieri, M., Horváth, A., Vicario, E.: Probabilistic model checking of regenerative concurrent systems. IEEE Trans. Software Eng. **42**(2), 153–169 (2015)

32. Resnick, S.: A Probability Path. Birkhäuser Boston (2019)

33. Roever, W.-P.: The need for compositional proof systems: a survey. In: de Roever, W.-P., Langmaack, H., Pnueli, A. (eds.) COMPOS 1997. LNCS, vol. 1536, pp. 1–22. Springer, Heidelberg (1998). https://doi.org/10.1007/3-540-49213-5_1

34. Segala, R.: A compositional trace-based semantics for probabilistic automata. In: Lee, I., Smolka, S.A. (eds.) CONCUR 1995. LNCS, vol. 962, pp. 234–248. Springer, Heidelberg (1995). https://doi.org/10.1007/3-540-60218-6_17

35. Slind, K., Norrish, M.: A brief overview of HOL4. In: Mohamed, O.A., Muñoz, C., Tahar, S. (eds.) TPHOLs 2008. LNCS, vol. 5170, pp. 28–32. Springer, Heidelberg (2008). https://doi.org/10.1007/978-3-540-71067-7_6

36. Stoelinga, M.: An introduction to probabilistic automata. Bull. EATCS **78**(176–198), 2 (2002)

37. Westman, J., Nyberg, M.: Conditions of contracts for separating responsibilities in heterogeneous systems. Formal Methods in System Design, September 2017

38. Wu, S.H., Smolka, S.A., Stark, E.W.: Composition and behaviors of probabilistic I/O automata. Theoret. Comput. Sci. **176**(1–2), 1–38 (1997)

Asynchronous Test Equivalence over Timed Processes

Puneet Bhateja[✉]

DA-IICT, Gandhinagar, India
puneet_bhateja@daiict.ac.in

Abstract. Each timed process exhibits a kind of input-output behaviour when subjected to asynchronous testing. This behaviour is called the asynchronous test behaviour of the process. Two processes exhibiting the same asynchronous test behaviour are called asynchronous test equivalent. In this paper, we first formalize the notion of asynchronous test behaviour of a timed process, and then address the following decision problem. Given two timed processes, determine whether they are asynchronous test equivalent or not. We prove this problem to be undecidable. The undecidability result holds even for processes with one clock.

1 Introduction

In theoretical computer science, a labelled transition system (LTS) is often used to model the operational semantics of a concurrent process [11]. Language equivalence, bisimulation, isomorphism, etc. are some of the well known notions of semantic equivalence, each defined as a binary relation over the set of all LTSs. A common feature among these equivalences is that they all are characterized by the intensional behaviour of a process [14].

Semantic equivalences can however also be characterized by the extensional observed behaviour of a process. In simple words, two LTS processes are regarded as equivalent if they cannot be distinguished by an observer (or a tester) interacting with them [8]. The communication between the tester and the process can be either synchronous or asynchronous. In synchronous testing, the two interact with each other directly, whereas in asynchronous testing they interact through a medium [5–7].

In [5] we formalized the notion of asynchronous test behaviour for an untimed processes. The medium there is comprised of a pair of FIFO queues, the input queue and the output queue. The asynchronous test behaviour of a process is a collection of input-output pairs (u, v). It means that when the process under test is fed with input u through the input queue, it consequently produces output v through the output queue. Recently we extended the same notion of asynchronous test behaviour to probabilistic processes [3,4]. The asynchronous test behaviour of a probabilistic process is a collection of triples (u, v, π). It means that when the process is fed with input u, it produces output v with probability π as a result.

C. David and M. Sun (Eds.): TASE 2023, LNCS 13931, pp. 114–125, 2023.
https://doi.org/10.1007/978-3-031-35257-7_7

In this paper, our contribution lies in extending the same ideas even further to timed systems. We first define the notion of asynchronous test behaviour of a timed process. We call two processes asynchronous test equivalent if they exhibit the same asynchronous test behaviour. Next, we address the issue of determining asynchronous test equivalence for two given timed processes. This is an important issue for the following reason. Suppose we are given a timed specification, and a timed implementation of some software system. We say that the implementation conforms to the specification, if it is the case that the two are asynchronous test equivalent. Now if this definition of conformance is to be adopted as a standard, there must be an algorithmic way to check it. We here however show that it is not possible to have such an algorithm. Basically, we prove that determining asynchronous test equivalence between two timed processes is an undecidable problem. Our proof of undecidability is based on reducing the classical Post correspondence problem [10] to this problem.

The rest of the paper is organised as follows. In Sect. 2, we explain, through an example, our setup for asynchronous testing. In Sect. 3, we formalize the notion of asynchronous test behaviour as well as asynchronous test equivalence. In Sect. 4, we rigorously prove that determining asynchronous test equivalence for timed processes is an undecidable problem. In Sect. 5, we relate our work with the existing work, especially the problem of determining synchronous test equivalence.

2   Asynchronous Testing Setup

A timed process to be tested is modelled by a timed automaton with input and output (TAIO). Formally TAIO is a tuple $A = (Q, Q_0, C, \Sigma, I, E)$ where:

- Q is a finite set of locations.
- $Q_0 \subseteq Q$ is the set of initial locations.
- C is a finite set of clocks.
- Σ is a set of actions called alphabet. It is further partitioned into input alphabet Σ_{in} and output alphabet Σ_{out}.
- $I : Q \to \Psi(C)$ is a function from the set of locations Q to the set of constraints $\Psi(C)$. Each constraint is of the form $c\#x$, where c ranges over C, x ranges over the set of non negative rational numbers, and $\# \in \{<, \leq, =, \geq, >\}$
- E is a finite set of edges $e = (q, q', \phi, r, a)$ where:
  - $q, q' \in Q$ are the source and the destination locations, respectively.
  - ϕ is called guard. It is a conjunction of finite number of constraints.
  - $r \subseteq C$ is a set of clocks to be reset to zero.
  - $a \in \Sigma$ is an action.

Note that our TAIO model differs from the standard timed automata model [1] in two respects. First, in TAIO the alphabet is partitioned. This actually helps in modelling reactive systems, i.e., systems which constantly interact with their environment. Secondly, there is no concept of final states in TAIO.

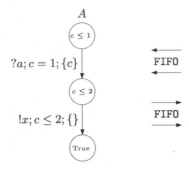

Fig. 1. TAIO A interacting asynchronously with its observer

It should be noted that each location of the TAIO is associated with a clock constraint called local invariant. The purpose of the local invariant is to ensure progress. Control can stay in a location only as long as the local invariant is satisfied. Mostly downwards closed constraints are chosen as local invariants, where a downwards closed constraint is of the form $c < x$ or $c \le x$.

We now draw distinction between the synchronous test behaviour and asynchronous test behaviour of a timed process. The synchronous test behaviour of a TAIO is defined through a set of timed words. A timed word is a sequence of pairs wherein each pair consists of an action and its real-valued time of occurrence. Formally, a timed word is defined as $\rho = (\sigma_1, \tau_1), (\sigma_2, \tau_2), \cdots, (\sigma_n, \tau_n)$. Here $\sigma = \sigma_1 \cdots \sigma_n$ is a finite sequence of symbols in Σ and $\tau = \tau_1 \cdots \tau_n$ is a monotonic sequence of real numbers representing the time stamps of the corresponding actions in σ.

Before explaining the asynchronous test behaviour, let us define some notations.

– The set of non negative real numbers will be denoted by $\mathbb{R}$.
– Symbols t, t_1, t_2, etc. will denote finite delays and will range over $\mathbb{R}$.
– Symbol t_∞ will always denote an infinite delay.

In our asynchronous testing setup, the TAIO is separated from its observer (or tester) by a pair of FIFO queues: the input queue and the output queue (see Fig. 1). What the input queue is for the tester is output queue for the process and vice versa. The tester initially puts some finite string $u = a_1 a_2 \cdots a_n$ into the input queue and waits for the TAIO to respond by putting some string $v = x_1 x_2 \cdots x_m$ into the output queue. This gives us an input-output pair (u, v). But this is not the pair we are interested in. We are rather interested in the pair (u, v') where $v' = t_1 x_1 t_2 x_2 \cdots t_m x_m t_\infty$. Here t_1 is the time elapsed before the arrival of x_1, t_2 is the time elapsed between the arrival of x_1 and x_2, and so on. Finally, t_∞ indicates that after the arrival of x_m there is an interminable delay.

The pair $(a_1a_2 \cdots a_n, t_1x_1t_2x_2 \cdots t_mx_mt_\infty)$ can be considered a legiti-mate asynchronous test behavior whenever (1) the TAIO has consumed the entire input string $a_1a_2 \cdots a_n$, (2) the TAIO has produced the output string $t_1x_1t_2x_2 \cdots t_mx_m$, and (3) the system is held up permanently with no new out-put coming. All such legitimate pairs constitute the asynchronous test behaviour of a timed process A which is denoted by $\mathcal{ATB}(A)$.

Another important point here is that the tester is not aware of the internal structure of the TAIO. Nor does it know how many or which all states the TAIO has. All it knows is the contents of the two queues. Metaphorically, the tester sees the TAIO as a black-box with two transparent ducts attached to it.

Example 1. *Figure 1 shows a TAIO A with input alphabet $\Sigma_{in} = \{a\}$, output alphabet $\Sigma_{out} = \{x\}$ and set of clocks $C = \{c\}$. The asynchronous test behaviour of the system is given as $\mathcal{ATB}(A) = \{(a, t_1.x.t_\infty)|t_1 \in [1, 3]\}$.*

Let us explain how we arrive at this behavior. To begin with, the observer puts a into the input queue of the TAIO. It takes precisely 1 time unit for the TAIO to extract the input from its input queue, and then another $t \in [0, 2]$ time units to release the output x into its output queue. Now for an observer located across the queues, it takes $t \in [1, 3]$ time units for the output x to appear in the output queue. After that there is an endless wait.

3   Asynchronous Test Equivalence over Timed Processes

In this section we first formalize the notion of asynchronous test behaviour of a timed process and then define a new semantic equivalence by the name asyn-chronous test equivalence. We begin by introducing some notations.

- γ denotes a mapping from the set of clocks C to the set of non negative real numbers $\mathbb{R}$. It is called clock valuation.
- $\mathbb{R}^C$ denotes the set of all possible clock valuations.
- $\gamma + t$ denotes a clock valuation wherein each clock is mapped to a value which is t units more that its value under the valuation γ. Formally, $\forall c \in C, \forall \gamma \in \mathbb{R}^C : \gamma + t(c) = \gamma(c) + t$.
- For any $r \subseteq C, \gamma[r]$ denotes a valuation which can be obtained from the valuation γ by assigning all clocks in r to zero and keeping others unchanged.
- $\gamma \models \phi$ denotes that clock valuation γ satisfies guard ϕ.
- γ_0 denotes the valuation under which each clock is assigned value zero.
- **T** denotes a guard which is always true.

For a given TAIO $A = (Q, Q_0, C, \Sigma, I, E)$, it is well known that its semantics can be defined by an infinite state labeled transition system $L = (S, \rightarrow, S_0)$, where:

- S is an infinite set of states $\{(q, \gamma)|q \in Q, \gamma \in \mathbb{R}^C$ and $\gamma \models I(q)\}$.

– → is a transition relation. There are two kinds of transitions: discrete and timed. A discrete transition $(q, \gamma) \xrightarrow{a} (q', \gamma[r])$ takes place whenever $\exists (q, q', \phi, r, a) \in E$ such that $\gamma \models \phi$ and $\gamma[r] \models I(q')$. We write $(q, \gamma) \xslashedrightarrow{a}$ to denote that there is no discrete transition from state (q, γ) on action a.

A timed transition $(q, \gamma) \xrightarrow{t} (q, \gamma + t)$ takes place whenever $\forall t' \leq t : \gamma + t' \models I(q)$. It means that the maximum wait allowed in the location q is until $I(q)$ is satisfied.

– S_0 is the set of initial states $\{(q_0, \gamma_0) | q_0 \in Q_0\}$.

Defintion 1. *A state (q, γ) is called deadlocked when no output action can emanate from it, or any of the states reachable from it solely through timed transitions. Formally, $\forall t \in \mathbb{R}, \forall x \in \Sigma_{out} :$ If $(q, \gamma) \xrightarrow{t} (q, \gamma + t)$, then $(q, \gamma + t) \xslashedrightarrow{x}\}$.*

Defintion 2. *Let A be a TAIO and let $\rho = (\sigma_1, \tau_1), (\sigma_2, \tau_2), \cdots, (\sigma_n, \tau_n)$ be a timed word. A run of the TAIO on the given timed word is a sequence of alternating timed and discrete transitions $(q_0, \gamma_0) \xrightarrow{\tau_1} (q_0, \gamma_0') \xrightarrow{\sigma_1} (q_1, \gamma_1) \xrightarrow{\tau_2 - \tau_1} (q_1, \gamma_1') \xrightarrow{\sigma_2} (q_2, \gamma_2) \cdots \xrightarrow{\sigma_n} (q_n, \gamma_n)$. We can also denote the same run as $(q_0, \gamma_0) \xrightarrow{w} (q_n, \gamma_n)$ where $w = \tau_1 \sigma_1 (\tau_2 - \tau_1) \sigma_2 \cdots (\tau_n - \tau_{n-1}) \sigma_n$.*

Defintion 3. *A run $(q_0, \gamma_0) \xrightarrow{\tau_1} (q_0, \gamma_0') \xrightarrow{\sigma_1} (q_1, \gamma_1) \xrightarrow{\tau_2 - \tau_1} (q_1, \gamma_1') \xrightarrow{\sigma_2} (q_2, \gamma_2) \cdots \xrightarrow{\sigma_n} (q_n, \gamma_n)$ is called deadlocked if (q_n, γ_n) is a deadlocked state. In simple words, a deadlocked run is one which begins in a start state and ends in a deadlocked state.*

For any deadlocked run $(q_0, \gamma_0) \xrightarrow{w} (q_n, \gamma_n)$, we are interested in two things. (1) The projection of string w on the input alphabet Σ_{in}. (2) The projection of string w on the output alphabet Σ_{out}. We now define them one by one.

The projection of string w on Σ_{in} is denoted by $w \downarrow \Sigma_{in}$ and is obtained by removing from w everything except input actions. For example, if $\Sigma_{in} = \{a, b\}$, $\Sigma_{out} = \{x, y, z\}$ and $w = 3a2x1a2b1y1z2a$, then $w \downarrow \Sigma_{in} = aaba$. We can also define this through induction as follows. Base case: $\epsilon \downarrow \Sigma_{in} = \epsilon$. Induction case: Suppose $w = t\alpha w'$ where $t \in \mathbb{R}$ and $\alpha \in \Sigma$. Now $w \downarrow \Sigma_{in} = \alpha(w' \downarrow \Sigma_{in})$ if it is the case that $\alpha \in \Sigma_{in}$. Otherwise, $w \downarrow \Sigma_{in} = w' \downarrow \Sigma_{in}$.

Likewise, the projection of string w on Σ_{out} is denoted by $w \downarrow \Sigma_{out}$ and is obtained by removing from w only input actions and nothing else. For the same example, $w \downarrow \Sigma_{out} = (3 \cdot 2)x(1 \cdot 2 \cdot 1)y1z2$. Since any two consecutive time lapses can be added, we therefore can also write $w \downarrow \Sigma_{out} = 5x4y1z2$. We now define it by induction. Base case: $\epsilon \downarrow \Sigma_{out} = \epsilon$. Induction case: Suppose $w = t\alpha w'$ where $t \in \mathbb{R}$ and $\alpha \in \Sigma$. Now $w \downarrow \Sigma_{out} = t\alpha(w' \downarrow \Sigma_{out})$ if it is the case that $\alpha \in \Sigma_{out}$. Otherwise, $w \downarrow \Sigma_{out} = t(w' \downarrow \Sigma_{out})$.

Defintion 4. *Given a TAIO A, its asynchronous test behavior $\mathcal{ATB}(A)$ is a set of pairs (u, vt_∞) such that the following two conditions hold simultaneously. (1) There is a deadlocked run $(q_0, \gamma_0) \xrightarrow{w} (q_d, \gamma_d)$. (2) $u = w \downarrow \Sigma_{in} \wedge v = w \downarrow \Sigma_{out}$.*

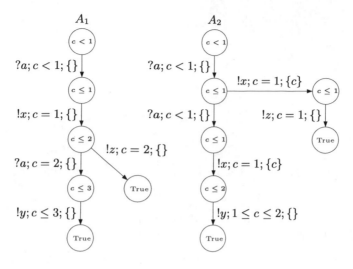

Fig. 2. A_1 and A_2 are asynchronous test equivalent

Suppose some TAIO A admits a deadlocked run $(q_0, \gamma_0) \xrightarrow{w} (q_d, \gamma_d)$ where the input alphabet, output alphabet and w are all the same as in the previous example. Then it is the case that pair $(aaba, 5x4y1zt_\infty)$, which is equal to the pair $(aaba, 5x4y1z2t_\infty)$, belongs to $\mathcal{ATB}(A)$.

We are now ready to define a new semantic equivalence called asynchronous test equivalence over the set of all TAIOs.

Defintion 5. *TAIOs A_1, A_2 are asynchronous test equivalent iff $\mathcal{ATB}(A_1) = \mathcal{ATB}(A_2)$.*

Example 2. *In Fig. 2 TAIOs A_1, A_2 are asynchronous test equivalent. Here $\mathcal{ATB}(A_1) = \mathcal{ATB}(A_2) = \{(a, t_1xt_2z)|t_1 = 1 \wedge t_2 = 1\} \cup \{(aa, t_1xt_2y)|t_1 = 1 \wedge t_2 \in [1, 2]\}$*

4   Undecidability of Asynchronous Test Equivalence

In this section, we prove that the problem of determining asynchronous test equivalence between two timed processes is an undecidable problem.

4.1   Our Proof Strategy

The proof of undecidabililty comprises reducing the Post's correspondence problem (PCP) to this problem. It is well known that PCP is an undecidable problem in the theory of computation [10]. In what follows, we define the PCP in terms of two morphisms f, g from the set Σ_1^+ to the set Σ_2^+. For each of these morphisms, we use the string concatenation operator.

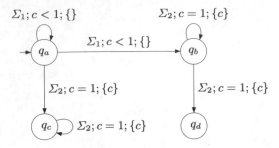

Fig. 3. Process P with input alphabet Σ_1 and output alphabet Σ_2

Defintion 6. *Given two finite alphabets Σ_1 and Σ_2 and two morphisms $f, g : \Sigma_1^+ \to \Sigma_2^+$, does there exist $u \in \Sigma_1^\star$ such that $f(u) = g(u)$?*

We basically construct three timed processes, namely P, P_f, and P_g from the given PCP instance (f, g). The three processes are to be constructed over the input alphabet $\Sigma_{in} = \Sigma_1$ and $\Sigma_{out} = \Sigma_2$. We next compare process P against the process $S = P_f \cup P_g$ and claim that the PCP instance has a solution if and only if $\mathcal{ATB}(P) \neq \mathcal{ATB}(S)$.

4.2   Structure of Process P

Figure 3 shows process P. It has four locations q_a, q_b, q_c and q_d. The initial location q_a has an arrow pointing to it. The process P makes use of the following notations:

- A transition labelled with Σ_1 is representative of the multiple transitions, each labelled differently. For example, the self loop on q_a labelled with Σ_1 actually means that there is a separate self loop for each $a \in \Sigma_1$. Similar explanation can be given for transitions labelled with Σ_2.
- We have not shown location invariants in the figure to avoid clutter. Note that the location invariant for each state is $c \leq 1$.

Lemma 1. *The asynchronous test behaviour of P in Fig. 3 is given by the set $\mathcal{ATB}(P) = \{(a_1 a_2 \cdots a_n, t_1 x_1 t_2 x_2 \cdots t_m x_m t_\infty | \forall i : a_i \in \Sigma_1, x_i \in \Sigma_2, t_i = 1\}$.*

Proof. It should be observed that all the deadlocked runs that process P admit end in location q_d. Each run is of the following kind. $(q_a, \gamma_0) \xrightarrow{t_1} (q_a, \gamma_0') \xrightarrow{a_1} (q_a, \gamma_1) \xrightarrow{t_2} (q_a, \gamma_1') \xrightarrow{a_2} (q_a, \gamma_2) \cdots \xrightarrow{a_n} (q_b, \gamma_n) \xrightarrow{t_{n+1}} (q_b, \gamma_n') \xrightarrow{a_{n+1}} (q_b, \gamma_{n+1}) \xrightarrow{t_{n+2}} (q_b, \gamma_{n+1}') \xrightarrow{a_{n+2}} (q_b, \gamma_{n+2}) \cdots \xrightarrow{a_{n+m}} (q_d, \gamma_{n+m})$, where

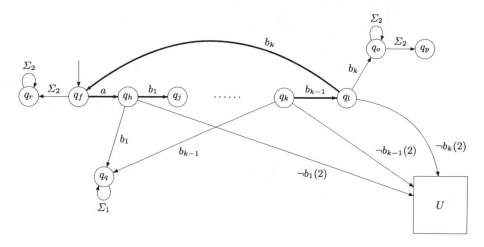

Fig. 4. Process P_f with input alphabet Σ_1 and output alphabet Σ_2

- $a_1 a_2 \cdots a_n \in \Sigma_1^+$
- $t_1 + t_2 + \cdots + t_{n+1} = 1$
- $a_{n+1} a_{n+2} \cdots a_{n+m} \in \Sigma_2^+$
- $\forall 1 < i \leq m : t_{n+i} = 1$

Now string $t_1 a_1 t_2 a_2 ... a_{n+m}$ projected onto the input alphabet Σ_1 gives us string $a_1 a_2 ... a_n$, and the same string projected onto the output alphabet Σ_2 gives us string $1 a_{n+1} 1 a_{n+2} ... 1 a_{n+m}$. If we choose to call $\forall 1 \leq i \leq m : a_{n+i} = x_i$ then $\mathcal{ATB}(P) = \{(a_1 a_2 \cdots a_n, t_1 x_1 t_2 x_2 \cdots t_m x_m t_\infty | \forall i : a_i \in \Sigma_1, x_i \in \Sigma_2, t_i = 1\}$. Hence proved.

4.3 Structure of Process P_f

Figure 4 shows the process P_f. The bottom right corner of P_f has a sub process U called the universal process. Its actual structure is shown in Fig. 5. It is called the universal process as it exhibits input-output behaviour $(a_1 a_2 .. a_n, 1 x_1 1 x_2 ... x_m t_\infty)$ for every possible $a_1 a_2 ... a_n \in \Sigma_1^\star$ and $x_1 x_2 ... x_m \in \Sigma_2^\star$. Note that the sub process U has two initial locations though none of these should be counted as an initial location of the main process P_f. The main process P_f has only one initial location, namely q_f.

Another prominent feature of P_f is the loop (shown in boldface) $a.b_1.b_2. \cdots b_k$. Actually this loop is a template for a set of loops, one for each $a \in \Sigma_1$. Note that each of the b_i in the loop is an element of the set Σ_2. So if $\Sigma_1 = \{a_1, a_2, \cdots, a_n\}$ then for each $a_j \in \Sigma_1$ we have a loop $a_j, b_1^j \cdot b_2^j \cdots b_{k_j}^j$ where $f(a_j) = b_1^j \cdot b_2^j \cdots b_{k_j}^j$. This way, we have n loops.

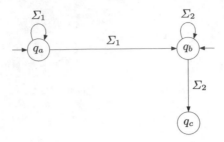

Fig. 5. The universal process U with input alphabet Σ_1 and output alphabet Σ_2

Let us name the locations of these n loops. $q_j(w)$ denotes the location in the jth loop corresponding to the prefix w of $a_j, b_1^j \cdot b_2^j \cdots b_{k_j}^j$. Since $\forall 1 \leq j \leq n$: $a_j, b_1^j \cdot b_2^j \cdots b_{k_j}^j$ is a loop, it is the case that $q_j(\epsilon) = q_j(a_j, b_1^j \cdot b_2^j \cdots b_{k_j}^j)$. All the loops have precisely one common location which is the location corresponding to the prefix ϵ. This is the location where all the n loops are fused together. Formally, $\forall 1 \leq j, l \leq n : q_j(\epsilon) = q_l(\epsilon)$. This way, the sum of number of locations in all the loops is $\sum_{j=1}^{n} k_j + 1$. It is the case that $\forall 1 \leq j \leq n$, there is an edge $q_j(w) \xrightarrow{\alpha} q_j(wa)$ in the jth loop.

We now discuss about the other edges of the process P_f. There is an edge from q_f to q_r labelled with Σ_2 which actually means that from q_f there is an edge for each $a \in \Sigma_2$ arriving at q_r. By the same logic there is a self loop at location q_q on each input symbol $a \in \Sigma_1$ and a self loop at location q_r on each output symbol $x \in \Sigma_2$.

From state q_h there is an edge on symbol b_1 to location q_j as well as q_q. What we also see in the figure is an edge from q_h arriving at sub process U. This edge is indicative of two edges for each $x \in \Sigma_2 \backslash \{b_1\}$. One of these two edges arrive at the initial location q_a, while the other arrive at the initial location q_b.

Note that in Figs. 4 and 5, we have labelled the edges with only actions. The guards and set of clocks to be reset are missing on every edge. Also missing are the location invariants. We have done so to avoid clutter. However, we strictly adhere to the following rules.

- Any edge labelled with an input action has the following guard: $c < 1$.
- Any edge labelled with an input action has the following set of clocks to be reset to zero: $\{\}$
- Any edge labelled with an output action has the following guard: $c = 1$.
- Any edge labelled with an output action has the following set of clocks to be reset to zero: $\{c\}$.
- Every state has the following local invariant: $c \leq 1$.

Hence, by the above rules, the edge from the location q_f to q_h is labelled as follows: $a; c < 1; \{\}$. Similarly, the edge from the location q_h to q_j is labelled as follows: $b_1; c = 1; \{c\}$.

The above rules ensure that the first output action happens after exactly one time unit, and any two consecutive output actions are separated by exactly one time unit.

Let us now calculate the asynchronous test behaviour of the process P_f. Hereafter $w \preceq w'$ will indicate that the string w is a prefix of the string w', and $w \prec w'$ will indicate that the string w is a proper prefix of the string w'.

Lemma 2. $\forall a_1 a_2 \cdots a_n \in \Sigma_1^+, x_1 x_2 \cdots x_m \in \Sigma_2^+$, it is the case that $(a_1 a_2 \cdots a_n, t_1 x_1 t_2 x_2 \cdots t_m x_m t_\infty) \in \mathcal{ATB}(P_f)$ iff $x_1 x_2 \cdots x_m \neq f(a_1 a_2 \cdots a_n)$ where $\forall i : t_i = 1$.

Proof. We first prove that if pair $(a_1 a_2 \cdots a_n, 1 x_1 1 x_2 \cdots 1 x_m t_\infty)$ belongs to $\mathcal{ATB}(P_f)$ then $f(a_1 a_2 \cdots a_n) \neq x_1 x_2 \cdots x_m$.

Suppose $(a_1 a_2 \cdots a_n, 1 x_1 1 x_2 \cdots 1 x_m t_\infty)$ belongs to $\mathcal{ATB}(P_f)$. This means that process P_f admits a deadlocked run $(q_f, \gamma_0) \xrightarrow{w} (q, \gamma)$ such that $(w \downarrow \Sigma_1 = a_1 a_2 \cdots a_n) \wedge (w \downarrow \Sigma_2 = 1 x_1 1 x_2 \cdots 1 x_m t)$. Now from the structure of the process P_f we can make out that a deadlocked run will end is one of the four locations q_p, q_q, q_a, q_c. In other words, the deadlocked state (q, γ) can be one of the states $(q_p, \gamma_p), (q_q, \gamma_q), (q_a, \gamma_a), (q_c, \gamma_c)$. We consider four cases, one for each possible deadlocked state.

Case 1: If $(q, \gamma) = (q_q, \gamma_q)$, then it should be the case that $x_1 x_2 \cdots x_m \prec f(a_1 u_2 \cdots a_n)$.

Case 2: If $(q, \gamma) = (q_p, \gamma_p)$, then it should be the case that $f(a_1 a_2 \cdots a_n) \prec x_1 x_2 \cdots x_m$

Cases 3 & 4: If $(q, \gamma) \in \{(q_a, \gamma_a), (q_c, \gamma_c)\}$. Now if $u = a_1 a_2 \cdots a_n$ and $v = x_1 x_2 \cdots x_m$, then it should be that $u = u_1.a.u_2 \wedge v = v_1.w.\neg b_g.v_2$ where $f(u_1) = v_1$ and $f(a) = w.b_g.w'$. This means that $f(u) \neq v$.

Conversely we can easily prove that for any pair $(a_1 a_2 \cdots a_n, x_1 x_2 \cdots x_m)$, if $f(a_1 a_2 \cdots a_n) \neq x_1 x_2 \cdots x_m$ then the process P_f admits a deadlocked run $(q_f, \gamma_0) \xrightarrow{w} (q, \gamma)$ where $(w \downarrow \Sigma_1 = a_1 a_2 \cdots a_n) \wedge (w \downarrow \Sigma_2 = 1 x_1 1 x_2 \cdots 1 x_m)$ $\wedge (q, \gamma) \in \{(q_p, \gamma_p), (q_q, \gamma_q), (q_a, \gamma_a), (q_c, \gamma_c)\}$. This run ensures that the pair $(a_1 a_2 \cdots a_n, 1 x_1 1 x_2 \cdots 1 x_m t_\infty)$ belongs to the set $\mathcal{ATB}(P_f)$.

4.4   Structure of Process P_g

The structure of process P_g will be same as that of the process P_f, except that the main loop (shown in boldface) will be based on the morphism g instead of morphism f. We therefore do not describe the structure of P_g. We, analogously, have the following lemma.

Lemma 3. $\forall a_1 a_2 \cdots a_n \in \Sigma_1^+, x_1 x_2 \cdots x_m \in \Sigma_2^+$, it is the case that $(a_1 a_2 \cdots a_n, t_1 x_1 t_2 x_2 \cdots t_m x_m t_\infty) \in \mathcal{ATB}(P_g)$ iff $x_1 x_2 \cdots x_m \neq g(a_1 a_2 \cdots a_n)$ where $\forall i : t_i = 1$.

4.5   Undecidability of Asynchronous Test Equivalence

We are now ready to state the main undecidability result of this paper. Let us recall that we have two mathematical objects to compare, namely P and $S = P_f \cup P_g$. Here process S is formed by the disjoint union of the processes P_f and P_g. It is also the case that $\mathcal{ATB}(S) = \mathcal{ATB}(P_f) \cup \mathcal{ATB}(P_g)$.

Theorem 1. $\mathcal{ATB}(P) \neq \mathcal{ATB}(S)$ *if and only if the PCP instance (f, g) has a solution.*

Proof. Suppose that the instance (f, g) has a solution. It means that there exists $a_1 a_2 \cdots a_n \in \Sigma_1^+$ such that $f(a_1 a_2 \cdots a_n) = g(a_1 a_2 \cdots a_n) = x_1 x_2 \cdots x_m$. Now by above observations, it must be the case that $(a_1 a_2 \cdots a_n, 1x_1 1x_2 \cdots 1x_m t_\infty) \notin \mathcal{ATB}(P_f) \wedge (a_1 a_2 \cdots a_n, 1x_1 1x_2 \cdots 1x_m t_\infty) \notin \mathcal{ATB}(P_g)$ However $(a_1 a_2 \cdots a_n, 1x_1 1x_2 \cdots 1x_m t_\infty) \in \mathcal{ATB}(P)$. It is therefore the case that $\mathcal{ATB}(P) \neq \mathcal{ATB}(S)$

Now let us prove the converse. Suppose it is the case that $\mathcal{ATB}(P) \neq \mathcal{ATB}(S)$. Again from the above observations we infer that there must be a pair $(a_1 a_2 \cdots a_n, 1x_1 1x_2 \cdots 1x_m t_\infty)$ which belongs to neither the set $\mathcal{ATB}(P_f)$ nor the set $\mathcal{ATB}(P_g)$. This is only possible when $x_1 x_2 \cdots x_m = f(a_1 a_2 \cdots a_n) = g(a_1 a_2 \cdots a_n)$. This implies that the given PCP instance (f, g) has a solution.

5   Related Work

In this paper, we have proposed a new semantic equivalence over the set of timed processes. Each timed process is modelled by a TAIO, a variant of the timed safety automata [9]. The semantic equivalence is defined through asynchronous testing of TAIO. Further, we have investigated the decidability issue of determining whether two processes are asynchronous test equivalent or not. It turns out that this problem is undecidable.

The synchronous test behaviour of a TAIO is comprised of all the timed words for which there is a valid run of the TAIO. It is well known that the problem of determining whether the two given TAIOs have the same synchronous test behaviour or not is an undecidable problem [2]. Interestingly, if the number of clocks in the each TAIO is restricted to one, then the same problem becomes decidable [12,13].

Our findings are all the more important, because in our undecidability proof we have used only one clock. This means that the problem of determining asynchronous test equivalence is undecidable even for the class of problems for which determining synchronous test equivalence is decidable.

References

1. Alur, R., Dill, D.L.: A theory of timed automata. Theor. Comput. Sci. **126**, 183–235 (1994)
2. Alur, R., Madhusudan, P.: Decision problems for timed automata: a survey. In: International School on Formal Methods for the Design of Computer, Communication and Software Systems, SFM-RT 2004, Bertinoro, Italy, 13–18 September 2004, pp. 1–24 (2004)
3. Bhateja, P.: Asynchronous test equivalence over probabilistic processes. In: 27th Asia-Pacific Software Engineering Conference, APSEC-2020, Singapore, 1–4 December 2020
4. Bhateja, P.: Determining asynchronous test equivalence for probabilistic processes. Inf. Process. Lett. **177**, 106269 (2022)
5. Bhateja, P., Gastin, P., Mukund, M.: A fresh look at testing for asynchronous communication. In: Graf, S., Zhang, W. (eds.) ATVA 2006. LNCS, vol. 4218, pp. 369–383. Springer, Heidelberg (2006). https://doi.org/10.1007/11901914_28
6. Boreale, M., De Nicola, R., Pugliese, R.: Trace and testing equivalence on asynchronous processes. Inf. Comput. **172**, 139–164 (2002)
7. Castellani, I., Hennessy, M.: Testing theories for asynchronous languages. In: Arvind, V., Ramanujam, S. (eds.) FSTTCS 1998. LNCS, vol. 1530, pp. 90–101. Springer, Heidelberg (1998). https://doi.org/10.1007/978-3-540-49382-2_9
8. De Nicola, R., Hennessy, M.: Testing equivalences for processes. Theor. Comput. Sci. **34**, 83–133 (1984)
9. Henzinger, T., Nicollin, X., Sifakis, J., Yovine, S.: Symbolic model checking for real-time systems. Inf. Comput. **111**(2), 193–244 (1994)
10. Hopcroft, J., Ullman, J.: Introduction to Automata Theory, Languages, and Computation. Adison-Wesley Publishing Company, Reading (1979)
11. Keller, R.M.: Formal verification of parallel programs. Commun. ACM **19**, 371–384 (1976)
12. Laroussinie, F., Markey, N., Schnoebelen, P.: Model checking timed automata with one or two clocks. In: Gardner, P., Yoshida, N. (eds.) CONCUR 2004. LNCS, vol. 3170, pp. 387–401. Springer, Heidelberg (2004). https://doi.org/10.1007/978-3-540-28644-8_25
13. Ouaknine, J., Worrell, J.: On the language inclusion problem for timed automata: closing a decidability gap. In: Proceedings of the 19th Annual IEEE Symposium on Logic in Computer Science, pp. 54–63 (2004)
14. van Glabbeek, R.J.: The linear time - branching time spectrum I. In: Bergstra, J.A., Ponse, A., Smolka, S.A. (eds.) Handbook of Process Algebra, pp. 3–99. North-Holland/Elsevier (2001)

Protocol Conformance
with Choreographic PlusCal

Darius Foo[(✉)] [iD], Andreea Costea[(✉)] [iD], and Wei-Ngan Chin[(✉)] [iD]

National University of Singapore, Singapore, Singapore
{dariusf,andreeac,chinwn}@comp.nus.edu.sg

Abstract. Distributed protocols, an essential part of modern computing infrastructure, are well-known to be difficult to implement correctly.
While lightweight formal methods such as TLA$^+$ can be effectively used
to verify abstract protocols, end-to-end validation of real-world protocol
implementations remains challenging due to their complexity. To address
this problem, we extend the TLA$^+$ toolset along two fronts. We propose several extensions to PlusCal – an algorithm language which compiles to TLA$^+$ – to allow writing distributed protocols as choreographies.
This enables more structured and succinct specifications for role-based
protocols. We also provide a methodology and toolchain for compiling
TLA$^+$ models into monitors, allowing them to be used to test existing
systems for conformance. The result is a lightweight testing method that
bridges specification and implementation. We demonstrate its benefits
with case studies of both classic and recent protocols and show it to be
readily applicable to existing systems with low runtime overhead.

1 Introduction

Distributed systems are an essential part of modern computing infrastructure.
They are well known to be hard to implement correctly: Faults and asynchrony
give rise to huge state spaces which make ad hoc testing ineffective. To alleviate
this, developers of distributed systems implement well-known distributed protocols and algorithms, e.g. Paxos and Raft, which provide strong guarantees,
e.g. solving consensus provided a quorum of nodes does not fail. Implementing
a protocol correctly transfers its guarantees to the implementation, but this is
easier said than done. In practice, production-ready consensus implementations
are large and complex, containing optimizations and low-level details that make
the correspondence with an abstract protocol difficult to establish. Moreover,
protocols must often be extended to meet real-world needs. It is thus difficult to
say if a protocol is correct, and if a system indeed implements a given protocol.

Developers working with such protocols today rely on *lightweight formal
methods* [6,27], best exemplified by TLA$^+$. Its combination of first-order temporal logic with explicit state-space model checking is simple, yet effective. Its
expressiveness makes it readily applicable, and its intended workflow of checking
protocol properties in a relatively low-commitment manner is compatible with
software engineering constraints [27]. However, TLA$^+$ has two shortcomings.

C. David and M. Sun (Eds.): TASE 2023, LNCS 13931, pp. 126–145, 2023.
https://doi.org/10.1007/978-3-031-35257-7_8

Distributed protocols are specified in TLA$^+$ as state machines, consisting of a set of *actions* (relations between states). This form is simple and explicit, but relatively unstructured. Control flow must be encoded in guard conditions, and it is generally difficult to see how actions relate: given two actions A and B, we must examine potentially all other actions to see that B follows A and is the *only* action that could follow A. Modifying protocols is in turn error-prone, as seemingly local protocol changes often require nonlocal specification changes. Even for experienced users, changing a large model in state machine form without introducing bugs takes several tries. TLA$^+$ has an algorithm language, PlusCal [22], that should solve these issues, but despite being more structured and apt, it is not often used[1]. We suggest that this is because it does not provide sufficiently high-level constructs for common patterns that occur in distributed protocols.

The TLA$^+$ toolset also does not contain a lightweight mechanism for checking an implementation's conformance to a specification. This is a pity given the ready availability of protocol specifications and the abundance of supposedly-conforming implementations. We thus extend TLA$^+$ along two fronts.

We first extend PlusCal with *choreographies* – global descriptions of communication protocols, and a natural fit for specifying distributed behavior. Choreographies are typically used for specifying communication protocols using multiparty session types [14], in security protocols ("Alice-and-Bob notation"), or writing distributed programs. As specifications, they read causally and resemble informal natural-language descriptions. Choreographies are *projected* into individual process declarations and subsequently translated to regular PlusCal. The translation is parametric in the choice of network semantics.

Secondly, we extend the TLA$^+$ tools with a source-to-source translator from TLA$^+$ into a *monitor* in an implementation language. This allows a system model to be linked into an implementation and executed in lockstep to check for protocol conformance, a lightweight testing method which does not require invasive changes. Given a TLA$^+$ model verified using the TLC model checker, an implementation which refines it thus inherits its safety properties.

We implement both of these extensions in the TLA$^+$ tools and demonstrate both the use of choreographies and monitors with case studies.

Our prototype, experimental data and results, and an extended technical report containing case studies and more detailed proofs are publicly available[2].

2   Overview

We highlight our proposed extensions and methodology using an instance of the classic two-phase commit protocol [23], in which a set of database replicas collectively agree on whether or not to commit a distributed transaction.

The two-phase commit protocol is initiated by the *coordinator*, a distinguished node which first sends requests to a set of *participant* nodes, asking

---

[1] Of the 99 TLA$^+$ models in the official examples repository, 61 could be called distributed protocols and only 15 of them use PlusCal.

[2] https://github.com/dariusf/tlaplus/tree/cpcal.

them to prepare to commit a transaction. The participants decide independently whether or not to commit and reply to the coordinator, which decides to commit the transaction provided *all* participants decided to commit. Entering the second phase of the protocol, the coordinator performs another multicast to inform the participants of the outcome, which end the protocol by acknowledging.

```
process (C \in coordinators)
  variables temp = participants,
            aborted = FALSE; {
    while (temp /= {}) {
      with (r \in temp) {
        Send(self, r, "prepare");
        temp := temp \ {r};
      } };
    temp := participants;
    while (temp /= {} \/ aborted) {
      with (r \in temp) {
        either {
        Receive(r, self, "prepared");
        } or {
        Receive(r, self, "abort");
        aborted := TRUE;
        };
        temp := temp \ {r};
      } };
    if (aborted) {
      temp := participants;
      while (temp /= {}) {
        with (r \in temp) {
        Send(coord, r, "abort");
        temp := temp \ {r};
      } };
      temp := participants;
      while (temp /= {}) {
        with (r \in temp) {
        Receive(r, coord, "aborted");
        temp := temp \ {r};
      } }
    } else {
      temp := participants;
      while (temp /= {}) {
        with (r \in temp) {
        Send(coord, r, "commit");
        temp := temp \ {r};
      } }
      temp := participants;
      while (temp /= {}) {
        with (r \in temp) {
        Receive(r, coord, "committed");
        temp := temp \ {r};
      } } } }
```

Fig. 1. Two-Phase Commit Coordinator (PlusCal)

```
process (P \in participants) {
  Receive(coord, self, "prepare");
  either {
  psend:
    Send(self, coord, "prepared");
  } or {
    Send(self, coord, "abort");
  };
  either {
    Receive(coord, self, "commit");
    Send(self, coord, "committed");
  } or {
    Receive(coord, self, "abort");
    Send(self, coord, "aborted");
  } }
```

Fig. 2. Two-Phase Commit Participant (PlusCal)

```
choreography
  (P \in participants),
  (C \in coordinators) {
  task coordinators "phase1" {
    all (p \in participants) {
      Transmit(coord, p, "prepare");
      either {
        Transmit(p, coord, "prepared");
      } or {
        Transmit(p, coord, "aborted");
        cancel "phase1";
      } } };
  if (aborted) {
    all (p \in participants) {
      Transmit(coord, p, "abort");
      Transmit(p, coord, "aborted");
    }
  } else {
    all (p \in participants) {
      Transmit(coord, p, "commit");
      Transmit(p, coord, "committed");
    } } }
```

Fig. 3. Two-Phase Commit Choreography

The protocol in PlusCal is shown in Fig. 1 and Fig. 2. It is parameterized by two *roles* (Definition 1), `participants` and `coordinators`: finite sets of identifiers (or *parties*) which represent protocol nodes. Intuitively, parties in a role enact the same unique pattern of interactions in a protocol. One PlusCal `process` per role is declared, and processes are replicated for each party in their role. `Send` and `Receive` are macros for communication. `P` and `C` are process names (Sect. 3.1).

Figure 1 shows the coordinator's process; `coordinators` is the singleton role `{coord}`. Within its body, `self` refers to the current party (which is always `coord` here). There are two locals: a set of participants `temp` and a boolean variable `aborted`. The initial multicast is modelled with a `while` loop which repeatedly selects a participant to send a `prepare` message to by iterating over `temp`.

The loop may seem a rather low-level construct to use, but while it is possible to define a TLA$^+$ operator to perform an atomic multicast and send a batch of messages at once, the loop lets us model possible reorderings of parallel sends. Unfortunately, PlusCal macros may only be parameterized by expressions, not blocks or statements, so this pattern of relying on loops and `temp` to communicate with the participants is repeated throughout the coordinator's model.

The second loop in the coordinator's process receives `prepared` messages from every participant, and stops at the first `abort`, ending the first phase. The second phase begins with the coordinator making a decision: if a participant aborted the transaction, the coordinator ensures that every participant acknowledges this; otherwise it solicits `committed` messages from everyone.

Moving on to the participant model in Fig. 2, we see that it mirrors the coordinator: the control flow is identical, sends are replaced with receives, loops with replicated processes, and `if` with `either`.

2.1   Choreographies

It may have seemed natural to break the specification of the two-phase commit protocol into two parts corresponding to the coordinator and participant, respectively. However, such a split compromises the readability and maintainability of the protocol: it is tedious to identify the matching receives and sends spread across different `process`es and keep them in sync. A better specification approach is a *choreography*, a global description of interactions. The entire two-phase commit protocol as a choreography is shown in Fig. 3. Like a program, a choreography has imperative and control flow constructs, but is written from a global perspective instead: statements like `Transmit` are now allowed to mention members of *multiple* roles. `Transmit` is intuitively a juxtaposed `Send` on one party and a `Receive` on another, and effectively halves the size of protocol specifications. A `choreography` is statically *projected* (Sect. 4) into multiple `process`es, recovering something close to what was written in Fig. 1 and Fig. 2.

2.2 Parallel Composition and all

There are still a number of problems with the PlusCal model. A glaring one is that the coordinator's model is overly sequential: despite our attempt to model parallelism with the while loop in Fig. 1, the coordinator is forced to send all its *prepare* messages before receiving a single response. To alleviate that, we could merge the first two loops, but that makes message transmission synchronous. To specify asynchronous transmissions in PlusCal, we could factor the sends and receives into separate processes and manually add variables and awaits to sequence them between phases, but this is, again, error-prone and tedious.

At this point one might be tempted to fall back to TLA$^+$, where having separate actions for sending and receiving messages is easy. The downside is that TLA$^+$ is *unstructured*. Any action may interact with any other, so it is difficult to see where new actions fit into an existing model without a global view. Furthermore, TLA$^+$ is no less verbose; the PlusCal translator's TLA$^+$ output is more than twice the size of Fig. 1 and Fig. 2 combined.

To overcome this, we extend PlusCal with two structuring mechanisms for intra-process concurrency, all and par; use of the former is illustrated in Fig. 3. The all statement may be thought of procedurally as a *fork-join* or nested process, and logically as universal quantification. Its body is executed once for each element in the given set, *possibly in parallel*.

all in combination with Transmit is particularly useful for modelling multicasts. The resulting model is more succinct, but more importantly, it is more *abstract*: the body of the all statement *need not* execute sequentially. Sends and receives to different participants may also occur asynchronously.

Parallel composition par { ... } and { ... } ... is similar: each of the given blocks executes in parallel and may differ, compared to what all does, where each element of the set gives rise to a copy of a single process.

2.3 Tasks and Cancellation

A second problem with the PlusCal model in Fig. 1 is that *cancellation*, a useful complement to timeouts, is done in an ad hoc manner. While we attempted an early abort in the first phase, we had to send all the prepare messages first.

To address this, we extend PlusCal with two constructs, task and cancel. task delimits a block of statements; anything within will *no longer execute* following the corresponding cancellation. cancel terminates its matching task.

The model finally expresses the desired behavior. Suppose we observe (a prefix of) a behavior where two prepare messages are sent, immediately after which a reply to abort comes back. In the final model, no more prepare messages will be sent, and no more prepared or abort messages will be *received*. In other words, the entire first phase has been cancelled early, and the decision in the second phase will be the very next thing following the cancellation.

With all these changes implemented, we see also that our choreographic specification is very succinct: the final model in Fig. 3 is less than half the size of its PlusCal counterpart while saying more.

2.4   Verification and Monitoring

Choreographic PlusCal projects and translates down to regular PlusCal, which in turn translates to TLA^+, so it fits naturally into the verification pipeline of the TLA^+ tools (Fig. 4).

Suppose we specify an invariant that the protocol must uphold and verify it with TLC, the TLA^+ model checker. For example, an invariant for two-phase commit is that participants all commit or all abort, i.e. we cannot observe one participant that has committed and another that has aborted.

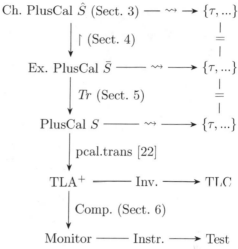

Fig. 4. Overview

We would like assurance that a given implementation of two-phase commit follows the protocol and satisfies the same invariant. The typical way to ensure this is to show that the implementation is a refinement of the model: for each of its behaviors, we find a corresponding behavior of the model that "justifies" the implementation behavior under a refinement mapping— a mapping of implementation states to model states. This in turn implies inheritance of safety properties.

We provide a lightweight way to gain this assurance for TLA^+ models via monitoring. As mentioned earlier, this supports the validation of the many hand-tuned implementations which already exist, not requiring major changes.

We illustrate monitor generation for the statement labelled psend in Fig. 2, where a participant sends a message to the coordinator, is shown in Fig. 5a. This translates down to an action which adds to a participant-local outbox, then advances a program counter pc to capture the protocol's progression.

Given a TLA^+ model satisfying some syntactic conditions[3] (e.g. that local variables are represented as records), we project it, removing non-local variables and actions and projecting local record variables. psend now looks as in Fig. 5b.

We then generate code to be linked with an implementation to enable the collection and validation of traces. Collection is done via the following function.

```
func (m *Monitor) Capture(s State, a Action, args ...TLA)
```

The State struct is generated from the variables of the model and represents its abstract state via a deep embedding of TLA^+. The user provides a refinement

---

[3] Choreographic PlusCal ensures these by construction, but they can also be satisfied in handwritten TLA^+ models, so this methodology applies to them equally.

```
psend(self) ==                              psend(self) ==
  /\ pc[self] = "psend"                       /\ pc = "psend"
  /\ outbox' = [outbox EXCEPT ![self] =       /\ outbox' = outbox \union
     outbox[self] \union                         {[To |-> coord, From |-> self,
        {[To |-> coord, From |-> self,            Type |-> "prepared"]}
         Type |-> "prepared"]}]               /\ pc' = "Lbl_2"
  /\ pc' = [pc EXCEPT ![self] = "Lbl_2"]
  /\ UNCHANGED << participants, temp,
                  aborted >>
```

(a) TLA$^+$ rendering of psend action   (b) Projection of psend action

Fig. 5. TLA$^+$ rendering and projection of psend action from Fig. 2

mapping by constructing it using the concrete state of the implementation, and placing it at appropriate *linearization points* to snapshot the state of the system.

With traces captured, validation is done by interpreting projected actions as assertions and using them to check traces, via generated code like in Fig. 6.

```
func psend(prev state, this state, self TLA) bool {
  if !(reflect.DeepEqual(prev.pc, Str("psend"))) {
    return false
  }
  // ... outbox check elided
  if !(reflect.DeepEqual(this.pc, Str("Lbl_2"))) {
    return false
  }
  return true
}
```

Fig. 6. Go rendering of psend in generated monitor

This gives us a pipeline for checking the correspondence of a high-level choreography with a lower-level implementation, supporting their evolution in tandem. As this is a testing approach, it finds only *violations* of refinement, but scales to real-world implementations.

In the following sections we describe a core fragment of PlusCal and define our extensions to it (Sect. 3). Section 4 and Sect. 5 define projection and translation, respectively, to this core fragment. Section 6 describes the generation and use of monitors. We evaluate the approach empirically in Sect. 7 before concluding.

3   Choreographic PlusCal

3.1   PlusCal

We begin by introducing the syntax (Fig. 7a) and semantics of a minimal subset of PlusCal, *Core PlusCal*, which extends TLA$^+$ with **process** declarations and control flow constructs such as conditionals and loops.

A model *pcal* is a sequence of global variable declarations, followed by one or more **process**es, sequential and replicated imperative programs. Processes are declared with an identifying expression of the form $v \in e$, where v is a name for the set of replicas collectively, and e is a set of indices for the individual replicas.

`skip` is a no-op. `await` blocks until a condition becomes true. `with` nondeterministically selects an element of the set e and binds it to v in its body, and `either` nondeterministically executes one of its branches. The rest are standard.

The semantics of a (Core) PlusCal model is a set of *behaviors*, sequences of *states*. A state is an assignment of variables to values; in each state global variables are assigned values, and each local is assigned one value *per process*. The execution of a process gives rise to a behavior by updating variables via assignments, nondeterminism allows several possible behaviors, and the execution of multiple processes interleaves their individual behaviors. Within process bodies, the special variable *self* refers to the current replica.

$$pcal ::= vardecl^* proc^* \qquad vardecl ::= v = e \qquad procid ::= v \in \{e^*\}$$
$$proc ::= \textbf{process } procid \; vardecl^* \; S$$
$$S ::= \textbf{skip} \mid \textbf{await } e \mid \textbf{while } e \; S \mid \textbf{if } e \; S \; S \mid \textbf{with } v \in e \; S \mid v := e$$
$$\mid S; \; S \mid \textbf{either } S \textbf{ or } S$$
$$e ::= string \mid v \mid e = e \mid e \neq e \mid \forall v \in e : e \mid \{e^*\} \mid e \setminus e \mid e \cup e$$
$$\mid \langle\langle e^* \rangle\rangle \mid e[e] \mid e[e] := e$$

(a) Core PlusCal

$$\bar{S} ::= S \mid \textsf{Send}(e,e,e)$$
$$\mid v := \textsf{Receive}(e,e)$$
$$\mid \textbf{all } v \in e \; \bar{S} \mid \textbf{par } \bar{S} \textbf{ and } \bar{S}$$
$$\mid \textbf{task } R \; e \; \bar{S} \mid \textbf{cancel } e$$

(b) Extended Core PlusCal

$$cpcal ::= vardecl^* \; chor \; proc^*$$
$$chor ::= \textbf{choreography } (procid \; vardecl^*)^* \; \hat{S}$$
$$\hat{S} ::= \bar{S} \mid \textbf{while } e^* \; \hat{S}$$
$$\mid \textsf{Transmit}(e,e,v = e)$$

(c) Choreographic PlusCal

Fig. 7. Syntax of Core PlusCal and its extensions

3.2 Extensions

We extend Core PlusCal with new statements (Fig. 7b), and a `choreography` top-level declaration in *cpcal* (Fig. 7c), which allows additional global statements.

A protocol implementation typically involves multiple sets of physical *nodes* (or replicas), where nodes within each set follow the same "pattern of interaction". We represent nodes by their identifiers (concretely, TLA$^+$ model values or short strings), and their interactions by PlusCal `processes`. These concepts are made explicit in all our PlusCal variants.

Definition 1 (Roles and parties). *A role R is a statically-declared set of node identifiers. A node identifier, as a member of a role, is called a* party.

The syntax of Extended Core PlusCal also contains explicit *send* and *receive* operations that parties use to exchange messages over the network [31,38].

with executes its body with a nondeterministically chosen element of some set, whereas all does so with *every* element of the set. There is no obligation that this be done sequentially, so each "subprocess" executes in parallel. Parallel composition is similar to all, but has a *fixed* number of child processes with *different* behavior. Unlike subprocesses in Distributed PlusCal [1], the translation scheme for both is compositional, allowing arbitrary nested trees of processes.

Finally, there are the paired constructs of *tasks* and *cancellation*. A task is a block of statements that may or may not execute to completion. Tasks are local to a given role R, and are uniquely named with an expression e. Correspondingly, cancellation is a local operation which terminates its task: the suffix of any behavior following a cancellation will not contain actions in the scope of its task. There is exactly one task for a given cancellation. A task may, however, be cancelled in multiple places. For example, in

$$\texttt{par (cancel } e\texttt{) and (task } \{p_1\} \ e \ \texttt{Transmit}(p_2, p_2, v = m))$$

if Transmit means that p_1 sends the message m asynchronously to p_2 and the network is reliable, then there are two outcomes: one where m is received by p_2, and one where it is sent but never received. Tasks and cancellation are thus useful for more fine-grained modeling of timeouts and aborted operations.

A choreography declaration *chor* (Fig. 7c) gives the roles involved in the protocol and their locals. Transmit allows for a name v to be given, which e will be bound to on the receiving party. A while loop must have a termination condition for each role its body involves, and is otherwise standard.

4   Projection

The first step in the translation to PlusCal is to split choreographies $\hat{S}$ into processes $\bar{S}$ via projection. As mentioned earlier, a choreography declares a number of roles, each with its own local variables. The body of the choreography $\hat{S}$ (Fig. 7c) allows two additional *global* statements (Transmit and global while) and may mention variables and members of all roles simultaneously in expressions, subject to well-formedness conditions detailed in this section.

A global while statement has a termination condition for every role involved in its body. We have seen Transmit before; a multicast is expressed as a Transmit inside all. Consider how the first multicast from Fig. 3 is projected:

$$coordinator : \ \texttt{all } p \in participants \ (\texttt{Send}(coord, p, prepare))$$
$$participants : \ v := \texttt{Receive}(p, coord)$$

The Transmit is split into a Send and Receive. As the set of participants is "quantified over", the all block vanishes when we view the protocol from the perspective of some p, which performs only a single Receive from *coord*.

Projection is a partial operation, requiring that variables and expressions used by non-global statements belong to only one role. For example, we cannot `await` a global condition involving multiple roles.

Choreographies are parametric in their choice of network semantics. The user can implement any network semantics they wish via the macros `Send` and `Receive`: reliable, ordered, etc. This is a more minimalistic solution than in Distributed PlusCal [1], which provides explicit `broadcast` and `multicast` operations and multiple kinds of channels, and Modular PlusCal [7,42], which adds constructs for separating the system from the environment of a model.

Definition 2 (Projection). *The projection of $\hat{S}$ onto a role R, $\hat{S} \upharpoonright R$, is defined inductively over the syntax of $\hat{S}$ in Fig. 8.*

Parties and roles are first-class citizens in Choreographic PlusCal, yet projection is done at translation time and must use only statically-known information. A number of auxiliary predicates which relate syntax with (approximations of) semantic information are used in its definition. $loc(v, R)$ is true if v is a local variable of R, $loc(e, R)$ is true if all variables in e are local to R; $role(e, R)$ and $party(e, R)$ allow interpreting expressions as roles and parties of the given role respectively; $task(e, R)$ holds if there is a task `task` R e S.

Projection is defined in Fig. 8. Assignments, `await` (elided), and `cancel` vanish if the variables, expressions, and/or tasks they mention are not local to the *current role* (the role being projected onto). Transmissions are projected depending on *how* the parties involved are related to the current role. Projection is "pushed through" sequential composition, `par`, and `either`.

`all` is slightly more subtle. If the set being "quantified over" is a role different from the current one, we project under the "quantifier". We do the same if the set is not a role but some data located on R. Otherwise we drop the quantifier. Note that due to the side condition on transmission, there is no use for nesting more than one `all` over the same role. `with` is similar to `all`, except that the set being selected from is not allowed to be a role, as the selection of an arbitrary party cannot be coordinated globally in a simple manner. `if` projects to an `either` depending on whether its condition can be tested by the current role.

To project `while`, a termination condition must be given for the role it is to be projected on, and it is carried through without changes. The body of the loop must not involve roles for which there is no termination condition.

Projection of a statement $\hat{S}$ with respect to a set of roles R^* results in a set of statements $\{\bar{S}_1, ...\}$. A given projection function is *sound* if every behavior of the parallel composition of $\{\bar{S}_1, ...\}$ is a behavior of $\hat{S}$, and *complete* if the converse is true. A sound and complete projection function thus splits a choreography into a set of processes with equivalent behavior. This may be expressed in the following statement, if $(\hat{S}, \sigma) \rightsquigarrow \tau$ denotes that $\hat{S}$ may give rise to the behavior τ from a starting state σ, where τ is a sequence of states.

Theorem 1. *Given $\hat{S} \upharpoonright R_1 = \bar{S}_1, ..., (\hat{S}, \sigma) \rightsquigarrow \tau \iff (\textbf{par } \bar{S}_1 \textbf{ and } ..., \sigma) \rightsquigarrow \tau.$*

$$(v := e) \restriction R \triangleq \begin{cases} v := e \text{ if } loc(v, R), loc(e, R) \\ \texttt{skip} \quad \text{otherwise} \end{cases} \qquad (\texttt{cancel } e) \restriction R \triangleq \begin{cases} \texttt{cancel } e \text{ if } task(e, R) \\ \texttt{skip} \qquad \text{otherwise} \end{cases}$$

$$\underset{party(s,R_s),party(r,R_r),R_s \neq R_r}{\texttt{Transmit}(s, r, v = m)) \restriction R} \triangleq \begin{cases} \texttt{Send}(s, r, m) \qquad \text{if } party(r, R) \\ v := \texttt{Receive}(s, r) \text{ if } party(s, R) \\ \texttt{skip} \qquad\qquad \text{otherwise} \end{cases}$$

$$(\texttt{task } Q \ e \ \hat{S}) \restriction R \triangleq \begin{cases} \texttt{task } Q \ e \ (\hat{S} \restriction R) \text{ if } Q = R \\ \hat{S} \restriction R \qquad\qquad \text{otherwise} \end{cases}$$

$$(\texttt{all } v \in e \ \hat{S}) \restriction R \triangleq \begin{cases} \texttt{all } v \in e \ (\hat{S} \restriction R) \text{ if } role(e, Q), Q \neq R \\ \texttt{all } v \in e \ (\hat{S} \restriction R) \text{ if } loc(e, R) \\ \hat{S} \restriction R \qquad\qquad \text{otherwise} \end{cases}$$

$$(\texttt{if } e \ \hat{S}_1 \ \hat{S}_2) \restriction R \triangleq \begin{cases} \texttt{if } e \ (\hat{S}_1 \restriction R) \ (\hat{S}_2 \restriction R) \qquad \text{if } loc(e, R) \\ \texttt{either } (\hat{S}_1 \restriction R) \texttt{ or } (\hat{S}_2 \restriction R) \text{ otherwise} \end{cases}$$

$$(\texttt{while } e^* \ \hat{S}) \restriction R \triangleq \begin{cases} \texttt{while } e_1 \ (\hat{S} \restriction R) \text{ if } loc(e_1, R), e_1 \in e^* \\ \hat{S} \restriction R \qquad\qquad \text{if } roles(\hat{S}, R^*), R \notin R^* \end{cases}$$

Fig. 8. Projection

5 Translation

Having projected a **choreography** $\hat{S}$ into a set of processes $\bar{S}$, we now cover the translation to Core PlusCal S. The overall translation is denoted by the function $Tr : \bar{S} \to S$, which is the composition of several functions $Tr_{task} \circ Tr_{par} \circ Tr_{all}$, each handling a specific construct orthogonally. We explain each translation scheme by example and then justify its correctness.

First is Tr_{task}, which handles tasks and cancellation. It instruments models with a global variable **cancelled**, a record whose domain is the set of all task identifiers. For each statement **task** $R \ e \ \bar{S}$, **cancelled[e]** is initially **FALSE**. **cancel** e translates to **cancelled[e] := TRUE**, and **task** $R \ e \ \bar{S}$ by transforming

```
process (p_main \in {main}) {
  fork: await \A p \in {S1, S2} :
    pc[p] = "Done";
}
process (p_S1 \in {S1}) {
  await pc[main] = "fork";
  (* body of S1 *)
}
(* S2 is similar *)
```

```
process (p_main \in {main}) {
  fork:
    await \A p \in {main} \X {p1, p2} :
      pc[p] = "Done"
}
process (p_S \in {main} \X {p1, p2}) {
  await pc[Head(self)] = "fork";
  (* S[Head(self)/v] *)
}
```

Fig. 9. Translation of **par** Translation of **par**

Fig. 10. Translation of **all**

every statement $\bar{S}_1$ in $\bar{S}$ to if cancelled[e] $\bar{S}_1$ skip. Intuitively, this translation is correct because it makes cancellation idempotent and prevents further actions in a task from occurring by making them skips.

The actual statement of semantic preservation is as follows, given that the target language S is a strict subset of the source language $\bar{S}$ and the behaviors produced by both are identical (hence they are equally expressive):

Theorem 2. *Given* $Tr_{task}(\bar{S}) = S$, $(S, \sigma) \rightsquigarrow \tau \iff (Tr_{task}(\bar{S}), \sigma) \rightsquigarrow \tau$.

(par $\bar{S}_1$ and $\bar{S}_2$) is translated as in Fig. 9. main is the process this "fork" is nested in, where control is initially (above). $\bar{S}_1$ and $\bar{S}_2$ expand into separate processes (below) which may only begin execution once main reaches the labelled fork point. $\bar{S}_1$ and $\bar{S}_2$ execute in parallel, and main awaits their completion at the "join" point before proceeding.

Theorem 3. *Given* $Tr_{par}(\bar{S}) = S$, $(S, \sigma) \rightsquigarrow \tau \iff (Tr_{par}(\bar{S}), \sigma) \rightsquigarrow \tau$.

Next, we cover all, which extends the approach (and justification) for par. The statement all $v \in e$ $\bar{S}$ expands as shown in Fig. 10, assuming $e = \{p_1, p_2\}$.

As before, there is a main process with a distinguished fork point. It awaits the completion of all the subprocesses whose identifiers are in e. Now, however, as the value of e may not be statically known, we create a set of processes whose identifiers come from the cartesian product of e and *any roles in enclosing all statements*; in this case, the only such role is the singleton set {main}. Each process body contains $\bar{S}$ with the bound variable v substituted.

This translation scheme is compositional: we can apply it recursively to support arbitrary nesting of all statements. This is in contrast to threads in Distributed PlusCal [1], which only allow one level of nesting due to the way program counters are extended. This gives Choreographic PlusCal much of the flexibility of a process calculus, allowing very direct expression of some protocols.

Theorem 4. *Given* $Tr_{all}(\bar{S}) = S$, $(S, \sigma) \rightsquigarrow \tau \iff (Tr_{all}(S), \sigma) \rightsquigarrow \tau$.

6 Monitoring

After progressively translating from Choreographic PlusCal to regular PlusCal to TLA$^+$, the next step of the pipeline compiles a TLA$^+$ model into a monitor in an implementation's language. We choose Go here because of its popularity for distributed protocol work, but our overall approach is language-agnostic.

To use a TLA$^+$ model as a monitor for a system, one instruments the system to collect behaviors. Each behavior is checked to see if it satisfies the temporal formula Init $\wedge \square$ Next of the model. As a testing approach, monitoring is sound but incomplete: failing assertion point to refinement violations and indicate bugs, but nothing can be said about assertions which are never executed.

Specifications of distributed protocols are satisfied by behaviors involving several roles, so traces must be collected from all of them and merged to obtain a behavior to check. This may be inconvenient (requiring events to be ordered using vector clocks) or impractical (if the behaviors of some roles cannot be observed directly). We would thus like to perform monitoring *locally*, checking the behaviors of individual parties in isolation, and deriving global guarantees from the assumption that *all* parties satisfy their specifications.

6.1 Projection of TLA$^+$ Models

This motivates projecting *TLA$^+$ models* – using only variables and actions relevant to a given role to monitor a party of that role. This in turn requires that models have a little more structure, satisfying additional syntactic conditions:

All variables are local to a role or to the Network (a distinguished, singleton role). Variables representing role-local state have record values with the role as domain. All actions are local and have an *initiating* party, intuitively the one which acts, e.g. performing a send, or reacting to a message. Actions take this initiating party as an argument and may modify only its variables. If an action involves communication, it must take the other party as an argument as well; all communication is via message-passing and we assume there is at most one other party. Non-Network actions may only modify variables belonging to the role of the party; Network actions must modify the variables of one other party as well.

Choreographic PlusCal ensures all of these by construction, but handwritten TLA$^+$ models may also satisfy them and thereby be usable as monitors.

With this additional structure, projecting a TLA$^+$ model on a role R leaves only R's actions. Variables for R are straightforwardly projected on the initiating party. Network actions are projected to remove state nonlocal to R.

```
CONSTANT Nodes
VARIABLES inbox, outbox, inflight

Init ==
  /\ inbox = [n \in Nodes |-> {}]
  /\ outbox = [n \in Nodes |-> {}]        CONSTANT Nodes
  /\ inflight = {}                        VARIABLES inbox, outbox

Send(n) ==                                Init ==
  /\ outbox' = [outbox EXCEPT ![n] =        /\ inbox = {}
     outbox[n] \union {"msg"}]              /\ outbox = {}

NetworkDeliver(n, m) ==                   Send(n) ==
  /\ inbox' = [inbox EXCEPT ![n] =          /\ outbox' = outbox \union {"msg"}
     inbox[n] \union {m}]
  /\ inflight' = inflight \ {m}           NetworkDeliver(n, m) ==
                                            /\ inbox' = inbox \union {m}
Next ==
  \/ \E n \in Nodes :
    \/ Send(n)
    \/ \E m \in inflight :
      NetworkDeliver(s, m)
  \/ ...
```

Fig. 11. Projection example

An example is in Fig. 11. On the left is a model for a set of communicating Nodes. There are two local variables, inbox and outbox, which have record values indexed by node. The set of inflight messages is local to the Network. Nodes can send the string "msg" across the network by putting it in their outbox. The Network delivers messages by moving them from the set of inflight messages into some node's inbox. The projection of this model for monitoring the Node role is shown on the right. Local variables are no longer records, but single values for a given node. Non-local variables (inflight) and actions (Next) have vanished. Network actions have been projected by removing conjuncts involving inflight.

6.2 Trace Collection

To facilitate collection of traces, we utilize a deep embedding of TLA$^+$ formulae. This avoids semantic mismatches, e.g. TLA$^+$'s dynamic value types vs Go's static value/interface types. Instrumentation of the system to expose its states as a trace is user-provided, and consists of calls to a function with the following signature, to record the current State and the Action that led to it.

```
func (m *Monitor) Capture(s State, a Action, args ...TLA)
```

The use of a *refinement mapping* to construct a State value from the system state and the placement of Capture at appropriate *linearization points*, where snapshots of system state can be observed, are crucial. Because the construction of a State value is decoupled from its use, it is possible to make use of arbitrary auxiliary state to build it, or to build it piecemeal if the state of the system cannot be easily snapshot [8]. We assume that this instrumentation produces traces which faithfully represent system behaviors.

6.3 Trace Validation

Checking if a concrete behavior satisfies the model's specification can be done in multiple ways (e.g. model-based trace checking [8,34]), with different tradeoffs.

Here we experiment with the approach of compiling the model into a monitor (in Go) and executing it on observed behaviors. Each action is interpreted as an assertion on pairs of consecutive states with additional information to make the failure cause clear (the user sees more than just an opaque assertion violation). An artificial example (Fig. 12) illustrates the compilation scheme.

```
A1(z) ==                    func CheckA1(prev State, this State, z Int) bool {
  /\ x = 1                     if !reflect.DeepEqual(prev.x, Int(1)) {
  /\ y' = z + 2                  return false
                              }
                              if !reflect.DeepEqual(this.y, Plus(z, Int(2))) {
                                return false
                              }
                              return true
                            }
```

Fig. 12. TLA$^+$ monitor compilation example

Table 1. Relative specification sizes (LoC)

Protocol	Ch. PlusCal	TLA$^+$
Two-phase commit [23]	23	66
Non-blocking atomic commit [35]	36	96
Raft leader election [32]	46	186

We benchmark the approach in Sect. 7. Compared to model-based trace checking, monitoring requires more engineering (a TLA$^+$ embedding and translations of required operators) but is more scalable (allowing validation of large numbers of traces from randomized testing) and may be done either online or offline, even enabled in production and used to e.g. block transactions if a bug is detected.

7   Evaluation

We answer the following research questions, divided along two broad axes:

1. What classes of protocols does Choreographic PlusCal express well? How concisely can it render them compared to existing specification languages?
2. How applicable is the monitoring approach to existing codebases? How much overhead does it impose at runtime?

7.1   Expressiveness

Choreographic PlusCal lends itself well to the concise expression of protocols with multiple roles. Our case studies focus on distributed consensus protocols, but protocols from other domains which are typically specified as choreographies or in Alice-and-Bob notation (networking, security) would also benefit.

We compare the sizes of such protocol models against handwritten TLA$^+$ in Table 1. Writing TLA$^+$ directly offers a great deal of flexibility, but Choreographic PlusCal builds in a lot of structure for the domain and juxtaposes communication, usually halving the sizes of specifications. While LoC is by no means a perfect measure of succinctness and clarity, the point of this comparison is to show that choreographies are an appropriate and promising paradigm for distributed protocols, and make them much easier specify and evolve.

7.2   Monitoring

To evaluate the scalability of the monitoring approach, we instrumented two systems to check their conformance to their protocols. *committer* was the largest implementation under the `two-phase-commit` GitHub tag in Go, while *etcd* is a key infrastructure piece for platforms such as Kubernetes. Neither project was

Table 2. Monitor overhead

Project	Protocol	LoC	Overhead
vadiminshakov/committer	2PC	3032	19% (5 ms)
etcd-io/raft	Raft leader election	21,064	2% (4 ms)

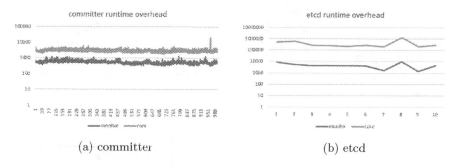

(a) committer   (b) etcd

Fig. 13. Runtime overhead measurements

designed for monitoring, and the models used to monitor them were taken from the public TLA$^+$ examples repository and were not written with them in mind.

For *committer*, we issued 1000 requests to write different keys (and trigger its commit protocol) in a blocking manner. For *etcd*, we waited for a cluster of newly created nodes to elect a leader and stabilize, repeating this 10 times. The overhead figures in Table 2 (distribution in Fig. 13, where the x-axis is the request number and the y-axis is time taken) represent the percentage (and absolute amount) of time spent in monitor code over the amount of time spent in their core consensus flows, per request. Experiments were carried out in clusters of size 3 (one coordinator and two replicas, and 3 servers), on a 2020 MacBook Pro with a 2.3 GHz CPU and 16 GB RAM, with Go 1.19.4. The runtime overhead was consistently low (up to two orders of magnitude for etcd), making monitoring readily usable for randomized testing and CI, possibly even in production as a sort of sanitizer. Monitoring also performs significantly better than model-based trace checking with a separate TLC process [8, 34]; I/O for such a task typically adds hundreds of ms, compared to 4–5 ms that in-process monitoring costs.

8   Related Work

8.1   Protocol Specifications

Protocols are classically specified as state machines [20] or automata [25], and early specification languages such as TLA$^+$ [21] and IOA [12] provided a concrete syntax for defining such models. While they are simple to manipulate symbolically, such specifications are unstructured (Sect. 1, Sect. 2) and are hard to extend and comprehend as they grow. Despite that, they are popular as a classical approach for embedding in general-purpose languages [4,10,11,17] and proof assistants [2,16,36,39], supporting extraction validation by model checking, testing, symbolic execution, or deductive verification.

Since protocols are essentially distributed algorithms which compute and branch, they are also naturally specified as imperative programs, in the spirit of "exhaustively testable pseudocode" [27]. DistAlgo [24] extends Python for this, adding queries over message history. Ivy [33] uses carefully constrained imperative programs to enable decidable reasoning. PlusCal [22], Distributed PlusCal [1] (which adds threads, channels, and communication primitives such as multicasts) and Modular PlusCal [7,42] (which separates system descriptions from their environment to support program extraction) are also in this category.

Choreographies make up a third family of specification styles, describing interactions globally and utilizing projection. Examples are Choral [13], a language for writing executable descriptions of protocols, and session-typed systems [9,14], many of which utilize monitoring [3,5,28–30].

Our work aims to combine the benefits of these three approaches. By integrating choreographies into PlusCal, a system for which transparency of the compilation to TLA$^+$ model is an explicit goal, we are able to support succinct and high-level specifications which also have a clear semantics, and for practical goals of model checking and conformance testing.

8.2 Testing Distributed Systems

We distinguish distributed systems testing approaches which require clean-room implementations [10,11,17,24,42] or extensive generated scaffolding [13,41] from those which aim to validate existing systems with minimal changes, like ours. Dealing with existing systems not originally designed with verification in mind is challenging, and falling back on testing is the usual compromise. Jepsen [18] is a well-known system for black-box testing of distributed databases. It exemplifies the offline monitoring approach: implementation traces are recorded, then analyzed later for indications of bugs using correctness conditions such as linearizability, serializability, and transaction isolation [19]. Model-based trace checking [15] is another similarly offline approach; specializations to TLA$^+$ [8,34] use TLC to determine conformance with a model. Online approaches include SPL [26], which uses imperative event-based specifications for monitoring, model-based test case generation [8,37], and stateless model checking [40].

9   Conclusion

We proposed Choreographic PlusCal, a suite of extensions to PlusCal to enable more abstract and succinct specifications of communication-centric algorithms. We hope that it may become for distributed protocols what PlusCal was to shared-memory concurrent algorithms. Separately, we extended the TLA$^+$ tools to enable monitoring implementations for protocol conformance, resulting in a practical and scalable approach for improving the robustness of existing systems.

Acknowledgments. We would like to thank Ilya Sergey for the insights that led to this work, George Pîrlea for contributing to an early implementation of it, and Markus Kuppe, Leslie Lamport, and the anonymous reviewers for their thoughtful suggestions and comments.

References

1. Alkayed, H., Cirstea, H., Merz, S.: An extension of PlusCal for modeling distributed algorithms. In: TLA+ Community Event 2020 (2020)
2. Athalye, A.: CoqIOA: a formalization of IO automata in the Coq proof assistant. Ph.D. thesis, Massachusetts Institute of Technology (2017)
3. Burlò, C.B., Francalanza, A., Scalas, A.: On the monitorability of session types, in theory and practice. In: 35th European Conference on Object-Oriented Programming (ECOOP 2021). Schloss Dagstuhl-Leibniz-Zentrum für Informatik (2021)
4. Biely, M., Delgado, P., Milosevic, Z., Schiper, A.: Distal: a framework for implementing fault-tolerant distributed algorithms. In: International Conference on Dependable Systems and Networks (DSN), pp. 1–8. IEEE (2013)
5. Bocchi, L., Chen, T.-C., Demangeon, R., Honda, K., Yoshida, N.: Monitoring networks through multiparty session types. In: Beyer, D., Boreale, M. (eds.) FMOODS/FORTE -2013. LNCS, vol. 7892, pp. 50–65. Springer, Heidelberg (2013). https://doi.org/10.1007/978-3-642-38592-6_5
6. Bornholt, J., et al.: Using lightweight formal methods to validate a key-value storage node in Amazon S3. In: Proceedings of the ACM SIGOPS 28th Symposium on Operating Systems Principles, pp. 836–850 (2021)
7. Costa, R.M.: Compiling distributed system specifications into implementations. Ph.D. thesis, University of British Columbia (2019)
8. Davis, A., Hirschhorn, M., Schvimer, J.: Extreme modelling in practice. arXiv preprint arXiv:2006.00915 (2020)
9. Deniélou, P.-M., Yoshida, N.: Dynamic multirole session types. In: ACM SIGPLAN-SIGACT Symposium on Principles of Programming Languages, pp. 435 446 (2011)
10. Desai, A., Gupta, V., Jackson, E., Qadeer, S., Rajamani, S., Zufferey, D.: P: safe asynchronous event-driven programming. ACM SIGPLAN Notices **48**(6), 321–332 (2013)
11. Desai, A., Phanishayee, A., Qadeer, S., Seshia, S.A.: Compositional programming and testing of dynamic distributed systems. (OOPSLA) **2**, 1–30 (2018)
12. Garland, S.J., Lynch, N.A., Vaziri, M.: IOA: A Language for Specifying, Programming, and Validating Distributed Systems. Unpublished Manuscript (1997)
13. Giallorenzo, S., Montesi, F., Peressotti, M.: Choreographies as objects. arXiv
14. Honda, K., Yoshida, N., Carbone, M.: Multiparty asynchronous session types. In: POPL, pp. 273–284 (2008)
15. Howard, Y., Gruner, S., Gravell, A., Ferreira, C., Augusto, J.C.: Model-based trace-checking. arXiv preprint arXiv:1111.2825 (2011)
16. Hsieh, C., Mitra, S.: DIONE: a protocol verification system built with DAFNY for I/O automata. In: Ahrendt, W., Tapia Tarifa, S.L. (eds.) IFM 2019. LNCS, vol. 11918, pp. 227–245. Springer, Cham (2019). https://doi.org/10.1007/978-3-030-34968-4_13
17. Killian, C.E., Anderson, J.W., Braud, R., Jhala, R., Vahdat, A.M.: Mace: language support for building distributed systems. ACM Sigplan Not. 179–188 (2007)

18. Kingsbury, K.: A framework for distributed systems verification, with fault injection (2022)
19. Kingsbury, K., Alvaro, P.: Elle: inferring isolation anomalies from experimental observations. arXiv preprint arXiv:2003.10554 (2020)
20. Lamport, L.: The temporal logic of actions. ACM Trans. Program. Lang. Syst. (TOPLAS) **16**(3), 872–923 (1994)
21. Lamport, L.: Specifying Systems, vol. 388. Addison-Wesley, Boston (2002)
22. Lamport, L.: The PlusCal algorithm language. In: Leucker, M., Morgan, C. (eds.) ICTAC 2009. LNCS, vol. 5684, pp. 36–60. Springer, Heidelberg (2009). https://doi.org/10.1007/978-3-642-03466-4_2
23. Lampson, B., Sturgis, H.E.: Crash recovery in a distributed data storage system (1979)
24. Liu, Y.A., Stoller, S.D., Lin, B., Gorbovitski, M.: From clarity to efficiency for distributed algorithms. Number OOPSLA, pp. 395–410 (2012)
25. Lynch, N.A., Tuttle, M.R.: Hierarchical correctness proofs for distributed algorithms. In: Proceedings of the Sixth Annual ACM Symposium on Principles of Distributed Computing, pp. 137–151 (1987)
26. Madhavapeddy, A.: Combining static model checking with dynamic enforcement using the Statecall policy language. In: Breitman, K., Cavalcanti, A. (eds.) ICFEM 2009. LNCS, vol. 5885, pp. 446–465. Springer, Heidelberg (2009). https://doi.org/10.1007/978-3-642-10373-5_23
27. Newcombe, C., Rath, T., Zhang, F., Munteanu, B., Brooker, M., Deardeuff, M.: How amazon web services uses formal methods. Commun. ACM 66–73 (2015)
28. Neykova, R., Bocchi, L., Yoshida, N.: Timed runtime monitoring for multiparty conversations. Formal Aspects Comput. **29**(5), 877–910 (2017). https://doi.org/10.1007/s00165-017-0420-8
29. Neykova, R., Yoshida, N.: Multiparty session actors. In: Kühn, E., Pugliese, R. (eds.) COORDINATION 2014. LNCS, vol. 8459, pp. 131–146. Springer, Heidelberg (2014). https://doi.org/10.1007/978-3-662-43376-8_9
30. Neykova, R., Yoshida, N.: Let it recover: multiparty protocol-induced recovery. In: Proceedings of the 26th International Conference on Compiler Construction, pp. 98–108 (2017)
31. Ongaro, D.: TLA+ specification for the raft consensus algorithm (2022)
32. Ongaro, D., Ousterhout, J.: In search of an understandable consensus algorithm. In: USENIX, pp. 305–319 (2014)
33. Padon, O., McMillan, K.L., Panda, A., Sagiv, M., Shoham, S.: Ivy: safety verification by interactive generalization. In: PLDI, pp. 614–630 (2016)
34. Pressler, R.: Verifying software traces against a formal specification with TLA+ and TLC (2018)
35. Raynal, M.: A case study of agreement problems in distributed systems: non-blocking atomic commitment. In: HASE, pp. 209–214 (1997)
36. Sergey, I., Wilcox, J.R., Tatlock, Z.: Programming and proving with distributed protocols. **2**(POPL), 1–30 (2017)
37. Tervoort, T., Prasetya, I.: Modeling and testing implementations of protocols with complex messages. arXiv preprint arXiv:1804.03927 (2018)
38. TLAplus. A collection of TLA+ specifications of varying complexities (2022)
39. Wilcox, J.R., et al.: Verdi: a framework for implementing and formally verifying distributed systems. In: PLDI, pp. 357–368 (2015)
40. Yang, J., et al.: MODIST: transparent model checking of unmodified distributed systems (2009)

41. Yoshida, N., Hu, R., Neykova, R., Ng, N.: The Scribble protocol language. In: International Symposium on Trustworthy Global Computing, pp. 22–41 (2013)
42. Zhang, B.: PGo: corresponding a high-level formal specification with its implementation. In: SOSP SRC, p. 3 (2016)

Verifying Chips Design at RTL Level

Wu Wang, Nan Zhang, Cong Tian, Zhenhua Duan$^{(\boxtimes)}$, Zhijie Xu, and Chaofeng Yu

Institute of Computing Theory and Technology, and ISN Laboratory,
Xidian University, Xi'an 710071, China
nanzhang@xidian.edu.cn, {ctian,zhhduan}@mail.xidian.edu.cn

Abstract. With the increasing complexity of chips design, the design errors or defects will inevitably increase. It is difficult to detect corresponding design logic problems with some conventional detection methods, such as testing and simulation. Further, the cost of such detection processes is also expensive. In contrast, formal verification methods based on mathematical logic reasoning about formal description capabilities can strictly prove whether a system meets the expected demand properties, so that it can effectively find out hidden defects or errors in chips design. Model checking is a widely used formal method for verifying chips design. However, model checking suffers from so called state space explosion problem. Although traditional model checking method alleviates the problem of state space explosion to a certain extent, there is still the problem of slow solution efficiency for large-scale chips design. Bounded model checking detects the limited path of a model to quickly determine the hidden problems of chips design, which can effectively alleviate the problem of system state space explosion. However, most of the logic languages such as LTL or CTL used in describing the desired properties cannot describe full regular properties of chips design. Further, the most of verification processes are based on symbolic model checking which is ineffective to detect design bugs in practice. Therefore, this paper focuses on the use of PPTL in bounded model checking to describe the properties to be verified and makes full use of SAT solvers to convert bounded model checking problems into SAT instances so that the scope and scale of verification of chips design can be reinforced and the efficiency of the verification processes can be also improved.

Keywords: bounded model checking · PPTL · SAT · chips design · reliability

1 Introduction

Chips are widely used in modern industry, from smart phones, tablets and computers, to precision machine tools, aircraft and high-speed rail; from medical equipment to aerospace equipment; from civilian fields to military fields. Chips are the heart of modern industry.

This research is supported by National Natural Science Foundation of China under Grant Nos. 62272359 and 62172322; Natural Science Basic Research Program of Shaanxi Province under Grant Nos. 2023JC-XJ-13 and 2022JM-367.

As chips become more integrated, the cost of manufacturing will also increase. Errors or hidden logic problems in chips design will cause serious consequences, and even re-spinning will bring unacceptable losses. Therefore, before a chip tape-out, it is important and necessary to find potential design defects and errors by means of simulation and verification.

At present, most of methods to improve chips reliability are by means of using EDA tools to test [1], simulate [2] and verify [3] chips design. It is difficult to detect the corresponding design logic problems by simulation and testing. In contrast, formal verification methods using mathematical logic reasoning about formal description capabilities can strictly prove whether a system meets the expected demand properties, and can effectively find out hidden defects or errors in chips design. Commonly used formal verification methods include theorem proving [4], equivalence verification [5] and model checking (MC) [6]. In this paper, we will study the reliability of chips design based on model checking.

Model checking was originally proposed by Clarke and Emerson, and Sifakis and Quelle in the early 1980s. It is an automatic verification method. However, it suffers from so called state space explosion problem. With the development of MC in recent decades, many model checking algorithms have been proposed successfully, including partial order model checking (PMC) [7], symbolic model checking (SMC) [8,11], abstract model checking (AMC) [9] and bounded model checking (BMC) [10].

All these methods have improved model checking algorithms which alleviate the state space explosion problems to a certain extent. In particular, there are some useful representative tools in practice: SPIN developed by Bell Laboratory, SMV developed by Carnegie Mellon University, CPAChecker developed by professor Dirk Beyer and others. However, there is still the problem of slow solution efficiency for large-scale chips design. Bounded model checking (BMC) is proposed by Biere et al. By detecting the limited path of a model, in order to quickly determine the relevant problems of model checking, it can effectively alleviate the problem of system state space explosion. The representative tool is NuSMV, jointly developed by Italian FBK-IRST and Carnegie Mellon University. Its typical application is the verification of chips design.

Bounded model checking considers a path with finite length, thereby it reduces the state space. Several tools such as CBMC, CPAChecker, ESBMC and others [12] use bounded model checking to verify the C language programs. However, bounded model checking suffers from incomplete problem because we know nothing when all finite paths have been checked, but no bugs could be found. In order to improve efficiency of verification, the BMC problem is often encoded into a SAT instance and making full use of SAT solvers to solve it [13]. Although SAT has been proved to be an NP Complete problem, SAT solvers have been greatly developed in recent years [14], and can be used to solve practical problems that arise in applications.

The existing bounded model checking algorithms based on SAT use LTL or CTL to describe desired properties. However, the expressiveness of LTL or CTL is not powerful enough. In fact, they are incapable of describing full regular properties and failed to verify these properties. Therefore, a more expressive temporal logic is needed to describe and verify full regular properties. The propositional projection temporal logic (PPTL) [16] is of full regular expressiveness and can be used to verify full regular properties of chips design. Therefore, this paper presents a bounded model checking approach based on SAT for PPTL to verify chips design at RTL(Register Transfer Level) level.

The main contributions of this paper are as follows:

(1) This paper proposes a SAT-based PPTL bounded model checking algorithm. With this method, a Verilog program is modeled as a Kripke structure and the desired property to be verified is described by a PPTL formula. Then, the negation of the property is transferred to an automaton. After that, the algorithm combines the two automata to produce a new automaton. With the help of Tseitin encoding and SAT solver, this algorithm completes the verification of the chips design.
(2) The proposed method has been realized. A tool called SAT-BMC4PPTL has been developed which can be used to verify full regular properties of Verilog programs by means of BMC with MiniSAT solver. Also, the tool is capable of improving the verification efficiency in a certain extent.

This paper is organized as follows: the next section introduces the basic knowledge related to our proposed algorithm including PPTL language, MiniSAT solver, Tseitin encoding, as well as basic BMC techniques. Section 3 focuses on the proposed bounded model checking approach for PPTL. First, modeling of a Verilog program into a Kripke structure is presented; then, transforming a desired property described by a PPTL formula into an Büchi automaton is illustrated; subsequently, combining the two automata to produce a final automaton is demonstrated. Section 4 presents the frame work of developed tool-kit SAT-BMC4PPTL. A short example is also given to show how to use the proposed approach in practice. Section 5 introduces the related work of the field. Finally, the conclusion is drawn in Sect. 6.

2   Preliminaries

This section mainly introduces several fundamental knowledge of SAT-based PPTL bounded model checking, including Kripke structure [15], the syntax and semantics of PPTL, Tseitin encoding technique and SAT solvers.

2.1   Kripke Structure

A Kripke structure is a quadruple $K = (S, I, R, L)$, here, $S = \{s_0, s_1, s_2, ...\}$ represents a finite state set; $I = \{s_0, ...\}$ represents an initial state set; $R \subset S \times S$ is a binary relation, representing a transition relation of a state; $L : S \rightarrow 2^{AP}$ represents a labeling function, and AP is the set of atomic propositions in the model. Labeling function L marks the set of propositions that need to be satisfied in the current state. A path of a Kripke structure is represented by a state sequence $< s_0, ..., s_j >$, where $s_0 \in I$ and $(s_i, s_{i+1}) \in R$. When there are loops in a path, it represents an infinite path.

2.2   PPTL

Our underlying logic is Propositional Projection Temporal Logic(PPTL) [16–20].

Syntax: PPTL comprises propositional logic and three modal constructs used to reason about systems over time intervals. Let *Prop* be a countable set of atomic propositions, and $\mathbb{N}_0$ the set of natural numbers. The formulas of PPTL are inductively defined as follows:

$$P ::= p \mid \bigcirc P \mid \neg P \mid P_1 \vee P_2 \mid (P_1, \ldots, P_m) \text{ prj } P$$

where $p \in Prop$ and $P, P_1, \ldots, P_i, \ldots, P_l, \ldots, P_m$ (for $1 \le i \le l \le m$) are well-formed PPTL formulas. PPTL formulas consist of two basic temporal operators: next ($\bigcirc$) and projection (prj). A formula is called a *state formula* if it contains no temporal operators, otherwise it is called a *temporal formula*.

Semantics: The meaning of $\neg$, $\vee$ and $\bigcirc$ is standard. However, the semantics of the projection constructs needs to be explained in detail.

The interpretation of $(P_1, \ldots, P_m)$ *prj* Q is that we need two sequences of clocks (states) running on different time scales: one is a local state sequence, over which $P_1; \ldots; P_m$ are interpreted, the other is a global state sequence over which Q is interpreted. Formula Q is interpreted in a parallel manner with the sequence of formulas $P_1; \ldots; P_m$. The interpretation proceeds as follows: First, Q and P_1 start at the first global state and P_1 is interpreted over a sequence of local states until its termination. Then (the remaining part of) Q and P_2 are executed at the second global state. Subsequently, P_2 is continuously interpreted over a sequence of local states until its termination, and so on. Although Q and P_1 start at the same time, $P_1; \ldots; P_m$ and Q may terminate at different time points. If Q terminates before some P_{h+1}, then, subsequently, $P_{h+1}; \ldots; P_m$ are interpreted sequentially. If $P_1; \ldots; P_m$ are finished before Q, then the execution of Q is continued until its termination. Note that the projection construct can be interpreted over an infinite interval. Projection can be thought of as a special parallel computation which is executed on different time scales.

The following are some derivation formulas.

Derived Formula:

NXN $\neg \bigcirc P \leftrightarrow \varepsilon \vee \bigcirc \neg P$

NXC $\bigcirc P; Q \leftrightarrow \bigcirc(P; Q)$

ECI $P \wedge \Diamond \neg P \rightarrow \Diamond(P \wedge \bigcirc \neg P)$

TRU $\Diamond \varepsilon \rightarrow (\bigcirc \varepsilon)^*$

AES $\square w \wedge \Diamond \varepsilon \leftrightarrow w \wedge (\bigcirc(w \wedge \varepsilon))^*$

CEL $(P_1; \bigcirc^n \varepsilon) \wedge (P_2; \bigcirc^n \varepsilon) \leftrightarrow (P_1 \wedge P_2); \bigcirc^n \varepsilon$

IDP $P^+; P^+ \rightarrow P^+$

ISP $P^+ \leftrightarrow P \vee (P \wedge 3; P^+)$

IST $P^+ \leftrightarrow P^*; P$

ADI $\square(P \rightarrow Q) \rightarrow (\square P \rightarrow \square Q)$

NDI $\bigcirc(P \rightarrow Q) \rightarrow (\bigcirc P \rightarrow \bigcirc Q)$

INA $\square(P \rightarrow \bigcirc P) \rightarrow (P \rightarrow \square P)$

PEB $P \text{ prj } \varepsilon \leftrightarrow P$

PEF $\varepsilon \text{ prj } P \leftrightarrow P$

PNX $(\bigcirc P, P_1, \ldots, P_m) \text{ prj } \bigcirc Q \leftrightarrow \bigcirc(P; (P_1, \ldots, P_m) \text{ prj } Q)$

PDF $(P_1,\ldots,(P_i \vee P_i'),\ldots,P_m) \; prj \; Q \leftrightarrow ((P_1,\ldots,P_i,\ldots,P_m) \; prj \; Q) \vee (P_1,\ldots,P_i', \ldots,P_m) \; prj \; Q$

PDB $(P_1,\ldots,P_m) \; prj \; (Q \vee Q') \leftrightarrow ((P_1,\ldots,P_m) \; prj \; Q) \vee ((P_1,\ldots,P_m) \; prj \; Q')$

PSM $(P_1,\ldots,w \wedge \varepsilon, P_i,\ldots,P_m) \; prj \; Q \leftrightarrow (P_1,\ldots,w \wedge P_i,\ldots,P_m) \; prj \; Q$

PSB $(P_1,\ldots,P_m) \; prj \; (w \wedge Q) \leftrightarrow w \wedge (P_1,\ldots,P_m) \; prj \; Q$

PSF $(w \wedge P_1,\ldots,P_m) \; prj \; Q \leftrightarrow w \wedge (P_1,\ldots,P_m) \; prj \; Q$

PEE $(P_1,\ldots,P_i \wedge \Diamond \varepsilon,\ldots,P_m) \; prj \; Q \leftrightarrow (P_1,\ldots,P_i,\varepsilon,\ldots,P_m) \; prj \; Q$

PEC $(P_1,P_2,\ldots,P_m) \; prj \; \varepsilon \leftrightarrow (P_1,(P_2,\ldots,P_m) \; prj \; \varepsilon) \; prj \; \varepsilon \leftrightarrow ((P_1,\ldots,P_{m-1}) \; prj \; \varepsilon, P_m) \; prj \; \varepsilon$

PIF $P \wedge \neg \Diamond \varepsilon \; prj \; Q \leftrightarrow P \wedge \neg \Diamond \varepsilon \; prj \; Q \wedge \varepsilon$

2.3 Tseitin Encoding

Tseitin encoding technique [21] is an algorithm that transforms propositional logic formulas into Conjunctive Normal Form (CNF) in linear time. CNF is a standard form of propositional logic formulas, which is connected by a series of disjunctive clauses with conjunction operation. Tseitin encoding technique provides a new Boolean variable expression for each disjunctive clause. Because any propositional logic formula can be represented by AND and NOT, a propositional logic formula can be transformed to another logic formula with only AND and NOT. Then, a new variable is introduced for each disjunctive clause and the relevant variables or combinations of variables in the original propositional logic formula are replaced, so as to obtain an equivalent formula of satisfiability. Finally, the Tseitin encoding transforms the converted disjunctive clause into CNF formula, and all CNF formulas are subjected to conjunction operation to obtain the final logic formula in CNF form.

AIGER [22] is one of tools based on Tseitin encoding technique. The propositional logic formula is easily transformed into CNF form by using AIGER. The basis of AIGER is the AIG. An and-inverter graph (AIG) is a directed, acyclic graph that represents a structural implementation of the logical functionality of a circuit or network. An AIG consists of two-input nodes representing logical conjunction, terminal nodes labeled with variable names, and edges optionally containing markers indicating logical negation. This representation of a logic function is rarely structurally efficient for large circuits, but is an efficient representation for manipulation of boolean functions. Typically, the abstract graph is represented as a data structure in software.

2.4 SAT Solvers

The SAT problem [23] is a classic decision problem and the first problem to be proved to be NP-complete. SAT-related search algorithms include two categories: complete algorithms [24] and incomplete algorithms [25].

The complete algorithm is based on the idea of traversing the entire state space and the backtracking search mechanism. The entire solution space is searched through a complete traversal. If the result is satisfiable, all solutions to the formula to be solved are given; if the formula is unsatisfiable, then an unsatisfiable counterexample is given. The representative algorithm is the DPLL [23] algorithm proposed by Davis and Putnam et al. The second-generation DPLL algorithms that introduce a heuristic search strategy on this basis, such as SAT0 [26], POSITE [24], GRASP [27], and zChaff [27] etc. After these improvements, the conflict clause learning technology CDCL (Conflict Driven Clause Learning) is introduced to form a more efficient SAT algorithm, such as Berk Min [28], CHAFF [29], BERKMINE [30], and Glucose [31,32].

The incomplete algorithm is also called the local search algorithm. Its basic idea is to reduce the number of unsatisfiable clauses based on a given random global assignment vector. In this way, the state space of the search is reduced and the efficiency of the solution is greatly improved. Classic local search algorithms include GSAT [33], WSAT [34], NSAT [35], TSAT [36], SDF [37], RANGERE [38] and GUNSAT [39]. The commonly used one is GSAT based on greedy search or WSAT based on noise model analysis.

The widely used SAT solvers are CryptoMiniSAT [40], Lingeling [41], MiniSAT [42], and ManySAT [43]. In this paper, we use MiniSAT to solve bounded model checking problem.

3 Verifying Chips Design Using SAT-based BMC for PPTL

The process of the SAT-based PPTL bounded model checking algorithm proposed in this paper is as shown in Fig. 1: (1) a Verilog program is modeled by a Kripke structure K, and a desired property is extracted from the requirement specification, and expressed in the form of the negation of the property to be verified by PPTL formula P; then formula P is transformed into an automaton model B. (2) the Kripke structure K and automaton B are composited to produce an automaton C. (3) the length of searching step size in BMC is set to an integer k, and the maximum step size set to $kk(k \leq kk)$. (4) Tseitin encoding is used to encode a path of the automaton C into a CNF formula. (5) an efficient SAT solver (MiniSAT) is invoked to solve the CNF formula. As a result, the satisfiability of the CNF formula is given. If the CNF formula is satisfiable, then a counterexample is found, otherwise a further search is required. With the current integer k, if all paths in model C are checked, k will plus one and the bounded model checking process starts the next loop. Notice that it is necessary to keep the integer k within the maximum step size kk. We are lucky when the BMC process is finished with a found counterexample otherwise we know nothing about checking results out of scope of the maximum step size kk. Therefore, the BMC algorithm is a typically semi-decidable one.

3.1 Modeling of Verilog Programs

A variant of AIG (And-Inverter Graph) is used in this paper, namely ASCII AIG, and its specific definition is given in [44]. An ASCII AIG is composed of input variables, latches, output variables, AND gates, and NOT gates. An example of ASCII AIG is shown in Fig. 2. Therefore, a circuit can be represented by an ASCII AIG.

In order to model a Verilog program, the program is first synthesised as a net-list (edif or blif) by an existing EDA tool, such as ABC [45] and Yosys [46]. The generated net-list is transformed to an ASCII AIG by using Yosys. The obtained ASCII AIG is then converted to a direct graph G through text processing, and finally converted to a Kripke structure by means of the A2K algorithm. The A2K algorithm is shown in Algorithm 1.

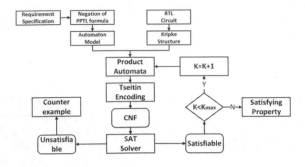

Fig. 1. The process of the SAT-based PPTL bounded model checking.

```
aag 6 1 3 3 2
2
4 12
6 4
8 6
4
6
8
10 7 5
12 10 9
```

Fig. 2. ASCII AIG file example.

For example, a Verilog program representing a counter is given in Fig. 5, the generated net-list is shown in Fig. 6, the transformed ASCII AIG is indicated in Fig. 7, and the converted directed graph G is demonstrated in Fig. 8. Finally, produced Kripke structure by the $A2K$ algorithm is generated in Fig. 9.

In the following, we describe the $A2K$ algorithm in detail. Here, input G is extracted from ASCII AIG using the $Extract$ algorithm. In fact, $Extract$ is merely an interpretive process to convert a text ASCII AIG to a direct graph. With $A2K$ algorithm, let each latch node be a starting point, $A2K$ uses the $GENERATE$ function to traverse all edges associated with it by reverse breadth first search, and a binary tree $expr$ representing and-invert logic expression is obtained. The leaf nodes of $expr$ are its corresponding variables denoted by $param$ array of (key,value) pairs. The non-leaf nodes of $expr$ are AND gates or NOT gates. $expr$ and $param$ are stored in the $MapR$ array of (key,value) pairs. All V_k and E_k are initialized to empty. All h latches are sorted and encoded so as to obtain the initial state I_k, which is a h-bits code. Thus, I_k is added to V_k. In the algorithm, $currentState$ and $nextState$ are employed to represent the current state's code and the next state's code respectively. For each latch, to obtain the value of $param$ (key,value) pair, a function Val is called. The $Post\text{-}Order\text{-}Traversal$ function is used to traverse the $expr$ so that each variable is assigned a corresponding value. Therefore, the value of the current latch is obtained and stored in $nextState$. After all the latches are processed, the next state's code $nextState$ and the state transition relationship ($currentState$, $nextState$) are obtained and stored in V_k and E_k respectively. Repeat the above process until all states and state transitions are found.

Algorithm 1. A2K(G, K) //it transforms a directed graph G into a Kripke structure K

Input: directed graph G=($V_i,V_o,V_l,V_a,V_n,E_{il},E_{ol},E_{nl},E_{al},E_{lo},E_{ln},E_{in},E_{ia},E_{on},E_{oa},E_{na},E_{an},E_{aa}$)

Output: Kripke structure K=(V_k,E_k,I_k)

1: $V_i=(v_{i1}, v_{i2},...,v_{if})$//$V_i$ is a set of input nodes of G
2: $V_o=(v_{o1}, v_{o2},...,v_{og})$//$V_o$ is a set of output nodes of G
3: $V_l=(v_{l1}, v_{l2},...,v_{lh})$//$V_l$ is a set of latch nodes of G
4: $V_a=(v_{a1},v_{a2},...,v_{al})$//$V_a$ is a set of AND gate nodes of G
5: $V_n=(v_{n1},v_{n2},...,v_{nm})$//$V_n$ is a set of NOT gate nodes of G
6: $E_{il}=\{eil_1,...,eil_n\} \subset V_i \times V_l$//$E_{il}$ is a set of edges from input to latch nodes
7: $E_{ol}=\{eol_1,...,eol_p\} \subset V_o \times V_l$//$E_{ol}$ is a set of edges from output to latch nodes
8: $E_{nl}=\{enl_1,...,en_q\} \subset V_n \times V_l$//$E_{nl}$ is a set of edges from NOT gate to latch
9: $E_{al}=\{eal_1,...,eal_u\} \subset V_a \times V_l$//$E_{al}$ is a set of edges from AND gate to latch
10: $E_{lo}=\{elo_1,...,elo_v\} \subset V_l \times V_o$//$E_{lo}$ is a set of edges from latch to output
11: $E_{in}=\{ein_1,...,ein_w\} \subset V_i \times V_n$//$E_{in}$ is a set of edges from input to NOT gate
12: $E_{ia}=\{eia_1,...,eia_s\} \subset V_i \times V_a$//$E_{ia}$ is a set of edges from input to AND gate
13: $E_{on}=\{eon_1,...,eon_t\} \subset V_o \times V_n$//$E_{on}$ is a set of edges from output to NOT gate
14: $E_{oa}=\{eoa_1,...,eoa_r\} \subset V_o \times V_a$//$E_{oa}$ is a set of edges from output to AND gate
15: $E_{na}=\{ena_1,...,ena_x\} \subset V_n \times V_a$//$E_{na}$ is a set of edges from NOT to AND gate
16: $E_{an}=\{ean_1,...,ean_y\} \subset V_a \times V_n$//$E_{an}$ is a set of edges from AND to NOT gate
17: $E_{aa}=\{eaa_1,...,eaa_z\} \subset V_a \times V_a$//$E_{aa}$ is a set of edges from AND to AND gate
18: $E_{ln}=\{eln_1,...,eln_o\} \subset V_l \times V_n$//$E_{ln}$ is a set of edges from latch to NOT gate
19: Begin
20: $V_k = \emptyset, E_k = \emptyset$ //V_k is a set of nodes. E_k is a set of edges
21: $I_k = \emptyset$ //I_k is a set of initial nodes
22: $currentState = nextState =$ "". //$currentState$ and $nextState$ are strings
23: $MapR$ is an array of (key,value) pairs, initialized with h empty elements.
24: $E = E_{il} \cup E_{ol} \cup E_{nl} \cup E_{al} \cup E_{lo} \cup E_{in} \cup E_{ia} \cup E_{on} \cup E_{oa} \cup E_{na} \cup E_{an} \cup E_{aa} \cup E_{ln}$
25: **for** ($i = 1; i \leq h; i++$) **do**
26:    let $expr$ be an empty binary tree representing an and-invert logic expression
27:    let $param$ be an array of (key,value) pairs , key is a logic variable appearing in the $expr$ and value is the variable's value.
28:    GENERATE($v_{li},E,expr,param$)//it constructs v_{li}'s $expr$ and $param$
29:    $MapR[i] =< expr, param >$
30: **end for**
31: I_k = initial(V_l) /* initial() is a function used to sort all latches, and encode them in order. So the initial state set I_k is obtained, each of which is a h-bits code, such as "001" */
32: $V_k = V_k \cup I_k$
33: **for** ($t = 1; t \leq len(I_k); t++$) **do**
34:    $currentState = i_{kt} \in I_k$
35:    **while** v_{clk} **do**
36:       //v_{clk} is the clock-related input, if v_{clk} reset, break
37:       $nextState =$ ""//$nextState$ is an empty string
38:       **for** ($i = 1; i \leq h; i++$) **do**
39:          $expr = \Pi_1(MapR[i]), param = \Pi_2(MapR[i])$
40:          **for** ($j = 1; j \leq len(param); j++$) **do**
41:             $Val(V_i,V_o,currentState,\Pi_1(param[j]),\Pi_2(param[j]))$
42:          **end for**

43:        Op is used to record an operation
44:        Stk is a stack used to record intermediate values (0 or 1)
45:        Post-Order-Traversal($expr,param,Op,Stk$)
46:        $nextState$.append(Stk.top())
47:     **end for**
48:     /*The loop termination condition*/
49:     **if** $nextState \in V_k$ and $(currentState, nextState) \in E_k$ and $nextState \notin I_k$ **then**
50:        break;
51:     **end if**
52:     let $e' = (currentState, nextState)$ // an edge from $currentState$ to $nextState$
53:        $E_k = E_k \cup e'$, $V_k = V_k \cup nextState$, $currentState = nextState$
54:   **end while**
55: **end for**
56: **return** K
57: End

Algorithm 2. GENERATE(v_{li},E,$expr$,$param$)//it constructs v_{li}'s $expr$ and $param$

Input: $v_{li} \in V_l$, E
Output: $expr$, $param$
 1: here v_{li} is a latch and E is all edges.
 2: $expr$ is an empty binary tree representing an and-invert logic expression.
 3: $param$ is an array of (key,value) pairs , key is a logic variable appearing in the $expr$
    and value is the variable's value
 4: Begin
 5: **for** $(j = 1; j \leq len(E); j++)$ **do**
 6:    **if** $e_j = (v_x, v_{li})$ **then**
 7:        //v_x is one of v_a and v_n and v_i and v_o
 8:        $expr$.value $= v_x$, break
 9:    **end if**
10: **end for**
11: Build-Tree(E,$expr$,$param$)
12: **return** $expr$,$param$
13: End

Algorithm 3. Build-Tree($E, T, param$)//it constructs a binary tree

Input: E
Output: T, $param$
 1: Begin
 2: tmp is an array of nodes
 3: **for** $(j = 1; j \leq len(E); j++)$ **do**
 4:    **if** $e_j = (v_x, T.value)$ **then**
 5:        tmp.addElement(v_x)//v_x is one of v_a and v_n and v_i and v_o
 6:    **end if**
 7: **end for**
 8: **if** len(tmp) = 0 **then**

```
 9:    param.addElement((T.value,0))
10:    return
11:  else if len(tmp) = 1 then
12:       T → left.value = tmp[1], Build-Tree(E,T → left,param)
13:  else
14:       T → left.value = tmp[1], Build-Tree(E,T → left,param)
15:       T → right.value = tmp[2], Build-Tree(E,T → right,param)
16:  end if
17:  End
```

Algorithm 4. Val(V_i, V_o, *currentState*, *key*, *value*)//it generates a *value*

Input: V_i, V_o, *currentState*, *key*
Output: *value*
```
 1: here V_i is a set of input nodes of G, V_o is a set of output nodes of G, and currentState
    is a string.
 2: key is a logic variable. value is 0 or 1.
 3: Begin
 4: if key ∈ V_i then
 5:    value = 0
 6:    return value
 7: end if
 8: for (k = 1; k ≤ len(currentState); k++) do
 9:    if key = v_{ok} ∈ V_o then
10:       value = currentState[k], break
11:    end if
12: end for
13: return value
14: End
```

Algorithm 5. Post-Order-Traversal(T, *param*, Op, *Stk*)//it calculates a value

Input: T, *param*
Output: Op, *Stk*
```
 1: Begin
 2: if T is empty then
 3:    return
 4: end if
 5: if T → left then
 6:    Post-Order-Traversal(T → left,param,Op,Stk)
 7: end if
 8: if T → right then
 9:    Post-Order-Traversal(T → right,param,Op,Stk)
10: end if
11: if T → left and T → right are empty then
12:    tmp is the value of T.value in param, Stk.push(tmp)
```

13: **else**
14:     $Op = T$.value
15: **end if**
16: **if** Op is And **then**
17:     $st_1 = Stk.\text{pop}()$, $st_2 = Stk.\text{pop}()$, $Stk.\text{push}(st_1 \ \& \ st_2)$
18: **else**
19:     $st = Stk.\text{pop}()$, $Stk.\text{push}(\neg st)$
20: **end if**
21: End

3.2 Describing Properties of Chips Design Using PPTL

To extract a desired property of chips design is a key process. This process is usually dominated by experienced engineers. However, in this paper we focus on how to describe the full regular properties of chips designs by using PPTL formulas and convert the properties into Büchi automata so that the properties can be verified by means of BMC with SAT. In order to transform a PPTL formula P into a Büchi automaton, we first convert P into its normal form $P \equiv P_\varepsilon \wedge \varepsilon \vee \bigvee_i P_{ci} \wedge \bigcirc P_i$ [16], then build a LNFG (labelled normal form graph) G [47] for P, and finally transform G into a Büchi automaton B. The details of above transforming processes can be found in [47].

3.3 Compound Kripke Structure and Büchi automaton

In order to verify whether the chips design satisfies the desired properties, composing Kripke structure and Büchi automaton is necessary. First, according to the described properties, we label each state of the Kripke structure K to obtain $K' = (V_k, E_k, I_k, L_k)$. L_k is a labeling function used to label the atomic propositions that each state satisfies. Then, composing K' and Büchi automaton B by Cartesian synchronous product can obtain a product automaton C. Consequently, we can get all paths of length k from C.

3.4 Tseitin Encoding and SAT Solving

For each path, we use the Tseitin encoding tool to encode it and obtain its CNF formula, and call the MiniSAT solver to determine the satisfiability of CNF. If the CNF formula is satisfiable, then we can find a counterexample, otherwise a further search is necessary. With the current integer k, if all paths of length k in C are checked, k will plus one and the model checking process starts the next loop.

4 Implementation of $A2K$ Algorithm

In this section, we briefly show the implementation of $A2K$ algorithm. In particular, the framework of a tool-kit called SAT-BMC4PPTL is presented.

4.1 The Framework of SAT-BMC4PPTL

SAT-BMC4PPTL is implemented by C++ code and about 10k line codes are developed. It contains 5 modules and about 30 functions. The user interface is implemented based on Qt5 [48]. With the characteristics of low coupling, easy maintenance and reusability, the MVC model meets the requirements of SAT-BMC4PPTL. So the MVC model, as well as the signal and slot mechanism of the Qt5 application development framework are used to build a layered architecture model, as shown in Fig. 3.

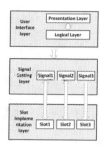 

Fig. 3. MVC model of SAT-BMC4PPTL.   **Fig. 4.** SAT-BMC4PPTL main interface.

As shown in Fig. 4, according to the hierarchical model of the architecture and the functional requirements, the structure of the SAT-BMC4PPTL tool is divided to several parts. It mainly includes menu bar, tool bar, resource management module, editing module, output module, compilation and execution module, etc.

4.2 A Verification Example

To illustrate how $A2K$ algorithm and SAT-BMC4PPTL work, an example of counter in Verilog is given. The code of the counter is shown in Fig. 5. First, the blif net-list is obtained by using Yosys as shown in Fig. 6. Then, the blif net-list is transformed to the ASCII AIG by also using Yosys, as shown in Fig. 7. The converted directed graph G is demonstrated in Fig. 8. It is generated by *Extract* algorithm. Figure 9 is the Kripke structure of the counter constructed by $A2K$ Algorithm 1.

According to the counter circuit, we define the following atomic proposition set $\{p,q,r,e\}$, where p denotes $count[0] = 1$, q $count[1] = 1$, r $count[2] = 1$, and e $count[3] = 1$. We can describe the periodic repetition property: p is true on state S_n, r is true on state S_{2n+1}, $1 \leq n \in N$ as a PPTL formula P: $(\bigcirc(p \wedge \varepsilon))^+ \wedge (\bigcirc^2(r \wedge \varepsilon))^+$. By using the method proposed in [47], $\neg P$ can be transformed into an automaton as shown in Fig. 10.

```
module counter(clk,count);
        input clk;
        output [3:0] count;
        reg [3:0] count;
        wire cin = ~count[0] & ~count[1] & ~count[2] & ~count[3];
        initial count=4'b0;
        always@(posedge clk) begin
        count[0]<=cin;
        count[1]<=count[0];
        count[2]<=count[1];
        count[3]<=count[2];
        end
endmodule
```

Fig. 5. The Verilog code of counter.

```
.model counter
.inputs i2
.outputs o0 o1 o2 o3
.latch a16 i4 0
.latch i4 i6 0
.latch i6 i8 0
.latch i8 i10 0
.names i6 i4 a12
00 1
.names a12 i8 a14
10 1
.names a14 i10 a16
10 1
.names i4 o0
1 1
.names i6 o1
1 1
.names i8 o2
1 1
.names i10 o3
1 1
.end
```

```
aag 8 1 4 4 3
2
4 16
6 4
8 6
10 8
4
6
8
10
12 7 5
14 12 9
16 14 11
```

Fig. 6. The blif net-list of counter.   **Fig. 7.** The ASCII AIG of counter.

$$V_i = \{x_1\}$$
$$V_o = \{x_2, x_3, x_4, x_5\}$$
$$V_l = \{L_0, L_1, L_2, L_3\}$$
$$V_g = \{x_6, x_7, x_8\}$$
$$V_n = \{!x_2, !x_1, !x_4, !x_5\}$$
$$E_{ol} = \{(x_2, L_1),(x_3, L_2),(x_4, L_3)\}$$
$$E_{lo} = \{(L_0, x_2),(L_1, x_3),(L_2, x_4),(L_2, x_5)\}$$
$$E_{ol} = \{(x_8, L_0)\}$$
$$E_{on} = \{(x_2, !x_2),(x_3, !x_3),(x_4, !x_4),(x_5, !x_5)\}$$
$$E_{na} = \{(!x_2, x_6),(!x_3, x_6),(!x_4, x_7),(!x_5, x_8)\}$$
$$E_{aa} = \{(x_6, x_7),(x_7, x_8)\}$$

Fig. 8. The directed graph G of counter.   **Fig. 9.** The Kripke structure of counter.

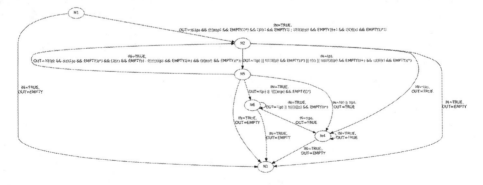

Fig. 10. The result of converting PPTL formula to automaton.

Now, we need to label each state in K with its corresponding atomic proposi-tions to obtain K'. $L_k = \{L(s_0), L(s_1), L(s_2), L(s_3), L(s_4)\}$ is obtained, in which $L(s_0) = \{\neg p \wedge \neg q \wedge \neg r \wedge \neg e\}$, $L(s_1) = \{p\}$, $L(s_2) = \{q\}$, $L(s_3) = \{r\}$, $L(s_4) = \{e\}$ and $s_0 =$ "0000", $s_1 =$ "0001", $s_2 =$ "0010", $s_3 =$ "0100", $s_4 =$ "1000". Let $k = 4$, and compos-ing K' and automaton B gets all paths of length 4, such as a path $(s_0, N_1) \rightarrow (s_1, N2) \rightarrow (s_2, N_5) \rightarrow (s_2, N_2) \rightarrow (s_2, N_3)$.

Fig. 11. The CNF formula.   **Fig. 12.** The result of MiniSAT.

We use the Tseitin encoding tool to encode above path to obtain its CNF formula, and call the MiniSAT solver to determine the satisfiability of CNF. The CNF formula and its solution result are shown in Fig. 11 and Fig. 12 respectively. So we know the CNF formula is unsatisfiable, and the chosen path is not a counterexample. After solv-ing all paths, if there is no counterexample path, increase k and enter the next cycle.

4.3 Testing and Analysis

Similar to the process of the verification example presented in Sect. 4.2, we also use BMC4PPTL tool-kit to verify more circuits and their properties shown in the Table 1.

5 Related Work

For model checking Verilog programs at RTL level, [49] presents a novel technique that combines IC3 with syntax-guided abstraction (SA) to allow scalable word-level model checking using SMT solvers [50] without any needs for additional solver queries or unrolling. It shows how to efficiently integrate IC3 with SA, and demonstrates its effectiveness on a suite of open-source and industrial Verilog RTL designs. However, SA only works for bitvector and the subset of data operations are short of hybrid data abstraction.

For Verilog designs, literature [51] studies the impact of various available abstrac-tion and refinement options on Reveal toolkit performance. It employs Counter Exam-ple Guided Abstraction Refinement (CEGAR) technique [52,53] to verify chips design. It is suitable for verifying complex control logic for designs with wide data paths. It performs automatically data path abstraction yielding an approximation of the original design with a much smaller state space. However, it may require some specific config-urations of the designs to ensure correctness and efficiency of verification.

For complex arithmetic circuits, literature [54] proposes the idea of hybrid verifi-cation to prove the correctness of advanced ALUs containing complex arithmetic units

Table 1. Other verification examples

Num	Circuit	Description	Property	Result
1	peterson	mutual exclusion algorithm	It is always impossible for process 1 and process 2 to be in the critical section at the same time	satisfiable
2	pci	bus control protocol	After a module obtains the right to use the bus, all modules continue to apply for and obtain the right to use the bus. This process is repeated periodically	unsatisfiable
3	deque	priority queue	The data stored first must be taken out first in the future queue	unsatisfiable
4	abp	interleaved bit protocol	If the sender's message bit is 1 and returns the correct acknowledgment, the receiver actually received a 1	unsatisfiable
5	dec4-16	4-16 decoder	For different inputs, there will be the same output	unsatisfiable
6	alu4	4-bit logical operation unit	There exists a state in the future where the output value is equal to the sum of the two addends	unsatisfiable

such as multipliers. It can efficiently verify large-scale addition circuits, especially when a large number of addition circuits need to be verified. However, it only works on finite fields, so it requires special handling when dealing with non-finite fields.

For abstracting away wide data paths of circuit systems while keeping the low-level details of their control logic, [55] describes a tool that automatically abstracts behavioral RTL Verilog to the CLU language used by the UCLID system. The tool performs a sound abstraction with emphasis on minimizing false errors, but it needs to abstract the model into a finite state machine first.

Compared with the above approaches, the verifying chips design at RTL level proposed in this paper is of two advantages: (1) our approach uses PPTL as a specification language, the fully regular properties can be verified; (2) we combine BMC with SAT solver to verify chips design. With this method, a Verilog program is first synthesized to a netlist file, and then modeled as a Kripke structure; a desired property is described by a PPTL formula. To verify whether or not the Kripke structure satisfies the property is to automatically execute the toolkit SAT-BMC4PPTL. This approach facilitates us to effectively and conveniently to verify chips design.

6   Conclusion

This paper proposes a SAT-based bounded model checking algorithm for PPTL. It models a Verilog circuit program as a Kripke structure K and the PPTL formula as an automaton B. Then, composing K and B get a product automaton C. Each path with length k from C is encoded and solved with the Tseitin encoding tool and SAT solver, the satisfiability of a desired property for a chip design circuit is verified. SAT-BMC4PPTL tool-kit allows us to verify chips design in an automatic way. However, the tool-kit is only a prototype, and needs to be improved in the future. Further, we will continue to study approaches for fighting state explosion problem of model checking so that the verification efficiency can be improved.

References

1. Weyuker, E.J., Ostrand, T.J.: Theories of program testing and the application of revealing subdomains. IEEE Trans. Software Eng. **3**, 236–246 (1980)
2. Frenkel, D., Smit, B.: Understanding Molecular Simulation: From Algorithms to Applications. Academic Press, New York (2001)
3. Wing, J.M.: A specifier's introduction to formal methods. Computer **23**(9), 8–22 (1990)
4. Hoare, C.A.R.: An axiomatic basis for computer programming. Commun. ACM **12**, 576–580 (1969)
5. Pnueli, A.: The temporal logic of programs. In: Symposium on Foundations of Computer Science, pp. 46–57. IEEE Xplore (1977)
6. Clarke, E.M., Emerson, E.A., Sifakis, J.: Model checking. Lect. Notes Comput. Sci. **164**(2), 305–349 (1999)
7. Holzmann, G.J.: The model checker SPIN. IEEE Trans. Software Eng. **23**(5), 279–295 (1997)
8. Burch, J.R., Clarke, E.M., Mc Millan, K.L., et al.: Symbolic model checking: 1020 states and beyond. Inf. Comput. **98**(2), 142–170 (1992)
9. Clarke, E.M., Grumberg, O., Long, D.E.: Model checking and abstraction. ACM Trans. Program. Lang. Syst. **16**(5), 1512–1542 (1994)
10. Cimatti, A., et al.: NuSMV 2: an OpenSource tool for symbolic model checking. In: Brinksma, E., Larsen, K.G. (eds.) CAV 2002. LNCS, vol. 2404, pp. 359–364. Springer, Heidelberg (2002). https://doi.org/10.1007/3-540-45657-0_29
11. Bryant, R.E.: Graph-Based Algorithms for Boolean Function Manipulation12 (1986)
12. Gadelha, M.Y.R., Ismail, H.I., Cordeiro, L.C.: Handling loops in bounded model checking of C programs via K-induction. Int. J. Softw. Tools Technol. Transfer **19**, 97–114 (2017)
13. Bicre, A., Cimatti, A., Clarke, E.M., Fujita, M., Zhu, Y.: Symbolic model checking using SAT procedures instead of BDDs. In: *Design Automation Conference, (DAC*1999), June 1999
14. Cai, S., Zhang, X.: Deep cooperation of CDCL and local search for SAT (Extended Abstract). In: IJCAI 2022, pp. 5274–5278 (2022)
15. Kripke, S.A.: Semantical analysis of modal logic I normal modal propositional calculi. Math. Log. Q. **9**(5–6), 67–96 (1963)
16. Duan, Z.: Temporal Logic and Temporal Logic Programming, Beijing (2005)
17. Duan, Z., Holcombe, M., Bell, A.: A logic for biosystems. Biosystems **55**(1–3), 93–105 (2000)
18. Duan, Z., Koutny, M., Holt, C.: Projection in temporal logic programming. In: Pfenning, F. (ed.) LPAR 1994. LNCS, vol. 822, pp. 333–344. Springer, Heidelberg (1994). https://doi.org/10.1007/3-540-58216-9_48
19. Duan, Z., Koutny, M.: A framed temporal logic programming language. J. Comput. Sci. Technol. **19**, 333–344 (2004)
20. Duan, Z., Yang, X., Koutny, M.: Semantics of framed temporal logic programs. In: Gabbrielli, M., Gupta, G. (eds.) ICLP 2005. LNCS, vol. 3668, pp. 356–370. Springer, Heidelberg (2005). https://doi.org/10.1007/11562931_27
21. Galesi, N., Itsykson, D., Riazanov, A., Sofronova, A.: Bounded-depth Frege complexity of Tseitin formulas for all graphs. In: MFCS 2019, pp. 49:1–49:15 (2019)

22. Chambers, B., et al.: Faster SAT solving with better CNF generation. In: 2009 Design, Automation and Test in Europe Conference and Exhibition, pp. 1590–1595 (2009)
23. Davis, M., Logemann, G., Lovelandn, D.: A machine program for theorem proving. Commun. ACM **5**(7), 394–397 (1962)
24. Freeman, J.W.: Improvements to Propositional Satisfiability Search Algorithms. University of Pennsylvania, Philadelphia, PA, USA (1995)
25. Een, N., Sorensson, N.: An extensible SAT solver. In: Theory and Applications of Satisfiability Testing. Santa Margherita Ligure, Italy, pp. 502–518 (2003)
26. Zhang, H.-T.: SATO: an efficient propositional prover. In: Proceedings of the 14th International Conference on Automated Deduction (CADE-1997), pp. 272–275, London, UK (1997)
27. Marques-Silva, J.P., Sakallah, K.A.: GRASP: a new search algorithm for satisfiability. In: Proceedings of the ACM/IEEE International Conference on Computer-Aided Design, pp. 220–227, Washington, DC, USA (1996)
28. Goldberg, E., Novikov, Y.: BerkMin: a fast and robust SAT-solver. Discret. Appl. Math. **155**(12), 1549–1561 (2007)
29. Moskewicz, M., Madigan, C., Zhao, Y., et al.: Chaff: engineering an efficient SAT solver. In: Proceedings of 38th Conference on Design Automation, pp. 530–535, Las Vegas, NV, USA (2001)
30. Goldberg, E., Novikov, Y.: BerMin: a fast and robust SAT-solver. In: Proceedings of Design Automation and Test in Europe (DATE), pp. 142–149, Paris, France (2002)
31. Audemard, G., Simon, L.: Refining restarts strategies for SAT and UNSAT formulae. In: Proceedings of the 18th International Conference on Principles and Practice of Constraint Programming (2012)
32. Cai, S., Zhang, X., Fleury, M., Biere, A.: Better decision heuristics in CDCL through local search and target phases. J. Artif. Intell. Res. **74**, 1515–1563 (2022)
33. Selman, B., Levesque, H., Mitchell, D.: A new method for solving hard satisfiability problems. In: Proceedings of the 10th AAAI 1992, pp. 440–446. AAAI Press, Menlo Park, CA (1992)
34. Selman, B., Kautz, H.A., Cohen, B.: Noise strategies for improving local search. In: Proceedings of the 12th AAAI-1994, pp. 337–343. AAAI Press, Menlo Park, CA (1994)
35. McAllester, D., Selman, B., Kautz, H.: Evidence for invariants in local search. In: Proceedings of the 14th AAAI 1997, pp. 321–326. AAAI Press, Menlo Park, CA (1997)
36. Mazure, B., Sais, L., Gregoire, E.: Tabu search for SAT. In: Proceedings of the 14th AAAI 1997, pp. 28–285. AAAI Press, Menlo Park, CA (1997)
37. Schuurmans, D., Southey, F.: Local search characteristics of incomplete SAT procedures. Artif. Intell. **132**(2), 121–150 (2001)
38. Prestwich, S., Lynce, I.: Local search for unsatisfiability. In: Proceedings of the 9th International Conference on Theory and Applications of Satisfiability Testing, Seattle, pp. 283–296, WA, USA (2006)
39. Audemard, G., Simon, L.: GUNSAT: a greedy local search algorithm for unsatisfiability. In: Proceedings of the 20th International Joint Conference of Artificial Intelligence, pp. 2256–2261, Hyderabad, India (2007)
40. Crypto MiniSat2 [CP/OL]. http://www.msoos.org/cryptominisat2/
41. Biere, A.: Lingeling, Plingeling and Treengeling entering the SAT competition 2013. In: Proceedings of SAT Competition (2013)
42. Een, N., Sorensson, N.: An extensible SAT solver. In: Theory and Applications of Satisfiability Testing, pp. 502–518, Santa Margherita Ligure, Italy (2003)
43. Guo, L., Hamadi, Y., Jabbour, S., Sais, L.: Diversification and intensification in parallel SAT solving. In: Proceedings of the 16th International Conference on Principles and Practices of Constraint Programming (2010)

44. Biere, A.: The AIGER And-Inverter Graph (AIG) Format Version 20070427 (2007)
45. Brayton, R., Mishchenko, A.: ABC: an academic industrial-strength verification tool. In: Touili, T., Cook, B., Jackson, P. (eds.) CAV 2010. LNCS, vol. 6174, pp. 24–40. Springer, Heidelberg (2010). https://doi.org/10.1007/978-3-642-14295-6_5
46. https://yosyshq.net/yosys/
47. Duan, Z., Tian, C., Zhang, N.: A canonical form based decision procedure and model checking approach for propositional projection temporal logic. Theoret. Comput. Sci. **609**, 544–560 (2016)
48. Pan, Y.: Development of image processing software based on QT creator. In: 2019 IEEE 3rd Information Technology, Networking, Electronic and Automation Control Conference (ITNEC), pp. 2667–2671. IEEE (2019)
49. Goel, A., Sakallah, K.: Model checking of verilog RTL using IC3 with syntax-guided abstraction. In: Badger, J.M., Rozier, K.Y. (eds.) NFM 2019. LNCS, vol. 11460, pp. 166–185. Springer, Cham (2019). https://doi.org/10.1007/978-3-030-20652-9_11
50. Irfan, A., Cimatti, A., Griggio, A., et al.: Verilog2SMV: a tool for word-level verification. In: 2016 Design, Automation & Test in Europe Conference & Exhibition (DATE), pp. 1156–1159. IEEE (2016)
51. Andraus, Z.S., Liffiton, M.H., Sakallah, K.A.: Reveal: a formal verification tool for verilog designs. In: Cervesato, I., Veith, H., Voronkov, A. (eds.) LPAR 2008. LNCS (LNAI), vol. 5330, pp. 343–352. Springer, Heidelberg (2008). https://doi.org/10.1007/978-3-540-89439-1_25
52. Ho, Y.S., Mishchenko, A., Brayton, R.: Property directed reachability with word-level abstraction. In: 2017 Formal Methods in Computer Aided Design (FMCAD), pp. 132–139. IEEE (2017)
53. Leucker, M., Markin, G., Neuhäußer, M.R.: A new refinement strategy for CEGAR-based industrial model checking. In: Piterman, N. (ed.) HVC 2015. LNCS, vol. 9434, pp. 155–170. Springer, Cham (2015). https://doi.org/10.1007/978-3-319-26287-1_10
54. Drechsler, R.: PolyAdd: polynomial formal verification of adder circuits. In: 2021 24th International Symposium on Design and Diagnostics of Electronic Circuits and Systems (DDECS), pp. 99–104. IEEE (2021)
55. Andraus, Z.S., Sakallah, K.A.: Automatic abstraction and verification of verilog models. In: Proceedings of the 41st annual Design Automation Conference, pp. 218–223 (2004)

Maximizing Reachability Probabilities in Rectangular Automata with Random Clocks

Joanna Delicaris[1(✉)] , Stefan Schupp[2(✉)] , Erika Ábrahám[3(✉)] ,
and Anne Remke[1(✉)]

[1] Westfälische Wilhelms-Universität, 48149 Münster, Germany
{joanna.delicaris,anne.remke}@uni-muenster.de
[2] TU Wien, Vienna, Austria
stefan.schupp@tuwien.ac.at
[3] RWTH Aachen, Aachen, Germany
abraham@informatik.rwth-aachen.de

Abstract. This paper proposes an algorithm to maximize reachability probabilities for rectangular automata with random clocks via a history-dependent prophetic scheduler. This model class incorporates time-induced nondeterminism on discrete behavior and nondeterminism in the dynamic behavior. After computing reachable state sets via a forward flowpipe construction, we use backward refinement to compute maximum reachability probabilities. The feasibility of the presented approach is illustrated on a scalable model.

1 Introduction

Hybrid automata [2] are a modeling formalism for systems whose evolution combines continuous dynamics interrupted by discrete steps. This work considers a subclass of rectangular automata [13], which we equip with stochasticity via random delays. The duration of a random delay in a hybrid automaton can be measured either (i) implicitly, via the semantics, or (ii) explicitly via a stopwatch and constraints on the syntax. While the first is user-friendly and intuitive, the latter makes restrictions on the modeling formalism explicit.

We follow the syntactical modeling variant and explicitly define the corresponding modeling restrictions. Similar to [7,20], we use stopwatches to model random delays on jumps. We propose an algorithm to optimize reachability probabilities in *rectangular automata with random clocks* (*RAR*).

Nondeterminism, which arises naturally, e.g., in concurrent systems, is often resolved probabilistically in stochastic models [1,4,17], and is usually not explicitly resolved in non-stochastic hybrid systems. Recently, *history-dependent* schedulers have been proposed to resolve *discrete* nondeterminism in hybrid Petri nets [19] and in singular automata with random clocks and urgent transitions either prophetically, or nonprophetically [20]. The prophetic scheduler knows the expiration times of random variables and is considered more powerful than the nonprophetic scheduler, who does not know these. Prophetic schedulers model the *worst/best case scenario* and induce maximal bounds on probabilities.

C. David and M. Sun (Eds.): TASE 2023, LNCS 13931, pp. 164–182, 2023.
https://doi.org/10.1007/978-3-031-35257-7_10

When adding random clocks to rectangular automata, the challenge lies in the correct handling of continuous nondeterminism to compute correct probabilities. We propose a measure-driven backward computation which partitions the infinite set of schedulers according to their ability to reach the goal set. Prophetic scheduling hence computes a symbolic refinement of schedulers when performing a backward analysis through the precomputed reachability tree. Maximizing reachability probabilities requires taking the union over the reachable states leading to the goal, whose transition delays have been refined by backward analysis. To compute the optimal reachability probabilities, that union is projected onto the integration domain of the corresponding probability densities, before performing a multidimensional integration over the joint probability density.

For a bounded number of jumps reachability is decidable for non-initialized rectangular automata [2,9]. Hence, flowpipe construction computes the exact reachable state-set for this model class, e.g. using a state representation of polytopes [9]. Backward refinement is then used to resolve the inherent continuous nondeterminism such that reachability probabilities are maximized. Consequently, the analysis approach presented here is exact up to numerical integration for the considered model formalism. To the best of our knowledge, the only approach able to compute reachability for this model class without resolving nondeterminism probabilistically computes a safe overapproximation via the tool ProHVer [12]. The feasibility of our approach is illustrated on a scalable model and validated by results computed in ProHVer.

Related Work. The application of model checking methods for probabilistic HA was enabled by CEGAR-style abstractions [26]. Extending decidable subclasses of HA by discrete probability distributions on jumps ([24,25]) preserves decidability of reachability. An extension of probabilistic timed automata is presented in [16], where continuously distributed resets are used and randomized schedulers resolve *discrete* nondeterminism for a discretized state-space. Further approaches for (networks of) stochastic timed automata ([3]) maintain the probabilistic approach of resolving nondeterminism. Approaches for more general classes either rely on stochastic approximation (also for nondeterminism) [21] or on a combination of discretization and randomness [15]. Several approaches that abstract to finite Markov decision processes have been proposed: In [23] abstractions for uncountable-state discrete-time stochastic processes are proposed for SHA, where all nondeterminism is resolved probabilistically. In [5] an abstraction to interval Markov decision processes is proposed. Both approaches feature a stochastic kernel, and can hence not be compared to our work.

The analysis proposed in [12] resolves *discrete* nondeterminism prophetically and *continuous* nondeterminism via a safe overapproximation (c.f. [26]). The same approach has been specified for stochastic timed automata in [11].

In [6], *discrete* nondeterminism is resolved (non-)prophetically for stochastic automata, where all continuous variables are random clocks. Similarly, scheduling of *discrete* nondeterminism is introduced for hybrid Petri nets in [19] and for singular automata with random clocks in [20], where a forward analysis without refinement is sufficient to compute maximal reachability probabilities.

Contribution. We propose both (i) the *modeling formalism* of rectangular automata with random clocks, which combines discrete and continuous non-determinism with stochastic delays; and (ii) an *analytical approach* which computes maximum reachability probabilities induced by a prophetic scheduler. We provide a feasibility study that shows that our computations are highly accurate.

Organization of the Paper. Section 2 introduces the considered model class. The computation of the maximum probabilities is explained in Sect. 3. The feasibility study is shown in Sect. 4 and the paper is concluded in Sect. 5.

2   Rectangular Automata with Random Clocks

Let $\mathbb{I}$ denote the set of all closed intervals $[a, b], [a, \infty), (-\infty, b], (-\infty, \infty) \subseteq \mathbb{R}$ with infinite or rational endpoints $a, b \in \mathbb{Q}$, with the standard set semantics.

For $distr : \mathbb{R}_{\geq 0} \rightarrow [0, 1] \subseteq \mathbb{R}$ let $supp(distr) = \{v \in \mathbb{R}_{\geq 0} \mid distr(v) > 0\}$. We call $distr$ a *continuous distribution* if it is absolute continuous with $\int_0^\infty distr(v) dv = 1$. We call $distr$ a *discrete distribution* if $supp(distr)$ is countable and $\sum_{v \in supp(distr)} f(v) = 1$. We use $\mathbb{F}_c$ and $\mathbb{F}_d$ to denote the set of all continuous resp. discrete distributions, and let $\mathbb{F} = \mathbb{F}_c \cup \mathbb{F}_d$ contain all *distributions*.

Hybrid automata [2] are a modeling formalism for systems whose evolution combines continuous dynamics (flow) interrupted by discrete steps (jumps). In this work we restrict ourselves to the subclass of *rectangular automata* [13].

Definition 1. *A* rectangular automaton (RA) *is a tuple* $R = (Loc, Var_C, Inv, Init, Flow_C, Edge_C)$ *with*

- *a finite set Loc of locations;*
- *a finite ordered set* $Var_C = \{x_1, \ldots, x_{d_C}\}$ *of variables; for* $\nu = (\nu_1, \ldots, \nu_{d_C}) \in \mathbb{R}^{d_C}$ *we define* $\nu_{x_i} = \nu_i$, *and for* $I = I_1 \times \ldots \times I_{d_C} \in \mathbb{I}^{d_C}$ *we set* $I_{x_i} = I_i$;
- *functions Inv, Init and* $Flow_C$, *all of type* $Loc \rightarrow \mathbb{I}^{d_C}$, *assigning an invariant, initial states resp. flow to each location; we call* $Flow_C(\ell)_x$ *the rate of* $x \in Var_C$ *in location* $\ell \in Loc$;
- *a finite set* $Edge_C \subseteq Loc \times \mathbb{I}^{d_C} \times \mathbb{I}^{d_C} \times 2^{Var_C} \times Loc$ *of non-stochastic jumps* $e = (\ell, pre, post, reset, \ell') \in Edge_C$ *with source (target) location* ℓ (ℓ'), *such that* $pre_x = post_x$ *for all* $x \in Var_C \setminus reset$ *and* $post \subseteq Inv(\ell')$;

R is non-blocking *if for each location* $\ell \in Loc$ *and each variable* $x \in Var_C$:

- *if* $Inv(\ell)_x$ *is lower-bounded by* $a \in \mathbb{Q}$ *(i.e. it has the form either* $[a, b]$ *or* $[a, \infty)$*) and* $Flow_C(\ell)_x \cap \mathbb{R}_{<0} \neq \emptyset$ *then there exists a non-stochastic jump* $e = (\ell, pre, post, reset, \ell') \in Edge_C$ *such that* $\{\nu \in Inv(\ell) \mid \nu_x = a\} \subseteq pre$,
- *if* $Inv(\ell)_x$ *is upper-bounded by* $b \in \mathbb{Q}$ *(i.e. it has the form either* $[a, b]$ *or* $(-\infty, b]$*) and* $Flow_C(\ell)_x \cap \mathbb{R}_{>0} \neq \emptyset$ *then there exists a non-stochastic jump* $e = (\ell, pre, post, reset, \ell') \in Edge_C$ *such that* $\{\nu \in Inv(\ell) \mid \nu_x = b\} \subseteq pre$.

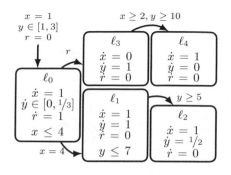

Fig. 1. RAR with $Var_R = \{r\}$.

We equip non-blocking RA with stochastic delays modeled by *random clocks*, which behave as stopwatches, i.e. having derivatives either 0 (*paused*) or 1 (*active*). Each random clock r is associated with a continuous distribution to sample random variables $S_{r,n}$, which determine at which value (*expiration time*) of the random clock certain jumps shall be taken. After expiration, the random clock is reset to 0 and a new random variable is used to determine the expiration time for the next event, yielding a sequence of random variables $S_{r,0}, S_{r,1}, S_{r,2}, \ldots$ for each random clock r. An illustrative example is depicted in Fig. 1.

Definition 2. *A rectangular automaton with random clocks (RAR) is a tuple* $\mathcal{A} = (Loc, Var_C, Var_R, Distr, Inv, Init, Flow_C, Flow_R, Edge_C, Edge_R)$ *with* ($Loc,$ $Var_C, Inv, Init, Flow_C, Edge_C$) *a non-blocking RA and:*

- *a finite ordered set* $Var_R = \{r_1, \ldots, r_{d_R}\}$ *of random clocks; we use analogously* $\mu_{r_i} = \mu_i$ *for* $\mu \in \mathbb{R}^{d_R}$ *and* $I_{r_i} = I_i$ *for* $I = I_1 \times \ldots \times I_{d_R} \in \mathbb{I}^{d_R}$;
- *a function* $Distr : Var_R \rightarrow \mathbb{F}_c$;
- *a function* $Flow_R : Loc \rightarrow \{0, 1\}^{|Var_R|}$;
- *a finite set* $Edge_R \subseteq Loc \times Var_R \times Loc$ *of stochastic jumps* $e = (\ell, r, \ell')$ *with* source (target) *location* ℓ (ℓ') *and random clock* r, *where (i) each two stochastic jumps* $e, e' \in Edge_R$, $e \neq e'$, *with the same source location* ℓ *have different random clocks, (ii) for all locations* $\ell \in Loc$ *and all random clocks* $r \in Var_R$, *if* $Flow_R(\ell)_r = 1$ *then* $(\ell, r, \ell') \in Edge_R$ *for some* $\ell' \in Loc$, *and (iii) for each stochastic jump* $(\ell, r, \ell') \in Edge_R$ *it holds that* $Inv(\ell) \subseteq Inv(\ell')$.

Let $\mathcal{A} = (Loc, Var_C, Var_R, distr, Inv, Init, Flow_C, Edge_C, Edge_R)$ with $Var_C = \{x_1, \ldots, x_{d_C}\}$ and $Var_R = \{r_1, \ldots, r_{d_R}\}$ be a RAR. A state $\sigma = (\ell, \nu, \mu, s) \in \mathcal{S} = Loc \times \mathbb{R}^{d_C} \times \mathbb{R}^{d_R} \times \mathbb{R}^{d_R}$ of $\mathcal{A}$ specifies the current location ℓ, the values ν of the continuous variables, and the values μ and expiration times s of the random clocks. The operational semantics [14] specifies the evolution of a state of $\mathcal{A}$, by letting time elapse or by taking a discrete jump (non-stochastic or stochastic):

$$\text{Flow} \frac{t \in \mathbb{R}_{\geq 0} \quad rate \in Flow_C(\ell) \quad \nu' = \nu + t \cdot rate \quad \nu' \in Inv(\ell) \\ \mu' = \mu + t \cdot Flow_R(\ell) \quad \forall r \in Var_R. \mu'_r \leq s_r}{(\ell, \nu, \mu, s) \xrightarrow{t, rate} (\ell, \nu', \mu', s)}$$

$$\text{Jump}_C \frac{e = (\ell, pre, post, reset, \ell') \in Edge_C \quad \nu \in pre \quad \nu' \in post \\ \forall x \in Var_C \setminus reset. \nu'_x = \nu_x \quad \nu' \in Inv(\ell')}{(\ell, \nu, \mu, s) \xrightarrow{e} (\ell', \nu', \mu, s)}$$

$$\text{Jump}_R \frac{\begin{array}{c} e = (\ell, r, \ell') \in Edge_R \quad \mu_r = s_r \quad \mu'_r = 0 \quad s'_r \in supp(Distr(r)) \\ \forall r' \in Var_R \setminus \{r\}.\mu'_{r'} = \mu_{r'} \wedge s'_{r'} = s_{r'} \end{array}}{(\ell, \nu, \mu, s) \xrightarrow{e} (\ell', \nu, \mu', s')}$$

For $\sigma \in \mathcal{S}$, let $EnabledJumps(\sigma) = \{e \in Edge_C \cup Edge_R \mid \exists \sigma' \in \mathcal{S}. \sigma \xrightarrow{e} \sigma'\}$ be the set of jumps $enabled$ in $\sigma \in \mathcal{S}$. We will also use $EnabledTime(\sigma) := \{(t, rate) \in \mathbb{R}_{\geq 0} \times \mathbb{R}^{d_C} \mid \exists \sigma' \in \mathcal{S}. \sigma \xrightarrow{t, rate} \sigma'\}$.

We set $\rightarrow = (\bigcup_{t \in \mathbb{R}_{\geq 0}, rate \in \mathbb{R}^{d_C}} \xrightarrow{t, rate}) \cup (\bigcup_{e \in Edge_C \cup Edge_R} \xrightarrow{e})$. A $path$ of $\mathcal{A}$ is a finite sequence $\pi = \sigma_0 \xrightarrow{a_0} \sigma_1 \xrightarrow{a_1} \ldots$ of states with $\sigma_0 = (\ell_0, \nu_0, \mu_0, s_0)$, $\nu_0 \in Inv(\ell_0)$, and $\sigma_i \xrightarrow{a_i} \sigma_{i+1}$ for all $i \in \mathbb{N}$; we call π $initial$ if $\nu_0 \in Init(\ell_0)$, $\mu_0 = 0 \in \mathbb{R}^{d_R}$ and $s_{0_r} \in supp(Distr(r))$ for all $r \in Var_R$. A state is $reachable$ if there is an initial path leading to it. Let $Paths$ denote the set of all paths.

For every reachable state, there is a path with alternating delays and jumps, as delays may have duration zero and consecutive delays can be combined. This holds even for consecutive delays with different rates, as flow sets are convex[1]:

Lemma 1. *Let* $\sigma_0 \xrightarrow{t_1, rate_1} \sigma_1 \xrightarrow{t_2, rate_2} \sigma_2$ *for* $\sigma_0, \sigma_1, \sigma_2 \in \mathcal{S}$ *with location* ℓ, $t_1, t_2 \in \mathbb{R}_{\geq 0}$ *and* $rate_1, rate_2 \in Flow_C(\ell)$. *Then there is* $rate \in Flow_C(\ell)$ *s.t.* $\sigma_0 \xrightarrow{t_1+t_2, rate} \sigma_2$.

The $duration$ of a path is defined as the sum of the durations of its steps, where jumps are considered instantaneous: $dur(\sigma) = 0$, $dur(\pi \xrightarrow{e} \sigma) = dur(\pi)$ and $dur(\pi \xrightarrow{t, rate} \sigma') = dur(\pi) + t$. Let the $jump$-$depth$ of a path be the number of jumps in it. We call a RAR $Zeno$-$free$ iff for all $t \in \mathbb{R}_{\geq 0}$ there exists a $k \in \mathbb{N}$ such that all initial paths of jump-depth at least k have duration at least t. We deviate from the standard definition, which requires that only finitely many jumps are possible in finite time. Our definition assures a *concrete bound on the number of jumps* per path for each time bound. In the following, we assume all considered models to be Zeno-free.

RAR allow for (i) *initial nondeterminism* in the choice of the initial state, (ii) *time nondeterminism* when time can elapse but also jumps are enabled during the whole flow, and (iii) *rate nondeterminism* when continuous variables can evolve with different rates. In addition to these continuous types of nondeterminism, we also consider (iv) *discrete nondeterminism* when different jumps are enabled simultaneously. We use prophetic schedulers to resolve nondeterminism, which have full information not only on the history but also on the future expiration times of all random clocks, as introduced in [20]. While prophetic scheduling may seem unrealistic, they are well-suited to perform a *worst-case* analysis, especially when uncontrollable uncertainties are modeled nondeterministically.

---

[1] For a proof of Lemma 1, we refer to [8].

Definition 3. *A* (prophetic history-dependent) scheduler *is a function* $\mathfrak{s} : Paths$
$\rightarrow \mathbb{F}$ *which assigns to every path* $\pi = \sigma_0 \xrightarrow{a_1} \ldots \xrightarrow{a_n} \sigma_n \in Paths$ *a distribution*
$distr = \mathfrak{s}(\pi)$, *such that if* $n \geq 1$ *and* $a_n \in Edge_C \cup Edge_R$ *is an edge then distr is*
continuous with $supp(distr) \subseteq EnabledTime(\sigma_n)$ *and otherwise distr is discrete*
with $supp(distr) \subseteq EnabledJumps(\sigma_n)$. *The set of schedulers is denoted* $\mathfrak{S}$.

We maximize the probability of *time-bounded* reachability, i.e., of reaching a
set of goal states $\mathcal{S}^{goal} \subseteq \mathcal{S}$ along initial paths π with $dur(\pi) \leq t_{max}$.

Resolving nondeterminism in a RAR $\mathcal{A}$ via the set of schedulers $\mathfrak{S}$ induces
an interval of *reachability probabilities* $[p_{min}^{\mathfrak{S}}(\mathcal{S}^{goal}, t_{max}), p_{max}^{\mathfrak{S}}(\mathcal{S}^{goal}, t_{max})]$, where
the bounds are referred to as minimum and maximum. We define $\mathfrak{S}_{goal} \subseteq \mathfrak{S}$ as
the set of schedulers that reach $\mathcal{S}^{goal}$ along initial paths π with $dur(\pi) \leq t_{max}$
and induce $p_{max}^{\mathfrak{S}}$. Let $\mathcal{V}^{\mathfrak{s}} \subseteq \mathbb{R}^{d_R}$ denote the sample values for all random variables
that allow scheduler $\mathfrak{s}$ to reach $\mathcal{S}^{goal}$. This yields the following definition:

Definition 4. *The prophetic maximum reachability probability is:*

$$p_{max}^{\mathfrak{S}}(\mathcal{S}^{goal}, t_{max}) = \int_{\bigcup_{\mathfrak{s} \in \mathfrak{S}_{goal}} \mathcal{V}^{\mathfrak{s}}} G(\mathbf{s}) \; d\mathbf{s}, \qquad (1)$$

where $G(\mathbf{s}) = \prod_{r_n} Distr(r)$ *is the joint probability density function for all ran-*
dom delays r_n *and random clocks* r.

Note that due to the independence of the random variables, $G(\mathbf{s})$ equals the
product over the probability density functions $Distr(r)$.

3   Computation of Maximum Reachability Probabilities

The inherent continuous nondeterminism in RAR leads to an uncountable number of choices and hence schedulers. We propose a measure-driven state space
construction, which partitions the infinite set of continuous schedulers w.r.t. their
ability to reach the set of goal states. We remark that our model class allows
resets on continuous variables, but our method does not yet support this.

Section 3.1 explains the forward flowpipe construction and Sect. 3.2 introduces the backward refinement. Sample domains are extracted in Sect. 3.3 and
maximum prophetic reachability probabilities are computed in Sect. 3.4.

3.1   Forward Flowpipe Construction

To compute reachability for rectangular automata, flowpipe construction has
been proposed in [2], which results in a geometric representation of all states
reachable up to a predefined time bound. To apply this method to RAR, we
disregard the stochasticity by removing all constraints on the sample values s
from the operational semantics. The resulting automaton is a regular rectangular
automaton, where the n-th random delay induced by random clock r in the original automaton is treated as a continuous variable r_n. Replacing every random

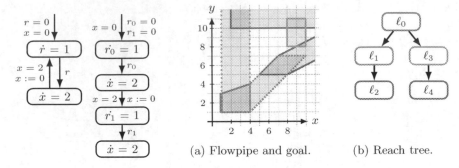

(a) Flowpipe and goal.   (b) Reach tree.

Fig. 2. Enrollment of RAR with $Var_R = \{r\}, t_{max} = 3$; rates are zero if not stated.

Fig. 3. Flowpipe (in 2D), goal set and an illustration of the reach tree for the RAR shown in Fig. 1.

clock r with one continuous variable for each possible delay corresponds to an enrollment of the automaton (c.f. Fig. 2). The set Var_R of the enrolled rectangular automaton then contains continuous variables $r_0, r_1, \ldots$ for each random clock r in the original automaton and d_R is the number of all random delays.

In the following, we omit the sampled values s from states $\sigma = (\ell, \nu, \mu, s)$. To simplify, we also combine the valuations of continuous variables ν and random clocks μ, such that we call $(\ell, \mathcal{V})$ *state set*, where $\mathcal{V}$ is a set of valuations and ν_x refers to the valuation of a variable $x \in Var_C \cup Var_R$. Even though formally we work on state sets $(\ell, \mathcal{V})$, for readability our notation restricts to valuation sets $\mathcal{V}$. We refer to valuation sets as *segments* and to the respective location of the state set as *corresponding* location.

We execute a forward flowpipe construction, i.e., starting with the initial states we alternate between computing the forward time closure and the jump successors until a predefined t_{max} is reached. The forward time closure $T_\ell^+(\mathcal{V})$ of $\mathcal{V}$ in ℓ (c.f. [2]), represents the set of states reachable from the set of entry states, i.e., computes states reachable via a time delay in location ℓ. Jumps are represented by the one-step relation $D_e^+(\mathcal{V})$, which defines the set of valuations reachable by choosing transition $e \in Edge_C \cup Edge_R$ from valuations $\mathcal{V}$ [2].

Our computation relies on a state representation via convex polytopes, usually in *H-representation*, defined as an intersection of multiple halfspaces. Some computations require the *V-representation*, defined as convex hull of a set of vertices (convex hull combined with convex cone for unbounded polytopes) [27].

The forward flowpipe construction then computes all reachable segments and stores them together with their corresponding location in the *reach tree* $\mathcal{R}$ according to their occurrence. We define a *reach tree*:

Definition 5. *For a rectangular automaton R and a time bound t_{max}, a reach tree is a tuple $\mathcal{R} = (N, E)$ with symbolic state sets $(\ell, \mathcal{V}) \in N$ as nodes and edges $e \in E = N \times (Edge_C \cup Edge_R) \times N$ annotated with jumps, where for each state*

$\sigma = (\ell, \nu) \in \mathcal{S}$ it holds that, if and only if σ is reachable in R before time t_{max}, there exists a node $n = (\ell, \mathcal{V}) \in N$, such that $\sigma \in \mathcal{V}$.

When performing qualitative analysis in the purely hybrid case, flowpipe construction ends as soon as the intersection of a computed segment with the set of goal states is non-empty. As we perform quantitative reachability analysis, we have to complete the flowpipe construction until the time bound t_{max} and collect all trajectories leading to goal states in order to fully resolve the nondeterminism present in the system. After computing the flowpipe up to t_{max}, the resulting segments are intersected with the goal set to determine reachability. We define goal states as $\mathcal{S}^{goal} = (L^{goal}, \mathcal{V}^{goal})$, where L^{goal} is a set of locations and $\mathcal{V}^{goal}$ is a set of valuations defined as a convex polytope, with constraints only for continuous variables $x \in Var_C$. Hence, $\mathcal{V}^{goal}$ is unbounded in the dimensions of random clocks $r \in Var_R$.

We define the set $\mathcal{S}^{goal}_{reach}$ of *reachable goal states*, such that it contains all subsets of the goal state set that can be reached via a trace in the reach tree:

$$(\ell, \mathcal{V}) \in \mathcal{S}^{goal}_{reach} \Leftrightarrow \ell \in L^{goal} \wedge \exists (\ell', \mathcal{V}') \in \mathcal{R}.\mathcal{V}' \cap \mathcal{V}^{goal} = \mathcal{V}(\neq \emptyset) \wedge \ell' = \ell. \quad (2)$$

We use $\mathcal{V}^i$ and $\mathcal{S}^i = (\ell, \mathcal{V}^i)$ to refer to these subsets of goal states and index i to refer to the trace of the reach tree leading to $\mathcal{S}^i$ (c.f. Fig. 4c). We define $I_\mathcal{S}$ as the set collecting all trace indices i. All segments $\mathcal{V}^i$, then serve as input for the backward refinement (c.f. Sect. 3.2).

Running Example. The forward time closure of the initial set in location ℓ_0 (c.f. Fig. 1) corresponds to the segment indicated by a gray solid line in Fig. 3a. Moving from location ℓ_0 to ℓ_3 corresponds to the expiration of the random clock r, which models the only random delay present in the automaton. In location ℓ_2, only y evolves (green dotted border). For states with $x \geq 2$ and $y \geq 10$, taking the transition to location ℓ_4 is possible (solid dark green border). Here, y is stopped and only x evolves. Alternatively, moving from ℓ_0 to ℓ_1 (blue dotted border) is possible for $x = 4$. All states with $y \geq 5$ can reach location ℓ_2, as long as $y \leq 7$ holds. This leads to overlapping segments for ℓ_1 and ℓ_2 (solid dark blue border). The goal states (yellow border) are defined by $\mathcal{S}^{goal} = \{(\ell, \nu) \in \mathcal{S} \mid \ell \in Loc \wedge \nu_x \in [8, 10] \wedge \nu_y \in [8, 11]\}$. Figure 3b illustrates the reach tree $\mathcal{R}$.

The goal can be reached both, via locations ℓ_1, ℓ_2 and via locations ℓ_3, ℓ_4. Hence, intersecting the forward flowpipe segments with the goal set results in two traces $i = 0, 1$, leading to state sets $\mathcal{S}^0 = (\ell_2, \mathcal{V}^0)$ and $\mathcal{S}^1 = (\ell_4, \mathcal{V}^1)$, where:

$$\mathcal{V}^0 = \{\nu \in \mathbb{R}^3 \mid \nu_x \leq 10 \wedge \nu_y \geq 8 \wedge \nu_y \leq 3.5 + 1/2 \cdot \nu_x \wedge \nu_r = 3\} \quad (3)$$

$$\mathcal{V}^1 = \{\nu \in \mathbb{R}^3 \mid \nu_x \in [8, 10] \wedge \nu_y \in [10, 11] \wedge \nu_r \in [0, 3]\}. \quad (4)$$

3.2 Backward Refinement

Starting from each $\mathcal{V}^i \subseteq \mathcal{V}^{goal}$, we perform a backward computation along the reach tree to refine state sets according to prophetic maximum schedulers until the root of the tree is reached. We refine backward by computing *refined segments*

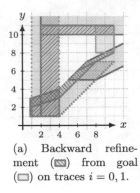
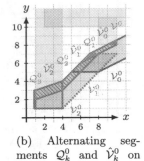
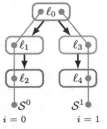

(a) Backward refinement (▧) from goal (▨) on traces $i = 0, 1$.

(b) Alternating segments $\mathcal{Q}_k^0$ and $\hat{\mathcal{V}}_k^0$ on trace $i = 0$.

(c) Reach tree with traces $i = 0, 1$ leading to $\mathcal{S}^i$ via refined segments $\hat{\mathcal{V}}_k^i$, $\mathcal{V}^i$.

Fig. 4. Backward refinement.

and *intermediate goal segments* for all forward flowpipe segments on trace i. The result of the backward refinement then is given by all refined segments and $\mathcal{V}^i$ in traces i along the reach tree, containing exactly the fragment of the reach tree that allows reaching the goal.

Backward propagation relies on the definitions of backward time closure $T_\ell^-(\mathcal{V})$ and backward one-step relation $D_e^-(\mathcal{V})$ (c.f. [2]). Similar to the forward time closure, $T_\ell^-(\mathcal{V})$ computes all states valid in location ℓ by regressing the time delay in that location, that are able to reach valuations in $\mathcal{V}$. $D_e^-(\mathcal{V})$ reverts the effects of transition e leading to $\mathcal{V}$, defined through guards and resets.

Starting from each segment $\mathcal{V}^i$, the backward time closure $T_\ell^-(\mathcal{V})$ is computed according to the activity of the corresponding location ℓ. This yields an unbounded cone, containing all states which can reach $\mathcal{V}^{goal}$ from an arbitrary state in location ℓ. We define the corresponding precomputed forward segment $\mathcal{V}_k^i$ as the flowpipe segment on trace i in the reach tree, which is encountered in step k going backward from $\mathcal{V}^i$ for $\mathcal{V}^i \subset \mathcal{V}_0^i$ (c.f. Fig. 4b). It is then intersected with the unbounded backward time closure to restrict the state set to states that are actually reachable in the hybrid automaton via a maximizing scheduler (c.f. Fig. 5a). This results in a so-called *refined segment* $\hat{\mathcal{V}}_k^i$, containing all states which can reach the goal set from location ℓ (in step k) on trace i:

Definition 6. *Given an intermediate goal segment $\mathcal{Q}_k^i$ within a segment $\mathcal{V}_k^i$ and its corresponding location ℓ, the* refined segment $\hat{\mathcal{V}}_k^i$ *on trace i is $\hat{\mathcal{V}}_k^i = T_\ell^-(\mathcal{Q}_k^i) \cap \mathcal{V}_k^i$. The first intermediate goal segment $\mathcal{Q}_0^i$ on trace i is $\mathcal{V}^i$ itself.*

Figure 5 illustrates refined segments computed from intermediate goal segments, corresponding to the running example. Given a transition e from ℓ_p to ℓ connecting segments $\mathcal{V}_{k+1}^i$ and $\mathcal{V}_k^i$, we compute the backward one-step relation of a refined segment $\hat{\mathcal{V}}_k^i$. By intersecting with the next forward segment $\mathcal{V}_{k+1}^i$ it is ensured, that the resulting segment $\mathcal{Q}_{k+1}^i$ is a subset of $\mathcal{V}_{k+1}^i$. This will be used as intermediate goal segment for the next computation step.

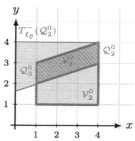

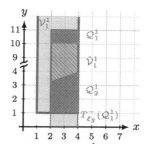

(a) Refined segment $\hat{\mathcal{V}}_2^0$ (▨) and intermediate goal segments $\mathcal{Q}_2^0, \mathcal{Q}_3^0$ (▦) on trace $i = 0$.

(b) Refined segment $\hat{\mathcal{V}}_1^1$ (▨) and intermediate goal segments $\mathcal{Q}_1^1, \mathcal{Q}_2^1$ (▦) on trace $i = 1$.

Fig. 5. Detailed backward refinement steps.

Definition 7. *For a refined segment $\hat{\mathcal{V}}_k^i$ and its corresponding location ℓ, the next intermediate goal segment $\mathcal{Q}_{k+1}^i$ on trace i is $\mathcal{Q}_{k+1}^i = D_e^-(\hat{\mathcal{V}}_k^i) \cap \mathcal{V}_{k+1}^i$. If $\hat{\mathcal{V}}_k^i$ corresponds to an initial location ℓ_0 (i.e., $Init(\ell_0) \neq \emptyset$), we use the initial set of ℓ_0 instead of $\mathcal{V}_{k+1}^i$ for the intersection, i.e., $\mathcal{Q}_{k+1}^i = D_e^-(\hat{\mathcal{V}}_k^i) \cap Init(\ell_0)$.*

Running Example. Backward refinement for the running example is illustrated in Fig. 4a and Fig. 4b. Figure 4c illustrates the two traces $i = 0, 1$. Starting from segments $\mathcal{V}^0$ and $\mathcal{V}^1$, the refined segments $\hat{\mathcal{V}}_k^0$ and $\hat{\mathcal{V}}_k^1$ can be computed iteratively. Figure 5 illustrates one refined segment on each trace. The refined segment $\hat{\mathcal{V}}_2^0$ and the next intermediate goal segment $\mathcal{Q}_3^0$ (c.f. Fig. 5a) can be computed from $\mathcal{Q}_2^0$. In addition to the constraints visible in Fig. 5a, $\hat{\mathcal{V}}_2^0$ then contains the constraint $\nu_r = \nu_x - 1$, stemming from the initial valuation of $\nu_x = 1$. Note that $\mathcal{Q}_3^0$ is computed via intersection with $Init(\ell_0)$.

The refined segment $\hat{\mathcal{V}}_1^1$ and the next intermediate goal segment $\mathcal{Q}_2^1$ (c.f. Fig. 5b) are computed from $\mathcal{Q}_1^1$. Again, $\hat{\mathcal{V}}_1^1$ and $\mathcal{Q}_2^1$ contain the constraint $\nu_r = \nu_x - 1$. Note that, since also $\nu_x \in [2, 4]$, ν_r is implicitly restricted to be contained by $[1, 3]$. These computation steps can also be found in [8].

3.3   Extracting the Sample Domain

Backward refinement results in refined segments $\hat{\mathcal{V}}_k^i$, from which the sample domain for all random variables is extracted as follows. Refined segments contain information on interdependencies between all variables and valuations leading to the goal in $\mathcal{V}^i$. The sample domain for each random variable $S_{r,n}$ is derived from the segment which corresponds to the n-th expiration of random clock r.

Polytopes $\mathcal{P}^i \subset \mathbb{R}^{d_R}$ collect the sample values which lead to the goal via trace i. Traversing the traces in a forward manner, for each segment we derive information on the sample domains from the constraints on the valuations of the random clocks which allow taking the next step on trace i (in the reach tree). Thus, we collect all valid values for each random delay on trace i.

For each segment, constraints on the samples are derived as follows. First, we project the segment onto the stochastic dimensions. Second, we collect information about all random delays, which are either already expired, about to expire in the next step on the trace, or not expired. (i) Random delays that are already expired cannot provide any new information, and hence do not have to be considered again. (ii) A step in the trace that corresponds to the expiration of a random delay, induces (upper) bounds on the sample domain. Each edge in the reach tree maps to exactly one jump in the automaton. In case of a stochastic jump, the step results in the upper bounds of exactly one random clock. (iii) To account for information on future expirations, the upper bounds of all other random delays have to be *lifted*.

Definition 8. *We define the* lifting *for a variable r in a polytope $P \subseteq \mathbb{R}^{d_R}$ as*
$$\Lambda_r(P) := \{(s_1, \ldots, s_r + c, \ldots, s_{d_R}) \in \mathbb{R}^{d_R} \mid (s_1, \ldots, s_r, \ldots, s_{d_R}) \in P \wedge c \in [0, \infty)\}.$$

This iterative collection of constraints on the sample domain leads to a polytope $\mathcal{P}^i$ that contains all sample values which allow to follow trace i. To compute maximum reachability probabilities, all possibilities of reaching the goal have to be included in the integration. This corresponds to taking the union over all $\mathcal{P}^i$ for $i \in I_S$.

Summarizing, this leads to a polytope $\mathcal{P}_{max} = \bigcup_{i \in I_S} \mathcal{P}^i$.

Running Example. The random delay r does not expire on trace 0, hence the lower constraints on the sample domain for s_r are iteratively collected, leading to the strongest lower constraint in $\mathcal{V}^0$. By projecting $\mathcal{V}^0$ onto $\mathbb{R}^{d_R}$ and lifting the resulting polytope in dimension r, the constraint $s_r \geq 3$ can be derived.

On trace 1, the expiration of the random clock corresponds to the transition from ℓ_0 to ℓ_3, i.e., r is about to expire in segment $\hat{\mathcal{V}}_2^1$. Hence, from $\hat{\mathcal{V}}_2^1$, the constraints $s_r \geq 1$ and $s_r \leq 3$ are derived, i.e. $\mathcal{P}^1 = [1, 3]$. This leads to $\mathcal{P}_{max} = [3, \infty) \cup [1, 3] = [1, \infty)$, which contains all values for random variable S_r for which the goal is reachable: for $s_r \geq 3$ via trace 0, and for $s_r \in [1, 3]$ via trace 1.

3.4   Maximum Prophetic Reachability Probabilities

To maximize continuous nondeterminism prophetically, we partition the potentially infinite set of prophetic schedulers $\mathfrak{S}_{goal}$ with respect to their ability to reach the goal. The backward refinement returns the fragment of the reach tree that leads to goal states $\mathcal{S}^{goal}$ (and specifically state sets $\mathcal{S}^i \in \mathcal{S}_{reach}^{goal}$), that allows extracting the sample domain. This process incorporates knowledge of future expiration times of random variables, leading to prophetic schedulers.

Reachability defines an equivalence relation on the set of schedulers $\mathfrak{S}_{goal}$ with respect to the state sets $\mathcal{S}^i$, reachable via trace i. This results in equivalence classes $[\mathfrak{s}]_i$, which contain all schedulers $\mathfrak{s}$ able to reach $\mathcal{S}^i$. Hence, $\bigcup_{i \in I_S} [\mathfrak{s}]_i = \mathfrak{S}_{goal}$. Via this equivalence relation, we are able to resolve different types of (continuous) nondeterminism. This is explained in the following for nondeterministic time delays on transitions, rectangular flow sets and conflicting transitions.

Initial and Time Nondeterminism. Taking a transition (from ℓ_p to ℓ) at different points in time leads to different states in the set, with which target location ℓ is entered. This set $\mathcal{Q}_{k+1}^i \subset \hat{\mathcal{V}}_k^i$ then contains all states corresponding to time delays which enable reaching $\mathcal{Q}_k^i$. Recall, that at the end of the trace, $\mathcal{Q}_0^i$ equals $\mathcal{V}^i$. This corresponds to a maximizing scheduler choosing (in a forward way) a time delay for that transition, such that from each state in $\mathcal{Q}_{k+1}^i$, entering location ℓ_p, it is possible to reach the intermediate goal segment $\mathcal{Q}_k^i$. Similarly, for a corresponding initial location, $\mathcal{Q}_{k+1}^i$ restricts the initial set. The scheduler then chooses an initial state, such that $\mathcal{Q}_k^i$ can be reached via $\hat{\mathcal{V}}_k^i$.

Figure 5b illustrates overlapping segments caused by a nondeterministic guard. The backward time closure from $\mathcal{Q}_1^1$ in segment $\mathcal{V}_1^1$ restricts the range of possible time delays: the (intermediate) goal segment can solely be reached from the pink fragment, i.e., from states with $\nu_y \leq 11$.

Rate Nondeterminism. The backward refinement results in restricted segments, which implicitly define a partitioning of the schedulers. For every state in $\mathcal{Q}_{k+1}^i$, a maximizing prophetic scheduler can pick at least one slope, which leads to the intermediate goal set $\mathcal{Q}_k^i$. In contrast, for all states outside of $\mathcal{Q}_{k+1}^i$, such a slope does not exist. Figure 5a illustrates that only initial states in $\hat{\mathcal{V}}_2^0$ (and hence in $\mathcal{Q}_3^0$) can reach the goal. The choice of the initial state restricts the possible rates. In this example, for initial state $\nu_x = 1, \nu_y = 2$, only the largest possible rate ($\dot{y} = 1/3$) leads to the intermediate goal segment $\mathcal{Q}_2^0$ and enables reaching $\mathcal{V}^0$.

Discrete Nondeterminism. Every discrete choice leads to a different trace in the forward flowpipe. The backward analysis starts from $\mathcal{S}_{reach}^{goal}$, i.e., only considers traces leading to goal states. Hence, the union of all $\mathcal{P}^i$ over all traces i, obtained from backward refinement, represents all discrete choices which reach the goal. Consequently, this maximizes discrete nondeterminism.

Summarizing, the valuations induced by all maximizing schedulers match the valuation sets computed by the backward refinement.

Lemma 2. *Given the set of valuations $\mathcal{V}^{\mathfrak{s}}$ over the space of the random variables that allow scheduler $\mathfrak{s}$ to reach the goal set $\mathcal{S}^{goal}$, and an equivalence relation over $\mathfrak{S}_{goal}$ defining equivalence classes $[\mathfrak{s}]_i$, $\bigcup_{\mathfrak{s} \in \mathfrak{S}_{goal}} \mathcal{V}^{\mathfrak{s}}$ can be computed as follows:*

$$\bigcup_{\mathfrak{s} \in \mathfrak{S}_{goal}} \mathcal{V}^{\mathfrak{s}} = \bigcup_{i \in I_S} \bigcup_{\mathfrak{s} \in [\mathfrak{s}]_i} \mathcal{V}^{\mathfrak{s}} = \bigcup_{i \in I_S} \mathcal{V}^{[\mathfrak{s}]_i} = \bigcup_{i \in I_S} \mathcal{P}^i = \mathcal{P}_{\max}, \tag{5}$$

where $\mathcal{V}^{[\mathfrak{s}]_i}$ is the union of valuations induced by schedulers $\mathfrak{s} \in [\mathfrak{s}]_i$.

For a proof of Lemma 2, we refer to [8]. We can now compute the maximum reachability probability by integration over $\mathcal{P}_{\max}$:

$$p_{\max}^{\mathfrak{S}}(\mathcal{S}^{goal}, t_{\max}) = \int_{\bigcup_{\mathfrak{s} \in \mathfrak{S}_{goal}} \mathcal{V}^{\mathfrak{s}}} G(\mathbf{s}) \, ds = \int_{\mathcal{P}_{\max}} G(\mathbf{s}) ds, \tag{6}$$

where $G(\mathbf{s}) = \prod_{r_n \in Var_R} Distr(r_n)$ is the joint probability density function.

The maximum reachability probability stems from all schedulers which can reach the goal. Hence, taking the union over all sample values $\mathcal{V}^{\mathfrak{s}}$ reached by $\mathfrak{s} \in \mathfrak{S}_{goal}$ results in the integration domain for maximum reachability probabilities. By construction, $\mathfrak{S}_{goal}$ contains all maximizing prophetic schedulers:

(i) All schedulers $\mathfrak{s}$ able to reach the goal $\mathcal{S}^{goal}$, reach a state set $\mathcal{S}^i$ and are hence represented by an equivalence class $[\mathfrak{s}]_i$, collectively reaching $\mathcal{S}^i$.

(ii) Schedulers $\mathfrak{s} \in \mathfrak{S} \setminus \mathfrak{S}_{goal}$ cannot reach the goal states $\mathcal{S}^{goal}$. In case a scheduler $\mathfrak{s} \in \mathfrak{S} \setminus \mathfrak{S}_{goal}$ could reach a goal state, the state(s) reachable by $\mathfrak{s}$ would belong to a flowpipe segment, and hence belong to a state set $\mathcal{S}^i$.

(iii) The combination of forward analysis and backward refinement results in prophetic schedulers $\mathfrak{S}_{goal}$. The former ensures that all sample values leading to goal states are known. The latter partitions the infinite set of schedulers w.r.t the reachability of different state sets $\mathcal{S}^i$ using this knowledge.

Integration Error. Multidimensional integration over unbounded polytopes is in practice not possible. Hence, we lift to a predefined *integration bound* $t_{int} \geq t_{max}$ and not to infinity, as stated in Sect. 3.3. This results in an overapproximation error:

$$e_\infty = 1 - \int_{[0,t_{int}]^{d_R}} G(\mathbf{s})d\mathbf{s}.$$

This error is exact if: (i) no random clock has ever expired upon reaching the goal set on all traces, or (ii) the support of all random clocks that have not expired upon reaching the goal is finite. Clearly, increasing t_{int} decreases e_∞. Integration is done statistically with Monte Carlo Vegas [18], which introduces an additional statistical error e_{stat}, depending on the number of integration samples.

Running Example. Maximizing schedulers form two equivalence classes, where $[\mathfrak{s}]_0$ contains all schedulers reaching $\mathcal{S}^0$ and $[\mathfrak{s}]_1$ contains all schedulers reaching $\mathcal{S}^1$. Schedulers in $[\mathfrak{s}]_0$ start with $\nu_y \geq 2$ in ℓ_0, then pick a rate of y that is at least $1 - \nu_y/3$ in ℓ_1. Finally, the time delay in ℓ_1 has to ensure $\nu_y \geq 3 + 1/2 \cdot \nu_x$. Schedulers in $[\mathfrak{s}]_1$ choose to leave ℓ_3 such that $\nu_y \leq 11$.

Assuming a folded normal distribution $\mathcal{N}(2, 1)$ for the stochastic delay, the maximum reachability probability to reach $\mathcal{S}^{goal}$ before $t_{max} = 10$ is computed by integration over $[1, \infty]$: $p_{max}^{\mathfrak{S}}(\mathcal{S}^{goal}, 10) = \int_{[1,\infty]} G(\mathbf{s})d\mathbf{s} = 1 - 0.2464 = 0.7536$.

Computational Complexity. The complexity of forward reachability analysis *fwra* is exponential in the state-space dimension and depends on the automaton, the set of initial states, and the number of jumps *jmp* depending on t_{max}. The complexity of computing one refined segment $\hat{\mathcal{V}}_k^i$ from its predecessor $\hat{\mathcal{V}}_{k-1}^i$ is denoted *bwra* with worst-case length $\mathcal{O}(jmp)$ of traces $i \in I_S$. We can then bound the complexity of the proposed analysis by $\mathcal{O}(fwra + |I_S| \cdot jmp \cdot bwra)$, where the number of sets used for numerical integration is in $\mathcal{O}(|I_S| \cdot jmp)$.

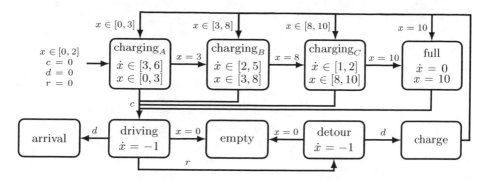

Fig. 6. Car model with detours. Random clock c is active ($\dot{c} = 1$) in the charging locations, d is active in locations *driving* and *detour* and r is active in location *driving*. The state of charge x is restricted to $[0, 10]$ in all locations unless stated otherwise. No time is spent in location *charge* due to invariants not shown.

4   Feasibility Study

Figure 6 illustrates our model of an electric car with different charging modes, which choose the charging rate nondeterministically from different intervals. Charging stops whenever the battery is full. The driving distances are sampled from random variables. See [8] for the automaton with all dynamics.

Locations *charging*$_A$, *charging*$_B$, *charging*$_C$ and *full* model decreasing charging rates, depending on the state of charge of the battery. The charging time is modeled by random clock c which follows a folded normal distribution, i.e. $\mathcal{N}(2, 2)$. In location *driving*, the battery decreases, where random clock d models the time spent driving. The expiration of d leads to location *arrival*, while draining the battery leads to location *empty*. The driving time follows a folded normal distribution ($\mathcal{N}(4, 1)$).

The model is scalable, as it includes the possibility of taking 0 or more detours. In location *driving*, the random delay until the next detour (r) competes with the end of the drive (d). Random clock r follows an exponential distribution with $\lambda = 2$. In the *detour* location, d is still active and the battery still decreases. The expiration of d corresponds to the end of the detour and the transition to location *charge* is taken, which marks the start of the next charging cycle. Depending on the current charge of the battery, the transition to the matching charging location is chosen immediately. By explicitly restricting the number of detours, we ensure that the model is Zeno-free. Performing a worst case analysis, we compute the maximum probability of reaching an *empty* battery.

Implementation and Reproducibility. We rely on a prototypical implementation of the tool REALYST[2] and use the library HYPRO [22] to compute flowpipe segments; particularly HYPRO is used to compute the forward flowpipe, the

---

[2] Tool and models: https://zivgitlab.uni-muenster.de/ag-sks/tools/realyst/.

Table 1. Max reachability probabilities for $\mathcal{S}^{goal} = \{(empty, \nu) \mid \nu_x = 0\}$, $t_{max} = (\#detours + 1) \cdot 21$ and $\#detours \in \{0, 1, 2\}$. Computation times t_{comp} provided for REALYST (R) with error e_{stat} and PROHVER (P). $K = (|Var_R|, |\mathcal{R}|, |I_S|)$.

			0 detours			1 detour			2 detours
		var.	A	AB	ABC	A	AB	ABC	A
		K	$(2,8,2)$	$(2,12,3)$	$(2,16,4)$	$(5,38,10)$	$(5,88,19)$	$(5,167,39)$	$(8,128,34)$
rectangular	R	p_{max}	0.050 354	0.064 824	0.066 698	0.407 864	0.426 210	0.429 555	0.402 105
		e_{stat}	$8.763 \cdot 10^{-5}$	$1.192 \cdot 10^{-4}$	$1.286 \cdot 10^{-4}$	$1.715 \cdot 10^{-3}$	$1.677 \cdot 10^{-3}$	$6.131 \cdot 10^{-4}$	$3.327 \cdot 10^{-3}$
		t_{comp}	4.49 s	10.75 s	15.31 s	484.50 s	1166.49 s	1800.63 s	35 570.30 s
	P	p_{max}	0.305 592	0.327 600	0.327 600	0.579 922	0.614 576	0.590 174	0.794 977
		t_{comp}	613.48 s	1202.66 s	1735.18 s	7890.29 s	15 247.25 s	28 533.80 s	1881.61 s
singular	R	p_{max}	0.026 673	0.026 534	0.026 600	0.406 624	0.424 759	0.429 528	0.408 268
		e_{stat}	$3.405 \cdot 10^{-5}$	$9.476 \cdot 10^{-5}$	$1.123 \cdot 10^{-4}$	$7.120 \cdot 10^{-4}$	$6.703 \cdot 10^{-4}$	$1.676 \cdot 10^{-3}$	$3.719 \cdot 10^{-3}$
		t_{comp}	2.47 s	11.66 s	19.38 s	245.21 s	518.30 s	1720.16 s	12 187.80 s
	P	p_{max}	0.305 592	0.327 600	0.327 600	0.442 959	0.467 916	0.523 958	0.758 034
		t_{comp}	348.09 s	500.19 s	546.56 s	6984.12 s	10 249.28 s	14 273.85 s	1461.85 s

reach tree, and the backward time closure and one-step relation as used in our backward refinement. Additionally, we use GNU SCIENTIFIC LIBRARY [10] to perform multi-dimensional integration. All experiments were run on a machine equipped with an Intel® Core™ i7 with 6×3.30 GHz and 32 GB RAM.

Results. We consider three different model variants, namely ABC, AB and A, that include exactly those charging locations indicated in the model name. If locations $charging_B$ and/or $charging_C$ are removed, the invariant in the last charging location is extended to $x \leq 10$ and the in- and outgoing transitions of that location are adapted accordingly. To further reduce model complexity, a singular version is created, where the rate of the continuous variables equals the lower bound of the corresponding rectangular interval. Continuous nondeterminism is maintained via the initial set, hence results cannot be compared with [20].

Table 1 contains maximum reachability probabilities and the corresponding computation time for the full model presented in Fig. 6 (indicated by ABC) and for reduced model versions (AB and A). We scale $t_{max} = (\#detours + 1) \cdot 21$, for $\#detours \in \{0, 1, 2\}$ and use $1 \cdot 10^5$, $2 \cdot 10^6$, $1 \cdot 10^7$ integration samples for $0, 1, 2$ detours. We validate results for different parameter settings computed by our prototype REALYST with results from PROHVER [12], which computes a safe overapproximation of the reachability probabilities via discretization.

Table 1 indicates for every considered number of detours the resulting size of the model as tuple $K = (|Var_R|, |\mathcal{R}|, |\mathcal{S}^{goal}_{reach}|)$, where $|Var_R|$ is the number of random variables, $|\mathcal{R}|$ the number of nodes in the reach tree and $|I_S| = |\mathcal{S}^{goal}_{reach}|$ the number of traces leading to the goal set. The dimension of the polytopes constructed by forward and backward analysis is $|Var_R| + 3$, and the dimension of integration equals $|Var_R|$.

REALYST computes maximum reachability probabilities for all model variants with 0 and 1 detour in at most 30 min. For 2 detours, the complexity of the model increases considerably. Computations in the singular model A take up to 3.5 h, and in the rectangular variant for 2 detours just below 10 h. The number of dimensions in variants AB and ABC with 2 detours becomes too large, such that flowpipe construction does not terminate or takes very long. REALYST is able to complete the singular variant of AB in slightly less than 83 h and results in probability 0.431 565 with $e_{stat} = 7.064 \cdot 10^{-3}$ statistical error.

The probability to reach an empty battery increases considerably with additional detours, as they introduce uncertainty to the state of charge of the battery. The scheduler can exploit this to maximize the probability of an empty battery.

Maximizing the reachability probability for an undesired goal yields a *worst case* probability. Reaching an empty battery is undesirable, hence, the computed probability to reach the goal provides an upper bound when everything goes wrong. The results indicate that modeling the charging process in more detail has a relatively low impact on the computed probability. This is expected, as the influence of charging on the state of charge of the battery (rates between 1 and 6) is in any case higher than the influence of driving on the state of charge of the battery (rate -1). Rectangular behavior gives a scheduler plenty opportunities to impact model evolution, which may increase the reachability probability.

As of 1 detour, the results for rectangular and singular models are close. This is due to the singular rates being equal to the lower bounds of the rectangular rate intervals. The scheduler aims to reduce the state of charge of the battery, hence, in most cases it will choose the lowest possible rate.

PROHVER computes safe overapproximations of maximum reachability probabilities. However, its precision highly depends on the chosen number of discretization intervals. A recent release of PROHVER automates the interval generation as well as a refinement thereof, w.r.t. to given parameters. For 0 detours, PROHVER computes a substantial overapproximation of the reachability probability obtained by REALYST. Computation times of PROHVER are between 28 and 140 times larger. For 1 detour, PROHVER takes up to 8 h and results in a better approximation of the reachability probabilities. For 2 detours, PROHVER is not able to perform a refinement on its discretization, yielding quick computation times with a substantial overapproximation. Running PROHVER with alternative parameters which enforce more discretization intervals does not terminate in less than 15 h. We refer to [8] for details on the parameter setting of PROHVER and for details on the computation times of REALYST.

REALYST indicates an error between 10^{-5} up to 10^{-3}, which due to Lemma 2, solely stems from integration. For the choice of $t_{int} = 100$ and the distributions $\mathcal{N}(4,1)$, $\mathcal{N}(2,2)$ and $Exp(2)$, the computed error $e_\infty = 0$, using IEEE 754 double precision. Hence, the probabilities computed by REALYST plus the indicated error e_{stat} agree with the overapproximations provided by PROHVER.

5   Conclusions and Future Work

We propose rectangular automata with random clocks as a new modeling formalism that combines discrete and continuous behavior with random delays. Nondeterminism is usually resolved probabilistically in stochastic hybrid systems. In contrast, this paper presents the first approach to compute maximum reachability probabilities for rectangular automata with random clocks, fully resolving all kinds of discrete and continuous nondeterminism prophetically. The computation requires a combination of forward flowpipe construction with a backward refinement to partition the potentially infinite set of schedulers. The resulting error solely stems from the multidimensional integration. The results of the feasibility study show that REALYST performs very well for up to five random variables. Reachability probabilities are highly accurate and obtained fast in comparison to PROHVER. Future work aims to improve scalability via other state set representations, and compute prophetic minimum reachability probabilities. We will provide an equivalent notion of RAR where restrictions on random delays are placed implicitly via the semantics to ease modeling; a transformation between both will maintain analyzability via REALYST.

References

1. Abate, A., Prandini, M., Lygeros, J., Sastry, S.: Probabilistic reachability and safety for controlled discrete time stochastic hybrid systems. Automatica **44**(11), 2724–2734 (2008). https://doi.org/10.1016/j.automatica.2008.03.027
2. Alur, R., et al.: The algorithmic analysis of hybrid systems. Theor. Comput. Sci. **138**(1), 3–34 (1995). https://doi.org/10.1016/0304-3975(94)00202-T
3. Ballarini, P., Bertrand, N., Horváth, A., Paolieri, M., Vicario, E.: Transient Analysis of Networks of Stochastic Timed Automata Using Stochastic State Classes. In: 10th Int. Conf. on Quantitative Evaluation of Systems. LNCS, vol. 8054, pp. 355–371. Springer (2013). https://doi.org/10.1007/978-3-642-40196-1_30
4. Betrand, N., et al.: Stochastic timed automata. Logical Methods Comput. Sci. **10**(4), 1–73 (2014). https://doi.org/10.2168/LMCS-10(4:6)2014
5. Cauchi, N., Abate, A.: StocHy: Automated verification and synthesis of stochastic processes. In: Proc. of TACAS'19, pp. 247–264. Springer, Cham (2019). https://doi.org/10.1145/3302504.3313349
6. D'Argenio, P.R., Gerhold, M., Hartmanns, A., Sedwards, S.: A Hierarchy of Scheduler Classes for Stochastic Automata. In: 21st Int. Conf. on Foundations of Software Science and Computation Structures. LNCS, vol. 10803, pp. 384–402. Springer (2018). https://doi.org/10.1007/978-3-319-89366-2_21
7. D'Argenio, P.R., Katoen, J.P.: A theory of stochastic systems part i: stochastic automata. Inform. Comput. **203**(1), 1–38 (2005). https://doi.org/10.1016/j.ic.2005.07.001
8. Delicaris, J., Schupp, S., Ábrahám, E., Remke, A.: Maximizing reachability probabilities in rectangular automata with random clocks (2023). https://doi.org/10.48550/arXiv.2304.14996
9. Frehse, G.: PHAVer: Algorithmic Verification of Hybrid Systems Past HyTech. In: 8th Int. Workshop on Hybrid Systems: Computation and Control. LNCS, vol. 3414, pp. 258–273. Springer (2005). https://doi.org/10.1007/s10009-007-0062-x

10. Galassi, M., Davies, J., Theiler, J., Gough, B.: GNU Scientific Library Reference Manual - Third Edition. Network Theory Ltd. (2009)
11. Hahn, E.M., Hartmanns, A., Hermanns, H.: Reachability and Reward Checking for Stochastic Timed Automata. Electron. Commun. EASST **70** (2014). https://doi.org/10.2168/LMCS-10(4:6)2014
12. Hahn, E.M., Hartmanns, A., Hermanns, H., Katoen, J.P.: A compositional modelling and analysis framework for stochastic hybrid systems. Formal Methods Syst. Design **43**(2), 191–232 (2013). https://doi.org/10.1007/s10703-012-0167-z
13. Henzinger, T.A.: The Theory of Hybrid Automata. In: Verification of Digital and Hybrid systems, NATO ASI Series, vol. 170, pp. 265–292. Springer (2000). https://doi.org/10.1007/978-3-642-59615-5_13
14. Henzinger, T.A., Kopke, P.W., Puri, A., Varaiya, P.: What's decidable about hybrid automata? J. Comput. Syst. Sci. **57**(1), 94–124 (1998). https://doi.org/10.1006/jcss.1998.1581
15. Koutsoukos, X.D., Riley, D.: Computational methods for verification of stochastic hybrid systems. IEEE Trans. Syst. Man, Cybern. - Part A: Syst. Humans **38**(2), 385–396 (2008). https://doi.org/10.1109/TSMCA.2007.914777
16. Kwiatkowska, M.Z., Norman, G., Segala, R., Sproston, J.: Verifying Quantitative Properties of Continuous Probabilistic Timed Automata. In: 11th Int. Conf. on Concurrency Theory. LNCS, vol. 1877, pp. 123–137. Springer (2000). https://doi.org/10.1007/3-540-44618-4_11
17. Lygeros, J., Prandini, M.: Stochastic hybrid systems: a powerful framework for complex, large scale applications. Europ. J. Contr. **16**(6), 583–594 (2010). https://doi.org/10.3166/ejc.16.583-594
18. Peter Lepage, G.: A new algorithm for adaptive multidimensional integration. J. Comput. Phys. **27**(2), 192–203 (1978). https://doi.org/10.1016/0021-9991(78)90004-9
19. Pilch, C., Hartmanns, A., Remke, A.: Classic and Non-Prophetic Model Checking for Hybrid Petri Nets with Stochastic Firings. In: 23rd ACM Int. Conf. on Hybrid Systems: Computation and Control, pp. 1–11. ACM (2020). https://doi.org/10.1145/3365365.3382198
20. Pilch, C., Schupp, S., Remke, A.: Optimizing reachability probabilities for a restricted class of stochastic hybrid automata via flowpipe-construction. In: 18th Int. Conference on Quantitative Evaluation of Systems, pp. 435–456 (2021). https://doi.org/10.1007/978-3-030-85172-9_23
21. Prandini, M., Hu, J.: A Stochastic Approximation Method for Reachability Computations. In: Stochastic Hybrid Systems: Theory and Safety Critical Applications, LNCS, vol. 337, pp. 107–139. Springer (2006). https://doi.org/10.1007/11587392_4
22. Schupp, S., Ábrahám, E., Ben Makhlouf, I., Kowalewski, S.: HyPro: A C++ Library of State Set Representations for Hybrid Systems Reachability Analysis. In: 9th Int. NASA Formal Methods Symposium. LNCS, vol. 10227, pp. 288–294. Springer (2017). https://doi.org/10.1007/978-3-319-57288-8_20
23. Soudjani, S.E.Z., Gevaerts, C., Abate, A.: FAUST2: Formal Abstractions of Uncountable-STate STochastic Processes. In: 21st Int. Conf. on Tools and Algorithms for the Construction and Analysis of Systems. LNCS, vol. 9035, pp. 272–286. Springer (2015). https://doi.org/10.1007/978-3-662-46681-0_23
24. Sproston, J.: Decidable Model Checking of Probabilistic Hybrid Automata. In: 6th Int. Symposium on Formal Techniques in Real-Time and Fault-Tolerant Systems. LNCS, vol. 1926, pp. 31–45. Springer (2000). https://doi.org/10.1007/3-540-45352-0_5

25. Sproston, J.: Verification and control for probabilistic hybrid automata with finite bisimulations. J. Log. Algebraic Methods Program. **103**, 46–61 (2019). https://doi.org/10.1016/j.jlamp.2018.11.001
26. Zhang, L., She, Z., Ratschan, S., Hermanns, H., Hahn, E.M.: Safety verification for probabilistic hybrid systems. Europ. J. Contr. **18**(6), 572–587 (2012). https://doi.org/10.3166/EJC.18.572-587
27. Ziegler, G.: Lectures on Polytopes, vol. 152. Springer Science & Business Media (1995). https://doi.org/10.1007/978-1-4613-8431-1

A Hierarchical Spatial Logic
for Knowledge Sharing and Fusion in
Intelligent Connected Vehicle
Cooperation

Shengyang Yao[1] and Qin Li[1,2(✉)] ⓘD

[1] Shanghai Key Laboratory of Trustworthy Computing,
East China Normal University, Shanghai, China
[2] Shanghai Institute of Intelligent Science and Technology, Tongji University,
Shanghai, China
qli@sei.ecnu.edu.cn

Abstract. Intelligent connected vehicles have attracted great concerns from researchers in intelligent transportation filed for recent years. The safety of a scenario involving multiple intelligent vehicles and infrastructures depends on delicate design of their collaboration. A unified and efficient representation for knowledge sharing and fusion is essential for such collaboration. However, the existing logical representation of spatial knowledge seldom considers integrating the knowledge from distributed agents with different granularities of views and data models. This paper designs a novel spatial logic based on a hierarchical spatial model, and provides a knowledge fusion method based on view and grained conversion between distributed agents. The spatial logic can be used to specify and share the key spatial knowledge in vehicle infrastructure cooperation scenarios. The converted knowledge shared by other agents is beneficial for an intelligent vehicle to improve its cognition and decision-making process. The effectiveness of our approach is illustrated with the case studies in path planning and cooperative cross-traffic turning.

Keywords: Intelligent connected vehicles · vehicle infrastructure cooperation · spatial logic · hierarchical spatial model · formal verification

1 Introduction

Autonomous vehicles have been researched and tested for a long time in the field of intelligent transportation. Compared with autonomous vehicles based on single-vehicle intelligence, the approach of vehicle infrastructure cooperation (VIC) can handle more complex scenarios and make better decisions for safety, which is one of the most promising commercial applications in autonomous

This work was supported by NKRDP (2020AAA0107800) and NSFC (62272165).

driving. The VIC scenario is an intelligent traffic scenario in which multiple intelligent traffic participants, such as intelligent vehicles, roadside units, etc., perform the interaction and collaboration on vehicle and road information. However, the existing approaches for information interaction are based on vehicle-to-everything (V2X) communication, transmitting by way of images [1] or video streams [2], which are unsuitable for unified knowledge representation and abstract reasoning. Additionally, many spatial logics focus solely on the perspective of host vehicles under global knowledge, neglecting the issue of knowledge conversion and fusion between vehicles and other agents in VIC scenarios. Therefore, there still needs an effective logical language that can unify knowledge representation, fusion, and reasoning for the information obtained by different intelligent traffic participants in VIC scenarios.

In industrial applications, the decision-making of autonomous driving has been explicitly divided into multiple layers, where path planning and behaviour planning are at different layers. However, existing spatial logic [3,4] matches either coarse-grained or fine-grained models to handle decisions at a specific layer. Path planning focuses on overall information, such as whether a road is congested. Behaviour planning such as right-turn requires detailed information, including the turning junction status and possible collision around its surrounding. However, caring about the driving behaviour of vehicles in the coarse-grained model may lead to insufficient information, while caring about the whole traffic conditions in the fine-grained model may accompany redundant data. At the same time, path planning formulated in the upper layer provides a reference for concrete behaviour planning, and a series of behaviour plannings executed in the lower layer determine the performance of path planning. These issues can be solved by a hierarchical model, which has the ability to distinguish decisions at different layers and retain the correlation between decisions at different layers.

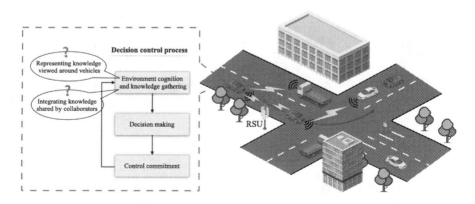

Fig. 1. Decision control process in vehicle-infrastructure cooperation scenarios

In this paper, we focus on collaborative decision-making through hierarchical models and multi-agent knowledge fusion in vehicle-infrastructure cooperation scenarios. As illustrated with Fig. 1, multiple intelligent vehicles and roadside units interact through spatial knowledge to assist the host vehicle in making reasonable decisions in VIC scenario, forming an intelligent vehicle infrastructure cooperation system. By sharing and fusing spatial knowledge with other agents, including collaborative overtaking, blind lane turning, parking station guidance, and other scenarios, this system can make better decisions than a single intelligent vehicle in terms of safety and efficiency. To address these concerns, we propose a novel hierarchical spatial model and logical framework, with examples demonstrating its effectiveness. Figure 2 is an overview of our research route. We abstract road and traffic information to build a hierarchical spatial model that captures the necessary environmental information for the autonomous vehicle's local view, and exploit the property of hierarchical spatial logic to solve spatial knowledge representation and fusion for autonomous vehicles in VIC scenarios. The contributions of this paper are as follows:

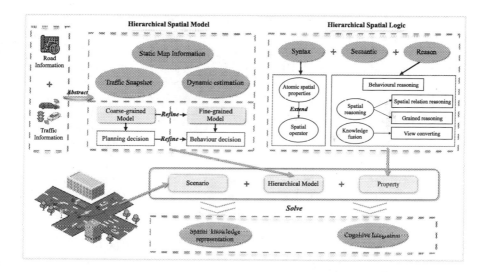

Fig. 2. Overview of the research route

- We propose a Hierarchical Spatial Logic (HSL) language and its semantic model for the abstract description and reasoning of spatial information from the autonomous vehicle's local view.
- We apply HSL to the VIC scenario for supporting cognitive fusion and cooperative behavioural reasoning between vehicles and other agents, implementing tools for automatically converting opendrive map files to our coarse-grained spatial models and spatial knowledge between distributed agents.
- We demonstrate the effectiveness of our approach in the case study, which enables the sharing and integration of spatial knowledge between distributed agents for driving scenarios with different granularity.

The rest of the paper is organized as follows: Section 2 reviews the related work. Section 3 presents the hierarchical spatial model to distinguish decisions at different granularity. Section 4 defines the syntax and semantics of HSL. Section 5 classifies the reasoning of HSL. Section 6 demonstrates how our approach works in detail with the VIC scenario. Section 7 concludes this paper.

2   Related Work

In the development process of autonomous driving, spatial logical language is considered as a convincing method to reason and make safety decisions in autonomous vehicles. The spatial logic [5] extended the one-dimensional interval temporal logic [6] to cover spatial information through two-dimensional features. Compass logic [7] introduced modal operators and viewed one-dimensional intervals as points on a plane to describe two-dimensional interval relationships. Randell et al. proposed region connection calculus [8] (RCC) by regarding the region as a basic element and calculating binary spatial relationships between regions. The Olderog's group proposed multi-lane spatial logic [3,9] by dividing spatial views to represent spatial information around the internet of vehicles for verifying the safety of changing lanes and overtaking on the motorway. Then they improved the road network model to make it applicable to urban traffic [10]. Xu et al. [11,12] defined the basic scene structure, and introduced modal operators on MLSL to describe the spatio-temporal information of the host vehicle in the driving scenario. However, most existing spatial logics representing languages are based on single-vehicle intelligence, and they will be stuck in a bottleneck [13] when dealing with scenarios such as blind spot turning, sensor failures, and cooperative overtaking. In VIC scenario, these issues can be solved by sharing and integrating the key spatial knowledge between vehicles and other agents. The method of machine learning algorithms [14,15] can be used for knowledge extraction and fusion, but they are difficult to conduct safety analysis due to their poor interpretability. Kamali et al. [16] introduce a spatial controller for knowledge representing in vehicle platoons to simulate the lane-changing behaviour with a hybrid agent structure. Xu et al. [17] proposed a multi-agent spatial logic with relative directions and multi-agent observations, by introducing operators for knowledge sharing and joint, and using the logic formula to ensure a queuing driving decision under UPPAAL [18]. However, the above works related to spatial logic extend the single-vehicle perspective to multi-agent for collaborative decision-making. They are limited to platoon systems with the same observation direction for moving vehicles, which avoids the issue of cognitive fusion under the view of different traffic participants.

3   Hierarchical Spatial Model

In order to model the spatial information on the map and present a unified knowledge specification framework for decision-making at different levels, we propose a hierarchical spatial model, including both coarse-grained and fine-grained models. The coarse-grained model is an upper-level structure that abstracts roads and crosses as sets of nodes, e.g., the set of roads $\mathbb{R} = \{r_0, r_1, r_2, r_3, r_4, r_5\}$

and the set of crosses $\mathbb{C} = \{c_0, c_1, c_2\}$ in Fig. 3 (a), which is used for path planning in autonomous driving, such as route planning and nearest parking choosing. The fine-grained model is a lower-level structure, which divides the nodes in the upper level into grids by the driveable direction and its vertical direction to form a detailed map. For example, node r_0 is divided into four grids $\{(r_0, 0), (r_0, 1), (r_0, 2), (r_0, 3)\}$, and $(r_0, 0)$ represents a grid in Fig. 3 (b). The fine-grained model is suitable for handling behavioural planning, such as right turning, lane changing etc.

3.1 Topology and Map

The three factors of a map are scale, direction, and symbol. In this paper, scale, direction, and spatial relationships between roads and crosses are represented by a topological network, while symbols are described by traffic snapshots captured by sensors. For a topological network, we have a direction set D, where $D = \{N, E, S, W, NE, SE, SW, NW\}$, which respectively indicates north, east, south, west, northeast, southeast, southwest, and northwest.

Definition 1 (Network). *Given a spatial direction D, a hierarchical topological network is a quadruplet consisting of regions and spatial relationships $HN = (R, E, RD, f_v)$, where*

- *R is the set of regions.*
- *$E \subseteq R \times R$ is the fundamental spatial relation determined by the adjacent regions in R.*
- *$RD : R \to 2^D$ is a function denoting the available driving directions of a region. E.g. for a region $r \in R$, $RD(r) = \{N\}$ means the region is available for cars to drive northward.*
- *$f_r : R \times R \to D$ is a function that determines spatial position relation between regions in R.*

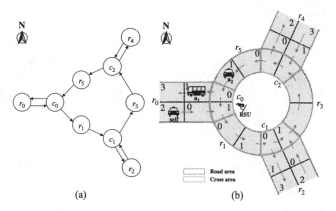

Fig. 3. Topology and map structure for a roundabout example (a) Road network (b) Gird network

Definition 2 (Road Network). *A Road network(RN) is a special network HN where its R is instantiated as a set $V = \mathbb{R} \cup \mathbb{C}$ consisting of abstract nodes for roads and crosses. It is served as the coarse-grained model in our framework.*

Figure 3 (a) depicts a transformed network model RN from a realistic road traffic map. The top-left corner of the figure indicates the north direction. The set of nodes, denoted as $\{r_0, ..., c_0, ...\}$, represents the roads and crosses, and the edge set E is the arrow line. For function f_r, c_0 is to the east of r_0 on the actual map. Therefore, we have $f_r(r_0, c_0) = E$ and $f_r(c_0, r_0) = W$.

Definition 3 (Grid Network). *A Grid network (GN) is a special network HN where its R is instantiated as a set $G = V \times L_d \times L_{vd}$ that represents the set of grids in the fine-grained network, where for each region abstracted as node x in V, L_d is the set of the driving direction lanes of node x and L_{vd} is the set of vertical direction lanes of node x. E.g. the grid $(r_0, 0)$ in Fig. 3 (b) is the intersection of eastbound lanes and northbound lanes.*

Figure 3 shows the illustration of a *Map* with RN and GN transformed from reality. The green and orange grids in (b) represent roads and crosses, respectively. The red arrow lines between grids denote the available driving directions. $self, a_1, a_2$ are traffic participants, and roadside unit RSU represents the video surveillance near cross c_0. The symbol in the upper left corner of (b) indicates the north direction on the map. We say a pair of (RN, GN) is a map when they satisfy the following property: (1) they share the same set V; (2) the information in GN is consistent with RN, i.e., RN is an abstraction of GN by projecting it to the set V.

3.2   Traffic Snapshot

Traffic snapshot records real-time dynamic information of vehicles and other participants on the map, such as their positions or signal states, which are usually collected by multiple sensors. In previous work, traffic snapshots have primarily focused on vehicle-related information, including position, speed, and driving direction within the host vehicle's view range. This paper also covers the traffic signal status to supplement decision-making, which can be used to judge the optimal path, turn behaviour planning, etc. In particular, we constraint that each autonomous vehicle and traffic light has a unique number, and the information of the same object obtained by different sensors is consistent.

Definition 4 (Traffic snapshot). *Given a Map, let I be the set of autonomous vehicles, and S be the set of signals. The variable $self$ indicates the host vehicle which belongs to I and for every AV $c \in I$, signal $t \in S$, the traffic snapshot $TS = (pos, dir, spd, left, right, ltl, lts, ltr)$, where*

- *$pos : I \cup S \to R$ is a function to get the position of car c or signal t. We define that each car or signal can only reserve one region.*
- *$dir : I \to D$ is a function to obtain the driving direction of car c, e.g., $dir(c) = E$ means the car c is driving towards east.*

– $spd : I \rightarrow 0 \cup \mathcal{R}^+$ is a function to calculate the movement distance of car c.
– $left, right : I \rightarrow bool$ is a function indicating the signals of car c to turn left or right. And the bool takes the value 0 or 1. For example, $left(c)$ means the left turn light of car c is on.
– $ltl, lts, ltr : S \rightarrow bool$ is a function to get the current state of traffic light t, where ltl, lts, ltr indicate that the traffic signal allows left turn, straight ahead, and right turn, respectively. For example, $ltl(t)$ means the signal t allows cars to turn left.

Since the generality of our hierarchical network model, the instances of traffic snapshots TS defined as TS_u for the road network and TS_l for the grid network are similar, we briefly give the difference between them. Only the *pos* function needs to be changed, where $pos : I \cup S \rightarrow V$ belongs to TS_u and $pos : I \cup S \rightarrow G$ belongs to TS_l. Other functions, such as dir, ltl, etc., are bound to vehicles or signal lights, and these functions are consistent at different layers.

3.3   Estimation Structure

The estimation structure supplements the insufficient information for traffic snapshots and forecasts possible situations based on current information. We take the vehicle's acceleration, claim area, and driving path as components of the estimation structure to assist autonomous vehicles in making decisions.

Definition 5 (Estimation structure). *Given a Map, let I be the set of autonomous vehicles, and S be the set of signals. For every AV $c \in I$, signal $t \in S$, the estimation structure $ES = (acc, clm, pth)$ is a structure maintained by c to estimate cars' driving motivation under the current cycle of TS, where*

– $acc : I \rightarrow \mathcal{R}$ is a function to estimate the acceleration of each car in I.
– $clm : I \rightarrow \mathcal{R}$ is a function to get the next possible positions of each car by its speed and turn signal.
– $pth : I \rightarrow R^{\mathcal{N}^+}$ is a function to estimate the route that other car intends to take according to its state, road conditions and communication content.

Similarly, for the estimation structure ES, function acc is consistent between models with different granularities. Under the coarse-grained model, the functions clm and pth are defined as $clm : I \rightarrow V$ and $pth : I \rightarrow V^{\mathcal{N}^+}$ to be part of ES_u. The functions of $clm : I \rightarrow G$ and $pth : I \rightarrow G^{\mathcal{N}^+}$ belong to ES_l under the fine-grained model.

4   Hierarchical Spatial Logic

In the previous section, we have formalised the road information into a hierarchical spatial model, which can describe the spatial states and spatial relationships at different granularities. In this section, we define the syntax and semantics of hierarchical spatial logic for specifying the spatial properties that an autonomous vehicle considers at different granularity models.

4.1 Syntax

Definition 6 (Syntax).

ϕ is the atomic spatial logic formulas, where ϕ_u or ϕ_l are the specific formulas under coarse-grained or fine-grained models, respectively, defined as follows:

$\phi ::= true \mid \phi_u \mid \phi_l \mid \alpha = \beta \mid free \mid cross \mid \neg\phi \mid \phi_1 \wedge \phi_2 \mid \phi_1 \rightarrow \phi_2 \mid \exists \alpha \bullet \phi$

where α, β are variables for car or signal identifiers.

$\psi ::= \phi \mid \psi_1 \Pi \psi_2 \mid \psi_1 \wedge \psi_2 \mid \neg\psi \mid \psi_1 \rightarrow \psi_2 \mid \exists \alpha \bullet \psi$

Π is a spatial relation operator defined as follows:

$$\Pi ::= \pi \mid \neg\pi \mid \pi^c \mid \Pi_1 \vee \Pi_2 \qquad \pi ::= F \mid B \mid L \mid R \mid LF \mid LB \mid RF \mid RB$$

In our hierarchical spatial road traffic model, the HSL formula characterizes regions' spatial state and spatial relationship. Atomic spatial logic ϕ is the primitive property of HSL, which represents the spatial state of a road or a grid, describing whether this region is occupied by cars or regarded as crosses or completely free, etc. And these spatial states are expressed by formulas ϕ_u, ϕ_l, $free, cross$, where ϕ_u and ϕ_l will be introduced in detail in the following definition. We extend ϕ to construct HSL with spatial operator Π and common logical connectives, describing a relative spatial relationship between spatial states through the formula $\phi_1 \Pi \phi_2$. The spatial operator has eight basic relative orientations: front, back, left, right, left-front, left-back, right-front and left-back. Notation $\neg\pi$ means the inversion of π, π^c means the regions are directly connected in the π direction, and $\Pi_1 \vee \Pi_2$ means either in the direction of Π_1 or Π_2. Note that we constraint the priority of spatial relation operation is greater than common logical connectives. Moreover, when a formula ψ contains spatial relation operation, we need to use parenthesis to separate the two sides of Π, such as $(\phi_1 \Pi_1 \phi_2)\Pi_2(\phi_3)$, where the parenthesis can be omitted if ψ only contains an atomic spatial formula, which ensures a unique interpretation of formula.

4.2 Semantics

In this subsection, we first give semantic model of atomic spatial logic and then extend it by introducing the semantics of spatial relation operators in the following definitions. Given a Map, let r be the observation view of an autonomous car c in the coarse-grained or fine-grained model, which relates to TS and ES. The satisfaction of the formula ϕ implies that the spatial property specified by ϕ holds within a given view r, and the ϕ is interpreted by the model $\mathcal{M} = (TS, ES, r, c, v)$, where

- TS *is a traffic snapshot, where* $TS = TS_u$ *in the coarse-grained model and* $TS = TS_l$ *in the fine-grained model.*
- ES *is an estimation structure, where* $ES = ES_u$ *in the coarse-grained model and* $ES = ES_l$ *in fine-grained model.*
- r *is a view area around car* c *under* TS *and* ES*, where* $r_u \subseteq V$ *and* $r_l \subseteq G$ *are for the coarse-grained and fine-grained models, respectively.*

- $c \in I$ is a car under current consideration.
- $v : Var \to I \cup S$ is a function that maps car variables or signal variables to an actual car ID or traffic signal ID.

Definition 7 (The semantics of atomic spatial logic). *The satisfaction relation between a context model $\mathcal{M} = (TS, ES, r, c, v)$ and an atomic spatial logic formula ϕ, $\mathcal{M} \vDash \phi$, is defined inductively over ϕ as follows:*

$$
\begin{array}{ll}
\mathcal{M} \vDash true \text{ iff } True & \mathcal{M} \vDash \alpha = \beta \quad \text{iff } v(\alpha) = v(\beta) \\
\mathcal{M} \vDash \phi_u \quad \text{iff } (TS_u, ES_u, r_u, c, v) \vDash \phi_u & \mathcal{M} \vDash \phi_l \qquad \text{iff } (TS_l, ES_l, r_l, c, v) \vDash \phi_l \\
\mathcal{M} \vDash free \text{ iff } \forall x \in r \bullet x \notin pos(I) \cup clm(I) & \mathcal{M} \vDash cross \quad \text{iff } r \subseteq \mathbb{C} \\
\mathcal{M} \vDash \neg\phi \quad \text{iff } \mathcal{M} \nvDash \phi & \mathcal{M} \vDash \phi_1 \wedge \phi_2 \text{ iff } \mathcal{M} \vDash \phi_1 \wedge \mathcal{M} \vDash \phi_2 \\
\mathcal{M} \vDash \phi_1 \to \phi_2 \text{ iff } \mathcal{M} \nvDash \phi_1 \vee \mathcal{M} \vDash \phi_2 & \mathcal{M} \vDash \exists\alpha \cdot \phi \text{ iff } \exists\gamma \bullet (TS, ES, r, c, v(\alpha \mapsto \gamma)) \vDash \phi
\end{array}
$$

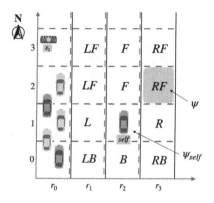

Fig. 4. Spatial relation observed by car $self$

In Definition 7, $\mathcal{M} \vDash free$ means the view area r is not reserved or claimed by any vehicle, for example, the road r_1 in Fig. 4 satisfies this property. $\mathcal{M} \vDash cross$ means the view area r belongs to crosses. Moreover, Definition 9 will introduce specific formulas ϕ_u and ϕ_l. For the atomic spatial logic, we limit r to either a node or a grid. To extend the atomic spatial logic, we introduce operator Π to describe spatial relations. Given a model $\mathcal{M}$, a formula $\psi_1 \Pi \psi_2$ is satisfied when a satisfying Π relation exists between ψ_1 and ψ_2. For instance, ψ_{self} RF ψ is satisfied in Fig. 4 when ψ is in RF direction of ψ_{self}. We define the function f_Π to describe the connection between the car $self$ and the eight directions, in terms of the relative and absolute positions. For example, the car $self$ is driving northward with $dir(self) = N$, then the front and right-front direction with car $self$ are calculated by the f_Π function $f_\Pi(F, dir(self)) = N, f_\Pi(RF, dir(self)) = NE$, which are N and NE.

- $f_\Pi(\pi, dir(c))$ calculates the absolute direction converting from π relative to the driving direction of car c, where π specifies the relative orientation and function $dir(c)$ returns the car c's absolute orientation.
- $r = \mathcal{F}(d, r_1, r_2) \Leftrightarrow r = r_1 \cup r_2 \wedge r_1 \cap r_2 = \emptyset \wedge \exists a, b \in r_1, r_2 \bullet d = f_r(a, b)$
- $r = \mathcal{F}_c(d, r_1, r_2) \Leftrightarrow r = \mathcal{F}(d, r_1, r_2) \wedge \exists a, b \in r_1, r_2 \bullet d = f_r(a, b) \wedge (a, b) \in E$

Let r be the view under TS and ES. Then we have $r = \mathcal{F}(d, r_1, r_2)$ to chop view r in the d direction for views r_1 and r_2. Notice that f_r is a spatial relation function of HN, and d is calculated by π through f_Π. This division ensures that at least one pair of elements (a, b) satisfy $d = f_r(a, b)$ in these two parts under the given *Map*. And $r = \mathcal{F}_c(d, r_1, r_2)$ is satisfied if and only if $r = \mathcal{F}(d, r_1, r_2)$ holds on with additional condition $(a, b) \in E$. Here, E represents the edge set. Moreover, function *inv* gets the opposite direction of π, as shown in Table 1.

Table 1. Inversion mapping table $inv(\pi)$

π	F	B	L	R	LF	RF	LB	RB
$inv(\pi)$	B	F	R	L	RB	LB	RF	LF

Definition 8 (The semantics of spatial relation operators). *Given a context model* $\mathcal{M} = (TS, ES, r, c, v)$ *with the driving direction of car* c, *the satisfaction of a formula with spatial relation operators are defined as follows:*

1) $\psi_1 \pi \psi_2$ *is satisfied iff an element in* ψ_2 *is in the* π *direction of an element in* ψ_1.

$$\mathcal{M} \vDash \psi_1 \pi \psi_2 \quad \textbf{iff} \quad \exists r_1, r_2 \bullet r = \mathcal{F}(f_\Pi(\pi, dir(c)), r_1, r_2)$$
$$\wedge (TS, ES, r_1, c, v) \vDash \psi_1 \wedge (TS, ES, r_2, c, v) \vDash \psi_2$$

2) $\psi_1(\neg\pi)\psi_2$ *is satisfied iff an element in* ψ_2 *is in the* $\neg\pi$ *direction of an element in* ψ_1.

$$\mathcal{M} \vDash \psi_1(\neg\pi)\psi_2 \quad \textbf{iff} \quad \exists r_1, r_2 \bullet r = \mathcal{F}(f_\Pi(inv(\pi), dir(c)), r_1, r_2)$$
$$\wedge (TS, ES, r_1, c, v) \vDash \psi_1 \wedge (TS, ES, r_2, c, v) \vDash \psi_2$$

3) $\psi_1 \pi^c \psi_2$ *is satisfied iff an element in* ψ_2 *is in the* π *direction of an element in* ψ_1 *and they are adjacent.*

$$\mathcal{M} \vDash \psi_1 \pi^c \psi_2 \quad \textbf{iff} \quad \exists r_1, r_2 \bullet r = \mathcal{F}_c(f_\Pi(\pi, dir(c)), r_1, r_2)$$
$$\wedge (TS, ES, r_1, c, v) \vDash \psi_1 \wedge (TS, ES, r_2, c, v) \vDash \psi_2$$

4) $\psi_1(\Pi_1 \vee \Pi_2)\psi_2$ *is satisfied iff an element in* ψ_2 *is in the* Π_1 *or* Π_2 *direction of an element in* ψ_1.

$$\mathcal{M} \vDash \psi_1(\Pi_1 \vee \Pi_2)\psi_2 \quad \textbf{iff} \quad \exists r_1, r_2 \bullet r = \mathcal{F}(f_\Pi(\Pi_1 \vee \Pi_2, dir(c)), r_1, r_2)$$
$$\wedge (TS, ES, r_1, c, v) \vDash \psi_1 \wedge (TS, ES, r_2, c, v) \vDash \psi_2$$

In the previous definitions, we gave the generalised semantics of HSL. And then, we define the concrete atomic formulas ϕ_u and ϕ_l under coarse-grained and fine-grained models, which can be extended for specific scenarios. In this paper, ϕ_u has terms $jam, ubt, st(\alpha), des(\alpha)$ and $lt(\beta)$, and these spatial states describe whether part of a region is traffic jam or an unobstructed road, or a car's starting position or destination position or traffic lights appear. ϕ_l has terms $re(\alpha)$ and $cl(\alpha)$; for a grid, the spatial states indicate whether a part of it is reserved or claimed by a car. The syntax of ϕ_u and ϕ_l are as follows:

$$\phi_u ::= jam \mid ubt \mid st(\alpha) \mid des(\alpha) \mid lt(\beta) \qquad\qquad \phi_l ::= re(\alpha) \mid cl(\alpha)$$

We define context models $\mathcal{M}_u$ and $\mathcal{M}_l$ at the specific granularity, where $\mathcal{M}_u = (TS_u, ES_u, r_u, c, v)$ interprets ϕ_u and $\mathcal{M}_l = (TS_l, ES_l, r_l, c, v)$ interprets ϕ_l. In Fig. 4, for formulas ϕ_u under the coarse-grained model, we say that $\mathcal{M}_u \models jam$ holds when the view area r is limited to road r_0, and formula ubt indicates that the road is unobstructed. Furthermore, if the position of s_1 obtained by function pos is r_0 and the view area r is also r_0, $\mathcal{M}_u \models lt(s_1)$ holds. In the fine-grained model, formula $re(self)$ is satisfied when the view area r is grid $(r_2, 1)$ reserved by vehicle $self$, while $cl(\alpha)$ indicates the view area r is claimed by car α. Note that the driving speed m and amount q of cars C for formula jam or ubt can be specified according to the actual road conditions. And we use the notation $\parallel$ in pth and car collections to return the length of variables.

Definition 9 (The semantics of ϕ_u and ϕ_l). *Given a traffic snapshot TS, estimation structure ES, and the vehicle self's observation area r under the specific granularity, the semantics of formulas ϕ_u and ϕ_l are defined as follows:*

$\mathcal{M}_u \models jam$	iff $\exists C \subseteq I, \exists q \le \lvert C \rvert, \forall x_i, x_j \in C \bullet$ $dir(v(x_i)) = dir(v(x_j)) \wedge spd(x_i)$ $\le m \wedge pos(v(x_i)) = r$	$\mathcal{M}_u \models ubt$	iff $\exists C \subseteq I, \forall x_i, x_j \in C \bullet dir(v(x_i))$ $= dir(v(x_j)) \wedge spd(x_i) > m \wedge pos$ $(v(x_i)) = r$
$\mathcal{M}_u \models st(\alpha)$	iff $r = pth(v(\alpha))_0$	$\mathcal{M}_u \models des(\alpha)$	iff $r = pth(v(\alpha))_{\lvert pth(v(\alpha)) \rvert - 1}$
$\mathcal{M}_u \models lt(\beta)$	iff $r = pos(v(\beta))$	$\mathcal{M}_l \models cl(\alpha)$	iff $r \in clm(v(\alpha))$
$\mathcal{M}_l \models re(\alpha)$	iff $r = pos(v(\alpha)) \wedge dir(v(\alpha)) \in RD(r)$		

5   Reasoning

In order to ensure the safety of decision-making and solve the issue of cognitive fusion, we propose two categories of reasoning based on the difference in granularity and mode. The first category involves multi-grained spatial reasoning, which includes both spatial relational reasoning and grained reasoning. The second category focuses on multi-source knowledge fusion, leveraging a view converting method to integrate knowledges from different agents. In this section, we first introduce primitive reasoning, and then present two classes of reasoning under the framework of HSL.

Behavioural Reasoning. Primitive reasoning in spatial logic refers to the evaluation of certain spatial properties when an intelligent vehicle making its driving decisions, we call it as behavioral reasoning for vehicles. Decision-making in VIC scenarios can generally be classified into safety and efficiency categories. The safety category includes collision warning decisions, turning decisions, and so on. The efficiency category includes cooperative lane decisions, vehicle platoon decisions, and so on, and we focus on decision-making under the safety category. For example, the car $self$ deciding to claim a turn in the ahead intersection can drive successfully if the following formula is satisfied.

$$re(self) \text{ F } (cross \wedge \neg cl(self)) \wedge re(self) \text{ F}^c \ free$$
$$\wedge \ re(self) \text{ F } (\neg \exists c \bullet c \ne self \wedge (re(c) \vee cl(c)))$$

$re(self)$ F $(cross \land \neg cl(self))$ indicates that the car $self$ is driving towards the intersection, which has not yet been claimed by itself. $re(self)$ F^c $free$ demonstrates that the front road on which the car $self$ next pass is currently no car. $re(self)$ F $(\neg \exists c \bullet c \neq self \land (re(c) \lor cl(c)))$ is a strong spatial constraint that indicates the road section the car $self$ will go straight for a turn, which will not be reserved or claimed by any other cars.

In the following subsections, we respectively give the multi-grained spatial reasoning and multi-source knowledge fusion under the HSL language, including spatial relation reasoning calculated with the spatial direction relationship under the same granularity, grained reasoning by using the hierarchical spatial model to distinguish the decision-making at different layers, and the view converting method for spatial knowledge fusion between vehicles and other agents.

5.1 Multi-grained Spatial Reasoning

Table 2. Spatial direction calculation (Lower case indicates a superset in that direction, e.g. l indicates LF|L|LB)

	F	B	L	R	LF	RF	LB	RB
F	F	F|B	LF	RF	LF	RF	l	r
B	F|B	B	LB	RB	l	r	LB	RB
L	LF	LB	L	L|R	LF	f	LB	b
R	RF	RB	L|R	R	f	RF	b	RB
LF	LF	l	LF	f	LF	f	l	all
RF	RF	r	f	RF	f	RF	all	r
LB	l	LB	LB	b	l	all	LB	b
RB	r	RB	b	RB	all	r	b	RB

Spatial Relation Reasoning. Spatial relation reasoning is the most basic logical reasoning and is widely used to understand, analyze and draw conclusions about the spatial environment. The spatial relation operator has properties such as negation law, transitivity and distributive law. Using the transitivity of spatial relations, we can deduce the direction from A to C by giving directions from A to B and B to C. Where rules **A1**, **A2**, **A3**, **A4** are the spatial properties, Table 2 shows the results of the spatial transfer calculations of all directions.

We restrict ψ in inference rules **A1** - **A4** to atomic spatial formula, where **A1** represents negative law, for example, ψ_2 on the right side of ψ_1 is equal to ψ_1 on the left side of ψ_2. **A2** is the distributive law that holds under $\land$. **A3** describes spatial transitive relations, where the relation between ψ_1 and ψ_3 can be determined using Table 2. For instance, if $re(self)$ R $re(c_1)$ and $re(c_1)$ F $re(c_2)$ hold, then the reasoning yields that $re(self)$ RF $re(c_2)$. **A4** is similar to conjunction elimination, e.g., if $\psi_1 \pi_1 \psi_2 \pi_2 \psi_3$ holds, then both $\psi_1 \pi_1 \psi_2$ and $\psi_2 \pi_2 \psi_3$ holds.

$$\mathbf{A1} : \psi_1 \pi \psi_2 \Leftrightarrow \psi_2 (\neg \pi) \psi_1 \qquad \mathbf{A2} : \psi_1 \pi (\psi_2 \land \psi_3) \Leftrightarrow \psi_1 \pi \psi_2 \land \psi_1 \pi \psi_3$$
$$\mathbf{A3} : \psi_1 \pi_1 \psi_2 \land \psi_2 \pi_2 \psi_3 \rightarrow \psi_1 \pi_3 \psi_3 \qquad \mathbf{A4} : \psi_1 \pi_1 \psi_2 \pi_2 \psi_3 ... \rightarrow \psi_i \pi_i \psi_{i+1}$$

Grained Reasoning. Grained reasoning is based on our hierarchical spatial model, which exploits a distinguishing feature of networks to divide decisions and retain the correlation and consistency between decisions at different layers. The coarse-grained model shows the overall state of the road, such as traffic jams, while the fine-grained model focuses on the situation inside the road, such as a car's position. We can choose a suitable grain of the model to fit the knowledge representing and reasoning for decision making at different levels to improve the efficiency. The coarse-grained reasoning related to path decisions includes driving path planning, nearest parking choosing, etc., and the fine-grained reasoning related to behavioural decisions includes right turn, lane change, etc. The decision-making is optimised through this approach, which divides the reasoning in specific cases into coarse-grained and fine-grained. This paper gives coarse-grained and fine-grained reasoning in Sect. 6, corresponding to *Case-A* and *Case-B*, respectively.

5.2 Multi-source Knowledge Fusion

View Converting Method. In the VIC scenarios, as the observation direction of the traffic participants changes continuously, the senders and receivers have different formulas for characterizing the same spatial information. In order to enable the autonomous vehicle to recognise the knowledge from different traffic participants, it is necessary to convert the formula of the sender into a formula that the receiver can recognise. Based on the correspondence between absolute and relative direction, this paper establishes a mapping relationship transition between the absolute direction observed by different traffic participants and the relative spatial direction that they currently confirm. Table 3 and Table 4 respectively show the mapping of the spatial view and the detailed transition of relative direction, where the **Init** direction is F|B|L|R|LF|LB|RF|RB.

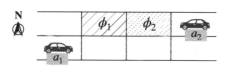

Fig. 5. View transition between cars in opposite direction

For example, we demonstrate how the view converting method works in Fig. 5. Assume that cars a_1 and a_2 drive towards east and west, respectively. The diagonal shadow and dotted shadow satisfy spatial properties ϕ_1 and ϕ_2, respectively, where ϕ_1 and ϕ_2 are not explicitly specified, they can be $re(\alpha)$ or $cl(\alpha) \wedge cross$, etc. As we regard car a_1 as the host view, the two shadows should satisfy property $\phi_1 F \phi_2$ or $\phi_2 B \phi_1$, and regard car a_2 as the host view, the spatial property should hold with $\phi_2 F \phi_1$ or $\phi_1 B \phi_2$. Since the relative spatial relation observed by host vehicle changes continuously with its driving direction, the spatial property satisfied under car a_2's view may not hold on for car a_1. According to view converting method, we should apply transition d_4 from the driving direction of a_2, $dir(a_2) = W$ to a_1, $dir(a_1) = E$, that is, F|B|L|R|LF|LB|RF|RB $\rightarrow$ B|F|R|L|RB|RF|LB|LF. Therefore, the spatial property satisfied in two shadows under car a_2's view is converted to $\phi_2 B \phi_1$ or $\phi_1 F \phi_2$ for car a_1's view, which is consistent with the properties that hold on car a_1.

Table 3. Trasition by eight directions

	N	NE	E	SE	S	SW	W	NW
N	d_0	d_1	d_2	d_3	d_4	d_5	d_6	d_7
NE	d_7	d_0	d_1	d_2	d_3	d_4	d_5	d_6
E	d_6	d_7	d_0	d_1	d_2	d_3	d_4	d_5
SE	d_5	d_6	d_7	d_0	d_1	d_2	d_3	d_4
S	d_4	d_5	d_6	d_7	d_0	d_1	d_2	d_3
SW	d_3	d_4	d_5	d_6	d_7	d_0	d_1	d_2
W	d_2	d_3	d_4	d_5	d_6	d_7	d_0	d_1
NW	d_1	d_2	d_3	d_4	d_5	d_6	d_7	d_0

Table 4. Detailed transition relation

d_i	Transition
d_0	**Init** $\rightarrow$ F|B|L|R|LF|LB|RF|RB
d_1	**Init** $\rightarrow$ LF|RB|RF|LB|L|B|F|R
d_2	**Init** $\rightarrow$ L|R|B|F|LB|RB|LF|RF
d_3	**Init** $\rightarrow$ LB|RF|RB|LF|B|R|L|F
d_4	**Init** $\rightarrow$ B|F|R|L|RB|RF|LB|LF
d_5	**Init** $\rightarrow$ RB|LF|RF|LB|R|F|B|L
d_6	**Init** $\rightarrow$ R|L|F|B|RF|LF|RB|LB
d_7	**Init** $\rightarrow$ RF|LB|LF|RB|F|L|R|B

After giving different reasoning classes of knowledge sharing and fusion under the HSL language, we implement tools to apply HSL better. One is a tool for converting opendirve map files of simulation software into coarse-grained spatial models, and the other is for converting spatial knowledge between distributed agents in VIC scenarios, which will be demonstrated in our *Case-A* and *Case-B*.

6   Case Study

To illustrate the effectiveness of our logic, this section presents two examples. *Case-A* shows that our logic is able to represent driving paths intuitively under the coarse-grained model with a tool to convert opendrive map files to road network models. *Case-B* describes VIC scenario in the fine-grained model, demonstrating that the participants' knowledge can be converted with logic formulas, which enriches the host vehicle's cognition to make precise decisions. Furthermore, we complete an automatic converting tool for logic formulas from different views to promote cognitive fusion.

Case-A Description

Case-A is an application of spatial logic in path planning, where the blue line is one of planning route in navigation software. Figure 6 represents a possible route navigated by car *self*, where the yellow line indicates that the road is unobstructed with fewer cars, and the red line indicates that the road is jammed with lots of cars. Car *self* describes the road conditions of the selected route from the start point to destination using a spatial logic formula.

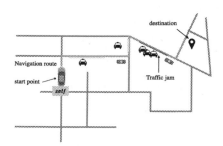

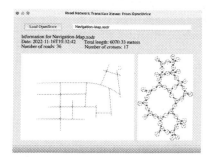

Fig. 6. A navigation route in map

Fig. 7. An example of converting open-drive file to RN

Apply Spatial Logic in Case-A

we can describe the navigation route within the view of car $self$ as formula:

$$st(self) \ \text{F}^c \ cross \ \text{R}^c \ [ubt \wedge lt(s_1)] \ \text{R}^c \ cross \ \text{F}^c \ ubt \ \text{F}^c cross \ \text{RB}^c$$
$$[jam \wedge lt(s_2)] \ \text{RB}^c \ cross \ \text{RF}^c \ des(self)$$

Further, we implement a tool to convert the opendrive file into road network. Figure 7 shows a conversion from opendrive map of Fig. 6 to the road network RN. In coarse-grained model, we only need to add road information to the node and allocate estimated driving time to formulas jam, ubt, and $lt(\beta)$. And then we can calculate several routes of driving time using graph theory. In addition, the number of traffic lights on the planned route can be calculated according to $lt(\beta)$ in a formula. $Case$-A shows that our logic can express the driving information simulated in opendrive and select an appropriate driving route according to the estimated driving time or traffic lights returned by the formula.

Case-B Description

$Case$-B is one of the critical scenarios in VIC, which is mentioned in white papers such as SAE-China, ETSI, and 5GAA. The traffic situation shown in Fig. 8 involves intelligent vehicle $self$, bus a_1, normal car a_2, and video surveillance RSU. The car $self$ intends to turn right into a roundabout and wants to know if any vehicle is driving on the left side of the intersection. Still, its view is blocked by obstacles to both sides of the road and the taller bus a_1. Using V2X communication, the car $self$ can query traffic participants in its vicinity that can provide spatial information to extend its field of view for obtaining obstructed information. Assume that bus a_1 or the video surveillance RSU can communicate with car $self$, sending the information they perceived or car $self$ requested through logic formulas. Since the viewing direction differs between the traffic participants, it is necessary to convert the spatial logic formula from the source entity to the target formula that car $self$ can recognise. Further, the car $self$ determines whether it can turn right into the roundabout with guard G_r based on safety and reasoning, where the right turn guard G_r of $self$ is:

$$G_r = re(self) \text{ F } (cross \wedge \neg cl(self)) \wedge re(self) \text{ F}^c \ free$$
$$\wedge \ re(self) \text{ F } (\neg \exists c \bullet c \neq self \wedge (re(c) \vee cl(c)))$$

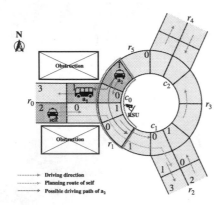

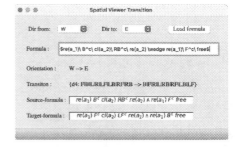

Fig. 8. A right turn decision scenario in roundabout

Fig. 9. An automatic view converting tool applied in $Case$-B

Apply Spatial Logic in Case-B

The Map in Fig. 8 depicts a right turn scenario, where $\{(c_0, 0), (c_0, 1)\}$ is a subset of the $cross$, $RD(pos(self)) = E$, $RD(pos(a_1)) = W$ and $RD(pos(a_2)) = WS$. The areas with green, blue, and red boxes are reserved by vehicles, claimed by vehicle a_2, and observed by RSU, respectively. The decision-making control process of autonomous vehicles based on V2X communication is simplified into the following four steps.

– **Collect spatial information through sensors**

We can obtain the information below for the current traffic snapshot $TS = (pos, dir, spd, left, right, ltl, lts, ltr)$ of car $self$.

$$pos(self) = \{(r_0, 2)\}, dir(self) = E, right(self)$$
$$pos(a_1) = \{(r_0, 1)\}, dir(a_1) = W, spd(a_1) = 2$$

The spatial logic formula of car $self$, ranging from its current position to the cross and a bus in front of the left.

$$re(self) \text{ F}^c \ free \text{ F}^c \ cross \wedge re(self) \text{ LF } re(a_1)$$

1) and **2)** are the spatial logic formulas for the car a_1 and the video surveillance RSU from their viewing directions, respectively. a_1 describes the area forward and backward from its position, and the area of RSU is the red box where we assume RSU observes toward the south.

$$\textbf{1)}\ re(a_1)\ \text{B}^c\ cl(a_2)\ \text{RB}^c\ re(a_2) \wedge re(a_1)\ \text{F}^c\ free$$
$$\textbf{2)}\ re(a_2)\ \text{RF}^c\ cl(a_2)\ \text{F}^c\ cross\ \text{LF}^c\ free$$

– Share knowledge through formula

According to the view converting method in Sect. 5.2, the relative direction transforms of bus a_1 and video surveillance RSU as follows:

$$d_4 : a_1(W) \rightarrow self(E) : \text{F|B|L|R|LF|LB|RF|RB} \rightarrow \text{B|F|R|L|RB|RF|LB|LF}$$
$$d_6 : RSU(S) \rightarrow self(E) : \text{F|B|L|R|LF|LB|RF|RB} \rightarrow \text{R|L|F|B|RF|LF|RB|LB}$$

Modify the formulas of **1)** and **2)** in step 1 as follows, where the formulas under different views can be converted by our tool, as shown in Fig. 9.

$$\textbf{3)}\ re(a_1)\ \text{F}^c\ cl(a_2)\ \text{LF}^c\ re(a_2) \wedge re(a_1)\ \text{B}^c\ free$$
$$\textbf{4)}\ re(a_2)\ \text{RB}^c\ cl(a_2)\ \text{R}^c\ cross\ \text{RF}^c\ free$$

– Reason spatial relation and update information

Car $self$ uses spatial relation reasoning to infer whether other vehicles on its left front intend to go through the intersection, where the same result can be obtained from bus a_1 and video surveillance RSU.

1	$re(a_1)$ F^c $cl(a_2)$ LF^c $re(a_2)$	**Pre**	$re(a_2)$ RB^c $cl(a_2)$ R^c $cross$ RF^c $free$	**Pre**
2	$re(self)$ LF $re(a_1)$	**Pre**	$free$ LB^c $cross$ L^c $cl(a_2)$ LF^c $re(a_2)$	**A1**
3	$re(a_1)$ F^c $cl(a_2)$	**A4**	$re(self)$ F $cross$	**Pre**
4	$cl(a_2)$ LF^c $rc(a_2)$	**A4**	$cross$ L^c $cl(a_2)$	**A4**
5	$re(a_1)$ LF $re(a_2)$	**A3**(3, 4)	$cl(a_2)$ LF^c $re(a_2)$	**A4**
6	$re(self)$ LF $re(a_2)$	**A3**(2, 5)	$cross$ LF $re(a_2)$	**A3**(4, 5)
7			$re(self)$ LF $re(a_2)$	**A3**(3, 6)

– Make decision based on updated spatial information

According to the spatial relation reasoning in the previous step, we know that car a_2 is in the left front of car $self$, approaching the intersection. The possible driving path of a_2 is estimated based on the current information as $pth(a_2) = \{(r_5, 1), (c_0, 0), (c_0, 1), (r_1, 0)\}$. We can infer that G_r is not satisfied when car $self$ claims grid $(c_0, 1)$ for a right turn at the current cycle. Because $re(self)$ F ($\neg \exists c \bullet$ $c \neq self \wedge (re(c) \vee cl(c))$) does not hold according to the estimated path $pth(a_2)$ that $cl(a_2)$ occurs at grid $(c_0, 1)$ in the driving path of car $self$. Based on the driving rules of the traffic circle, the car entering the traffic circle needs to yield to the car already inside the traffic circle, so car $self$ should stop and wait for safety until car a_2 goes through the intersection.

7   Conclusion

In this paper, we propose a hierarchical spatial model for HSL with view converting method. The innovation of our approach is to provide a unified logical language for knowledge representing and cognitive fusion at different layers. In addition, our view converting method expands the observed information of traffic participants from same view to multi-directional view. Compared with the transmitting way of images or video streams, using logical language to describe spatial information can retain knowledge and improve runtime efficiency. Moreover, the case study demonstrates our approach's effectiveness in the VIC scenarios with hierarchical spatial model. We also implement automatic tools for view converting and transformation from opendrive files to coarse-grained models, which help better apply HSL. In future work, we attempt to introduce temporal operations and present a complete decision-making control process of VIC scenarios.

References

1. Yamazato, T.: V2X communications with an image sensor. J. Commun. Inf. Netw. **2**(4), 65–74 (2017)
2. Gyawali, S., Xu, S., Qian, Y., Hu, R.Q.: Challenges and solutions for cellular based V2X communications. IEEE Commun. Surv. Tutorials **23**(1), 222–255 (2020)
3. Hilscher, M., Linker, S., Olderog, E.-R., Ravn, A.P.: An abstract model for proving safety of multi-lane traffic Manoeuvres. In: Qin, S., Qiu, Z. (eds.) ICFEM 2011. LNCS, vol. 6991, pp. 404–419. Springer, Heidelberg (2011). https://doi.org/10.1007/978-3-642-24559-6_28
4. Xu, B., Li, Q.: A spatial logic for modeling and verification of collision-free control of vehicles. In: 2016 21st International Conference on Engineering of Complex Computer Systems (ICECCS), pp. 33–42. IEEE (2016)
5. Aiello, M., Pratt-Hartmann, I., Benthem, J.V.: What is spatial logic? In: Aiello, M., Pratt-Hartmann, I., Van Benthem, J. (eds.) Handbook of Spatial Logics, pp. 1–11. Springer (2007). https://doi.org/10.1007/978-1-4020-5587-4_1
6. Moszkowski, B.: A temporal logic for multi-level reasoning about hardware. Technical report, Stanford University, CA (1982)
7. Venema, Y.: Expressiveness and completeness of an interval tense logic. Notre Dame J. Formal Logic **31**(4), 529–547 (1990)
8. Randell, D.A., Cui, Z., Cohn, A.G.: A spatial logic based on regions and connection. KR **92**, 165–176 (1992)
9. Hilscher, M., Linker, S.: Proof theory of a multi-lane spatial logic. Logical Methods Comput. Sci. **11** (2015)
10. Schwammberger, M.: An abstract model for proving safety of autonomous urban traffic. Theoret. Comput. Sci. **744**, 143–169 (2018)
11. Xu, B., Li, Q., Guo, T., Du, D.: A scenario-based approach for formal modelling and verification of safety properties in automated driving. IEEE Access **7**, 140566–140587 (2019)
12. Xu, B., Li, Q.: A bounded multi-dimensional modal logic for autonomous cars based on local traffic and estimation. In: 2017 International Symposium on Theoretical Aspects of Software Engineering (TASE), pp. 1–8. IEEE (2017)

13. Gong, Y., Feng, H., Zhang, C.: Research on the development strategy of the internet of vehicles. J. Phys. Conf. Ser. **1907**, 012063 (2021)
14. Ma, Y., Wang, Z., Yang, H., Yang, L.: Artificial intelligence applications in the development of autonomous vehicles: a survey. IEEE/CAA J. Automatica Sinica **7**(2), 315–329 (2020)
15. Chen, S., Dong, J., Ha, P., Li, Y., Labi, S.: Graph neural network and reinforcement learning for multi-agent cooperative control of connected autonomous vehicles. Comput. Aided Civ. Infrastruct. Eng. **36**(7), 838–857 (2021)
16. Kamali, M., Linker, S., Fisher, M.: Modular verification of vehicle platooning with respect to decisions, space and time. In: Artho, C., Ölveczky, P.C. (eds.) FTSCS 2018. CCIS, vol. 1008, pp. 18–36. Springer, Cham (2019). https://doi.org/10.1007/978-3-030-12988-0_2
17. Xu, J., Huang, Y., Shi, J., Qin, S.: A multi-agent spatial logic for scenario-based decision modeling and verification in platoon systems. J. Comput. Sci. Technol. **36**(6), 1231–1247 (2021)
18. Behrmann, G., David, A., Larsen, K.G.: A tutorial on UPPAAL. In: Bernardo, M., Corradini, F. (eds.) SFM-RT 2004. LNCS, vol. 3185, pp. 200–236. Springer, Heidelberg (2004). https://doi.org/10.1007/978-3-540-30080-9_7

VeriLin: A Linearizability Checker for Large-Scale Concurrent Objects

Qiaowen Jia[1,2(✉)], Yi Lv[1,2(✉)], Peng Wu[1,2(✉)], Bohua Zhan[1,2(✉)],
Jifeng Hao[3(✉)], Hong Ye[3(✉)], and Chao Wang[4(✉)]

[1] State Key Laboratory of Computer Science, Institute of Software, Chinese
Academy of Sciences, Beijing, China
{jiaqw,lvyi,wp,bzhan}@ios.ac.cn
[2] University of Chinese Academy of Sciences, Beijing, China
[3] Aeronautics Computing Technique Research Institute, Xi'an, China
{haojifeng1187,mr_yehong}@163.com
[4] Southwest University, Chongqing, China
wangch1@swu.edu.cn

Abstract. Linearizability is an important correctness criterion for concurrent objects, and there have been several existing tools for checking linearizability. However, due to the inherent exponential complexity of the problem, existing tools have difficulty scaling up to large, industrial-sized concurrent objects. In this paper, we introduce VeriLin, a new linearizability checker that incorporates a more general checking algorithm as well as associated testing strategies, that allow it to continue to be effective for large-scale concurrent objects and long histories. For evaluation, we apply VeriLin to checking linearizability of student implementations of a train ticketing system, as well as the task management and scheduling module of a proprietary multicore operating system.

1 Introduction

Concurrent programming has been an important area of research in both academia and industry, resulting in increasingly complex designs and implementations of concurrent programs. Hence, there is a continuing need for more effective and scalable techniques to ensure the correctness of concurrent programs.

Linearizability [1,2] has been the *de facto* criterion for the correctness of a concurrent object (implementation). It concerns histories of the concurrent object, which characterize the concurrent object's run-time behaviors as sequences of invocation and response events of operations (a.k.a., method calls). A concurrent object is *linearizable* with respect to a sequential specification, if for each history of the concurrent object, there exists a sequential permutation of the history that is admitted by the specification, and preserves the partial order between non-overlapping operations in the history. Linearizability has been proved to be equivalent to the property of observational refinement [3]. Hence, for a linearizable concurrent object, calling its methods concurrently yields the same results as calling them sequentially, and in particular, the usual concurrency defects such as non-benign data races and atomicity violations will never occur.

C. David and M. Sun (Eds.): TASE 2023, LNCS 13931, pp. 202–220, 2023.
https://doi.org/10.1007/978-3-031-35257-7_12

Linearizability has attracted attention from the formal methods community, and many approaches of verifying linearizability have been proposed based on theorem proving [4–6] and model checking [7,8]. However, the complexity of model checking of linearizability is known to be fundamentally high, while theorem proving approaches usually involve a large amount of manual intervention.

Efforts have also been devoted to testing or monitoring of linearizability for finite, observed histories of a concurrent object. A classical algorithm for checking linearizability of a finite history is presented in [9]. It works by enumerating exhaustively all the possible sequential permutations of the history, and checking the validity of each permutation with respect to the given specification. The history is linearizable if a valid permutation is found; otherwise, the history is not linearizable, which implies that the concurrent object itself is not linearizable.

The linearizability checking problem has been shown to be NP-complete [10] in general. Hence, the state-of-the-art linearizability checkers mostly support finite histories with just 2–4 threads and up to about 100 operations per thread; while longer histories, with 10,000 or more operations per thread, are only supported for simple objects or specific ones that can be considered as collections [11,12]. It is rather difficult to scale these algorithms up to large-scale concurrent objects, which may contain thousands of lines of implementation code and consist of multiple small components.

We propose in this paper that with the use of practical testing strategies, it is possible to scale up linearizability checking, allow it to continue to be effective for large-scale objects and long histories in real-world scenarios. We first present a general framework that expresses linearizability checking as permutation search for a topological ordering that preserves the happen-before relation among the operations. During the search, we can follow different orders for choosing the next operation.

We also present a testing strategy by adding some waiting time before or after each operation when generating a history. By adjusting the waiting time, we can adjust the number and size of regions in the history, in order to balance between checking time and detection of interesting concurrency defects. These testing strategies allow for linearizability checking that can handle large-scale concurrent objects that cannot be decomposed into small components, and also detect subtle concurrency defects that do not show in short executions.

Another contribution of our paper is to incorporate testing the sequential specification of a concurrent object as an integral preparatory part of linearizability checking. Prior to checking the linearizability of a large-scale, complex concurrent object, we first validate whether its sequential specification satisfies certain logical constraints or assertions.

We implement the above approaches as the linearizability checker VeriLin. Then, we evaluate VeriLin on a number of typical concurrent objects in comparison with state-of-the-art linearizability checkers. The experimental results show that VeriLin exhibits a comparable performance as state-of-the-art checkers on small-scale cases.

We further apply VeriLin in the following two large-scale examples. One is the concurrent implementations of a train ticketing system, submitted by graduate students in a course project we assigned. The other is a real-world application to the task management and scheduling module of a proprietary multi-core operating system kernel, which is examined as a single but complex concurrent object. For both scenarios, VeriLin finds previously unknown concurrency bugs that can be confirmed by hand.

The rest of the paper is organized as follows. Section 2 reviews related work on linearizability checking and verification techniques. Section 3 shows the preliminary definitions, using the train ticketing system as an example. Section 4 presents the generic linearizability checking algorithm with different choices of ordering. Section 5 presents the testing strategies. Section 6 presents the implementation of the VeriLin checker. Section 7 evaluates the performance of VeriLin in comparison with other linearizability checkers, as well as the large-scale case studies. Finally, Sect. 8 concludes the paper with future work.

2   Related Work

Linearizability was introduced by Herlihy and Wing in the early 1990s [1], and adopted as the most prevalent correctness criterion for concurrent systems [2]. Many concurrent objects have been designed following this criterion, such as Michael-Scott queue [13] (implemented as class `ConcurrentLinkedQueue` in the `java.util.concurrent` package) and the time-stamped stack [14].

Many approaches of ensuring the linearizability of concurrent systems have been proposed based on theorem proving, model checking or testing strategies. Model checking of linearizability has been studied in [7,8,15]. Vafeiadis et al. introduced in [4] one of the first approaches for verifying linearizability through theorem proving, making use of rely-guarantee reasoning. Further work on the use of rely-guarantee reasoning for verifying concurrent data structures includes [5,6]. In [16], forward and backward simulations are adapted to reason about linearizability of concurrent algorithms. While theorem proving approaches can be applied to verify highly-complex concurrent objects, it has the disadvantage of requiring substantial manual intervention.

The classical algorithm for testing linearizability is introduced by Wing and Gong [9]. VeriTrace [17] takes the inner events of each operation into consideration in a fine-grained model. It uses segmentation for fine-grained histories and delays the read-only operations to accelerate the checking process. Lowe gave in [18] just-in-time linearization algorithms to optimize the classical algorithm so that operations can be linearized as late as possible. Similar to our approach, the algorithms in [18] consider a set of concurrent operations simultaneously. However these algorithms only decide a next operation according to its invocation time, while our approach chooses a next operation according to both its invocation time and response time. To the best of our knowledge, this is the first work to take advantage of response time order. Horn et al. [19] substantially improves the implementation of the algorithm in [9], extending the locality principle in [1] into the concept of P-compositionality. Recently, lincheck [20] has been presented to test concurrency on the JVM with respect to linearizability and other correctness criterion, e.g., interval linearizability.

All of the above testing algorithms have worst-case exponential complexity, making them not scalable to large and complex cases. The problem of testing linearizability for a single history was shown to be NP-Complete [10]. There have been efforts to find polynomial-time testing algorithms, either for an approximation of the problem or for specific types of concurrent data structures. Bouajjani et al. introduced in [21] an approximation of linearizability testing based on a parameter k, representing the degree to which refinement violations are visible. Checking the approximated problem for each k can then be done in polynomial time. Emmi et al. [11,12] designed polynomial-time algorithms for collection-type concurrent data structures, such as stacks, queues, sets and maps. In contrast to these works, we focus on testing linearizability of more complex data structures that are not simply collections, and using various testing strategies rather than approximations for scalable performance.

Emmil and Enea presented an observational refinement (linearizability) testing tool Violat [22–24], which conducts stress tests on concurrent objects with small and simple harnesses to achieve a high level of parallelism. It checks linearizability or weaker consistency properties using a precomputed set of possible outcomes. While other approaches enumerate exponentially many linearizations per execution, Violat enumerates exponentially many linearizations for the precomputed outcomes per harness schema. Ozkan et al. showed that linearizable histories can be established efficiently by through a prioritization of the search space of possible witnesses using the notion of linearizability depth [25]. The feasibility of their approach has been demonstrated by checking the linearizability of the java.util.concurrent package with small linearizability depth in small harness. However, it is not known yet whether or how their approach may apply for large-scale objects such as multi-core OS kernels.

For typical concurrency defects, other categories of testing approaches have also been developed, such as systematic testing [26–28] and active testing [29–33]. Systematic testing explores all possible interleaving executions under a given input, or within a bounded number of context switches. However, it inevitably encounters the scalability issue [26–28]. Active testing [29] first predicts suspicious interleaving executions with respect to certain types of concurrency bugs, e.g., data races [30,32] and concurrency-memory bugs [31,33], and then enforces the potential buggy interleaving executions actively to reveal bugs. Instead of tackling particular concurrency defects, in this paper we focus on a general framework for detecting any potential concurrency defects through linearizability checking.

3   Linearizability

We present in this section the basic terminologies about concurrent objects, and the formal definition of linearizability [1], followed by the train ticketing system as the running example.

Without loss of generality, we consider object-oriented concurrent programs. A concurrent datatype contains several methods. We assume we are given the concrete implementations of these methods, and possibly also an abstract specification. The abstract specification may also include assertions constraining the behavior of the methods.

An execution of a method is called an *operation*. In the coarse-grained model considered in this paper, each operation consists of two *events*: invocation (*inv*) and response (*rsp*). An invocation event has the form $O.inv(m, arg, t)$, where m is the name of the method invoked on the object O, arg is the argument provided to this method, and t is the thread number. A response event has the form $O.rsp(m, res, t)$, where O, m and t are the same as before, and res is the return value. The operation (combination of invocation and response events) is denoted $O.op(m, arg, res, t)$.

A *history* for a concurrent execution of an object consists of a sequence of invocation and response events. Event e_1 *happens before* event e_2 in history h, denoted $e_1 \prec e_2$, if e_1 appears in front of e_2 in h. In a history, each response event of an operation must happen after the corresponding invocation event. Operation op_1 *happens before* operation op_2, denoted $op_1 \prec op_2$, if the response event of op_1 happens before the invocation event of op_2. Operations op_1 and op_2 *overlap* if neither $op_1 \prec op_2$ nor $op_2 \prec op_1$.

Each response event is *matched* with its corresponding invocation event with the same method name and thread number. An invocation event is *pending* if no response event can be matched with it. History h is *complete* if all invocation events have their matched response events in h. Let $h \mid t$ be the projection of h on thread t, i.e. a sequence of operations of thread t only.

A history h is *sequential* if it starts with an invocation event and, for each operation, its response event appears right next to its invocation event in h. History h is *well-formed* if $h \mid t$ is sequential for each thread t. In this paper, we consider the well-formed and complete history.

A *sequential specification* S is a set of allowed sequential histories (subject to, e.g., the abstract specification). A *sequential witness* of history h is a permutation of h that is sequential and preserves all the happen-before relations between the operations in the history. A complete history h of an object is *linearizable* with respect to a sequential specification S if there exists a sequential witness s of h such that $s \in S$. An object is *linearizable* with respect to a sequential specification S if all of its histories are linearizable with respect to S. For a linearizable history, each operation can be considered as taking effect at a linearization point, located between its invocation and response events.

3.1   Train Ticketing System

We now introduce the train ticketing system as an example to demonstrate the concepts presented above. The train ticketing system models an application for buying and selling tickets for $m > 0$ trains. Each train has $l > 0$ coaches and each coach has $k > 0$ seats. Moreover, each train travels a sequence of stations. A *ticket* consists of a train number, a coach number, a seat number, a departure station and an arrival station. Suppose n clients run on separate threads, and access the train ticketing system concurrently to buy tickets (`buyTicket`), refund tickets (`refundTicket`), and inquire the number of the remaining tickets (`inquiry`).

The challenge is to implement the functions of the train ticketing system with fine-grained concurrency, so that it can (when deployed on a multi-core computer) simultaneously handle multiple requests for different trains. Implementing this system is assigned as a course project in a class about concurrent programming. Students can choose to implement the system using various synchronization techniques, such as fine-grained locks for each train and coach, or lock-free concurrent data structures. The linearizability checker introduced in this paper is used to automatically grade the students' submissions by attempting to find sequential and concurrency bugs in their submissions.

We now give an example illustrating the definitions. Consider the history shown in Fig. 1. Thread t_1 has three operations: buying a ticket twice and refunding the first one bought. They are named op_1, op_2 and op_3. Thread t_2 has one operation op_4 inquiring the number of available tickets. All the operations are for train 1, departure station 1, and arrival station 5. We assume train 1 has only one coach with two seats `1A` and `1B`. On thread t_1, the first purchase returns ticket T_1 with seat `1B`; the second purchase returns ticket T_2 with seat `1A`; and the refund of T_1 is successful. On thread t_2, the inquiry returns that the number of available tickets is 2. The relations among the operations are: $op_1 \prec op_2$, $op_1 \prec op_3$, $op_1 \prec op_4$, $op_2 \prec op_3$, and op_4 overlaps with both op_2 and op_3. This history cannot be linearized: however we order op_4 in the candidate witness of that history (subject to the restriction that it comes after op_1), the number of available tickets should be either 0 or 1. One possible cause of this error is a data-race defect: when the inquiry operation starts, it first looks up the availability of seat `1A`, and finds it available. Then seat `1A` is purchased followed by the refund of seat `1B`, the inquiry resumes looking up the availability of seat `1B` and also finds it available. One solution to this problem is to place a lock on access to the entire train during the inquiry operation.

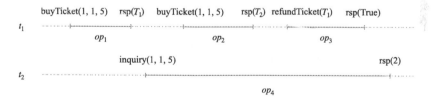

Fig. 1. A non-linearizable history. Here T_1 is `Ticket(1,1,1B,1,5)` and T_2 is `Ticket(1,1,1A,1,5)`. We assume there is only one coach with seats `1A` and `1B`.

4   Checking Algorithm

We first review the linearizability testing method of Wing & Gong [9] and further developed by Lowe [18]. For each history H to be tested, this method enumerates sequential witnesses of the history and checks validity of each sequential witness.

For this method, checking time on a linearizable history depends heavily on the order of enumerating sequential witnesses. Both [9] and [18] use a relatively simple strategy: the next operation is chosen in the order of invocation time.

We now present a more general algorithm for linearizability checking. The main idea of this algorithm is similar to topological sorting, as a given history can be modelled as a directed acyclic graph (DAG), in which operations can be seen as nodes and happen-before relations can be as edges. A topological order, which is an essential part of topological sorting, will determine the choice of a next operation. The topological order of operations varies and depends on the concrete implementation of each concurrent object, e.g., in the order of their invocation or response time, or by making a random choice, while in the literature a fixed order of their invocation time, are only adopted for linearizability checking. The main work-flow of this topological ordering based algorithm is presented as Algorithm 1. Although its time complexity remains the same as in the literature, by applying an appropriate order, it is more likely to establish a linearization of a given history with better efficiency, i.e., less time consumption.

Algorithm 1. Main Algorithm of Checking Linearizability

Require: cur ▷ currently enumerating sequence, on the top
Require: DAG ▷ graph of operations by happen-before order
Require: S ▷ specification object
1: **function** CHECK_LINEARIZABILITY(DAG, cur, S)
2:    **if** $DAG = \emptyset$ **then**
3:        **return** true
4:    **end if**
5:    **for** node in DAG whose in-degree is 0 by a pre-specified topological order **do**
6:        res ← run node's operation in S
7:        **if** res = return value of node **then**
8:            cur.push(node)
9:            delete node and all its edges from DAG
10:            **if** CHECK_LINEARIZABILITY(DAG, cur, S) **then**
11:                **return** true ▷ found a valid sequence.
12:            **else**
13:                recover node and its edges in DAG
14:                recover operation in S
15:                cur.pop()
16:            **end if**
17:        **end if**
18:    **end for**
19:    **return** false
20: **end function**

This algorithm will check the linearizability of a given history h. The input to the algorithm is the currently enumerating sequence cur, the graph of remaining operations DAG, and the specification object S. We assume that no valid sequential witness has been found prior to cur. The returned value of the algorithm indicates whether the history is linearizable. In the algorithm, if DAG is empty, then return true (Line 1,2), since the current sequence cur forms a linearization of h. Otherwise, for each node in DAG, we search over nodes whose in-degree is 0 (Line 5), based on the pre-specified topological order. For each node, we run the corresponding operation in S and get the result res (Line 6). If res equals the result of node (Line 7), meaning the current operation does not violate validity, then update cur and DAG (Line 8,9), and recursively check linearizability on their new values (Line 10). If this results in a valid sequential history, return true (Line 11); otherwise we recover cur and DAG (Line 13–15) and continue to the next node in the search. If all nodes are exhausted, meaning there is no valid sequential witness for the input value of cur and DAG, return false (Line 19). The algorithm is initially called on the DAG containing all operations in h, and the empty sequence for cur, and returns whether h is linearizable.

Intuitively, the order of picking the next operation in the valid sequential witness depends on the linearization point of each operation, which relies on the implementation of the concurrent object. Hence, different searching order may be more effective for different concurrent objects, or even different histories of a single concurrent object. In the evaluation in Sect. 7, we will show that trying both invocation and response time will improve the searching time overall in a large case study.

Regions. In our implementation, a history is divided into a sequence of *regions*. Each pair of consecutive regions is separated by a quiescence period where no operation takes place. The use of regions shows clearly the division of the history into non-overlapping parts. For example, in Fig. 2, the history can be divided into three regions. The division into regions does not affect the algorithm itself in a significant way. For example, if no valid sequential witness is found during a search in Region 2 and 3 in Fig. 2, it is necessary to backtrack and try other orderings of operations in Region 1. Hence, we do not show the division of regions in Algorithm 1. However, the sizes of regions (in terms of the number of operations) affect the actual amount of search done by the algorithm, and we will use this size as a measure of complexity of the search problem in the following sections.

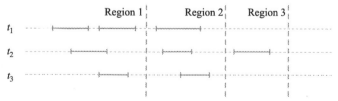

Fig. 2. Example where the history is segmented into three regions.

5   Testing Strategies for Large-Scale Objects

The techniques described in Sect. 4 serve to speed up linearizability checking, especially for linearizable histories. However, without further techniques, the checking process will still run out of time on the more complex cases. In this section, we describe one testing strategy that is effective for adjusting the difficulty of linearizability checking in terms of region size. We further describe the combination of linearizability checking with testing of sequential specifications in VeriLin.

In practice it is rather vital for a linearizability checker to be able to handle long histories, especially for detecting subtle hidden bugs in large-scale objects. Although short histories may be exploited to mimic corner cases (e.g., a shared container object is full) by limiting the parameters (e.g., size) of the concurrent object under test, this does not work for third-party concurrent objects with immutable parameters. For example, the error of a fixed size buggy bounded queue happens only when this queue is full but more than one thread tries to enqueue elements into this queue concurrently. Furthermore, even when a concurrency bug can be detected and fixed through short histories, it remains uncertain in general whether the revised implementation can function correctly along long histories. Hence, it is still necessary to certifying the linearizability of these long histories for a more robust validation.

5.1 Control of Waiting Time

The efficiency of linearizability checking algorithms on a history depends very much on the size of regions in the history (or more precisely, on the amount of overlaps between operations in each region of the history). Larger regions mean more overlaps between operations, which lead to bigger search space in looking for a sequential witness. On the other hand, smaller regions make testing less effective for finding concurrency defects. Hence, it is desirable to have some way to tune the size of a region when generating the history from execution of the concurrent object.

We propose a strategy for this purpose that works generally for any concurrent object. It works by inserting extra waiting time before, during, or after the execution of some operation. When there are too many operations in a region, extra waiting time before the invocation events and after the response events of operations help reduce the overlaps between operations, and hence the size of the region. When there are too few operations in a region, extra waiting time within some operation (e.g. before or after a write instruction) help increase the possibility of overlaps between operations. VeriLin provides a simple method to insert wait instructions into the program under test, after the user provides the desired waiting times. These waiting times can then be tuned to achieve the desired region size.

5.2 Validation of Sequential Specification

Sequential specification is a necessary input for checking linearizability. The work [17] takes sequential execution of the tested concurrent object as the specification. When the concurrent object is too complex, the sequential specification itself may be error-prone, and should be tested on its own. Clearly, there is little point checking for concurrency defects when the sequential specification of the program is wrong.

To address this problem, VeriLin offers a mechanism for validating the sequential specification on user-inserted constraints. After inserting constraints as assertions in the program, VeriLin checks sequential histories generated in a random manner for system faults and violations of assertions. If any errors are found, this error can be reproduced using a replay-and-check mechanism.

6 Implementation

We implemented the techniques presented in previous sections as a Java-based linearizability checker VeriLin. The implementation code, together with the evaluations on the benchmark examples and the train ticketing system implementations, are available at https://github.com/Qiaowen-Jia/VeriLin. The evaluation on the multicore OS kernel module is available as jar packages due to proprietary reason.

In this section, we describe the architecture and implementation of VeriLin in detail. First, we give an overview for the architecture of the tool. Then we describe its two working modes: manual mode and automatic mode. Finally, we describe how to set and debug specifications.

6.1 Overview

Figure 4 shows the overall architecture of VeriLin. To adapt to different testing requirements, VeriLin provides a flexible interface supporting two different modes: manual and automatic mode. Moreover, VeriLin supports various kinds of specifications, and methods for debugging specifications using the replay mechanism (Fig. 3).

Input/Output. The input to VeriLin consists of three files in the general case: object file, specification file and configuration file. The object file is always necessary, containing the code for the concurrent object to be tested. The configuration file contains basic settings such as file name, method list, properties of methods such as reversibility and classification into read/write methods, etc. The specification file can also be omitted if built-in specification or the object file is used.

The output of VeriLin is the result of linearizability checking: whether the generated history is linearizable or not. If the history is not linearizable, the shortest non-linearizable prefix is provided for debugging purposes.

6.2 Manual Mode

In the manual mode, the user is involved in providing and tuning the configurations, as well as detailed instrumentation of the object file, during the checking process. Checking in this mode consists of the following stages.

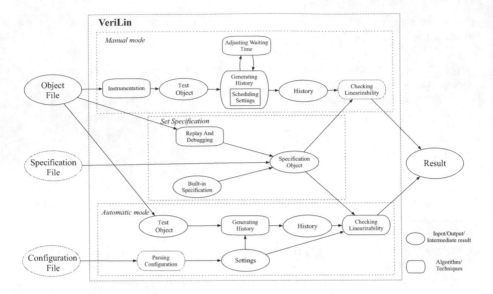

Fig. 3. The Main Structure of VeriLin

- **Instrumentation.** The user can instrument arbitrary positions of the object file to provide more information for the latter stages. These instrumentations serve at least two purposes. First, the user can specify custom call and return locations for methods (overriding the default of beginning and end of each method). Second, the user can print information about the state into the history. These are ignored by the linearizability checker but can be helpful for debugging the non-linearizable cases.
- **Generating history.** Various configurations are provided and adjusted by the user during the generating history stage. In particular, extra waiting times before, after, and within operations can be adjusted at this time in order to tune the size of regions in the resulting history, for a balance between checking time and the ability to find defects. In this stage, VeriLin does not rely on other stress testing or model checking tools to explore histories, but simply picks up randomly a given number of operations for each given number of threads.
- **Checking linearizability.** This stage implements the algorithm and techniques introduced in Sect. 4 to perform linearizability checking.

6.3   Automatic Mode

In the automatic mode, VeriLin performs generating history and linearizability checking steps fully automatically from the given object file and configuration file. VeriLin has a built-in parser for parsing configuration and generate settings for testing, the parser also uses Java Parser to parse the test object and specification object.

6.4 Setting and Debugging Specifications

Obtaining the correct sequential specification for the concurrent object to be tested is an important part of the testing process. VeriLin provides three ways to set the specification: built-in specification, the object file itself, and a separate executable specification.

- **Built-in specification.** These are used for concurrent data structures with standard interfaces. VeriLin provides five built-in specifications: queue, stack, list, set and double-ended queue (deque).
- **Object file.** User can choose to treat the sequential-executing test object as the specification in order to focus on finding concurrency defects.
- **User-provided specification.** User can provide an abstract executable specification. More specifically, the specification is a Java implementation of the sequential version of the object. In addition to the executable implementation, the specification may also contain assertions that constrain its behavior. These assertions will be checked during sequential correctness checking.

In the latter two cases, VeriLin provides a replay mechanism to help users test and debug the specification, as described in Sect. 5.2. After a sequential bug is detected, VeriLin allows replaying the sequence of operations on the user interface, so that the user can see the results of operations step-by-step. Only after the sequential test is passed, VeriLin proceeds to the linearizability checking stage.

7 Experimental Evaluation

In this section, we evaluate VeriLin on typical concurrent objects, train ticketing system implementations, and a multi-core OS kernel module, in comparison with the state-of-the-art linearizability checkers: lincheck [20], VeriTrace [17], and Lowe's implementation of TFL in [18]. Among these tools, lincheck and TFL are developed in Kotlin and Scala, respectively, while VeriTrace and VeriLin are developed in Java. Hence, these tools can handle concurrent objects in different languages, and use different implementations of histories that are not compatible with each other. Thus we can only run each tool with histories generated by itself. The evaluation runs on a Ubuntu 18.04 machine with Intel Xeon CPU E7-8850, 2TB memory and Java 11, while the tools comparison runs on a Ubuntu 20.04 machine with Intel Xeon CPU E5-2673, 512G memory and Java 14.

7.1 Evaluation on Typical Concurrent Objects

We first use five typical concurrent objects: an optimistic list, a lazy list, the Treiber's *Lock-free Stack*, the Michael-Scott *Lock-free Queue* [13] from Herlihy et al.'s textbook [2], and the concurrent linked double-ended queue `Concurrent-LinkedDeque` implemented in the Java concurrency package, to demonstrate

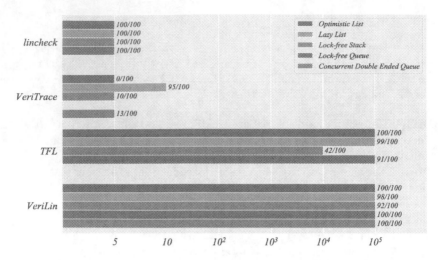

Fig. 4. Comparison results on the typical concurrent objects. The x-axis shows the largest scale, of which a concurrent object can be handled with a definite answer within 10 min.

the comparable basic performance of VeriLin, in comparison with other related tools.

Figure 4 shows the performance of VeriLin and the other three checkers in terms of the ratio $X/100$ of the number of successful runs among a total of 100 runs, with a time limit of 10 min. A run is successful if it returns a definite answer. Histories are generated for four concurrent threads, with the number of operations per thread ranging in 5, 10, 10^2, 10^3, 10^4 and 10^5. The missing cases in Fig. 4 are due to lack of implementations in the corresponding tools' artifacts. The setting for VeriLin are default ones: response-time ordering and no delays.

It can be seen in Fig. 4 that neither lincheck nor VeriTrace can handle more than 10^2 operations per thread, while TFL can scale up to 10^4 or 10^5 operations per thread. VeriLin scales up to 10^5 operations per thread on all of the above examples. Note that TFL in [18] has been optimized specially for lists and queues, while VeriLin treated such concurrent objects uniformly, and still obtained the best performances.

7.2   Evaluation on Train Ticketing System Implementations

In total 103 Java implementations of the train ticketing system have been collected from students in a graduate course project. The sizes of the implementations range from 250 to 1,700 lines of code. We build a straightforward sequential specification object with a coarse-grained lock to check the linearizability of these implementations. Histories are generated for 4 concurrent threads, with the number of operations per thread chosen to be 250, 500, 1000 and 2000 (hence for a total of $4 \times 103 = 412$ sets of experiments). Most checks terminated successfully within 5 min, while some run out of time (30 min).

Table 1. Invocation Time vs. Response Time

Size	$r \geq 10$	$r \in [2, 10)$	$r \in (0.5, 2)$	$r \in (0.1, 0.5]$	$r \leq 0.1$	InvTO	RespTO	DualTO
4 × 250	7/103	15/103	63/103	13/103	5/103	202	177	136
4 × 500	6/103	15/103	64/103	10/103	8/103	207	182	141
4 × 1,000	7/103	17/103	68/103	4/103	7/103	215	178	142
4 × 2,000	8/103	15/103	68/103	9/103	3/103	207	181	138

Invocation Time vs. Response Time. Table 1 compares the performances of VeriLin on various size scales when choosing ordering by either invocation time or response time. Three strategies are evaluated for this comparison: the invocation-only and response-only strategy use only operations' invocation time and response time, respectively; while the dual strategy tries ordering by invocation time and response time simultaneously in parallel, and takes the run that terminates first, with the other run halted immediately.

Table 2. Linearizability checking of all the train ticketing system implementations

Size	Delay	#Non-linearizable Histories	#Buggy Implementations	Time
4 × 250	0 ms	2,034	40/103	3d 5 h 51 m 59 s
	1 ms	2,024	31/103	4 h 25 m 33 s
	10 ms	2,007	26/103	10 h 37 m 41 s
4 × 500	0 ms	2,038	40/103	3d 4 h 40 m 59 s
	1 ms	2,027	33/103	5 h 55 m 34 s
	10 ms	2,026	26/103	18 h 43 m 22 s
4 × 1,000	0 ms	2,052	46/103	3d 18 h 10 m 33 s
	1 ms	2,062	33/103	8 h 45 m 2 2 s
	10 ms	2,065	28/103	1d 10 h 18 m 50 s
4 × 2,000	0 ms	2,078	46/103	4d 9 h 13 m 52 s
	1 ms	2,085	35/103	14 h 3 m 50 s
	10 ms	2,137	27/103	2d 17 h 11 m 53 s

The inv-resp ratio r is the ratio between the time taken by the invocation-time ordering to the time taken by the response-time ordering. Columns 2–6 in Table 1 report the numbers of implementations, for which the values of r fall in the corresponding ranges.

It can be seen that for more than 36% (149/412) of the experiments, one order outperforms the other by more than 2-fold (i.e. the four columns in Table 1 with $r \geq 2$ or $r \leq 0.5$), and for more than 12% (51/412) of the experiments, one order outperforms the other by more than 10-fold (i.e. the two columns with $r \geq 10$ or $r \leq 0.1$). For some histories, the inv-resp ratio can even reach 10,000. Hence, the dual strategy can dynamically reduce the testing time, although it requires twice the amount of testing resources. More importantly, as shown in Table 1, the number DualTO of timeouts under the dual strategy is much less than the number RespTO of timeouts under the response-only strategy, which is in turn much less than the number InvTO of timeouts under the invocation-only strategy. Therefore, more errors may be potentially found with the dual strategy. So the following tests all use the dual strategy.

Waiting Time. Sequential histories of these 103 implementations are examined 100 times at size $4 \times 1,000$, and we find 19 buggy implementations. Then, we examined their concurrent histories with sizes as in Table 1, and found 40 more implementations with concurrency faults, as shown in Table 2. We rerun these tests with time delays introduced explicitly, and found 4 more implementations with subtle concurrency faults: 3 found with 1ms delay at size $4 \times 2,000$, and 1 found with 10ms delay at size $4 \times 1,000$. This suggests that introducing explicit time delays can help detect fresh unknown bugs, although the total number of bugs detected is reduced noticeably, thanks to the reduced testing time consumption in most cases.

7.3   Evaluation on a Multicore OS Kernel Module

As another case study, we consider the task management and scheduling module in a proprietary multi-core operating system kernel, which adopts preemptive scheduling based on task priorities. Interrupts are used for inter-core communications, including notifying other cores to reschedule or perform another task management operation.

We implement a Java model of the task management and scheduling module, where executions on different cores are modeled using threads, and the interrupt mechanism is modeled using shared objects. The size of the model is about 3,000 lines of code. We consider the whole model as a single concurrent object, with top-level methods for creating, starting, stopping, resuming, deleting a task, setting the priority or affinity of a task, and so on.

We generate histories with four concurrent threads, and the number of operations per thread ranges over 125, 250, 500 and 1,000. For each test, 100 random histories are generated. The linearizability checking results of a buggy version are reported in Table 3. Column "#Regions" shows the average number of distinct regions in a history. Column "Max Region Size" shows the average size of the largest region in a history. Column "#Solved" shows the number of successful runs of VeriLin within 30 min. Column "Time" shows the total testing time of the 100 runs. It can be seen that with explicit time delays before and after operations, the average maximum size of a region decreases significantly, and more runs of linearizability checking terminates successfully within a reasonable amount of time.

VeriLin found 8 bugs in the Java model in total. 5 of these bugs are due to the Java model itself, e.g., language difference, boundary error, initialization or synchronization errors. The remaining 3 bugs correspond to real defects in the original module implementation, which are confirmed by checking the original C programs by hand. For example, one of these bugs is a linearizability violation as follows.

Task $task_1$ on thread t_1 requests a resource res, which is occupied by task $task_2$ on another thread t_2. Then, $task_1$ finds that the resource's lock is locked,

Table 3. Linearizability checking of a Multicore OS Kernel Module

Size	Delay	#Regions	Max Region Size	#Solved	Time
4×125	0 ms	74	45	28/100	1d 12 h 0 m 23 s
	1 ms	162	6	41/100	1d 7 h 41 m 49 s
	10 ms	188	3	88/100	7 h 22 m 15 s
4×250	0 ms	141	66	10/100	1d 21 h 27 m 15 s
	1 ms	339	7	30/100	1d 14 h 2 m 26 s
	10 ms	375	3	72/100	15 h 42 m 50 s
4×500	0 ms	183	49	7/100	1d 23 h 22 m 55 s
	1 ms	694	5	26/100	1d 15 h 58 m 22 s
	10 ms	754	3	71/100	16 h 40 m 3 s
$4 \times 1,000$	0 ms	818	57	3/100	2d 0 h 38 m 38 s
	1 ms	1,356	7	21/100	1d 17 h 56 m 48 s
	10 ms	1,529	3	70/100	16 h 44 m 22 s

points its resource queue to the resource waiting queue of res and prepares to enter this resource waiting queue. At this time, the resource waiting queue of res is still empty. Then, the kernel schedules t_2 to proceed to release res. Task $task_2$ first queries the resource waiting queue of res, and finds it empty, indicating that no task is waiting for the resource. So, $task_2$ releases the lock of res directly and finishes releasing the resource. Then, the kernel schedules t_1 to proceed to place itself in the resource waiting queue and to finish its request for the resource. At the end of this request, $task_1$ does not get the resource.

However, there is no valid sequential history for the above concurrent history. In an sequential execution, there are only two possible permutations: either $task_1$ requests res first and $task_2$ releases res later, or vice versa. In both cases, $task_1$ would always obtain res successfully at the end of both operations.

8 Conclusion

In this paper, we presented VeriLin, an integrated environment for checking linearizability of concurrent objects. We developed several strategies to help VeriLin finish linearizability checking in more cases, especially for linearizable histories. We further developed testing strategies that make VeriLin applicable to large-scale objects. Finally, we compared VeriLin with several other linearizability checkers on typical concurrent objects, and applied it on student implementations of the train ticketing system and a module of a proprietary multi-core operating system kernel. The experimental results show that VeriLin is highly effective as a linearizability checking tool for industry-level concurrent objects.

Currently, the waiting time between or within operations can only be adjusted manually in order to tune the size of a region. In future work, we plan to study automated tuning techniques through, e.g., placing more control on thread scheduling, so as to control the region size more precisely. We also plan to extend VeriLin to check other large-scale concurrent systems and correctness criteria.

Acknowledgements. We sincerely thank the anonymous reviewers for their insightful comments. We also thank all the students participating in our UCAS graduate course project. This work is supported in part by the National Natural Science Foundation of China (62002298, 62072443, 62032019, and 61732019), the National Key R&D Program of China (2022YFA1005100, 2022YFA1005101, and 2022YFA1005104), the Fundamental Research Funds for the Central Universities (SWU019036), and the Capacity Development Grant of Southwest University (SWU116007).

References

1. Herlihy, M.P., Wing, J.M.: Linearizability: a correctness condition for concurrent objects. ACM Trans. Program. Lang. Syst. (TOPLAS) **12**, 463–492 (1990)
2. Herlihy, M., Shavit, N., Luchangco, V., Spear, M.: The art of multiprocessor programming. Newnes (2020)
3. Filipovic, I., O'Hearn, P.W., Rinetzky, N., Yang, H.: Abstraction for concurrent objects. Theor. Comput. Sci. **411**, 4379–4398 (2010)
4. Vafeiadis, V., Herlihy, M., Hoare, T., Shapiro, M.: Proving correctness of highly-concurrent linearisable objects. In: Proceedings of the ACM SIGPLAN Symposium on Principles and Practice of Parallel Programming, PPOPP 2006, New York, New York, USA, 29–31 March 2006, pp. 129–136 (2006)
5. Liang, H., Feng, X.: Modular verification of linearizability with non-fixed linearization points. In: Proceedings of the 34th ACM SIGPLAN Conference on Programming Language Design and Implementation, pp. 459–470 (2013)
6. Vafeiadis, V.: Modular fine-grained concurrency verification. Technical report, University of Cambridge, Computer Laboratory (2008)
7. Alur, R., McMillan, K., Peled, D.: Model-checking of correctness conditions for concurrent objects. Inf. Comput. **160**, 167–188 (2000)
8. Bouajjani, A., Emmi, M., Enea, C., Hamza, J.: Verifying concurrent programs against sequential specifications. In: Felleisen, M., Gardner, P. (eds.) ESOP 2013. LNCS, vol. 7792, pp. 290–309. Springer, Heidelberg (2013). https://doi.org/10.1007/978-3-642-37036-6_17
9. Wing, J.M., Gong, C.: Testing and verifying concurrent objects. J. Parallel Distrib. Comput. **17**, 164–182 (1993)
10. Gibbons, P.B., Korach, E.: Testing shared memories. SIAM J. Comput. **26**, 1208–1244 (1997)
11. Emmi, M., Enea, C., Hamza, J.: Monitoring refinement via symbolic reasoning. In: Proceedings of the 36th ACM SIGPLAN Conference on Programming Language Design and Implementation, Portland, OR, USA, 15–17 June 2015, pp. 260–269 (2015)
12. Emmi, M., Enea, C.: Sound, complete, and tractable linearizability monitoring for concurrent collections. Proc. ACM Program. Lang. **2**, 25:1–25:27 (2018)
13. Michael, M.M., Scott, M.L.: Simple, fast, and practical non-blocking and blocking concurrent queue algorithms. In: Proceedings of the Fifteenth Annual ACM Symposium on Principles of Distributed Computing, pp. 267–275 (1996)

14. Dodds, M., Haas, A., Kirsch, C.M.: A scalable, correct time-stamped stack. ACM SIGPLAN Not. **50**, 233–246 (2015)
15. Burckhardt, S., Dern, C., Musuvathi, M., Tan, R.: Line-up: a complete and automatic linearizability checker. In: Proceedings of the 31st ACM SIGPLAN Conference on Programming Language Design and Implementation, pp. 330–340 (2010)
16. Schellhorn, G., Wehrheim, H., Derrick, J.: How to prove algorithms linearisable. In: Madhusudan, P., Seshia, S.A. (eds.) CAV 2012. LNCS, vol. 7358, pp. 243–259. Springer, Heidelberg (2012). https://doi.org/10.1007/978-3-642-31424-7_21
17. Long, Z., Zhang, Y.: Checking linearizability with fine-grained traces. In: Proceedings of the 31st Annual ACM Symposium on Applied Computing, pp. 1394–1400 (2016)
18. Lowe, G.: Testing for linearizability. Concurrency Comput. Pract. Experience **29**, e3928 (2017)
19. Horn, A., Kroening, D.: Faster linearizability checking via P-compositionality. In: Graf, S., Viswanathan, M. (eds.) FORTE 2015. LNCS, vol. 9039, pp. 50–65. Springer, Cham (2015). https://doi.org/10.1007/978-3-319-19195-9_4
20. Koval, N., Sokolova, M., Fedorov, A., Alistarh, D., Tsitelov, D.: Testing concurrency on the JVM with lincheck. In: Proceedings of the 25th ACM SIGPLAN Symposium on Principles and Practice of Parallel Programming, pp. 423–424 (2020)
21. Bouajjani, A., Emmi, M., Enea, C., Hamza, J.: Tractable refinement checking for concurrent objects. In: Proceedings of the 42nd Annual ACM SIGPLAN-SIGACT Symposium on Principles of Programming Languages, POPL 2015, Mumbai, India, 15–17 January 2015, pp. 651–662 (2015)
22. Emmi, M., Enea, C.: Violat: generating tests of observational refinement for concurrent objects. In: Dillig, I., Tasiran, S. (eds.) CAV 2019. LNCS, vol. 11562, pp. 534–546. Springer, Cham (2019). https://doi.org/10.1007/978-3-030-25543-5_30
23. Emmi, M., Enea, C.: Monitoring weak consistency. In: Chockler, H., Weissenbacher, G. (eds.) CAV 2018. LNCS, vol. 10981, pp. 487–506. Springer, Cham (2018). https://doi.org/10.1007/978-3-319-96145-3_26
24. Emmi, M., Enea, C.: Weak-consistency specification via visibility relaxation. Proc. ACM Program. Lang. **3**, 60:1–60:28 (2019)
25. Ozkan, B.K., Majumdar, R., Niksic, F.: Checking linearizability using hitting families. In: Hollingsworth, J.K., Keidar, I. (eds.) Proceedings of the 24th ACM SIGPLAN Symposium on Principles and Practice of Parallel Programming, PPoPP 2019, Washington, DC, USA, 16–20 February 2019, pp. 366–377. ACM (2019)
26. Godefroid, P.: Model checking for programming languages using VeriSoft. In: Proceedings of the 24th ACM Symposium on Principles of Programming Languages (POPL 1997), pp. 174–186 (1997)
27. Musuvathi, M., Qadeer, S.: CHESS: systematic stress testing of concurrent software. In: Puebla, G. (ed.) LOPSTR 2006. LNCS, vol. 4407, pp. 15–16. Springer, Heidelberg (2007). https://doi.org/10.1007/978-3-540-71410-1_2
28. Musuvathi, M., Qadeer, S., Ball, T., Basler, G., Nainar, P.A., Neamtiu, I.: Finding and reproducing heisenbugs in concurrent programs. In: Proceedings of the 8th USENIX Conference on Operating Systems Design and Implementation (OSDI 2008), pp. 267–280 (2008)
29. Yu, J., Narayanasamy, S., Pereira, C., Pokam, G.: Maple: A coverage-driven testing tool for multithreaded programs. In: Proceedings of ACM International Conference on Object Oriented Programming Systems Languages and Applications (OOPSLA 2012), pp. 485–502 (2012)

30. Sen, K.: Race directed random testing of concurrent programs. In: Proceedings of the 29th ACM International Conference on Programming Language Design and Implementation (PLDI 2008), pp. 11–21 (2008)

31. Zhang, W., Sun, C., Lu, S.: ConMem: detecting severe concurrency bugs through an effect-oriented approach. In: Proceedings of the 15th ACM International Conference on Architectural Support for Programming Languages and Operating Systems (ASPLOS XV), pp. 179–192 (2010)

32. Yue, H., Wu, P., Chen, T.Y., Lv, Y.: Input-driven active testing of multi-threaded programs. In: Proceedings of 2015 Asia-Pacific Software Engineering Conference (APSEC 2015), pp. 246–253 (2015)

33. Ma, L., Wu, P., Chen, T.Y.: Diversity driven adaptive test generation for concurrent data structures. Inf. Softw. Technol. **103**, 162–173 (2018)

Identifying Minimal Changes in the Zone Abstract Domain

Kenny Ballou$^{(\boxtimes)}$ (ID) and Elena Sherman (ID)

Boise State University, Boise, USA
kennyballou@u.boisestate.edu, elenasherman@boisestate.edu

Abstract. Verification techniques express program states as logical formulas over program variables. For example, symbolic execution and abstract interpretation encode program states as a set of linear integer inequalities. However, for real-world programs these formulas tend to become large, which affects scalability of analyses. To address this problem, researchers developed complementary approaches which either remove redundant inequalities or extract a subset of inequalities sufficient for specific reasoning, *i.e.,* formula slicing. For arbitrary linear integer inequalities, such reduction approaches either have high complexities or over-approximate. However, efficiency and precision of these approaches can be improved for a restricted type of logical formulas used in relational numerical abstract domains. While previous work investigated custom efficient redundant inequality elimination for Zones states, our work examines custom semantic slicing algorithms that identify a minimal set of changed inequalities in Zones states.

The client application of the minimal changes in Zones is an empirical study on comparison between invariants computed by data-flow analysis using Zones, Intervals and Predicates numerical domains. In particular, evaluations compare how our proposed algorithms affect the precision of comparing Zones vs. Intervals and Zones vs. Predicates abstract domains. The results show our techniques reduce the number of variables by more than 70% and the number of linear inequalities by 30%, comparing to those of full states. The approach refines the granularity of comparison between domains, reducing incomparable invariants between Zones and Predicates from 52% to 4%, and increases equality of Intervals and Zones, invariants from 27% to 71%. Finally, the techniques improve the comparison efficiency by reducing total runtime for all subject comparisons for Zones and Predicates from over four minutes to a few seconds.

Keywords: Abstract domains · Abstract interpretation · Static analysis · Program analysis

1 Introduction

Many verification techniques express a program state as a logical formula over program variables. For example, symbolic execution uses a logical formula to describe a path constraint; in abstract interpretation, relational domains such

C. David and M. Sun (Eds.): TASE 2023, LNCS 13931, pp. 221–239, 2023.
https://doi.org/10.1007/978-3-031-35257-7_13

as Zones or Polyhedra use a set of linear integer inequalities to describe program invariants. While expressive, this logical representation can become quite difficult to handle efficiently. For example, when symbolic execution traverses deep paths, or when relational domains encode numerous program variables. The increase in formula size causes verification tasks to run out of memory or timeout. Thus, to improve scalability, verification techniques need to efficiently handle these large logical formulas.

To overcome this predicament, researchers consider two complementary approaches. The first one focuses on eliminating the number of redundant constraints using techniques such as Motzkin-Chernikova-Le Verge [6,21] algorithm for linear integer inequalities. Previous work, for example, used it to minimize path constraints in symbolic execution [22].

The second approach focuses on identifying a minimal set of constraints necessary to reason about a specific task, for example, identifying a set of linear inequalities affected by state change. Green [33] performs the slicing operation on a path constraint formula to determine a set of linear inequalities affected by a newly added constraint. Identifying relevant constraints reduces the query size sent to an SMT solver to check for satisfiability.

However, these minimization techniques assume a general format of linear inequalities, which for a logical formula over linear integer inequalities of restricted types, may incur complexity cost or obtain a non-optimal solution. In abstract interpretation, most popular abstract relational domains such as Zones [24] or Octagons [26] restrict the type of linear inequalities they encode. Researches noted that Motzkin-Chernikova-Le Verge algorithm has a high complexity and in some cases exponential complexity [34] when applied to eliminate redundant linear inequalities. Leveraging the efficient encoding for the Zones domain, Larsen *et al.* [19] developed a more efficient algorithm which removes redundant constraints, with cubic complexity with respect to the number of program variables.

The slicing technique proposed in Green uses syntax-based rules to compute transitive dependencies of constraints. While sound, this approach might over-approximate the set of affected linear inequalities. Applying a precise "semantic-based" slicing for a general linear inequality is a difficult problem. However, as this work shows for Zones domain, it reduces to quadratic complexity. In this work we propose several specialized algorithms for computing a minimal changed set of linear inequalities for the Zones domain. For efficient encodings and operations, relational numerical domains use rewriting rules [28] to convert linear constraints into a canonical form. We also identify challenges such a canonical representation causes in identifying minimal changes in an abstract state.

We evaluate our approach in the context of a data-flow analysis framework [18], where abstract interpretation computes invariants over program variables. Researchers in areas such as program verification [5,35] or program optimization [1,17] use the computed invariants to accomplish their respective goals.

The goal is to improve the precision of comparing invariants of Zones against ones of Interval and Predicate abstract domains by comparing only the part of

Zone state that changed. The importance of empirically evaluating domains has been suggested previously [25] since domains differ in their expressiveness and efficiency, and thus, finding an optimal domain is an important problem.

Evaluating our techniques to study the difference between incomparable domains, *e.g.,* Zones and Predicate domains [14], allows us to determine its effect on decreasing the number of incomparable comparisons results. For example, Zones can compute more precise values for some variables at the beginning of a method, but later on, Predicates domain computes more precise values for another set of variables. If analyses are compared using the entire state of each, then results would be incomparable for the later part. However, using our approach, the comparison would indicate that the Predicates domain computes more precise invariants in the latter part of the program.

Our main contributions for this work are:

- A problem definition and a collection of efficient algorithms to identify minimal changes for the Zones abstract domain.
- A demonstration of the effectiveness of our techniques at increasing precision when comparing Zones to comparable and incomparable domains. Similarly, demonstration that our techniques improve efficiency of domain comparison.

2   Background and Motivation

We illustrate problems with finding the minimal changed set of linear inequalities for the Zones domain on a code example in Fig. 1a and focus on changes to the abstract state after taking the true branch in statement 4, *i.e.,* changes to the incoming state of 4 to the outgoing state of the true branch of state 4.

To better conceptualize the idea of the minimal changed state, we first consider abstract states computed by an analyzer over the Intervals [8] domain. The incoming state is $x \mapsto [0,0], w \mapsto (-\infty, 2], y \mapsto \top$, where the interval for x comes from line 2; w comes from taking the true branch on line 3; and y, at this point, is unbounded. After applying the transfer function for the true branch of line 4, the analyzer updates the value of y to $(-\infty, 0]$ without affecting values of x and w. To identify changed variables, the analyzer simply checks the difference in updated variable values between the two states since changes to one variable do not induce changes in other variables.

2.1   Finding a Minimal Subset in Relational Domains

For a relational numerical domain, the analyzer produces the formula $x = 0 \land w - x \leq 2$ for the incoming state to line 4, the absence of the y variable means it is a free variable. Interpreting the true branch of 4, the analyzer introduces: $y - x \leq 0$, resulting in a new outgoing state: $x = 0 \land w - x \leq 2 \land y - x \leq 0$. Here, the minimal subset of inequalities contains $x = 0$ and $y - x \leq 0$. Indeed, only these two inequalities are sufficient to reason about the changed part of the state.

```
1 int example(int w, int y) {
2    int x = 0;
3    if (w <= x + 2) {
4        if (y <= x) {
5            assert y <= 0;
6        }
7    }
8    return x;
9 }
```

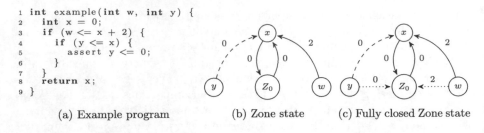

(a) Example program   (b) Zone state   (c) Fully closed Zone state

Fig. 1. Example program and two equivalent Zones

Such a minimal subset is not easily identifiable. Green's slicing technique over-approximates it by including all inequalities through a syntax-based transitive closure. However, since x has not changed and is only used in $y - x \leq 0$ to restrict y's values, *no changes occurred with respect to* w, and hence, the $w - x \leq 2$ inequality remains the same. In our work, we show algorithms for reasoning about such "semantic-based" slicing for the Zones domain. Before we provide an overview of our approach, we present a brief background on the Zones domain.

2.2 Zones Domain

The Zones abstract domain expresses specific relations between program variables. Zones limits its relations to unitary difference inequalities such as $x - y \leq b$, and interval inequalities such as $x \leq b$ and $x \geq b$, where $b \in \mathbb{Z}$. Equality relations are rewritten into a pair of two inequalities. For example, an $x = y + b$ relation results in $x - y \leq b$ and $y - x \leq -b$. To encode an interval value such as $x = [1, 2]$, Zones use the following inequalities $x \geq 1$ and $x \leq 2$. To encode interval valued variables as unitary difference constraints, Zones introduces a special "zero" variable, denoted here as Z_0, and rewriting rules. These rules change the inequalities for the interval $[1, 2]$ into $x - Z_0 \leq 2$ and $Z_0 - x \leq -1$ where the value of Z_0 always equals 0. In this way, the Zones domain represents all inequality constraints in a uniform $x - y \leq b$ template.

Inequalities in the Zones domain have an isomorphic representation as a weighted, directed graph, which is efficiently encoded as a 2D matrix [9,24]. In this graph, variables are nodes, the source and the sink of an edge identify variables in the first and the second positions of the difference template, respectively, and the weight is the coefficient b.

To illustrate this representation, consider the graph in Fig. 1b, which encodes the constraints from the running example. The solid lines denote the inequalities of the incoming state to statement 4; and the dashed line is the additional inequality after interpreting the true branch of line 4. Here, the edge from x to Z_0 is for $x - Z_0 \leq 0$ and the edge from Z_0 to x is for $Z_0 - x \leq 0$ of the rewritten $x = 0$ term. The edge from w to x represents $w - x \leq 2$. Similarly, the dashed edge from y to x represents the additional $y - x \leq 0$ term.

2.3   Finding Affected Inequalities

In graph terms, the problem reduces to finding affected edges when an edge is changed in the state graph. Naively, all edges reachable from the changed variables are affected, *i.e.*, a connected component (with undirected edges).

However, we should exclude nodes connected only through Z_0 as a part of the connected component since it might introduce *spurious* dependencies. Consider, the state also has an edge from a variable w to Z_0 with weight 2, which encodes inequality $w \le 2$ represented as $w - Z_0 \le 2$ in the canonical unitary difference form. If Z_0 is treated as a regular variable, then the technique would include $w - Z_0 \le 2$ in the set of affected inequalities. Our approach considers Z_0 a singularity and stops at Z_0 when it transitively computes predecessors R^- and successors R^+ of a node, for example, to identify connected components.

To improve on the connected component approach, our algorithms reason about the directions of the edges in the graph. The outgoing edges from one node to another means the second one restricts the first. In our example, w has an outgoing edge to x, meaning x restricts w. The only changes that can be propagated to w from an additional inequality, if x's value would be further restricted, manifests as a new or updated outgoing edge. However, after adding $y - x \le 0$ inequality (the dashed edge), the only new outgoing transitions are associated with y. Thus, in order to determine the affected inequalities we transitively compute the predecessors and successors of y, *i.e.*, $R^-(y) = \{y\}$ and $R^+(y) = \{x, y, Z_0\}$. The union of the two sets results in the subgraph of dependent variables to y. In the next section we present formal algorithms and prove their correctness.

2.4   Dealing with Spurious Inequalities

Relational numerical domains possess a powerful ability to infer new relations between variables. In the Zones domain, it happens through computing transitive closures for each variable. For example, since w can reach Z_0, one can establish that $w \le 2$. Later, when the x variable gets reassigned, $w \le 2$ remains in place. Since inequalities describing a bounded region are not unique, Zones require a canonical representation to enable operations such as equality comparisons. In order to determine whether two Zones are equal, as needed in DFA's fixed-point algorithms, these states should be *fully closed*. That is, all inferred, transitive constraints should be explicitly stated. Figure 1c shows the fully closed version of the same graph as in Fig. 1b, where dotted lines depict inferred edges.

Applying the previously described technique identifies three inequalities $y \le x$, $x = 0$ and $y \le 0$. Clearly, the first two constraints do not add any additional information to the third. In fact, after closing, the newly added edge (y, x) becomes what we call a *spurious* edge since it falsely implies that y and x make up a relational constraint, while in fact, since x is a constant, this is not the case.

Therefore, before finding affected inequalities, we identify such spurious edges and remove them from the graph. The algorithm checks for a given connected component containing changed variables whether an edge between two nodes connected to Z_0 carries additional information, otherwise it removes the direct edge. In our example, the connected component containing potentially changed variables are all nodes with an edge to Z_0.

In our example, the algorithm removes edges (y, x) and (w, x). Now, node x is no longer reachable from y, making $R^+(y) = \{y, Z_0\}$. For a fully closed state the algorithm determines a single affected inequality: $y \leq 0$. Thus, removing spurious constraints helps with identifying smaller, truly connected components.

3   Finding the Minimal Changed Set of Inequalities

In this section, we first formally define the problem of finding a minimal changed set of inequalities from Zones. We continue with a series of algorithms starting with spurious constraint elimination, followed by different minimization approaches for arbitrary and fully closed Zones.

3.1   Problem Definition

Let $\mathcal{N}_1$ and $\mathcal{N}_2$ be sets of inequalities in the initial and updated states, respectively. An inequality n of a Zone state can be uniquely identified by its first n_1 and the second n_2 variables in the unitary difference formula template. Let u be the node representing n_1 and similarly $w = n_2$, then the corresponding edge n in the state graph has u as its source and w as its target nodes.

For a given variable v, we define its dependent inequalities in $\mathcal{N}_1$ as

$$S_1 = \{n \in \mathcal{N}_1 \mid n_1 \in R_{\mathcal{N}_1}^-(v) \vee n_2 \in R_{\mathcal{N}_1}^+(v)\}$$

where $R_{\mathcal{N}_1}^-(v) = P(v) \cup \{v\}$, and similarly, $R_{\mathcal{N}_1}^+(v) = S(v) \cup \{v\}$. S_2 is dually constructed for $\mathcal{N}_2$.

Let dv be a nonempty set of updated variables that change $\mathcal{N}_1$ to $\mathcal{N}_2$. Then, the problem of finding the minimal changed set of inequalities is equivalent to finding the smallest $S \subseteq \mathcal{N}_2$ such that

$$S \cap \{n \in \mathcal{N}_2 \mid \forall v \in dv : n_1 \in R_{\mathcal{N}_2}^-(v) \vee n_2 \in R_{\mathcal{N}_2}^+(v)\} \neq \emptyset \text{ and } S_2 \setminus_{id} S \Leftrightarrow S_1 \setminus_{id} S$$

Here, the first term ensures that the set S includes only affected inequalities. The second term ensures that the set of remaining inequalities after removing updated ones should be logically equivalent between the initial and updated states. The equality in the set minus operation is determined by inequality IDs, i.e., n_1 and n_2. That is, if two inequalities have the same order of variables, then they are considered equivalent for set operations.

3.2   Minimization Algorithms

A straightforward solution to identify such an S would be to compare $\mathcal{N}_1$ and $\mathcal{N}_2$ directly, which would require an exhaustive search. Instead, our approaches only take $\mathcal{N}_2$ as a graph Z, a set of updated variables dv, and a set of updated edges de. A DFA framework can directly provide the sets dv and de when it invokes a transfer function. Using these three input values and a choice of minimization $Method$, the pseudocode in Algorithm 1 computes the smallest set of changed inequalities which it returns as a graph G.

Algorithm 1 Minimal Changed Set

1: **function** MINCHANGEDSET(Z, dv, de, $Method$)
2:     $G \leftarrow$ REMOVESPURIOUS(Z)
3:     **switch** $Method$ **do**
4:         **case** CC
5:             $G \leftarrow$ CONNECTEDCOMPONENTS(G, dv)
6:         **case** NN
7:             $G \leftarrow$ NODENEIGHBORS(G, dv)
8:         **case** MN
9:             $G \leftarrow$ MINIMALNEIGHBORS(G, de)
10:     **return** G
11: **end function**

On line 2, the algorithm invokes `RemoveSpurious` on the updated state Z. The purpose of this method is to remove spurious dependencies in Z inferred through Z_0, thus creating smaller connected components in G. Next, on line 3, the algorithm switches on $Method$. The rest of the algorithm computes minimal changed sets based on the method selected: CC approach– `ConnectedComponents`; NN approach– `NodeNeighbors`, and lastly MN– `MinimalNeighbors`. These algorithms approximate S differently and have different computational complexity, which are varied based on the Zones representation. Gs of these algorithms create a total order on the number of inequalities in the reduced state $G_{CC} \preceq_{|E|} G_{NN} \preceq_{|E|} G_{MN}$. The runtime complexity of Algorithm 1 is $O(n^2)$,[1] which is dominated by the quadratic complexity of `RemoveSpurious`.

Algorithm 2 Removal of spurious dependences in G

1: **function** REMOVESPURIOUS(G)
2:     $C \leftarrow \{\}$
3:     **for** $s \in$ V(G) **do**
4:         **if** $(s, Z_0) \neq \top \vee (Z_0, s) \neq \top$ **then**
5:             $C \leftarrow C \cup \{s\}$
6:         **end if**
7:     **end for**
8:     **for** $s \in C$ **do**
9:         **for** $t \in C$ **do**
10:             **if** $s \neq t \wedge (s, t) \geq (s, Z_0) + (Z_0, t)$ **then**
11:                 $(s, t) \leftarrow \top$
12:             **end if**
13:         **end for**
14:     **end for**
15:     **return** G
16: **end function**

---

[1] The average is usually less due to sparsity in graphs.

Spurious Connections. The goal of the spurious constraint removal step is to deal with inferences through Z_0. Our approach for identifying spurious edges is a special case of the reduction proposed by Larsen *et al.* [19]. That is, an edge between two nodes can be removed from a Zone if the weight between them is greater or equal to any path between them. Instead of applying this reduction to the entire state, our algorithm considers only the path *through* Z_0. This reduces the runtime complexity from $O(n^3)$ to $O(n^2)$. We define a spurious directed edge between s and t variables when $(s, t) \geq (s, Z_0) + (Z_0, t)$.

Algorithm 2 details the steps for this spurious edge removal. The algorithm determines candidate pairs by selecting variables with connections to or from Z_0, line 1. Nodes not connected to the zero node can be excluded because any edge is, by definition, non-spurious. It iterates over the candidate node pairs, line 9 and for each pair, it checks the spurious edge criterion on line 10. If the criterion is satisfied, the edge is removed, line 11. The correctness of the algorithm comes from the spurious edge criterion: it never removes an edge inferred by Z_0 that is not redundant. Furthermore, spurious edges represent redundant constraints, therefore, removing them does not cause precision loss.

Connected Components. For an arbitrary Zone, we can safely over-approximate all affected inequalities from dv by identifying a connected component containing dv. Note, that changed variables are always in one component, since an update to a Zone creates an edge between them. Identifying dv's connected component reduces to discovering the undirected, reachable nodes of each $v \in dv$ in the spurious reduced Zone. The CC algorithm is a modified depth-first search algorithm, with $O(n^2)$ runtime complexity. In the beginning, the algorithm marks the special Z_0 node as visited, thus, preventing discovery of new paths through it, lest we undo the reduction of Algorithm 2.

The CC algorithm is the same for arbitrary, non-closed Zones and fully closed Zones. The resulting sets of changed variables, however, may differ. The set of inequalities of fully closed Zones are minimized but often more connected. However, more connections enables more spurious reductions, therefore, leading to smaller connected components.

Algorithm 3 Algorithm for node neighbor selection for arbitrary Zones.

```
1: function NODENEIGHBORS(G, dv)
2:     variables ← {}
3:     for v ∈ dv do
4:         variables ← variables ∪ FORWARDREACHABLE(G, v)
5:         variables ← variables ∪ BACKWARDREACHABLE(G, v)
6:     end for
7:     return variables
8: end function
```

Node Neighbors. The Node Neighbors (NN) algorithm for an arbitrary Zone state is presented in Algorithm 3. In essence, the algorithm searches for the successor and predecessor of each changed variable, line 3. `ForwardReachable` returns the set of all reachable successor variables for each changed variable, $v \in dv$, using a typical depth-first search. `BackwardReachable` is similarly defined for reachable predecessor variables. In both cases, the zero variable receives special consideration. That is, we specially treat the zero variable as a sink with no outgoing edges during traversal.

The complexity of NN is $O(4n^2)$ because there are at most 2 changed variables from the DFA framework, and we do DFS twice per variable.

When given a fully closed Zone, the NN complexity is reduced. The form of a fully closed Zones makes explicit all transitively related variables. That is, the set of successors and predecessors of a variable in a fully closed Zone is equivalent to the local neighborhood of the variable, $R_G^-(v) \cup R_G^+(v) = N_G^\pm(v)$. Therefore, NN for the fully closed Zones simply returns the inequalities incident to the neighbor set of the requested variable.

The complexity and accuracy of finding a minimized state can be reduced for Zones in fully closed canonical form, where all dependencies are explicit. Thus, to identify affected inequalities by dv, we need to find incoming and outgoing edges of dv since they are potentially affected by those updates. The NN algorithm takes dv and a reduced state graph G, and retrieves all incoming and outgoing edges of dv, then uses them to identify its neighbors. The local subgraphs for each $v \in dv$ represent the identified changed inequalities. The runtime complexity of NN is linear $O(n)$, since it only considers each associated edge of dv.

The correctness of NN relies on the dependency information encoded in the successors and predecessors set. If a variable u is not in the $R_G^-(v) \cup R_G^+(v)$ set for v, then v does not depend on or relate to u. Furthermore, since u is not in this dependency set, it has not changed from the previous state. Therefore, the variable u can be removed from the dependent inequality set returned by NN.

Algorithm 4 Minimize Changed Variables Algorithm

```
1: function MinNeighbors(G, de)
2:     variables ← {}
3:     for (s, t) ∈ de do
4:         if s = Z₀ then
5:             variables ← variables ∪ {t}
6:         else if t = Z₀ then
7:             variables ← variables ∪ {s}
8:         else if s ≠ Z₀ ∧ t ≠ Z₀ then
9:             variables ← variables ∪ {s}
10:        end if
11:    end for
12:    return NodeNeighbors(G, variables)
13: end function
```

Minimal Neighbors. The previous CC and NN minimization algorithms assume that all updated variables, dv, modify inequalities within a Zone state, however, that may not always be the case. An updated variable might not induce changes to the state. The Minimal Neighbors (MN) technique improves upon this over-approximation by considering the set of updated edges de in a Zone state. DFA framework can provide this information when processing a statement, *e.g.,* an assignment or a conditional statement. Notice, that sources and targets of an edge in de are always in dv, but additional computation is required to identify de.

Algorithm 4 shows the pseudocode for identifying the changed variables among updated edges. Specifically, the algorithm takes as input G produced by RemoveSpurious and a set of updated edges, de. It starts by iterating over the set of updated edges, line 3. For each edge, the algorithm checks whether the source or target is the zero node, Z_0. If so, then the other node from the edge pair is added to the variables set, lines 5 and 7. This case handles when updates are on intervals because we must always include the non Z_0 variable in the filtered set of changed variables.

If neither source nor target is Z_0, then the source of the edge is added to the variables set, line 9, since this corresponds to the target variable restricting the source node, while the former remains unchanged for that edge. Finally, on line 12, the algorithm invokes NN procedure on G and the computed changed set of variables, and returns the minimized graph. The runtime complexity of MN is equivalent to NN: $O(4n^2)$. Similarly, if G is fully closed, the complexity is $O(n)$.

Below we provide a proof sketch that shows that for a given G from RemoveSpurious algorithm and an updated edge (s, t), the variable of its target, t does not change if the edges (t, s) and (Z_0, s) do not exist. That is, the target variable is never added to the variable set in Algorithm 4.

Proof. Given G with an updated edge (s, t) corresponding to the additional constraint $s - t \leq c$, for some $c \in \mathbb{Z}$. For the purpose of contradiction, let us assume t has changed as a result of the update from $s - t \leq c$. This means either there exists a path from t to s or that there exists a path (Z_0, s). But existence of such paths violates our assumption that $t, Z_0 \notin R_G^-(s)$. Therefore, t remains unchanged by the addition of the edge (s, t).

3.3   Widening and Merges

A few situations require special treatment for state updates in DFA. First, widening and merge points in the CFG of the analysis may induce more changed variables. Second, conditional transfers tend to modify more than a single variable, *e.g.,* two variables in three address form. Therefore, to ensure accurate and minimal comparisons, our techniques and comparisons must handle these situations. However, this is easily accomplished by each of our techniques since the parameter, dv for Algorithm 1 is a set of changed variables.

4   Experiments Methodology

To determine if the proposed minimization algorithms are efficient and effective, we evaluate them using subject programs within an existing DFA analyzer.

For each subject program, we compute invariants at each statement for each abstract domain. Over the corpus of methods, we compute 4529 total invariants. The invariants are stored as logical formulas in SMT format. We run analysis on three domains: Zones, Intervals and Predicates, and compare the first with the last two using queries to an SMT solver. Since previous research demonstrates advantages of using fully closed Zone states [4], our experiments evaluate minimization algorithms for that canonical representation.

To evaluate the efficacy of CC, NN and MN, each after computing spurious constraint reduction, we compute the reduction in the number of variables and inequalities in the SMT formula of Zone invariants over the preceding techniques in $\preceq$, i.e., CC vs. full state (FS), NN vs. CC, and MN vs. NN. That is, we compute the percentage of change per program statement and then average them over all methods. We use percentage, and not absolute values since the number of variables changes from statement to statement. Similarly, we compute the average percentage change for inequalities. Since program branches compute possibly different sized sets of variables and inequalities, we take the maximum number of variables and inequalities between the two.

Using the invariants computed for Zones, Intervals, and Predicates, we entail the invariants to compare the precision of Zones vs. Intervals and Zones vs. Predicates for each minimization algorithm. The results for Interval's invariants are classified as less precise $\prec$ or equal $=$. Predicates extend these categories to include more precise $\succ$ or incomparable $\prec\succ$ to Zones.

Subject Programs. Subject programs consist of 127 Java methods used in previous research [3,31]. Methods from the DFA benchmark suite [31] were extracted from a wide range of open-source projects and have a high number of integer operations. The subject programs range from 4 to 412 Jimple instructions, a three address intermediate representation.

The EQBench suite [3] consists of method pairs for testing differential symbolic execution tools [2,30]. We sampled only original methods and excluded renamed equivalent methods.

Experimental Setup. We execute each of the analyses on a single GNU/Linux machine, running Linux kernel version 5.15.89, equipped with an AMD Ryzen Threadripper 1950X 16-Core Processor and 64 GB of system memory. We use an existing DFA static analysis tool [31] implemented in the Java programming language. The analysis framework uses Soot [29] version 4.2.1. Similarly, we use Z3 [27], version 4.8.17 with Java bindings to compare SMT expressions from the abstract domain states. Finally, we use Java version 11 to execute the analyses, providing the following JVM options: -Xms4g, -Xmx32G, -XX:+UseG1GC, -XX:+UseStringDeduplication, and -XX:+UseNUMA.

Implementation. We use the reduction from Larsen *et al.* [19] to create an equivalent, but reduced invariant expression at each program point. We combine the output states via logical entailment to compare Zones to Intervals and to Predicates. The set of variables in a minimized Zone state determines what variables are extracted from the corresponding full states of Intervals and Predicates. After entailment, we use Z3, using the linear integer arithmetic (LIA) logic, to decide model behavior of each domain. Using the GNU `time` [13] command, version 1.9, we capture the walk-clock execution time of Z3.

Evaluations. Intervals and Zones perform widening operations after two iterations over widening program points. We do not preform narrowing for either domain because narrowing is program specific. The lack of narrowing does not affect our results since we are evaluating techniques for identifying minimal subsets of changes, not techniques for improving precision.

We use a generic disjoint Predicate domain, which does not affect generality of the results. The Predicate domain's elements are influenced by Collberg *et al.'s* [7] study on Java programs and numerical constants. Consequently, the domain elements use several of the most common integer constants found in Java programs. The specific Predicate domain used in this study consists of the following set of disjoint elements: $\{(-\infty, -5], (-5, -2], -1, 0, 1, [2, 5), [5, +\infty)\}$.

5   Evaluation Results and Discussions

To empirically evaluate efficiency and effectiveness of the state minimization algorithms, we answer the following research questions:

RQ1 How well do the minimization algorithms reduce the size of a Zone state and improve runtime of domain comparisons?

RQ2 How do the minimization algorithms affect categorization of domain comparison results?

5.1   Impact of Minimization on State Size and Comparison Efficiency

Table 1 contains data for efficiency evaluation, split over the two benchmark suites. The table shows the average percentage reduction in vertices and edges in Zones, comparing to the preceding minimization algorithm (columns 2–4); and as a reduction in total runtime for all comparisons between Zones and Interval states (column 5) and between Zones and Predicates (column 6).

We aggregate the relative change in vertices and edges over all subject methods for a more tractable comparison. We use the percentage change to answer the first part of **RQ1** related to state sizes. The data show a large reduction in the number of vertices between FS and after applying CC algorithm. The number of edges features a similarly significant, though less dramatic reduction since they are compared without spurious constraints. On average, we see small reductions in the rest of the comparisons. The difference in vertex reductions versus edge reductions is due to the reduced number of vertices required, contrasted with edge sparsity arising from widening and merge operations which affects all representations. However, as the small reduction of edges between MN and NN shows that after removing more vertices from the subgraph, we remove more edges as well.

Table 1. Average percentage changes in V and E between each technique (columns 2–4), and average total runtime of state comparisons (columns 5,6).

DFA Subject Programs					
State Type	**vs.**	**↓ Δ % V**	**↓ Δ % E**	**~ Inter, sec.**	**~ Pred, sec.**
FS	-	-	-	4.03	265.91
CC	FS	70.37	29.47	1.41	4.09
NN	CC	0.02	0.01	1.41	4.04
MN	NN	0.10	0.05	1.35	4.05
EQBench Subject Programs					
FS	-	-	-	0.79	5.56
CC	FS	43.0	2.1	0.63	0.87
NN	CC	0.0	0.0	0.58	0.9
MN	NN	0.13	0.13	0.58	0.9

The EQBench results mirror the reduction of edges and variables. In the EQBench benchmark suite, we see no reduction between CC to NN. However, our final approach does remove vertices and edges from the previous techniques of CC and NN. This reduction is attributable to the bisection enabled by our final technique which further reduces sparse graphs based on the semantics of the changed constraint.

Addressing the second part of **RQ1**, we compare the average total runtime of comparisons over the corpus of subject programs. Columns 5 and 6 of Table 1 show the total runtime to execute all domain comparisons, averaged over 5 executions, and broken down by benchmark suite. Between FS and CC, we see dramatic reductions in total time. As expected the remaining techniques show small improvements in comparison time due to the minor reductions of vertices and edges shown in columns 2–4. The increase in time for Zone and Predicate comparison for the EQBench subject programs is attributable to execution variance. Overall, our minimization algorithms reduce the size of Zone states and, in turn, improve the efficiency of domain comparisons.

5.2   Impact on Domain Comparison

Comparable Domains. We compare Zones and Intervals invariants to answer **RQ2**. We break down the results by benchmark suites in Table 2. Columns 2 and 3 show the precision summary of invariants between Zones and Intervals.

In the DFA suite, using FS to compare each domain, Zones compute more precise invariants for approximately 3/4 of the total number of invariants. However, the ratio drops significantly to less than a third, (31%), when using the CC technique. Our final technique MN lowers the percentage of invariants where Zones are more precise to about 30% of all computed invariants. Furthermore,

Table 2. Summary of comparison between Zones and Intervals(2, 3), and between Zones and Predicates (4–7).

State	≻ Intervals	= Intervals	≻ Pred	= Pred	≺ Pred	≺≻ Pred
DFA Subject Programs						
FS	2898	1002	1464	237	167	2032
CC	1194	2706	1324	1930	473	173
NN	1191	2709	1322	1933	473	172
MN	1164	2736	1305	1960	473	162
EQBench Subject Programs						
FS	374	255	307	135	46	141
CC	131	498	217	322	72	18
NN	131	498	217	322	72	18
MN	131	498	217	322	72	18

our techniques demonstrate the preponderance of invariants where Zones and Intervals are equivalent. We see similar results when considering the methods of the EQBench suite. Using the full state to compare Zones and Intervals, we see Zones compute a majority of more precise invariants, about 59%. However, using any one of our minimization techniques moves the proportion of more precise invariants to 21%. We attribute the lack of further reduction with later techniques to the preponderance of non-integer operations in the EQBench suite.

Incomparable Domains. Additionally, with respect to **RQ2**, we compare Zones to Predicates to evaluate whether our techniques minimize the number of incomparable invariants computed between the two domains. Since Zones and Predicates are incomparable, we consider all comparison categories denoted here as: ≻ *Pred* for Zones more precise than Predicates; = *Pred* for Zones equivalent to Predicates; ≺ *Pred* for Zones less precise than Predicates; and ≺≻ *Pred* for Zones and Predicates being incomparable.

Columns 4–6 of Table 2 summarizes the distribution of relative precision for Zones and Predicates over the computed invariants of the subject programs. Unlike Zones, Predicates cannot represent arbitrary integer constants; Predicates are limited to the *a priori* chosen predicate elements. However, Predicates can represent disjoint ranges of values which Zones, and other numerical domains, cannot. As such, when using FS, we see a high percentage of invariants fall into either ≻ *Pred* and ≺≻ *Pred*. The ≻ *Pred* makes up about 38% of invariants. Similarly, ≺≻ *Pred* weighs in at ∼ 52% of invariants.

When, applying CC, the percentage of incomparable invariants drops significantly to 4%. ≺ *Pred* comprise 12% of invariants, up from 4%. Similarly, the percentage of ≻ *Pred* drops from 38% to 34%. Finally, equality between the two domains significantly increased from 6% to about 49%. These trends continue for each technique. Each technique shifts the distributions of invariants from $\succ Pred$ and $\prec\succ Pred$ to $= Pred$ and $\prec Pred$. In MN state, Zones are more precise for about 33% of invariants, down from 38%; Zones are equal to Predicates for about 50% of invariants, up from 6%; and Zones and Predicates are incomparable for about 4% of invariants, down from 52%. For each technique, Zones less precise than Predicates remained at 12%, up from 4% compared to FS, between the techniques. Considering the EQBench methods, we observe similar results for Zones and Predicates. Using the CC technique, we see a significant shift in the distribution of invariants. However, we do not see any further distribution shifts in this program set. We attribute this to the fact that the EQBench methods consist of many non-integer operations.

Clearly, our techniques reduce the percentage of incomparable invariants, enabling, for example, more accurate comparison between Zones and incomparable domains, such as Predicates. While not the goal of this study, the comparable results confer merit to previous research which anecdotally mentions: the majority of computed invariants are interval valued [10,16]. This improved accuracy would be especially valuable in adaptive analysis approaches where a heuristic decides which abstract domain to utilize for a specific block of code.

5.3   Threats to Validity

External Threats. The subject programs from previous research [3,31] were extracted from real, open-source projects, each with a high number of integer operations. The EQBench suite consists of predominately numerical programs but demonstrate the generalizability of our results. Other concerns include the choice of Predicate elements and lack of narrowing which could influence the precision counts between Zones and Predicates and between Zones and Intervals, respectively. However, since we examine only the trend of the different categories, the exact precision does not affect our conclusions.

Internal Threats. To mitigate internal threats to validity, we developed a large test suite, 703 unit tests, to ensure our implementation is correct. The test suite contains numerous tests which check the consistency of the partial order over Zones and Intervals. Furthermore, we developed and manually verified tests to check comparison between Zones and Predicates. Specifically, the test suite contains manually verified tests which use real subject programs to test the correctness of the analyses and their comparisons.

6   Related Work

We have mentioned our spurious reduction technique is based on the work by Larsen *et al.* [19]. Their algorithm removes all redundant constraints without removing variables, reducing the overall number of linear integer inequalities but it does not reduce the number of variables. Along similar lines, Giacobazzi *et al.* [12] proposed techniques for abstract domain compression for complete finite abstract domains. That is, it reduces the number of constraints within the logical formula without altering the approximation of the abstract domain. Our techniques extract subsets of the state for specific verification tasks.

Our approach, Connected Components (CC), resembles the slicing technique of the Green solver interface [33] and split normal form introduced by Gange *et al.* [10,11]. Our approach differs from Green in application and restriction to Zone constraints. Slicing can extract connected constraints by what variables are present in the set of constraints. However, we can exclude transitive relations between variables because within Zones, not all variables are modified by the introduction of a new constraint.

We base our methodology on previous work on new abstract domains which provide a comparison of the new domain against other known similar or comparable domains. These comparisons can be categorized into two predominate strategies. The first, domains are compared via a known set of properties over benchmark programs [10,15,16,20,23]. The second, domains are compared via logical entailment of the invariants computed at program points [25,31]. In the first case, the comparison is straightforward. In the latter case, as this work demonstrates, the precision between two domains can depend on the set of invariants used to perform the comparison.

7   Conclusion and Future Work

We proposed several techniques which identify a minimal set of changed inequalities for the Zones abstract domain. Our techniques improve upon existing techniques such as Green's slicing [33] technique which further reduces the number of dependent variables within a changed set of inequalities. We empirically evaluated our techniques and showed improvements of efficacy and efficiency. Concretely, the changed subgraph of Zones is equivalent to Intervals in more than 70% of computed invariants, a result commented on but never demonstrated in previous research [10,16]. Moreover, our techniques significantly reduced the incomparable invariants found when comparing two incomparable domains, resulting in a clearer picture of the relative precision between the two domains. Furthermore, the reduction in variables improved the efficiency of domain comparison, reducing average total runtime of incomparable domain comparisons by 98%. While evaluated within the context of DFA frameworks, we presented general algorithms which, we believe, are applicable in other areas of formal methods such as model checking and symbolic execution.

Future Work. We intend to extend this work to include additional relational domains. Specifically, enabling comparison between two relational domains, such as Zones and Octagons, is an interesting avenue to pursue. Since the techniques improve accuracy in comparison between domains they could be beneficial for adaptive static analysis techniques which selectively use the best abstraction. We believe this work also opens up possibilities of comprehensive studies which empirically validate several abstract domains and their partial ordering. Specifically, it would be interesting to see comprehensive comparisons between Predicate domains and Zones.

Acknowledgments. The work reported here was supported by the U.S. National Science Foundation under award CCF-19-42044.

References

1. Abate, C., et al.: An extended account of trace-relating compiler correctness and secure compilation. ACM Trans. Programm. Lang. Syst. **43**(4), 1–48 (Dec 2021). https://doi.org/10.1145/3460860
2. Badihi, S., Akinotcho, F., Li, Y., Rubin, J.: Ardiff: scaling program equivalence checking via iterative abstraction and refinement of common code. In: Proceedings of the 28th ACM Joint Meeting on European Software Engineering Conference and Symposium on the Foundations of Software Engineering (11 2020). https://doi.org/10.1145/3368089.3409757
3. Badihi, S., Li, Y., Rubin, J.: Eqbench: A dataset of equivalent and non-equivalent program pairs. In: 2021 IEEE/ACM 18th International Conference on Mining Software Repositories (MSR) (May 2021). https://doi.org/10.1109/msr52588.2021.00084
4. Ballou, K., Sherman, E.: Incremental transitive closure for zonal abstract domain. In: NASA Formal Methods, pp. 800–808 (2022). https://doi.org/10.1007/978-3-031-06773-0_43
5. Blanchet, B., et al.: A static analyzer for large safety-critical software. In: Proceedings of the ACM SIGPLAN 2003 Conference on Programming Language Design and Implementation - PLDI '03 (2003). https://doi.org/10.1145/781131.781153
6. Chernikova, N.: Algorithm for finding a general formula for the non-negative solutions of a system of linear inequalities. USSR Comput. Math. Math. Phys. **5**(2), 228–233 (1965). https://doi.org/10.1016/0041-5553(65)90045-5, https://www.sciencedirect.com/science/article/pii/0041555365900455
7. Collberg, C., Myles, G., Stepp, M.: An empirical study of java bytecode programs. Software: Pract. Experience **37**(6), 581–641 (2007). https://doi.org/10.1002/spe.776
8. Cousot, P., Cousot, R.: Static determination of dynamic properties of programs. In: Proceedings of the Second International Symposium on Programming, pp. 106–130. Dunod, Paris, France (1976)
9. Dill, D.L.: Timing assumptions and verification of finite-state concurrent systems. Lecture Notes in Computer Science pp. 197–212 (1990). https://doi.org/10.1007/3-540-52148-8_17
10. Gange, G., Ma, Z., Navas, J.A., Schachte, P., Søndergaard, H., Stuckey, P.J.: A fresh look at zones and octagons. ACM Trans. Programm. Lang. Syst. **43**(3), 1–51 (2021). https://doi.org/10.1145/3457885
11. Gange, G., Navas, J.A., Schachte, P., Søndergaard, H., Stuckey, P.J.: Exploiting sparsity in difference-bound matrices. Lecture Notes in Computer Science, pp. 189–211 (2016). https://doi.org/10.1007/978-3-662-53413-7_10
12. Giacobazzi, R., Mastroeni, I.: Domain compression for complete abstractions. Verification, Model Checking, and Abstract Interpretation pp. 146–160 (Dec 2002). https://doi.org/10.1007/3-540-36384-x_14

13. Gordon, A.: Gnu time, https://www.gnu.org/software/time/
14. Graf, S., Saidi, H.: Construction of abstract state graphs with pvs. Lecture Notes in Computer Science, pp. 72–83 (1997). https://doi.org/10.1007/3-540-63166-6_10
15. Gurfinkel, A., Chaki, S.: Boxes: A symbolic abstract domain of boxes. Lecture Notes in Computer Science, pp. 287–303 (2010). https://doi.org/10.1007/978-3-642-15769-1_18
16. Howe, J.M., King, A.: Logahedra: A new weakly relational domain. Lecture Notes in Computer Science, pp. 306–320 (2009). https://doi.org/10.1007/978-3-642-04761-9_23
17. Katz, S.: Program optimization using invariants. IEEE Trans. Softw. Eng. SE-**4**(5), 378–389 (Sep 1978). https://doi.org/10.1109/tse.1978.233858
18. Kildall, G.A.: A unified approach to global program optimization. In: Proceedings of the 1st Annual ACM SIGACT-SIGPLAN Symposium on Principles of Programming Languages - POPL '73 (1973). https://doi.org/10.1145/512927.512945
19. Larsen, K., Larsson, F., Pettersson, P., Yi, W.: Efficient verification of real-time systems: Compact data structure and state-space reduction. In: Proceedings Real-Time Systems Symposium, pp. 14–24. IEEE Comput. Soc (1997). https://doi.org/10.1109/real.1997.641265
20. Laviron, V., Logozzo, F.: Subpolyhedra: A (more) scalable approach to infer linear inequalities. In: Verification, Model Checking, and Abstract Interpretation, pp. 229–244 (2008). https://doi.org/10.1007/978-3-540-93900-9_20
21. Le Verge, H.: A Note on Chernikova's algorithm. Research Report RR-1662, INRIA (1992), https://hal.inria.fr/inria-00074895
22. Lloyd, J., Sherman, E.: Minimizing the size of path conditions using convex polyhedra abstract domain. ACM SIGSOFT Softw. Eng. Notes **40**(1), 1–5 (Feb 2015). https://doi.org/10.1145/2693208.2693244
23. Logozzo, F., Fähndrich, M.: Pentagons: A weakly relational abstract domain for the efficient validation of array accesses. Sci. Comput. Programm. **75**(9), 796–807 (9 2010). https://doi.org/10.1016/j.scico.2009.04.004
24. Miné, A.: A new numerical abstract domain based on difference-bound matrices. In: Lecture Notes in Computer Science, pp. 155–172 (2001). https://doi.org/10.1007/3-540-44978-7_10
25. Miné, A.: Weakly Relational Numerical Abstract Domains (12 2004), https://pastel.archives-ouvertes.fr/tel-00136630
26. Miné, A.: The octagon abstract domain. Higher-Order Symbolic Comput. **19**(1), 31–100 (3 2006). https://doi.org/10.1007/s10990-006-8609-1
27. de Moura, L., Bjørner, N.: Z3: An efficient SMT solver. In: Lecture Notes in Computer Science pp. 337–340 (2008). https://doi.org/10.1007/978-3-540-78800-3_24
28. Nötzli, A., Reynolds, A., Barbosa, H., Niemetz, A., Preiner, M., Barrett, C., Tinelli, C.: Syntax-guided rewrite rule enumeration for SMT solvers. In: Janota, M., Lynce, I. (eds.) SAT 2019. LNCS, vol. 11628, pp. 279–297. Springer, Cham (2019). https://doi.org/10.1007/978-3-030-24258-9_20
29. OSS, S.: Soot (2020), https://soot-oss.github.io/soot/
30. Person, S., Dwyer, M.B., Elbaum, S., Păsăreanu, C.S.: Differential symbolic execution. In: Proceedings of the 16th ACM SIGSOFT International Symposium on Foundations of Software Engineering - SIGSOFT '08/FSE-16 (2008). https://doi.org/10.1145/1453101.1453131
31. Sherman, E., Dwyer, M.B.: Exploiting domain and program structure to synthesize efficient and precise data flow analyses (t). In: 2015 30th IEEE/ACM International Conference on Automated Software Engineering (ASE) (11 2015). https://doi.org/10.1109/ase.2015.41

32. Tange, O.: Gnu parallel 20221222 ('chatgpt') (Dec 2022). https://doi.org/10.5281/zenodo.7465517 GNU Parallel is a general parallelizer to run multiple serial command line programs in parallel without changing them
33. Visser, W., Geldenhuys, J., Dwyer, M.B.: Green: Reducing, reusing and recycling constraints in program analysis. In: Proceedings of the ACM SIGSOFT 20th International Symposium on the Foundations of Software Engineering (Nov 2012). https://doi.org/10.1145/2393596.2393665
34. Yu, H., Monniaux, D.: An efficient parametric linear programming solver and application to polyhedral projection. In: Chang, B.Y.E. (ed.) Static Analysis, pp. 203–224. Springer International Publishing, Cham (2019)
35. Zhu, H., Magill, S., Jagannathan, S.: A data-driven chc solver. In: Proceedings of the 39th ACM SIGPLAN Conference on Programming Language Design and Implementation (Jun 2018). https://doi.org/10.1145/3192366.3192416

idDL2DL – Interval Syntax to $d\mathcal{L}$

Jaime Santos[1,2($\boxtimes$)], Daniel Figueiredo[2,3], and Alexandre Madeira[2]

[1] Universidade do Minho, Braga, Portugal
`jaimepereirasantos123@gmail.com`
[2] CIDMA - Department of Mathematics, University of Aveiro, Aveiro, Portugal
[3] Association for Biomedical Research and Innovation in Light and Image,
Coimbra, Portugal

Abstract. A wide range of methods from computer science are being applied to many modern engineering domains, such as synthetic biology. Most behaviors described in synthetic biology have a hybrid nature, in the sense that both discrete or continuous dynamics are observed. Differential Dynamic Logic ($d\mathcal{L}$) is a well-known formalism used for the rigorous treatment of these systems by considering formalisms comprising both differential equations and discrete assignments. Since the many systems often consider a range of values rather than exact values, due to errors and perturbations of observed quantities, recent work within the team proposed an interval version of $d\mathcal{L}$, where variables are interpreted as intervals. This paper presents the first steps in the development of computational support for this formalism by introducing a tool designed to models based on intervals, prepared to translate them into specifications ready to be processed by the `KeYmaera X` tool.

Keywords: Synthetic biology · Formal verification · Dynamic Logic

1 Introduction and Preliminaries

Hybrid systems – those composed of continuous and discrete components – are everywhere, from the medical devices to the aerospace artifacts we have. Due to the critical role that some of them play in our life, the scientific community was pushed to develop theories and tools to support the trustworthy conception of these systems, not only via simulation techniques (e.g. with `Simulink`) but also using program verification techniques and logic.

Differential Dynamic Logic [1], with its supporting tool `KeYmaera X` (KX) [2], represents a core formalism in this context. This approach brings principles and techniques from program verification to hybrid systems developers, namely from dynamic logic [3]. The formalism has been successfully applied to several computational hybrid systems scenarios [1]; but also in other less obvious domains, including the specification and analysis of models in biology [4].

This work is supported by FCT, the Portuguese funding agency for Science and Technology with the projects PTDC/CCI-COM/4280/2021, UIDB/50014/2020 and UIDB/04106/2020.

C. David and M. Sun (Eds.): TASE 2023, LNCS 13931, pp. 240–247, 2023.
https://doi.org/10.1007/978-3-031-35257-7_14

Differential dynamic logic is a quantified dynamic logic with two kinds of atomic programs: assignments (discrete state transitions); and continuous evolutions. The syntax combines both kinds of atomic programs to express and prove the correctness of assertions of the so-called cyber-physical or hybrid systems. Because of this, a $d\mathcal{L}$ program is called a *hybrid program*. With the sound proof calculus for $d\mathcal{L}$, and the KX tool – a semi-automatic prover – one can prove the correctness of such systems. When the user provides a formula of $d\mathcal{L}$ as input, KX either generates its proof or retrieves some simpler formulas - preconditions that are required to be valid - to prove the formula.

We follow with a brief description of $d\mathcal{L}$ syntax.

Definition 1. *Let Σ be a signature containing n-ary functions, propositions, and state variables; and X be a set of logical variables.*

- *The set $Trm(X, \Sigma)$ of terms is the least set containing X such that $f(t_1, ..., t_n) \in Trm(X, \Sigma)$ iff $f \in \Sigma$ is a n-ary function and $t_1, ..., t_n \in Trm(X, \Sigma)$;*
- *$p(t_1, ..., t_n)$ is a predicate if $p \in \Sigma$ is a n-ary proposition and $t_1, ..., t_n \in Trm(\Sigma, X)$;*
- *$Fml_{FOL}(X, \Sigma)$ is the least set containing every predicate, and such that $\varphi \vee \psi$, $\varphi \wedge \psi$, $\neg\varphi$, $\forall\varphi$, $\exists\varphi \in Fml_{FOL}(X, \Sigma)$ whenever $\varphi, \psi \in Fml_{FOL}(X, \Sigma)$.*

Note that constants are 0-ary functions and other Boolean operators can be introduced as usual abbreviations. Also, Σ_{fl} denotes the set of state variables.

Definition 2. *The set of hybrid programs $HP(X, \Sigma)$ is defined as follows:*

- *$(x_1 := t_1, ..., x_n := t_n)$, $(x_1' = t_1, ..., x_n' = t_n \,\&\, \psi)$, $?\psi \in HP(X, \Sigma)$ for every state variables $x_1, ..., x_n \in \Sigma$, $t_1, ..., t_n \in Trm(X, \Sigma)$ and $\psi \in Fml_{FOL}(X, \Sigma)$;*
- *$\alpha; \beta$, $\alpha \cup \beta$, $\alpha^* \in HP(X, \Sigma)$ whenever $\alpha, \beta \in HP(X, \Sigma)$.*

Definition 3. *The set $Fml(X, \Sigma)$ of formulas of $d\mathcal{L}$ is defined recursively as the least set containing $Fml_{FOL}(X, \Sigma)$ and such that:*

- *$[\alpha]\varphi$, $\langle\alpha\rangle\varphi \in Fml(X, \Sigma)$ whenever $\varphi \in Fml(X, \Sigma)$ and $\alpha \in HP(X, \Sigma)$*
- *$\varphi \vee \psi$, $\varphi \wedge \psi$, $\neg\varphi$, $\forall\varphi$, $\exists\varphi \in Fml(X, \Sigma)$ whenever $\varphi, \psi \in Fml(X, \Sigma)$.*

The truth of a formula in the scope of a modality embedding a hybrid program is evaluated in a scenario obtained after the hybrid program is run. The semantics of $d\mathcal{L}$ are defined over the reals, and a strict interpretation of formulas and propositions from Σ is imposed. Thus, Σ only contain symbols such as $+$ or $\leq$ that are interpreted as "sum" or "less or equal", respectively. The full semantics can be found in [1].

In [5], an interval syntax is developed for $d\mathcal{L}$, regarding its application in contexts where variables are presented in terms of intervals, namely due to errors or uncertainty. This can be useful, for instance, to model a physical system under some measure uncertainties or whenever we want to make an assignment of an irrational number without machine representation. Apart from replacing real numbers for closed intervals, the interval syntax is the same as in $d\mathcal{L}$, and the semantics presented are adapted to an interval context, namely following the work of Moore [6]. In this context real numbers are considered as degenerated intervals. For instance the value $a \in \mathbb{R}$ is represented by the interval $[a, a]$. Under this perspective, the semantics for this adapted syntax considers a "strict" interpretation over closed intervals, *i.e.* a symbol like $+ \in \Sigma$ is interpreted as "interval sum" , for instance (check [6] for additional information in interval arithmetics). Also, logical and state variables are evaluated over $\mathcal{I}(\mathbb{R})$. Thus, the interpretation of each predicate P (defined for reals) must be adapted to intervals. Particularly, denoting by $P^{\mathcal{I}}(\mathbb{R})$ the interval interpretation of P, a predicate $P^{\mathcal{I}}(\mathbb{R})(X_1, ... X_n)$ is said to be *true* if $P(x_1, ..., x_n)$ holds for every $(x_1, ..., x_n) \in X_1 \times ... \times X_n$. With this definition, we expand the valuation for the full set of formulas, by keeping the coherence, so that the semantics of $d\mathcal{L}$ can be seen as a particular case of the interval one since the interpretation of its formulas is done over real numbers (the set of degenerated intervals).

This paper presents a parser and a translator which accepts interval $d\mathcal{L}$ formulas and retrieves equivalent ones in standard $d\mathcal{L}$. In this way, we take advantage of the sound $d\mathcal{L}$ proof calculus. In particular, we can use KX and try to obtain proof for the original interval $d\mathcal{L}$ formula. We illustrate the framework by modeling a biological regulatory network [7] – where there are variables like concentration of a protein are rather expressed in intervals than with a determined value. For this example, we consider a formula in the interval syntax of $d\mathcal{L}$, describing a property of the system, and use our parser and translator to obtain its equivalent formula in $d\mathcal{L}$ standard syntax. We then use the automatic tactic of KX to prove the correctness of this example.

2   The idDL2dDL Tool

This section introduces a tool to parse and translate specifications from interval $d\mathcal{L}$ to specifications in standard $d\mathcal{L}$, following the theoretical work in [5]. The implementation, developed in Python, is structured in five main parts – the *lexer*, the *parser*, the *translator*, a *graphical user interface* (GUI), and the *interpreter*. Detailed user instructions are available in the GitHub repository[1].

We first perform lexical analysis to convert the input text into tokens, contained in a list of predefined symbols, whose order is maintained through a Position attribute. Then, we use a parser to analyze the syntax of these tokens and generate an abstract syntax tree (AST) as output. The priority of operations in the AST is determined by the depth of the nodes, which are constructed with unary, and binary operations according to Definition 2 of hybrid programs [1]. This was one of the core challenges with the parser, since it required some language design and testing to ensure the legality of the nodes.

---

[1] https://github.com/JaimePSantos/idDL2DL.

The translator converts interval dynamic logic expressions into regular $d\mathcal{L}$ formulas using `visit` methods for each type of node. These methods evaluate tokens and preserve the priority degree of the AST. For instance, when an interval token is detected, a `TranslatedInterval` object creates an in equation between a fresh variable and the interval bounds. To comply with `KX` syntax, many other expressions are converted according to its specifications. Ensuring each interval generates a unique variable and that the final expression maps the variable to the correct interval came at a surprising performance cost, indicating that our method for generating infinite strings requires improvement.

The user interface was created using `Python`'s `Tkinter` library and has two pages: a translation page and a translation history page. On the translation page, shown in Fig. 2, users can load a file containing multiple formulas and save the resulting translations as *.kyx* files. If only one formula is translated, the user can specify a file name and location. For multiple translations, users can choose to save them in a single *.kyx* file or multiple files. The history page saves all translated statements, which is useful for analyzing complex models step by step. Displaying errors in a user-friendly way is still a work in progress for this component.

Interpreter and Performance. The latest feature of the software is an initial version of an interpreter. This component, similarly to the translator, converts an AST into a string. The implementation logic is to visit each node and apply one of the interval arithmetic rules from [6, 8], depending on the type of operation associated with the node

$$[a, b] + [c, d] = [a + c, b + d] \tag{1}$$

$$[a, b] - [c, d] = [a - d, b - c] \tag{2}$$

$$[a, b] \times [c, d] = [min(P), max(P)] \text{where} P = \{a \times c, a \times d, b \times c, b \times d\} \tag{3}$$

$$[a, b] \div [c, d] = [min(P), max(P)] \text{where} P = \{\frac{a}{c}, \frac{a}{d}, \frac{b}{c}, \frac{b}{d}\}, 0 \notin [c, d]. \tag{4}$$

As we visit and interpret the nodes of the AST, the resulting output must be used to rebuild the structure of the AST. Thus, the current version of the program recreates and re-parses the tokens before feeding them to the translator, which results in an inherent performance cost. Figure 1 shows the performance comparison between a simple translation and an interpreted translation of a formula that involves the sum of consecutive divisions between two intervals. Each formula was sampled 100 times to calculate the mean of each execution. Despite the interpreter adding a small performance

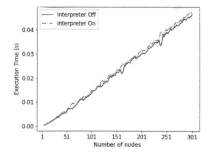

Fig. 1. Execution time with and without the interpreter vs the number of nodes.

cost, it was expected to be significantly larger due to the second round of lexing and parsing. This suggests that the true bottleneck is indeed in the translation process, most likely due to an inefficient method of generating unique variables.

This component posed several challenges during implementation, particularly in ensuring that the visit methods properly apply the defined operations while ignoring and preserving nodes containing operations between intervals and non-intervals. However, a limitation of the current version is that operations between intervals and expressions inside parentheses are kept separate, which will be addressed in the future. Another limitation of the software is the recursion limits imposed by `Python`, which can be extended but is not recommended. In the future, this limitation can be resolved by replacing recursion with a stack.

An illustration. We illustrate the application of the `idDL2dDL` tool with the analysis of a *PieceWise linear (PWL) model* of a biological regulatory network [9]. Biological regulatory networks are complex systems describing biological phenomena such as cell metabolism. This kind of model describes the physical and chemical interaction between cell proteins, mRNA, and other cell organelles.

$\begin{cases} x' = -x \\ y' = -y \end{cases}$ $x \le 2$ $2 \le y$	$\begin{cases} x' = -x \\ y' = -y \end{cases}$ $2 \le 4$ $2 \le y$	$\begin{cases} x' = -x \\ y' = 3 - y \end{cases}$ $4 \le x$ $2 \le y$
$\begin{cases} x' = -x \\ y' = -y \end{cases}$ $x \le 2$ $y \le 2$	$\begin{cases} x' = 5 - x \\ y' = -y \end{cases}$ $2 \le x \le 4$ $0 \le y \le 2$	$\begin{cases} x' = 5 - x \\ y' = 3 - y \end{cases}$ $4 \le x$ $0 \le y \le 2$

Table 1. PWL model.

The more detailed deterministic formalism used to model these systems are nonlinear differential equations. Numerical methods, such as simulations, are then applied to study the complex behavior and interactions between the components of a cell. These systems of differential equations often are subjected to a preliminary study to fully understand the major dynamics of a biological process. They are firstly simplified by proper methods, resulting in models such as PWL models that preserve the major dynamics of the original one and are easier to study. A PWL model is composed of several domains containing a system of linear differential equations which are obtained by proper simplifications of the (nonlinear) original one (cf. [9] for details). In [7] we can found an example of a PWL model, illustrated in Table 1.

This system is characterized by having continuous dynamics within each domain but discrete reconfigurations when we move from one domain to another. Continuous variables describe the concentration of intracellular components, such as proteins and RNA. This hybrid dynamics can be expressed by a hybrid program of $d\mathcal{L}$.

Making the same for the other five domains (and aggregating bio_{00} and bio_{01} in bio_0), we have:

$$bio_0 \equiv ?(x \le 2); (x' = -x, y' = -y \& (x \le 2))$$

$bio_{10} \equiv ?(2 \leq x \wedge x \leq 4 \wedge 0 \leq y \wedge y \leq 2); (x' = 5 - x, y' = -y \& (2 \leq x \wedge x \leq 4 \wedge 0 \leq y \wedge y \leq 2))$

$bio_{20} \equiv ?(4 \leq x \wedge 0 \leq y \wedge y \leq 2); (x' = 5 - x, y' = 3 - y \& (4 \leq x \wedge 0 \leq y \wedge y \leq 2))$

$bio_{11} \equiv ?(2 \leq x \wedge x \leq 4 \wedge 2 \leq y); (x' = -x, y' = -y \& (2 \leq x \wedge x \leq 4 \wedge 2 \leq y))$

$bio_{21} \equiv ?(4 \leq x \wedge 2 \leq y); (x' = -x, y' = 3 - y \& (4 \leq x \wedge 2 \leq y))$

The hybrid program describing the full dynamics of the biological system is:

$$bio \equiv (bio_0 \bigcup bio_{10} \bigcup bio_{20} \bigcup bio_{11} \bigcup bio_{21})^*$$

Then we can take advantage of the interval syntax to express biological properties like "when the concentrations x and y are around 5.5 and 3.5, the biological system will never reach a state where $x < 2$".

$$[x := [5,6]\,;\, y := [3,4]]\,[bio]\, x > 2$$

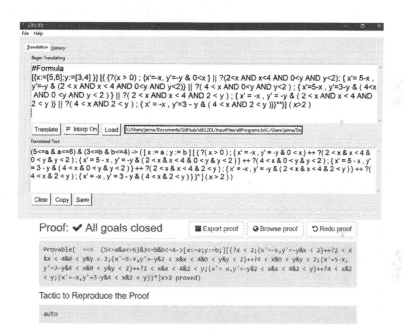

Fig. 2. The translation of the biological regulatory network example in idDL2dDL and the respective proof in KX.

This example was then translated and proven in KX version 4.9.5, using the default automatic proof tactic according to Fig. 2. Note that, although the example presented is representative of biological scenarios treatable with KX in real biological systems, human intervention may be required while using the semi-automatic prover, to aid the closing of the proof goals.

3 Discussion and Conclusion

This paper introduces idDL2DL, a parser and translator from interval dynamic logic formulas to $d\mathcal{L}$. An example of how to use the tool is presented with a case study for the synthetic biology field. As aforementioned, the formalism introduced consists of a syntax directed to interval contexts along with adapted semantics, to inherit the soundness from $d\mathcal{L}$ (see [1,5]). We note that interval arithmetic has already been considered in $d\mathcal{L}$, through a different approach, in [10]. In that work, a third truth-value U is considered for uncertain statements like $[0,2] < [1,3]$. These kinds of propositions are evaluated as $false$ in the present work, to carry a conservative approach. Consequently, our semantical interpretation of continuous evolutions was adapted, not being so restrictive to catch every punctual n-dimension initial state. This allows KX to consider every possible continuous evolution as in $d\mathcal{L}$ and, in this way, preserve the soundness (see [5] for details). This tool still has room for multiple improvements, mainly when it comes to extending its pre-processing capabilities. With this user-friendly interface, we aim to develop a user-friendly tool for those without experience in formal verification, as is the case of synthetic biology.

References

1. Platzer, A.: Virtual substitution & real arithmetic. In: Logical Foundations of Cyber-Physical Systems, pp. 607–628. Springer, Cham (2018). https://doi.org/10.1007/978-3-319-63588-0_21
2. Müller, A., Mitsch, S., Schwinger, W., Platzer, A.: A component-based hybrid systems verification and implementation tool in KeYmaera X (tool demonstration). In: Chamberlain, R., Taha, W., Törngren, M. (eds.) CyPhy/WESE -2018. LNCS, vol. 11615, pp. 91–110. Springer, Cham (2019). https://doi.org/10.1007/978-3-030-23703-5_5
3. Harel, D., Tiuryn, J., Kozen, D.: Dynamic Logic. MIT Press, Cambridge (2000)
4. Figueiredo, D., Martins, M.A., Chaves, M.: Applying differential dynamic logic to reconfigurable biological networks. Math. Biosci. **291**, 10–20 (2017)
5. Figueiredo, D.: Introducing interval differential dynamic logic. In: Hojjat, H., Massink, M. (eds.) FSEN 2021. LNCS, vol. 12818, pp. 69–75. Springer, Cham (2021). https://doi.org/10.1007/978-3-030-89247-0_5
6. Moore, R.E.: Interval arithmetic and automatic error analysis in digital computing. PhD thesis, Stanford University (1962)
7. Figueiredo, D., Barbosa, L.S.: Reactive models for biological regulatory networks. In: Chaves, M., Martins, M.A. (eds.) MLCSB 2018. LNCS, vol. 11415, pp. 74–88. Springer, Cham (2019). https://doi.org/10.1007/978-3-030-19432-1_5
8. Kubica, B.J.: Interval Methods for Solving Nonlinear Constraint Satisfaction, Optimization and Similar Problems. SCI, vol. 805. Springer, Cham (2019). https://doi.org/10.1007/978-3-030-13795-3
9. De Jong, H.: Modeling and simulation of genetic regulatory systems: a literature review. J. Comput. Biol. **9**(1), 67–103 (2002)
10. Bohrer, B., Tan, Y.K., Mitsch, S., Myreen, M.O., Platzer, A.: VeriPhy: verified controller executables from verified cyber-physical system models. In: Proceedings of the 39th ACM SIGPLAN Conference on Programming Language Design and Implementation, pp. 617–630. Association for Computing Machinery (2018)

11. Sanfelice, R., Copp, D., Nanez, P.: A toolbox for simulation of hybrid systems in Matlab/Simulink: hybrid equations (HyEQ) toolbox. In: Belta, C., Ivancic, F. (eds.) Proceedings of the 16th International Conference on Hybrid Systems: Computation and Control, HSCC 2013, pp. 101–106. ACM (2013)

12. Santiago, R., Bedregal, B., Madeira, A., Martins, M.A.: On interval dynamic logic: introducing quasi-action lattices. Sci. Comput. Program. **175**, 1–16 (2019)

13. Bohrer, B., Tan, Y.K., Mitsch, S., Myreen, M.O., Platzer, A.: VeriPhy: verified controller executables from verified cyber-physical system models. SIGPLAN Not. **53**(4), 617–630 (2018)

Safety Verification for Neural Networks Based on Set-Boundary Analysis

Zhen Liang[1] , Dejin Ren[2,3] , Wanwei Liu[4] , Ji Wang[1] , Wenjing Yang[1] , and Bai Xue[2,3(✉)]

[1] Institute for Quantum Information and State Key Laboratory of High Performance Computing, National University of Defense Technology, Changsha, China
{liangzhen,wj,wenjing.yang}@nudt.edu.cn
[2] State Key Laboratory of Computer Science, Institute of Software, Chinese Academy of Sciences, Beijing, China
{rendj,xuebai}@ios.ac.cn
[3] University of Chinese Academy of Sciences, Beijing, China
[4] College of Computer Science and Technology, National University of Defense Technology, Changsha, China
wwliu@nudt.edu.cn

Abstract. Neural networks (NNs) are increasingly applied in safety-critical systems such as autonomous vehicles. However, they are fragile and are often ill-behaved. Consequently, their behaviors should undergo rigorous guarantees before deployment in practice. In this paper, we propose a set-boundary reachability method to investigate the safety verification problem of NNs from a topological perspective. Given an NN with an input set and a safe set, the safety verification problem is to determine whether all outputs of the NN resulting from the input set fall within the safe set. In our method, the homeomorphism property of NNs is mainly exploited, which establishes a relationship mapping boundaries to boundaries. The exploitation of this property facilitates reachability computations via extracting subsets of the input set rather than the entire input set, thus controlling the wrapping effect in reachability analysis and facilitating the reduction of computation burdens for safety verification. The homeomorphism property exists in some widely used NNs such as invertible NNs. Notable representations are invertible residual networks (i-ResNets) and Neural ordinary differential equations (Neural ODEs). For these NNs, our set-boundary reachability method only needs to perform reachability analysis on the boundary of the input set. For NNs that do not feature this property with respect to the input set, we explore subsets of the input set for establishing the local homeomorphism property and then abandon these subsets for reachability computations. Finally, some examples demonstrate the performance of the proposed method.

Keywords: Safety verification · Neural networks · Boundary analysis · Homeomorphism

C. David and M. Sun (Eds.): TASE 2023, LNCS 13931, pp. 248–267, 2023.
https://doi.org/10.1007/978-3-031-35257-7_15

1   Introduction

Machine learning has seen rapid growth due to the high amount of data produced in many industries and the increase in computation power. NNs have emerged as a leading candidate computation model for machine learning, which promotes the prosperity of artificial intelligence in various fields, such as computer vision [7, 39], natural language processing [23, 50] and so on. Recently, NNs are increasingly applied in safety-critical systems. Consequently, to gain users' trust and ease their concerns, it is of vital importance to ensure that NNs are able to produce safe outputs and satisfy the essential safety requirements before the deployment.

Safety verification of NNs, which determines whether all outputs of an NN satisfy specified safety requirements via computing output reachable sets, has attracted huge attention from different communities such as machine learning [1, 30], formal methods [19, 29, 40], and security [11, 42]. Because NNs are generally large, nonlinear, and non-convex, exact computation of output reachable sets is challenging. Although there are some methods on exact reachability analysis such as SMT-based [24] and polyhedron-based approaches [41, 44], they are usually time-consuming and do not scale well. Moreover, these methods are limited to NNs with ReLU activation functions. Consequently, over-approximate reachability analysis, which mainly involves the computation of super sets of output reachable sets, is often resorted to in practice. The over-approximate analysis is usually more efficient and can be applied to more general NNs beyond ReLU ones. Due to these advantages, increasing attention has been attracted and thus a large number of computational techniques have been developed for over-approximate reachability analysis [28].

Overly conservative over-approximations, however, often render many safety properties unverifiable in practice. This conservatism mainly results from the wrapping effect, which is the accumulation of over-approximation errors through layer-by-layer propagation. As the extent of the wrapping effect correlates strongly with the size of the input set [45], techniques that partition the input set and independently compute output reachable sets of the resulting subsets are often adopted to reduce the wrapping effect, especially for the cases of large input sets. Such partitioning may, however, produce a great number of subsets, which is generally exponential in dimensionality. This will induce extensive demand on computation time and memory, often rendering existing reachability analysis techniques not suitable for the safety verification of complex NNs in real applications. Therefore, exploring subsets of the input set rather than the entire input set could help reduce computation burdens and thus accelerate the safety verification tremendously.

In this work, we investigate the safety verification problem of NNs from the topological perspective and extend the set-boundary reachability method, which is originally proposed for verifying the safety properties of systems modeled by ODEs in [46], to the safety verification of NNs. In [46], the set-boundary reachability method only performs over-approximate reachability analysis on the initial set's boundary rather than the entire initial set to address safety verification problems. It was built upon the homeomorphism property of ODEs. This nice property also widely exists in NNs, and representative NNs are invertible NNs such as neural ODEs [5] and invertible residual networks [4]. Consequently, it is straightforward to extend the set-boundary reachability method to safety verification of these NNs, just using the boundary of the input set for reachability analysis which does not involve reachability computations of interior points and thus reducing computation burdens in safety verification. Furthermore, we extend the set-boundary reachability method to general NNs (feedforward NNs) by exploiting the local homeomorphism property with respect to the input set. This exploitation is instrumental for constructing a subset of the input set for reachability computations, which is gained via removing a set of points in the input set such that the NN is a homeomorphism with respect to them. The above methods of extracting subsets for performing reachability computations can also be applied to intermediate layers of NNs rather than just between the input and output layers. Finally, we demonstrate the performance of the proposed method on several examples.

Main contributions of this paper are listed as follows.

- We investigate the safety verification problem of NNs from the topological perspective. More concretely, we exploit the homeomorphism property and aim at extracting a subset of the input set rather than the entire input set for reachability computations. To the best of our knowledge, this is the first work on the utilization of the homeomorphism property to address the safety verification problems of NNs. This might on its own open research directions on digging into insightful topological properties of facilitating reachability computations for NNs.
- The proposed method is able to enhance the capabilities and performances of existing reachability computation methods for the safety verification of NNs via reducing computation burdens. Based on the homeomorphism property, the computation burdens of solving the safety verification problem can be reduced for invertible NNs. We further show that the computation burdens can also be reduced for more general NNs by exploiting this property on subsets of the input set.

The remainder of this paper is structured as follows. First, an overview of the closely relevant research is introduced in Sect. 2. Afterward, we formulate the safety verification problem of interest on NNs in Sect. 3 and then elucidate our set-boundary reachability method for addressing the safety verification problem with the homeomorphism property in Sect. 4. Following this, we demonstrate the performance of our set-boundary reachability method and compare it with existing methods on several examples in Sect. 5. Finally, we summarize the paper and discuss potential future work in Sect. 6.

2   Related Work

There have been a dozen of works on the safety verification of NNs. The first work on DNN verification was published in [36], which focuses on DNNs with Sigmoid activation functions via a partition-refinement approach. Later, Katz et al.

[24] and Ehlers [10] independently implemented Reluplex and Planet, two SMT solvers to verify DNNs with ReLU activation function on properties expressible with SMT constraints.

In recent years, methods based on abstract interpretation attracts much more attention, which are to propagate sets layer by layer in a sound (i.e., over-approximate) way [6] and are more efficient. There are many widely used abstract domains, such as intervals [42], and star-sets [40]. A method based on zonotope abstract domains is proposed in [11], which works for any piece linear activation function with great scalability. Then, it is further improved [37] for obtaining tighter results via imposing abstract transformation on ReLU, Tanh and Sigmoid activation functions. [37] proposed specialized abstract zonotope transformers for handling NNs with ReLU, Sigmoid and Tanh functions. [38] proposes an abstract domain that combines floating point polyhedra with intervals to over-approximate output reachable sets. Subsequently, a spurious region guided approach is proposed to infer tighter output reachable sets [49] based on the method in [38]. [9] abstracts an NN by a polynomial, which has the advantage that dependencies can in principle be preserved. This approach can be precise in practice for small input sets. [25] completes NN verification with non-convex polynomial zonotope domains, obtaining tighter reachable sets. Afterward, [18] approximates Lipschitz-continuous neural networks with Bernstein polynomials. [20] transforms a neural network with Sigmoid activation functions into a hybrid automaton and then uses existing reachability analysis methods for the hybrid automaton to perform reachability computations. [45] proposed a maximum sensitivity based approach for solving safety verification problems for multi-layer perceptrons with monotonic activation functions. In this approach, an exhaustive search of the input set is enabled by discretizing input space to compute the output reachable set which consists of a union of reachtubes.

Neural ODEs were first introduced in 2018, which exhibit considerable computational efficiency on time-series modeling tasks [5]. Recent years have witnessed an increased use of them on real-world applications [17,27]. However, the verification techniques for Neural ODEs are rare and still in infancy. The first reachability technique for Neural ODEs appeared in [16], which proposed Stochastic Lagrangian reachability, an abstraction-based technique for constructing an over-approximation of the output reachable set with probabilistic guarantees. Later, this method was improved and implemented in a tool GoTube [15], which is able to perform reachability analysis for long time horizons. Since these methods only provide stochastic bounds on the computed over-approximation and thus cannot provide formal guarantees on the satisfaction of safety properties, [31] presented a deterministic verification framework for a general class of Neural ODEs with multiple continuous- and discrete-time layers.

Based on entire input sets, all the aforementioned works focus on developing computational techniques for reachability analysis and safety verification of appropriate NNs. In contrast, the present work shifts this focus to topological analysis of NNs and guides reachability computations on subsets of the input set rather than the entire input set, reducing computation burdens and thus increasing the power of existing safety verification methods for NNs. Although there are studies on topological properties of NNs [4,8,35], there is no work on the utilization of homeomorphism property to analyze their reachability and safety verification problems, to the best of our knowledge.

3   Preliminaries

In this section, we give an introduction on the safety verification problem of interest for NNs and homeomorphisms. Throughout this paper, given a set Δ, Δ°, $\partial\Delta$ and $\overline{\Delta}$ respectively denotes its interior, boundary and the closure.

NNs, also known as artificial NNs, are a subset of machine learning and are at the heart of deep learning algorithms. It works by using interconnected nodes or neurons in a layered structure that resembles a human brain, and is generally composed of three layers: an input layer, hidden layers and an output layer. Mathematically, it is a mathematical function $N(\cdot) : \mathbb{R}^n \to \mathbb{R}^m$, where n and m respectively denote the dimension of the input and output of the NN.

3.1   Problem Statement

Given an input set $\mathcal{X}_{in}$, the output reachable set of an NN $N(\cdot) : \mathbb{R}^n \to \mathbb{R}^m$ is stated by the following definition.

Definition 1. *For a given neural network $N(\cdot) : \mathbb{R}^n \to \mathbb{R}^m$, with an input set $\mathcal{X}_{in} \subseteq \mathbb{R}^n$, the output reachable set $\mathcal{R}(\mathcal{X}_{in})$ is defined as*

$$\mathcal{R}(\mathcal{X}_{in}) = \{y \in \mathbb{R}^m \mid y = N(x),\ x \in \mathcal{X}_{in}\}.$$

The safety verification problem is formulated in Definition 2.

Definition 2 (Safety Verification Problem).   *Given a neural network $N(\cdot) : \mathbb{R}^n \to \mathbb{R}^m$, an input set $\mathcal{X}_{in} \subseteq \mathbb{R}^n$ which is compact, and a safe set $\mathcal{X}_s \subseteq \mathbb{R}^m$ which is simply connected, the safety verification problem is to verify that*

$$\forall x_0 \in \mathcal{X}_{in}.\ N(x_0) \in \mathcal{X}_s.$$

In topology, a simply connected set is a path-connected set where one can continuously shrink any simple closed curve into a point while remaining in it. The requirement that the safe set $\mathcal{X}_s$ is a simply connected set is not strict, since many widely used sets such as intervals, ellipsoids, convex polyhedra and zonotopes are simply connected.

Obviously, the safety property that $\forall x_0 \in \mathcal{X}_{in}.\ N(x_0) \in \mathcal{X}_s$ holds if and only if $\mathcal{R}(\mathcal{X}_{in}) \subseteq \mathcal{X}_s$. However, it is challenging to compute the exact output reachable set $\mathcal{R}(\mathcal{X}_{in})$ and thus an over-approximation $\Omega(\mathcal{X}_{in})$, which is a super set of the set $\mathcal{R}(\mathcal{X}_{in})$ (i.e., $\mathcal{R}(\mathcal{X}_{in}) \subseteq \Omega(\mathcal{X}_{in})$), is commonly resorted to in existing literature for formally reasoning about the safety property. If $\Omega(\mathcal{X}_{in}) \subseteq \mathcal{X}_s$, the safety property that $\forall x_0 \in \mathcal{X}_{in}.\ N(x_0) \in \mathcal{X}_s$ holds.

3.2   Homeomorphisms

In this subsection, we will recall the definition of a homeomorphism, which is a map between spaces that preserves all topological properties.

Definition 3. *A map* $h : \mathcal{X} \to \mathcal{Y}$ *with* $\mathcal{X}, \mathcal{Y} \subseteq \mathbb{R}^n$ *is a homeomorphism with respect to* $\mathcal{X}$ *if it is a continuous bijection and its inverse* $h^{-1}(\cdot) : \mathcal{Y} \to \mathcal{X}$ *is also continuous.*

Homeomorphisms are continuous maps that preserve topological properties, which map boundaries to boundaries and interiors to interiors [33], as illustrated in Fig. 1.

Proposition 1. *Suppose sets* $\mathcal{X}, \mathcal{Y} \subseteq \mathbb{R}^n$ *are compact. If a map* $h(\cdot) : \mathcal{X} \to \mathcal{Y}$ *is a homeomorphism, then* h *maps the boundary of the set* $\mathcal{X}$ *onto the boundary of the set* $\mathcal{Y}$, *and the interior of the set* $\mathcal{X}$ *onto the interior of the set* $\mathcal{Y}$.

(a) A homeomorphic map   (b) A non-homeomorphic map

Fig. 1. Homeomorphic and non-homeomorphic maps

Based on this property, [46] proposed a set-boundary reachability method for safety verification of ODEs, via only propagating the initial set's boundary. Later, this method was extended to a class of delay differential equations [48].

4   Safety Verification Based on Boundary Analysis

In this section, we introduce our set-boundary reachability method for addressing the safety verification problem in the sense of Definition 1. We first consider invertible NNs in Subsect. 4.1, and then extend the method to more general NNs in Subsect. 4.2.

4.1   Safety Verification on Invertible NNs

In this subsection, we introduce our set-boundary reachability method for safety verification on invertible NNs, which relies on the homeomorphism property of these NNs.

Generally, invertible NNs, such as i-RevNets [21], RevNets [13], i-ResNets [4] and Neural ODEs [5], are NNs with invertibility by designed architectures, which are extensively used in flow model and can reconstruct inputs from their outputs. These NNs are continuous bijective maps. Based on the facts that $\mathcal{X}_{in}$ is compact,

Algorithm 1. Safety Verification Framework for Invertible NNs Based on Boundary Analysis

---

Input: an invertible NN $N(\cdot) : \mathbb{R}^n \to \mathbb{R}^n$, an input set $\mathcal{X}_{in}$ and a safe set $\mathcal{X}_s$.
Output: **Safe** or **Unknown**.

1: extract the boundary $\partial \mathcal{X}_{in}$ of the input set $\mathcal{X}_{in}$;
2: apply existing methods to compute an over-approximation $\Omega(\partial \mathcal{X}_{in})$;
3: **if** $\Omega(\partial \mathcal{X}_{in}) \subseteq \mathcal{X}_s$ **then**
4:     return **Safe**
5: **else**
6:     return **Unknown**
7: **end if**

---

they are homeomorphisms [Corollary 2.4, [22]][1]. In the existing literature, many invertible NNs are constructed by requiring their Jacobian determinants to be non-zero [3]. Consequently, based on the inverse function theorem [26], these NNs are homeomorphisms. In the present work, we also use Jacobian determinants to justify the invertibility of some NNs. It is noteworthy that Jacobian determinants being non-zero is a sufficient but not necessary condition for homeomorphisms and the reason that we resort to this requirement lies in the simple and efficient computations of Jacobian determinants with interval arithmetic. However, this demands the differentiability of NNs. Thus, this technique of computing Jacobian determinants to determine homeomorphisms is not applicable to NNs with ReLU activation functions.

Based on the homeomorphism property of mapping the input set's boundary onto the output reachable set's boundary, we propose a set-boundary reachability method for safety verification of invertible NNs, which just performs the over-approximate reachability analysis on the input set's boundary. Its computation procedure is presented in Algorithm 1.

Remark 1. In the second step of Algorithm 1, we may take the partition operator on the input set's boundary to refine the computed over-approximation for addressing the safety verification problem. The computations can be accelerated via parallel techniques.

Theorem 1 (Soundness). *If Algorithm 1 returns* **Safe**, *the safety property in the sense of Definition 1 holds.*

Proof. It is equivalent to show that if $\mathcal{R}(\partial \mathcal{X}_{in}) \subseteq \mathcal{X}_s$,

$$\forall \boldsymbol{x}_0 \in \mathcal{X}_{in}. \ N(\boldsymbol{x}_0) \in \mathcal{X}_s.$$

The conclusion holds by Lemma 3 in [46].

In order to enhance the understanding of Algorithm 1 and its benefits, we use a sample example to illustrate it.

---

[1] A continuous bijection from a compact space onto a Hausdorff space is a homeomorphism. (Euclidean space and any subset of Euclidean space is Hausdorff.).

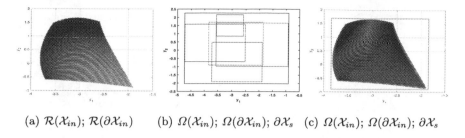

(a) $\mathcal{R}(\mathcal{X}_{in})$; $\mathcal{R}(\partial\mathcal{X}_{in})$ (b) $\Omega(\mathcal{X}_{in})$; $\Omega(\partial\mathcal{X}_{in})$; $\partial\mathcal{X}_s$ (c) $\Omega(\mathcal{X}_{in})$; $\Omega(\partial\mathcal{X}_{in})$; $\partial\mathcal{X}_s$

Fig. 2. Illustrations on Example 1 (Color figure online)

Example 1. Consider an *NN* from [45], which has 2 inputs, 2 outputs and 1 hidden layer consisting of 5 neurons. The input set is $\mathcal{X}_{in} = [0,1]^2$. Its boundary is $\partial\mathcal{X}_{in} = \cup_{i=1}^{4}\mathcal{B}_i$, where $\mathcal{B}_1 = [0,0] \times [0,1]$, $\mathcal{B}_2 = [1,1] \times [0,1]$, $\mathcal{B}_3 = [0,1] \times [0,0]$ and $\mathcal{B}_4 = [0,1] \times [1,1]$. The activation functions for the hidden layer and the output layer are `Tanh` and `Purelin` functions, respectively, whose weight matrices and bias vectors can be found in Example 1 in [45]. For this neural network, based on interval arithmetic, we can show that the determinant of the Jacobian matrix $\frac{\partial y}{\partial x_0} = \frac{\partial N(x_0)}{\partial x_0}$ is non-zero for any $x_0 \in \mathcal{X}_{in}$. Therefore, this NN is invertible and the map $N(\cdot) : \mathcal{X}_{in} \to \mathcal{R}(\mathcal{X}_{in})$ is a homeomorphism with respect to the input set $\mathcal{X}_{in}$, leading to $\mathcal{R}(\partial\mathcal{X}_{in}) = \partial\mathcal{R}(\mathcal{X}_{in})$. This statement is also verified via the visualized results in Fig. 2(a) ($\mathcal{R}(\mathcal{X}_{in})$ in blue; $\mathcal{R}(\partial\mathcal{X}_{in})$ in red).

The homeomorphism property facilitates the reduction of the wrapping effect in over-approximate reachability analysis and thus reduces computation burdens in addressing the safety verification problem in the sense of Definition 1. For this example, with the safe set $\mathcal{X}_s = [-3.85, -1.85] \times [-0.9, 1.7]$ (in green), we first take the input set and its boundary for reachability computations. Based on interval arithmetic, we respectively compute over-approximations $\Omega(\mathcal{X}_{in})$ (blue) and $\Omega(\partial\mathcal{X}_{in})$ (red), which are illustrated in Fig. 2(b). Although the approximation $\Omega(\partial\mathcal{X}_{in})$ is indeed smaller than $\Omega(\mathcal{X}_{in})$, it still renders the safety property unverifiable. We next take the partition operator for more accurate reachability computations. If the entire input set is used, we can successfully verify the safety property when the entire input set is divided into 10^4 small intervals of equal size. In contrast, our set-boundary reachability method just needs 400 equal partitions on the input set's boundary, significantly reducing the computation burdens. The reachability results, i.e., the computation of $\Omega(\partial\mathcal{X}_{in})$, are illustrated in Fig. 2(c), with the same color remarks in Fig. 2(b).

4.2 Safety Verification on Non-invertible NNs

When an NN has the homeomorphism property, we can use Algorithm 1 to address the safety verification problem in the sense of Definition 1. However, not all of NNs have such a nice property. In this subsection, we extend the set-boundary reachability method to safety verification of non-invertible NNs, via analyzing the homeomorphism property of NNs with respect to subsets of the input set $\mathcal{X}_{in}$.

Example 2. Consider an NN from [43], which has 2 inputs, 2 outputs and 1 hidden layer consisting of 7 neurons. The input set is $\mathcal{X}_{in} = [-1, 1]^2$. The activation functions for the hidden layer and the output layer are `Tanh` and `Purelin`, whose weight matrices and bias vectors can be found in Example 4.3 in [43]. For this neural network, the boundary of the output reachable set (the blue region), i.e., $\partial\mathcal{R}(\mathcal{X}_{in})$, is not included in the output reachable set of the input set's boundary $\mathcal{R}(\partial\mathcal{X}_{in})$ (in red). This statement is visualized in Fig. 3(a).

Example 2 presents us an NN, whose mapping does not admit the homeomorphism property with respect to the input set and the output reachable set. However, the NN may feature the homeomorphism property with respect to a subset of the input set. This is illustrated in Example 3.

Example 3. Consider the NN in Example 2 again. We divide the input set $\mathcal{X}_{in}$ into 4×10^4 small intervals of equal size and verify whether the NN is a homeomorphism with respect to each of them based on the use of interval arithmetic to determine the determinant of the corresponding Jacobian matrix $\frac{\partial y}{\partial x_0} = \frac{\partial N(x_0)}{\partial x_0}$. The blue region in Fig. 3(b) is the set of intervals, which features the NN with the homeomorphism property. The number of these intervals is 31473. For simplicity, we denote these intervals by set $\mathcal{A}$.

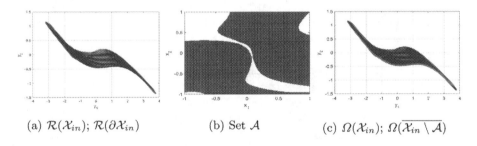

(a) $\mathcal{R}(\mathcal{X}_{in})$; $\mathcal{R}(\partial\mathcal{X}_{in})$ (b) Set $\mathcal{A}$ (c) $\Omega(\mathcal{X}_{in})$; $\Omega(\overline{\mathcal{X}_{in} \setminus \mathcal{A}})$

Fig. 3. Illustrations on Example 2, 3 and 4

It is interesting to find that the safety verification in the sense of Definition 1 can be addressed by performing reachability analysis on a subset of the input set $\mathcal{X}_{in}$. This subset is obtained via removing subsets in the input set $\mathcal{X}_{in}$, which features the NN with the homeomorphism property.

Theorem 2. *Let $\mathcal{A} \subseteq \mathcal{X}_{in}$ and $\mathcal{A} \cap \partial\mathcal{X}_{in} = \emptyset$, and $N(\cdot) : \mathcal{A} \to \mathcal{R}(\mathcal{A})$ be a homeomorphism with respect to the input set $\mathcal{A}$. Then, if the output reachable set of the closure of the set $\mathcal{X}_{in} \setminus \mathcal{A}$ is a subset of the safe set $\mathcal{X}_s$, i.e., $\mathcal{R}(\overline{\mathcal{X}_{in} \setminus \mathcal{A}}) \subseteq \mathcal{X}_s$, the safety property that $\forall x_0 \in \mathcal{X}_{in}. \ N(x_0) \in \mathcal{X}_s$ holds.*

Algorithm 2.. Safety Verification Framework for Non-Invertible NNs

---

Input: a non-invertible NN $N(\cdot) : \mathbb{R}^n \to \mathbb{R}^n$, an input set $\mathcal{X}_{in}$ and a safe set $\mathcal{X}_s$.
Output: **Safe** or **Unknown**.
1: determine a subset $\mathcal{A}$ of the set $\mathcal{X}_{in}$ such that $N(\cdot) : \mathbb{R}^n \to \mathbb{R}^n$ is a homeomorphism
   with respect to it;
2: apply existing methods to compute an over-approximation $\Omega(\overline{\mathcal{X}_{in} \setminus \mathcal{A}})$;
3: **if** $\Omega(\overline{\mathcal{X}_{in} \setminus \mathcal{A}}) \subseteq \mathcal{X}_s$ **then**
4:     return **Safe**
5: **else**
6:     return **Unknown**
7: **end if**

Proof. Obviously, if $\mathcal{R}(\mathcal{A}) \subseteq \mathcal{X}_s$ and $\mathcal{R}(\overline{\mathcal{X}_{in} \setminus \mathcal{A}}) \subseteq \mathcal{X}_s$, the safety property that $\forall \boldsymbol{x}_0 \in \mathcal{X}_{in}.\ N(\boldsymbol{x}_0) \in \mathcal{X}_s$ holds.

According to Theorem 1, we have that if $\mathcal{R}(\partial \mathcal{A}) \subseteq \mathcal{X}_s$, the safety property that $\forall \boldsymbol{x}_0 \in \mathcal{A}.\ N(\boldsymbol{x}_0) \in \mathcal{X}_s$ holds.

According to the condition that $\mathcal{A} \subseteq \mathcal{X}_{in}$ and $\mathcal{A} \cap \partial \mathcal{X}_{in} = \emptyset$, we have that $\mathcal{A} \subseteq \mathcal{X}_{in}^\circ$ and thus $\partial \mathcal{A} \subseteq \overline{\mathcal{X}_{in} \setminus \mathcal{A}}$. Therefore, $\mathcal{R}(\overline{\mathcal{X}_{in} \setminus \mathcal{A}}) \subseteq \mathcal{X}_s$ implies that $\forall \boldsymbol{x}_0 \in \mathcal{X}_{in}.\ N(\boldsymbol{x}_0) \in \mathcal{X}_s$. The proof is completed.

Theorem 2 tells that it is still possible to use a subset of the input set for the safety verification problem in Definition 1, even if the given NN is not a homeomorphism w.r.t. the entire input set $\mathcal{X}_{in}$. This is shown in Example 4.

Example 4. Consider the situation in Example 3 again. If the entire input set is used for computations, all of 4×10^4 small intervals participate in calculations. However, Theorem 2 tells us that only 9071 intervals (i.e., subset $\overline{\mathcal{X}_{in} \setminus \mathcal{A}}$) are needed, which is much smaller than 4×10^4. The computation results based on interval arithmetic are illustrated in Fig. 3(c) ($\Omega(\mathcal{X}_{in})$ in blue; $\Omega(\overline{\mathcal{X}_{in} \setminus \mathcal{A}})$ in red). It is noting that 9071 intervals rather than 8527 ($= 4 \times 10^4 - 31473$) intervals are used since some intervals, which have non-empty intersection with the boundary of the input set $\mathcal{X}_{in}$ (since Theorem 2 requires $\mathcal{A} \cap \partial \mathcal{X}_{in} = \emptyset$), should participate in calculations.

Remark 2. According to Theorem 2, we can also observe that the boundary of the output reachable set $\mathcal{R}(\mathcal{X}_{in})$ is included in the output reachable set of the input set $\overline{\mathcal{X}_{in} \setminus \mathcal{A}}$, i.e., $\partial \mathcal{R}(\mathcal{X}_{in}) \subseteq \mathcal{R}(\overline{\mathcal{X}_{in} \setminus \mathcal{A}})$. This can also be visualized in Fig. 3(c). Consequently, this observation may open new research directions of addressing various problems of NNs [12]. For instance, it may facilitate the generation of adversarial examples, which are inputs causing the NN to falsify the safety property, and the characterization of decision boundaries of NNs, which are a surface that separates data points belonging to different class labels.

Therefore, we arrive at an algorithm for the safety verification of non-invertible NNs, which is formulated in Algorithm 2.

Theorem 3 (Soundness). *If Algorithm 2 returns* **Safe**, *the safety property that* $\forall \boldsymbol{x}_0 \in \mathcal{X}_{in}.\ N(\boldsymbol{x}_0) \in \mathcal{X}_s$ *holds.*

Proof. This conclusion can be assured by Theorem 2.

Remark 3. The set-boundary reachability method can also be applied to intermediate layers in a given NN, rather than just the input and output layers. Suppose that there exists a sub-NN $\boldsymbol{N}'(\cdot) : \mathbb{R}^{n'} \to \mathbb{R}^{n'}$, which maps the input of the l-th layer to the output of the k-th layer, in the given NNs, and its input set is $\mathcal{X}'_{in}$ which is an over-approximation of the output reachable set of the $(l-1)$-th layer. If $\boldsymbol{N}'(\cdot) : \mathbb{R}^{n'} \to \mathbb{R}^{n'}$ is a homeomorphism with respect to $\mathcal{X}'_{in}$, we can use $\partial \mathcal{X}'_{in}$ to compute an over-approximation $\Omega'(\partial \mathcal{X}'_{in})$ of the output reachable set $\{\boldsymbol{y} \mid \boldsymbol{y} = \boldsymbol{N}'(\boldsymbol{x}_0), \boldsymbol{x}_0 \in \partial \mathcal{X}'_{in}\}$; otherwise, we can apply Theorem 2 and compute an over-approximation $\Omega'(\overline{\mathcal{X}'_{in} \setminus \mathcal{A}})$ of the output reachable set $\{\boldsymbol{y} \mid \boldsymbol{y} = \boldsymbol{N}'(\boldsymbol{x}_0), \boldsymbol{x}_0 \in \overline{\mathcal{X}'_{in} \setminus \mathcal{A}}\}$. In case that the k-th layer is not the output layer of the NN, we need to construct a simply connected set, like convex polytope, zonotope or interval, to cover $\Omega'(\partial \mathcal{X}'_{in})$ or $\Omega'(\overline{\mathcal{X}'_{in} \setminus \mathcal{A}})$ for the subsequent layer-by-layer propagation. This set is an over-approximation of the output reachable set of the k-th layer, according to Lemma 1 in [47].

Remark 4. Any existing over-approximate reachability methods such as interval arithmetic- [42], zonotopes- [37], star sets [40] based methods, which are suitable for given NNs, can be used to compute the involved over-approximations, i.e., $\Omega(\partial \mathcal{X}_{in})$ and $\Omega(\overline{\mathcal{X}_{in} \setminus \mathcal{A}})$, in Algorithm 1 and 2.

5   Experiments

In this section, several examples of NNs are used to demonstrate the performance of the proposed set-boundary reachability method for safety verification. Experiments are conducted on invertible NNs and general ones respectively. Recall that the proposed set-boundary method is applicable for any reachability analysis algorithm based on set representation, resulting in tighter and verifiable over-approximations when existing approaches fail. Thus, we compare the set-boundary method versus the entire set based one on some existing reachability tools in terms of effectiveness and efficiency.

Experiment Setting. All the experiments herein are run on MATLAB 2021a with Intel (R) Core (TM) i7-10750H CPU@2.60 GHz and RAM 16 GB. The codes and models are available from https://github.com/DejinRen/BoundaryNN.

5.1   Experiments on Invertible NNs

In this subsection, we carry out some examples involving neural ODEs and invertible feedforward neural networks.

Neural ODEs. We experiment on two widely-used neural ODEs in [32], which are respectively a nonlinear 2-dimensional spiral [5] with the input set $\mathcal{X}_{in} = [1.5, 2.5] \times [-0.5, 0.5]$ and the safe set $\mathcal{X}_s = [-0.08, 0.9] \times [-1.5, -0.3]$ and a 12-dimensional controlled cartpole [14] with the input set $\mathcal{X}_{in} = [-0.001, 0.001]^{12}$

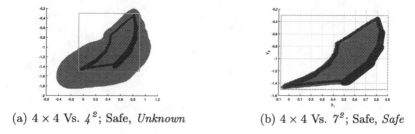

(a) 4×4 Vs. 4^2; Safe, *Unknown*   (b) 4×4 Vs. 7^2; Safe, *Safe*

Fig. 4. Verification on N_1

and the safe set $\mathcal{X}_s = \{y \in \mathbb{R}^{12} \mid y_1 \in [0.0545, 0.1465], y_2 \in [0.145, 0.725]\}$. For simplicity, we respectively denote them by N_1 and N_2.

Here, we take zonotopes as abstract domains and compare the output reachable sets computed by the set boundary reachability method and the entire input set based method. The over-approximate reachability analysis is performed by the continuous reachability analyzer CORA [2], with minor modifications [32].

The time horizon and the time step are respectively $[0, 6]$ and 0.01 for verification computations on N_1. The performance of our set-boundary reachability method and the comparison with the entire input set based method are summarized in Table 1. The number n in the 'Partition' column denotes that the entire input set is divided into equal n^2 subsets, and the boundary of the input set into $4n$ subsets. During each partition, if we fail to verify the safety property, we continue the use of the partition operator to obtain smaller subsets for computations. Otherwise, we terminate the partition. In each partition-verification round, the corresponding computation time from the entire input set based method and our set-boundary reachability method are respectively listed in the 'Entire set' and 'Boundary' column of Table 1, which shows their ratios as well. We also present the total verification time in the last row, i.e., the sum of computation times

Table 1. Time consumption of safety verification on N_1 and N_3

Partition	Network N_1			Network N_3		
	Entire set	Boundary	Ratio	Entire set	Boundary	Ratio
1	3.3417	29.8787	8.941	1.5080	5.6662	3.757
2	31.9848	106.0663	3.316	5.9560	11.4954	1.930
3	111.6617	159.6125	1.429	13.5740	17.1452	1.263
4	235.0475	**220.8258**	0.939	23.9392	22.9996	0.961
5	325.2500	–	–	37.2290	**28.4822**	0.765
6	477.5187	–	–	54.4542	–	–
7	*671.3200*	–	–	73.9100	–	–
8	–	–	–	*95.5307*	–	–
Total	*1856.1240*	**516.3833**	0.278	*306.0975*	85.7886	0.280

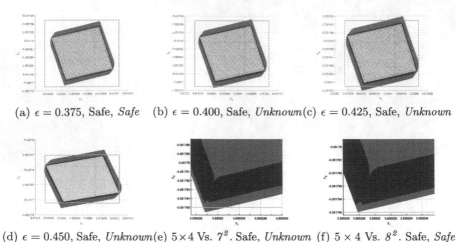

(a) $\epsilon = 0.375$, Safe, *Safe*   (b) $\epsilon = 0.400$, Safe, *Unknown*(c) $\epsilon = 0.425$, Safe, *Unknown*

(d) $\epsilon = 0.450$, Safe, *Unknown*(e) 5×4 Vs. 7^2. Safe, *Unknown* (f) 5×4 Vs. 8^2. Safe, *Safe*

Fig. 5. Safety verification on N_3

in all rounds. These statements also apply to other tables. Our set-boundary reachability method for N_1 returns 'Safe' when the boundary of the input set is partitioned into 16 equal subsets (blue regions and Roman style texts). However, the safety property for N_1 is verified until the entire input set is partitioned into 49 equal subsets (red regions and *Italic* style texts). The computed output reachable sets for N_1 are displayed in Fig. 4(a) and 4(b). It is observed from Table 1 that the computation time from the set-boundary reachability method is reduced by 72.2%, compared to the entire input set based method.

For network N_2, when the time horizon is $[0.0, 1.1]$ and the time step is 0.01, we first use the entire set based method to verify the safety property. Unfortunately, it fails. Consequently, we have to partition the entire input set into small subsets for the verification. In this case, the boundary of the input set is a good choice and thus we utilize the set-boundary reachability method for the safety verification. Without further splitting, our set-boundary reachability method returns 'Safe' with the time consumption of around 7400.5699 s.

Feedforward NNs. Rather than considering neural ODEs, we instead take more general invertible NNs, such as feedforward NNs, into account. The invertibility of NNs used here, i.e., N_3 and N_4, are assured by their Jacobian determinant not being zero. The NN N_3 is fully connected with `Sigmoid` activation functions, having an input/output layer with dimension 2 and 5 hidden layers with size 10. The NN N_4 is similar to N_3, consisting 5 hidden layers with size 5 and its input/output dimensions are 3. The results of safety verification of N_3 and N_4 are demonstrated in Fig. 5 and 6. The input sets in Fig. 5 are $[-0.375, 0.375]^2$, $[-0.4, 0.4]^2$, $[-0.425, 0.425]^2$, $[-0.45, 0.45]^2$ and $[-1.0, 1.0]^2$ (Fig. 5(e)–5(f).) respectively and those of Fig. 6 are $[-0.45, 0.45]^3$, $[-0.475, 0.475]^3$, $[-0.5, 0.5]^3$. Their safe sets $\mathcal{X}_s$

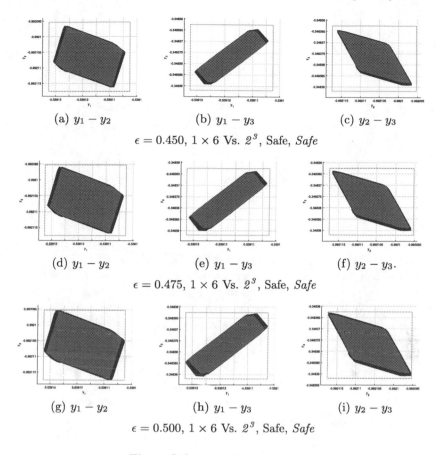

(a) $y_1 - y_2$ (b) $y_1 - y_3$ (c) $y_2 - y_3$

$\epsilon = 0.450$, 1×6 Vs. 2^3, Safe, *Safe*

(d) $y_1 - y_2$ (e) $y_1 - y_3$ (f) $y_2 - y_3$.

$\epsilon = 0.475$, 1×6 Vs. 2^3, Safe, *Safe*

(g) $y_1 - y_2$ (h) $y_1 - y_3$ (i) $y_2 - y_3$

$\epsilon = 0.500$, 1×6 Vs. 2^3, Safe, *Safe*

Fig. 6. Safety verification on N_4

are respectively $[0.835237, 0.835517] \times [-0.0517100, -0.0515511]$ (Fig. 5(a)–5(d)), $[0.835078, 0.83567] \times [-0.051795, \quad 0.05146]$ (Fig. 5(e)–5(f)) and $[-0.5391325, -0.5391025] \times [-0.9921175, -0.99209530] \times [-0.348392, -0.3483625]$ (Fig. 6), whose boundaries are shown in green color. The over-approximate reachability analysis is implemented with polynominal zonotope domains [25], which is a recently proposed NN verification tool via propagating polynominal zonotopes through networks and is termed OCNNV for brevity herein.

The output reachable sets from our set-boundary reachability method and the entire set based method are displayed in blue and red in Fig. 5 and 6, respectively. Further, we also show the exact output reachable sets estimated via the Monte-Carlo simulation method in Fig. 5, which corresponds to the yellow regions. The visualized results show that the set-boundary reachability method can generate tighter output reachable sets than the entire set based method. As a result, our set-boundary reachability method can verify the safety properties successfully when $\epsilon \in \{0.375, 0.400, 0.425, 0.450\}$, as shown in Fig. 6(a)–6(d). In contrast,

Table 2. Time consumption of safety verification on N_4

Partition	$\epsilon = 0.450$		$\epsilon = 0.475$		$\epsilon = 0.500$	
	Entire set	Boundary	Entire set	Boundary	Entire set	Boundary
1	0.7215	**4.1115**	0.7246	**4.2466**	0.7353	**4.3676**
2	*5.7110*	–	*5.7957*	–	*5.9281*	–
Total	*6.4325*	**4.1115**	*6.5203*	**4.2466**	*6.6634*	**4.3676**

the entire set based method fails for cases with large input sets, demonstrated in Fig. 6(b)–6(d), since the computed output reachable sets are not included in safe sets. Furthermore, when the safety property cannot be verified with respect to the input set $[-1.0, 1.0]^2$, we impose the uniform partition operator on both the entire input set and its boundary. When the boundary is divided into 20 equal subsets, the safety verification can be verified using the set-boundary reachability method (zoomed in, Fig. 6(e)) with the total verification time of 85.7886 s. However, when the entire input set is used, it should be partitioned into 64 equal subsets (zoomed in, Fig. 6(f)) and the total verification time is 306.5307 s. Consequently, the computation time from the set-boundary reachability method is reduced by 72.0%, as opposed to the entire input set based method. These times are also listed in Table 1. For N_4, the entire set based method fails to verify the safety property with respect to all the input sets, whose output reachable sets are shown in Appendix. It succeeds with partitioning each input set into 2^3 equal subsets, while the set-boundary reachability method succeeds without partitioning, as shown in Fig. 6. It also can be observed from Table 2, which shows the time consumption for safety verification on N_4, that our set-boundary reachability method reduces the time consumption by around 35% in all the cases.

5.2 Experiments on General Feedforward NNs

When the homeomorphism property cannot be assured with respect to the given input region, our method is also able to facilitate the extraction of subsets from the input region for safety verification, as done in Algorithm 2. In this subsection, we experiment on a non-invertible NN N_5, which shares a similar structure with N_3, with 3 hidden layers. The input set $\mathcal{X}_{in}$ and safe set $\mathcal{X}_s$ are $[-9.5, -9] \times [9.25, 9.5]$ and $[0.16294, 0.16331] \times [-0.1393, -0.13855]$, respectively. For verifying the safety property successfully, the entire set based method implemented on the tool OCNNV has to divide the input set into 50 equal subsets and the time consumed is about 47.3114 s. The corresponding output reachable set is displayed in Fig. 7(b) with the red region, which also shows the boundary of the safe region in green. Then, based on the tool OCNNV, we follow the computational procedure in Algorithm 2 to verify the safety property. The subset $\mathcal{A} = [-9.4, -9.05] \times [9.3, 9.45] \cup [-9.45, -9.4] \times [9.35, 9.45]$ rendering the NN homeomorphic is visualized in Fig. 7(a) with the orange region, and the subset $\overline{\mathcal{X}_{in} \setminus \mathcal{A}}$ is shown with the blue region in Fig. 7(a), which covers only 54%

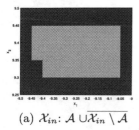

(a) $\mathcal{X}_{in}$: $\mathcal{A} \cup \overline{\mathcal{X}_{in} \setminus \mathcal{A}}$

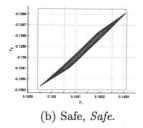

(b) Safe, *Safe*.

Fig. 7. Safety verification on N_5

of the initial input set and of which the corresponding output reachable set is illustrated in Fig. 7(b) with the blue region. It is noting to point out that the blue region overlaps with the boundary of the red region exactly. In this verification computation, the homeomorphism analysis takes around 10.3737 seconds and the output reachable set computations take 25.2487 s, totalling 35.6224 s. Therefore, our method reduces the time consumption of verification by 24.7%, compared with the entire set based method.

6   Conclusion

In this paper, we proposed a set-boundary reachability method to verify the safety property of neural networks. Different from existing works on developing computational techniques for output reachable sets estimation of NNs, the set-boundary reachability method analyzed the reachability from the topology point of view. Based on homeomorphism property, this analysis took a careful inspection on what happens at boundaries of input sets, and uncovered that the homeomorphism property facilitates the reduction of computational burdens on the safety verification of NNs. Several examples demonstrated the performance of our method and the comparison with existing methods. The experimental results showed that our method is indeed able to promote computation efficiency of existing verification methods on certain NNs.

There are a lot of works remaining to be done in order to render the proposed approach more practical. In the future we will develop more efficient and accurate methods (including the use of parallel computing techniques) for calculating Jacobian matrices. Besides, the homeomorphism property may be strict. Different from homeomorphisms, open maps, mapping open sets to open sets [34], can also ensure that the output reachable set's boundary corresponds to the input's boundary. Moreover, the open mapping condition is weaker than the one for homeomorphism. Consequently, in future work, we would exploit the open mapping property to facilitate reachability computations for safety verification.

Acknowledgement. This work is supported by the National Key R&D Program of China No. 2022YFA1005101, the National Natural Science Foundation of China under Grant No. 61836005, No. 61872371 and No. 62032024 and the CAS Pioneer Hundred Talents Program.

Appendix

For a better understanding of the safety verification on network N_4, we supplement some omitted verification details in the body part due to space limitation. For N_4 the entire set based method without partitioning fails to verify the safety property with respect to all the given input sets while our proposed set-boundary reachability method succeeds the verification. The output reachable sets of both methods are shown in Fig. 8. Also, the verification processes herein are run on MATLAB 2021a with Intel (R) Core (TM) i7-10750H CPU@2.60 GHz and RAM 16 GB.

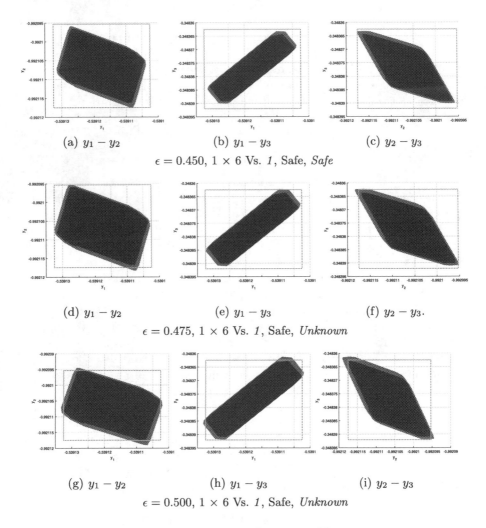

(a) $y_1 - y_2$ (b) $y_1 - y_3$ (c) $y_2 - y_3$

$\epsilon = 0.450$, 1×6 Vs. *1*, Safe, *Safe*

(d) $y_1 - y_2$ (e) $y_1 - y_3$ (f) $y_2 - y_3$.

$\epsilon = 0.475$, 1×6 Vs. *1*, Safe, *Unknown*

(g) $y_1 - y_2$ (h) $y_1 - y_3$ (i) $y_2 - y_3$

$\epsilon = 0.500$, 1×6 Vs. *1*, Safe, *Unknown*

Fig. 8. Safety verification on N_4

References

1. Akintunde, M.E., Kevorchian, A., Lomuscio, A., Pirovano, E.: Verification of rnn-based neural agent-environment systems. In: Proceedings of the AAAI Conference on Artificial Intelligence, vol. 33, pp. 6006–6013 (2019). https://doi.org/10.1609/aaai.v33i01.33016006
2. Althoff, M.: An introduction to CORA 2015. In: Proceedings of the Workshop on Applied Verification for Continuous and Hybrid Systems, pp. 120–151 (2015)
3. Ardizzone, L., Kruse, J., Rother, C., Köthe, U.: Analyzing inverse problems with invertible neural networks. In: International Conference on Learning Representations (2018)
4. Behrmann, J., Grathwohl, W., Chen, R.T., Duvenaud, D., Jacobsen, J.H.: Invertible residual networks. In: International Conference on Machine Learning, pp. 573–582. PMLR (2019)
5. Chen, R.T., Rubanova, Y., Bettencourt, J., Duvenaud, D.K.: Neural ordinary differential equations. In: Advances in Neural Information Processing Systems, vol. 31 (2018)
6. Cousot, P., Cousot, R.: Abstract interpretation: a unified lattice model for static analysis of programs by construction or approximation of fixpoints. In: Proceedings of the 4th ACM SIGACT-SIGPLAN Symposium on Principles of Programming Languages, pp. 238–252 (1977). https://doi.org/10.1145/512950.512973
7. Dahnert, M., Hou, J., Nießner, M., Dai, A.: Panoptic 3D scene reconstruction from a single RGB image. In: Advances in Neural Information Processing Systems, vol. 34 (2021)
8. Dupont, E., Doucet, A., Teh, Y.W.: Augmented neural odes. In: Advances in Neural Information Processing Systems, vol. 32 (2019)
9. Dutta, S., Jha, S., Sanakaranarayanan, S., Tiwari, A.: Output range analysis for deep neural networks. arXiv preprint arXiv:1709.09130 (2017)
10. Ehlers, R.: Formal verification of piece-wise linear feed-forward neural networks. In: D'Souza, D., Narayan Kumar, K. (eds.) ATVA 2017. LNCS, vol. 10482, pp. 269–286. Springer, Cham (2017). https://doi.org/10.1007/978-3-319-68167-2_19
11. Gehr, T., Mirman, M., Drachsler-Cohen, D., Tsankov, P., Chaudhuri, S., Vechev, M.: AI2: safety and robustness certification of neural networks with abstract interpretation. In: 2018 IEEE Symposium on Security and Privacy (SP), pp. 3–18. IEEE (2018). https://doi.org/10.1109/SP.2018.00058
12. Ghorbani, A., Abid, A., Zou, J.: Interpretation of neural networks is fragile. In: Proceedings of the AAAI Conference on Artificial Intelligence, vol. 33, pp. 3681–3688 (2019). https://doi.org/10.1609/aaai.v33i01.33013681
13. Gomez, A.N., Ren, M., Urtasun, R., Grosse, R.B.: The reversible residual network: backpropagation without storing activations. In: Advances in Neural Information Processing Systems, vol. 30 (2017)
14. Gruenbacher, S., Cyranka, J., Lechner, M., Islam, M.A., Smolka, S.A., Grosu, R.: Lagrangian Reachtubes: the next generation. In: 2020 59th IEEE Conference on Decision and Control (CDC), pp. 1556–1563. IEEE (2020). https://doi.org/10.1109/CDC42340.2020.9304042
15. Gruenbacher, S., et al.: GoTube: scalable stochastic verification of continuous-depth models. arXiv preprint arXiv:2107.08467 (2021)
16. Grunbacher, S., Hasani, R., Lechner, M., Cyranka, J., Smolka, S.A., Grosu, R.: On the verification of neural odes with stochastic guarantees. In: Proceedings of the AAAI Conference on Artificial Intelligence, vol. 35, pp. 11525–11535 (2021). https://doi.org/10.1609/aaai.v35i13.17372

17. Hasani, R., Lechner, M., Amini, A., Rus, D., Grosu, R.: A natural lottery ticket winner: reinforcement learning with ordinary neural circuits. In: International Conference on Machine Learning, pp. 4082–4093. PMLR (2020)
18. Huang, C., Fan, J., Li, W., Chen, X., Zhu, Q.: ReachNN: reachability analysis of neural-network controlled systems. ACM Trans. Embed. Comput. Syst. (TECS) **18**(5s), 1–22 (2019). https://doi.org/10.1145/3358228
19. Huang, X., Kwiatkowska, M., Wang, S., Wu, M.: Safety verification of deep neural networks. In: Majumdar, R., Kunčak, V. (eds.) CAV 2017. LNCS, vol. 10426, pp. 3–29. Springer, Cham (2017). https://doi.org/10.1007/978-3-319-63387-9_1
20. Ivanov, R., Carpenter, T.J., Weimer, J., Alur, R., Pappas, G.J., Lee, I.: Verifying the safety of autonomous systems with neural network controllers. ACM Trans. Embed. Comput. Syst. (TECS) **20**(1), 1–26 (2020). https://doi.org/10.1145/3419742
21. Jacobsen, J.H., Smeulders, A., Oyallon, E.: i-RevNet: deep invertible networks. arXiv preprint arXiv:1802.07088 (2018)
22. Joshi, K.D.: Introduction to General Topology. New Age International, New Delhi (1983)
23. Karch, T., Teodorescu, L., Hofmann, K., Moulin-Frier, C., Oudeyer, P.Y.: Grounding spatio-temporal language with transformers. arXiv preprint arXiv:2106.08858 (2021)
24. Katz, G., Barrett, C., Dill, D.L., Julian, K., Kochenderfer, M.J.: Reluplex: an efficient SMT solver for verifying deep neural networks. In: Majumdar, R., Kunčak, V. (eds.) CAV 2017. LNCS, vol. 10426, pp. 97–117. Springer, Cham (2017). https://doi.org/10.1007/978-3-319-63387-9_5
25. Kochdumper, N., Schilling, C., Althoff, M., Bak, S.: Open-and closed-loop neural network verification using polynomial zonotopes. arXiv preprint arXiv:2207.02715 (2022)
26. Krantz, S.G., Parks, H.R.: The Implicit Function Theorem: History, Theory, and Applications. Springer, New York (2002). https://doi.org/10.1007/978-1-4614-5981-1
27. Lechner, M., Hasani, R., Amini, A., Henzinger, T.A., Rus, D., Grosu, R.: Neural circuit policies enabling auditable autonomy. Nat. Mach. Intell. **2**(10), 642–652 (2020). https://doi.org/10.1038/s42256-020-00237-3
28. Liu, C., Arnon, T., Lazarus, C., Strong, C., Barrett, C., Kochenderfer, M.J., et al.: Algorithms for verifying deep neural networks. Found. Trends® Optim. **4**(3–4), 244–404 (2021). https://doi.org/10.1561/2400000035
29. Liu, W.-W., Song, F., Zhang, T.-H.-R., Wang, J.: Verifying ReLU neural networks from a model checking perspective. J. Comput. Sci. Technol. **35**(6), 1365–1381 (2020). https://doi.org/10.1007/s11390-020-0546-7
30. Lomuscio, A., Maganti, L.: An approach to reachability analysis for feed-forward ReLU neural networks. arXiv preprint arXiv:1706.07351 (2017)
31. Lopez, D.M., Musau, P., Hamilton, N., Johnson, T.T.: Reachability analysis of a general class of neural ordinary differential equations. arXiv preprint arXiv:2207.06531 (2022)
32. Manzanas Lopez, D., Musau, P., Hamilton, N., Johnson, T.T.: Reachability analysis of a general class of neural ordinary differential equations. arXiv e-prints pp. arXiv-2207 (2022)
33. Massey, W.S.: A Basic Course in Algebraic Topology. GTM, vol. 127. Springer, New York (1991). https://doi.org/10.1007/978-1-4939-9063-4
34. Mendelson, B.: Introduction to Topology. Courier Corporation, Massachusetts (1990)

35. Naitzat, G., Zhitnikov, A., Lim, L.H.: Topology of deep neural networks. J. Mach. Learn. Res. **21**(184), 1–40 (2020)
36. Pulina, L., Tacchella, A.: An abstraction-refinement approach to verification of artificial neural networks. In: Touili, T., Cook, B., Jackson, P. (eds.) CAV 2010. LNCS, vol. 6174, pp. 243–257. Springer, Heidelberg (2010). https://doi.org/10.1007/978-3-642-14295-6_24
37. Singh, G., Gehr, T., Mirman, M., Püschel, M., Vechev, M.: Fast and effective robustness certification. In: Advances in Neural Information Processing Systems, vol. 31 (2018)
38. Singh, G., Gehr, T., Püschel, M., Vechev, M.: An abstract domain for certifying neural networks. Proc. ACM Program. Lang. **3**(POPL), 1–30 (2019). https://doi.org/10.1145/3290354
39. Tian, Y., Yang, W., Wang, J.: Image fusion using a multi-level image decomposition and fusion method. Appl. Opt. **60**(24), 7466–7479 (2021). https://doi.org/10.1364/ao.432397
40. Tran, H.-D., et al.: Star-based reachability analysis of deep neural networks. In: ter Beek, M.H., McIver, A., Oliveira, J.N. (eds.) FM 2019. LNCS, vol. 11800, pp. 670–686. Springer, Cham (2019). https://doi.org/10.1007/978-3-030-30942-8_39
41. Tran, H.D., et al.: Parallelizable reachability analysis algorithms for feed-forward neural networks. In: 2019 IEEE/ACM 7th International Conference on Formal Methods in Software Engineering (FormaliSE), pp. 51–60. IEEE (2019). https://doi.org/10.1109/FormaliSE.2019.00012
42. Wang, S., Pei, K., Whitehouse, J., Yang, J., Jana, S.: Efficient formal safety analysis of neural networks. In: Advances in Neural Information Processing Systems, vol. 31 (2018)
43. Xiang, W., Johnson, T.T.: Reachability analysis and safety verification for neural network control systems. arXiv preprint arXiv:1805.09944 (2018)
44. Xiang, W., Tran, H.D., Johnson, T.T.: Reachable set computation and safety verification for neural networks with ReLU activations. arXiv preprint arXiv:1712.08163 (2017)
45. Xiang, W., Tran, H.D., Johnson, T.T.: Output reachable set estimation and verification for multilayer neural networks. IEEE Trans. Neural Netw. Learn. Syst. **29**(11), 5777–5783 (2018). https://doi.org/10.1109/tnnls.2018.2808470
46. Xue, B., Easwaran, A., Cho, N.J., Fränzle, M.: Reach-avoid verification for nonlinear systems based on boundary analysis. IEEE Trans. Autom. Control **62**(7), 3518–3523 (2016). https://doi.org/10.1109/TAC.2016.2615599
47. Xue, B., She, Z., Easwaran, A.: Under-approximating backward reachable sets by polytopes. In: Chaudhuri, S., Farzan, A. (eds.) CAV 2016. LNCS, vol. 9779, pp. 457–476. Springer, Cham (2016). https://doi.org/10.1007/978-3-319-41528-4_25
48. Xue, B., Wang, Q., Feng, S., Zhan, N.: Over-and underapproximating reach sets for perturbed delay differential equations. IEEE Trans. Autom. Control **66**(1), 283–290 (2020). https://doi.org/10.1109/TAC.2020.2977993
49. Yang, P., et al.: Improving neural network verification through spurious region guided refinement. In: TACAS 2021. LNCS, vol. 12651, pp. 389–408. Springer, Cham (2021). https://doi.org/10.1007/978-3-030-72016-2_21
50. Yuan, W., Neubig, G., Liu, P.: BARTScore: evaluating generated text as text generation. arXiv preprint arXiv:2106.11520 (2021)

Approximately Learning Quantum Automata

Wenjing Chu[1](✉), Shuo Chen[2], Marcello Bonsangue[1](✉), and Zenglin Shi[3]

[1] Leiden University, Leiden, The Netherlands
w.chu@liacs.leidenuniv.nl, marcello@liacs.nl
[2] University of Amsterdam, Amsterdam, The Netherlands
[3] I2R, Agency for Science, Technology and Research, Singapore, Singapore

Abstract. In this paper, we provide two methods for learning measure-once one-way quantum finite automata using a combination of active learning and non-linear optimization. First, we learn the number of states of a measure-once one-way quantum automaton using a heuristic binary tree representing the different variations of a Hankel matrix. Then we use two optimization methods to learn the unitary matrices representing the transitions of the automaton. When comparing the original automaton with the one learned, we provide a new way to compute the distance on the base of the language of the combined quantum automata. Finally, we show, using experiments on a set of randomly generated quantum automata, which method performs better.

Keywords: Automata learning · quantum automata · non-linear optimization · quantum computing

1 Introduction

Automata learning is the process of inferring a finite model of a system from information about its behavior. It has become an essential part of machine learning and has been found in diverse applications over the past decade, such as smartcard readers [12], describing the errors in a program [13] and implementations of network protocols [14,17,19].

Gold introduced the concept of "identification in the limit" [21] and showed that regular languages cannot be learned precisely using only positive samples. Instead, they can only be approximately learned [36]. Learning the smallest deterministic finite automaton (DFA) consistent with an arbitrary set of positive and negative samples is NP-hard [1,22]. However, it is still possible to approach specific sub-classes of regular languages [4]. A similar situation also holds for regular probabilistic languages and learning probabilistic automata, which can be weakly polynomially identified in the limit with probability one [3]. Consequently, several learning methods have been developed for learning, for example, locally testable languages [15,20], deterministic probabilistic language [11], and residual probabilistic language [16,18].

Given the initial negative results, researchers have investigated other ways of learning, based on more active interactions between the oracle and the learner,

C. David and M. Sun (Eds.): TASE 2023, LNCS 13931, pp. 268–285, 2023.
https://doi.org/10.1007/978-3-031-35257-7_16

by, for example, asking questions to acquire knowledge instead of passively using the given data. This mathematical setting is called active learning or learning with queries, represented by Angluin's famous L^* algorithm [2]. This algorithm works with membership queries (MQs) and equivalence queries (EQs). With membership queries, the learner asks if one string belongs to the language, and the oracle answers yes or no. Equivalence queries are used by the learner to check if the learned model is correct (i.e., language equivalent to the target one). Angluin's approach triggered a lot of subsequent research on active automata learning, with notable contributions from Bergadano and Varricchio, who used a similar model to learn weighted finite automata [7], and Bollig *et al.* who provided a nondeterministic finite automata version of L^* algorithm [9]. In practice, equivalence queries are often hard to implement and can be substituted by a large enough set of randomly chosen labeled examples [32] so that the learning algorithm is probably approximately correct [35].

In this paper, we present an approximate learning algorithm based on active learning quantum automata. Quantum automata are a model of computation based on quantum mechanics and differ from classical automata in their ability to process the superposition of states. Quantum finite automata are the quantum version of the deterministic finite automaton and have been introduced by Kondacs and Watrous in 1997 [27]. The most basic models of quantum automata are the measure-once quantum automata [30] and the measure-many quantum automata [27]. Quantum automata can model certain problems more efficiently and compactly than their classical counterparts [24], but they are more powerful. In fact, there exist measure-once quantum automata that accept languages with cut point 0 that are not regular [8].

Quantum learning theory is not new and has attracted a lot of attention since the end of the last century [6], developing quantum analogs of classical learning theory, such as quantum exact learning [6], quantum PAC model [10], and quantum agnostic model [5]. However, to the best of our knowledge, there is only one work on quantum automata learning [33], where an algorithm to learn quantum finite automata with queries is presented. In this algorithm, the oracle has to answer with the amplitude of each state instead of the probability of the string being in an accepting state. Moreover, the learner should already have all information about the number of states, including which one is accepted. In other words, the learner knows the structure of the automaton in advance and has been informed of the information about non-halting states [33].

In this paper, we provide a different approach combining active learning and non-linear optimization methods for learning measure-once quantum automata. Our method consists of two steps: In the first step, we use a Hankel matrix to learn the number of states. Then we use two state-of-the-art optimization methods to learn the weights labeling the transitions of the automaton. The resulting approximation is not necessarily a quantum automaton, as the learned operators need not be unitary. The second step starts after orthonormalizing the operators and consists in checking if the learned automaton is close enough to the target one. To this end, we define a new method to compute the L_1 distance between two quantum automata based on the basis of the language recognized by a suitable combination of the two automata. Our method can be used, for example, to construct a noise-free model from a photon optical experiment that manipulates laser through linear optical elements.

We proceed as follows: We first introduce the background knowledge in Sect. 2. In Sect. 3, we design a learning algorithm for active learning quantum automata. In Sect. 4, we first present an algorithm for calculating the L_1 distance of two quantum automata. Finally, in Sect. 5, we present some experimental results comparing the methods proposed.

2   Preliminaries

A (finite) Hilbert space $\mathcal{H}_n$ is an $n-$dimension complex vector space equipped with an inner product. The inner product of two vectors $|\phi\rangle = (\alpha_1 \ldots \alpha_n)^\mathsf{T}$ and $|\psi\rangle = (\beta_1 \ldots \beta_n)^\mathsf{T}$ is defined as $\langle\phi|\psi\rangle = \sum_{i=1}^{n} \alpha_i^* \beta_i$, where $\langle\phi|$ is the conjugate transpose of vector $|\phi\rangle$ and α_i^* is the conjugate of the complex number α_i. Vector $|\phi\rangle$ and $|\psi\rangle$ are said to be orthogonal if their inner product is zero. For example, the qubits $|0\rangle = (1, 0)^\mathsf{T}$ and $|1\rangle = (0, 1)^\mathsf{T}$ are orthogonal as their inner product $\langle 0|1\rangle$ is 0.

We use $\mathcal{B}_n = \{q_1, \ldots, q_n\}$ to denote the standard bases of $\mathcal{H}_n$. A pure quantum state is a unit column vector $|\phi\rangle$ in $\mathcal{H}_n$, that is, a linear combination

$$|\phi\rangle = \alpha_1|q_1\rangle + \cdots + \alpha_n|q_n\rangle,$$

such that its norm $|||\phi\rangle|| = 1$, that is the positive square root $\sqrt{\langle\phi|\phi\rangle} = 1$ (or equivalently, $|\alpha_1|^2 + \cdots + |\alpha_n|^2 = 1$). For a pure quantum state, we call $\alpha_i \in \mathbb{C}$ the probability amplitude, for any $i \in \{1, \ldots, n\}$. In this paper, we have only focused on rational numbers as they are computable. We do not consider complex numbers for simplicity and because we use off-the-shelf search methods. However, at the cost of increased time complexity, there is no theoretical problem in handling complex numbers.

The evolution of a closed quantum system is expressed by the multiplication of the pure quantum state vector by a unitary matrix. A matrix $U \in \mathbb{C}^{n \times n}$ is unitary if its conjugate transpose $U^\dagger$ is also its inverse, that is:

$$U^\dagger U = UU^\dagger = UU^{-1} = I$$

Any unitary operator on complex numbers is norm-preserving, thus $|\phi'\rangle = U|\phi\rangle$ is also a pure quantum state with norm 1 if $|\phi\rangle$ is.

A quantum measurement is a projection of a pure quantum state $|\phi\rangle$ in a perpendicular manner on a subspace of $\mathcal{H}_n$. Formally, a measurement is a positive $n \times n$ matrix M that is idempotent (i.e. $M^2 = M$) and Hermitian (i.e. $M^\dagger = M$). A projection matrix M is in a one-to-one correspondence with the subspace the Hilbert space $\mathcal{H}_n$, which consists of all $|\phi\rangle$ such that $|\phi\rangle = M|\phi\rangle$. Given a system in a pure quantum state $|\phi\rangle$, the probability to be in the subspace characterized by a measurement M is:

$$P(|\phi\rangle, M) = ||M|\phi\rangle||^2 = (M|\phi\rangle)^\dagger M|\phi\rangle = \langle\phi|M^\dagger M|\phi\rangle = \langle\phi|M|\phi\rangle .$$

After measurement, the new state $|\phi'\rangle$ of the system is normalized to $\frac{M|\phi\rangle}{\sqrt{\langle\phi|M|\phi\rangle}}$.

2.1 Quantum Automata

A quantum automaton is a generalization of a Markov decision process to quantum systems. Here we will consider only measure-once one-way quantum finite automata [27].

Definition 1. *A measure-once one-way quantum finite automaton (QFA) is a $5-tuple$ $\langle Q, \Sigma, \{U_\sigma | \sigma \in \Sigma\}, q_1, A\rangle$, where Q is a finite set of states, Σ is a finite alphabet, $\{U_\sigma | \sigma \in \Sigma\}$ is a set of unitary matrices describing the evolution of the system when reading an input symbol in Σ, $q_1 \in Q$ is the initial state, and $A \subseteq Q$ is the set of accepting states.*

Intuitively, the system starts from the quantum state $|q_1\rangle$. The system evolves from a state $|\phi\rangle$ to a state $U_\sigma|\phi\rangle$ when the symbol σ is read. After reading a string $x \in \Sigma^*$, the state of the automata is measured using the diagonal projector matrix M having 1 on the diagonal in position i, i if $q_i \in A$ and 0 otherwise. This assigns to every string $x \in \Sigma^*$ a probability $P(x)$ of being in an accepting state. Formally, let $|\phi_\epsilon\rangle$ be the vector representing the initial state, and $x = \sigma_1 \ldots \sigma_n \in \Sigma^*$. After reading x, the system will be in the quantum state:

$$|\phi_x\rangle = U_x|q_1\rangle = U_{\sigma_n} \cdots U_{\sigma_1}|q_1\rangle\,.$$

By projecting it into the subspace generated by the accepting states A the probability of accepting the string x is:

$$P(x) = ||M|\phi_x\rangle||^2 = \langle\phi_x|M|\phi_x\rangle\,.$$

A language $L \subseteq \Sigma^*$ is said to be accepted by a quantum finite automaton M with probability at least λ if $P(x) > \lambda$ for all $x \in L$.

Example 1. Consider the QFA M shown in Fig. 1a. The probabilities of the strings a and aa to be in an accepting state are:

$$P(a) = ||MU_a|\phi_\epsilon\rangle||^2$$

$$= ||\begin{pmatrix} 0 & 0 \\ 0 & 1 \end{pmatrix} \begin{pmatrix} \frac{\sqrt{3}}{2} & \frac{1}{2} \\ -\frac{1}{2} & \frac{\sqrt{3}}{2} \end{pmatrix} \begin{pmatrix} 1 \\ 0 \end{pmatrix}||^2$$

$$= ||\begin{pmatrix} 0 & 0 \\ 0 & 1 \end{pmatrix} \begin{pmatrix} \frac{\sqrt{3}}{2} \\ -\frac{1}{2} \end{pmatrix}||^2$$

$$= |-\frac{1}{2}|^2$$

$$= \frac{1}{4},$$

$$P(aa) = ||MU_{aa}|\phi_\epsilon\rangle||^2$$

$$= ||\begin{pmatrix} 0 & 0 \\ 0 & 1 \end{pmatrix} \begin{pmatrix} \frac{\sqrt{3}}{2} & \frac{1}{2} \\ -\frac{1}{2} & \frac{\sqrt{3}}{2} \end{pmatrix}^2 \begin{pmatrix} 1 \\ 0 \end{pmatrix}||^2$$

$$= ||\begin{pmatrix} 0 & 0 \\ 0 & 1 \end{pmatrix} \begin{pmatrix} \frac{1}{2} \\ -\frac{\sqrt{3}}{2} \end{pmatrix}||^2$$

$$= |-\frac{\sqrt{3}}{2}|^2$$

$$= \frac{3}{4}.$$

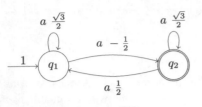

$$|\phi_\epsilon\rangle = \begin{pmatrix} 1 \\ 0 \end{pmatrix}, \quad M = \begin{pmatrix} 0 & 0 \\ 0 & 1 \end{pmatrix}$$

$$U_a = \begin{pmatrix} \frac{\sqrt{3}}{2} & \frac{1}{2} \\ -\frac{1}{2} & \frac{\sqrt{3}}{2} \end{pmatrix}$$

(a) A given QFA.

(b) The corresponding initial vector $|\phi_\epsilon\rangle$, projector M, and transition matrix U_a

Fig. 1. An example of a QFA.

Structurally, a QFA $\langle Q, \Sigma, \{U_\sigma | \sigma \in \Sigma\}, q_1, A\rangle$, can be seen as a weighted finite automaton over the semiring $(\mathbb{R}, +, \times, 0, 1)$, assigning a 'weight' $w(x)$ to each string $x = \sigma_1 \ldots \sigma_n \in \Sigma^*$ as follows:

$$w(x) = \sum_{q \in A} w(x, q)$$

where

$$w(x, q) = \langle q | U_x | q_1 \rangle = \langle q | U_{\sigma_n} \cdots U_{\sigma_1} | q_1 \rangle.$$

Note that if the string x is the empty string, its weight is 1 if and only if $q_1 \in A$. In the sequel we denote by $\beta_A^\mathsf{T} = \sum_{q \in A} \langle q|$ and by U_x the matrix obtained by the product $U_{\sigma_n} \cdots U_{\sigma_1}$. This way, $w(x) = \beta_A^\mathsf{T} U_x | q_1 \rangle$.

Differently from $P(x)$, the weight $w(x)$ of a string x is the sum of the weight of the paths with input x from the initial state to each accepting state in A. This will be useful for learning the number of states of a quantum automaton, that is related to the rank to its Hankel matrix. Here recall that the rank of a matrix is the maximal number of linearly independent rows (or, equivalently, columns). Furthermore, in the context of matrices indexed by strings in Σ^*, recall that a Hankel matrix is a square matrix H such that its element $\alpha_{u,v} = \alpha_{u',v'}$ for all $u, u', v, v' \in \Sigma^*$ with $uv = u'v'$. For example, the Hankel matrix H_f of a function $f : \Sigma^* \to \mathbb{R}$ is defined by setting $\alpha_{u,v} = f(uv)$, for all $u, v \in \Sigma^*$.

Theorem 1. *Given a QFA $\langle Q, \Sigma, \{U_\sigma | \sigma \in \Sigma\}, q_1, A\rangle$, and its associated weight function $w : \Sigma^* \to \mathbb{R}$ then the rank of H_w is smaller or equal than the number of states $|Q|$. Furthermore, this rank is minimal, meaning that there is no other QFA having the same weight function w with fewer states than the rank of H_w.*

Proof. Given a QFA $\langle Q, \Sigma, \{U_\sigma | \sigma \in \Sigma\}, q_1, A\rangle$ with a weight function w and $u, v \in \Sigma^*$, we have:

$$w(uv) = (\beta_A^\mathsf{T} U_v)(U_u | q_1 \rangle), \tag{1}$$

where $\beta_A^\mathsf{T} U_v$ is a row vector in $\mathbb{R}^{1 \times Q}$ and $U_u | q_1 \rangle$ is a column vector in $\mathbb{R}^{Q \times 1}$. Define two matrices P and S in $\mathbb{R}^{\Sigma^* \times Q}$, by setting $P(v, \cdot) = \beta_A^\mathsf{T} U_v$ for all $v \in \Sigma^*$ and $S_A(u, \cdot) = (U_u | q_1 \rangle)^\mathsf{T}$ for all $u \in \Sigma^*$. We then have:

$$w(uv) = (\beta_A^\mathsf{T} U_v)(U_u | q_1 \rangle) = (PS^\mathsf{T})(v, u). \tag{2}$$

This means that $H_w = PS^\mathsf{T}$. Since the rank of P and S is bounded by the number of states $|Q|$, we have that $rank(H_w) \leq |Q|$.

Next, assume $rank(H_w) = n$ and consider a QFA $A = \langle S, \Sigma, \{V_\sigma | \sigma \in \Sigma\}, s_0, A \rangle$, assigning a weight $f(x) = w(x)$ to strings $x \in \Sigma^*$. We need to prove that $rank(H_w) \leq |S|$. Using the same reasoning as before, we get that rank $rank(H_f) \leq |S|$. But since $f = w$, we have $rank(H_w) \leq |S|$.

More specifically, given H_w, one can construct a weighted finite automaton (not necessarily a QFA) with exactly n states such that the weight $f(x)$ associated with each string x is $w(x)$. To this end we need to give an initial vector α and an accepting vector β both in $\mathbb{R}^{n \times 1}$, and transition matrices U_σ in $\mathbb{R}^{n \times n}$, for every $\sigma \in \Sigma$. Since $rank(H_w) = n$, let $H_w(\cdot, v_i)$ be the n linear independent $v-$indexed column vectors in H_w. There exist $\alpha_1, \cdots, \alpha_n \in \mathbb{R}$ such that $H_w(\cdot, \epsilon) = \sum_{i=1}^{n} \alpha_i H_w(\cdot, v_i)$. Together they define the weight vector α of the initial state. Note that this need not be of the form $(1, 0, \cdots, 0)$ for a QFA.

Similarly, for all $1 \leq i \leq n$ and $\sigma \in \Sigma$ we have $H_w(\cdot, \sigma v_i) = \sum_{j=1}^{n} \beta_{j,i}^\sigma H_w(\cdot, v_i)$. For all σ, all $\beta_{j,i}^\sigma$ define the weight of the transition matrix U_σ, that in general needs not to be unitary. As usual, for a string $x = \sigma_1 \cdots \sigma_k \in \Sigma^*$ we let $U_x = U_{\sigma_k} \cdots U_{\sigma_1}$ and get $H_w(\cdot, x v_i) = \sum_{j=1}^{n} (U_x)_{j,i} H_w(\cdot, v_j)$. Thus,

$$w(x) = H_w(\epsilon, x) = H_w(x, \epsilon) = \sum_{i=1}^{n} \alpha_i H_w(x, v_i)$$

$$= \sum_{i=1}^{n} \alpha_i \sum_{j=1}^{n} (U_x)_{ji} H_w(\epsilon, v_j) = \beta^\mathsf{T} U_x \alpha = f(x),$$

where $\beta_j = H_f(\epsilon, v_j)$ and $\alpha = (\alpha_1, \ldots, \alpha_n)$. □

3 Approximately Learning Quantum Automata

In active automata learning, contrary to passive one, the learning algorithm can query the target system for additional information. The most famous method for active learning is Angluin's L^* algorithm [2], which learns exactly the minimal deterministic finite automaton recognizing a target regular language by means of two types of queries: membership queries and equivalence queries.

When learning quantum automata, a variation of the L^* algorithm should implement both queries. Equivalence of measure once (and also measure many) quantum automata is decidable [28, 29], so equivalence queries do not pose any problem. As for probabilistic automata, constructing a quantum automaton from membership queries, however, is not easy. With a membership query, the learner asks the oracle for the target value of a string x. This value represents the probability that the automaton is in the superposition of the accepting states after reading the string x. While this information will be enough to extract the structural information of the automaton, it does not tell us how it evolves at each step. Our approach will be to learn the unitary matrices representing the evolution of the system by solving a non-linear (but polynomial) system of equations in real values variables. Such a solution, however, can only be approximate, and we will use two different optimization algorithms for that. Consequently, we will only approximately learn quantum automata, and the equivalence queries will be replaced by measuring how close the learned automaton is to the target.

Our goal is to find a quantum automaton that assigns probabilities arbitrarily close to those assigned by the target language for each string in the membership queries so that they are identified in the limit [36]. Furthermore, similar to the approximately correct version of the L^* algorithm [32], we substitute the equivalence query with a large enough set of strings that are used to measure the distance from the target. When this distance is greater than a fixed threshold parameter δ, the algorithm will offer a new string with an associated probability that will be used to improve the resulting automaton. In this context, we use two novel ways to calculate the distance between the learned automaton and the target one, as will be shown in Sect. 4.

Next, we present our approximate learning algorithm for quantum automata. We first learn the structure, assuming that the target automaton has only one accepting state. We will relax this assumption to more accepting states later, but it requires the oracle to associate as many probabilities to each string as the accepting states of the target automaton. We conclude the section by showing how to define the unitary operators for the automaton given the strings received from the membership queries so far.

3.1   Learning the Structure

In order to learn the structure of a quantum automaton, we need to learn how many states it has. Because of Theorem 1, the number of states is given by the rank of the Hankel matrix that we build by means of the membership queries.

We start by asking the oracle the probability $P(x_1)$, where x_1 is the empty string ϵ, and build the 1×1 Hankel matrix (p_1). Because of the way probabilities are calculated in quantum automata, here p_1 is the amplitude of the unique final state, and thus $p_1 = \pm\sqrt{P(x_1)}$. Recall that an $n \times n$ Hankel matrix is defined by only $2n - 1$ elements since the Hankel matrix is symmetric, thus given an $n \times n$ Hankel matrix, if it has rank $r = n$, then to extend its size by 1 we need to ask the probabilities $P(x_{2n})$ and $P(x_{2n+1})$ of the next two strings x_{2n} and x_{2n+1} with respect to the length-lexicographic order. The example below shows a 3×3 Hankel matrix that is extended to a 4×4 one by adding the two elements p_6 and p_7 (here in red):

$$\begin{pmatrix} p_1 & p_2 & p_3 \\ p_2 & p_3 & p_4 \\ p_3 & p_4 & p_5 \end{pmatrix} \rightarrow \begin{pmatrix} p_1 & p_2 & p_3 & p_4 \\ p_2 & p_3 & p_4 & p_5 \\ p_3 & p_4 & p_5 & p_6 \\ p_4 & p_5 & p_6 & p_7 \end{pmatrix}$$

In the matrices above, $p_i = \pm\sqrt{P(x_i)}$ is the possible amplitude of the final state after reading the string x_i, for all i. This process of extending the current matrix using membership queries is repeated until the rank r of the current Hankel matrix is strictly smaller than its size n. In this case, $1, \ldots, r$ are the states of the proposed learned automaton, with 1 the initial state. If $p_1 \neq 0$, then 1 is also the accepting state. Otherwise, we set 2 to be the accepting one. This choice is arbitrary but does not influence the result because of the symmetry of the transitions of the automaton.

Each element p_i above can have two values, namely $\sqrt{P(x_i)}$ or $-\sqrt{P(x_i)}$. This implies that we have $(2n - 1)(2n - 1)$ different Hankel matrices given the first $2n-1$ membership queries. To avoid an exponential explosion in the number of matrices that we have to treat in parallel, we organize all variations of the above Hankel matrix as two binary trees, where each node is either the positive or negative value of p_i, having as children the two values of p_{i+1}. We have two trees instead of one because of the two values of p_1 at the root. Each tree has depth $2n - 1$, and a path in the tree represents a Hankel matrix. In fact, we have in total $(2n - 1)^2$ paths.

We use a few heuristics to be more efficient by cutting some of the paths. First, we can remove the tree with the negative value at the first node because any path of that tree can be obtained by one starting from the positive root by multiplying it by -1. So any matrix represented by a path in the tree with the negative root will have the same rank as one represented in the other tree. Second, if the root $p_1 = 0$, then we can prune the subtree rooted in its child $-\sqrt{P(x_2)}$ with a negative value because any path passing through this subtree can be obtained as one from the remaining part of tree multiplying it by -1. Third, for any other node with value 0, there is no need to calculate the subtree starting from the sibling since, for each represented matrix, we can find one the same rank in the remaining tree.

We implemented a binary search based on these three heuristics in Algorithm 1 (lines 16 to 18). The algorithm stops when the rank of the Hankel matrix is smaller than its size. We can start directly by building a 3 Hankel matrix using 5 membership queries (lines 1 to 4) because the size 1 Hankel matrix can only have rank 1. If the rank is smaller than a Hankel Matrix of size 2, then it must be equal to 1, meaning that we have only a one-state finite automaton. We can immediately notice this when asking the first $|\Sigma|+1$ membership queries because all those strings will need to have probability 1. We first build the heuristic binary tree (lines 2 to 26), and then we construct one Hankel matrix at a time for each path until the rank of this matrix is strictly smaller than its size (line 28 to line 33). If this is not the case for all paths in the tree, then we repeat the process by increasing the size of the matrix by 1. The worst-case time complexity of the algorithm is $\mathbf{O}(n * (2n - 1))$, where $n = n_{max}$ and is the maximal number of states allowed for the automaton.

The next example shows an example where we learn the number of states of a quantum finite automaton over a single letter alphabet $\Sigma = \{a\}$:

Example 2. We start by constructing a 3×3 Hankel matrix asking the oracle for the probability of being in the unique final state when reading the strings $\epsilon, a, aa, aaa, aaaa$. Assume the oracle returns $P(\epsilon) = 0$, $P(a) = 0.23$, $P(aa) = 0.13$, $P(aaa) = 0.97$ and $P(aaaa) = 0.06$. We use the positive and negative

---

Algorithm 1: Heuristic binary tree to find the number of states in QFA

Input: S: the probabilities of strings and n_{max}
Output: the Hankel matrix and the number of states
1: $n = 3$
2: **while** $n < n_{max}$ **do**
3:     T is an empty tree
4:     $A = S[: 2n - 1]$
5:     $root \leftarrow$ Node(A[0]) {Use the first element as the root of T}
6:     $queue$ is a First-In-First-Out queue
7:     $i = 0$
8:     $queue \leftarrow root$
9:     **while** $queue$ is not empty **do**
10:         $i = i + 1$
11:         **if** $i \geq \text{len}(A)$ **then**
12:             break
13:         **end if**
14:         **for** $j = 0$ **to** len($queue$) **do**
15:             $node \leftarrow$ Pop $queue$
16:             **if** $A[i] == 0$ or ($A[0] == 0$ and $i == 1$) **then**
17:                 $node.left \leftarrow$ Node($\sqrt{A[i]}$)
18:                 Add $node.left$ to $queue$
19:             **else**
20:                 $node.left \leftarrow$ Node($\sqrt{A[i]}$)
21:                 $node.right \leftarrow$ Node($-\sqrt{A[i]}$)
22:                 Add $node.left$ to $queue$
23:                 Add $node.right$ to $queue$
24:             **end if**
25:         **end for**
26:     **end while**
27:     **for** $path$ in T **do**
28:         construct Hankel matrix H using $path$
29:         $r = rank(H)$
30:         **if** $r < n$ **then**
31:             return H, r
32:         **end if**
33:         remove $path$
34:     **end for**
35:     $n = n + 1$
36: **end while**

---

values of the square root of all these probabilities as elements of our Hankel matrices. All paths of our heuristic binary tree denote the following 8 Hankel matrices:

$$\begin{pmatrix} 0 & 0.48 & \pm 0.36 \\ 0.48 & \pm 0.36 & \pm 0.98 \\ \pm 0.36 & \pm 0.98 & \pm 0.25 \end{pmatrix}. \tag{3}$$

Simple calculations show that the rank of all these 8 matrices is 3 as the rank is not smaller than the size. We continue with two membership queries, namely the probability of $aaaaa$ and $aaaaaa$. Let us assume the oracle returns $P(aaaaa) = 0.25$ and $P(aaaaaa) = 0.01$. Next, we construct a heuristic binary tree representing the following 32 Hankel matrices:

$$\begin{pmatrix} 0 & 0.48 & \pm 0.36 & \pm 0.98 \\ 0.48 & \pm 0.36 & \pm 0.98 & \pm 0.25 \\ \pm 0.36 & \pm 0.98 & \pm 0.25 & \pm 0.50 \\ \pm 0.98 & \pm 0.25 & \pm 0.50 & \pm 0.11 \end{pmatrix}. \tag{4}$$

Among them there are four 4×4 matrices having rank 3, including the following one:

$$\begin{pmatrix} 0 & 0.48 & -0.36 & -0.98 \\ 0.48 & -0.36 & -0.98 & -0.25 \\ -0.36 & -0.98 & -0.25 & 0.50 \\ -0.98 & -0.25 & 0.50 & -0.11 \end{pmatrix}.$$

This one can be used to construct a 3 states quantum automaton with 1 as the initial state and 2 as the final one.

3.2   Learning the Operators

Once we know the number of states of the quantum automaton, we construct a $n \times n$ symbolic matrix U_σ for each $\sigma \in \Sigma$ with variables $x^\sigma_{q_i,q_j}$ as elements. Here n is the number of states of the automaton. We will use all those variables in a non-linear system of equations that we will then solve using two different optimization methods.

The system of equations includes constraints about the property of the matrices U_σ to be unitary for each $\sigma \in \Sigma$. To this end, we add for each $q_i, q_j \in Q$ the following equation:

$$\sum_{q \in Q} (x^\sigma_{q_i,q})^* x^\sigma_{q_j,q} = \begin{cases} 1 & q_i = q_j \\ 0 & q_i \neq q_j \end{cases}$$

where $(x^\sigma_{q_i,q_j})^*$ is the complex conjugate of $x^\sigma_{q_i,q_j}$.

Next, for each string $w = \sigma_0 \ldots \sigma_m$ used for the membership queries, we write the equation $E(w)$, which represents the symbolic calculation of the probability of being assigned to the string w:

$$M \begin{pmatrix} x^{\sigma_m}_{q_1,q_1} & \cdots & x^{\sigma_m}_{q_n,q_1} \\ \vdots & \ddots & \vdots \\ x^{\sigma_m}_{q_1,q_n} & \cdots & x^{\sigma_m}_{q_n,q_n} \end{pmatrix} \cdots \begin{pmatrix} x^{\sigma_0}_{q_1,q_1} & \cdots & x^{\sigma_0}_{q_n,q_1} \\ \vdots & \ddots & \vdots \\ x^{\sigma_0}_{q_1,q_n} & \cdots & x^{\sigma_0}_{q_n,q_n} \end{pmatrix} \begin{pmatrix} 1 \\ \vdots \\ 0 \end{pmatrix} = p_w, \tag{5}$$

where p_w is one of the $2k - 1$ elements in the Hankel matrix of rank n we used to find the number of states of the automaton, and M is the projector matrix associated with the set of accepting states (i.e., with all zero elements except for either the element at position $1, 1$ or $2, 2$ that is set to 1).

In order to use optimization methods, we rewrite the system of equations as a set of functions for which we want to find its zero values. We use two different existing optimization methods. The first one is based on a genetic algorithm (GA) [23, 26], whereas the second one uses the covariance matrix adaptation evolution strategy (CMA-ES). The latter is a stochastic method for real-valued parameter optimization of non-linear, non-convex functions. Adaptation of the covariance matrix amounts to learning a second-order model of the underlying objective function similar to the approximation of the inverse Hessian matrix in the quasi-Newton method in classical optimization [25, 31].

Since the solution resulting from both the GA and CMA-ES methods is only an approximation, the values we find for the operators will, in general, not satisfy the unitary condition but will be close to that. Therefore, we need to adapt the operators via the Gram-Schmidt process to orthonormalize them.

The Gram-Schmidt Process

For two vectors u and v of the same size, let $proj_u(v)$ be the projection operator defined as:

$$proj_u(v) = \frac{\langle u, v \rangle}{\langle u, u \rangle} u,$$

where $\langle u, v \rangle$ is the inner product of the two vectors. Assume $v_1, \cdots, v_n$ are the columns of an $n \times n$ matrix that we want to orthonormalize. Define $u_1 = v_1$ and for all $2 \leq i \leq n$ and $1 \leq k \leq n$ let

$$u_i = v_i - \sum_{j=1}^{n-1} proj_{u_j}(v_i), \quad \text{and} \quad e_i = \frac{u_i}{||u_i||}.$$

where $||u||$ is the norm of vector u. Then the vectors e_i will form the column of an $n \times n$ orthogonal matrix with the property that each vector e_i generate the same subspace as the original vector v_i. Moreover, if the original matrix is unitary, then it is not changed by The Gram-Schmidt process [34].

Example 3. Assume the target automaton we want to learn is the one given in Fig. 2a. When asking the membership queries for the strings ϵ, a, aa, aaa and $aaaa$ the oracle returns $P(\epsilon) = 0$, $P(a) = 0.96884649$, $P(aa) = 0$, $P(aaa) = 0.968981$ and $P(aaaa) = 0$. These values form the following 3×3 Hankel matrix:

$$\begin{pmatrix} 0 & 0.9843 & 0 \\ 0.9843 & 0 & 0.984368 \\ 0 & 0.984368 & 0 \end{pmatrix}.$$

The rank of this matrix is 2, so we can construct a 2-state automaton with q_1 as the initial state and the other state q_2 as the accepting (because $P(\epsilon) = 0$). To calculate the unitary operator U_a, we associate variables to each transition as shown in Fig. 2b.

From the unitary constraints on U_a we derive four equations of degree two:

$$\begin{cases} (x^a_{q_1,q_1})^* x^a_{q_1,q_1} + (x^a_{q_1,q_2})^* x^a_{q_1,q_2} = 1 \\ (x^a_{q_2,q_1})^* x^a_{q_2,q_1} + (x^a_{q_2,q_2})^* x^a_{q_2,q_2} = 1 \\ (x^a_{q_1,q_1})^* x^a_{q_1,q_2} + (x^a_{q_2,q_1})^* x^a_{q_2,q_2} = 0 \\ (x^a_{q_1,q_2})^* x^a_{q_1,q_1} + (x^a_{q_2,q_2})^* x^a_{q_2,q_1} = 0 \end{cases}$$

The non-empty strings used in the membership query give four more equations, with a degree smaller or equal to the length of the longest string:

$$\begin{cases} 1 \cdot x^a_{q_1,q_2} \cdot 1 = 0.9843 \\ 1 \cdot (x^a_{q_1,q_2} x^a_{q_2,q_2} + x^a_{q_1,q_1} x^a_{q_1,q_2}) \cdot 1 = 0 \\ 1 \cdot (x^a_{q_1,q_1} x^a_{q_1,q_1} x^a_{q_1,q_2} + x^a_{q_1,q_1} x^a_{q_1,q_2} x^a_{q_2,q_2} \\ \quad + x^a_{q_1,q_2} x^a_{q_2,q_1} x^a_{q_1,q_2} + x^a_{q_1,q_2} x^a_{q_2,q_2} x^a_{q_2,q_2}) \cdot 1 = 0.984368 \\ 1 \cdot (x^a_{q_1,q_1} x^a_{q_1,q_1} x^a_{q_1,q_1} x^a_{q_1,q_2} + x^a_{q_1,q_1} x^a_{q_1,q_1} x^a_{q_1,q_2} x^a_{q_2,q_2} \\ \quad + x^a_{q_1,q_1} x^a_{q_1,q_2} x^a_{q_2,q_1} x^a_{q_1,q_2} + x^a_{q_1,q_1} x^a_{q_1,q_2} x^a_{q_2,q_2} x^a_{q_2,q_2} \\ \quad + x^a_{q_1,q_2} x^a_{q_2,q_1} x^a_{q_1,q_1} x^a_{q_1,q_2} + x^a_{q_1,q_2} x^a_{q_2,q_1} x^a_{q_1,q_2} x^a_{q_2,q_2} \\ \quad + x^a_{q_1,q_2} x^a_{q_2,q_2} x^a_{q_2,q_1} x^a_{q_1,q_2} + x^a_{q_1,q_2} x^a_{q_2,q_2} x^a_{q_2,q_2} x^a_{q_2,q_2}) \cdot 1 = 0 \end{cases}$$

We find an approximation to the solution of this system of 8 equations in 4 variables using the GA and CMA-ES methods and by choosing 0.1 as the threshold value for the equivalence query (see below). The result after the Gram-Schmit process for each method is shown in Figs. 2c and d, respectively.

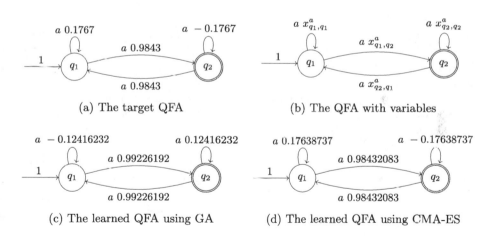

(a) The target QFA

(b) The QFA with variables

(c) The learned QFA using GA

(d) The learned QFA using CMA-ES

Fig. 2. An example of learning QFA.

3.3   Learning with More Accepting States

In the framework above, we assumed to learn a quantum automaton having only one accepting state. If there is more than one accepting state when asking membership queries, we need the oracle to answer with a fixed number of probabilities, one for each accepting state separately. This is reasonable and physically realizable, as the probability of the automata accepting a string is the sum of all probabilities of accepting the string in each accepting state, meaning that we can (and actually physically must by the third postulate of quantum mechanics) measure this probability independently on each accepting state. Of course, this way, the oracle indirectly reveals a minimum number of states needed by the automaton, i.e., the number of accepting states. This information can be used when constructing the starting Hankel matrix that can now be of a size equal to the number of accepting states. Furthermore, the variants of Hankel matrices we have to consider will increase exponentially with the number of accepting states. For example, given a quantum automaton with two accepting states, when asking the membership query for a string x, the oracle should give probabilities $P_1(x)$ and $P_2(x)$, such that $P(x) = P_1(x) + P_2(x)$. As a result, there are now 4 entries instead of 2 in the Hankel matrix, namely i) $\sqrt{P_1(x)} + \sqrt{P_2(x)}$, ii) $\sqrt{P_1(x)} - \sqrt{P_2(x)}$, iii) $-\sqrt{P_1(x)} + \sqrt{P_2(x)}$, and iv) $-\sqrt{P_1(x)} - \sqrt{P_2(x)}$.

As before, once we find a Hankel matrix with a rank smaller than its size, then the rank r is the number of states of our automaton. If $P(\epsilon) = 0$, then the initial state is one of the accepting states, and the next $r - 1$ states are the others. Otherwise, $P(\epsilon) > 0$ and the accepting states are $q_2, ... q_r$.

4   Distance Between Quantum Automata

In the previous section, we concentrated on constructing a quantum automaton from membership queries. Such an automaton is then given to the oracle to check for equivalence. Even if the equivalence of measure-once quantum automata is decidable [28], the learned automata is an approximation of the target one. So we need to substitute the equivalence query with a set of strings to measure the distance of the learned automata from the target. The algorithm terminates when this distance is smaller than a given threshold parameter δ. Otherwise, a new sequence of strings with associated probabilities is used to improve the resulting automaton.

In this section, we present two methods to calculate the distance between the learned and the target automata: one based on the two automata and another based on a testing sample.

L_1 Distance Based on the Automata

Let $A_1 = \langle Q_1, \Sigma, \{U_{1,\sigma} | \sigma \in \Sigma\}, q_1, F_1\rangle$ and $A_2 = \langle Q_2, \Sigma, \{U_{2,\sigma} | \sigma \in \Sigma\}, q_2, F_2\rangle$ be two quantum finite automata. Let $L(A_1)$ and $L(A_2)$ be the languages accepted by A_1 and A_2, respectively, with probability greater than 0. Since these two languages are infinite, it is impossible to calculate the L_1 distance between them. Therefore, our strategy is to calculate the distance only between those strings that form a base of the language recognized by the combination of the two automata.

We define, for each string $x \in \Sigma^*$, the matrix

$$W_{A_1 \oplus A_2}(x) = \begin{pmatrix} W_1(x) & O \\ O & W_2(x) \end{pmatrix}.$$

where $W_i(x) = U_{i,x}^* \otimes U_{i,x}$ for $i = 1, 2$, respectively. Further, let

$$D_{A_1 \oplus A_2}(x) = W_{A_1 \oplus A_2}(x) \begin{pmatrix} q_1 \otimes q_1 \\ q_2 \otimes q_2 \end{pmatrix},$$

where q_i is the vector of dimension $|Q_i|$ with 1 in the first position and the rest all 0's representing the initial state q_i for $i = 1, 2$. Finally, for $q \in F_i$, let q be the vector of size $|Q_i|$ with 1 at the q-th position and zero in all other. We define $\eta_i = \sum_{q \in F_i} q^* \otimes q$ for $i = 1, 2$. By the above definitions, we then have that

$$|(\eta_{F_1}, -\eta_{F_2})^\mathsf{T} D_{A_1 \oplus A_2}(x)| = |P_{A_1}(x) - P_{A_2}(x)|.$$

Let $H(A_1, A_2) = \{D_{A_1 \oplus A_2}(x) : x \in \Sigma^*\}$ and V be a basis for $span(H(A_1, A_2))$. Note that the dimension of the vector space $span(H(A_1, A_2))$ is at most $2|Q_1| + 2|Q_2|$. We can finally calculate the normalized L_1 distance using only vectors from the basis V by:

$$d_1(A_1, A_2) = \frac{\sum_{x \in V} |P_{A_1}(x) - P_{A_2}(x)|}{dim(V)} = \frac{\sum_{v \in V} |[(\eta_{F_1}, -\eta_{F_2})^\mathsf{T}]v|}{dim(V)},$$

where $dim(V)$ is the number of columns of V. This distance can be calculated in polynomial time using the pseudo-code shown in Algorithm 2.

In the beginning, we set V to be the empty set. In order to find a basis V of $H(A_1, A_2) = \{D_{A_1 \oplus A_2}(x) : x \in \Sigma^*\}$ we use a breadth-first search on a tree T with strings in Σ^* as nodes. The root node is ϵ. For any string $x \in \Sigma^*$, every $\sigma \in \Sigma$, the node x has $|\Sigma|$ children, namely all strings $x\sigma$ for $\sigma \in \Sigma$. Then, we visit the tree T in breadth-first order from the root node. When visiting each node x, we check whether $D_{A_1 \oplus A_2}(x)$ is linear-independent of V. If it is linear-independent, we add $D_{A_1 \oplus A_2}(x)$ to set V and continue to search the tree T. If it is not, we truncate all children nodes of node (x). (line 2 - line 8). We stop searching when every node in T is visited or pruned. Note that the vectors in the set V are all linearly independent and lexicographically minima. In the worst case, the time complexity of this algorithm is $\mathbb{O}(m * dim(V)^3)$ using Gaussian elimination, where m is the length of the queue (bounded by $dim(V) * |\Sigma|$) and $dim(V)$ is bounded by the size of automaton, which is $dim(V) \leqslant 2|Q_1| + 2|Q_2|$.

L_1 Distance Computing over Testing Sample

Instead of using the target quantum automata, we could simply calculate the L_1 distance between the learned automaton A and a finite testing sample T of strings in Σ^*. In this case, the normalized L_1 distance is given by

$$d_1(T, A) = \frac{\sum_{x \in T} |P_T(x) - P_A(x)|}{|T|},$$

where $P_T(x)$ is the probability of string x given by the oracle and $P_A(x)$ is the probability of string x calculated using the learned automaton A.

Algorithm 2: Normalized L_1 distance on the base of two quantum automata

Input: $A_1 = \langle Q_1, \Sigma, \{U_{1,\sigma} | \sigma \in \Sigma\}, q_1, F_1 \rangle$ and $A_2 = \langle Q_2, \Sigma, \{U_{2,\sigma} | \sigma \in \Sigma\}, q_2, F_2 \rangle$

Output: $d_1(A_1, A_2)$

1: $V = \emptyset$
2: $queue \leftarrow \text{Node}(\epsilon)$
3: **while** $queue$ is not empty **do**
4:     take a $\text{Node}(x)$ from $queue$
5:     **if** $D_{A_1 \oplus A_2}(x) \notin span(V)$ **then**
6:        $\forall \sigma \in \Sigma$, $queue \leftarrow \text{Node}(x\sigma)$
7:        $V \leftarrow D_{A_1 \oplus A_2}(x)$
8:     **end if**
9: **end while**
10: $\forall v \in V$, $d_1(A_1, A_2) = \frac{\sum_v |[(\eta_{F_1}, \eta_{F_2})^\top] v|}{dim(V)}$
11: **return** $d_1(A_1, A_2)$

---

5   Experimental Results

In this section, we conclude with some experiments on the performance of our algorithm when we consider the different optimization methods GA and CMA-ES and the two different distances described above. We use randomly generated quantum automata varying from 2 to 7 states. For each size of the state, we generate 10 automata on one letter alphabet and 10 on a two letters alphabet. For simplicity, we only generate one single accepting state. We use either 0.1 or 0.2 as the threshold for accepting distance. For calculating the normalized L_1 distance using a testing sample, the oracle returns a sample of strings in lexicographic order that is 5 times bigger than what has already been asked for the membership queries. In our experiments, we use Hankel matrices to determine the number of states for each symbol in the alphabet of the automata under consideration. The largest number of states found across all symbols is then chosen as the final structure for the automata.

Table 1 shows the average normalized L_1 distance calculated using the testing sample method and the variances with respect to using GA or CMA-ES as an optimization method. The latter has, on average, the smallest distance from the target automaton and the smallest variance, too (except for the case of 7−state automata that has a greater variance). Interestingly, the CMA-ES based algorithm is up to 30 times quicker than the one based on GA.

Table 2 does a similar experiment but with the oracle using a normalized L_1 distance calculated using the target and the learned automata. Also, in this case, CMA-ES has the smallest average distance and variance, confirming the results of the previous table.

Table 1. Averages and variances of normalized L_1 distance over testing samples between different sizes target automata and learned automata respectively.

Optimization method	2 states		3 states		4 states		5 states		6 states		7 states	
	Avg.	Var	Avg.	Var	Avg.	Var	Avg	Var	Avg.	Var	Avg.	Var
GA	0.0068	9.98e-05	0.0699	0.0015	0.1254	0.0069	0.1615	0.0046	0.1857	0.0042	0.1518	0.0014
CMA-ES	0.0003	1.05e-07	0.0003	5.63e-07	0.0003	3.58e-07	0.0021	3.76e-05	0.0181	0.0014	0.0885	0.0035

Table 2. Averages and variances of normalized L_1 distance on the base of the language between different sizes target automata and learned automata respectively.

Optimization method	2 states		3 states		4 states		5 states		6 states		7 states	
	Avg.	Var.	Avg.	Var.	Avg.	Var.	Avg	Var.	Avg.	Var.	Avg.	Var.
GA	0.0028	8.81e-06	0.0775	0.0104	0.1262	0.0106	0.1751	0.0040	0.1878	0.0058	0.1454	0.0033
CMA-ES	5.28e-05	1.98e-09	7.03e-05	3.83e-09	0.0007	4.81e-06	0.0052	0.0003	0.0290	0.0020	0.1093	0.0032

When considering only the CMA-ES method, we note that the distance calculated using the two automata is better for a small number of states (2 and 3), while the testing sample is better for a larger number of states. However, this is not the case when we use the GA method, as the automata-based distance is better for the 7−state case.

6 Conclusion

In this paper, we learn quantum automata using a combination of active learning and two non-linear optimization methods based on genetic and evolutionary algorithms. We experimentally compared the results from these two methods using randomly generated automata. The evolutionary CMA-ES method has the smallest distance from the target and the smallest variance in general. It also runs much quicker compared to the genetic algorithm. The scalability of our algorithm depends very much on the scalability of the non-linear optimization method we use.

In the future, we want to investigate an extension of this work to measure-many quantum automata, for which we already know how to compute equivalence queries [29], and a more general PAC version of the L^* algorithm [32] applied to quantum automata. Furthermore, it would be interesting to have a deeper analysis of the distance algorithm between two combined quantum automata.

References

1. Angluin, D.: On the complexity of minimum inference of regular sets. Inf. Control **39**(3), 337–350 (1978)
2. Angluin, D.: Learning regular sets from queries and counterexamples. Inf. Comput. **75**(2), 87–106 (1987)
3. Angluin, D.: Identifying languages from stochastic examples. Yale University, Department of Computer Science (1988)

4. Angluin, D., Smith, C.H.: Inductive inference: theory and methods. ACM Comput. Surv. (CSUR) **15**(3), 237–269 (1983)
5. Arunachalam, S., De Wolf, R.: Optimal quantum sample complexity of learning algorithms. J. Mach. Learn. Res. **19**(1), 2879–2878 (2018)
6. Arunachalam, S., de Wolf, R.: Guest column: a survey of quantum learning theory. ACM SIGACT News **48**(2), 41–67 (2017)
7. Bergadano, F., Varricchio, S.: Learning behaviors of automata from multiplicity and equivalence queries. SIAM J. Comput. **25**(6), 1268–1280 (1996)
8. Bertoni, A., Carpentieri, M.: Analogies and differences between quantum and stochastic automata. Theor. Comput. Sci. **262**(1–2), 69–81 (2001)
9. Bollig, B., Habermehl, P., Kern, C., Leucker, M.: Angluin-style learning of NFA. In: IJCAI. vol. 9, pp. 1004–1009 (2009)
10. Bshouty, N.H., Jackson, J.C.: Learning DNF over the uniform distribution using a quantum example oracle. In: Proceedings of the Eighth Annual Conference on Computational Learning Theory, pp. 118–127 (1995)
11. Carrasco, R.C., Oncina, J.: Learning stochastic regular grammars by means of a state merging method. In: Carrasco, R.C., Oncina, J. (eds.) ICGI 1994. LNCS, vol. 862, pp. 139–152. Springer, Heidelberg (1994). https://doi.org/10.1007/3-540-58473-0_144
12. Chalupar, G., Peherstorfer, S., Poll, E., De Ruiter, J.: Automated reverse engineering using {Lego®}. In: 8th USENIX Workshop on Offensive Technologies (WOOT 14) (2014)
13. Chapman, M., Chockler, H., Kesseli, P., Kroening, D., Strichman, O., Tautschnig, M.: Learning the language of error. In: Finkbeiner, B., Pu, G., Zhang, L. (eds.) ATVA 2015. LNCS, vol. 9364, pp. 114–130. Springer, Cham (2015). https://doi.org/10.1007/978-3-319-24953-7_9
14. Cho, C.Y., Babi ć, D., Shin, E.C.R., Song, D.: Inference and analysis of formal models of botnet command and control protocols. In: Proceedings of the 17th ACM Conference on Computer and Communications Security, pp. 426–439 (2010)
15. Chu, W., Bonsangue, M.: Learning probabilistic languages by k-testable machines. In: 2020 International Symposium on Theoretical Aspects of Software Engineering (TASE), pp. 129–136. IEEE (2020)
16. Chu, W., Chen, S., Bonsangue, M.: Non-linear optimization methods for learning regular distributions. In: Riesco, A., Zhang, M. (eds.) Formal Methods and Software Engineering. ICFEM 2022. LNCS, vol. 13478, pp. 54–70. Springer, Cham (2022). https://doi.org/10.1007/978-3-031-17244-1_4
17. De Ruiter, J., Poll, E.: Protocol state fuzzing of {TLS} implementations. In: 24th USENIX Security Symposium (USENIX Security 2015), pp. 193–206 (2015)
18. Esposito, Y., Lemay, A., Denis, F., Dupont, P.: Learning probabilistic residual finite state automata. In: Adriaans, P., Fernau, H., van Zaanen, M. (eds.) ICGI 2002. LNCS (LNAI), vol. 2484, pp. 77–91. Springer, Heidelberg (2002). https://doi.org/10.1007/3-540-45790-9_7
19. Fiterău-Broştean, P., Janssen, R., Vaandrager, F.: Combining model learning and model checking to analyze TCP implementations. In: Chaudhuri, S., Farzan, A. (eds.) CAV 2016. LNCS, vol. 9780, pp. 454–471. Springer, Cham (2016). https://doi.org/10.1007/978-3-319-41540-6_25
20. Garcia, P., Vidal, E., Oncina, J.: Learning locally testable languages in the strict sense. In: ALT, pp. 325–338 (1990)
21. Gold, E.M.: Language identification in the limit. Inf. Control **10**(5), 447–474 (1967)
22. Gold, E.M.: Complexity of automaton identification from given data. Inf. Control **37**(3), 302–320 (1978)

23. Grefenstette, J.J.: Genetic algorithms and machine learning. In: Proceedings of the Sixth Annual Conference on Computational Learning Theory, pp. 3–4 (1993)

24. Gruska, J., Qiu, D., Zheng, S.: Potential of quantum finite automata with exact acceptance. Int. J. Found. Comput. Sci. **26**(03), 381–398 (2015)

25. Hansen, N.: The CMA evolution strategy: a tutorial. arXiv preprint arXiv:1604.00772 (2016)

26. Holland, J.H.: Genetic algorithms. Sci. Am. **267**(1), 66–73 (1992)

27. Kondacs, A., Watrous, J.: On the power of quantum finite state automata. In: Proceedings 38th Annual Symposium on Foundations of Computer Science, pp. 66–75. IEEE (1997)

28. Koshiba, T.: Polynomial-time algorithms for the equivalence for one-way quantum finite automata. In: Eades, P., Takaoka, T. (eds.) ISAAC 2001. LNCS, vol. 2223, pp. 268–278. Springer, Heidelberg (2001). https://doi.org/10.1007/3-540-45678-3_24

29. Lin, T.: Another approach to the equivalence of measure-many one-way quantum finite automata and its application. J. Comput. Syst. Sci. **78**(3), 807–821 (2012)

30. Moore, C., Crutchfield, J.P.: Quantum automata and quantum grammars. Theor. Comput. Sci. **237**(1–2), 275–306 (2000)

31. de Nobel, J., Vermetten, D., Wang, H., Doerr, C., Bäck, T.: Tuning as a means of assessing the benefits of new ideas in interplay with existing algorithmic modules. In: Proceedings of the Genetic and Evolutionary Computation Conference Companion, pp. 1375–1384 (2021)

32. Parekh, R., Nichitiu, C., Honavar, V.: A polynomial time incremental algorithm for learning DFA. In: Honavar, V., Slutzki, G. (eds.) ICGI 1998. LNCS, vol. 1433, pp. 37–49. Springer, Heidelberg (1998). https://doi.org/10.1007/BFb0054062

33. Qiu, D.: Learning quantum finite automata with queries. arXiv preprint arXiv:2111.14041 (2021)

34. Schmidt, E.: Zur theorie der linearen und nichtlinearen integralgleichungen. Math. Ann. **63**(4), 433–476 (1907)

35. Valiant, L.G.: A theory of the learnable. Commun. ACM **27**(11), 1134–1142 (1984)

36. Wharton, R.M.: Approximate language identification. Inf. Control **26**(3), 236–255 (1974)

View-Based Axiomatic Reasoning for PSO

Lara Bargmann$^{(\boxtimes)}$ and Heike Wehrheim$^{(\boxtimes)}$

Department of Computing Science, University of Oldenburg, Oldenburg, Germany
{lara.bargmann,heike.wehrheim}@uol.de

Abstract. Weak memory models describe the semantics of concurrent programs on modern multi-core architectures. Reasoning techniques for concurrent programs, like Owicki-Gries-style proof calculi, have to be based on such a semantics, and hence need to be freshly developed for every new memory model. Recently, a more uniform approach to reasoning has been proposed which builds correctness proofs on the basis of a number of core *axioms*. This allows to prove program correctness *independent* of memory models, and transfers proofs to specific memory models by showing these to instantiate all axioms required in a proof. The axiomatisation is built on the notion of thread *views* as first class elements in the semantics.

In this paper, we investigate the applicability of this form of axiomatic reasoning to the *Partial Store Order* (PSO) memory model. As the standard semantics for PSO is not based on views, we first of all provide a view-based semantics for PSO and prove it to coincide with the standard semantics. We then show the new view-based semantics to satisfy all but one axiom. The missing axiom refers to message-passing (MP) abilities of memory models, which PSO does not guarantee. As a consequence, only proofs without usage of the MP axiom are transferable to PSO. We illustrate the reasoning technique by proving correctness of a litmus test employing a fence to ensure message passing.

Keywords: Weak memory models · Axiomatic reasoning · View-based semantics · Owicki-Gries proof calculus

1 Introduction

On multi-core architectures, the semantics of concurrent programs deviates from the often assumed *sequential consistency* (Lamport [29]). Sequential consistency guarantees that a concurrent program executes as an interleaving of statements following program order within threads. In contrast, the behaviour of concurrent programs on modern multi-core architectures looks like program statements have been reordered, e.g. allowing for write-write reorderings (on disjoint variables). A *weak memory model* details the semantics of programs on such architectures.

Today, weak memory models exist for a number of different architectures (e.g. TSO [33], PSO and Power [2], ARM [18]) as well as for programming

Bargmann and Wehrheim are supported by DFG project WE2290/14-1.

languages (e.g. C11 [9]). The semantics is either specified in an *axiomatic* or an *operational* style. The operational style is more suitable for verification approaches like Hoare-style proof calculi [21] and their extensions to parallel programs by Owicki and Gries [32] which need to construct proof outlines and reason about program statements. Recently, a number of operational semantics based on the concept of *views* have been proposed [10–12,17,23,24]. Views are specific to threads in concurrent programs and – simply speaking – specify the values of shared variables a thread can read (i.e., view) in some particular state[1]. View-based semantics lend itself well to Owicki-Gries style reasoning [32], by replacing standard assertions on program variables by view-based assertions speaking about potential views of threads on shared variables. Still, with every new weak memory model, a new proof calculus for reasoning needs to be built.

To alleviate this problem, Doherty et al. [16] proposed a *generic* reasoning technique for weak memory models with a view-based operational semantics. The core of this technique are a number of axioms on the transition systems generated by the memory model. The axioms detail properties of read and write actions (e.g., semi-commutativity of actions operating on different program variables) as well as fence instructions. Correctness proofs of concurrent programs can then be done on the basis of axioms only, independent of a concrete memory model. Proofs can be *transferred* to a specific memory model once the memory model has been shown to *instantiate* all axioms employed within the proof.

In this paper, we investigate the applicability of this approach to the memory model *Partial Store Ordering* (PSO) [22]. A number of works have studied this memory model, proposing stateless model checking [1], proving the decidability of reachability [7] or the NP-hardness of the testing (or consistency) problem [19]. Besides an axiomatic semantics [3], PSO also has an operational semantics, however, not easily lending itself to the definition of views, in particular not for defining *view maximality*, the core concept underlying axiomatic reasoning in [16]. Our first step is thus to develop a new semantics definition for PSO and prove it to coincide with the standard semantics via forward and backward simulations [31]. Equipped with the new semantics, we prove PSO to instantiate all but one axiom of [16]. The missing axiom refers to the ability of some memory models to provide *message passing* (MP) facilities, i.e. to transfer the view of one thread t_1 to another thread t_2 when t_2 reads a value written by t_1. This property does not hold for PSO. Hence, only correctness proofs using the axioms other than MP are valid in PSO. Besides the already existing proofs in [16], we provide a new correctness proof for a message passing example with a fence, required to guarantee correctness for weak memory models without message passing facilities, i.e. requiring a proof without use of the MP axiom. On this, we exemplify the technique of axiomatic proving.

2 Background

Before looking at PSO and its view-based semantics, we define our program syntax and semantics partly following the notation of [16].

---

[1] Note that in contrast to sequentially consistent execution, threads might be able to see different values of a shared variable in one state.

$$\text{EXP}\frac{v = [\![e]\!]_{ls}}{(r := e, ls) \xrightarrow{\tau} (skip, ls[r := v])}$$

$$\text{READ}\frac{a = rd(x, r, v)}{(r := x, ls) \xrightarrow{a} (skip, ls[r := v])}$$

$$\text{WRITE}\frac{a = wr(x, v) \;\; v = [\![e]\!]_{ls}}{(x := e, ls) \xrightarrow{a} (skip, ls)}$$

$$\text{FENCE}\frac{a = fence}{(fnc, ls) \xrightarrow{a} (skip, ls)}$$

$$\text{PARCOM}\frac{(C_1, ls) \xrightarrow{a} (C_1', ls')}{(C_1; \; C_2, ls) \xrightarrow{a} (C_1'; \; C_2, ls')}$$

$$\text{SKIP}\frac{}{(skip; \; C_2, ls) \xrightarrow{\tau} (C_2, ls)}$$

$$\text{IF1}\frac{[\![b]\!]_{ls}}{(\text{if } b \text{ then } C_1 \text{ else } C_2, ls) \xrightarrow{\tau} (C_1, ls)}$$

$$\text{IF2}\frac{\neg[\![b]\!]_{ls}}{(\text{if } b \text{ then } C_1 \text{ else } C_2, ls) \xrightarrow{\tau} (C_2, ls)}$$

$$\text{WHILE1}\frac{[\![b]\!]_{ls}}{(\text{while } b \text{ do } C, ls) \xrightarrow{\tau} (C; \text{ while } b \text{ do } C, ls)}$$

$$\text{WHILE2}\frac{\neg[\![b]\!]_{ls}}{(\text{while } b \text{ do } C, ls) \xrightarrow{\tau} (skip, ls)}$$

Fig. 1. Local program semantics

2.1 Program Syntax and Semantics

We define a concurrent program as a parallel composition of sequential programs. Each thread $t \in$ Tid runs a sequential program Com and with the function $\Pi : $ Tid $\rightarrow Com$ we model a concurrent program over threads Tid. We let Var_G be the set of global variables and Var_L the set of local variables (or registers) with $\text{Var}_G \cap \text{Var}_L = \varnothing$ and $\text{Var} = \text{Var}_G \cup \text{Var}_L$. We assume that initially all variables have the value 0.

For $x \in \text{Var}_G$, $r \in \text{Var}_L$ and value $v \in$ Val we define the following grammar

$$E ::= v \mid e \quad com ::= skip \mid fnc \mid r := E \mid r := x \mid x := E$$

$$Com ::= com \mid Com; Com \mid \text{if } b \text{ then } Com \text{ else } Com \mid \text{while } b \text{ do } Com$$

where $e \in Exp$ and $b \in BExp$ are expressions over local variables, e arithmetic and b boolean.

Alike a number of recent approaches for weak memory model semantics [16,17,27], we define the semantics of a concurrent program running on a weak memory model by defining the semantics of programs *independent* of the memory model and later combining them with the memory model semantics. The program semantics first of all assumes that *any* value can be read for variables and the memory model later restricts these values. We will describe the operational rules for the memory model PSO (Fig. 3) below.

First, we start with the set of actions

$$\text{Act} = \{rd(x, r, v), wr(x, v), fence \mid x \in \text{Var}_G \wedge r \in \text{Var}_L \wedge v \in \text{Val}\}$$

and add the read $r := v$ and a silent action τ such that $\text{Act}_{\text{ext}} = \text{Act} \cup \{r := v, \tau \mid r \in Var_L \wedge v \in \text{Val}\}$. For an action $a \in$ Act we will need the functions

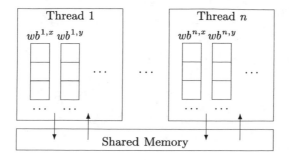

Fig. 2. PSO architecture

var, $rdval$ and $wrval$, where $var(a) \in \mathsf{Var_G}$ describes the global variable of the action. If a is a read action $rd(x, r, v)$, then $rdval(a) = v \in \mathsf{Val}$ describes its value, otherwise we set $rdval(a) = \bot \notin \mathsf{Val}$. $wrval(a)$ is similarly defined for write actions. With these functions we can define the subsets of Act: $Rd = \{a \in \mathsf{Act} | wrval(a) = \bot \wedge rdval(a) \neq \bot\}$ and $Wr = \{a \in \mathsf{Act} | rdval(a) = \bot \wedge wrval(a) \neq \bot\}$. For a value v, we assume $Rd[v] = \{a \in Rd | rdval(a) = v\}$ and $Wr[v] = \{a \in Wr | wrval(a) = v\}$. We let $\mathsf{Act}_{|x}$ be the set of all actions a with $var(a) = x$. Hence $Rd_{|x}$ is the set of all reads in $\mathsf{Act}_{|x}$ and $Wr_{|x}$ the set of all writes.

The operational semantics for a sequential program is given by the transition rules in Fig. 1. Therein $ls : \mathsf{Var_L} \to \mathsf{Val}$ defines the local state, which maps each local variable to its value, and $[\![e]\!]_{ls}$ is the value of the expression e in the local state ls. By $ls[r := v]$ we denote the local state which is equal to ls for every local variable except for r and the value of r in $ls[r := v]$ is v. Note in particular that the READ rule allows to use arbitrary values for v. To lift the sequential program of one thread to a concurrent program ($\Pi : \mathsf{Tid} \to Com$) we in addition employ the following rule

$$\text{PAR} \frac{(\Pi(t), lst(t)) \xrightarrow{a} (C, ls) \; a \in \mathsf{Act_{ext}}}{(\Pi, lst) \xrightarrow{a}_t (\Pi[t := C], lst[t := ls])}$$

where $lst : \mathsf{Tid} \to (\mathsf{Var_L} \to \mathsf{Val})$ maps each thread to its local state.

2.2 PSO Semantics

Next, we give the operational semantics of PSO. This semantics is of an architectural style as it directly models architecture specific details. The PSO memory model contains a shared memory plus a write buffer per thread and per variable (see Fig. 2 for an illustration). The per-variable write buffers distinguish PSO from the TSO memory model [1] which contains just one write buffer per thread. A write buffer $wb^{t,x}$ of a thread t and a global variable x is a FIFO ordered list with values as entries. Each write buffer can flush its first entry to the shared memory at any time. If a thread t wants to read the value of a variable x, it either reads the last entry of $wb^{t,x}$ or, if $wb^{t,x}$ is empty, it reads from shared memory. Next, we formally define the PSO semantics describing this behaviour.

$$\text{PSO-READ} \frac{a = rd(x, r, v) \quad v = val_\sigma(t, x)}{\sigma \overset{a,t}{\leadsto}_{PSO} \sigma}$$

$$\text{PSO-WRITE} \frac{a = wr(x, v) \quad wb' = \sigma.wb[(t, x) := \sigma.wb^{t,x} \cdot \langle v \rangle]}{\sigma \overset{a,t}{\leadsto}_{PSO} (s, wb')}$$

$$\text{PSO-FENCE} \frac{a = fence \quad \sigma.wb^{t,x} = \langle \, \rangle \text{ for all } x \in \mathsf{Var_G}}{\sigma \overset{a,t}{\leadsto}_{PSO} \sigma}$$

$$\text{PSO-FLUSH} \frac{wb^{t,x} = \langle v \rangle \cdot w \quad s' = \sigma.s[x := v] \quad wb' = \sigma.wb[(t, x) := w]}{\sigma \overset{flush,t}{\leadsto}_{PSO} (s', wb')}$$

Fig. 3. PSO semantics

In the PSO semantics, each state $\sigma = (s, wb) \in \Sigma_{PSO}$ contains a shared memory $s : \mathsf{Var_G} \to \mathsf{Val}$ and a write buffer map $wb : (\mathsf{Tid} \times \mathsf{Var_G}) \to \mathsf{Val}^*$, which maps each thread $t \in \mathsf{Tid}$ and each global variable $x \in \mathsf{Var_G}$ to a write buffer list $wb^{t,x}$. With $I_{PSO} \subseteq \Sigma_{PSO}$ we denote the initial states, in which we assume $s(x) = 0$ for all x and write buffers to be empty. The rule PSO-WRITE in Fig. 3 tells us that whenever a program writes some value $v \in \mathsf{Val}$ to a global variable x in a thread t, we add v to the write buffer $wb^{t,x}$. If we flush a write buffer $wb^{t,x}$ (rule PSO-FLUSH), we change the entry of x in the shared memory s to the first entry of $wb^{t,x}$ and delete it from the write buffer. When a program wants to read the value v of a variable x to a register r in a thread t (rule PSO-READ), it reads the last value of $wb^{t,x}$ in case the write buffer is not empty. Otherwise, the program reads the entry of x directly from the shared memory. In the rule, this is described by the function val_σ. If the write buffer $wb^{t,x}$ is empty, then $val_\sigma(t, x) = \sigma.s(x)$, otherwise $val_\sigma(t, x) = last(\sigma.wb^{t,x})$. To pass a fence statement in a thread t (i.e., to apply rule PSO-FENCE) we first need to flush all write buffers of that thread until $wb^{t,x}$ is empty for every x.

To integrate the operational semantics of PSO in the program semantics, we will need to define the transition system TS_{PSO} generated by programs running on PSO. Formally we write $TS_{PSO} = (\mathsf{Act}, \Sigma_{PSO}, I_{PSO}, T_{PSO})$ with the set of states $\Sigma_{PSO} = (\mathsf{Var_G} \to \mathsf{Val}) \times ((\mathsf{Tid} \times \mathsf{Var_G}) \to \mathsf{Val}^*)$, the set of initial states $I_{PSO} = \{(s, wb) \in \Sigma_{PSO} | \forall t \in \mathsf{Tid} \, \forall x \in \mathsf{Var_G} : wb^{t,x} = \langle \, \rangle \wedge s(x) = 0\}$ and the set of transitions $T_{PSO} \in \mathsf{Tid} \times \mathsf{Act} \to 2^{\Sigma_{PSO} \times \Sigma_{PSO}}$. For an action $a \in \mathsf{Act}$ in a thread $t \in \mathsf{Tid}$, we set $T_{PSO}(t, a) = FL_{PSO} \, \overset{a,t}{\varsigma} \leadsto_{PSO}$ where $FL_{PSO} = \left(\bigcup_{t \in \mathsf{Tid}} \overset{flush,t}{\leadsto}_{PSO} \right)^*$ and ς is the relational composition.

2.3   Combined Semantics

Program and weak memory semantics are combined using the following three lifting rules.

$$\text{SILENT} \frac{(\Pi, lst) \overset{\tau}{\to}_t (\Pi', lst')}{(\Pi, lst, \sigma) \Rightarrow_t (\Pi', lst', \sigma)} \qquad \text{LOCAL} \frac{(\Pi, lst) \overset{r:=v}{\to}_t (\Pi', lst')}{(\Pi, lst, \sigma) \overset{r:=v}{\Longrightarrow}_t (\Pi', lst', \sigma)}$$

Init: $x := 0;\ y := 0;$

Thread 1	**Thread 2**
$1 : x := 1;$	$3 : r_1 := y;$
$2 : y := 1;$	$4 : r_2 := x;$

$$\{r_1 \in \{0,1\} \wedge r_2 \in \{0,1\}\}$$

Fig. 4. MP without fence

Init: $x := 0;\ y := 0;$

Thread 1	**Thread 2**
$1 : x := 1;$	$4 : r_1 := y;$
$2 : fnc;$	$5 : r_2 := x;$
$3 : y := 1;$	

$$\{r_1 = 1 \Rightarrow r_2 = 1\}$$

Fig. 5. MP with fence

$$\text{MEMORY} \frac{(\Pi, lst) \overset{a}{\to}_t (\Pi', lst') \quad a \in \mathsf{Act} \quad (\sigma, \sigma') \in T(t, a)}{(\Pi, lst, \sigma) \overset{a}{\Rightarrow}_t (\Pi', lst', \sigma')}$$

The MEMORY-rule combines the rules for $a \in \mathsf{Act}$ of the local program semantics (READ, WRITE, FENCE and PARCOM) with the ones of the PSO semantics. It is used for actions which affect the global memory. Here, lst changes only if we read a value of a global variable to a register. We use the LOCAL-rule to read a value directly to a register (READ), which changes lst, but since there is no global variable involved σ stays the same. For the remaining rules of the local semantics we use the SILENT-rule, which changes lst only if we read an expression to a register (EXP). We exemplify the semantics of PSO in the so-called *message passing* litmus test [6] in Fig. 4. It is called "message passing" as the expected behaviour is the following: when thread 2 reads y to be 1, then it will afterwards read x to be 1 as well. Thus, the message of x to be 1 is passed from thread 1 to thread 2 upon reading y to be 1. However, PSO also allows the outcome $r_1 = 1 \wedge r_2 = 0$ (no message passing). This can be explained as follows. First, thread 1 writes the value 1 to x, so $wb^{1,x} = \langle 1 \rangle$. After that the same happens for y and therefore $wb^{1,y} = \langle 1 \rangle$. Then just one write buffer is flushed before the reads, namely $wb^{1,y}$. In that case, thread 1 reads y to be 1 from shared memory and x to be 0. On the other hand, the outcome $r_1 = 1 \wedge r_2 = 0$ is not allowed in the message passing with fence example (Fig. 5). There we can only write the value of y after the fence action, for which all write buffers of thread 1 have to be flushed. Hence thread 2 can only read the value 1 for y, if it also reads 1 for x. We will use the MP with fence example later to illustrate how our reasoning technique works. But first we explain axiomatic reasoning in the next section.

3   Axiomatic Reasoning

The axioms of [16] reason about arbitrary transition systems $TS \mathrel{\widehat{=}} (\mathsf{Act}, \Sigma, I, T)$ such as those of PSO, where Act is a set of actions, Σ a set of states, $I \subseteq \Sigma$ a set of initial states and $T \in \mathsf{Tid} \times \mathsf{Act} \to 2^{\Sigma \times \Sigma}$ a set of transitions. The axiomatisation makes use of the *weakest liberal precondition transformer* [15], as a basis for property specification and verification. For a relation R and set of states P (representing a predicate), let $\mathsf{wlp} : 2^{\Sigma \times \Sigma} \times 2^{\Sigma} \to 2^{\Sigma}$ be

$$\mathsf{wlp}(R, P) \mathrel{\widehat{=}} \{\sigma \in \Sigma \mid \forall \sigma' : (\sigma, \sigma') \in R \implies \sigma' \in P\}$$

$$\Sigma = \mathsf{wlp}(R, \Sigma) \qquad \text{(Non-aborting)}$$
$$R' \subseteq R \wedge P \subseteq P' \Rightarrow \mathsf{wlp}(R, P) \subseteq \mathsf{wlp}(R', P') \qquad \text{((Anti)-Monotonicity)}$$
$$\mathsf{wlp}(R, \mathsf{wlp}(R', P)) = \mathsf{wlp}(R \,\mathring{,}\, R', P) \qquad \text{(Composition)}$$
$$R[\mathsf{wlp}(R, P)] \subseteq P \qquad \text{(Relation Application)}$$
$$\mathsf{wlp}(R, P) \cap \mathsf{wlp}(R, Q) = \mathsf{wlp}(R, P \cap Q) \qquad \text{(Conjunctivity)}$$
$$\mathsf{wlp}(R, P) \cup \mathsf{wlp}(R, Q) \subseteq \mathsf{wlp}(R, P \cup Q) \qquad \text{(Disjunctivity)}$$

Fig. 6. Properties of wlp

Some standard properties of wlp are given in Fig. 6, where $\mathring{,}$ again denotes relational composition and $R[S]$ relational image.

In this work, R is typically instantiated to the relation $T(t, a)$, where T is the transition relation, t a thread and a an action. We say R is *disabled* in a state σ iff $\sigma \in \mathsf{dis}(R)$ holds, where $\mathsf{dis}(R) \mathrel{\hat{=}} \mathsf{wlp}(R, \varnothing)$.

Next, we give the axioms of [16]. The axioms are structured in a hierarchy in which every level adds a set of axioms to the axioms of lower levels. Figure 7 gives the hierarchy. When instantiating a memory model, parameters $vmax, interf$ (of level CORE) and $sync$ (of level MSGPASSING) have to be concretised. Their meaning is described below.

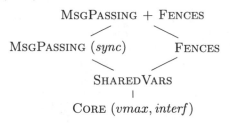

Fig. 7. Axiom Hierarchy

Level CORE. The lowest level contains basic axioms describing core properties of view-based memory model semantics. The key concept here is that of *view maximality*: a thread is view maximal (on an action operating on a variable $x \in \mathsf{Var_G}$) if it has the "most up-to-date" view on this variable. In PSO, a thread t is view maximal on e.g. reading x, if either x is in shared memory and in no write buffer or t's write buffer for x has an entry which will be flushed to shared memory "later" than all other values for x. This means, while non view maximal threads might be able to read older values of x, thread t reads the most up-to-date value. However, as this concept of "being flushed later" is not present in the semantics of PSO we will later need to define an alternative semantics. This will enable us to instantiate $vmax$ for PSO.

The core ingredient of the axiom system are view-preserving simulations.

Definition 1. *For a transition system* $TS = (\mathsf{Act}, \Sigma, I, T)$, *a* view-preserving simulation, *denoted* β, *is the weakest relation* R *satisfying the following, for all threads* $t \in \mathsf{Tid}$ *and all actions* $a \in \mathsf{Act}$

$$R \,\mathring{,}\, T(t, a) \subseteq T(t, a) \,\mathring{,}\, R \qquad \text{(semi-commutation)}$$
$$vmax(t, a) \subseteq \mathsf{wlp}(R, vmax(t, a)) \qquad \text{(view maximality)}$$

View-preserving simulations conceptionally include all sorts of system steps changing the state without executing visible actions like read and write. In PSO,

C1 : $\forall\, t \in \mathsf{Tid}, a \in \mathsf{Act} : I \subseteq vmax(t, a)$

C2 : $\forall\, \sigma, \sigma' \in \Sigma, t, t' \in \mathsf{Tid}, a \in \mathsf{Act}$:

$\quad \sigma \in vmax(t, a) \wedge (\sigma, \sigma') \in T(t, a) \Rightarrow \exists\, \tau \in \Sigma : \; (\sigma', \tau) \in \beta \wedge (\sigma, \tau) \in T(t', a) \,\mathring{,}\, \beta$

C3 : $\forall\, t \in \mathsf{Tid}, a \in \mathsf{Act} : T(t, a) \subseteq \beta \,\mathring{,}\, interf(t, a) \,\mathring{,}\, \beta$

C4 : $\forall\, t \in \mathsf{Tid}, a, b \in \mathsf{Act} : vmax(t, a) \subseteq \mathsf{wlp}(interf(t, b), vmax(t, a))$

Fig. 8. The axioms of level CORE

these would be flushes. In order for these steps to not mess up the proofs, the relation associated with these steps should keep view maximality of threads and should semi-commute with the transition relation.

Furthermore, the core axioms make use of an *interference relation* $inter f \in \mathsf{Tid} \times \mathsf{Act} \to 2^{\Sigma \times \Sigma}$ which (together with β) provides an overapproximation of the transition relation $T(t, a)$ in order to abstract from details of the memory model and to regain standard properties of reasoning (like writes and reads on different variables commuting). Figure 8 gives all core axioms.

For reasoning we will later employ the following *view-based* assertions.

Definition 2. *For a thread t, a variable $x \in \mathsf{Var_G}$ and a value $v \in \mathsf{Val}$ we define*

$\quad [x \not\approx v]_t \,\hat{=}\, \mathsf{dis}(T(t, Rd_{|x}[v]))$ *(Impossible value)*

$\quad [x \equiv v]_t \,\hat{=}\, \bigcap_{u \neq v} [x \not\approx u]_t$ *(Definite value)*

$\quad\quad x_{\uparrow t} \,\hat{=}\, \bigcap_{a \in \mathsf{Act}_{|x}} vmax(t, a)$ *(Maximal view)*

$\quad [x = v]_t \,\hat{=}\, [x \equiv v]_t \cap x_{\uparrow t}$ *(Synced value)*

Assertions should be (and indeed are) stable under β.

Definition 3. *Predicate $P \in 2^{\Sigma}$ is β-stable iff $P \subseteq \mathsf{wlp}(\beta, P)$.*

In fact, the four assertions introduced above are β-stable. Furthermore, the following property is derivable from the axioms.

Lemma 1 ([16]). *For any $a \in \mathsf{Act}$, thread t and β-stable predicate P, if $P \subseteq \mathsf{wlp}(inter f(t, a), P)$, then $P \subseteq \mathsf{wlp}(T(t, a), P)$.*

Level SHAREDVARS. The next level of the axiom hierarchy deals with axioms about actions with respect to the shared variables they access. The level SHARED VARIABLES contains all axioms of the level CORE plus those given in Fig. 9. We exemplarily look at two of them, namely **SV1** and **RW6**. The axiom **SV1** states a semi-commutation property of actions (i.e., reads and writes) on *different* variables. This is a property commonly expected for programming languages, e.g. if we first write 4 to x and then 5 to y and $y \neq x$, then we should reach the same state if we first write 5 to y and then 4 to x. However, this does not necessarily hold for weak memory models. For instance, in TSO [33] with just one write buffer for all locations we would reach two different states. To regain this property for axiomatic reasoning, the axiom uses $inter f(t', b)$ (instead of

SV1 $: \forall\, a, b \in \mathsf{Act}, t, t' \in \mathsf{Tid}$ s.t. $var(a) \neq var(b)$:

$interf(t', b) \,\mathbf{\S}\, T(t, a) \subseteq T(t, a) \,\mathbf{\S}\, interf(t', b)$

SV2 $: \forall\, a, b \in \mathsf{Act}, t, t' \in \mathsf{Tid}$ s.t. $var(a) \neq var(b)$:

$vmax(t, a) \subseteq \mathsf{wlp}(interf(t', b), vmax(t, a))$

RW1 $: \forall\, t, t' \in \mathsf{Tid}, x \in \mathsf{Var_G}, a_r \in Rd_{|x}, a_w \in Wr_{|x}$ s.t. $rdval(a_r) \neq wrval(a_w)$:

$interf(t', a_w) \,\mathbf{\S}\, T(t, a_r) \subseteq T(t, a_r) \,\mathbf{\S}\, interf(t', a_w)$

RW2 $: \forall a \in \mathsf{Act}, t, t' \in \mathsf{Tid}, a_r \in Rd_{|var(a)} : interf(t', a_r) \,\mathbf{\S}\, T(t, a) \subseteq T(t, a) \,\mathbf{\S}\, interf(t', a_r)$

RW3 $: \forall a \in \mathsf{Act}, t, t' \in \mathsf{Tid}, a_r \in Rd_{|var(a)} : vmax(t, a) \subseteq \mathsf{wlp}(interf(t', a_r), vmax(t, a))$

RW4 $: \forall\, x \in \mathsf{Var_G}, t \in \mathsf{Tid} : \Sigma \subseteq \mathrm{dom}(T(t, Rd_{|x}))$

RW5 $: \forall\, x \in \mathsf{Var_G}, a_w \in Wr_{|x}, v = wrval(a_w) : \Sigma \subseteq \mathsf{wlp}(T(t, a_w), \mathrm{dom}(T(t, Rd_{|x}[v])))$

RW6 $: \forall\, x \in \mathsf{Var_G}, t \in \mathsf{Tid}, v \in \mathsf{Val} : x_{\uparrow t} \subseteq \bigcup_{v \in \mathsf{Val}} [x \equiv v]_t$

RW7 $: \forall x \in \mathsf{Var_G}, a_w, a_r, a \in \mathsf{Act}_{|x}, t, t' \in \mathsf{Tid}, a_r \in Rd$ s.t. $wrval(a_w) = rdval(a_r) \wedge t \neq t'$:

$vmax(t, a_w) \cap \mathsf{dis}(T(t', a_r)) \subseteq \mathsf{wlp}(T(t, a_w), \mathsf{wlp}(T(t', a_r), vmax(t', a)))$

Fig. 9. The axioms of level SHAREDVARS

$T(t', b)$). Axiom **RW6** uses the notion of *maximal view* of a thread t on a variable $x \in \mathsf{Var_G}$. **RW6** states that a thread being maximal wrt. x has to know a definite value for x.

When the axioms **C3**, **SV1** and **SV2** hold, we get the following property for β-stable predicates:

Lemma 2. *For all* $P \subseteq \Sigma$ *and threads* t, *if* $P \subseteq \mathsf{wlp}(\beta, P)$, *then* $P \subseteq \mathsf{wlp}(T(t, fence), P)$.

If additionally **RW2** and **RW3** hold, we can show the same for read actions.

Lemma 3 ([16]). *For all* $P \subseteq \Sigma$, *threads* t *and* $a_r \in Rd$, *if* $P \subseteq \mathsf{wlp}(\beta, P)$, *then* $P \subseteq \mathsf{wlp}(T(t, a_r), P)$.

Levels MSGPASSING *and* FENCES. Finally, we have two levels with just one additional axiom (plus a level MSGPASSING + FENCES uniting these two). Level MSGPASSING contains all axioms of SHAREDVARS plus the following message passing axiom.

MP For $a_w, a_r, b \in \mathsf{Act}$ and $t, t' \in \mathsf{Tid}$ such that $(a_w, a_r) \in sync$, $var(a_w) = var(a_r)$, $wrval(a_w) = rdval(a_r)$, $var(b) \neq var(a_w)$, and $t \neq t'$, we have

$$vmax(t, b) \cap \mathsf{wlp}(T(t', a_r), vmax(t', b))$$
$$\subseteq \mathsf{wlp}(T(t, a_w), \mathsf{wlp}(T(t', a_r), vmax(t', b))).$$

Intuitively, **MP** states the following property: we consider two actions a_w and a_r, the first a write and the second a read reading the value written by a_w.

$$\text{PP-Read} \frac{a = rd(x, r, v) \quad v = val_\sigma(t, x)}{\sigma \overset{a,t}{\leadsto}_{PP} \sigma}$$

$$\text{PP-Write} \frac{a = wr(x, v) \quad fresh_\sigma(t, x, q) \quad wb' = \sigma.wb[(t, x) := \sigma.wb^{t,x} \cdot \langle(v, q)\rangle]}{\sigma \overset{a,t}{\leadsto}_{PP} (s, wb')}$$

$$\text{PP-Fence} \frac{a = fence \quad \sigma.wb^{t,x} = \langle \, \rangle \text{ for all } x \in \mathsf{Var_G}}{\sigma \overset{a,t}{\leadsto}_{PP} \sigma}$$

$$\text{PP-Flush} \frac{wb^{t,x} = \langle(v, \cdot)\rangle \cdot w \quad s' = \sigma.s[x := v] \quad nextFlush_\sigma(t, x) \quad wb' = \sigma.wb[(t, x) := w]}{\sigma \overset{flush,t}{\leadsto}_{PP} (s', wb')}$$

Fig. 10. PPSO semantics

Furthermore, $(a_w, a_r) \in sync$ means that reading provides synchronisation with writing. The relation $sync$ is a parameter to the axiomatisation which – like $interf$ and $vmax$ – needs to be instantiated for a concrete memory model. For example, in TSO, any write is in $sync$ with any read; in C11 RAR [17] we only have writes marked as Releasing in sync with reads marked as Acquiring.

The axiom then requires the following: if thread t is view maximal on action b, say on variable x, and the read action a_r would make thread t' view maximal on b as well, then after performing the write a_w and the read a_r thread t' actually becomes view maximal on b^2.

Note that this axiom does not hold for PSO (or, rather we could make it hold by setting $sync$ to $\varnothing$ and then not being able to apply it anywhere). The reason for this is the use of separate write buffers per variable as already explained on the example in Fig. 4.

The last axiom of level Fences deals with fence instructions. It states that a thread t being view maximal on a makes all other threads view maximal on a when executing a fence instruction.

FNC $\forall a \in \mathsf{Act}, t, t' \in \mathsf{Tid}: vmax(t, a) \subseteq \mathsf{wlp}(T(t, fence), vmax(t', a))$.

Finally, to reason about assignments to local registers $r \in \mathsf{Var_L}$ a standard wlp rule is required:

$$e[r := v] \subseteq \mathsf{wlp}(T(t, rd(x, r, v)), e) \tag{1}$$

Here, $e[r := v]$ is the replacement of r by v within expression e. This completes the axiom set. Next, we look at PSO again, instantiate the parameters $vmax$ and $interf$ for PSO and then prove PSO to satisfy all axioms of level SharedVars plus axiom **FNC**.

---

[2] This is akin to the Shared-Memory Causality Principle of Lahav and Boker [26].

4   Prophetic PSO

To use our axiomatisation, we need to instantiate the parameters $vmax$ and $interf$ for the concrete memory model. However, this is not straightforward for PSO as we cannot see view maximality from the state; we do not know for which thread the entries of the write buffers are being flushed last, so we do not know which thread has the "most up-to-date" view on a variable. To still be able to use the axioms for reasoning on PSO, we thus first provide an alternative semantics for PSO called *Prophetic PSO* (PPSO). It is "prophetic" in the sense of knowing the order of flushing entries of write buffers. To this end, we directly assign a timestamp to every entry when writing and only flush entries in order of timestamps. PPSO is then shown to be trace equivalent to PSO.

The semantics of PPSO is given in Fig. 10. PSO and PPSO only differ in the type of write buffers. In the prophetic version, they do not only contain the values written, but also a timestamp $q \in \mathbb{Q}$ for each write. Therefore, we can only write a value v to a variable x in a thread t, if the condition $fresh_\sigma(t, x, q) = true$ in the current state σ. Formally $fresh_\sigma(t, x, q)$ is defined as

$$(\forall t' \in \mathsf{Tid}\ \forall x' \in \mathsf{Var_G} : (\cdot, q) \notin \sigma.wb^{t', x'}) \wedge (\forall (\cdot, q') \in \sigma.wb^{x, t} : q > q')$$

This means that none of the write buffers contains the timestamp q and all timestamps in $wb^{t,x}$ are smaller than q. In that case, we can add the pair (v, q) to $wb^{t,x}$. To flush the first entry (v, q) of a write buffer $wb^{t,x}$ the condition $nextFlush_\sigma(t, x)$ has to be $true$. That is the case if

$$(\exists q : (\cdot, q) = wb^{t,x}(0)) \wedge (\forall t' \forall x' \forall (\cdot, q') \in wb^{t', x'} : t' \neq t \vee x' \neq x \Rightarrow q' > q)$$

Then q is smaller then every timestamp from every other write buffer. In this case we can delete the entry and change the memory as before. The read and fence rules are the same as the ones in the PSO semantics. Only $val_\sigma(t, x)$ is now the value of the last entry of $\sigma.wb^{t,x}$, if $wb^{t,x}$ is not empty. In this case we write $val_\sigma(t, x) = val(last(\sigma.wb^{t,x}))$, otherwise $val_\sigma(t, x)$ is still $\sigma.s(x)$.

We define the transition system T_{PP} that is generated by programs running on PPSO analogous to TS_{PSO}. Hence we set $TS_{PP} = (\mathsf{Act}, \Sigma_{PP}, I_{PP}, T_{PP})$ with the set of states $\Sigma_{PP} = (\mathsf{Var_G} \to \mathsf{Val}) \times ((\mathsf{Tid} \times \mathsf{Var_G}) \to (\mathsf{Val} \times \mathbb{Q})^*)$, the set of initial states $I_{PP} = \{(s, wb) | s \in \mathsf{Var_G} \to \mathsf{Val} \wedge \forall t \in \mathsf{Tid}\ \forall x \in \mathsf{Var_G} : wb^{t,x} = \langle\ \rangle\}$ and the set of transitions $T_{PP} \in \mathsf{Tid} \times \mathsf{Act} \to 2^{\Sigma_{PP} \times \Sigma_{PP}}$. Similarly to T_{PSO}, we set $T_{PP}(t, a) = FL_{PP} \overset{a,t}{\leadsto}_{PP}$ where $FL_{PP} = \left(\bigcup_{t \in \mathsf{Tid}} \overset{flush,t}{\leadsto}_{PP}\right)^*$.

For PPSO we know whether a state $\sigma \in \Sigma_{PP}$ has the maximal view for an action a in a thread t. With that we can define $vmax$ and $interf$ for PPSO and investigate which axioms from Sect. 3 hold. First we however prove that PSO and PPSO (or more precisely TS_{PSO} and TS_{PP}) are *trace equivalent*. Every correctness proof for a program running on PPSO then also holds for PSO, because the reasoning technique only considers finial states.

For showing trace equivalence, we first need some definitions. We partly follow the notation of Lynch and Vaandrager [31]. Let $TS_A = (\mathsf{Act}, \Sigma_A, I_A, T_A)$ and

$TS_C = (\mathsf{Act}, \Sigma_C, I_C, T_C)$ be two transition systems. A trace of TS_A is a finite sequence of actions $\alpha \in \mathsf{Act}^*$ with $\exists \sigma_0 \in I_A, \sigma \in \Sigma_A : \sigma_0 \overset{\alpha}{\Rightarrow} \sigma$. Here $\sigma_0 \overset{\alpha}{\Rightarrow} \sigma$ means $(\sigma_0, \sigma) \in T_A(t_1, a_1) \, \overset{\circ}{\circ} ... \overset{\circ}{\circ} \, T_A(t_n, a_n)$ for $\alpha = a_1...a_n \in \mathsf{Act}^*$ and $t_1, ..., t_n \in$ Tid. By $traces(TS_A)$ we note all traces of TS_A. We call two transition systems TS_A and TS_C *trace equivalent* if $traces(TS_A) = traces(TS_C)$. Hence, to show that TS_{PSO} and TS_{PP} are trace equivalent, we prove that (i) $traces(TS_{PP}) \subseteq traces(TS_{PSO})$ and (ii) $traces(TS_{PSO}) \subseteq traces(TS_{PP})$. To do so, we employ forward and backward simulations. We start with forward simulations and the proof of (i).

Definition 4 ([31]). *A forward simulation from TS_A to TS_C is a relation $F \subseteq \Sigma_A \times \Sigma_C$ with $F(\sigma_0) \cap I_C \neq \varnothing$ for all $\sigma_0 \in I_A$ such that for every $a \in \mathsf{Act}$*

$$(\sigma_1, \sigma_2) \in F \wedge (\sigma_1, \sigma_1') \in T_A(t, a) \Rightarrow \exists \sigma_2' : (\sigma_2, \sigma_2') \in T_C(t, a) \wedge (\sigma_1', \sigma_2') \in F.$$

Lynch and Vaandrager [31] tell us that whenever there exists a forward simulation from TS_{PP} to TS_{PSO}, then $traces(TS_{PP}) \subseteq traces(TS_{PSO})$. Therefore, we need the following theorem:

Theorem 1. *There exists a forward simulation from TS_{PP} to TS_{PSO}.*

In the proof of this theorem, we choose a relation $F \subseteq \Sigma_{PP} \times \Sigma_{PSO}$ and show that F is a forward simulation. For $\sigma_1 = (s_1, wb_1)$ and $\sigma_2 = (s_2, wb_2)$ we say

$$(\sigma_1, \sigma_2) \in F :\Leftrightarrow s_1 = s_2 \wedge \forall t \in \mathsf{Tid} \ \forall x \in \mathsf{Var_G} : wb_2^{t,x} = wb_1^{t,x}.val$$

With $wb^{t,x}.val$ we describe a write buffer which contains only the values of $wb^{t,x}$. This means our relation contains only pairs that have the same shared memory and the same values in every write buffer. The full proof can be found in the extended version [8]. (i) follows directly from this theorem. Next we look at backward simulations to prove (ii).

Definition 5 ([31]). *A backward simulation from TS_A to TS_C is a relation $B \subseteq \Sigma_A \times \Sigma_C$ with $B(\sigma_0) \subseteq I_C$ for all $\sigma_0 \in I_A$ such that for every $a \in \mathsf{Act}$*

$$(\sigma_1', \sigma_2') \in B \wedge (\sigma_1, \sigma_1') \in T_A(t, a) \Rightarrow \exists \sigma_2 : (\sigma_2, \sigma_2') \in T_C(t, a) \wedge (\sigma_1, \sigma_2) \in B$$

and B is total on Σ_A.

In the next theorem we show that there exists a backward simulation from TS_{PSO} to TS_{PP}. Since we only look at finite traces, [31] proved that then $traces(TS_{PSO}) \subseteq traces(TS_{PP})$.

Theorem 2. *There exists a backward simulation from TS_{PSO} to TS_{PP}.*

We prove this theorem by choosing the relation $B \subseteq \Sigma_{PSO} \times \Sigma_{PP}$ analogous to the forward simulation with

$$(\sigma_1, \sigma_2) \in B :\Leftrightarrow s_1 = s_2 \wedge \forall t \in \mathsf{Tid} \ \forall x \in \mathsf{Var_G} : wb_1^{t,x} = wb_2^{t,x}.val$$

for $\sigma_1 = (s_1, wb_1) \in \Sigma_{PSO}$ and $\sigma_2 = (s_2, wb_2) \in \Sigma_{PP}$. To show that B is a backward simulation, we use the following invariant:

Lemma 4. *Let* $t \in Tid$, $x \in Var_G$, $\sigma_0 \in I_{PP}$ *and* $\sigma \in \Sigma_{PP}$ *with* $\sigma_0 \overset{\alpha}{\Rightarrow} \sigma$ *for* $\alpha \in traces(TS_{PP})$. *If* $q = ts(last(\sigma.wb^{t,x}))$ *we have*

$$\forall t' \in Tid \forall x' \in Var_G, t' \neq t \vee x' \neq x : (\cdot, q) \notin \sigma.wb^{t',x'}$$
$$\wedge \forall (\cdot, q') \in \sigma.wb^{x,t}, (\cdot, q') \neq last(\sigma.wb^{t,x}) : q > q'$$

We will need that lemma to ensure that $fresh_\sigma(t, x, q) = true$ for the last timestamp q of every write buffer $wb^{t,x}$ in every reachable state $\sigma \in \Sigma_{PP}$. Hence, we can execute a write action under PPSO for every variable in every thread at any time. Both proofs can be found in the extended version [8].

Corollary 1. TS_{PSO} *and* TS_{PP} *are trace equivalent.*

$$vmax_{PP}(t, a) = \begin{cases} maxTS(t, var(a)), & \text{if } a \in Wr \cup Rd \\ \Sigma_{PP}, & \text{else} \end{cases}$$

$$interf_{PP}(t, a) = \begin{cases} id, & \text{if } a \in Rd \cup \{fence\} \\ T_{PP}(t, a) \, \natural \, FL_{PP}, & a \in Wr \end{cases}$$

$$maxTS(t, x) = \{\sigma \mid \sigma.wb^{t,x} \neq \langle \, \rangle \wedge (\forall \, t', q : (\cdot, q) \in \sigma.wb^{t',x} \Rightarrow ts(last(\sigma.wb^{t,x})) \geq q)\}$$
$$\cup \{\sigma \mid \forall \, t' : \sigma.wb^{t',x} = \langle \, \rangle\}$$

Fig. 11. PPSO definitions

With that equivalence we can show on which level PSO fits in the axiom hierarchy, by showing which axioms hold for PPSO. To do so, we first need to instantiate the parameters mentioned in Sect. 3. Figure 11 gives an overview of these definitions. The set of states with maximal view $vmax_{PP}(t, a)$ for instance contains all states when $a = fence$. For an action $a \in Wr \cup Rd$, $vmax_{PP}(t, a)$ contains all states σ with maximal timestamp for thread t and variable $x = var(a)$. This either means all write buffers for x are empty or the last timestamp in $\sigma.wb^{t,x}$ is larger than any other timestamp in the write buffers for x. Also note that FL_{PP} fulfils the properties of Definition 1 and therefore FL_{PP} is at least a subset of the view-preserving simulation β.

Theorem 3. *PSO satisfies the axioms of* CORE, SHAREDVARS *and* FENCES, *but not the axiom of* MSGPASSING.

In the extended version [8] we prove that PPSO fulfils the axioms of CORE, SHAREDVARS and FENCES. Because of Corollary 1 the axioms then also hold for PSO. We can show that MP does not hold for PPSO by looking at Fig. 4. A possible outcome of the example is $r_1 = 1 \wedge r_2 = 0$ (see Sect. 2.3). Let $a_w = wr(y, 1)$, $a_r = rd(y, r_1, 1)$, $b = wr(x, 1)$, $t = 1$ and $t' = 2$. We choose σ to be the state after the write $x := 1$ in thread 1, such that $\sigma.wb^{1,x} = \langle (1, 2) \rangle$. Hence $\sigma \in vmax_{PP}(1, b)$ and since $\sigma \notin dom(T_{PP}(2, a_r))$, we also get $\sigma \in wlp(T_{PP}(2, a_r), vmax_{PP}(2, b))$. Now we need to show, that $\sigma \notin \mathsf{wlp}(T_{PP}(1, a_w), \mathsf{wlp}(T_{PP}(2, a_r), vmax(2, b)))$. For that let σ' be a state after $y := 1$, such that $\sigma'.wb^{1,x} = \langle(1, 2)\rangle$ and $\sigma'.wb^{1,y} = \langle(1, 1)\rangle$. After a flush of $wb^{1,y}$ we get to a state σ'' for which $\sigma''.s(y) = 1$ and still $\sigma''.wb^{1,x} = \langle(1, 2)\rangle$. Then $(\sigma, \sigma') \in T_{PP}(1, a_w)$ and $(\sigma', \sigma'') \in T_{PP}(2, a_r)$, but $\sigma'' \notin vmax_{PP}(2, b)$. Hence, $\sigma \notin \mathsf{wlp}(T_{PP}(1, a_w), \mathsf{wlp}(T_{PP}(2, a_r), vmax_{PP}(2, b)))$ and PSO does not satisfy MP.

5 Example Proof

In this section we want to apply this form of axiomatic reasoning to prove the correctness of the message passing with fence litmus test (see Fig. 5). For that we use Owicki-Gries reasoning for concurrent programs [32]. Like [16] we prove the holding of Hoare-triples [21] of the form $\{P\}com_t\{Q\}$ by showing that

$$P \subseteq \mathsf{wlp}(T(t, a), Q)$$

holds for all actions a belonging to com_t. Here com_t is the program command of a thread t and we call P the *pre-assertion* and Q the *post-assertion*. These assertions occur in proof outlines of programs as in Owicki-Gries reasoning [32]. The assertion above a command is its pre-assertion and the one below its post-assertion. To check if a proof outline is valid we differentiate between local and global correctness (interference-freedom). A proof outline is valid when every thread is locally correct and the proof outline itself is globally correct.

Definition 6 ([16])
A thread t is locally correct *in a proof outline if $\{P\}com_t\{Q\}$ holds for every program command com in t with pre-assertion P and post-assertion Q.*

A proof outline is globally correct *if for every pair of threads t, t' $\{R \cap P\}com_{t'}\{R\}$ holds for every assertion R in the proof outline of t and command com with pre-assertion P in thread t'.*

Init: $x := 0; \quad y := 0;$
$$\{[x = 0]_1 \cap [y = 0]_1 \cap [x = 0]_2 \cap [x = 0]_2\}$$

Thread 1	**Thread 2**
$\{[x = 0]_1 \cap [x = 0]_2 \cap [y \not\approx 1]_2\}$	$\{\langle y = 1\rangle[x = 1]_2\}$
$1 : x := 1;$	$4 : r_1 := y;$
$\{[x = 1]_1 \cap [y \not\approx 1]_2\}$	$\{r_1 \neq 1 \cup [x = 1]_2\}$
$2 : fnc;$	$5 : r_2 := x;$
$\{[x = 1]_1 \cap [x = 1]_2 \cap [y \not\approx 1]_2\}$	$\{r_1 \neq 1 \cup r_2 = 1\}$
$3 : y := 1;$	
$\{true\}$	

$$\{r_1 \neq 1 \cup r_2 = 1\}$$

Fig. 12. Proof outline for MP with fence

Next we look at the MP with fence example. In the proof outline, we use a type of assertion additionally to the ones defined in Def. 2. For $t \in \mathsf{Tid}$, $x, y \in \mathsf{Var_G}$ and $u, v \in \mathsf{Val}$ we call

$$\langle y = u \rangle [x = v]_t = \mathsf{wlp}(T(t, rd(y, r, u)), [x = v]_t)$$

the *conditional observation assertion*. It holds for all states in which the synced value assertion $[x = v]_t$ holds, if t can read the value u for y first. Since the assertion contains only β-stable predicates, it is β-stable itself. The reasoning technique only uses the axioms holding for PSO. The proof outline given thus holds for all memory models satisfying these axioms.

Lemma 5. *The proof outline in Fig. 12 is valid under* FENCES.

To prove this lemma, we need to show local and global correctness of the proof outline.(Note that in [16] such proofs are done in Isabelle/HOL.) We illustrate how the proof looks like in detail by proving a Hoare-triple for the global correctness of thread 2. For that we choose the assertion $\langle y = 1 \rangle [x = 1]_2$ from the proof outline of thread 2 and the command $y := 1$ of thread 1 with its pre-assertion $[x = 1]_1 \cap [x = 1]_2 \cap [y \not\approx 1]_2$:

$$\{ \langle y = 1 \rangle [x = 1]_2 \cap [x = 1]_1 \cap [x = 1]_2 \cap [y \not\approx 1]_2 \} y :=_1 1 \{ \langle y = 1 \rangle [x = 1]_2 \}$$

This means we show that

$$\mathsf{wlp}(T(2, rd(y, r_1, 1)), [x = 1]_2) \cap [x = 1]_1 \cap [x = 1]_2 \cap [y \not\approx 1]_2$$
$$\subseteq \mathsf{wlp}(T(1, wr(y, 1)), \mathsf{wlp}(T(2, rd(y, r_1, 1)), [x = 1]_2))$$

Since $\mathsf{wlp}(T(2, rd(y, r_1, 1)), [x = 1]_2) \cap [x = 1]_1 \cap [x = 1]_2 \cap [y \not\approx 1]_2 \subseteq [x = 1]_2$, $[x = 1]_2 \subseteq \mathsf{wlp}(T(2, rd(y, r_1, 1)), [x = 1]_2)$ (see Lemma 3) and the monotonicity rule from Fig. 6, we only need to prove that

$$[x = 1]_2 \subseteq \mathsf{wlp}(T(1, wr(y, 1)), [x = 1]_2)$$

We divide this into two parts: (i) $[x \equiv 1]_2 \subseteq \mathsf{wlp}(T(1, wr(y, 1)), [x \equiv 1]_2)$ and (ii) $x_{\uparrow 2} \subseteq \mathsf{wlp}(T(1, wr(y, 1)), x_{\uparrow 2})$. Then with the conjunctivity rule from Fig. 6 the Hoare-triple is proven.

For (i), we need to show for every value $v \neq 1$:

$$\mathsf{dis}(T(2, rd(x, r_2, v))) \subseteq \mathsf{wlp}(T(1, wr(y, 1)), \mathsf{dis}(2, rd(x, r_2, v)))$$

Using the rules of Fig. 6 and the definition of dis we get

$$\mathsf{dis}(T(2, rd(x, r_2, v))) \subseteq \mathsf{wlp}(T(2, rd(x, r_2, v)), \varnothing)$$
$$\subseteq \mathsf{wlp}(T(2, rd(x, r_2, v)), \mathsf{wlp}(interf(1, wr(y, 1)), \varnothing))$$
$$\subseteq \mathsf{wlp}(T(2, rd(x, r_2, v)) \, {}_{9}^{\circ} \, interf(1, wr(y, 1)), \varnothing)$$

After applying **SV1**, we get

$$\mathsf{wlp}(T(2, rd(x, r_2, v)) \, {}_{9}^{\circ} \, interf(1, wr(y, 1)), \varnothing)$$

$$\subseteq \mathsf{wlp}(interf(1, wr(y, 1)) \; \fatsemi \; T(2, rd(x, r_2, v)), \varnothing)$$
$$\subseteq \mathsf{wlp}(interf(1, wr(y, 1)), \mathsf{wlp}(T(2, rd(x, r_2, v)), \varnothing))$$
$$\subseteq \mathsf{wlp}(interf(1, wr(y, 1)), \mathsf{dis}(T(2, rd(x, r_2, v))))$$

Now (i) follows from Lemma 1 and the conjunctivity rule.

For (ii), we use **SV2** and get for every action $a \in \mathsf{Act}_{|x}$

$$vmax(2, a) \subseteq \mathsf{wlp}(T(1, wr(y, 1)), vmax(2, a))$$

Hence (ii) follows from the conjunctivity rule.

6   Related Work

The work closest to us is that of Doherty et al. [16] who gave a generic approach to Owicki-Gries based axiomatic reasoning and applied that to a number of weak memory models (SC, C11 RAR and TSO). Since we show where PSO fits in their axiomatic hierarchy, our program semantics and the axiomatic reasoning are based on their work. We supplement that by giving a PSO specific semantics, showing which axioms hold for PSO and using them on a correctness proof of the MP with fence litmus test.

Other Owicki-Gries related approaches on reasoning for weak memory models were made by [10,12,13,28]. While Bila et al. [10] present an Owicki-Gries based logic for the persistent TSO memory model, Dalvandi et al. [12,13] and Lahav and Vafeiadis [28] looked at the C11 memory model. None of them introduce a generic proof calculus or a PSO specific one.

There are however other approaches regarding verification specific to PSO [1,5,14,34]. Abdulla et al. [1] for instance introduce a technique for stateless model checking under TSO and PSO. It is based on chronological traces, defining a partial order relation on program executions. Alglave et al. [5] present a transformation technique to verify programs under weak memory model by using SC tools. For different memory models (TSO, PSO,...) they define an abstract machine which is equivalent to its axiomatic semantics. They identify so-called unsafe pairs in the program and linearise it. The SC analyser then verifies the new program. Dan et al. [14] abstract store buffers of TSO and PSO to bounded arrays. For both models, they are able to translate a given program into one with over-approximately the same behaviour on SC and then also use SC Tools for its verification. Xiao et al. [34] formalise the PSO memory model with the process algebra Communicating Sequential Processes and use this formalisation for a model checker. Some of these techniques do not only work for PSO. Still, they are not generic as they cannot be easily applied to a different memory model.

More generic approaches were made by [4,20,25,30]. Alglave and Cousot [4] present an invariance proof method which shows that a given program is correct w.r.t. a given memory model and an invariant specification of that program. It does so by first proving that a so-called communication specification is sufficient for the program's invariant. If a memory model guarantees the communication, the program is correct under that model. Their method differs from the one we are using. Since every memory model needs its own communication specification, each step of the long proof has to be redone for a different model. This makes their proofs more complex. The other work focusses on model checking. Ponce de Leon et al. [30] and Gavrilenko et al. [20] present generic bounded model checkers which translate a given program under a given memory model into an SMT formula. They are generic because their input contains not only the program but also the memory model, formalised in CAT as a set of relations. Finally, Kokologiannakis et al. [25] developed a generic model checker that transforms a given program into an execution graph to check its correctness under a given memory model with an axiomatic semantics.

7   Conclusion

In the paper, we have shown the weak memory model PSO to instantiate the axioms of [16] for all but one axiom, thereby enabling memory-model independent reasoning. We have exemplified the reasoning technique on a litmus test for message passing achieved via the insertion of a fence.

As future work, we see the lifting of these low-level axioms to the level of view-based assertions as to provide a more abstract level for reasoning. We also plan to look at other weak memory models to check whether they fulfil the axioms.

References

1. Abdulla, P.A., Aronis, S., Atig, M.F., Jonsson, B., Leonardsson, C., Sagonas, K.: Stateless model checking for TSO and PSO. Acta Info. **54**(8), 789–818 (2016). https://doi.org/10.1007/s00236-016-0275-0
2. Adve, S.V., Gharachorloo, K.: Shared memory consistency models: a tutorial. Computer **29**(12), 66–76 (1996). https://doi.org/10.1109/2.546611
3. Alglave, J.: A formal hierarchy of weak memory models. Formal Methods Syst. Des. **41**(2), 178–210 (2012). https://doi.org/10.1007/s10703-012-0161-5
4. Alglave, J., Cousot, P.: Ogre and pythia: an invariance proof method for weak consistency models. In: Castagna, G., Gordon, A.D. (eds.) POPL, pp. 3–18. ACM (2017). https://doi.org/10.1145/3009837.3009883
5. Alglave, J., Kroening, D., Nimal, V., Tautschnig, M.: Software verification for weak memory via program transformation. In: Felleisen, M., Gardner, P. (eds.) ESOP 2013. LNCS, vol. 7792, pp. 512–532. Springer, Heidelberg (2013). https://doi.org/10.1007/978-3-642-37036-6_28
6. Alglave, J., Maranget, L., Sarkar, S., Sewell, P.: Litmus: running tests against hardware. In: Abdulla, P.A., Leino, K.R.M. (eds.) TACAS 2011. LNCS, vol. 6605, pp. 41–44. Springer, Heidelberg (2011). https://doi.org/10.1007/978-3-642-19835-9_5
7. Atig, M.F., Bouajjani, A., Burckhardt, S., Musuvathi, M.: On the verification problem for weak memory models. In: Hermenegildo, M.V., Palsberg, J. (eds.) POPL, pp. 7–18. ACM (2010). https://doi.org/10.1145/1706299.1706303
8. Bargmann, L., Wehrheim, H.: View-Based Axiomatic Reasoning for PSO (Extended Version) (2023). https://doi.org/10.48550/ARXIV.2301.07967

9. Batty, M., Owens, S., Sarkar, S., Sewell, P., Weber, T.: Mathematizing C++ concurrency. In: POPL, pp. 55–66 (2011).https://doi.org/10.1145/1926385.1926394
10. Bila, E.V., Dongol, B., Lahav, O., Raad, A., Wickerson, J.: View-based owicki-gries reasoning for persistent x86-TSO. In: ESOP 2022. LNCS, vol. 13240, pp. 234–261. Springer, Cham (2022). https://doi.org/10.1007/978-3-030-99336-8_9
11. Cho, K., Lee, S., Raad, A., Kang, J.: Revamping hardware persistency models: View-based and axiomatic persistency models for Intel-x86 and Armv8. In: Freund, S.N., Yahav, E. (eds.) PLDI, pp. 16–31. ACM (2021). https://doi.org/10.1145/3453483.3454027
12. Dalvandi, S., Doherty, S., Dongol, B., Wehrheim, H.: Owicki-Gries reasoning for C11 RAR. In: Hirschfeld, R., Pape, T. (eds.) ECOOP, pp. 11:1–11:26. LIPIcs, Schloss Dagstuhl - Leibniz-Zentrum für Informatik (2020). https://doi.org/10.4230/LIPIcs.ECOOP.2020.11
13. Dalvandi, S., Dongol, B., Doherty, S., Wehrheim, H.: Integrating owicki–gries for C11-style memory models into isabelle/HOL. J. Autom. Reason. (8), 1–31 (2021). https://doi.org/10.1007/s10817-021-09610-2
14. Dan, A., Meshman, Y., Vechev, M., Yahav, E.: Effective abstractions for verification under relaxed memory models. In: D'Souza, D., Lal, A., Larsen, K.G. (eds.) VMCAI 2015. LNCS, vol. 8931, pp. 449–466. Springer, Heidelberg (2015). https://doi.org/10.1007/978-3-662-46081-8_25
15. Dijkstra, E.W.: A Discipline of Programming. Prentice-Hall, Upper Saddle River (1976). https://www.worldcat.org/oclc/01958445
16. Doherty, S., Dalvandi, S., Dongol, B., Wehrheim, H.: Unifying operational weak memory verification: an axiomatic approach. ACM Trans. Comput. Log. **23**(4), 27:1–27:39 (2022). https://doi.org/10.1145/3545117
17. Doherty, S., Dongol, B., Wehrheim, H., Derrick, J.: Verifying C11 programs operationally. In: PPoPP, pp. 355–365 (2019). https://doi.org/10.1145/3293883.3295702
18. Flur, S., et al.: Modelling the ARMv8 architecture, operationally: concurrency and ISA. In: Bodík, R., Majumdar, R. (eds.) POPL, pp. 608–621. ACM (2016). https://doi.org/10.1145/2837614.2837615
19. Furbach, F., Meyer, R., Schneider, K., Senftleben, M.: Memory-model-aware testing: a unified complexity analysis. ACM Trans. Embed. Comput. Syst. **14**(4), 63:1–63:25 (2015). https://doi.org/10.1145/2753761
20. Gavrilenko, N., Ponce-de-León, H., Furbach, F., Heljanko, K., Meyer, R.: BMC for weak memory models: relation analysis for compact SMT encodings. In: Dillig, I., Tasiran, S. (eds.) CAV 2019. LNCS, vol. 11561, pp. 355–365. Springer, Cham (2019). https://doi.org/10.1007/978-3-030-25540-4_19
21. Hoare, C.A.R.: An axiomatic basis for computer programming. Commun. ACM **12**(10), 576–580 (1969). https://doi.org/10.1145/363235.363259
22. Inc., S.I.: The SPARC Architecture Model, Version 8 (1994)
23. Kaiser, J., Dang, H., Dreyer, D., Lahav, O., Vafeiadis, V.: Strong logic for weak memory: reasoning about release-acquire consistency in Iris. In: ECOOP, pp. 17:1–17:29 (2017). https://doi.org/10.4230/LIPIcs.ECOOP.2017.17
24. Kang, J., Hur, C., Lahav, O., Vafeiadis, V., Dreyer, D.: A promising semantics for relaxed-memory concurrency. In: Castagna, G., Gordon, A.D. (eds.) POPL, pp. 175–189. ACM (2017). https://doi.org/10.1145/3009837.3009850
25. Kokologiannakis, M., Raad, A., Vafeiadis, V.: Model checking for weakly consistent libraries. In: McKinley, K.S., Fisher, K. (eds.) PLDI, pp. 96–110. ACM (2019). https://doi.org/10.1145/3314221.3314609

26. Lahav, O., Boker, U.: What's decidable about causally consistent shared memory? ACM Trans. Program. Lang. Syst. **44**(2), 8:1–8:55 (2022). https://doi.org/10.1145/3505273
27. Lahav, O., Giannarakis, N., Vafeiadis, V.: Taming release-acquire consistency. In: Bodík, R., Majumdar, R. (eds.) POPL, pp. 649–662. ACM (2016). https://doi.org/10.1145/2837614.2837643
28. Lahav, O., Vafeiadis, V.: Owicki-Gries reasoning for weak memory models. In: Halldórsson, M.M., Iwama, K., Kobayashi, N., Speckmann, B. (eds.) ICALP 2015. LNCS, vol. 9135, pp. 311–323. Springer, Heidelberg (2015). https://doi.org/10.1007/978-3-662-47666-6_25
29. Lamport, L.: How to make a multiprocessor computer that correctly executes multiprocess programs. IEEE Trans. Comput. **28**(9), 690–691 (1979). https://doi.org/10.1109/TC.1979.1675439
30. de León, H.P., Furbach, F., Heljanko, K., Meyer, R.: BMC with memory models as modules. In: Bjørner, N.S., Gurfinkel, A. (eds.) FMCAD, pp. 1–9. IEEE (2018). https://doi.org/10.23919/FMCAD.2018.8603021
31. Lynch, N.A., Vaandrager, F.W.: Forward and backward simulations: I. untimed systems. Inf. Comput. **121**(2), 214–233 (1995). https://doi.org/10.1006/inco.1995.1134
32. Owicki, S.S., Gries, D.: An axiomatic proof technique for parallel programs I. Acta Inf. **6**, 319–340 (1976). https://doi.org/10.1007/BF00268134
33. Sarkar, S., et al.: The semantics of x86-CC multiprocessor machine code. In: Shao, Z., Pierce, B.C. (eds.) POPL, pp. 379–391. ACM (2009). https://doi.org/10.1145/1480881.1480929
34. Xiao, L., Zhu, H., Xu, Q., Vinh, P.C.: Modeling and verifying PSO memory model using CSP. Mob. Netw. Appl. **27**(5), 2068–2083 (2022). https://doi.org/10.1007/s11036-022-01989-5

A Static Analyser for Resource Sensitive Workflow Models

Muhammad Rizwan Ali$^{(\boxtimes)}$ and Violet Ka I Pun

Western Norway University of Applied Sciences, Bergen, Norway
{mral,vpu}@hvl.no

Abstract. Cross-organisational workflows involve multiple concurrently running workflows across organisations, and are in general more complex and unpredictable than single individual ones. Minor modifications in a collaborating workflow may be propagated to other concurrently running ones, leading to negative impacts on the cross-organisational workflow as a whole, e.g., deadline violation, which can be disastrous for, e.g., healthcare organisations. Worst-case execution time (WCET) is a metric for detecting potential deadline violation for a workflow. In this paper, we present a tool, $\mathcal{R}$PLTool, which helps planners model and simulate cross-organisational workflows in a resource-sensitive formal modelling language $\mathcal{R}$PL. The tool is equipped with a static analyser to approximate the WCET of workflows, which can provide decision support to the workflow planners prior to the implementation of the workflow and to help estimate the effect of changes to avoid deadline violation.

Keywords: worst-case execution time · cross-organisational workflows · resource planning · formal modelling · static analysis

1 Introduction

Corporations nowadays often engage with others beyond their organisational borders, e.g., supply chain management, and the business workflows can therefore be cross-organisational to restructure business processes outside an organisation [2]. Such workflows typically involve multiple concurrent workflows that run concurrently in different departments within the same or different organisations, and sometimes share resources.

Analysing cross-organisational workflows is challenging as they are generally more complex and unpredictable than a single individual workflow because of the inter-workflow dependencies and shared resources. Minor changes in the workflow of a collaborative partner can be propagated to other concurrently running tasks, which may result in negative impact on the collaborating workflows, e.g., longer execution time in one process in one collaborative workflow may eventually lead to deadline violation in another.

This work is part of the CROFLOW project: Enabling Highly Automated Cross-Organisational Workflow Planning (grant no. 326249) and *SIRIUS – Centre for Scalable Data Access* (grant no. 237898), funded by the Research Council of Norway.

Worst-case execution time (WCET) is a metric that can be used to predict whether a workflow may violate its deadline. The WCET of a workflow refers to the maximum amount of time that it takes to execute all its tasks under any possible scheduling conditions with a finite pool of resources. It would be useful for workflow planners to approximate the WCET of cross-organisational workflows prior to the actual implementation and estimate the effect of changes in the workflows before any changes are carried out.

Analyses and tools, e.g., [10] and [12], have been developed for workflow modelling and WCET analysis. However, as per our knowledge, cross-organisational workflow analysis remains a somewhat manual process as current tools and techniques often lack domain-specific knowledge to support the task dependencies and shared resources across collaborating workflows.

This paper focuses on workflows developed with the notion of time and resource descriptions, as well as task dependency, where multiple concurrently running workflows compete for shared resources and their tasks may depend on the others. Various metrics, including WCET and deadline violations, can be approximated statically to optimise the planning of such workflows. The contribution of paper is $\mathcal{R}$PLTool[1], a tool for workflows modelled in $\mathcal{R}$PL, a resource-sensitive workflow modelling language [8]. The tool comprises two modules, one allows simulating workflows modelled in $\mathcal{R}$PL, while the other provides a static WCET analyser for $\mathcal{R}$PL workflow models.

The rest of the paper is organised as follows: Sect. 2 briefly presents the formal modelling language $\mathcal{R}$PL with a simple example, and describes the functionalities and implementation of $\mathcal{R}$PLTool. Section 3 shows the experimental results, and Sect. 4 discusses the related work. Finally, we summarise the paper and discuss possible future work in Sect. 5.

2 $\mathcal{R}$PLTool

The $\mathcal{R}$PLTool has two main functionalities: (1) to simulate workflows modelled in $\mathcal{R}$PL, and (2) to statically analyse WCET for $\mathcal{R}$PL workflows models. In the following, we first briefly introduce the formal modelling language $\mathcal{R}$PL and we describe the structure of the tool afterwards.

2.1   Formal Workflow Modelling Language $\mathcal{R}$PL

We use a simple example to briefly present the formal modelling language $\mathcal{R}$PL, which is inspired by the

```
1  [r₁ ↦ (true, {Pizzaiolo,1}),
2   r₂ ↦ (true, {Pizzaiolo,3}), ...]
3  class Customer implements Customer
4  { Unit orderPizza(PizzaShop pz, Int pizza)
5    {
6      Fut<Int> f;
7      f = !bakePizza(pz,pizza) after dl 60;
8      await f?;
9      pizza = f.get; } }
10
11 class PizzaShop implements PizzaShop
12 { Int bakePizza(Int pizza)
13   {
14     List<Int> rid = Nil;
15     rid = hold(list[set[Pizzaiolo,Efficiency(3)]]);
16     //.... Pizzaiolo is baking pizza ....
17     rel(rid);
18     return pizza; } }
```

Fig. 1. A simple example in $\mathcal{R}$PL.

---

[1] https://github.com/razi236/Rpl-Tools.

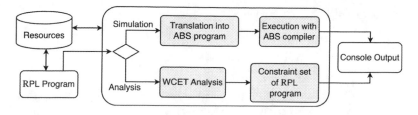

Fig. 2. The overview of the $\mathcal{R}$PLTool.

active object language ABS [17]. It has a Java-like syntax and actor-based concurrency model [3]. We refer the readers to [8] for the full syntax and semantics of the language.

The code snippet in Fig. 1 captures a simple pizza ordering workflow. Lines 1–2 model a map of resources available for the workflow, where r_i refers to the resource identifier, which maps to a tuple indicating the resource availability (true if available and false otherwise) and quality, e.g., a Pizzaiolo with one year of experience. The rest of the code defines two classes Customer and PizzaShop. When Customer orders a pizza, an asynchronous request is sent to the PizzaShop to bake the pizza within 60 time units (Line 7). Afterwards, while waiting for the pizza (until the method bakePizza returns a value), the Customer can continue with his other tasks (Line 8). Upon receiving an order, the PizzaShop first acquires a Pizzaiolo having three years of experience (efficiency) on 15 to bake the pizza. When pizza becomes ready, the PizzaShop releases the Pizzaiolo on Line 17 to bake other pizzas and notifies the Customer on Line 18. Afterwards, the Customer gets the pizza on Line 9.

2.2   Implementation

We present in this section the implementation of $\mathcal{R}$PLTool. An overview of the structure of $\mathcal{R}$PLTool is illustrated in Fig. 2. The tool comprises two modules, simulation and WCET analysis, which respectively correspond to the two main functionalities. The former allows simulating workflows modelled in $\mathcal{R}$PL, while the latter analyses the source code of the cross-organisational workflow modelled in $\mathcal{R}$PL compositionally and returns a set of cost equations that can be fed to an off-the-shelf constraint solver.

Simulation. The $\mathcal{R}$PLTool also allows simulating workflows modelled in $\mathcal{R}$PL. The simulation functionality is implemented by using the ABS compiler [1] and two additional libraries, ResourceManager and AwaitFut, which handle the incompatibility between the two languages. The ResourceManager library adds

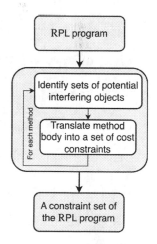

Fig. 3. Static Analysis of $\mathcal{R}$PL programs

Table 1. Experimental Results (time in milliseconds)

$\mathcal{R}$PL	Simulation				WCET
Programs	t_t	t_s	t_a	eq	*Upper bound*
Retailer	2183	8302	1611	5	$max(k1 + k2, k1 + max(c_{sale_f}, k2))$
Pathology	2035	8554	1723	6	$max(k1 + k2, k1 + max(c_{reg_{f_1}}, k2) + c_{reg_{f_2}} + c_{reg_{f_3}})$
Restaurant	2048	7793	1790	16	$max(k1, k1 + c_{start_f}) + k2$
MapReduce	2115	7333	1756	42	$max(c_{map_{f_{11}}} + k1 + c_{red_{f_{21}}}, c_{map_{f_{12}}} + k1 + c_{red_{f_{22}}}) + k2$
ProdCons	2035	7905	1770	6	$k1 + c_{p_{f_1}} + c_{p_{f_2}} + k2 + max(c_{c_{f_3}}, c_{c_{f_4}})$

functionality of resources handling in $\mathcal{R}$PL to ABS, including adding new resources, acquiring and releasing resources. In addition, to handle possible disjunctive paths in task dependencies in workflows, $\mathcal{R}$PL allows disjunction in future return tests, which checks if one or more paths in the workflow are active. We add this feature to ABS by implementing the AwaitFut library. With these two libraries, we can translate an $\mathcal{R}$PL program into a corresponding ABS program for simulation.

Static Analysis. The tool provides a static WCET analyser[2] for cross-organisational workflows modelled in $\mathcal{R}$PL, which is depicted in Fig. 3. Given an $\mathcal{R}$PL program, the analysis first identifies all the objects whose processes may have implicit dependencies, i.e., the processes of these objects may in turn influence the process pools of other objects through method invocations and synchronisations. With these sets of interfering objects, the analysis will translate each method body, including main, into a set of cost constraints, which can then be fed into an off-the-shelf constraint solver (e.g., [5,13]). The solution to the constraint set of each method over-approximates the method's WCET. As a result, the solution to the constraint set of the $\mathcal{R}$PL program's main method refers to the WCET of the workflow modelled as the $\mathcal{R}$PL program.

3   Experimental Results

In this section, we present the preliminary results of the efficiency and functionalities of $\mathcal{R}$PLTool, by running five examples modelled in $\mathcal{R}$PL[3]. The experiments were conducted on a MacBook Pro (Apple M1) with 8 cores and 16GB of RAM, running macOS Ventura 13.2.

Table 1 summarises the experimental results. The first column refers to the examples modelled in $\mathcal{R}$PLTool. While the first three, Retailer, Pathology and Restaurant model cross-organisational workflows in which concurrently running workflows collaborate through task dependency and shared resources, the other two, MapReduce and Prod-Cons, model the typical concurrency scenarios of

---

[2] A detailed WCET analysis can be found in [8].
[3] The codes can be found here: https://github.com/razi236/Rpl-Tools.

MapReduce and Producer/Consumer. For the simulation module of the tool, we use t_t to refer to the time taken for the translation from an $\mathcal{R}$PL program to the corresponding ABS program, and t_s for the time taken for simulating the program. Since the simulation functionality is developed on top of the ABS compiler, simulating an $\mathcal{R}$PL model always has an overhead t_t for translating the model into an ABS program.

As for the module of WCET analysis, we use t_a for the time taken to perform the analysis, *eq* for the number of cost equations generated by the static analysis, and *Upper bound* to represent the constraint equations of the main method of each example modelled in $\mathcal{R}$PL. Note that the solution to such equations correspond to the worst-case execution time of the $\mathcal{R}$PL program, where task dependencies, availability of resources and task scheduling are considered. For clarity, we manually simplified the redundant expressions of the presented upper bound. The time taken for WCET analysis t_a in general is shorter than the translation overhead t_t. The number of cost equations can be higher for some large or complex programs. For instance, in our experiments, the MapReduce example has the most complex distributed model and it can be observed in Table 1 that it has the highest number of cost equations.

4   Related Work

Tools have been developed for WCET analysis for embedded systems, e.g., Chronos [19], a static WCET analysis tool, models various architectural features (including branch prediction, instruction cache, and out-of-order execution) for embedded systems. Open Tool for Adaptive WCET Analyses (OTAWA) [9] is a framework of C++ classes for static analysis of machine code and WCET calculation. In addition to a set of tools for computing WCET, OTAWA offers a framework for developing new analyses for new hardware or for experimental needs. To the best of our knowledge, these tools lack advanced control flow mechanisms required for workflow modelling. In contrast to these tools, our presented tool supports a more expressive language allowing modelling workflows with task dependencies, synchronisation, and shared resources.

Various techniques have been prototyped to calculate the WCET. For example, the authors in [16] present a static analysis prototyped in Resource Aware ML (RAML) [15] for deriving bounds on the worst-case evaluation cost of parallel first-order functional programs. Compared to RAML, our approach is object-oriented and supports both kinds of synchronisation, blocking and non-blocking. Two approaches have been proposed in [11] for resource allocation and execution time computation for BPMN processes, one static and one dynamic. While the static approach is based on Maude's rewriting logic, the dynamic one requires instrumentation of existing platform for BPMN process execution. Compared to their approaches, which allows computing average execution time for BPMN processes based on simulation in Maude and monitoring in BPMN platform, our approach approximates the WCET of $\mathcal{R}$PL workflow models by considering all the possible task dependency and scheduling conditions.

COSTA [6] is an abstract-interpretation-based COSt and Termination Analyser for Java bytecode and presents the first static approach to the automatic cost analysis of object-oriented bytecode programs. [7] present a cost analysis that targets a language with the same concurrency model as $\mathcal{R}$PL. The analysis is prototyped within the SACO system [4], a static analyser for distributed concurrent programs. However, the analysis is not compositional and does not identify the objects that can interfere with the execution of the tasks running on other objects. The analysis takes the entire program and computes the components that may execute in parallel. In our earlier work [18], a static analysis is prototyped in SACO to compute the WCET for concurrent programs compositionally by identifying the set of potential interfering objects. Compared to this prototype, our tool supports a richer language that targets workflow modelling.

Several formal method tools have also been used for WCET analysis. For example, UPPAAL [10] is being used to model, simulate and verify workflows modelled in timed automata. SWEET [12] can generate models using UPPAAL syntax [20]. The functions in UPPAAL syntax are intended to be very small and simple [14]. Compared to these tools and techniques, $\mathcal{R}$PLTool estimates WCET for more complex workflows modelled in a language that is sensitive to resource and task dependency.

5   Conclusion

In this paper, we have presented a tool, $\mathcal{R}$PLTool, that aims to be used for simulating and analysing cross-organisational workflows modelled in the formal modelling language $\mathcal{R}$PL. The simulation module is built on top of the existing ABS Tools, it translates an $\mathcal{R}$PL program into a corresponding ABS program, with the help of two additional libraries to handle the incompatibilities between the two languages. The other module of the tool statically analyses the WCET of a workflow modelled as an $\mathcal{R}$PL program by translating the program code into a set of cost equations. The solution to this constraint set corresponds to the over-approximation of the execution time of the workflow. We have also presented a preliminary experimental evaluation of the tool to show the functionalities of the tool, and to provide a better understanding of the tool with respect to the efficiency and the complexity of the cost equations.

The presented tool is intended to be the first step towards the automation of cross-organisational workflow analysis. To achieve this long-term goal, we plan to implement a graphical user interface for $\mathcal{R}$PLTool that will allow planners to design workflows graphically that can be translated to $\mathcal{R}$PL models. In addition, we plan to implement a translator to translate the cost equations into the input format of an existing constraint solver. By connecting the cost analysis to a constraint solver, the analyst can estimate the overall execution time of collaborative workflows and see the effect of any changes in resource allocation and task dependency. Furthermore, we intend to develop verification techniques to ensure the correctness of cross-organisational workflows modelled in $\mathcal{R}$PL. We foresee that such extensions can eventually contribute to automating cross-organisational workflows analysis.

Acknowledgements. We would like to thank Einar Broch Johnsen and Rudolf Schlatte for providing insights into the ABS Tools and suggestions on the implementation of the $\mathcal{R}$PLTool.

References

1. ABS Tools. https://github.com/abstools/abstools. Accessed 11 Jan 2023
2. van der Aalst, W.M.: Loosely coupled interorganizational workflows: modeling and analyzing workflows crossing organizational boundaries. Inf. Manag. **37**(2), 67–75 (2000)
3. Agha, G.: Actors: a model of concurrent computation in distributed systems. MIT Press, Cambridge (1986)
4. Albert, E., et al.: SACO: static analyzer for concurrent objects. In: Ábrahám, E., Havelund, K. (eds.) TACAS 2014. LNCS, vol. 8413, pp. 562–567. Springer, Heidelberg (2014). https://doi.org/10.1007/978-3-642-54862-8_46
5. Albert, E., Arenas, P., Genaim, S., Puebla, G.: Closed-form upper bounds in static cost analysis. J. Autom. Reasoning **46**(2), 161–203 (2011)
6. Albert, E., Arenas, P., Genaim, S., Puebla, G., Zanardini, D.: Cost analysis of object-oriented bytecode programs. Theor. Comput. Sci. **413**(1), 142–159 (2012)
7. Albert, E., Correas, J., Johnsen, E.B., Román-Díez, G.: Parallel cost analysis of distributed systems. In: Blazy, S., Jensen, T. (eds.) SAS 2015. LNCS, vol. 9291, pp. 275–292. Springer, Heidelberg (2015). https://doi.org/10.1007/978-3-662-48288-9_16
8. Ali, M.R., Lamo, Y., Pun, V.K.I.: Cost analysis for a resource sensitive workflow modelling language. Sci. Comput. Program. **225**, 102896 (2023)
9. Ballabriga, C., Cassé, H., Rochange, C., Sainrat, P.: OTAWA: an open toolbox for adaptive WCET analysis. In: Min, S.L., Pettit, R., Puschner, P., Ungerer, T. (eds.) SEUS 2010. LNCS, vol. 6399, pp. 35–46. Springer, Heidelberg (2010). https://doi.org/10.1007/978-3-642-16256-5_6
10. David, A., et al.: UPPAAL 4.0. In: Proceedings of the 3rd International Conference on the Quantitative Evaluation of Systems (QEST), pp. 125–126. IEEE Computer Society Press (2006)
11. Durán, F., Falcone, Y., Rocha, C., Salaün, G., Zuo, A.: From static to dynamic analysis and allocation of resources for BPMN processes. In: Bae, K. (ed.) Rewriting Logic and Its Applications, pp. 3–21. Springer International Publishing, Cham (2022)
12. Ermedahl, A.: A Modular Tool Architecture for Worst-Case Execution Time Analysis. Ph.D. thesis, Uppsala University Uppsala University, Division of Computer Systems, Computer Systems (2003)
13. Flores-Montoya, A., Hähnle, R.: Resource analysis of complex programs with cost equations. In: Garrigue, J. (ed.) APLAS 2014. LNCS, vol. 8858, pp. 275–295. Springer, Cham (2014). https://doi.org/10.1007/978-3-319-12736-1_15
14. Gustavsson, A., Ermedahl, A., Lisper, B., Pettersson, P.: Towards WCET analysis of multicore architectures using UPPAAL. In: Lisper, B. (ed.) Proceedings of the 10th International Workshop on Worst-Case Execution Time Analysis (WCET). OASIcs. vol. 15, pp. 101–112. Schloss Dagstuhl-Leibniz-Zentrum fuer Informatik (2010)
15. Hoffmann, J., Aehlig, K., Hofmann, M.: Resource aware ML. In: Madhusudan, P., Seshia, S.A. (eds.) CAV 2012. LNCS, vol. 7358, pp. 781–786. Springer, Heidelberg (2012). https://doi.org/10.1007/978-3-642-31424-7_64

16. Hoffmann, J., Shao, Z.: Automatic static cost analysis for parallel programs. In: Vitek, J. (ed.) ESOP 2015. LNCS, vol. 9032, pp. 132–157. Springer, Heidelberg (2015). https://doi.org/10.1007/978-3-662-46669-8_6

17. Johnsen, E.B., Hähnle, R., Schäfer, J., Schlatte, R., Steffen, M.: ABS: a core language for abstract behavioral specification. In: Aichernig, B.K., de Boer, F.S., Bonsangue, M.M. (eds.) FMCO 2010. LNCS, vol. 6957, pp. 142–164. Springer, Heidelberg (2011). https://doi.org/10.1007/978-3-642-25271-6_8

18. Laneve, C., Lienhardt, M., Pun, K.I., Román-Díez, G.: Time analysis of actor programs. J. Logical Algebraic Methods Program. **105**, 1–27 (2019)

19. Li, X., Liang, Y., Mitra, T., Roychoudhury, A.: Chronos: a timing analyzer for embedded software. Sci. Comput. Program. **69**(1), 56–67 (2007)

20. Sundmark, D.: Structural System-Level Testing of Embedded Real-Time Systems. Ph.D. thesis, Mälardalen University, Department of Computer Science and Electronics (2008)

MTCD: An Efficient Cloning Detection Technique Based on Method Table

Fangting Liao, Shun Long, Weiheng Zhu[✉], Wenzhu Chen, Silei Cao, and Xinyi Guan

School of Information Science and Technology, Jinan University, Guangzhou 510632, China
tzhuwh@jnu.edu.cn

Abstract. Code cloning is an effective approach to accelerate software development, but may leave potentially significant pitfalls for maintenance. State-of-the-art clone detection techniques rely heavily on accurate syntax and semantic features which are difficult to identify and extract, making them hard to deploy in practice. This paper presents a simple but efficient approach called MTCD which extracts from a Java method (in its Java class file) the method table section of the code as its feature, and then transforms the feature into a decimal series for comparison. MTCD significantly simplifies feature identification and extraction. Experimental results on BigCloneBench suggested that MTCD clearly outperformed other established approaches by achieving an average F1-score of 0.95 with a modest training cost of 181 s for a 60 k dataset.

Keywords: Code cloning · Clone detection · Bytecode · Method table

1 Introduction

Modern software development practice encourages developers to reuse existing code by copying or modifying it for new projects in order to improve efficiency and reduce cost. This inevitably leads to code cloning, i.e. the existence of some identical or similar code segments in software systems. Prior studies have found that large software systems contain 20–50% clone code [1,2]. Despite its contribution to efficiency and cost reduction, code cloning has disadvantages that should not be ignored, for instance, a significantly higher maintenance cost to find and repair the errors and vulnerabilities spread to different parts of the software system.

Various approaches have been proposed to solve these problems. Most of them are based on text [6,7,14], token [8,11,15], abstract syntax tree (AST) [3,5,19,23], program dependency graph (PDG) [10,22] or index [12,13]. They attempt to detect code clones by building from source code syntactic and/or semantic feature vectors. Typically, text-based and token-based approaches show low complexity but are poor at detecting semantic similarity, and undoubtedly fail to detect codes that are semantically similar but syntactically different.

C. David and M. Sun (Eds.): TASE 2023, LNCS 13931, pp. 313–326, 2023.
https://doi.org/10.1007/978-3-031-35257-7_19

AST- or PDG-based approaches convert source code to AST or PDG before turning it into feature sequences through complex processing, which greatly increases the cost of analysis. Index-based techniques generate a lot of false positives because various code segments may result in a common index.

Bytecode(a sequence of the instructions) in the Java class file has also been used to achieve clone detection [9,18,20,21]. Java class file is a binary sequence of numeric constants, references, bytecode, and so on. It is formed from low-level instructions with lexical information eliminated, giving itself a higher level of abstraction than other code representations. Java class file is generated in a specified format which consists of a constant pool, some interface information, field tables, method tables, and additional attribute tables. A method table is a description of the internal methods of a class in the form of a set of tables, consisting of access_flags, method_name_index, descriptor_index, attributes_count, as well as attributes such as Code, Deprecated, and RuntimeVisibleAnnotations. It is worth noting that these above semantic information are fixed at their predefined positions in a Java class file, making it possible for functionally similar code pairs to produce similar Java class file after compilation, despite being syntactically different.

We present in this paper a straightforward clone detection approach called MTCD at method level. Given the Java class file of a method, MTCD directly extracts its full method table section (and ignores all the rest) as its feature for clone detection. Unlike prior works which consider only the bytecode within, MTCD is motivated by the fact that each byte in a method table has a specific meaning, as explained above, and therefore the entire method table should be considered.

In order to evaluate the effectiveness of MTCD, we have conducted an empirical experiment with the BigCloneBench [17] benchmark dataset. The results show that the full method table sequence is a better feature than its bytecode sequence segment for clone detection, by yielding average 2.4% higher F1 scores on all five types of code clones. Furthermore, the results suggest that whether or not the bytecode sequence contains any operand makes no impact on the result, and that irrelevant information in feature sequences can be used as noise to help train the classifier, as it does not affect its outcome.

The rest of this article is organized as follows. The background is outlined in Sect. 2, our approach is presented in depth in Sect. 3, with the experimental results and threats to its effectiveness in Sect. 4, before some concluding remark on Sect. 5.

2   Related Work

2.1   Code Clone Types

Traditional code cloning is roughly divided into four categories [13]. T1: Both code snippets are identical except for spaces, layout, and comments; T2: Both snippets are identical except for spaces, layout, comments, text, type, and identifiers; T3: Two snippets are syntactically similar but have differences in space, layout, comments, text, type, and identifiers, and with statements changed, added, or deleted; T4: Two code snippets share a common functionality, but not syntactically similar.

Because there is no consensus among researchers on the minimum syntactic similarity of T3 clones, it is difficult to distinguish between T3 and T4 pairs of clones that perform the same function. Svajlenko et al. [17] further divide T3 and T4 into strong type 3 (ST3), medium type 3 (MT3) and weak type 3/4 (WT3/4) according to grammatical similarity.

2.2   Prior Code Clone Detection Techniques

Various source-based cloning detection approaches have been proposed over the past decade or so. Nicad [14] detects code clones by a line-wise comparison of text difference, and SourcererCC [15] is a token-based clone detector that uses filtering heuristics to create indexes in order to reduce code block comparisons. It can be extended to large code repositories. Zeng [23] proposed a fast cloning detection approach which is based on weighted recursive autoencoder (RAE) and uses weighted RAE in its AST analysis in order to extract program features and encode them into vectors. Approximate nearest neighbor search (ANNS) is adopted to detect code clones in large software systems. Yuan [22]developed a graph representation method based on intermediate code for clone detection. Graph embedding technique is used to extract syntactic and semantic feature from AST, CFG, and DFG generated from intermediate code, before a Softmax classifier is adopted. DeepSim [24] encodes the control flow and data flow of code snippet into a semantic matrix which is used as feature in the training of a DNN classifier. Li et al. [12] used the distance in the metric space to measure code similarity. Hybrid code representations are also considered for clone detection. Tufano et al. [18] proved that deep learning can automatically learn code similarity from different representations. Identifiers, AST, CFG, and bytecode were adopted to train the model separately, and proper combination of these different representations yielded better results. FCCA [4] extracts the features of code from the code text, AST as well as CFG and applies the attention mechanism to these code representations respectively in order to capture important information. Finally, multiple code representations are fused into a mixed representation as the feature of the code segment for clone detection.

In the area of Java bytecode clone detection, SeByte [9] applies semantic-enabled token matching. It divides the input into three dimension (namely instruction, method call and type) and uses the Jaccard similarity coefficient in its multi-dimensional comparison. Yu et al. [20] encoded the instruction sequence and method call sequence extracted from bytecode, and calculated the similarity in between during its clone detection process. They [21] used Smith-Waterman algorithm to align the instruction sequence and calculated the cosine similarity of the sequence. Tufano et al. [18] extracted code features from bytecode to study how deep learning can automatically learn code similarity from different code representations. They put the opcodes in bytecode into a recursive autoencoder to learn embedding. The code similarity is measured by calculating the spatial distance between different embeddings. They found that bytecode- and CFG-based models outperformed other models in detection of semantically similar clones, but they also caused more false positives results on syntactically similar clones. They believed that the AST-based model provides the best balance between accuracy and recall.

2.3   BigCloneBench

There was once no large-scale datasets suitable for clone detection evaluation until Svajlenko et al. constructed BigCloneBench, which is a manually verified subset of IJaDataset-2.0 (25000 open source Java systems) that containing 43 functional Java files, including a total of 8,584,153 real clone pairs from T1 to T4 and 279,032 fake clone pairs. However, the Java source codes in BigCloneBench cannot be directly compiled due to a lack of required dependencies. Schafer et al. [16] developed the Stubber tool to compile Java sources code into Java class files without dependencies, which can retain more than 92.5% code clone pairs within.

3   Method Table for Clone Detection

Unlike other clone detection techniques which considers only the bytecode of a method, we believe that its access flag, attribute counter, max_stack, max_locals, code_length, etc. are all useful information to help distinguish whether or not methods are similar. Therefore, the whole sequence of the method table is used as the feature of the method for clone detection. Other information are ignored.

   To demonstrate that the full method table is a more suitable feature for efficient clone detection, we present it as three phases, namely *Code preprocessing*, *Feature extraction* and *Clone detection*, as illustrated in Fig. 1. The first phase (*Code preprocessing*) is trivial, where Java source codes are first compiled into Java class files. The second and third phases are explained below.

3.1   Feature Extraction

Normally, Java class file is presented as a byte sequence of hexadecimal codes which usually contain letters. They are first converted to a sequence of decimal numbers in order to enable efficient numeric-based processing at the latter phase, as illustrated in Fig. 2. It shows a segment of Java source code of an add function (left), its information obtained by parsing the Java class file via the javap command (top center), and its method table sequence in hexadecimal form as converted (center bottom, as explained on the right).

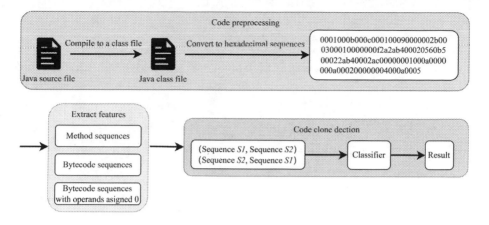

Fig. 1. Cloning detection framework

It is worth noting that each section of the method table not only has a specific meaning for the content defined by the JVM, but also is of a fixed length (one or a few bytes). For instance two bytes for access flags, method name indexes, descriptor indexes and so on, and four bytes for the lengths of the attribute segments and the bytecode. For example, the first two bytes in the method table sequence (middle bottom of Fig. 2) represent the access type of the function (0001 indicates Public, as specified by JVM). At the green section on the right of Fig. 2, the value of code length is $0000000f_{HEX}$ suggesting the bytecode section is of 15_{DEC} bytes long. The yellow section in Fig. 2 is the bytecode sequence composed of both opcodes and operands, each of which is of one byte and they are indexed from 0 to 14. Some opcodes are followed by operands to be processed. For example, the opcode b4 (indexed by 2) is followed by two operands 00 and 02 as (indexed by 3 and 4) (not explicitly shown).

The resulting hexadecimal method table of this add function is then converted to decimal numbers in a byte-wise manner, as shown in Fig. 3, and the resulting sequence is a description of the function which contains most of its information.

To facilitate a straightforward comparison between the feature used by our approach and by prior works, a similar algorithm has been implemented to extract the sequence of beytecode. In addition, most prior works use only the opcodes in the bytecode sequence and discard the operands. However, the operands are references to the constant pool, and may be considered as equivalent to random numbers. We believe keeping them in training will not affect the training of our classifier, but may instead enhance its robustness by playing the role of noise within the whole sequence. To verify this, we provide another variant which modifies the original bytecode sequence by changing all operands within to 0, as shown in the lower part of Fig. 3.

In brief, we extract three different features from a method, A) its method table sequence (our plan, extracted by Algorithm 1 as specified below), B) the bytecode sequence (prior works), and C) a modified bytecode sequence with all operands assigned zero. Algorithm 1 is applied to the entire dataset to get A) of all methods, before B) and C) are obtained.

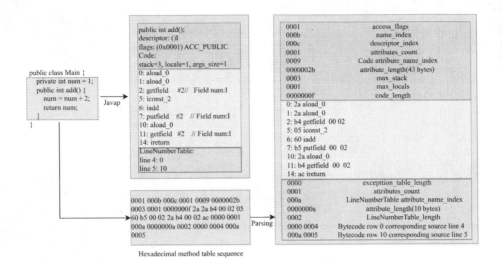

Fig. 2. Extraction method table

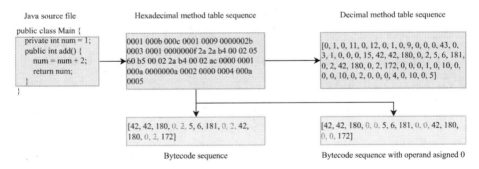

Fig. 3. Feature sequence extraction

Algorithm 1. Feature Extraction Algorithm

Input: $CodeFileSet$: a set of Java class files
Output: $MTSSet$: a set of method table sequences, $BSSet$: a set of bytecode sequences,
    $BSWOAOSet$: a set of bytecode sequences with operands assigned 0

```
 1: for each class file f in CodeFileSet do
 2:      A sequence S_HEX ← f
 3:      MTSSet ← ∅, BSSet ← ∅, BSWOAOSet ← ∅
 4:      MethodNum ← getMethodNum(S_HEX)
 5:      for each i in MethodNum do
 6:          MethodTableSeq_HEX ← getMethodTableSeq(S_HEX)
 7:          if MethodTableSeq_HEX is not the default constructor then
 8:              MTS_DEC ← MethodTableSeq_HEX
 9:              MTSSet.add(MTS_DEC)
10:              AttributeName, AttributeLength ← getAttributeName&Length(MethodTableSeq)
11:              if AttributeName is Code then
12:                  BytecodeSeq ← getBytecodeSeq(MethodTableSeq)
13:                  BS_DEC ← BytecodeSeq
14:                  BSSet.add(BS_DEC)
15:                  for j in AttributeLength do
16:                      if BytecodeSeq[j] is operand then
17:                          BytecodeSeq[j] ← 0
18:                      end if
19:                  end for
20:                  BSWOAOSet.add(BytecodeSeq)
21:              end if
22:          end if
23:      end for
24: end for
25: return MTSSet, BSSet, BSWOAOSet
```

3.2 Clone Detection

Clone detection is a typical similarity-based classification problem where one or more classifiers are trained must undergo supervised training before deployed. The three feature sequences discussed above are used to train classifiers such as deep neural network(DNN), support vector machine(SVM), logistic regression(LR) and decision tree(DT) in order to evaluate their effectiveness and efficiency.

Classifiers cannot deal with inputs of varied length. Based on the observation that more than 70% of the method table sequence in BigCloneBench is shorter than 512 bytes, and more than 70% of the bytecode sequences is shorter than 256 bytes, we set a fixed method table sequence length as 512. Those shorter than 512 bytes are filled with 0 and those longer then that are cut. Similarly, 256 is set as the fixed bytecode sequence length. During training, the feature pairs are concatenated into a sample, so that the length of the method table sequence samples and that of the bytecode sequence samples is set 1024 and 512 respectively.

4   Experiments and Analysis

4.1   Setup

Data. We obtained feature sequences of 7,945,129 true clone pairs (as positive samples) and 261,206 false clone pairs (as negative samples) from Big-CloneBench, i.e. more than 92.5% and 95% of the true and false clone pairs it contains have been included to lay a solid foundation of our claim. BigCloneBench contains Java source code for 43 functions. Considering that function 4 contains almost as many clones as all the rest combined do, we split the dataset into two parts and used those in function 4 for training and the other for testing, as DeepSim has done. The number of samples in the BigCloneBench is shown in Table 1.

Table 1. Number of feature sequences of different clone pairs

Type	T1	T2	ST3	MT3	WT3/4	Positive sample	Negative sample
In function 4	13770	3108	5681	22431	4284131	4329121	–
In the other functions	34229	1026	15439	57324	3507990	3616008	–
Total	47999	4134	21120	79755	7792121	7945129	261206

Considering the fact positive and negative sample pairs is highly unbalanced in BigCloneBench, we select for training a same number of positive and negative samples from true and false clone pairs from those in function 4, as summarised in Table 2. In addition, because of the commutativity (i.e. $Sim(m_i, m_j) = Sim(m_j, m_i)$), we can easily double the training samples by swapping the feature sequence. By swapping the sequence order, we double the training set to 650,636 samples, with 325,318 positive and negative samples.

In order to test the classifiers' performance for different types of clones, we divide the test set into five subsets as shown in Table 2. No swapping has been applied.

Methodology. Our experiment consists of two parts. First, comparisons are made 1) between using as feature the full method table sequence (as we propose in this paper) and using only the bytecode sequence extracted from the method table (prior work), and 2) between using the original bytecode sequence and using its modified version with all operands assigned 0. The latter aims to verify that operand has no impact on the detection result. Then, comparisons have been made between our proposed approach with four state-of-the-art clone detection tools, including FCCA [4], CDLH [19], SourcererCC [15], and DeepSim [24]. Since we can reproduce none of them except SourcererCC for a strictly fair comparison, we obtained the the results by applying our approach to a testset

Table 2. Number of different types of samples in the training set and test set

	Type	T1	T2	ST3	MT3	WT3/4	total
Trainset	+ve sample	13770	3108	5681	22431	117669	162659
	-ve sample	13770	3108	5681	22431	117669	162659
Testset	+ve sample	34229	1026	15439	57324	3507990	3616008
	-ve samples	27360	1026	15439	27361	27361	98547

of the same size as used in FCCA but from BigCloneBench in the FCCA case, directly referring to the results provided in [4] and [19], and applying our dataset to SourcererCC.

Evaluation Metrics. We used P, R, F1 score as evaluation metrics to evaluate clone detectors, which are widely adopted in classification tasks and are defined as follows (where TP, FN and FP denote true positive, false negative and false positive respectively):

$$Recall, R = \frac{TP}{TP + FN} \tag{1}$$

$$Precision, P = \frac{TP}{TP + FP} \tag{2}$$

$$F1\ Score = \frac{2 \times P \times R}{P + R} \tag{3}$$

We introduced two metrics, the rate of training time to training data size ($Rate_{Training}$) and the rate of prediction time to data size ($Rate_{Prediction}$), to quantitatively evaluate different clone detection methods in concern of both training and use. They are defined as:

$$Rate_{Training} = \frac{\text{Training usage time (s)}}{\text{Training dataset size (k)}} \tag{4}$$

$$Rate_{Prediction} = \frac{\text{Test usage time (s)}}{\text{Test dataset size (k)}} \tag{5}$$

A higher $Rate_{Training}$ suggests higher training cost, and a lower $Rate_{Prediction}$, suggests faster prediction.

Environment. All experiments are carried out on a platform of Linux 5.4.0-97-generic x86_64 with Intel(R) Core(TM) i7-8700 CPU, NVIDIA GeForce RTX3060Ti, 32GB of RAM, and 1TB SSD.

4.2   Results and Evaluation

Comparison of Features. By training the DNN classifiers separately, comparisons are made between using the method table extracted directly from Java class file and using only the bytecode sequence within, and the results are listed in Table 3.

Table 3. Performance comparison between using the method table and its bytecode sequence as feature

| Clone Type | Method table/Bytecode sequence only | | |
	P	R	F1
T1	**0.99**/0.96	1.00/1.00	**0.99**/0.98
T2	**0.94**/0.90	**0.94**/0.90	**0.94**/0.90
ST3	**0.95**/0.92	**0.96**/0.92	**0.95**/0.92
MT3	**0.94**/0.91	**0.93**/0.90	**0.93**/0.90
WT3	**0.95**/0.94	**0.95**/0.94	**0.95**/0.94

Table 3 shows that using the full method table as the feature for clone detection outperforms using only its bytecode sequence for all five types of code clone. This suggests that other information in the method table provides useful hints to distinguish whether the methods are similar.

Comparison of Classifiers. We then compare the performance of various classifiers which use the original bytecode sequence and its modified version with all operands assigned 0, and the results are summarized in Table 4.

Table 4. F1 scores of different classifiers on various clone types

| Classifier | Original bytecode sequence/Modified bytecode sequence with all operands assigned 0 | | | | |
	T1	T2	ST3	MT3	WT3/4
DNN	0.99/0.99	0.90/**0.92**	**0.92**/0.90	**0.90**/0.88	**0.94**/0.93
SVM	0.91/**0.93**	**0.80**/0.62	**0.80**/0.65	**0.82**/0.72	**0.91**/0.86
LR	0.95/**0.96**	0.79/**0.84**	0.76/**0.80**	**0.80**/0.77	0.89/0.89
DT	0.99/0.99	0.79/**0.89**	**0.90**/0.80	**0.91**/0.86	**0.93**/0.91

Table 4 shows that these two feature options lead to similar results on all four classifiers, suggesting that operands in the bytecode sequence do not affect clone detection. Although the effect of the original bytecode sequence on the T1 and T2 clones is worse than its variant, it yields clearly better performance on more practical and challenging types of clone of semantic similarity (ST3, MT3 and WT3/4), except for LR classifier on ST3.

Considering that DNN yield the best and most stable performance among the four classifiers (minimum difference between the two features used, as suggested in Table 4), we pick DNN as the clone detector for the following evaluations and present its results only. Its parameters are set as follows: layers size: 1024–256, epoch: 10, batch size: 512, dropout: 0.5, initial learning rate: 0.01, λ for L2 regularization: 0.02, and Momentum: 0.01.

Comparison Against Established Approaches. Comparison on P, R and F1 scores then is made among our approach and baseline approaches FCCA, CDLH, SourcererCC and DeepSim, and the results are summarized in Table 5.

Table 5. P, R and F1 scores of MTCD and four other baseline approaches

Method	P	R	F1
SourcererCC	0.85	0.01	0.02
CDLH	0.92	0.74	0.82
DeepSim	0.97	0.98	0.98
FCCA	0.98	0.97	0.98
MTCD	0.94	0.95	0.94

Table 6 presents a comparison (F1 score) of various approaches on different types of clone.

Table 6. F1 scores of MTCD and the other four baseline approaches on different clone types

Approach	T1	T2	ST3	MT3	WT3/T4
SourcererCC	0.93	0.91	0.70	0.08	0.00
CDLH	1.0	1.0	0.93	0.80	0.86
DeepSim	0.99	0.99	0.99	0.99	0.97
FCCA	1.0	1.0	0.95	0.97	0.98
MTCD	0.99	0.93	0.95	0.94	0.95

Table 5 and 6 show that, concerning detection of MT3 and WT3/T4 clone pairs, MTCD yields better performance than CDLH and SourcererCC, but a bit worse than DeepSim and FCCA. This suggests that method table has an advantage over token and AST in the detection of semantic similarity. Table 6 suggests that MTCD performed worse than CDLH in the detection of T1 and T2 clone pairs. This is because our approach retained only the first 512 bytes and directly truncated the rest during feature processing. But 30% of feature sequences in the whole dataset are in fact longer than 512. In addition, the dataset contains far fewer clone pairs of T2 than those of other types, which significantly biased the resulting classifier. Overall, MTCD has good performance in detecting code clones, but it is still slightly inferior to the most advanced cloning detectors in terms of P, R and F1 score.

However, MTCD has its significant advantage in terms of time consumption in training and detection, as summarised in Table 7. It is worth noting that a large amount of time is needed for training for all other methods except Sourcer-erCC. Training for FCCA with 30K code pairs took about 13 h, for CDLH, it was roughly 12 h. In the case of DeeepSim, it took about 4 h to train with 1.26M code pairs. Our approach took only roughly 3 min to trains with 60K code pairs, i.e. a $Rate_{Training}$ of 3.0 which clearly outran the others. For prediction, our approach took only 8 s to complete a testset of 10 k code pairs, whilst FCCA, CDLH, and Sourcerer took 91 s, 90 s, and 44 s respectively, while DeepSim spent 34 s on 140 k code pairs. In brief, MTCD clearly outperformed DeepSim in term of $Rate_{Training}$, despite second to it in term of $Rate_{Prediction}$.

Table 7. Time cost comparison of our method and other four baselines

Method	$Rate_{Training}$ (s/k)	$Rate_{Prediction}$ (s/k)
SourcererCC	–	5.1 (51 s/10 k)
CDLH	1510.6 (45317 s/30 k)	9.0(90 s/10 k)
DeepSim	10.8 (13545 s/1260 k)	0.2 (34 s/140 k)
FCCA	15559.0 (46769 s/30 k)	9.1 (91 s/10 k)
MTCD	3.0 (181 s/60 k)	0.8 (8 s/10 k)

4.3   Discussion

The experimental results given above suggest that our proposed clone detection approach has great advantages when compared with the others based on other code representations. First, the method table can be easily extracted from Java class file, without further processing such as operands removal or encoding. More complex and time-consuming preprocessing is inevitably needed for approaches based on other code representations. Secondly, method table is a very effective feature for clone detection, helping to achieve F1 score of 0.93 or higher on clones of all five types. When it comes to detection of semantic similarity, it clearly outperforms token-based detectors which simply fail and AST-based detectors whose performance is far from satisfactory. Finally, the overhead of MTCD is modest (only a simple classifier must be trained using extracted method table sequences), while other techniques based on AST, graph, control flow and data flow need a lot of computing resources on feature extraction steps and/or model training. In short, the method table sequence extracted from Java class file is a promising feature for efficient code clone detection, because it is easy to extract and yields good performance.

5   Conclusions

This paper suggests that the method table sequence extracted from Java class file is a simple-to-extract and efficient feature for clone detection. Experimental results suggest it can achieve a high F1 score (0.95) on average for five types of clone on the BigCloneBench dataset and its training is very efficient. Our approach achieves high accuracy with a modest time overhead, clearly outperforming other established approaches.

References

1. Baker, B.: On finding duplication and near-duplication in large software systems. In: Proceedings of 2nd Working Conference on Reverse Engineering, pp. 86–95 (1995). https://doi.org/10.1109/WCRE.1995.514697
2. Ducasse, S., Rieger, M., Demeyer, S.: A language independent approach for detecting duplicated code. In: Proceedings IEEE International Conference on Software Maintenance - 1999 (ICSM 1999). Software Maintenance for Business Change (Cat. No.99CB36360), pp. 109–118 (1999). https://doi.org/10.1109/ICSM.1999.792593
3. Feng, C., Wang, T., Yu, Y., Zhang, Y., Zhang, Y., Wang, H.: Sia-RAE: a siamese network based on recursive autoencoder for effective clone detection. In: 2020 27th Asia-Pacific Software Engineering Conference (APSEC), pp. 238–246 (2020). https://doi.org/10.1109/APSEC51365.2020.00032
4. Hua, W., Sui, Y., Wan, Y., Liu, G., Xu, G.: FCCA: hybrid code representation for functional clone detection using attention networks. IEEE Trans. Reliab. **70**(1), 304–318 (2021). https://doi.org/10.1109/TR.2020.3001918
5. Jiang, L., Misherghi, G., Su, Z., Glondu, S.: DECKARD: scalable and accurate tree-based detection of code clones. In: 29th International Conference on Software Engineering (ICSE 2007), pp. 96–105 (2007). https://doi.org/10.1109/ICSE.2007.30
6. Johnson: Substring matching for clone detection and change tracking. In: Proceedings 1994 International Conference on Software Maintenance, pp. 120–126 (1994). https://doi.org/10.1109/ICSM.1994.336783
7. Johnson, J.H.: Identifying redundancy in source code using fingerprints. In: Proceedings of the 1993 Conference of the Centre for Advanced Studies on Collaborative Research: Software Engineering. vol. 1, p. 171–183. CASCON 1993, IBM Press (1993)
8. Kamiya, T., Kusumoto, S., Inoue, K.: CCFinder: a multilinguistic token-based code clone detection system for large scale source code. IEEE Trans. Softw. Eng. **28**(7), 654–670 (2002). https://doi.org/10.1109/TSE.2002.1019480
9. Keivanloo, I., Roy, C.K., Rilling, J.: SeByte: scalable clone and similarity search for bytecode. Sci. Comput. Program. **95**, 426–444 (2014). https://doi.org/10.1016/j.scico.2013.10.006, https://www.sciencedirect.com/science/article/pii/S0167642313002773, special Issue on Software Clones (IWSC 2012)
10. Krinke, J.: Identifying similar code with program dependence graphs. In: Proceedings Eighth Working Conference on Reverse Engineering, pp. 301–309 (2001). https://doi.org/10.1109/WCRE.2001.957835
11. Li, L., Feng, H., Zhuang, W., Meng, N., Ryder, B.: CCLearner: a deep learning-based clone detection approach. In: 2017 IEEE International Conference on Software Maintenance and Evolution (ICSME), pp. 249–260 (2017). https://doi.org/10.1109/ICSME.2017.46
12. Li, Z.O., Sun, J.: A metric space based software clone detection approach. In: 2010 2nd IEEE International Conference on Information Management and Engineering, pp. 393–397 (2010). https://doi.org/10.1109/ICIME.2010.5478099

13. Rattan, D., Bhatia, R., Singh, M.: Software clone detection: a systematic review. Inf. Softw. Technol. **55**(7), 1165–1199 (2013). https://doi.org/10.1016/j.infsof.2013.01.008, https://www.sciencedirect.com/science/article/pii/S0950584913000323

14. Roy, C.K., Cordy, J.R.: NICAD: accurate detection of near-miss intentional clones using flexible pretty-printing and code normalization. In: 2008 16th IEEE International Conference on Program Comprehension, pp. 172–181 (2008). https://doi.org/10.1109/ICPC.2008.41

15. Sajnani, H., Saini, V., Svajlenko, J., Roy, C.K., Lopes, C.V.: SourcererCC: scaling code clone detection to big-code. In: 2016 IEEE/ACM 38th International Conference on Software Engineering (ICSE), pp. 1157–1168 (2016). https://doi.org/10.1145/2884781.2884877

16. Schäfer, A., Amme, W., Heinze, T.S.: STUBBER: compiling source code into bytecode without dependencies for java code clone detection. In: 2021 IEEE 15th International Workshop on Software Clones (IWSC), pp. 29–35 (2021). https://doi.org/10.1109/IWSC53727.2021.00011

17. Svajlenko, J., Roy, C.K.: Evaluating clone detection tools with BigCloneBench. In: 2015 IEEE International Conference on Software Maintenance and Evolution (ICSME), pp. 131–140 (2015). https://doi.org/10.1109/ICSM.2015.7332459

18. Tufano, M., Watson, C., Bavota, G., Di Penta, M., White, M., Poshyvanyk, D.: Deep learning similarities from different representations of source code. In: 2018 IEEE/ACM 15th International Conference on Mining Software Repositories (MSR), pp. 542–553 (2018)

19. Wei, H.H., Li, M.: Supervised deep features for software functional clone detection by exploiting lexical and syntactical information in source code. In: Proceedings of the 26th International Joint Conference on Artificial Intelligence, pp. 3034–3040. IJCAI 2017, AAAI Press (2017)

20. Yu, D., et al.: Detecting java code clones with multi-granularities based on bytecode. In: 2017 IEEE 41st Annual Computer Software and Applications Conference (COMPSAC). vol. 1, pp. 317–326 (2017). https://doi.org/10.1109/COMPSAC.2017.104

21. Yu, D., Yang, J., Chen, X., Chen, J.: Detecting java code clones based on bytecode sequence alignment. IEEE Access **7**, 22421–22433 (2019). https://doi.org/10.1109/ACCESS.2019.2898411

22. Yuan, D., Fang, S., Zhang, T., Xu, Z., Luo, X.: Java code clone detection by exploiting semantic and syntax information from intermediate code-based graph. IEEE Trans. Reliab. 1–16 (2022). https://doi.org/10.1109/TR.2022.3176922

23. Zeng, J., Ben, K., Li, X., Zhang, X.: Fast code clone detection based on weighted recursive autoencoders. IEEE Access **7**, 125062–125078 (2019). https://doi.org/10.1109/ACCESS.2019.2938825

24. Zhao, G., Huang, J.: DeepSim: deep learning code functional similarity. In: Proceedings of the 2018 26th ACM Joint Meeting on European Software Engineering Conference and Symposium on the Foundations of Software Engineering, pp. 141–151. ESEC/FSE 2018, Association for Computing Machinery, New York, USA (2018). https://doi.org/10.1145/3236024.3236068, https://doi.org/10.1145/3236024.3236068

Stepwise Development of Paraconsistent Processes

Juliana Cunha[1]([✉]), Alexandre Madeira[1]([✉]), and Luís Soares Barbosa[2]([✉])

[1] CIDMA, Department of Mathematics, Aveiro University, Aveiro, Portugal
juliana.cunha@live.ua.pt, madeira@ua.pt
[2] INESC TEC & Department of Informatics, Minho University, Braga, Portugal
lsb@di.uminho.pt

Abstract. The development of more flexible and robust models for reasoning about systems in environments with potentially conflicting information is becoming more and more relevant in different contexts. In this direction, we recently introduced paraconsistent transition systems, i.e. transition systems whose transitions are tagged with a pair of weights, one standing for the degree of evidence that the transition exists, another weighting its potential non existence. Moreover, these structures were endowed with a modal logic [3] that was further formalised as an institution in [5]. This paper goes a step further, proposing an approach for the structured specification of paraconsistent transition processes, i.e. paraconsistent transition systems with initial states. The proposed approach is developed along the lines of [12], which introduced a complete methodology for (standard) reactive systems development building on the Sannella and Tarlecki stepwise implementation process. For this, we enrich the logic with dynamic modalities and hybrid features, and provide a pallet of constructors and abstractors to support the development process of paraconsistent processes along the entire design cycle.

1 Introduction

The development of more flexible and robust models for reasoning about systems in environments with potentially conflicting information is becoming more and more relevant in different contexts. Applications scenarios where these patterns emerge range from robotics (e.g. specifying a controller that has to react to collected conflicting data due faulty or imprecise sensors), to diagnostic support systems for the health domain (e.g. often dealing with contradictory marks). Moreover, it is not uncommon that along a development process, engineering

The present study was developed in the scope of the Project Agenda ILLIANCE [C644919832-00000035 — Project n 46], financed by PRR - Plano de Recuperação e Resiliência under the Next Generation EU from the European Union.
FCT, the Portuguese funding agency for Science and Technology suports the second author with the project UIDB/04106/2020 and the third with the project IBEX PTDC/CCI-COM/4280/2021.

C. David and M. Sun (Eds.): TASE 2023, LNCS 13931, pp. 327–343, 2023.
https://doi.org/10.1007/978-3-031-35257-7_20

teams make design decisions on often imprecise and contradictory requirements, elicited from stakeholders with distinct perspectives.

This entails the need for the design of new models and logics resilient to conflict, as well as methods prepared to assist the rigorous development and analysis of such complex systems. Following this direction, we introduced in [4] the notion of a paraconsistent transition system, where transitions are labelled with a pair of weights, one weighting the degree of evidence that the transition exists, another weighting its potential non existence. Then, in [3] these structures were endowed with a modal logic, that was further extended to a multi-modal logic, and formalised as an institution, in [5]. The latter reference, also discusses preliminary steps towards the structured specification of these structures, by characterizing a set of CASL-like operators.

The present paper contributes to this agenda along two main edges. Firstly, we adjust the models and extend the logic to express and reason about paraconsistent processes, i.e. processes with paraconsistent weighted transitions with specified initial states. Moreover, the multi-modal logic described in [5] is extended to a dynamic logic [10]. This involves bringing into the picture structured modalities, to express abstract properties such as safety and liveness, as well as hybrid logic constructs [2], such as binders and state-variables to express some other properties of paraconsistent processes as concrete transitions within concrete states. In the end, we end up with a paraconsistent version of the logic introduced in [12], which we also formalise as a logical institution.

Secondly, we introduce a method for the structured specification of paraconsistent transition processes starting from their abstract design down to the concrete implementation stage. More precisely, we fully instantiate the (generic) Sannella and Tarlecki's stepwise implementation process [15] for the case of development of paraconsistent processes. On the base of the approach of Sannella and Tarlecki is the notion of a specification as a syntactic representation of a class of possible implementations of the envisaged system. Conceptually, the implementation process corresponds to a chain of refinement steps in the sense that a specification refines another one if every model of the latter is a model of the former. This is complemented by the concepts of *constructor* and *abstractor* implementations, conveying the idea that a specification may resort to one or several given specifications applying a specific construction on top of them to meet the envisaged requirements. Thus, this paper also considers abstractor implementations to capture situations whose relevant requirements just need to be satisfied up to some suitable abstraction (e.g. freed from some implementation details). Note that this is not a trivial step since even the notion of a specification characterized by a class of models has to be adjusted to the proposed paraconsistent framework.

Finally, a pallet of constructors and abstracts was defined to support the whole development process. We revisited the pallet of process constructors and abstractors discussed in [12] for the development of (standard) processes, redefining their semantics in the paraconsistent setting. This includes operators to relabel and hidden actions, but also to compose specification using the product constructor. Bisimulation of paraconsistent transition structures introduced in [4] is used to support abstractor implementations.

The rest of the paper is organised as follows: Sect. 2 introduces some background definitions for the development of the work. Then, Sect. 3 introduces $P(\mathcal{A})$, an institution suitable to express and reason about paraconsistent transition systems. Section 4 depicts a complete formal development *à la* Sannella and Tarlecki for these systems. Finally, Sect. 5 concludes.

2   Preliminaries

Let us start by recalling what an institution is. Then, we will introduce a specific algebraic structure over which the logical system to support our specification will be defined. Such a structure is basically a particular class of residuated lattices in which the lattice meet and the monoidal composition coincide, equipped with a metric which measures the "distance" between specification which may be fully consistent (in which case the weights in the double transitions considered are complementary), vague (when their "sum" remains below the entire universe of discourse, typically sum less than 1), or paraconsistent (when sums above).

Institutions. Informally, an institution abstractly defines a logic system by describing through its spectrum of signatures, corresponding models and a satisfaction relation between models and sentences.

Definition 1 ([9]). *An institution I is a tuple $I = (\mathsf{Sign}_I, \mathsf{Sen}_I, \mathsf{Mod}_I, \models_I)$ consisting of*

- *a category Sign_I of signatures*
- *a functor $\mathsf{Sen}_I : \mathsf{Sign}_I \to \mathbb{S}\mathrm{et}$ giving a set of Σ-sentences for each signature $\Sigma \in |\mathsf{Sign}_I|$. For each signature morphism $\sigma : \Sigma \to \Sigma'$ the function $\mathsf{Sen}_I(\sigma) : \mathsf{Sen}_I(\Sigma) \to \mathsf{Sen}_I(\Sigma')$ translates Σ-sentences to Σ'-sentences*
- *a functor $\mathsf{Mod}_I : \mathsf{Sign}_I^{op} \to \mathbb{C}at$ assigns to each signature Σ the category of Σ-models. For each signature morphism $\sigma : \Sigma \to \Sigma'$ the functor $\mathsf{Mod}_I(\sigma) : \mathsf{Mod}_I(\Sigma') \to \mathsf{Mod}_I(\Sigma)$ translates Σ'-models to Σ-models.*
- *a satisfaction relation $\models_I^{\Sigma} \subseteq |\mathsf{Mod}_I(\Sigma)| \times \mathsf{Sen}_I(\Sigma)$ determines the satisfaction of Σ-sentences by Σ-models for each signature $\Sigma \in |\mathsf{Sign}_I|$.*

such that satisfaction is preserved under change of signature, that is for any signature morphism $\sigma : \Sigma \to \Sigma'$, for any $\varphi \in \mathsf{Sen}_I(\Sigma)$ and $M' \in |\mathsf{Mod}_I(\Sigma')|$

$$\left(M' \models_I^{\Sigma'} \mathsf{Sen}_I(\sigma)(\varphi) \right) \;\Leftrightarrow\; \left(\mathsf{Mod}_I(\sigma)(M') \models_I^{\Sigma} \varphi \right) \tag{1}$$

When formalising multi-valued logics as institutions, the equivalence on the satisfaction condition (1) can be replaced by an equality [1]:

$$\left(M' \models_I^{\Sigma'} \mathsf{Sen}_I(\sigma)(\varphi) \right) \;=\; \left(\mathsf{Mod}_I(\sigma)(M') \models_I^{\Sigma} \varphi \right) \tag{2}$$

(Metric) Twisted Algebras. Metric twisted algebras are introduced to deal with weights in paraconsistent transition systems.

A residuated lattice $\langle A, \sqcap, \sqcup, 1, 0, \odot, \rightarrow, e \rangle$, over a nonempty set A, is a complete lattice $\langle A, \sqcap, \sqcup \rangle$, equipped with a monoid $\langle A, \odot, e \rangle$ such that $\odot$ has a right adjoint, $\rightarrow$, called the residuum. We will focus on a class of complete residuated lattices that are bounded by a maximal element 1 and a minimal element 0 and that are *integral*, that is $1 = e$. Additionally, we want the lattice meet ($\sqcap$) and the monoidal composition ($\odot$) to coincide. Hence, the adjunction is stated as $a \sqcap b \leqslant c$ iff $b \leqslant a \rightarrow c$. A pre-linearity condition is also enforced

$$(a \rightarrow b) \sqcup (b \rightarrow a) = 1 \tag{3}$$

A residuated lattice obeying prelinearity is known as a MTL-algebra [7], with a slight abuse of nomenclature, the designation iMTL-algebra, from *integral MTL-algebra*, will be used in the sequel for the class of semantic structures considered. Examples of iMTL-algebras are:

- the Boolean algebra $\mathbf{2} = \langle \{0, 1\}, \wedge, \vee, 1, 0, \rightarrow \rangle$

- $\mathbf{3} = \langle \{\top, u, \bot\}, \wedge_3, \vee_3, \top, \bot, \rightarrow_3 \rangle$, where

$\wedge_3$	$\bot$	u	$\top$
$\bot$	$\bot$	$\bot$	$\bot$
u	$\bot$	u	u
$\top$	$\bot$	u	$\top$

$\vee_3$	$\bot$	u	$\top$
$\bot$	$\bot$	u	$\top$
u	u	u	$\top$
$\top$	$\top$	$\top$	$\top$

$\rightarrow_3$	$\bot$	u	$\top$
$\bot$	$\top$	$\top$	$\top$
u	$\bot$	$\top$	$\top$
$\top$	$\bot$	u	$\top$

- $\ddot{G} = \langle [0, 1], \min, \max, 1, 0, \rightarrow \rangle$, with implication defined as
$$a \rightarrow b = \begin{cases} 1 & if\, a \leqslant b \\ b & otherwise \end{cases}$$

We focus on iMTL-algebras $\mathbf{A}$ whose carrier A supports a metric space (A, d), with suitable choice of d. Where $d \colon A \times A \rightarrow \mathbb{R}^+$ such that $d(x, y) = 0$ iff $x = y$ and $d(x, y) \leqslant d(x, z) + d(z, y)$. The notion of a $\mathbf{A}$-twisted algebra, was introduced in [3] to operate with pairs of truth weights, which consists of an enrichment of a twist-structure [11] with a metric. This metric is necessary to the characterization of the consistency of these pairs of values, relevant on the interpretation of the consistency operator $\circ$ in the logic (see [3] for details).

Definition 2 ([3]). *Given a iMTL-algebra $\mathbf{A}$ enriched with a metric d, a $\mathbf{A}$-twisted algebra $\mathcal{A} = \langle A \times A, \sqcap\!\!\!\sqcap, \sqcup\!\!\!\sqcup, \Rightarrow, /\!\!/, D \rangle$ is defined as: $(a, b) \sqcap\!\!\!\sqcap (c, d) = (a \sqcap c, b \sqcup d)$, $(a, b) \sqcup\!\!\!\sqcup (c, d) = (a \sqcup c, b \sqcap d)$, $(a, b) \Rightarrow (c, d) = (a \rightarrow c, a \sqcap d)$, $/\!\!/(a, b) = (b, a)$ and $D((a, b), (c, d)) = \sqrt{d(a, c)^2 + d(b, d)^2}$. The order in $\mathbf{A}$ is lifted to $\mathcal{A}$ as $(a, b) \preceq (c, d)$ iff $a \leqslant c$ and $b \geqslant d$.*

3 An Institution for Paraconsistent Transitions Processes

This section introduces $\mathbf{P}(\mathcal{A})$, a logic for paraconsistent processes formalized as a (many-valued) institution. $\mathbf{P}(\mathcal{A})$ starting point is the logic for paraconsistent systems presented in [5]. However, in $\mathbf{P}(\mathcal{A})$ modalities can be indexed by regular expressions of actions, as in dynamic logic, and a binder $\downarrow x$ and identification $@_x$ operator, borrowed from hybrid logic, are introduced.

Let us fix any twisted algebra $\mathcal{A}$ to introduce all the necessary ingredients for an institution $\boldsymbol{P}(\mathcal{A}) = (\mathsf{Sign}, \mathsf{Sen}, \mathsf{Mod}, \models)$. Whenever the choice of $\mathcal{A}$ is not essential, $\boldsymbol{P}(\mathcal{A})$ will be abbreviated to $\boldsymbol{P}$. Note here that all constructions of $\boldsymbol{P}(\mathcal{A})$ are parametrically defined, thus admitting different instances according to the structure of the truth values domain relevant for the application at hands.

Firstly we introduce the signatures:

Definition 3. *A signature is a tuple* $\langle \mathsf{Act}, \mathsf{Prop} \rangle$ *where* Act *is a finite set of action symbols and* Prop *is a set of propositions.*

The set of actions $\mathsf{Act} = \{a_1, \ldots, a_n\}$ will induce a set of structured actions, $Str(\mathsf{Act})$, defined by $\alpha := a \mid \alpha ; \alpha \mid \alpha + \alpha \mid \alpha^*$ where $a \in Act$. As usual, we use $-a_i$ to denote the structured action $a_1 + \cdots + a_{i-1} + a_{i+1} + \cdots + a_n$ and, given a set of atomic actions $B = \{b_1, \ldots b_k\} \subseteq \mathsf{Act}$, we write B to refer to the structured action $b_1 + \cdots + b_k$.

Let $\Sigma, \Sigma' \in \mathsf{Sign}$ be signatures. A signature morphism $\sigma : \Sigma \to \Sigma'$ involves two functions $\sigma_{\mathsf{Prop}} : \mathsf{Prop} \to \mathsf{Prop}'$ and $\sigma_{\mathsf{Act}} : \mathsf{Act} \to \mathsf{Act}'$, where σ_{Act} extends to $Str(\mathsf{Act})$ as follows:

- $\widehat{\sigma}_{\mathsf{Act}}(a) = \sigma_{\mathsf{Act}}(a)$
- $\widehat{\sigma}_{\mathsf{Act}}(\alpha ; \alpha') = \widehat{\sigma}_{\mathsf{Act}}(\alpha) ; \widehat{\sigma}_{\mathsf{Act}}(\alpha')$
- $\widehat{\sigma}_{\mathsf{Act}}(\alpha + \alpha') = \widehat{\sigma}_{\mathsf{Act}}(\alpha) + \widehat{\sigma}_{\mathsf{Act}}(\alpha')$
- $\widehat{\sigma}_{\mathsf{Act}}(\alpha^*) = \widehat{\sigma}_{\mathsf{Act}}(\alpha)^*$

$$
\begin{array}{ccc}
\mathsf{Act} & \xrightarrow{\;\sigma_{\mathsf{Act}}\;} & \mathsf{Act}' \\[4pt]
\Big\uparrow & & \Big\uparrow \\[4pt]
Str(\mathsf{Act}) & \xrightarrow{\;\widehat{\sigma}_{\mathsf{Act}}\;} & Str(\mathsf{Act}')
\end{array}
$$

for all $a \in \mathsf{Act}$ and $\alpha, \alpha' \in Str(\mathsf{Act})$. The category of signatures and their morphisms form category Sign.

Now, let us introduce the models:

Definition 4. *A* $\langle \mathsf{Act}, \mathsf{Prop} \rangle$-*paraconsistent transition process, abbreviated to PTP, is a tuple* $P = (W, w_0, R, V)$ *such that,*

- W *is a non-empty set of states,*
- $w_0 \in W$ *is called the initial state*
- $R = (R_a : W \times W \to A \times A)_{a \in \mathsf{Act}}$ *is an* Act-*indexed family of functions;* $R_a(w_1, w_2) = (tt, ff)$ *means that there is the evidence degree* tt *that there exists a transition from* w_1 *to* w_2 *by* a*, and the evidence degree* ff *that this transition does not exists.*
- $V : W \times \mathsf{Prop} \to A \times A$ *is a valuation function;* $V(w, p) = (tt, ff)$ *means that in state* w *there is the evidence degree* tt *that the proposition* p *holds, and* ff *that it does not hold.*

For any pair $(tt, ff) \in A \times A$*,* $(tt, ff)^+$ *denotes* tt *and* $(tt, ff)^-$ *denotes* ff*.*

The interpretation of $\alpha \in Str(\mathsf{Act})$ in a model (W, w_0, R, V) extends the relation R to a relation $\widehat{R}$ defined for states $w, w' \in W$ as:

- $\widehat{R}_a(w, w') = R_a(w, w')$, for $a \in \mathrm{Act}$
- $\widehat{R}_{\alpha+\alpha'}(w, w') = \widehat{R}_\alpha(w, w') \sqcup \widehat{R}_{\alpha'}(w, w')$
- $\widehat{R}_{\alpha;\alpha'}(w, w') = \bigsqcup_{v \in W} \left(R_\alpha(w, v) \sqcap R_{\alpha'}(v, w') \right)$
- $\widehat{R}_{\alpha*}(w, w') = \bigsqcup_{i \geqslant 0} \widehat{R}_\alpha^i(w, w')$. Where,

  - $\widehat{R}_\alpha^0 = \begin{cases} (1, 0) & \text{if } w = w' \\ (0, 1) & \text{otherwise} \end{cases}$
  - $\widehat{R}_\alpha^{k+1}(w, w') = (\widehat{R}_\alpha^k; \widehat{R}_\alpha)(w, w')$

where $\sqcap$ and $\sqcup$ are the distributed versions of $\sqcap$ and $\sqcup$, respectively.

Definition 5. *A morphism connecting two* $\langle \mathrm{Act}, \mathrm{Prop} \rangle$*-PTPs* (W, w_0, R, V) *and* (W', w_0', R', V') *is a function* $h : W \to W'$*, such that: for each* $a \in \mathrm{Act}$*,* $R_a(w_1, w_2) \leqslant R_a'(h(w_1), h(w_2))$*; for any* $p \in \mathrm{Prop}$*,* $w \in W$*,* $V(w, p) \leqslant V'(h(w), p)$*; and* $h(w_0) = w_0'$*.*

We say that P and P' are isomorphic, in symbols $P \cong P'$, whenever there are morphisms $h : W \to W'$ and $h^{-1} : W' \to W$ such that $h' \circ h = id_{W'}$, $h \circ h' = id_W$.

Models and their corresponding morphisms form a category, denoted by Mod, which acts as the model category for our institution $\boldsymbol{P}$.

Definition 6. *For any signature morphism* $\sigma : \langle \mathrm{Act}, \mathrm{Prop} \rangle \to \langle \mathrm{Act}', \mathrm{Prop}' \rangle$ *and* $P = (W', w_0', R', V')$ *a* $\langle \mathrm{Act}', \mathrm{Prop}' \rangle$*-PTP, the* σ*-reduct of* P' *is a* $\langle \mathrm{Act}, \mathrm{Prop} \rangle$*-PTP* $P|_\sigma = (W, w_0, R, V)$ *such that* $W = W'$*,* $w_0 = w_0'$*; for* $p \in \mathrm{Prop}$*,* $w \in W$*,* $V(w, p) = V'(w, \sigma(p))$*; and for* $w, v \in W$ *and* $a \in \mathrm{Act}$*,* $R_a(w, v) = R'_{\sigma(a)}(w, v)$*.*

Therefore, each signature morphism $\sigma : \Sigma \to \Sigma'$ defines a functor $\mathsf{Mod}(\sigma) : \mathsf{Mod}(\Sigma') \to \mathsf{Mod}(\Sigma)$ that maps processes and morphisms to the corresponding reducts. This lifts to a functor, $\mathsf{Mod} : (\mathsf{Sign})^{op} \to \mathsf{CAT}$, mapping each signature to the category of its models, and each signature morphism to its reduct functor.

Definition 7. *Given a signature* $\Sigma = \langle \mathrm{Act}, \mathrm{Prop} \rangle$ *the set* $\mathsf{Sen}(\Sigma)$ *of sentences is given by the following grammar*

$$\varphi := p \mid \bot \mid \neg\varphi \mid \varphi \to \varphi \mid \varphi \lor \varphi \mid \varphi \land \varphi \mid [\alpha]\,\varphi \mid \langle\alpha\rangle\,\varphi \mid [\![\alpha]\!]\,\varphi \mid \langle\!\langle\alpha\rangle\!\rangle\,\varphi \mid \circ\varphi \mid x \mid {\downarrow} x.\varphi \mid @_x\varphi$$

where $p \in \mathrm{Prop}$*,* $\alpha \in \mathrm{Str}(\mathrm{Act})$ *and* $x \in X$*, with* X *being an infinite set of variables.*

Each signature morphism $\sigma : \langle \mathrm{Act}, \mathrm{Prop} \rangle \to \langle \mathrm{Act}', \mathrm{Prop}' \rangle$ induces a sentence translation scheme $\mathsf{Sen}(\sigma)$ recursively defined as follows:

- $\mathsf{Sen}(\sigma)(p) = \sigma_{\mathrm{Prop}}(p)$
- $\mathsf{Sen}(\sigma)(\bot) = \bot$
- $\mathsf{Sen}(\sigma)(\neg\varphi) = \neg\mathsf{Sen}(\sigma)(\varphi)$
- $\mathsf{Sen}(\sigma)(\varphi \odot \varphi') = \mathsf{Sen}(\sigma)(\varphi) \odot \mathsf{Sen}(\sigma)(\varphi')$, $\odot \in \{\lor, \land, \to\}$
- $\mathsf{Sen}(\sigma)([\alpha]\varphi) = [\widehat{\sigma}_{\mathrm{Act}}(\alpha)]\,\mathsf{Sen}(\sigma)(\varphi)$

- $\mathsf{Sen}(\sigma)(\langle\alpha\rangle\varphi) = \langle\widehat{\sigma}_{\mathrm{Act}}(\alpha)\rangle\,\mathsf{Sen}(\sigma)(\varphi)$
- $\mathsf{Sen}(\sigma)([\alpha]\varphi) = [\widehat{\sigma}_{\mathrm{Act}}(\alpha)]\,\mathsf{Sen}(\sigma)(\varphi)$
- $\mathsf{Sen}(\sigma)(\langle\!\langle\alpha\rangle\!\rangle\varphi) = \langle\!\langle\widehat{\sigma}_{\mathrm{Act}}(\alpha)\rangle\!\rangle\,\mathsf{Sen}(\sigma)(\varphi)$
- $\mathsf{Sen}(\sigma)(\circ\varphi) = \circ\,\mathsf{Sen}(\sigma)(\varphi)$
- $\mathsf{Sen}(\sigma)(x) = x$
- $\mathsf{Sen}(\sigma)(\downarrow x.\varphi) = \downarrow x.\mathsf{Sen}(\sigma)(\varphi)$
- $\mathsf{Sen}(\sigma)(@_x\varphi) = @_x\mathsf{Sen}(\sigma)(\varphi)$

Entailing a functor $\mathsf{Sen} : \mathsf{Sign} \to \mathsf{Set}$ mapping each signature to the set of its sentences, and each signature morphism to the corresponding translation of sentences.

Definition 8. *Let $\Sigma = \langle\mathrm{Act}, \mathrm{Prop}\rangle$ be a signature, $P = (W, w_0, R, V)$ a Σ-PTP and φ a Σ-sentence, the satisfaction relation*

$$(P \models \varphi) = \prod_{g \in W^X}(P, g, w_0 \models \varphi)$$

where $g : X \to W$ is a valuation function such that, for $x \in X$, $g[x \mapsto w]$ denotes the valuation given by $g[x \mapsto w](x) = w$ and $g[x \mapsto w](y) = g(y)$ for any $y \neq x \in X$. If φ is a formula without free variables then the valuation function g is irrelevant, that is, $(M, g, w \models \varphi) = (M, w \models \varphi)$. The relation $\models$ is recursively defined as follows

- $(M, w \models p) = V(w, p)$
- $(M, w \models \bot) = (0, 1)$
- $(M, w \models \neg\varphi) = /\!\!/(M, w \models \varphi)$
- $(M, w \models \varphi \to \varphi') = (M, w \models \varphi) \Rightarrow (M, w \models \varphi')$
- $(M, w \models \varphi \vee \varphi') = (M, w \models \varphi) \sqcup (M, w \models \varphi')$
- $(M, w \models \varphi \wedge \varphi') = (M, w \models \varphi) \sqcap (M, w \models \varphi')$
- $(M, w \models \circ\varphi) = \begin{cases} (1, 0) & \text{if } (M, w \models \varphi) \in \Delta_C \\ (0, 1) & \text{otherwise} \end{cases}$
- $(M, g, w \models [\alpha]\varphi) = ([\alpha^+](M, g, w, \varphi^+), \langle\alpha^+\rangle(M, g, w, \varphi^-))$
- $(M, g, w \models \langle\alpha\rangle\varphi) = (\langle\alpha^+\rangle(M, g, w, \varphi^+), [\alpha^+](M, g, w, \varphi^-))$
- $(M, g, w \models [\![\alpha]\!]\varphi) = (\langle\alpha^-\rangle(M, g, w, \varphi^-), [\alpha^-](M, g, w, \varphi^+))$
- $(M, g, w \models \langle\!\langle\alpha\rangle\!\rangle\varphi) = ([\alpha^-](M, g, w, \varphi^-), \langle\alpha^-\rangle(M, g, w, \varphi^+))$
- $(M, g, w \models x) = (1, 0)$ iff $g(x) = w$
- $(M, g, w \models \downarrow x.\varphi) = (M, g[x \mapsto w], w \models \varphi)$
- $(M, g, w \models @_x\varphi) = (M, g, g(x) \models \varphi)$

where

- $[\alpha^+](M, g, w, \varphi^*) = \prod_{w' \in W}(\widehat{R}_\alpha^+(w, w') \rightharpoonup (M, g, w' \models \varphi)^*)$
- $[\alpha^-](M, g, w, \varphi^*) = \prod_{w' \in W}(\widehat{R}_\alpha^-(w, w') \rightharpoonup (M, g, w' \models \varphi)^*)$
- $\langle\alpha^+\rangle(M, g, w, \varphi^*) = \bigsqcup_{w' \in W}(\widehat{R}_\alpha^+(w, w') \sqcap (M, g, w' \models \varphi)^*)$
- $\langle\alpha^-\rangle(M, g, w, \varphi^*) = \bigsqcup_{w' \in W}(\widehat{R}_\alpha^-(w, w') \sqcap (M, g, w' \models \varphi)^*)$

- $\Delta_C = \{(a,b) \mid D((a,b),(0,0)) \leqslant D((a,b),(1,1))\}$

with $* \in \{^+,^-\}$, $\alpha \in Str(\text{Act})$ and $\bigsqcup$ and $\bigsqcap$ are the distribuited versions of $\sqcup$ and $\sqcap$, respectively.

Proposition 1. Let $\Sigma = \langle \text{Act}, \text{Prop} \rangle$ and $\Sigma' = \langle \text{Act}', \text{Prop}' \rangle$ be signatures and $\sigma : \Sigma \to \Sigma'$ be a signature morphism. For any $P' = (W', w_0', R', V') \in \text{Mod}(\Sigma')$ and $\varphi \in \text{Sen}(\Sigma)$,

$$(P'|_\sigma \models \varphi) = (P' \models \text{Sen}(\sigma)(\varphi)) \tag{4}$$

Proof. For any $w \in W$ $(P'|_\sigma, g, w \models \varphi) = (P', g, w \models \text{Sen}(\sigma)(\varphi))$. The proof of this statement is done by induction over the structure of sentences. Cases $\bot$ is trivial $(P'|_\sigma, g, w \models \bot) = (P', g, w \models \text{Sen}(\sigma)(\bot)) = (0,1)$ and for any $p \in \text{Prop}$, by the defn of σ-reduct, $V(w,p) = V'(w, \sigma_{\text{Prop}}(p))$ which is equal to $(P'|_\sigma, g, w \models p) = (P', g, w \models \text{Sen}(\sigma)(p))$. For Boolean connectives $\neg$, $\wedge$, $\vee$, $\to$ and $\circ$ the proof boils down to first using the defn of Sen, followed by the defn of $\models$, the induction hypothesis and finally the defn of $\models$ again. For more details regarding this part of the proof we refer to [5] where a similar proof is done. For $[\alpha]\,\varphi$ the proof is similiar to the other modal connectives.

$P', g, w \models \text{Sen}(\sigma)([\alpha]\,\varphi)$

$= \{\text{defn of Sen}\}$

$P', g, w \models [\hat{\sigma}(\alpha)]\,\text{Sen}(\sigma)(\varphi)$

$= \{\text{defn of} \models\}$

$([\hat{\sigma}(\alpha)^+](P', g, w, \text{Sen}(\sigma)(\varphi)^+), \langle\hat{\sigma}(\alpha)^+\rangle(P', g, w, \text{Sen}(\sigma)(\varphi)^-))$

$= \{\text{defn of } [\alpha^+] \text{ and } \langle\alpha^+\rangle\}$

$$\Big(\bigsqcap_{w' \in W'} (R'^+_{\hat{\sigma}(a)}(w, w') \to (P', g, w' \models \text{Sen}(\sigma)(\varphi))^+),$$

$$\bigsqcup_{w' \in W'} (R'^+_{\hat{\sigma}(a)}(w, w') \sqcap (P', g, w' \models \text{Sen}(\sigma)(\varphi))^-) \Big)$$

$= \{(\text{step } \star)\}$

$$\Big(\bigsqcap_{w' \in W} (R^+_\alpha(w, w') \to (P'|_\sigma, g, w \models \varphi)^+), \bigsqcup_{w' \in W} (R^+_\alpha(w, w') \sqcap (P'|_\sigma, g, w \models \varphi)^-) \Big)$$

$= \{\text{defn } [\alpha^+] \text{ and } \langle\alpha^+\rangle\}$

$([\alpha^+](P'|_\sigma, g, w, \varphi^+), \langle\alpha^+\rangle(P'|_\sigma, g, w, \varphi^-))$

$= \{\text{defn of} \models\}$

$P'|_\sigma, g, w \models [\alpha]\,\varphi$

(step $\star$) By the definition of reduct we have that $W = W'$ and for any $w, w' \in W$, $R'_{\hat{\sigma}(\alpha)}(w, w') = R_\alpha(w, w') = (\mathit{tt}, \mathit{ff})$. Also by the induction hypothesis, $(P', g, w \models \text{Sen}(\sigma)(\varphi)) = (P'|_\sigma, g, w \models \varphi)$, which is equivalent to writing:

$$\Big((P', g, w \models \text{Sen}(\sigma)(\varphi))^+, (P', g, w \models \text{Sen}(\sigma)(\varphi))^-\Big) =$$

$$= \Big((P'|_\sigma, g, w \models \varphi)^+, (P'|_\sigma, g, w \models \varphi)^-\Big) \tag{5}$$

Therefore $P', g, w \models \mathsf{Sen}(\sigma)(\varphi))^+ = (P'|_\sigma, g, w \models \varphi)^+$ and $(P', g, w \models \mathsf{Sen}(\sigma)(\varphi))^- = (P'|_\sigma, g, w \models \varphi)^-$.

For the case of state variables we have that $P', g, w \models \mathsf{Sen}(\sigma)(x)$ is either $(1, 0)$ or $(0, 1)$. We illustrate the proof is it is equal to $(1, 0)$ then, if $(P', g, w \models \mathsf{Sen}(\sigma)(x)) = (1, 0)$, by definition of Sen, we have $(P', g, w \models x) = (1, 0)$. Thus, by induction hypothesis, $(P'|_\sigma, g, w \models x) = (1, 0)$.

The case $M', g, w \models \mathsf{Sen}(\sigma)(\downarrow x.\varphi)$ using the defn of Sen and $\models$, $M', g[x \mapsto w], w \models \mathsf{Sen}(\sigma)(\varphi)$ by the induction hypothesis and defn of $\models$, $M'|_\sigma, g, w \models\downarrow x.\varphi$. Similarly, for $M', g, w \models \mathsf{Sen}(\sigma)(@_x.\varphi) = M', g, w \models @_x.\mathsf{Sen}(\sigma)(\varphi)$ using the defn of $\models$, $M', g, g(x) \models \mathsf{Sen}(\sigma)(\varphi)$ followed by using the induction hypothesis and defn of $\models$, $M'|_\sigma, g, w \models @_x\varphi$.

In conclusion we have proven for any $w \in W$, $(P'|_\sigma, g, w \models \varphi) = (P', g, w \models \mathsf{Sen}(\sigma)(\varphi))$ if w is replaced by w_0, $(M'|_\sigma \models \varphi) = (M' \models \mathsf{Sen}(\sigma)(\varphi))$.

The following theorem is a consequence of this subsection where all the ingredients of institution **P** are formalized in a categorical manner.

Theorem 1. $P(\mathcal{A}) = (\mathsf{Sign}_{P(\mathcal{A})}, \mathsf{Sen}_{P(\mathcal{A})}, \mathsf{Mod}_{P(\mathcal{A})}, \models_{P(\mathcal{A})})$ *is an institution, for any fixed twisted algebra* $\mathcal{A}$.

4 Formal Development Method *à la* Sannella and Tarlecki

Once set a suitable institution to reason about specifications of paraconsistent processes, we turn to the methodological level. Therefore, the notions of a *simple*, *constructor* and *abstract* implementation for paraconsistent specifications are presented below.

A paraconsistent specification consists of a pair $SP = (Sig(SP), Mod(SP))$ where $Sig(SP)$ is a signature in Sign and $Mod(SP) : \mathsf{Mod}(Sig(SP)) \to A \times A$ is a mapping that associates to any process $P \in \mathsf{Mod}(Sig(SP))$ a pair $(tt, ff) \in A \times A$ such that tt represents the evidence degree of P satisfying the requirements of SP and ff represents the evidence degree of P not satisfying the requirements of SP.

Definition 9. *A flat specification is a pair* $SP = (\Sigma, \Phi)$ *where* $\Sigma \in \mathsf{Sign}$ *is a signature and* $\Phi \subseteq \mathsf{Sen}(\Sigma)$ *is a set of axioms. Hence,* $Sig(SP) = \Sigma$ *and*

$$Mod(SP)(P) = \left(\prod_{\varphi \in \Phi} (P \models \varphi) \right).$$

Flat specifications, that consist of a signature and a set of axioms, are suitable to capture requirements that can be easily expressed by a set of axioms. A simple refinement of specifications is classically seen as a restriction of the class of models. For paraconsistent specifications refinement is defined as follows

Definition 10. *A paraconsistent specification* SP' *is said to simple refine, or implement, another paraconsistent specification* SP, *in symbols* $SP \rightsquigarrow SP'$, *if both are over the same signature and for all* $P \in \mathsf{Mod}(Sig(SP))$, $Mod(SP')(P) \leqslant Mod(SP)(P)$.

Transitivity of $\leqslant$ ensures that vertical composition of simple implementations is well defined, that is, if $SP \rightsquigarrow SP'$ and $SP' \rightsquigarrow SP''$ then $SP \rightsquigarrow SP''$.

The running example in this work is adapted from the examples documented in [12] of a file compressing service. It consists of a compressing service of text files whose information regarding inputs and outputs can admit contradictions, for example because some components of the service are malfunctioning or subject to malicious manipulation.

Example 1. Let $\ddot{G}$ be the underlying iMTL-algebra, that is weights are a real number in the interval $[0, 1]$. Consider the specification SP_0 over signature $\langle \{in, out\}, \varnothing \rangle$ where the set of propositions is empty and the set of actions is Act $= \{in, out\}$ with $\{in\}$ standing for the input of a text file and $\{out\}$ standing for the output of a zip-file. SP_0 is a very loose specification, whose only requirement is $\langle in \rangle \top \wedge [out] \bot$, i.e. at the beginning of a computation only an input action is allowed. Let $P_0 = (W, w_0, R, V)$ be the following process:

$$out | (0.7, 0.4)$$
$$\curvearrowleft$$
$$w_0 \rightleftharpoons in | (1, 1)$$

Notice that[1],

$$Mod(SP_0)(P_0)$$
$$= P_0 \models (\langle in \rangle \top \wedge [out] \bot)$$
$$= P_0, w_0 \models (\langle in \rangle \top \wedge [out] \bot)$$
$$= (P_0, w_0 \models \langle in \rangle \top) \sqcap (P_0, w_0 \models [out] \bot)$$
$$= (\langle in^+ \rangle (P_0, w_0, \top^+), [in^+](P_0, w_0, \top^-)) \sqcap$$
$$\quad ([out^+](P_0, w_0, \bot^+), \langle out^+ \rangle (P_0, w_0, \bot^-))$$
$$= \left(\min(R_{in}^+(w_0, w_0), (P_0, w_0 \models \top)^+), R_{in}^+(w_0, w_0) \rightarrow (P_0, w_0 \models \top)^- \right) \sqcap$$
$$\quad \left(R_{out}^+(w_0, w_0) \rightarrow (P_0, w_0 \models \bot)^+, \min(R_{out}^+(w_0, w_0), (P_0, w_0 \models \bot)^-) \right)$$
$$= (\min(1, 1), 1 \rightarrow 0) \sqcap (0.7 \rightarrow 0, \min(0.7, 1)) = (1, 0) \sqcap (0, 0.7)$$
$$= (\min(1, 0), \max(0, 0.7)) = (0, 0.7)$$

Since there is some evidence degree that the computation may start with an output action, P_0 has an evidence degree 0 of satisfying the requirements of SP_0 and an evidence degree 0.7 of not satisfying them. Notice that $Mod(SP_0)(P_0)^-$ is equal to the evidence degree of action out occurring, that is, $R_{out}^+(w_0, w_0)$.

If we now consider a more concrete specification SP_1 over the same signature, whose requirement is $\downarrow x_0.(\langle in \rangle \downarrow x_1(\langle out \rangle x_0 \wedge [in] \bot) \wedge [out] \bot)$, meaning that at the beginning only an input action is allowed, after every input the next action must be an output action, and after any output action the system must go on with an input returning to the initial state. Consider the following $P_1 = (W', w_0', R', V')$ process where all transitions represent consistent information except for $R_{out}(w_1', w_2')$ that conveys inconsistent information.

---

[1] Valuation g is omitted since $\langle in \rangle \top \wedge [out] \bot$ is a sentence without free variables.

$$w_0' \xrightarrow{\ in|(1,0)\ } w_1'$$

$$out|(1,0) \uparrow \qquad\qquad \downarrow out|(0.7, 0.4)$$

$$w_3' \xleftarrow{\ in|(1,0)\ } w_2'$$

The requirement of SP_0 is also a requirement of SP_1. Therefore, $SP_0 \rightsquigarrow SP_1$ and $Mod(SP_1)(P_0) = (0,1) \leqslant (0,0.7) = Mod(SP_0)(P_0)$ and $Mod(SP_1)(P_1) = (0,1) \leqslant (1,0) = Mod(SP_0)(P_1)$. As expected, $Mod(SP_1)(P_1) = (0,1)$ since in P_1 after an initial input action followed by an output action the initial state is not reached.

For one specification to implement another (i.e. $SP \rightsquigarrow SP'$) they both need to have the same signature. Such definition of implementation can be too strict since some practices in software development often require implementation decisions, such as introducing new features or reusing previously defined features, which entail the need to deal with different signatures along the development process. The notion of a function called *constructor* that transforms models into other models, possible with different signatures. In such cases *constructor implementations* are the tools to be used.

Given signatures $\Sigma_1, \ldots, \Sigma_n, \Sigma$, a constructor is a function $k : \mathsf{Mod}(\Sigma_1) \times \cdots \times \mathsf{Mod}(\Sigma_n) \to \mathsf{Mod}(\Sigma)$. For a constructor k and a set of constructors $k_i : \mathsf{Mod}(\Sigma_i^1) \times \cdots \times \mathsf{Mod}(\Sigma_i^{k_i}) \to \mathsf{Mod}(\Sigma_i)$ for $1 \leqslant i \leqslant n$, the constructor, $k(k_1, \ldots, k_n) : \mathsf{Mod}(\Sigma_1^1) \times \ldots \times \mathsf{Mod}(\Sigma_1^{k_1}) \times \ldots \times \mathsf{Mod}(\Sigma_n^1) \times \ldots \times \mathsf{Mod}(\Sigma_n^{k_n}) \to \mathsf{Mod}(\Sigma)$ is obtained by the usual composition of functions.

Definition 11. *Let $SP, SP_1, \ldots, SP_n$ be paraconsistent specifications over signatures $\Sigma, \Sigma_1, \ldots, \Sigma_n$, respectively, and $k : \mathsf{Mod}(\Sigma_1) \times \cdots \times \mathsf{Mod}(\Sigma_n) \to \mathsf{Mod}(\Sigma)$ a constructor. We say that $(SP_1, \ldots, SP_n)$ is a constructor implementation via k of SP, in symbols $SP \rightsquigarrow_k (SP_1, \ldots, SP_n)$ if for any $P_i \in \mathsf{Mod}(\Sigma_i)$*

$$\bigsqcap_{i=1}^{n} Mod(SP_i)(P_i) \leqslant Mod(SP)(k(P_1, \ldots, P_n))$$

The implementation is said to involve decomposition if $n > 1$.

We illustrate the concept of a constructor by redefining the constructors documented in reference [12] to suit our paraconsistent logic.

Definition 12. *Let $\Sigma = \langle \mathrm{Act}, \mathrm{Prop} \rangle$ and $\Sigma' = \langle \mathrm{Act}', \mathrm{Prop}' \rangle$ be signatures such that $\mathrm{Prop} \subseteq \mathrm{Prop}'$ and $\mathrm{Act} \subseteq \mathrm{Act}'$. The signature extension constructor is $k_{ext} : \mathsf{Mod}(\Sigma) \to \mathsf{Mod}(\Sigma')$. Let $P = (W, w_0, R, V)$ be a process. Then, $k_{ext}(P) = (W, w_0, R', V')$ with*

$$- \ R_a'[w] = \begin{cases} R_a[w] & \text{if } a \in \mathrm{Act} \\ \{(w, w', 0, 1) \text{ for all } w' \in W\} & \text{otherwise} \end{cases}$$

$$- V'(w,p) = \begin{cases} V(w,p) & \text{if } p \in \text{Prop} \\ (0,1) & \text{otherwise} \end{cases}$$

Definition 13. *Let $\Sigma_1 = \langle \text{Act}, \text{Prop} \rangle$ and $\Sigma_2 = \langle \text{Act}', \text{Prop}' \rangle$ be signatures. The parallel composition constructor is $k_\otimes : \text{Mod}(\Sigma_1) \times \text{Mod}(\Sigma_2) \to \text{Mod}(\Sigma^\otimes)$ where $\Sigma^\otimes = \langle \text{Act} \cup \text{Act}', \text{Prop} \cup \text{Prop}' \rangle$. The parallel composition of $P = (W, w_0, R, V)$ and $P' = (W', w'_0, R', V')$ is $P \otimes P' = (W^\otimes, (w_0, w'_0), R^\otimes, V^\otimes)$ with*

- *$W^\otimes = W \times W'$*
- *for any $(w, w') \in W^\otimes$*
    - *if $a \in \text{Act} \cap \text{Act}'$, $R_a(w, v) = (\alpha, \beta)$ and $R'_a(w', v') = (\alpha', \beta')$, then $(v, v') \in W^\otimes$ and $R_a^\otimes((w, w'), (v, v')) = (\alpha \sqcap \alpha', \beta \sqcup \beta')$*
    - *if $a \in \text{Act} \setminus \text{Act}'$, $R_a(w, v) = (\alpha, \beta)$, then $(v, w') \in W^\otimes$ and $R_a^\otimes((w, w'), (v, w')) = (\alpha, \beta)$*
    - *if $a \in \text{Act}' \setminus \text{Act}$, $R'_a(w', v') = (\alpha', \beta')$, then $(w, v') \in W^\otimes$ and $R_a^\otimes((w, w'), (w, v')) = (\alpha', \beta')$*
- *for any $(w, w') \in W^\otimes$*
    - *if $p \in \text{Prop} \cap \text{Prop}'$, $V^\otimes((w, w'), p) = V(w, p) \sqcap V'(w', p)$*
    - *if $p \in \text{Prop} \setminus \text{Prop}'$, $V^\otimes((w, w'), p) = V(w, p)$*
    - *if $p \in \text{Prop}' \setminus \text{Prop}$, $V^\otimes((w, w'), p) = V'(w', p)$*

Example 2. A specification interface for SP_1 is now built from two components. One is $Ctrl$ with actions $\text{Act}_{Ctrl} = \{in, txt, zip, out\}$. It receives an input, action in, from the user, to be given with action txt to the other component $GZip$, and receives a zip-file, action zip, that is returned with action out. This behaviour is specified by

$$\downarrow x_0.(\langle in \rangle \downarrow x_1.(\langle txt \rangle \downarrow x_2.(\langle zip \rangle \downarrow x_3.(\langle out \rangle x_0 \wedge [-out]\bot)$$
$$\wedge [-zip]\bot) \wedge [-txt]\bot) \wedge [-in]\bot)$$

The other component is $GZip$ with actions $\text{Act}_{GZip} = \{txt, comp, zip\}$. First it receives action txt from $Ctrl$, then with action $comp$ compresses it, and finally delivers a zip-file with action zip. This behaviour is specified as

$$\downarrow x_0.(\langle txt \rangle \downarrow x_1.(\langle comp \rangle \downarrow x_2.(\langle zip \rangle x_0 \wedge [-zip]\bot) \wedge [-comp]\bot) \wedge [-txt]\bot)$$

Let P and P' be models of $Ctrl$ and $GZip$, respectively.

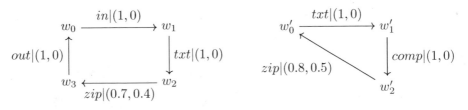

The parallel composition of process P and P' is the process $P \otimes P'$:

$$(w_0, w_0') \xrightarrow{in|(1,0)} (w_1, w_0') \xrightarrow{txt|(1,0)} (w_2, w_1')$$

$$out|(1,0)$$

$$comp|(1,0)$$

$$(w_3, w_0') \xleftarrow{zip|(0.7,0.5)} (w_2, w_2')$$

The models of specification $Ctrl \otimes GZip$, by the definition of $\otimes$, consist of all the possible parallel compositions of the models of $Ctrl$ and $GZip$. Therefore, $Ctrl \otimes GZip \rightsquigarrow_{k_\otimes} (Ctrl, GZip)$ is a constructor implementation with decomposition, with the requirements of $Ctrl \otimes GZip$ being similar to the previous ones. Thus,

$$Mod(Ctrl)(P) \sqcap Mod(GZip)(P') = (0.7, 0) \sqcap (0.8, 0) = (0.7, 0)$$
$$= Mod(Ctrl \otimes GZip)(P \otimes P')$$

Definition 14. *A signature morphism* $\sigma : \Sigma \rightarrow \Sigma'$ *between signatures* $\Sigma = \langle \text{Act}, \text{Prop} \rangle$ *and* $\Sigma' = \langle \text{Act}', \text{Prop}' \rangle$ *defines a constructor* $k_\sigma : \text{Mod}(\Sigma') \rightarrow \text{Mod}(\Sigma)$ *that maps any* $P' \in \text{Mod}(\Sigma')$ *to its reduct* $k_\sigma(P') = P'|_\sigma$.

If σ is bijective then k_σ is a relabelling constructor; if σ is injective then k_σ is a restriction constructor.

Definition 15. *Let* $\Sigma = \langle \text{Act}, \text{Prop} \rangle$, $\Sigma' = \langle \text{Act}', \text{Prop}' \rangle$ *be signatures and* $\Sigma_D' = \langle D, \text{Prop}' \rangle$ *also be a signature such that* $D \subseteq Str(\text{Act}')$ *is a finite subset and* $f : \Sigma \rightarrow \Sigma_D'$ *is a signature morphism. Then, the action refinement constructor* $k_f : \text{Mod}(\Sigma_D') \rightarrow \text{Mod}(\Sigma)$ *maps any* $P' \in \text{Mod}(\Sigma_D')$ *to its reduct* $\text{Mod}(f)(P')$.

Example 3. Let us define an action signature morphism $f : \{in, out\} \rightarrow Str(\text{Act}_{Ctrl} \cup \text{Act}_{GZip})$ with $f(in) = in; txt; comp$ and $f(out) = zip; out$. The following process $P = (W, w_0, R, V)$ is the f-reduct of $P \otimes P'$, with $R_{out}(w_1'', w_0'') = R_{zip;out}^{\otimes}((w_2, w_2'), (w_0, w_0'))$

$$in|(1,0)$$
$$w_0'' \xleftrightarrow{\quad\quad} w_1''$$
$$out|(0.7, 0.5)$$

We are now able to define an action refinement step $SP_1 \rightsquigarrow_{|_f} Ctrl \otimes GZip$. Notice that, $Mod(Ctrl \otimes GZip)(P \otimes P') = (0.7, 0) = Mod(SP_1)((P \otimes P')|_f)$. Thus, we are now able to define a refinement chain: $SP_0 \rightsquigarrow SP_1 \rightsquigarrow_{|_f} Ctrl \otimes GZip \rightsquigarrow_{k_\otimes} (Ctrl \otimes GZip)$. That can be written as $SP_0 \rightsquigarrow SP_1 \rightsquigarrow_{|_f \circ k_\otimes} (Ctrl, GZip)$.

Often in software development some model does not satisfy exactly the requirements of a specification because of certain implementation details. In this situations a model may still satisfy them abstractly if it exhibits the desired observable behaviour. Abstractor implementations aim at defining what precisely it means for two models to be identical from an observational perspective. This will be expressed by the use of an equivalence relation $\equiv$ between models, which, as one might expect, comes from a suitable notion of bisimulation between paraconsistent processes. Next definition generalises the bisimulation notion introduced in [3] to multi-modalities:

Definition 16. *Let* $\Sigma = \langle \text{Act}, \text{Prop} \rangle$ *be a signature and* $P = (W, w_0, R, V)$, $P' = (W', w_0', R', V')$ *be* Σ-*processes. A relation* $B \subseteq W \times W'$ *is a* bisimulation *between* P *and* P' *if for any* $(w, w') \in B$:

> **(Atom)** *for any* $p \in \text{Prop}$, $V(w, p) = V'(w', p)$
> **(Zig)** *for any* $v \in W$ *such that* $R_a(w, v) = (\alpha, \beta)$, *there is* $v' \in W'$ *such that* $R_a'(w', v') = (\alpha, \beta)$ *and* $(v, v') \in B$
> **(Zag)** *for any* $v' \in W'$ *such that* $R_a'(w', v') = (\alpha, \beta)$, *there is* $v \in W$ *such that* $R_a(w, v) = (\alpha, \beta)$ *and* $(v, v') \in B$

If there is a bisimulation B such that $(w, w') \in B$ for some $w \in W$, $w' \in W'$, we say that w and w' are bisimilar states and write $w \sim w'$. Given two paraconsistent processes $P = (W, w_0, R, V)$ and $P' = (W', w_0', R', V')$ over the same signature, we say that P and P' are *behaviourally equivalent*, in symbols $P \equiv P'$, if and only if $w_0 \sim w_0'$. Clearly, $\equiv$ is an equivalence relation.

Let SP be a paraconsistent specification over Σ then, $Mod(\textbf{abstractor } SP)$ is the closure of $Mod(SP)$ under $\equiv$. Thus,

$$Mod(\textbf{abstractor } SP)(M) = \bigsqcup_{N \in [M]_\equiv} Mod(SP)(N)$$

where $[M]_\equiv = \{N \in \text{Mod}(\Sigma) \mid N \equiv M\}$.

Definition 17. *Let* SP, SP' *be paraconsistent specifications over* Σ *and* $\equiv \subseteq Mod(\Sigma) \times Mod(\Sigma)$. *We write* $SP \leadsto^\equiv SP'$ *when* SP' *is a* simple abstractor implementation *of* SP, *that is, for any* $M \in \text{Mod}(\Sigma)$

$$Mod(SP')(M) \leqslant Mod(\textbf{abstractor } SP)(M)$$

The next definition combines abstractor implementation with constructor for paraconsistent specifications, generalizing [12, Definition 5].

Definition 18. *Let* $SP, SP_1, \dots, SP_n$ *be paraconsistent specifications over signatures* $\Sigma, \Sigma_1, \dots, \Sigma_n$, *respectively,* $k : \text{Mod}(\Sigma_1) \times \cdots \times \text{Mod}(\Sigma_n) \to \text{Mod}(\Sigma)$ *a constructor and* $\equiv \subseteq \text{Mod}(\Sigma) \times \text{Mod}(\Sigma)$ *an equivalence relation. We say that* $(SP_1, \dots, SP_n)$ *is an* abstractor implementation *of* SP, *in symbols* $SP \leadsto_k^\equiv (SP_1, \dots, SP_n)$ *if for any* $P_i \in \text{Mod}(\Sigma_i)$,

$$\prod_{i=1}^{n} Mod(SP_i)(P_i) \leqslant Mod(\textbf{abstractor } SP)(k(P_1, \dots, P_n))$$

Let k : $\mathsf{Mod}(\varSigma_1) \times \cdots \times \mathsf{Mod}(\varSigma_n) \rightarrow \mathsf{Mod}(\varSigma)$ be a constructor and, for each $1 \leqslant i \leqslant n$, $\equiv_i$ an equivalence relation between $\varSigma_i$-models and $\equiv$ an equivalence relation between $\varSigma$-models. We say that a constructor k *preserves abstractions* $\equiv_i$ if for any $M_i, N_i \in \mathsf{Mod}(\varSigma_i)$ such that $M_i \equiv_i N_i$, $k(M_1, .., M_n) \equiv k(N_1, \ldots, N_n)$.

Proposition 2. *The alphabet extension, parallel composition, reduct and action refinement constructors perverse behavioural equivalences, that is,*

- *for any $P \equiv P'$, $k_{ext}(P) \equiv k_{ext}(P')$*
- *for any $P_1 \equiv P_1'$ and $P_2 \equiv P_2'$, $P_1 \otimes P_2 \equiv P_1' \otimes P_2'$*
- *let $\sigma : \varSigma \rightarrow \varSigma'$ be a signature morphism. For any $P, P' \in \mathsf{Mod}(\varSigma')$, if $P \equiv P'$ then $P|_\sigma \equiv P'|_\sigma$*
- *let $\varSigma, \varSigma'$ be signatures. Consider the subset $D \subseteq Str(\mathrm{Act}')$ and signature $\varSigma_D = \langle D, \mathrm{Prop}' \rangle$ and let $f : \varSigma \rightarrow \varSigma_D$ be a signature morphism. For any $P, P' \in \mathsf{Mod}(\varSigma_D)$, if $P \equiv P'$ then $P|_f \equiv P'|_f$*

The proof of Proposition 2 is omitted since it is similar to the ones found in [12] for Theorems 4, 5 and 6. Analogously to [12, Theorem 3], next theorem states vertical composition for constructors and abstractor implementations:

Theorem 2. *Consider specifications $SP, SP_1, \ldots, SP_n$ over signatures $\varSigma, \varSigma_1, \ldots, \varSigma_n$ respectively, a constructor k : $\mathsf{Mod}(\varSigma_1) \times \cdots \times \mathsf{Mod}(\varSigma_n) \rightarrow \mathsf{Mod}(\varSigma)$ and an equivalence relation $\equiv \subseteq \mathsf{Mod}(\varSigma) \times \mathsf{Mod}(\varSigma)$ such that $SP \rightsquigarrow_k^{\equiv} (SP_1, \ldots, SP_n)$. For each $i \in \{1, \ldots, n\}$ let $SP_i \rightsquigarrow_{k_i}^{\equiv_i} (SP_i^1, \ldots, SP_i^{r_i})$ with specifications $SP_i^1, \ldots, SP_i^{r_i}$ over signatures $\varSigma_i^1, \ldots, \varSigma_i^{r_i}$ respectively, constructors k_i : $\mathsf{Mod}(\varSigma_i^1) \times \cdots \times \mathsf{Mod}(\varSigma_i^{r_i}) \rightarrow \mathsf{Mod}(\varSigma_i)$ and equivalence relations $\equiv_i \subseteq \mathsf{Mod}(\varSigma_i) \times \mathsf{Mod}(\varSigma_i)$. Suppose that k preserves the abstractions $\equiv_i$. Then,*

$$SP \rightsquigarrow_{k(k_1,\ldots,k_n)}^{\equiv} (SP_1^1, \ldots, SP_1^{r_1}, \ldots, SP_n^1, \ldots, SP_n^{r_n})$$

With $k(k_1, \ldots, k_n)$: $\mathsf{Mod}(\varSigma_1^1) \times \cdots \times \mathsf{Mod}(\varSigma_1^{r_1}) \times \cdots \times \mathsf{Mod}(\varSigma_n^1) \times \cdots \times \mathsf{Mod}(\varSigma_n^{r_n}) \rightarrow \mathsf{Mod}(\varSigma)$ being a constructor defined by the composition of constructors k_i and k.

Proof. For each $1 \leqslant i \leqslant n$ and for all $1 \leqslant j \leqslant r_i$, let $M_i^j \in \mathsf{Mod}(\varSigma_i^j)$. For each i, by hypothesis, $SP_i \rightsquigarrow_{k_i}^{\equiv_i} (SP_i^1, \ldots, SP_i^{r_i})$,

$$\overset{r_i}{\underset{j=1}{\sqcap}} Mod(SP_i^j)(M_i^j) \leqslant Mod(\textbf{abstractor } SP_i \textbf{ w.r.t } \equiv_i)(k_i(M_i^1, \ldots, M_i^{r_i}))$$

$$= \underset{N_i \in [k_i(M_i^1, \ldots, M_i^{r_i})]_{\equiv_i}}{\sqcup} Mod(SP_i)(N_i)$$

For each i, let M_i be a $\varSigma_i$-model such that

$$\overset{r_i}{\underset{j=1}{\sqcap}} Mod(SP_i^j)(M_i^j) \leqslant Mod(\textbf{abstractor } SP_i \textbf{ w.r.t } \equiv_i)(k_i(M_i^1, \ldots, M_i^{r_i}))$$

$$= Mod(SP_i)(M_i) \tag{6}$$

By definition of M_i, we have that $M_i \in [k_i(M_i^1, \ldots, M_i^{r_i})]_{\equiv_i}$, that is, $M_i \equiv_i k_i(M_i^1, \ldots, M_i^{r_i})$. Since k preserves abstraction $\equiv_i$,

$$k(M_1, \ldots, M_n) \equiv k(k_1, \ldots, k_n)(M_1^1, \ldots, M_1^{r_1}, \ldots, M_n^1, \ldots, M_n^{r_n}) \tag{7}$$

By hypothesis, $SP \rightsquigarrow_k^{\equiv} (SP_1, \ldots, SP_n)$,

$$\prod_{i=1}^{n} Mod(SP_i)(M_i) \leqslant Mod(\textbf{abstractor } SP \textbf{ w.r.t } \equiv)(k(M_1, \ldots, M_n))$$
$$= \bigsqcup_{N \in [k(M_1, \ldots, M_n)]_{\equiv}} Mod(SP)(N) \tag{8}$$

By Eq. 7, we have that:

$$k(k_1, \ldots, k_n)(M_1^1, \ldots, M_1^{r_1}, \ldots, M_n^1, \ldots, M_n^{r_n}) \in [k(M_1, \ldots, M_n)]_{\equiv} \tag{9}$$

Since $\equiv$ is transitive, in Eq. 8, $[k(M_1, \ldots, M_n)]_{\equiv}$ can be replaced with $[k(k_1, \ldots, k_n)(M_1^1, \ldots, M_1^{r_1}, \ldots, M_n^1, \ldots, M_n^{r_n})]_{\equiv}$. Considering Eq. 6, we know that for each i,

$$\prod_{j=1}^{r_i} Mod(SP_i^j)(M_i^j) \leqslant Mod(SP_i)(M_i)$$

Since $\prod$ is monotone,

$$\prod_{i=1}^{n} \prod_{j=1}^{r_i} Mod(SP_i^j)(M_i^j) \leqslant \prod_{i=1}^{n} Mod(SP_i)(M_i) \tag{10}$$

With (9) and Eq. 10 we can rewrite Eq. 8 as:

$$\prod_{i=1}^{n} \prod_{j=1}^{r_i} Mod(SP_i^j)(M_i^j) \leqslant$$
$$Mod(\textbf{abst. } SP \textbf{ w.r.t } \equiv)(k(k_1, \ldots, k_n)(M_1^1, \ldots, M_1^{r_1}, \ldots, M_n^1, \ldots, M_n^{r_n}))$$

Thus, $SP \rightsquigarrow (SP_1^1 \ldots SP_1^{r_1}, \ldots, SP_n^1, \ldots, SP_n^{r_n})$.

5   Conclusions

This paper is part of on-going research agenda on the (pragmatical) use of paraconsistency in a discipline of software design. Building on previous contributions [3,5] detailed in the Introduction, we define *i)* an institution to frame modelling and reasoning about paraconsistent processes, and *ii)* develop a formal, step-wise development method *à la* Sannella and Tarlecki for this sort of systems. In particular constructor and abstractor implementations were addressed in detail.

There are, of course, several directions for future work. One certainly worth to be explored consists in framing the logics discussed here under the paradigm of asymmetric combination of logics, where the features of a specific logic are developed on top of another one (see e.g. [14]). More precisely, we intend to introduce a systematic way to build paraconsistent modal logics on top of a (base) logic, used to represent the state space. This can be done along the lines of the so-called temporalization [8], and hybridisation of logics [13] processes. A detailed discussion of our method with respect to the approach introduced by Costa [6] to convert classic into paraconsistent logics is also in order.

References

1. Agustí-Cullell, J., Esteva, F., Garcia, P., Godo, L.: Formalizing multiple-valued logics as institutions. In: Bouchon-Meunier, B., Yager, R.R., Zadeh, L.A. (eds.) IPMU 1990. LNCS, vol. 521, pp. 269–278. Springer, Heidelberg (1991). https://doi.org/10.1007/BFb0028112
2. Brauner, T.: Hybrid Logic and its Proof-Theory. Springer, Applied Logic Series (2010)
3. Cruz, A., Madeira, A., Barbosa, L.S.: A logic for paraconsistent transition systems. In: Indrzejczak, A., Zawidzki, M., (eds.) 10th International Conference on Non-Classical Logics. Theory and Applications, vol. 358. EPTCS, pp. 270–284 (2022)
4. Cruz, A., Madeira, A., Barbosa, L.S.: Paraconsistent transition systems. In: Workshop on Logical and Semantic Frameworks, with Applications, EPTCS (in print)
5. Cunha, J., Madeira, A., Barbosa, L.S.: Structured specification of paraconsistent transition systems. In: Fundamentals of Software Engineering. LNCS (in print)
6. de Souza, E.G., Costa-Leite, A., Dias, D.H.B.: On a paraconsistentization functor in the category of consequence structures. J. Appli. Non-Class. Logi. **26**(3), 240–250 (2016)
7. Esteva, F., Godo, L.: Monoidal t-norm based logic: Towards a logic for left-continuous t-norms. Fuzzy Sets Syst. **124**, 271–288 (2001)
8. Finger, M., Gabbay, D.M.: Adding a temporal dimension to a logic system. J. Logic Lang. Inform. **1**(3), 203–233 (1992)
9. Goguen, J.A., Burstall, R.M.: Institutions: Abstract model theory for tpecification and programming. J. ACM **39**(1), 95–146 (1992)
10. Harel, D., Tiuryn, J., Kozen, D.: Dynamic Logic. MIT Press, Cambridge, MA, USA (2000)
11. Kracht, M.: On extensions of intermediate logics by strong negation. J. Philos. Log. **27**(1), 49–73 (1998)
12. Madeira, A., Barbosa, L.S., Hennicker, R., Martins, M.A.: A logic for the stepwise development of reactive systems. Theor. Comput. Sci. **744**, 78–96 (2018)
13. Martins, M.A., Madeira, A., Diaconescu, R., Barbosa, L.S.: Hybridization of institutions. In: Corradini, A., Klin, B., Cîrstea, C. (eds.) CALCO 2011. LNCS, vol. 6859, pp. 283–297. Springer, Heidelberg (2011). https://doi.org/10.1007/978-3-642-22944-2_20
14. Neves, R., Madeira, A., Barbosa, L.S., Martins, M.A.: Asymmetric combination of logics is functorial: a survey. In: James, P., Roggenbach, M. (eds.) WADT 2016. LNCS, vol. 10644, pp. 39–55. Springer, Cham (2017). https://doi.org/10.1007/978-3-319-72044-9_4
15. Sannella, D., Tarlecki, A.: Foundations of Algebraic Specification and Formal Software Development. Monographs on TCS, EATCS. Springer, Heidelberg (2012). https://doi.org/10.1007/978-3-642-17336-3

Detecting API-Misuse Based on Pattern Mining via API Usage Graph with Parameters

Yulin Wu[1], Zhiwu Xu[1(✉)], and Shengchao Qin[2]

[1] College of Computer Science and Software Engineering, Shenzhen University, Shenzhen, China
xuzhiwu@szu.edu.cn

[2] School of Computer Science and Technology, Xidian University, Xian, China

Abstract. API misuse is a common issue that can trigger software crashes, bugs, and vulnerabilities. To address this problem, researchers have proposed pattern-based violation detectors that automatically extract patterns from code. However, these detectors have demonstrated low precision in detecting API misuses. In this paper, we propose a novel API misuse detector. Our proposed detector initially extracts API usages from the code and represents them as API Usage Graphs with Parameters (AUGPs). Utilizing the association rule algorithm, it then mines the binary rules, which are subsequently employed to detect the possible violations. The experimental results show that, comparing against five state-of-the-art detectors on the public dataset MuBench, our detector achieves the highest precision (1x more precise than the second-best one) and the highest F1-score (50% higher than the second-best one).

Keywords: API-Misuse Detection · API Pattern · Static Analysis

1 Introduction

Modern software development relies heavily on Application Programming Interfaces (APIs) that enable developers to expedite project development. However, APIs often have usage limitations, such as call ordering and conditions. For instance, in Java cryptography APIs, cipher objects must be initialized by using the API *init()* before invoking the API *doFinal()* for encryption. Deviation from API usage restrictions are referred to as API misuses. Unfortunately, API misuses are prevalent in software development, and may yield software crashes, bugs, and vulnerabilities. Zhang et al. [25] conducted a thorough analysis of $217k$ Stack Overflow posts, revealing potential API misuses in 31% of them.

To address this problem, researchers have proposed pattern-based violation detectors. CrySL [10], for instance, is a API misuse detector relying on hand-crafted patterns. However, it poses a challenge for users to manually draft API usage patterns. Moreover, utilizing these patterns for detection frequently renders an excessive amount of false positives (incorrect patterns) or false negatives

© The Author(s), under exclusive license to Springer Nature Switzerland AG 2023
C. David and M. Sun (Eds.): TASE 2023, LNCS 13931, pp. 344–363, 2023.
https://doi.org/10.1007/978-3-031-35257-7_21

(incomplete patterns) [11]. Therefore, automated detectors [2,15,19,22,23] are proposed, where patterns are first extracted from the code and then utilized to detect violations. Nevertheless, these detectors currently demonstrate a high rate of false positives. Thus, more effective detectors are required.

In this paper, we propose a novel approach to detect API misuses. Specifically, we utilize data flow analysis to extract API usages from code and represent them as our proposed graph model called API usage graph with parameters (AUGP). To enrich the API usages, we also perform the inter-procedural analysis to capture the relevant APIs that are encapsulated in some functions from the client code, which are referred to as *client functions* in this paper. Then we use the association rule algorithm FP-growth to mine the binary relationships between APIs, yielding API usage rules. Guided by these usage rules, we propose the violation detection and the order detection to detect API misuses. Finally, we also provide a scoring mechanism to filter and rank the reported violations.

We have implemented our approach as a tool APDetect, based on WALA. To evaluate APDetect, we conducted experiments on the publicly available dataset MuBench [1] as well as to compare against five state-of-the-art detectors. The results show that APDetect achieves the highest precision rate 56.00% (31.5% larger than the second-best one) and the highest F1-score 0.54 (0.18 larger than the second-best one) on the 10 projects selected for manual analysis. Further-more, APDetect reports the fewest number 102 of violations (114 fewer than the second-fewest one and 20276 fewer than the most one) on all the 31 projects. These findings demonstrate that our approach is highly effective and outperforms several existing detectors.

The remainder of this paper is organized as follows. Section 2 introduces some preliminaries. Section 3 describes our approach, followed by the experi-mental results in Sect. 4. Section 5 presents the related work, followed by some concluding remarks in Sect. 6.

2 Preliminaries

In this section, we present data flow analysis and association rule learning used in the paper.

2.1 Data Flow Analysis

Data flow analysis is an analysis technique used to capture the flow of relevant data along a program. A classic way for data flow analysis, given in Algorithm 1, is to generate data flow equations for the nodes of a Control Flow Graph (CFG) and then solve them by iterative computation until the fixed point is reached. In this paper, we use reachable definitions to trace the data flow of relevant data.

2.2 Association Rule Learning

Let $I = \{i_1, i_2, ..., i_m\}$ be a non-empty set of items and $D = \{t_1, t_2, ...t_n\}$ be a non-empty set of transactions, where a transaction t is a non-empty subset of I, that is, $t \subseteq I$. An association rule [7] is an implication of the form $X \to Y$, where $\emptyset \subset X, Y \subseteq I$, $X \cap Y = \emptyset$, and X and Y are called the antecedent (or left-hand-side, LHS) and consequent (or right-hand-side, RHS) of the association rule, respectively. The support of the association rule $X \to Y$ in D is the percentage of transactions in D that contain both X and Y (i.e., the probability $P(X \cup Y | D)$), and the confidence is the percentage of transactions that contain both X and Y in the ones that contain X (i.e., the conditional probability $P(Y|X)$). An association rule is considered favorable or useful if both the minimum support threshold and the minimum confidence threshold are satisfied.

Association rule learning (ARL) is a machine learning technique to discover interesting relationships between variables in large databases. It aims to identify strong association rules found in a database using some interesting measures. In this paper, we use the association rule algorithm FP-growth [8] to mine the relationships between APIs.

Algorithm 1: Data flow analysis

Input: CFG
Output: INPUT[B] and OUTPUT[B] for each basic block B in CFG

1 **for** *basic block B in CFG* **do**
2 | OUTPUT[B] $\leftarrow \emptyset$;
3 **end**
4 **while** *OUTPUT has any changes* **do**
5 | **for** *basic block B in CFG* **do**
6 | | INPUT[B] $= \bigcup_P OUTPUT[P]$ // P is a predecessor of B
7 | | OUTPUT[B] $= gen_B \cup (INPUT[B] - kill_B)$ // gen_B and $kill_B$
   | | denotes the variable sets generated or killed by B,
   | | respectively
8 | **end**
9 **end**

---

3   Methodology

Fig. 1. Framework of Our Approach

In this section, we will present our approach to detect API misuses. Figure 1 shows the framework of our approach, which consists of three steps: AUGP extraction, pattern mining, violation detection.

3.1   AUGP Model

Graph-based Object Usage Models (GROUM) [19] and API Usage Graphs (AUG) [2] are graph models commonly used to represent API usages. However, both models are generated based on individual functions, which may result in irrelevant information or lack of critical information, undermining the effectiveness of pattern mining and violation detection. To address this issue, we propose a new graph model, called API Usage Graphs with Parameters (AUGP). AUGP focuses specifically on the APIs of interest (referred to as target APIs in this paper), their associated parameters, and the data relations between them. This enables us to effectively capture relevant APIs by filtering out irrelevant information to achieve better performance in pattern mining and violation detection.

AUGP are directed graphs with labels. Nodes in AUGP are classified into two types: instruction nodes and data nodes. Instruction nodes are used to represent the IR instructions of WALA as well as some generated PHI nodes during the construction of AUGP. According to the instruction kinds of WALA, instruction nodes can be further classified into method call nodes, field access nodes, PHI nodes, and so on. Data nodes, on the other hand, represent parameters, variables or input/output data used in the IR instructions. Adding data nodes to AUGP ensures the logical integrity of the API usages and facilitates the inter-procedural construction.

Edges in AUGP are classified into two types: use edges and parameter edges. Use edges are used to capture the arguments used by an instruction node. An instruction may have several arguments, which will been marked by different numbers starting from 1, indicating their different orders (i.e., positions). In particular, we use *object* to denote the object of the function (i.e., functions that require a special argument *self*) if the instruction is a function call. Parameter edges are generated to connect graphs of functions during the inter-procedural construction. Likewise, numbers are marked for different parameters.

3.2   AUGP Extraction

The key idea to construct AUGP for target APIs is to trace the data flow for each non-trivial parameters of the APIs, which are non-constant and whose types are non-primitive, such as user-defined classes.

Given a (Java) project and some target APIs (such as from a library), prior to constructing AUGPs, we build a API location tree to record the client functions in the project that invoke at least one of the target APIs and their invoking orders of APIs. The API location tree allows a quick and efficient check to determine the presence of a client function invoking a target API or another API usage after some AUGPs have been extracted.

Listing 1.1. Java encryption code examples

```
 1  public byte[] encrypt(String content, String slatKey, String vectorKey)
        throws Exception {
 2    Cipher cipher = Cipher.getInstance("AES/CBC/PKCS5Padding");
 3    initWithAES(cipher, slatKey, vectorKey);
 4    byte[] encrypted = cipher.doFinal(content.getBytes());
 5    return encrypted;
 6  }
 7
 8  public void initWithAES(Cipher cipher, String slatKey, String vectorKey)
 9        throws InvalidKeyException, InvalidAlgorithmParameterException {
10    SecretKey secretKey = new SecretKeySpec(slatKey.getBytes(), "AES");
11    IvParameterSpec iv = new IvParameterSpec(vectorKey.getBytes());
12    cipher.init(Cipher.ENCRYPT_MODE, secretKey, iv);
13  }
```

To build the API location tree, we just simply perform a text search on the given project function by function and line by line. We also consider the inter-procedural analysis, as some programmers may wrap APIs with inter-procedural as a client function of their projects. For example, as shown in Listing 1.1, the initialization of cipher with AES is encapsulated as the client function *initWith-AES*. And to avoid the recursive functions as well as too much information leading to the interference, we limit the depth of the function call. The location tree is easily extended to support inter-procedural analysis: to mark each API with its depth and order. Take the code in Listing 1.1 for example. Assume 'javax.crypto' is the target library (all its APIs are of interesting). The API location tree starting from the function *encrypt* (with depth 2) is shown in Fig. 2, where the numbers in the blue circles and in the red circles respectively denote the depths and the orders of the corresponding APIs (and functions).

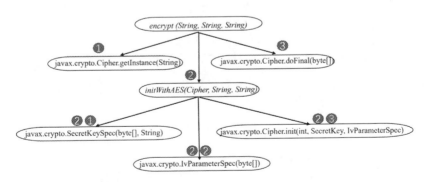

Fig. 2. API Location Tree Starting from Function *encrypt*

Then we construct AUGPs for each non-empty API location tree starting a function in the given project. Different from GROUM and AUG, we focus on the data flows between the target APIs. So we perform data flow analysis on the corresponding functions, guided by the API location tree. The algorithm for our AUGP construction is given in Algorithm 2, which takes an API location tree T as input, and returns a set of AUGPs GS.

Generally, the rightmost leaf of an API location tree starting from function f is the last target API called by the function f. From this API, we are more likely to be able to extract the possibly full usage of the target APIs. So we start with an empty graph G (line 3) and the rightmost (unvisited) leaf of the given location tree (line 4), which is added into the current graph G (line 5). Then we perform an intra-procedural (backward) data flow analysis on the client functions where the starting API locates (lines 6–12) and expand the graph G accordingly, yielding an intra-procedural AUGP. In detail, we start with an instruction set IS containing only the stating API. For each instruction I in IS, we resolve its parameters (line 9) and add them into the graph G (line 10). Moreover, these parameters can be instructions, variables or constants and some instructions can be further traced (line 11). In particular, if the instruction parameter involves the target APIs or an object is typed of some specific class of the target library (referred to as a target object), then it will be added in the instruction set IS for further analysis. During the analysis, for function call instructions, it is difficult to know exactly whether the called function modifies the target objects or not. So we conservatively consider all the functions would modify the target objects. Besides, if a target object is created by this instruction parameter, we will stop the trace of this target object, that is, the parameter would not be added into the instruction set IS.

Afterwards, we consider the inter-procedural analysis. For that, we check whether there are some client functions in T occurring in G as well (line 13). If so, we resolve the information of all the client functions (line 14), that is, the starting points (*i.e.*, calling sites) of the client functions, the target object considered by the analysis, and the IR instructions of the client functions. Then for each client function, we expand the current graph with its program slice with respect to the target object (lines 15–16), which can be done via an intra-procedural analysis on the client function as well.

We continue on the client function checking, until no client functions are found (lines 13–18). In that case, the graph G is a possibly full usage, as no more statements within the location tree T can be added into G. And, apparently, the graph G is an inter-procedural AUGP. We add G into GS (line 19) and mark the target API that occur in both T and G as visited (line 20). Finally, we continue on checking there are still some unvisited target APIs in T, and if so, we repeat to construct AUGPs for the unvisited APIs (lines 2–20).

Algorithm 2: BuildAUGP

Input: API location tree T
Output: AUGP set GS

1 $GS \leftarrow \emptyset$;
2 **while** T *contains some unvisited leaves* **do**
3     $G \leftarrow$ an empty graph;
4   APICall $\leftarrow$ the rightmost unvisited leaf of T;
5   add(G.nodes, APICall);
6     $IS \leftarrow \{APICall\}$;
7   **while** IS *is not empty* **do**
8        $I \leftarrow$ pop IS;
       // get parameters from data flow analysis results
9   paras $\leftarrow$ getParameters(I);
10   add(G, paras);
11   add_nontrivial(IS, paras);
12   **end**
13   **while** G *contains some client functions in* T **do**
14   funs $\leftarrow$ getClientFuns(G, T);
15   **for** $fun \in funs$ **do**
         // building AUGP for fun and expend G
16   expand(G, fun.start, fun.object, fun.body);
17   **end**
18   **end**
19    $GS \leftarrow GS \cup \{G\}$;
20   mark(T, G);
21 **end**

Consider the code in Listing 1.1 again and one of its API location trees is given in Fig. 2. We start with the rightmost API *doFinal* (line 4) and perform a data flow analysis on the client function *encrypt()* containing *doFinal*.

We first resolve two parameters *cipher* and *content.getBytes()*[1] from *doFinal*. Then we trace backward with respect to *cipher* and get the function call instruction (line 3). As we conservatively consider the function call instruction is a write for *cipher*, so *cipher* is "killed" (*i.e.*, the value of the object has been modified). But we will continue on the data flow analysis with the parameters of this function call instruction. And similar to *content.getBytes()*. The top-level graph is shown in the left part of Fig. 3, where the square nodes represent the instruction ones (such as function/API call), the oval nodes represent the data ones (such as the arguments of functions), edges labelled by *object* indicate the parameter is used as the instance object calling the corresponding function, edges labelled by *used_n* indicate the n-th argument of a target API or a client function not occurring in the location tree, edges labelled by *parameter_n* indicate the n-th argument of a client function occurring in the location tree.

---

[1] In WALA, there would be a temporary variable for this expression.

After that, we found a client function *initWithAES()* related to the target object *cipher*. So we expand the graph with this function, and get the final graph, which is shown in Fig. 3. Note that, with inter-procedural analysis, we are able to extract the data relation between *Cipher.doFinal* and *Cipher.init*. AUGP retains the package name, class name, parameter type, and return type. For presentation convenience, the functions in Fig. 3 omit the parameter type and return type.

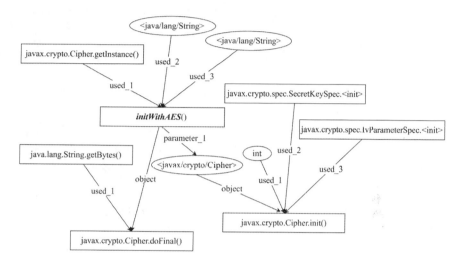

Fig. 3. AUGP for code in Listing 1.1

Concerning the target APIs, they can be provided by the users. But we also present a method to obtain the target APIs automatically for a given project: we scan the given project function by function and record the number of the classes of the APIs that are called in the project, then we take the classes whose numbers are larger than a given threshold and generate their corresponding APIs as the target ones. The more occurrences of (the classes of) APIs, the more probability of mining valid patterns.

3.3   Pattern Mining

AUGPs can capture API usages. We can use graph mining on AUGPs directly, but the result seems not good: only a small number of API usage patterns are obtained, this is because API usages are flexible, such as an API usage may have different conditional branches or wrap in different function with different inter-procedural, making the different usages interfere with each other. Moreover, applying graph patterns on violation detection prones to yield more false positives.

Therefore, we employ a looser data structure (i.e., set) and focus on binary relations between APIs. We convert each graph to a set via simply removing the edges and preserving only non-client functions. Next, we use the association rule algorithm FP-growth [8] to mine the relationships between two APIs. Our rule is an implication expression of the form $API_1 \rightarrow API_2$, which indicates that the antecedent API_1 occurring in a code snippet, then the consequent API_s should occur as well, no matter the orders between them. For example, a rule for the example code in Listing 1.1 may be *javax.crypto.Cipher.doFinal* $\rightarrow$ *javax.crypto.Cipher.init*, stating that if *javax.crypto.Cipher.doFinal* is called, then *javax.crypto.Cipher.init* should be called as well.

Prior to pattern mining, some graphs are filtered: (1) graphs with too fewer nodes or edges (which contains little information); (2) graphs with fields of some classes (it is not easy to trace all statements that involve this field); (3) graphs with depth larger than 3 (which are found to be expandable and more likely to be incomplete).

To facilitate violation detection, we summarize several properties for each association rule:

- **Relevance.** A function is said to be relevant if one of its class name, parameters or return type is consistent with the target API class. A rule $API_1 \rightarrow API_2$ is said to be high relevant (or low relevant or irrelevant, resp.) if both (or one or none, resp.) of API_1 and API_2 are relevant.
- **Order.** A rule $API_1 \rightarrow API_2$ is said to be in positive (or negative, resp.) order if API_1 should appear before (or after, resp.) API_2. If the order can not be determined, we said the rule is a unordered one.
- **Conditional Rule.** A rule $API_1 \rightarrow API_2$ is said to be conditional if one of API_1 and API_2 returns a Boolean value.

The relevance of a rule is easy to determine. The conditional property is helpful, as several APIs need to pass some conditional check before calling, such as the APIs *hasNext* and *next* in the class *Iterator*. We conservatively consider the rules wherein one of their APIs returns a Boolean value are conditional ones. Finally, we estimate the orders of APIs in terms of reachability. For each AUGP, we first remove the loops in it via disconnecting the end of loop statement and its corresponding begin, and calculate the reachabilities (i.e., transitive closure) between all non-client functions. Then for f_1 and f_2, we count the number n_{f_1,f_2} (n_{f_2,f_1}, resp.) of graphs wherein f_1 can reach f_2 (f_2 can reach f_1 resp.). If $n_{f_1,f_2} > 0$ and $n_{f_1,f_2} > 4 * n_{f_1,f_2}$, then the order of f_1 and f_2 is f_1, f_2. Similar for the order f_2, f_1. Otherwise, they are unordered.

3.4   Violation Detection

In this section, we present two kinds of violation detection, that is, co-occurrence detection and order detection, and the ranking of violations.

Co-Occurrence Detection. As mentioned above, if the antecedent of a rule occurs, then does the consequent. In other words, once the antecedent is called in a code snippet but the consequent is not, then the code snippet is considered as a suspicious violation. For the conditional rules, we perform a further check on a suspicious violation: whether there exists another condition check that involves an API sharing the same object/class with the missing one. This is because there may be some other APIs that can achieve the equivalent conditional check. For example, *list.size() == 0* and *list.isEmpty() == true* achieve the equivalent conditional check.

Order Detection. The order detection is a complement to the co-occurrence detection. When both APIs of an association rule occur and the association rule is ordered, we will perform the order detection. Generally, there are four possible orders in (the AUGP of) the code snippet: API_1, API_1, API_1, API_2, API_2, API_1, and API_2, API_2, assuming that either API_1 or API_2 may occur multiple times. The order that matches the rule is called consistent, while the other cases are inconsistent. Clearly, according to the estimation of order in Sect. 3.3, the consistent order should occur many times. But the inconsistent ones may not be a misuse. Consequently, we set a minimum threshold. If the frequency of an inconsistent order is smaller than this threshold, we consider it as a suspicious violation.

Nevertheless, after analyzing a large amount of code, we found that two cases are more likely to lead to a false positive:

- The frequency of the antecedent in the code snippet and the one of the consequent are almost the same;
- When the rule is conditional, the frequency of the conditional API in the code snippet is greater than the one of the other API of the rule.

So we exclude them. One can also think that the order check is unnecessary for these two cases.

Filtering and Ranking. After the co-occurrence detection and order detection, we get a list of suspicious violations. To evaluate these suspicious violations, we score the rules they violate, yielding a ranking for them.

Table 1. Scores for Association Rules

Properties	Score
Positive Ordered	5
Negative Ordered, Conditional	4
Positive Ordered, Conditional	3
Negative Ordered	2
Unordered	1
High Relevant	5
Low Relevant	2
Irrelevant	−5
Too Many Violations	−5

Table 1 shows the scores for the association rules. We focus on the positive ordered rules and high-relevant rules, so they are assigned the highest score. While the irrelevant rules and the ones that are violated too many times should be rejected by one vote (i.e., assigned the lowest score), so as not to lead to a false positive. The unordered rules are more likely to have little effect, so they would have lower scores. The conditional rules are a bit special: the negative order have higher score than the positive one, as the conditional API always appears as a consequent of a association rule.

A violation may violate several rules, we score it by the highest score among its violated rules. A violation is considered as a misuse if its score is not smaller than 6, in other words, all suspicious violations with scores smaller than 6 will be filtered out. After filtering, we can rank the list of violations.

4   Evaluation

In this section, we will introduce the data set used in the experiments as well as the experimental results.

4.1   Dataset

We implemented our approach as a detector *APDetect*, based on WALA[2]. So APDetect requires the projects in Java compiled bytecode. APDetect targets at the detection of a single project. Existing detectors of the same type in Java are DMMC [15], JADET [23] , TIKANGE [22], GROUMINER [19], and MUDDE-TECT [2]. However, some of these detectors require Java source code as input. Therefore, for comparison, we need projects that have both source code and bytecode. MuBench [1] is a dataset for evaluating the API misuse detector. We take 31 projects in total from MuBench that can be successfully compiled into bytecode as our experimental dataset.

Table 2. Type and number of violations

Violation	Number
missing/call	68
missing/condition/null_check	5
missing/condition/synchronization	1
missing/condition/value_or_state	35
Missing/violation_handling	20
redundant/call	10
redundant/violation_handling	1
Total	140

---

[2] https://wala.sourceforge.net/wiki/index.php/UserGuide:Technical_Overview.

Table 2 shows the statistics of the dataset, which contains a total of 140 known violations. The classification of violation types follows the one of Mubench. The API missing/call violation has the highest number, accounting for 48.5% of the total.

4.2   Experiments

For evaluating violation detection, soundness and completeness are two important criteria. Soundness indicates the accuracy of the detector, i.e., the number of false positives should be as low as possible; completeness requires that the detector can find as many violations as possible. Therefore, in this section, we design the precision experiment and the recall experiment. To evaluate the effectiveness of inter-procedural analysis, we also design the ablation experiment.

Precision Experiment. In this experiment, we need to check whether a reported violation is a true misuse or not. Moreover, some detectors may report thousands of violations. However, it is impractical to manually verify the correctness of all the reported violations on too many projects. Therefore, following the experiments of Amann et al.'s work [2], we selected 10 projects from the dataset for this experiment, on which all detectors were run on to detect violations, and took the TOP-20 reports as output for each project for manual verification.

Recall Experiment. This experiment aims to find the known violations. It is easy to manually check whether a known violation is reported or not. So we performed this experiment on all the 31 projects and checked whether the 140 known violations are contained in the output list reported by each detector. We also considered the 25 newly found violations in the above precision experiment, yielding a list of known violations with a total 165. In addition, we also performed the recall experiment with TOP-20 reports on the 10 projects selected for the precision experiment, so as to get the F1-scores.

Ablation Experiment. In order to evaluate the effectiveness of inter-procedural AUGP, we performed the precision experiment with the intra-procedural AUGP (i.e., without the inter-procedural analysis).

4.3   Results of Precision Experiment

Table 3. Precision and Recall Results on 10 selected projects

Detector	Correct	Report	Precision	Recall	F1-score
JADET	8	111	7.21%	16.48%	0.10
TIKANGA	12	105	11.43%	24.18%	0.16
DMMC	12	141	8.51%	34.07%	0.14
GROUMINER	4	150	2.67%	7.69%	0.04
MUDETECT	38	151	25.00%	62.64%	0.36
APDetect	42	75	56.00%	51.65%	0.54

The results of precision experiment are shown in Table 3, where **Correct** indicates the number of violations that are reported correctly for each detector.

Table 3 reveals that APDetect achieves the highest precision rate 56.00%, which is 31.00% more than the second-best detector. Furthermore, APDetect reports the highest number of true violations, correctly identifying a total of 42, which is 4 more than the second-best detector. Notably, the detectors also detected 25 new violations that are not previously recorded in the dataset MuBench, out of which 11 were identified by APDetect. These findings demonstrate that our approach is highly effective and outperforms several existing detectors in terms of precision.

Table 4. Reasons for false positives

Reason	Number	Ratio
Uncommon Usage	20	60.61%
Alternative Call	10	30.30%
Inter-procedural Disruption	2	6.06%
Insufficient Control Flow Analysis	1	3.03%

However, there are 33 false positives in this experiment reported by APDetect. After a manual analysis on these reports as well as the rules, we summarize the reasons in Table 4 and discuss them in the following:

- The uncommon usage in this section can be interpreted as that the mined rule is not very strict such that both APIs much appear at the same time. In other words, one of them can be appear separately. Take the iterator *Iterator* for example. *hashNext()* can be called separately to determine whether there are still some elements in the iterator without necessarily calling *next()* to get them. This reason causes the most false positives for APDetect, with a total of 20 cases, accounting for 60.61%.
- Alternative calls means that the functionality of the API can be replaced by other APIs. For example, in the class *java.util.StringTokenizer*, *nextElement()* and *nextToken()* have the same functionality and can be used interchangeably. This would make one usage being considered a rule while the others being considered as a violation. There are 10 cases due to this reason, accounting for 30.30%.
- A client function that is detected by APDetect with a violation may make its client callers to be detected with a violation, leading to a redundant false positive. We call this reason as inter-procedural disruption, which causes 2 cases.
- Insufficient control flow analysis, such as the infeasible paths, can also lead APDetect to some false positives, which is left for future work.

Similar to the analysis result reported in Amann et al. [2,3], our study found that the main reasons behind the low precision rates in the precision experiment for the other detectors were uncommon usage, alternative call and inadequate program analysis.

Table 5. Recall Results on 31 projects

Detector	Hits	Report	Recall
JADET	15	355	9.09%
TIKANGA	22	216	13.33%
DMMC	33	8,097	20.00%
GROUMINER	7	710	4.24%
MUDETECT	60	20,378	36.36%
APDetect	48	102	29.09%

4.4   Results of Recall Experiment

Table 5 gives the statistical results of the recall experiment, where **hits** indicates the number of known violations that are reported by each detector. The detail results are given in Table 6.

Among the tested detectors, MuDetect identified a total of 60 violations and achieved the highest recall rate 36.36%. APDetect, on the other hand, detected a total of 48 violations and ranked second, achieving a recall rate of 29.70%, only 7.27% smaller than the top detector MuDetect. DMMC demonstrated a recall rate of 20.00% and ranked third. Notably, APDetect reported the fewest number of violations at 102, while MuDetect and DMMC reported 20,378 and 8,097 violations, respectively, which are considerably higher than that reported by our detector APDetect.

We also have a quick check on the rankings of the known violations reported by the detectors and found that some known violations reported by MuDetect and DMMC are ranked far behind. For example, the violation named by *tikanga11-4* is ranked 324-th, 58-th and 12-th by MuDetect, DMMC and APDetect, respectively. Clearly, the too-low ranking will make the programmer miss the violation.

In addition, our co-occurrence detection reports 71 violations, among which 34 ones are correct, with a precision rate 47.88%; and our order detection reports 29 violations, among which 12 ones are correct, with a a precision rate 41.38%. The above results show that both co-occurrence detection and order detection are effective.

As the projects and the reported numbers are different from the precision experiment, we cannot get the F1-scores from these two experiments. For that, we also performed the recall experiment with TOP-20 reports on the 10 projects selected for the precision experiment, so as to get the F1-scores. The results are

Table 6. Detail Results of Recall Experiment

Project	Vresion	Number of Findings					
		DMMC	GROUMINER	JADET	TIKANGA	MUDETECT	APDetect
aclang	587	157	13	0	0	103	0
acmath	998	685	–	17	17	2666	0
alibaba-druid	e10f28	517	–	17	5	798	7
apache-gora	bb09d89	0	15	0	1	193	1
argouml	026	1669	–	73	48	9128	33
asterisk-java	304421c	114	10	0	1	6	2
battleforge	878	171	3	0	0	76	2
bcel	24014e5	322	87	21	3	315	2
chensun	cf23b99	49	50	8	2	66	21
closure	319	1944	95	176	45	2567	7
corona-old	0d0d18b	146	8	0	0	45	1
hoverruan-weiboclient4j	6ca0c73	29	0	0	0	6	0
itext	5091	1173	137	17	55	1304	13
ivantrendafilov-confucius	2c30287	4	0	0	0	0	0
jigsaw	205	0	130	12	20	1525	0
jodatime	1231	1	0	0	0	9	0
jriecken-gae-java-mini-profiler	80f3a59	4	0	0	0	0	0
lucene	1918	–	72	2	4	334	5
minecraft-launcher	e62d1bb	95	0	0	0	2	1
mqtt	f438425	43	4	0	0	1	0
rhino	286251	258	43	–	–	156	0
saavn	e576758	–	0			0	0
secure-tcp	aeba19a	1	0	0	0	0	0
synthetic_java8-misuses	96d0ccb	–	0	–	–	0	0
synthetic_jca	jsl	0	0	0	0	0	0
synthetic_survey	jsl	5	0	0	0	0	0
tbuktu-ntru	8126929	60	1	0	0	0	0
technic-launcher-sp	7809682	138	4	0	0	0	1
testng	677302c	473	37	12	15	1075	6
thomas-s-b-visualee	410a80f	30	1	0	0	3	0
yapps	1ae52b0	9	0	0	0	0	0
Total		8097	710	355	216	**20378**	102

also shown in Table 3, which are similar to the ones for the 31 projects shown in Table 5. Table 3 demonstrates that APDetect achieves the best F1-score.

Finally, we study the violations involving API calls that are missed by APDetect for the 31 projects, and summarize the following possible reasons:

– Little data. Little data can be reflected in too few code files in a project, too few occurrences of the target classes, or too few occurrences of the target API. Any of these may cause the pattern mining unable to mine a valid rule, and then make the violation detection fail to the violations.
– Client-side functions. Client-side functions are written by the project developers and are generally more flexible to use in the projects. Our detector did not consider these client-side functions. However, there are some violations involving client-side functions in MuBench, which could be missed by our detector.

– Graph filtering. Graphs with only one target API are filtered by our approach. But in MuBench, there are some violations involving only one API. For example, a StringBuilder object is constructed by two redundant calls, wherein only one (i.e., the last one) call is useful.

Similar to the analysis result reported in Amann et al. [2,3], our study found that the low recall rates for the other detectors were mainly due to two factors: insufficient API usage cases for mining (*i.e.*, litter data) and inadequate detector functionality.

4.5 Results of Ablation Experiment

Table 7. Results for Intra-Detection and Inter-Detection

Project	Intra-Detection		Inter-Detection	
	Correct	Report	Correct	Report
closure	5	7	5	7
itext	2	3	6	13
jodatime	0	0	0	0
lucene	3	4	4	5
asterisk-java	0	2	0	2
bcel	0	0	0	2
chensun	0	3	12	20
jigsaw	0	0	0	0
testng	1	3	1	6
argouml	14	20	14	20
Total	25	42	42	75

Table 7 shows the results of the intar-procedural detection and the inter-procedural detection in the precision experiments. There are 17 more violations found by the inter-procedural detection then the one found by the intra-procedural detection, and their precisions are pretty close. This demonstrates the effectiveness and the necessary of the inter-procedural analysis.

There is no difference between the results on some projects, such as *closure* and *argouml*, for the intra-procedural detection and the inter-procedural detection. This is because these target APIs, such as *hasNext()* and *next()*, are called in the same client functions.

While on the project *chensun*, the results are significant different for these two detections. The reason is that *chensun* provides several client functions to encapsulate java database APIs, such as *java.sql.PreparedStatement.close()*. Without the inter-procedural analysis, it is unable to capture the usages of these APIs. In other words, building AUGP with the inter-procedural analysis can enrich the API usages, leading to a higher probability of mining (more) patterns.

5   Related Work

5.1   API Pattern Mining

An API Pattern defines a type of legal API usages [26] and API pattern mining is a technique for mining API usages from existing codes. Researchers have proposed various API pattern mining techniques. In this section, we briefly introduce existing mining techniques according to the following categories:

Frequent Itemset Mining. Li and Zhou [12] proposed PR-Miner to automatically extract the implied patterns from the code by hashing the functions in the source codes into integer itemsets, and then using the frequent subitem algorithm FPclose in data mining techniques to automatically extract the patterns of function calls from them. Bin Liang et al. [13] proposed a mining method based on frequent itemsets dependent on the quality of the dataset. As the presence of irrelevant interfering items in the code during the mining of API patterns can lead to incorrect API patterns, they proposed a novel mining tool, AntMiner.

Sequential Pattern Mining. Xie and Pei [27] proposed MAPO, a tool for extracting API usage patterns from source code. MAPO first extracts API call sequences from code fragments and then performs hierarchical clustering by similarity of API names, class names, etc., and the most frequent API call sequence obtained in each cluster is considered as an API usage pattern. UP-Miner [21] improved MAPO in extracting API invocation sequences from source code. UP-Miner uses a similar strategy as MAPO, which improves MAPO by reducing redundancy and interference in API invocation sequences by clustering twice, and it uses the BIDE nearest frequent sequence mining algorithm to obtain only API sequences without more frequent substrings, and finally presents the API statute using probabilistic graphs.

Frequent Subgraph Mining. Nguyen et al [19] proposed a method to construct a graph model GROUM from source code. The GROUM graph mainly retains function calls, WHILE loops, IF branches, etc. as nodes, and establishes basic directed edges first by the order of nodes occurring in the code, and then by the proximity and usage relationships of nodes, and finally obtains a graph model for code fragments. When the variable nodes are included in the graph, the graph model can represent the usage of some parameters, but some parameters for specific fetching values are still ignored. In the usage pattern mining, they determine whether a subgraph is a legitimate API statute based on the frequency of its occurrence in the graph. In 2018, Mover et al. [16] proposed BIGGROUM based on GROUM. They explicitly define the types of nodes and edges in the graph, where the data node represents the type of the parameter being used, again ignoring the specific fetching of the parameter. In mining pattern, they classify graphs by clustering frequent itemsets in order to reduce the computational space of isomorphic subgraphs, using a similar approach to GROUM, which identifies graph models that occur more frequently than a threshold as pattern.

Besides the above techniques, researchers have proposed other techniques to mine API patterns, such as probabilistic model mining [5,18], grammatical inference [4], template mining [6], etc.

5.2 Pattern-Based Detectors

Pattern-based detectors commonly mine usage patterns (*i.e.*, equivalent API usages that occur frequently) and then reports deviations from these patterns as potential misuses [2]. Amann et al. [3] have presented a detailed survey and comparison of detectors and their capabilities, so we briefly discuss the related detectors here.

JADET [23] keeps the function names, call orders, and instance objects in the code, extracts the directed graph from codes, and then extracts the relationship pairs of APIs from the graph. The relationship pairs that satisfy the minimum support are considered as the API usage patterns. A usage is considered as a violation if it misses at least 2 attributes of the pattern being violated as well as it occurs at least 10 times less than the pattern. Violations are ranked by $u \times s \div v$, where s is the violated pattern's support, v is the number of violations of the pattern, and u is a uniqueness factor of the pattern.

TIKANGA [22] builds on JADET and it replaces API call-order pair with Computation Tree Logic (CTL). TIKANGA looks through all the objects used as actual arguments and identifies those that violate the operational preconditions. Violations are ranked by elevation in association rules.

DMMC [15] is a missing method call detector for Java. It extracts usages from codes then compares their similarity. Two usages are exactly similar if their respective sets match and are almost similar if one of them contains exactly one additional method. If a usage has high strangeness score, then it is considered a violation and ranked by the score.

GROUMINER [19] creates a graph-based object-usage representation (GROUM) for each target function. It performs frequent subgraph mining on GROUMs to mine usage patterns and then uses them to detect violations. When at least 90% of, but not, all occurrences of a subgraph can be extended to a larger graph, these rare non-extendable graphs are considered as violations and are ranked by their rareness.

MUDETECT [2] represents each target (client) function as an API Usage Graph (AUG), and then uses a frequent subgraph mining algorithm to mine usage patterns with a minimum support of 6. A subgraph is considered abnormal if it does not match any usage pattern and the confidence score is less than the threshold. Violations are ranked by their confidence scores, which are computed by $p \div v \times o$, where p is the support of the violated pattern, v is the number of times that the violation occurs, o is violation-overlap.

The above detectors take a single Java project as input to mine patterns and detect violations. Besides, PR-Miner, AntMiner, CHRONICLER [20], COLIB-RI/ML [14] are designed for C programming language. DROIDASSIST [17] is designed for Android Java Bytecode. MuDetectXP, CL-Detector [24], ALP [9] add additional inputs to enhance the detection.

6   Conclusion

In this paper, we have proposed a graph model AUGP for intermediate representation of API usages and an approach to extract AUGPs from code. Based on AUGP, we have proposed a detector APDetect that mines the API usage rules first and then detects the possible violations guided by the rules. We have performed experiments to evaluate our detector, and the results shows that, comparing against five state-of-the-art detectors on the public dataset MuBench, our detector achieves the highest precision and the highest F1-score. In future work, we will add exception handling and conditional branching to AUGP and explore more experiments to evaluate our detector.

Acknowledgements. This work was supported in part by the National Natural Science Foundation of China (Nos. 61836005 and 61972260).

References

1. Amann, S., Nadi, S., Nguyen, H.A., Nguyen, T.N., Mezini, M.: Mubench: a benchmark for api-misuse detectors. In: MSR, pp. 464–467. ACM (2016)
2. Amann, S., Nguyen, H.A., Nadi, S., Nguyen, T.N., Mezini, M.: Investigating next steps in static api-misuse detection. In: Proceedings of the 16th International Conference on Mining Software Repositories, MSR 2019, 26–27 May 2019, Montreal, Canada, pp. 265–275. IEEE / ACM (2019)
3. Amann, S., Nguyen, H.A., Nadi, S., Nguyen, T.N., Mezini, M.: A systematic evaluation of static api-misuse detectors. IEEE Trans. Software Eng. 45(12), 1170–1188 (2019)
4. Ammons, G., Bodík, R., Larus, J.R.: Mining specifications. In: POPL, pp. 4–16. ACM (2002)
5. Fowkes, J.M., Sutton, C.: Parameter-free probabilistic API mining across github. In: SIGSOFT FSE, pp. 254–265. ACM (2016)
6. Gabel, M., Su, Z.: Online inference and enforcement of temporal properties. In: ICSE (1), pp. 15–24. ACM (2010)
7. Han, J., Kamber, M.: Data Mining: Concepts and Techniques. Morgan Kaufmann (2000)
8. Han, J., Pei, J., Yin, Y.: Mining frequent patterns without candidate generation. In: SIGMOD Conference, pp. 1–12. ACM (2000)
9. Kang, H.J., Lo, D.: Active learning of discriminative subgraph patterns for api misuse detection. IEEE Trans. Software Eng. 48(8), 2761–2783 (2022)
10. Krüger, S., Späth, J., Ali, K., Bodden, E., Mezini, M.: Crysl: an extensible approach to validating the correct usage of cryptographic apis. IEEE Trans. Software Eng. 47(11), 2382–2400 (2021)
11. Legunsen, O., Hassan, W.U., Xu, X., Rosu, G., Marinov, D.: How good are the specs? a study of the bug-finding effectiveness of existing java API specifications. In: ASE, pp. 602–613. ACM (2016)

12. Li, Z., Zhou, Y.: Pr-miner: automatically extracting implicit programming rules and detecting violations in large software code. In: ESEC/SIGSOFT FSE, pp. 306–315. ACM (2005)
13. Liang, B., Bian, P., Zhang, Y., Shi, W., You, W., Cai, Y.: Antminer: mining more bugs by reducing noise interference. In: ICSE, pp. 333–344. ACM (2016)
14. Lindig, C.: Mining patterns and violations using concept analysis. In: The Art and Science of Analyzing Software Data, pp. 17–38. Morgan Kaufmann / Elsevier (2015)
15. Monperrus, M., Bruch, M., Mezini, M.: Detecting missing method calls in object-oriented software. In: D'Hondt, T. (ed.) ECOOP 2010. LNCS, vol. 6183, pp. 2–25. Springer, Heidelberg (2010). https://doi.org/10.1007/978-3-642-14107-2_2
16. Mover, S., Sankaranarayanan, S., Olsen, R.B.P., Chang, B.E.: Mining framework usage graphs from app corpora. In: SANER, pp. 277–289. IEEE Computer Society (2018)
17. Nguyen, T.T., Pham, H.V., Vu, P.M., Nguyen, T.T.: Recommending API usages for mobile apps with hidden markov model. In: ASE, pp. 795–800. IEEE Computer Society (2015)
18. Nguyen, T.T., Pham, H.V., Vu, P.M., Nguyen, T.T.: Learning API usages from bytecode: a statistical approach. In: ICSE, pp. 416–427. ACM (2016)
19. Nguyen, T.T., Nguyen, H.A., Pham, N.H., Al-Kofahi, J.M., Nguyen, T.N.: Graph-based mining of multiple object usage patterns. In: ESEC/SIGSOFT FSE, pp. 383–392. ACM (2009)
20. Ramanathan, M.K., Grama, A., Jagannathan, S.: Path-sensitive inference of function precedence protocols. In: 29th International Conference on Software Engineering (ICSE'07), pp. 240–250 (2007). https://doi.org/10.1109/ICSE.2007.63
21. Wang, J., Dang, Y., Zhang, H., Chen, K., Xie, T., Zhang, D.: Mining succinct and high-coverage API usage patterns from source code. In: MSR, pp. 319–328. IEEE Computer Society (2013)
22. Wasylkowski, A., Zeller, A.: Mining temporal specifications from object usage. Autom. Softw. Eng. **18**(3–4), 263–292 (2011)
23. Wasylkowski, A., Zeller, A., Lindig, C.: Detecting object usage anomalies. In: ESEC/SIGSOFT FSE, pp. 35–44. ACM (2007)
24. Zeng, H., Chen, J., Shen, B., Zhong, H.: Mining api constraints from library and client to detect api misuses. In: 2021 28th Asia-Pacific Software Engineering Conference (APSEC), pp. 161–170 (2021)
25. Zhang, T., Upadhyaya, G., Reinhardt, A., Rajan, H., Kim, M.: Are code examples on an online q&a forum reliable?: a study of API misuse on stack overflow. In: ICSE, pp. 886–896. ACM (2018)
26. Zhong, H., Mei, H.: An empirical study on API usages. IEEE Trans. Software Eng. **45**(4), 319–334 (2019)
27. Zhong, H., Xie, T., Zhang, L., Pei, J., Mei, H.: MAPO: mining and recommending API usage patterns. In: Drossopoulou, S. (ed.) ECOOP 2009. LNCS, vol. 5653, pp. 318–343. Springer, Heidelberg (2009). https://doi.org/10.1007/978-3-642-03013-0_15

Author Index

C. David and M. Sun (Eds.): TASE 2023, LNCS 13931, pp. 365–366, 2023.
https://doi.org/10.1007/978-3-031-35257-7

Printed in the United States
by Baker & Taylor Publisher Services